$11.50

Marketing □

a contemporary

analysis

□

ROBERT D. BUZZELL

Harvard Business School

□

ROBERT E. M. NOURSE

University of Western Ontario

□

JOHN B. MATTHEWS, JR.

Harvard Business School

□

THEODORE LEVITT

Harvard Business School

Marketing □ a contemporary analysis

SECOND EDITION

McGRAW-HILL BOOK COMPANY

New York St. Louis San Francisco Düsseldorf Johannesburg Kuala Lumpur London Mexico Montreal New Delhi Panama Rio de Janeiro Singapore Sydney Toronto

Library of Congress Cataloging in Publication Data
Main entry under title:

Marketing: a contemporary analysis.

1964 ed. published under title: Marketing, an introductory analysis.
Includes bibliographical references.
1. Marketing. 2. Sales management. I. Buzzell, Robert Dow, 1933–
HF5415.M296 1972 658.8 78-39102
ISBN 0-07-009477-2

MARKETING: A CONTEMPORARY ANALYSIS

234567890MURM798765432

This book was set in Optima by Progressive Typographers, printed by The Murray Printing Company, and bound by Rand McNally & Company. The designer was Betty Binns; the drawings were done by Vantage Art, Inc. The editors were Jack R. Crutchfield and James R. Belser. Peter D. Guilmette supervised production.

CONTENTS

To the student

Marketing is exciting. No other area of business activity offers greater opportunity for imagination, analytical skill, and the willingness to take risks. The problems that marketing managers face spring from the ever-changing needs and desires of the consuming public and the activities of individual firms and their competitors. Marketing managers solve these problems by insight, analysis, and experience. The results of their decisions have much to do with competitive success or failure, both for themselves and for their organizations—whether business firms or nonprofit agencies. Because marketing activities and their costs represent a major element of the economy, marketing decisions also have significant effects on standards of living and rates of economic growth.

This book is an introduction to marketing. Its focus throughout is on problem solving and decision making in marketing. It is organized around the problems that confront marketing managers and emphasizes the dynamics of decision making. The book takes as its starting points the nature of marketing and the need for a careful and systematic analysis of customer behavior. Next, it proceeds to an examination of the institutional system of marketing; then, it outlines the types of problems involved in marketing management. Finally, it concludes with a discussion of major public policy issues related to marketing.

We expect the student who takes a course based on this book to achieve the following:

1. An appreciation of what is involved in marketing
2. A feeling for the excitement that marketing offers
3. An insight into the many skills involved in marketing management
4. The development of some of the knowledge and skills that are helpful in analyzing marketing problems
5. Some understanding of the importance of marketing to business success
6. An understanding of the issues involved in developing public policies regarding marketing

This book is intended for students who have had no prior courses in marketing and is designed for use in introductory courses at either the undergraduate or graduate level. Where terminology or concepts from economics and other sciences or disciplines are used, we have defined them and made apparent their relevance to marketing.

Although this is an introductory book, it covers a wide spectrum of marketing problems, thereby reflecting the vital relationships among the various aspects of marketing. A thorough understanding of the interacting effects of such factors as selling, advertising, pricing, and channels of distribution on customer and marketing behavior is an essential part of a student's introduction to marketing. This book is intended to develop an understanding of the nature and importance of those relationships.

In many problem areas, some factual and background information about marketing institutions is presented to enhance student familiarity with, and insight into, marketing problems. For example, the information about retailing and wholesaling institutions in Chapters 10 to 12 is extensive enough to provide a basis for understanding the management problems of these types of institutions, but it does not purport to be a comprehensive treatment of the subject. That objective and others similar to it are left for more specialized books. Thus no attempt is made to present a "complete" narrative and statistical description—which in any case would soon be out of date—of current marketing institutions and methods. In this regard this book differs from some marketing textbooks.

Overview of the book

This book begins with an introductory chapter, "What Is Marketing?" As the reader will find, marketing means many different things. Paul Mazur's comment that marketing is "the delivery of a standard of living" conveys an important idea. Other, more "standard," definitions are given in the text. But we prefer to introduce the world of marketing by a brief description of some of the decisions that face marketers and by some examples of the dynamics involved in the marketing process.

In the discussion of the marketing system in Chapter 2, marketing activity is related to the total business and social system, and attention is paid to the role of marketing in other societies. The total costs of marketing and some of the social criticisms that have been raised about marketing are also discussed. Part 2 consists of seven chapters relating to customer behavior. Many marketing books make the point that customer behavior is important. We agree. But we believe it is necessary to go beyond that and to help the beginning marketing student develop an understanding of the behavior of customers, both individuals and business firms. The rationale for both the organization and content of Part 2 is that marketing managers must, to a considerable extent, base their marketing decisions and programs on an analysis of customer behavior, using the best analytical tools and research findings that are available. Our objective, then, is to provide a guide to the analysis of customer behavior that is useful in the development of marketing policy and strategy. This is in contrast to merely furnishing large masses of statistical and behavioral data that the student would be hard put to remember, let alone apply.

Part 3 comprises three chapters dealing with retailing and wholesaling institutions. Our goal in this section is to provide an understanding of the role played by various types of firms engaged in retail and wholesale distribution, and of the process through which these institutions compete with each other. In these chapters, we briefly discuss the historical evolution of major kinds of retail and wholesale institutions, and we present some statistical data describing their sales, costs, and profits. We hope that you will *use* this information—but we do not expect or intend that you will feel obliged to memorize it. Descriptive data constitute a means, not an end in themselves.

Part 4 is concerned with the major functional areas of marketing policy and decision making. It covers the areas that are found in most marketing texts, but its distinguishing characteristic is an emphasis on (1) the kinds of decisions and problems that confront marketing men in developing policies and strategy and (2) the practical methods of analyzing problems and making decisions. Part 4 offers some descriptions of contemporary business practices but only to the extent necessary to permit understanding of the areas of decision and to give a perspective for the analysis of problems.

Part 5 deals with marketing information and analysis as aids to decision making. The topics treated in these chapters—marketing research and the measurement and analysis of marketing performance—involve some very complex techniques, which we cannot discuss fully. Our purpose is, rather, to give you some appreciation of the types of information and analytical techniques that are available and of the ways in which marketing decision makers combine formal analysis with intuition to define and resolve their problems.

Part 6, consisting of just one chapter, is devoted to a discussion of public policy issues related to marketing. Such questions as "Does marketing cost too much?" and the conflict between "private wants and public needs" are covered, and a variety of viewpoints is presented.

In an Appendix, we present accounting concepts and techniques that are useful in marketing analysis. With the assumption that the student has had little or no accounting training, this appendix introduces him to income statements and balance sheets, cost classifications, ratio analysis, and break-even calculations. We suggest that students study and thoroughly understand the Appendix before they reach Part 4.

We hope that you will find this introduction to marketing challenging and exciting, and that you will be stimulated to explore some aspects of the subject further. There is an extensive literature dealing with consumer behavior, marketing institutions, methods of advertising and selling, and many other subjects that are treated only briefly in this book. We believe that you will enjoy and benefit from learning about all these topics, whether or not you pursue a career in marketing.

Robert D. Buzzell
Robert E. M. Nourse
John B. Matthews, Jr.
Theodore Levitt

To the teacher

This book is an introductory marketing text designed for use in beginning courses at the graduate or undergraduate level. It can be used by itself or supplemented with case and/or readings. Suggested course outlines, recommended casebooks and individual cases, recommended readings, and detailed teaching suggestions are available to interested teachers in the Instructor's Manual, which can be obtained from the publisher.

All introductory marketing texts have many features in common since they cover the same basic ground. But we think our presentation differs from that of other books in several important respects.

1. Throughout the book, we have tried to put primary emphasis on marketing management and to view the marketing process from the perspective of the decision maker. Of course, many other texts also claim a managerial orientation; but, in some instances at least, management problems are presented by other authors in a rather abstract or idealized fashion, similar to that used in building for "model" in operations research. For the most part, we have chosen to depict and illustrate management problems as realistically as possible—frequently by using actual examples.

2. We have devoted a substantial part of the text to a discussion of customer behavior—7 of the 27 chapters deal specifically with various aspects of household, industry, and institutional purchasing behavior, and the discussion

of management problems is related, wherever possible, to applicable concepts and generalizations about customer needs and buying patterns.

3. While we provide questions and short "caselets" at the end of each chapter, we have specifically designed the text to be used in conjunction with case studies, either in the form of a published casebook or of individual cases available through the Intercollegiate Case Clearing House. We believe that this approach—as opposed to that of combining text with cases and/or readings in a single volume—offers the teacher maximum flexibility in designing a course to meet the particular needs of his own students and to fit into his school's curriculum most effectively.

Teachers who are familiar with the previous edition of the book, published in 1964, may wonder about the relationship between the two texts—especially in light of the long interval separating them. This book is far more than a "revision" of the earlier work—it is, essentially, a new book altogether. We have tried to emphasize this by changing the title from *Marketing: An Introductory Analysis* to *Marketing: A Contemporary Analysis*. Some features of the first edition have been retained—but more have been altered. Whereas the earlier version had only one chapter on retailing and wholesaling institutions, this edition has three. Entirely new chapters on "Marketing and Business Management" (Chapter 13), "International Marketing" (Chapter 24), and "Marketing and Public Policy" (Chapter 27), have been added. The discussions of product policy, pricing, and promotion have all been expanded—and, we hope, improved.

All the modifications reflect the many changes that have occurred in the field of marketing during the past eight years. Our students, and yours, are better prepared, more critical, and more socially concerned than their predecessors. We have tried to adapt our "product" to these new dimensions of "customer needs."

It is not possible for us to acknowledge the individual contributions of the many people who have influenced our work. We have been aided greatly by the suggestions and ideas of businessmen as well as those of our academic colleagues. Some of the materials in the book have been used in different form in our own teaching programs, and the reactions of students have been helpful in the book's evolution. We are greatly indebted to many members of both the administration and faculty of the Harvard Graduate School of Business Administration. Most particularly, we wish to thank Dean Lawrence E. Fouraker and Associate Dean George F. F. Lombard for their permission to undertake this text and for their appreciation of the many problems that beset authors.

We gratefully acknowledge the contributions of Professor Ronald E. Frank, who was a coauthor of the first edition. Many of his ideas have been retained in our revision, although he is not responsible for any shortcomings in our treatment of them.

Professor Phillip R. McDonald of Northeastern University prepared the Instructor's Manual and also made valuable suggestions for improvement in the text itself.

We appreciate the assistance of Cecile Landrum in the research done for the revision and of Maria E. Covell, Meredith McAfee, and Nonie Robinson in typing various portions of the manuscript. Sylvia Kolb made a major contribution by preparing the Index with meticulous care.

Finally, we thank our wives. Edith, Jennifer, Margaret, and Joan have been patient and understanding throughout the preparation of the original text and of the revision. It is to them that we dedicate the book.

Robert D. Buzzell
Robert E. M. Nourse
John B. Matthews, Jr.
Theodore Levitt

Introduction

PART ONE

About half of every dollar spent by American consumers is expended on marketing. There is general agreement that marketing has played a major role in the expansion of the American economy and other industrialized economies, and marketing is accepted as the mechanism through which new products and services are developed to meet the continuously changing needs and desires of the consuming public. As marketing plays its role in these developments, it follows that new and better jobs are created and that living standards rise. Marketing thus is capable of making a major contribution both to society and to those business firms that perform it effectively.

Marketing: A Contemporary Analysis *is concerned with what marketing is all about. What does "marketing" mean? How does it perform its role in relation to firms and their customers? Does marketing function within specific parameters? What does the marketing manager need to know in order to perform his job, and how does he go about getting this information? As you read and study, you will gain an appreciation for and an understanding of marketing problems and their solutions, in the context of the marketing management process.*

In the first chapter, some of the basic concepts behind marketing are developed. You will take a look at the role of research in marketing, and evaluate some general criteria for a successful marketing program. Cases of marketing management in action, illustrating several approaches to marketing problems, highlight the various elements of a marketing program which must be coordinated to solve them effectively.

In Chapter 2, the essential functions of marketing are described. You will learn what elements make up a marketing system, and how they are interrelated. This discussion analyzes the framework in which the marketing manager reaches decisions. Beyond these specific and traditional elements, there are peripheral environmental factors which influence and are influenced by the decisions of the marketer. Basic functions as a constant, with the continually changing environment, then, will be your touchstone in moving to Part 2, an in-depth study of customer and market behavior.

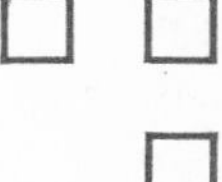

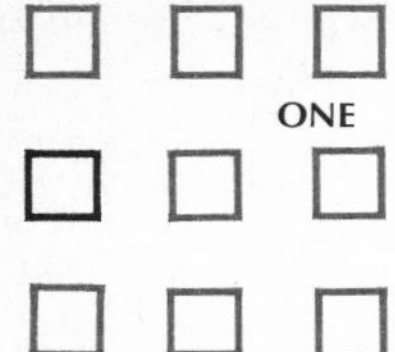

ONE

What is marketing?

It might seem reasonable to begin a book on marketing by defining it. There are a number of possible definitions—indeed, one of the interesting aspects of the study of marketing is to see how definitions of the subject have changed over the years, for the changes reflect some of the dynamism of the field itself. Nevertheless, we shall forgo definitions for the moment. Instead, you may wish to develop a definition of your own by thinking about some of the examples of business activity, successful and unsuccessful, that are presented below.

The mousetrap theory

"If you make a better mousetrap, the world will beat a path to your door." Chester M. Woolworth, president of the Woodstream Corporation, has probably heard this bit of homespun philosophy more often than anyone else in the world.[1] The company, which had been founded in 1928, produced millions of the well-known flat wooden mousetraps, originally pricing them at 5 cents.

Whenever Mr. Woolworth got together with business associates for social or business purposes, the conversation frequently produced the familiar question,

[1] Until 1966, the company was known as the Animal Trap Company of America.

"How's business?" No matter how Mr. Woolworth answered, he received the inevitable advice: "Make a better mousetrap, and the world will beat a path to your door."

So he did, and he has been sorry every since.[2]

The number of customers that came to his door would never have kept the weeds down, let alone beat a path. The better mousetrap became the worst shelf warmer in the company's history. Although every means of artificial respiration was tried, the "great new product" gradually expired and had to be removed from the line. Meanwhile the old-fashioned wooden mousetrap went right on selling in the millions, and it still is.

WHAT WENT WRONG?

Seemingly nothing could have gone wrong. The company did not embark on its new product rashly. It carefully researched mouse habits: eating habits, crawling habits, resting habits, and preferred sizes of holes. After many experimental models, all of which were carefully tested with mice of various shapes and sizes and given to groups of consumers to try out, Mr. Woolworth decided on the mousetrap he would finally offer to the market.

The new trap was called "Little Champ." It was a slick-looking little gadget with the appearance of an inverted miniature baby's bathtub with tapered sides and rounded corners. It had a modern, streamlined look and was molded in black plastic. It had a hole just the right size for the mouse to go in, leaving nothing but perhaps his tail outside. When he nibbled on the easily installed bait, a spring would snap smoothly upward and catch him neatly by the throat, causing almost instant death by strangulation. It then remained only for somebody to press the spring from the top so that the dead mouse would easily drop out.

The new trap worked like a charm. It never missed. It was clean, noiseless, sanitary, and relatively cheap (12 cents). It was modern. It was simple and safe to operate. A cross section of consumers who pretested it said it was splendid. For the first time in his life, Mr. Woolworth looked forward to hearing that tired old advice about making a better mousetrap. This time he would have not only an answer, but the profits to prove it.

But it turned out to be a colossal flop—the better mousetrap was a commercial failure. In spite of the fact that it seemed so perfect and that consumers had liked it so much in the testing stage, subsequent research showed where the advice of Mr. Woolworth's friends had gone wrong.

It was learned, first of all, that most mousetraps are bought by urban dwellers who have only an occasional mouse or two in the house. The traps are generally bought by the husband. But because of the presence of children

[2] Mr. Woolworth tells his sad tale "So We Made a Better Mousetrap" in *The Presidents' Forum,* Fall 1962, pp. 26–27.

who might be injured by playing with a set trap, and because mice tend to roam only when people are not present, the traps are generally set before retiring for the night. Because a trap is a mechanical gadget about which women are supposed to know very little, because men are the traditional "hunters" in society, and because women are more afraid of injuring their hands on a spring-set trap, the man of the house generally sets it.

If a mouse is caught, the housewife is eager to dispose of it quickly the next morning. But the typical household has a problem in the morning. There is an urgent rush to get the husband off to work on time and the children off to school. The husband seems never to have time to empty the trap he set so carefully the night before. And since the wife does not like to have a dead mouse around all day, it falls to her to remove it right after the morning rush subsides.

But she is afraid of both the spring and the mouse, even a dead mouse. Since the mouse that has been caught is probably the only one in the house anyhow, and since the conventional trap costs so little, she does not try to remove the mouse. She throws both the trap and the mouse into a paper bag and then into the trash barrel. Quick as a wink the problem is solved.

But housewives would not do this with the new trap. Even though it cost only 12 cents, it *looked* entirely too expensive to throw away. Hence it had to be emptied, and that got her entirely too close to, and involved with, the mouse. Then the trap had to be cleaned. And then it had to be stored. Just storing it was unpleasant, because every time she saw it on the shelf, it reminded her of the possible awful presence of another crawling and perhaps diseased intruder. Thus, while husbands bought the new "better mousetrap," their wives either would not let them use it or would not let them buy it a second time.

Perhaps the adage was sound in the days when the mouse was a common and constant household pest, when men did not have to rush off in the mornings to catch a train for work or fight the rush-hour traffic, or when women lived a hardy bucolic existence and mice did not frighten them so much. But by the 1950s, the times, conditions, and people had changed. The result was red ink for the company in spite of its seemingly careful product research, in spite of pretesting with customers, and in spite of an obviously "better" mousetrap.

What went wrong becomes painfully obvious. The product was indeed better—but not by the standards, problems, needs, and living habits of the urban household in the middle of the twentieth century. The better mousetrap was a commercial failure because, in spite of great care, an incomplete marketing job was done. The company had researched the mouse. It had designed a seemingly perfect trap. It had pretested various models with consumers. Everybody agreed that the product was splendid, and people said they would buy it. But they did not. In retrospect an important reason was that the conditions under which people actually *used* the product involved standards and problems entirely different from those in the pretests.

There are, fortunately, a number of success stories that stand in contrast to Mr. Woolworth's experience. Let us consider some of them and, as we do, try to put our finger on the significant differences between each and the Woodstream Company's better mousetrap.

Marketing in action

□

THE MUSTANG

The Ford Motor Company's Mustang has been one of the automobile industry's great success stories. Introduced in the spring of 1964, approximately one million Mustangs were sold before the car reached its second birthday. The unparalleled success of the Mustang reflects a combination of research, creativity, and aggressive marketing.[3]

In the late 1950s, foreign imports and the American Motors Corporation's Rambler succeeded in capturing over 15 percent of the automobile market in the United States. Led by the Volkswagen, these cars seemed to herald a new concept: the compact economy car. In response, the Big Three (General Motors, Ford, and Chrysler) of the United States automotive industry produced their own lines of compact cars which were introduced in the fall of 1959. Ford's Falcon and Chevrolet's Corvair were among the new brands.

During this same period, Ford's competitive analyses and consumer research began to detect what seemed to be some potentially significant developments in the market. The year 1960 was economically prosperous. The number of two-car families continued to increase at the rate of one million per year. The teenage segment of the population was also on the increase, and seemed to be playing a growing role in the buying decisions of older people. Young adults were characterized by rising incomes and rising expectations.

These developments were accompanied by changes in buying patterns in the American automobile market. Ford's marketing researchers noted several things. Sales of European sports cars were greater than might have been expected in a market with a strong economy-car orientation, and many buyers of compacts were making heavy purchases of such optional installations as automatic transmissions, bigger engines, and glamorous accessories. Convertibles and hard tops were capturing a larger share of automobile sales, and such items as four-speed manual transmissions were becoming more popular.

[3] For a more detailed description of the development and introduction of the Mustang, see Seymour Marshak, *The Mustang Story,* New Products: Concepts Development, and Strategy, Michigan Business Papers Number 43, Bureau of Business Research, Graduate School of Business Administration, The University of Michigan, Ann Arbor, 1967.

Ford's marketing managers believed, therefore, that they could "sense a stirring, subtle, undefined change in the automobile market."[4] Discussions led to a concept of a new car for the marketplace, one with style and flair, having strong appeal for young people, and priced so that the increasing numbers of young and young adult buyers could easily afford it.

In the automobile business, it takes a long time and prodigious effort to translate a concept into a car. For a major addition to the product line, such as the Mustang, the costs of tooling, dies, production facilities, and financing may well range between $200 and $300 million. In addition, a myriad of decisions are required on styling, engineering, design, pricing, product features and accessories, promotion, and all the other factors necessary to make, distribute, and sell the new car. At the same time, in order to reduce the chances of failure of what is essentially a multimillion dollar gamble, researchers must continuously test the likes and dislikes, and possible changes therein, of the car-buying public.

In 1960 and 1961, Ford's marketers and marketing planners translated their concept into a physical product in terms of size, weight, price, engineering features, and general configuration. The Mustang, hopefully, was to be a car with a Falcon's price tag and a Thunderbird's grace and performance. By July 1962, a number of clay models had been developed and one, with a long hood and short rear deck, seemed close to what was wanted. Because of the lead time necessary if the Mustang was to be introduced at the New York World's Fair in the spring of 1964, a crash design and styling program was instituted to turn July's "almost" model into a fully acceptable, life-sized model. The job was done in 20 days, and on August 16, 1962, the Mustang was born. Only minor design changes were made later—resulting from engineering, production, and consumer-acceptance studies.[5]

While Ford was gearing for production and the 1964 introduction of the Mustang, marketing executives continued to test the market regarding price, styling, and operating characteristics. These continuing studies indicated that style and low price should be the predominant selling themes, and that original estimates of potential volume could be expanded; it also seemed apparent that the Mustang could be offered with a range of options broad enough to permit it to appeal to luxury, sports, or economy-minded buyers.

The Mustang was unveiled to the public at the World's Fair in April 1964, accompanied by a carefully planned and integrated marketing campaign. To create dealer enthusiasm, live and filmed shows were held in 50 major cities and trading areas. The press was invited to the Ford Pavilion at the Fair, and

[4] Marshak, *op. cit.*, p. 35.

[5] New car models are closely guarded secrets prior to their introduction; consumer-acceptance studies at this stage typically consist of such things as silhouette-choice patterns.

the company's advertising was supplemented by cover stories and editorial spreads in such magazines as *Look, Life, Time,* and *Newsweek*. For the first time in the history of television advertising, all three major television networks were used simultaneously and Mustang commercials were seen in 29 million homes. Advertisements were placed in 2,600 newspapers, all emphasizing the high style, low price ($2,368 f.o.b. Detroit), and range of options. Special promotions were undertaken with women, young people, and young adults as targets. Mustang models were displayed at airports, 200 Holiday Inns, and other high-traffic locations throughout the country. The Mustang was an overnight success—within a short time production capacity had to be raised to 50,000 units per month.

□

HEUBLEIN, INC.

Heublein produces and markets a variety of packaged foods and beverages, including Smirnoff vodka. Vodka is a tasteless and odorless liquor that enjoyed a rapid upward trend in consumption during the 1960s, far outpacing any other major type of alcoholic beverage. A major portion of the credit for the growth of vodka sales can be attributed to Heublein and its aggressive and insightful marketing policies regarding Smirnoff. When it began its campaign to increase Smirnoff sales and make Smirnoff the top-selling brand of vodka, Heublein saw that there was an increasing tendency on the part of the buying public to prefer "lighter" alcoholic beverages with less pronounced taste, such as the lighter brands of Scotch whisky and vodka. Given the colorless, odorless, and tasteless character of vodka, Heublein's problem was to take advantage of the general market trend by finding ways to distinguish Smirnoff from competing brands.

Heublein viewed the development of a larger market for Smirnoff as essentially a marketing problem.[6] It was decided that heavy advertising and promotion would be the keys to consumer acceptance, and the price of Smirnoff was established at a level that would yield substantial funds for advertising. The consuming public was carefully analyzed by Heublein's marketing management, and it appeared that the most likely targets for advertising were young affluent adults to whom gaiety and modernity were important. An advertising campaign was developed that effectively conveyed the desired appeals, and Smirnoff sales began to skyrocket.

While developing its advertising campaigns, Heublein had been equally attentive to the need for acquiring and retaining widespread distribution in the nation's liquor stores, and to the development of posters and other point-of-sale devices to evoke the attention and interest of in-store customers.

[6] The manufacture of vodka, unlike other alcoholic beverages, is essentially an uncomplicated and rapid process. Aging, for example, is not required, and tastelessness is easily achieved.

The price of Smirnoff was also an important consideration, not only as a potential source of advertising dollars, but because it seemed to marketing management that a high price would stamp Smirnoff as a quality vodka. The quality image would, in turn, appeal to the kinds of people whom Heublein considered to be the most likely source of vodka sales and take advantage of evident upward national trends in incomes and discretionary spending. So convinced was Heublein that high price was an integral part of its successful marketing strategy for Smirnoff that at one point it raised Smirnoff's case price by one dollar in response to a competitor's price cut—thereby enhancing Smirnoff's image and, of course, increasing the profits available both to itself and to its channels of distribution.

Heublein's Smirnoff program is a major success story in marketing. In 1971, Smirnoff is both the number-one brand of vodka and the number-two brand among all liquors (beer excluded). The success of Smirnoff was brought about by marketing management's ability to see and understand trends in the consuming public and to take advantage of their opportunities.

□ HEAD SKI COMPANY

By the late 1960s, probably every skier and would-be skier in the United States had seen or heard of the black metal Head ski. "Heads," as they are called by skiers, had become for most people both the epitome of quality and the hallmark of social acceptance on the ski slopes.

A dozen years earlier, metal skis were little used and regarded as unsafe and inferior in performance. The change, which resulted in the sale of over 130,000 pairs of Head skis in 1968, compared with fewer than 8,000 pairs 12 years before, is a tribute to the vision and marketing acumen of Howard Head, founder of the Head Ski Company.

Mr. Head was the man responsible for the development of the first successful metal ski. An aircraft engineer and devoted ski enthusiast, he became convinced that it was possible to make metal skis which would represent the ultimate in skiing pleasure and performance. He spent years developing, testing, and perfecting a metal ski, and put the first ones on the market in the early 1950s. Mr. Head's main emphasis was on quality, and he believed that performance and durability would more than offset price advantages that might be enjoyed by competitive skis.

For that reason, Head skis were priced from the outset at around $100 per pair. Wooden skis, which typically sold at considerably below $100 and sometimes well below $50, were regarded as so different as to appeal to an entirely different type of customer. Fiberglas skis, though more expensive than wooden skis for the most part, were typically sold in price ranges below the Head skis. The Head metal ski, then, was priced to reflect its quality, reliability, and performance, and Howard Head assumed that skiers would be willing to pay premium prices for Head skis. In passing, it should be noted that Mr. Head's assumption was *not* based on the kind of research data available to Heublein in our previous example, but stemmed from his own personal assessment of the factors that were important to many buyers of skis.

The high-priced line of Head skis came to the market at precisely the right time. The leisure-time market was growing rapidly in the 1950s and 1960s, and skiing was one of the most dynamic segments of that market. The ski industry trade association estimated, for example, that expenditures related to skiing grew from $280 million in 1960 to $750 million in 1966–1967, and would be over $1 billion by 1970. The skiing public was expected to grow from about 1.5 million persons in 1960 to about 5 million by the 1970s. It also seemed clear that skiers were, for the most part, people of at least moderate incomes. In 1965, *The New York Times* said that the United States skier had a median age of 26.2 years and a median family income of $11,125, and that two-thirds of all skiers were college graduates. A high-priced, high-quality ski was therefore not too extravagant a purchase for customers with rising incomes in an expanding leisure-time market, particularly when the brand of the ski connoted a degree of social acceptance and importance.

The company worked hard to ensure both the quality and what can be termed the "social image" of its line of skis. It is worthwhile to spend a few moments in considering the mix of Head's marketing policies for its line of skis.

Product Every effort was made to ensure that each ski was of top quality; to this end, much of the production work done in the Head factory was handwork and subjected to exhaustive inspection and testing. Continuous research was undertaken on product improvement so that the company's line would continue to be a quality leader. As a further part of its product policy, Head's management strove to develop a line that would meet the needs of various kinds of skiers, ranging from the beginner to the expert racer, as well as the technical needs of various kinds of skiing such as downhill, slalom, and giant slalom.

Price All Head skis were priced at the high end of the price range for skis, ranging by 1968 from $115 to $175. Price promotions were not a part of the company's marketing strategy.

Promotion and advertising The company spent about 2 percent of gross sales on advertising, dividing its effort between skiing magazines and such publications as *The New Yorker, Yachting,* and *Sports Illustrated.* A "soft-sell" approach was used in advertising, and although not using personal endorsements, news pictures of famous skiers using Head skis were employed when possible. Posters featuring Head equipment were used in the shops that carried the Head line in order to catch the attention of people browsing or buying. Though the company did not believe in price promotions to ultimate customers, it lent skis to well-known skiers and gave discounts to ski area shops engaged in the ski-rental business.

Channels of distribution The company's insistence on quality applied to its choice of retail outlets. By the late 1960s Head's marketing organization had succeeded in building a network of 900 carefully selected dealers, of which 85 percent were specialty ski shops, 12 percent were full-line sporting goods stores, and the remainder department stores. Each dealer was franchised, and had to convince the Head company that his personnel knew a lot about skiing and skis. Howard Head believed that only good skiers had the potential to become good ski salesmen, and the company tried to put this philosophy into practice in selecting and working with its retail accounts.

Personal selling Head used its own salesmen to reach the 900 ski retail outlets. The company sought to employ salesmen who were knowledgeable about skis and skiing, interested in working with retail accounts on a continuing low-pressure basis, and willing to put in the time necessary to make the company's extensive service program effective.

Service An essential part of Head's marketing strategy was a service program thought by management to be better than those offered by competitors. The company assisted its dealers in maintaining facilities for minor ski repairs, and the Head factory in Maryland was geared for sharpening edges, rebuilding broken skis, and matching a single ski if its mate had been irreparably broken. Management worked hard to make sure that service time was kept at or below three weeks, even in the busiest part of the ski season.

THE INGREDIENTS OF SUCCESSFUL MARKETING

It is worthwhile to pause and think back over the three examples of successful marketing management activity just described. The three companies were different in many respects: size, product type and line, and number and kind of customers reached, for example. But each company was highly successful. Why?

Three broad themes seem to underlie each success story. In each case, there was an *opportunity* in the marketplace: a consumer want or need was being met either imperfectly or not at all. Each company, using research information, experience, or "feel" (luck sometimes plays a part), moved to meet the need by developing a clear notion as to what *kinds of people* it wanted to interest in its product and how. Finally, each marketing effort was implemented through a *program* of specific policies and operating activities. In each of these programs, the individual elements, such as pricing and advertising, in the Heublein example, were consistent with each other, and thus added up to an effective *total* marketing approach. In essence, the totality of each program made a sum greater than its parts.

Note, too, that timing played a key role in each case. Mr. Head's concept of a high-quality metal ski was "right" in the 1960s. But there may have been unsung champions of the same idea earlier, who were simply ahead of their times. (Can you think of some other illustrations of the importance of timing?)

It should be emphasized that these observations on "how to succeed" are generalizations, expressed in terms appropriately broad for an introductory chapter. The concepts and methods used by organizations to identify market opportunities and develop marketing programs will be dealt with in subsequent chapters. To obtain an insight into these areas, let us consider some other ways of thinking about marketing.

The framework of marketing

The United States and most other Western nations are basically free-market economies. In a free-market system, people are free to purchase whatever goods and services they wish within the limits of their purchasing power (after paying their taxes), and they are free to refrain from purchasing if they wish. Similarly, business firms are free to offer in the marketplace, in competition with one another, whatever goods and services they wish. These freedoms are made available to the business community and the consuming public by the society of which both are a part, subject only to the laws that society itself has seen fit to pass to regulate the actions of its members.

In a free-market economy, it can be said that a business has a number of responsibilities[7]:

To serve the buying public by offering goods or services that provide satisfaction for the public's needs and desires

To serve those members of the buying public who choose to become its customers by ensuring that its goods and services meet fairly the representations made about them

To serve its owners by providing a return on the capital that they have invested

To serve its employees by providing them with satisfactory working conditions and adequate compensation

To serve society as a whole by efficiently and effectively carrying out the responsibilities to the specific groups cited, and by doing so in ways that meet the legal requirements and social policies of the society or societies in which the company operates

A look at these responsibilities clearly indicates that over time none can be effectively discharged if the firm cannot market its goods or services.

[7] Some might prefer to use "opportunities" or "privileges" in place of the word "responsibilities."

It follows, then, that a prime task of every business is to get and keep *customers*. It is the customers who decide the fate of every business. Will they buy the product or service offered? Will they buy it at the price asked? Will they buy it in the places where it is available: hardware stores versus dime stores versus grocery stores versus drugstores; or New England or the Deep South or the Midwest? Will they buy it in the package it comes in and the size that is offered? Will the advertising appeals used convince them to buy? Will they buy it from the particular salesman who calls on them? Will they pay cash or prefer credit? Will they buy it if it cannot be delivered in less than three weeks? Will they buy it if the family next door has one? Will they buy it again and again?

The list of possible questions regarding the attitudes and actions of potential customers might be stretched out endlessly, and the answers would vary from product to product, from service to service. But one thing is sure: the answers depend on far more than the quality of the product or service itself. The potential success of a product depends on much more than what laboratory tests indicate about it, or on what potential users may *say*. The issue is resolved, finally, by what potential users *do*. And what they do may vary from one time to another and from one place to the next.

□

CUSTOMERS AND COMPETITORS

Getting and keeping customers depends on whether a company does the right thing in terms of what customers think, value, and do; and it depends on what the competition does. Assume the case of an industry where competing products are identical, such as basic chemicals. Why should a prospect want to buy particularly from this company rather than from a competitor? If the quality, prices, delivery, credit arrangements, and technical services are identical to his, the customer might just as well prefer the supplier who offers the best free lunch or the biggest Christmas turkey. To avoid lowering its prices and to make a customer want to deal with this company in preference to another, it must offer him tangible benefits which he values but cannot get elsewhere. To do that, the company must make a greater effort to find out what he really wants and values in addition to the quality, price, and technical service that it now offers him. The company's entire operation must be oriented toward discovering the customer's *total* needs and problems and toward attempting to satisfy them, even if it means going beyond the company's present range of abilities and interests.

An illustration of what this kind of thoroughgoing customer orientation really involves can be seen in what was done by one chemical company selling to the fertilizer industry. Note that our three "success stories," described earlier, all dealt with products sold to individuals or families. This example shows that the same basic ideas apply equally to products bought by industry.

Marketing chemicals to the fertilizer industry There are numerous fertilizer companies all over the country. Most of them are small and serve about a 15- to 20-county area. Few make their own raw materials or ingredients. They buy these in bulk from big chemical manufacturers, mix them in the right proportions, and then package and sell them as ready-to-use fertilizers to farm supply stores, nurseries, and farmers' cooperative buying organizations.

The fertilizer companies buy their ingredients—raw potash, phosphate rock, and superphosphates—from a handful of big bulk chemical companies. Raw material prices charged by the suppliers tend to be identical. The range and quality of their technical services to fertilizer companies are about the same.

In the late 1950s, A. E. Cascino, marketing vice-president of one of these suppliers, International Minerals and Chemical Corporation, wondered how he could successfully get and keep more fertilizer companies as customers. He decided that he would have to offer prospective customers some solid reasons for dealing with his company, reasons that his competitors could not duplicate very quickly. But what was a solid reason? He decided to find out by commissioning a nationwide study of the problems of fertilizer companies. The research firm he hired was told to study everything, not just production or packaging problems. After several months of interviews with fertilizer companies, the answers came. The biggest problems fertilizer companies seemed to have were estimating potential county-by-county sales in their areas; determining how good a credit risk a customer was and how to get customers to pay their bills on time; hiring, training, motivating, and paying salesmen; training and motivating retailers who sold their products; determining efficient shipping routes and freight costs; in-transit breakage and insurance; and advertising and sales promotion.

After considering these findings, International established within its own company a management consulting organization which was made available gratis to its customers, to help them with their management problems. In addition, it developed an easy-to-use self-help manual from which its customers could find solutions for some of their problems. Furthermore, it carefully trained its salesmen to explain and promote the company's new services.

The result was that the nation's many small fertilizer companies were given a solid reason for wanting and preferring to do business with this particular supplier, and sales promptly soared.

Now the critical question is this: What is the "product" which International was selling? To say that it is just phosphates and other raw materials is not correct. Those are its generic product line. But what made the company so successful was not its generic product. What really mattered was the whole *cluster* of benefits offered, of which the generic product was only one. Even if competitive suppliers had lowered their prices by a reasonable amount, they would probably not have substantially cut into International's sales because International offered an entirely different product from that of its competitors.

The result of International's brilliant innovation was this: instead of the company's having to go out and chase customers, the customers turned around and, in effect, chased International. It was offering a cluster of value satisfactions they wanted. They wanted to do business with International, not because its prices were lower, not because its quality was better, not because its salesmen were nicer, but because it offered a product its competitors were not offering. And International did all this because it deliberately set out to discover what the total needs and major problems of its potential customers really were. When it found out, it did not say, "That's too bad. Management consulting isn't our business; we know nothing about it." Instead it said, "Let's do what we have to do to help these people, because if we do, we will help ourselves."

THE DIFFERENCE BETWEEN SELLING AND MARKETING

What International Minerals and Chemical did is a perfect illustration of the profound difference between *selling* and *marketing*. Had International merely continued to have salemen periodically call on fertilizer plants and try to get business by being especially friendly with prospects, giving them expensive Christmas gifts, and generally trying to do a better job on the same kind of things its competitors were doing, this would have been referred to as "doing a good selling job"—trying to get the customer to buy its product.

But International did much more. Instead of merely trying by various devices to get the customer to buy what International had (potash, phosphate rock, superphosphates), International reversed the procedure and tried to have what the customer wanted, even though customers had not really been aware that they wanted or needed the services that were finally provided, and had no notion that a present supplier could be a source of these services.

Selling is generally concerned with the plans and tactics of trying to get the consumer to exchange what he has (money) for what you have (goods or services). In some extreme situations it boils down to little more than trying to separate the unwary consumer from his loose change.

Marketing is primarily concerned with the much more sophisticated strategy of trying to *have* what the consumer wants. Selling focuses on the needs of the seller, marketing on the needs of the buyer. Selling is preoccupied with the seller's need to convert his product into cash; marketing with the idea of satisfying the needs of the customer by means of the product as well as the whole cluster of customer value satisfactions associated with creating, delivering, and finally consuming the product.

A truly marketing-minded firm tries to create value-satisfying goods and services that customers will want to buy. What it provides includes not only the generic product or service, but also how the product or service is made available to the customer (mail order, types of stores, delivery), in what form (frozen, six-pack, size of package, colored or plain, bucket-seat options or not), when (seasonally, immediate delivery, or delivery next week), under what conditions (rain or shine, written order, or telephone order), and at what terms of trade (cash, credit, 30 days to pay, 2 percent discount for quick payment). Most important, what a genuinely marketing-minded firm offers for sale is determined less by the seller than by the buyer. The seller takes his cue from the buyer in such a way that the product becomes a consequence of the total marketing effort, and not vice versa.

The marketing concept and the marketing mix

The United States has become a "consumption economy," where once it was a production economy. That is a way of saying that while the energy and thought of the business community were once devoted to developing and improving ways of manufacturing products, we now take for granted our ability to manufacture and our skill at improving the manufacturing process; the emphasis has shifted to a marketing orientation, and energy and thought start with the customer.

This change has given rise to what is known as the *marketing concept.* The marketing concept has been defined "as a way of life in which all resources of an organization are mobilized to create, stimulate, and satisfy the customer at a profit."[8] The General Electric Company is generally regarded as having pioneered the marketing concept in industry after World War II. The company tried to make the concept explicit throughout its various product-market activities by defining the concept as a way of integrating the plans and actions of management toward the profitable marketing of products to the company's customers. Management's key responsibility under the marketing concept becomes one of (1) determining the nature and extent of changes in the company's various markets, (2) identifying and cultivating customers for the company's existing or potential products, (3) so planning the use of existing or to-be-secured resources that customer needs and wants are satisfactorily met, and (4) carrying out its marketing and related activities in such a fashion as to maintain the company in a profitable position.[9]

The marketing concept, then, applies to the totality of a company's effort. It becomes operational for marketing management through the development of specific objectives and the marketing programs necessary to achieve those objectives. It is meaningful to think about objectives and their implementing programs as the *marketing mix.* The words imply a mingling of factors, or to use a more formal notion, a systems approach. That is what the marketing mix is (or

[8] Edward J. Green, "The Concept of Marketing Planning," *Handbook of Modern Marketing,* McGraw-Hill Book Company, New York, 1970, p. 7-3.
[9] Adapted from a speech made by J. Stanford Smith, vice-president, Marketing and Public Relations, Nov. 12, 1964.

should be) — a system of interrelated and interdependent marketing activities designed to meet customer desires and company objectives.

Many different versions of the marketing mix have been offered by businessmen and marketing authorities.[10] One view, which might be considered traditional, puts forth the mix in a convenient, easily remembered literary shorthand known as the "4 Ps":

Product Making sure that the product (or service) is the right one, for a specific group of customers, in terms of quality, other operating and physical characteristics, packaging, brand, and relationship to other items in the company's line.

Price Establishing a price that makes the product as attractive as possible to customers and channels of distribution, while observing whatever legal restrictions may apply, and yielding a satisfactory profit.

Promotion Communicating to customers or potential customers whatever it is that marketing management has decided can effectively be said about a product. Promotion consists, in brief, of communicating through advertising, through the efforts of company salesmen, via catalogs and exhibits, and through various types of messages located at point of sale.

Place Putting the product where it can be most effectively available to customers is another key marketing task. The American economy, like that of most industrial nations, has available a variety of channels of distribution at both the intermediate (wholesale) and ultimate (retail store) levels. The proper choice of channels of distribution can make or break a company's product line.

Though the 4 Ps are often viewed as comprising the marketing mix, we believe it desirable to round out the latter by including two additional factors which, though perhaps obvious, are nonetheless important. We shall call them the "2 Cs":

Customers Central, of course, to the design of a mix that operates effectively is knowledge about a company's customers and consumers. Who are they? Where are they? How many are there, and might there be? What are their needs and wants? What changes are taking place? The more accurately marketing management answers these and related questions, the more likely its marketing policies are to succeed. Marketing information, from research or from company salesmen or from other sources, is indispensable to the long-run market acceptance of any good or service.

[10] See James W. Culliton, "The Concept of the Marketing Mix," *Handbook of Modern Marketing*, McGraw-Hill Book Company, New York, 1970, pp. 11-3 to 11-12, for a detailed discussion.

Costs All the aspects of a marketing program must be tied together in a framework of costs that permits the company to secure a profit on the good or service that it offers. Costs may include both those which are incurred directly because of the manufacture and marketing of the product and those which are allocated to it, such as administrative or manufacturing overhead. As a general rule, one can say that any product or service must have a price-cost relationship that yields a profit unless the product or service is deemed essential to the profitable sale of other goods or services in the company's product line, or unless it is subsidized by society because it is deemed essential for other reasons.

The marketing concept, then, views marketing as something more than a business function. It is, rather, a view of the entire business process. It affects everything a company does, how it is organized, how it allocates its money to such areas as manufacturing or scientific research and development, the number and operation of its warehouses, the delivery fleet, the advertising, the accounting department, and so forth. Thus, if the big, powerful Hollywood movie companies had had a realistic marketing view of their business in the 1950s, they would now be in a different financial shape. Television destroyed most of them because they consistently ignored it when it first started to attract wide interest in 1947 and 1948. The motion picture companies believed that they were in the *movie* business rather than the *entertainment* business. They were organized and operated to produce a specific kind of product: full-length movies. They were not organized and operated to think in terms of the entertainment and convenience preferences of their customers. They were product-oriented, not customer-oriented. Instead of looking carefully out the window at their customers, they looked narcissistically into the mirror at themselves, at their own needs and their investments in huge sound stages, in big-time writers, directors, and producers, and in costly big-name stars. They produced what their needs dictated, not what customers preferred.

As a result, a whole new breed of entertainment entrepreneurs emerged to give the customer what he wanted—entertainment through television—and the powerful old motion picture companies (United Artists, Twentieth Century Fox, Paramount, Metro-Goldwyn-Mayer) found that dominance shifted to, or was shared with, entirely new companies such as Desilu, Revue, Four Star, and MCA. Those movie companies which did survive were forced into drastic and costly reorganizations.

Marketing: a definition

□ *Marketing involves those business activities which are concerned with (1) identifying and stimulating demand for a company's goods or services, (2) meeting that demand by making available the goods or services in the most effective manner, and (3) achieving the profit and other objectives related to the identification, stimulation, and satisfaction of demand.**

Our definition of marketing□* goes somewhat beyond the American Marketing Association's: *the performance of business activities that direct the flow of goods and services from producer to consumer or user.*[11] The important differences are that the definition suggested here emphasizes the role that marketing managers play in identifying and stimulating demand and makes explicit the need for marketing managers to achieve profit and other objectives. Though these factors can be tacitly assumed in the Association's definition, we believe it important to be specific about them in a book that is concerned with the totality of marketing management functions.

There are, additionally, other ways of defining marketing. Legally, it is the process by which changes are effected in the ownership and possession of goods and services; this concept, however, takes too legalistic an approach to "what is essentially a commercial subject."[12]

We might have suggested a definition more closely related to the discipline of economics by describing marketing either as the creation of time, place, and possession utilities or as the sector of business activity that deals with the exchange of goods and services for considerations of value.

The alternative definitions, to be sure, are useful descriptions of marketing from specialized standpoints. But our concern is with what marketing is from the viewpoint of a manager. We hope that our definition, together with the examples and discussions in earlier portions of the chapter, has begun to give the reader a feeling for marketing and for the breadth and significance of the areas covered in the rest of this book. By grasping the substance of the field and wrestling with its diversity and complexity, the excitement and challenge that marketing offers the manager can be sensed. Before moving ahead, however, a final point needs to be made regarding the perspective from which marketing activities are viewed.

□

MARKETING IS NOT CONFINED TO BUSINESS FIRMS

Although this book is concerned almost exclusively with the marketing management activities of business firms, it should be recognized that marketing is an activity that is important in the affairs of many other kinds of organizations. Kotler and Levy point out that such disparate organizations as the United Auto Workers, the U.S. Department of Defense, the Ford Foundation, and the Catholic Church have marketing problems.[13] Thus, when union leaders are deciding on a package of benefits for negotiation, they must make sure that in-

* In this and future chapters, important definitions and concepts appear in the margin and are indicated in the text by an open-box superior symbol.

[11] Committee on Definitions, American Marketing Association, *Marketing Definitions,* American Marketing Association, Chicago, 1963, p. 15.

[12] *Ibid.,* p. 15.

[13] Philip Kotler and Sidney Levy, "Broadening the Concept of Marketing," *Journal of Marketing,* vol. 33, no. 1, American Marketing Association, Chicago, January, 1969, pp. 10–15.

sofar as possible those benefits meet the wishes of union members—who are the "customers" in our context. Later, when the package of benefits has been publicized and is in the negotiation stage, union management has a continuing "selling" job to make sure that the membership retains its commitment to the union's objective. Kotler and Levy cite an example from the field of education, in which the public school system of Oklahoma City, in an attempt to secure greater public support, used television to make the public more familiar with its work in such fields as new teaching techniques and the high school dropout problem.[14] In this context, marketing in *any* organization is the activity "that can keep in constant touch with the organization's consumers, read their needs, and build a program of communications to express the organization's purposes."[15]

Questions

1. Thinking of the examples presented in the chapter, define marketing in your own words.

2. Compare and contrast the approaches followed by Ford, Heublein, and Head with that followed by the Woodstream Company in marketing its "better" mousetrap. What are the significant differences in their approaches? Could the mousetrap's failure have been avoided? How?

3. Name some industries or companies whose fate and prosperity have been seriously undermined by changes in customer preferences and behavior patterns. Can you suggest how each might have avoided its plight?

4. Can you think of some companies that use different marketing strategies for products that are quite similar? What are the reasons for the differing strategies?

5. Heublein, Inc. acquired a large regional brewery in the mid 1960s. Do you think that the Smirnoff marketing skills can be transferred to beer and ale? Would you predict any problems? Head Ski Company has gone into the manufacture and sale of clothing for skiers. Will Head have to develop any new marketing skills to be successful with ski clothing?

6. While metal skis, especially "Heads," dominated the high-price segment of the market during most of the 1960s, by 1970 the dominance of metal skis was being seriously challenged by high-price Fiberglas skis. Why do you think this change was taking place? What action would you suggest to the Head company?

7. How would you expect the importance of each of the "4 Ps" to differ for the following products? Why?

[14] *Ibid.*, p. 11. [15] *Ibid.*, p. 15.

a. Furniture
b. Automobiles
c. Greeting cards
d. Headache remedies
e. Prescription drugs
f. Plate glass
g. Cans for beer and soft drinks

8. Do you agree with the statement that the United States is a "marketing economy" rather than a "production economy"?

9. At the end of the chapter, it was pointed out that business firms are not the only organizations that have marketing problems. Consider some of the organizations of which you are a member—what marketing problems do they have, and how would you solve them if you were asked to do so?

10. For many years, Pan American World Airways held air supremacy in international travel. In 1970, however, along with many other airlines, Pan Am incurred substantial losses. For Pan Am, these losses exceeded $48 million dollars.

Subsequently, the company realigned its marketing approach along "product manager" lines and formed a new marketing development group. An *Advertising Age* article in early 1971, based on an interview with Pan Am's vice-president for marketing development, Mr. Dan A. Colussy, described some of these changes as follows:

> The whole attempt is to localize problems and get them solved quickly before they spread. Beyond getting into a "product manager" concept, the carrier is counting on "product innovations" to ring up passenger sales. "We have a whole stable of product innovations ready and we'll be releasing them at a rate of about one a month," said Mr. Colussy.
>
> The product innovation pitch originally got started at Pan Am last fall with the introduction of Pan Am tours on tape, a series of pre-recorded tapes for travelers to play while they tour. Since then the carrier has introduced a weather-proof vacation plan, offering travelers insurance against rained-out vacations, and a homes-exchange service plan that allows European-bound travelers a chance to swap their homes with U.S.-bound European travelers during their respective vacations.
>
> "It's hard to be different and you really can't be that different," said Mr. Colussy of the Pan Am product innovation approach. "You have to focus on things that add up to give consumers more service for their money. Some are big and some are small but they're all aimed at setting us apart from the competition," he added.
>
> Destination advertising will be getting "more attention" this year, said the Pan Am exec, who added that the carrier will also continue its program of restating Pan Am's leadership role. The carrier bills itself as "the world's most experienced airline."
>
> . . . The principal problems facing the airline industry are seen by Pan Am's Mr. Colussy as "environmental problems beyond the control of management." The problems include, he said, "overcapacity situations" and the "proliferation of foreign-based carriers," a fact of life that has given the international United States carriers some hard competition on foreign routes.[16]

Outside observers differed in their view of the plight of the airlines. The purchase of new equipment, particularly large passenger jets such as Boeing 747s, had undoubtedly brought on a severe drain of airline capital. Ironically, the resulting increase in airline seat capacity coincided with a decline in business travel brought on by the depressed economic conditions of 1970 and 1971. In the opinion of many observers, the airlines were powerless to stimulate business travel as long as economic conditions remained depressed.

Some commentators felt, nonetheless, that airlines *could* take steps to encourage air travel. Typical was the following statement encouraging greater use of marketing communications:

> Being on the map is what airlines need these days. And that means marketing, a business skill that package-goods manufacturers have been employing for decades but that has been sought by airlines only in recent years.
>
> After all, it wasn't until most of the technical problems were ironed out and enough seats were available that the need for marketing arose. It is here now, though, and the marketing mix of most carriers includes media advertising (to consumers, to travel agents and to employees), direct mail, salesmen (who call on major corporate customers and travel agents), and product publicity.[17]

The latter viewpoint was a contentious one for, it was argued, an airline had very little to say about itself that was truly distinctive. All operated similar equipment, showed movies on long flights, served meals that differed very little from one airline to the next, or were in the process of rearranging seat configurations to give greater passenger comfort. None of these efforts, it was alleged, resulted in appreciably unique benefits to the consumer. They did little to change the essential character of air travel.

a. Why do you think airlines such as Pan Am incurred large losses in 1970–1971?

b. How would you appraise the action being taken by Pan Am to build sales and generate profits?

c. Evaluate the different views of outside observers on the plight of the airlines.

d. Do you think it is possible for Pan Am to expand business travel? How?

e. Based on the information presented above and any of your own observations, do you believe Pan Am and other airlines are production-oriented or market-oriented? Why? What should "marketing" mean in the airline industry?

[16] "Airlines Fight to Avoid Stalling in Economic Downdraft," *Advertising Age*, March 29, 1971, pp. 1,102.

[17] "Ad Agency Seeks to Improve Pan Am's Marketing," *The New York Times*, Nov. 8, 1970, Financial Section, p. 13.

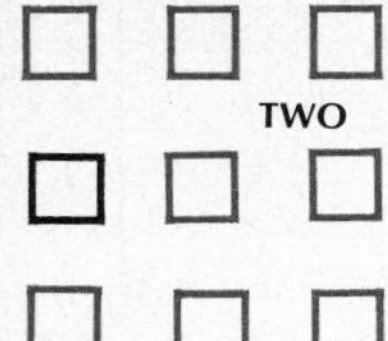

The marketing system

In Chapter 1, we have shown what marketing management involves and how important marketing decisions are to the business firm. To view these decisions in perspective, we must bear in mind that the firm is affected by the decisions of other businesses and by the customers with whom it deals. A manufacturer of electrical appliances, faced with a price increase by his raw materials suppliers, may be tempted to revise his own price schedules. But some wholesalers and retailers may drop the appliance line if prices are raised; customers may buy competing brands, or none at all; and government legislation may limit freedom to change prices. "No firm is an island" – it is only part of a total network of *interdependent* business firms, other institutions, and customers which combine to perform marketing functions in the economy.

MARKETING AS A SYSTEM

The network which performs marketing functions is commonly referred to as a "system," that is, an assemblage of interacting elements which affect and are affected by each other. The marketing system is one of many systems in a society. Political, monetary, and judicial systems, for example, each service other needs of a society.

The problems faced by a marketing executive are largely determined by the functioning of the total marketing system. Conversely, the actions of the numerous decision makers in the system, taken collectively, determine how the system performs. This two-way relationship between individual business firms and the total marketing system imposes a dual responsibility on the marketing executive. He must first understand his job within a company so that he recognizes its problems and deals with them effectively. In order to do this, he must *also* know enough about the marketing system and its functioning to see how it shapes and limits his task.

As background for the more detailed treatment of marketing activities and institutions in subsequent chapters, a brief overview of the marketing system is presented in this chapter. The discussion is confined primarily to the contemporary marketing system of the United States. But it should be emphasized that marketing institutions and activities are not just American idiosyncrasies. Every nation—advanced or underdeveloped, democratic or totalitarian, large or small—has a marketing system. The basic functions performed by the system are the same in *all* societies as we will see later in this chapter.

FUNCTIONS OF THE MARKETING SYSTEM

It is sometimes said that marketing is a process of *double search*. On one hand, customers are searching for goods and services to satisfy their needs. At the same time, suppliers are looking for customers. The marketing system is designed to ensure that customers and suppliers "find each other." Stated in more precise terms, the system must make goods and services available to customers in the right places, at the right times, and in the desired forms. It sounds like an elementary assignment. But the tasks or *functions* that must be performed to achieve these ends are very complex.

There are many variations in marketing functions, depending on the type of products, services, and customers involved as well as on the economic and social environment in which the tasks must be carried out. But irrespective of specific circumstances, certain basic functions must be performed, including:

1. The adjustment of supply to demand
2. The process of exchange
3. The physical distribution
4. The transmittal of market-related information

Perhaps the best way to explain these basic functions is through a specific (hypothetical) example set in our contemporary American system. The Creswell Corporation is a manufacturer of toys. What must be done to market these toys? In the first place, the manufacturer must somehow determine what kinds of toys to produce, when to produce them, and what quantities to produce. The company's survival depends on how effectively these decisions are made, since its products must be sold to customers in relatively free and open competition with those of other producers. All raw material producers, manufacturers, and processors must make similar decisions. In this way, the system as a whole performs the function of *adjusting the production of goods and services to the needs of customers*. As Adam Smith noted long ago, "consumption is the sole end and purpose of all production."[1] A basic function of the marketing system is to permit production to be directed to its purpose, that is, to adjust to demand.

The Creswell Corporation cannot, in all likelihood, sell its products directly to ultimate or household consumers. Some raw material producers and manufacturers do sell "direct" by mail, through door-to-door salesmen, or through their own retail stores, but usually large-scale direct selling is not feasible. Consequently, appropriate retail outlets—toy stores, department stores, variety stores, etc.—must be identified and induced to handle the products. If a large number of outlets is desired, it may also be necessary to use one or more kinds of wholesale outlets. If so, then the Creswell Corporation may employ salesmen to solicit business both from larger retailers and from wholesale outlets who, in turn, sell to retailers. The wholesale and the retail outlets, as well as the consumers who purchase the toys, must buy the products. This involves selection of specific items from those available, negotiation, determination of purchase quantities and timing, and so forth. These basic functions of selling and buying are referred to as the *process of exchange*. They are present in the marketing of any product or service.

Besides exchanging title to products, the marketing system must perform tasks necessary for their *physical distribution*. The Creswell Corporation's toys must be transported from factories to consumers' homes, with intermediate stops at warehouses and retail stores. Similarly, since the timing of production and of demand does not coincide exactly, especially in the light of the heavy demand at Christmas, the toys must be stored until needed. In connection with physical distribution, the toys must also be packaged to prevent damage and to facilitate efficient handling.

Still another important task of the marketing system is that of *transmitting market-related information*. The manufacturer must inform retailers and wholesalers of the products available, their prices, and terms of sale, perhaps through catalogs and trade shows in addition to the solicitation of salesmen. Consumers must also be informed, through advertising, display, and personal selling in retail stores. Finally, information must flow in the other direction: there must be "feedback" so that manufacturers, wholesalers, and retailers can learn what to produce, buy, and display.

Thus, we come full circle in this illustration of the functions performed by the marketing system. Even this simple illustration should make it clear that the job of the marketing system—covering, as it does, thousands of different kinds

[1] Adam Smith, *The Wealth of Nations*, Edwin Cannan (ed.), Modern Library, Inc., New York, 1937, p. 625.

of products and services, and serving a widely dispersed and heterogeneous market—is truly an immense undertaking. The elements involved in the system, and the relationships among them, are varied and complex.

□

ELEMENTS OF THE MARKETING SYSTEM

Just what makes up the marketing system? Like so many other commonly used words, *system* is hard to define precisely.□ Elements comprising the system include:

□ *A marketing system refers to the network of elements which, acting together, perform the marketing functions of an economy.*

1. Business institutions engaged in the performance of marketing functions, and the customers they serve. Because these institutions possess the capacity to make decisions and to initiate action affecting one another, they are designated as *active elements*.
2. *Flows* of products, information, and money between different business institutions, and between business institutions and customers.

The major components of the marketing system are depicted in Figure 2-1. The system's active elements—business institutions and their customers—are represented by blocks in this figure. Raw materials producers, manufacturers and processors, service industries, wholesale intermediaries, retail stores, and service establishments are all active elements in the system. So too are their customers, be they households, government, professional, and institutional users, or other business firms.

Marketing system flows can be thought of as similar to the electrons that flow among various components of an electronic circuit. The three classes of flow elements—product, information, and money—are also depicted in Figure 2-1.

The performance of the marketing system is affected by some institutions which are not part of the system itself. For example, federal, state, and municipal governments regulate competition and trade practices. Government fiscal and monetary policies may affect business firms' cash flows and decisions on capital expenditures. The attitudes and practices of financial institutions such as banks may be determining influences in decisions made by business institutions and customers within the system. These *influencing institutions* are not engaged directly in the performance of marketing functions, and are not formally part of the marketing system. But they are important environmental influences to which the marketing system must continually react and adapt.

Business institutions and customers

The major categories of institutions in the contemporary American marketing system are also found in other highly developed economies. Each type of institution *specializes* in different kinds of activities. To illustrate how specialized types of businesses enter into the marketing process, consider the steps in the

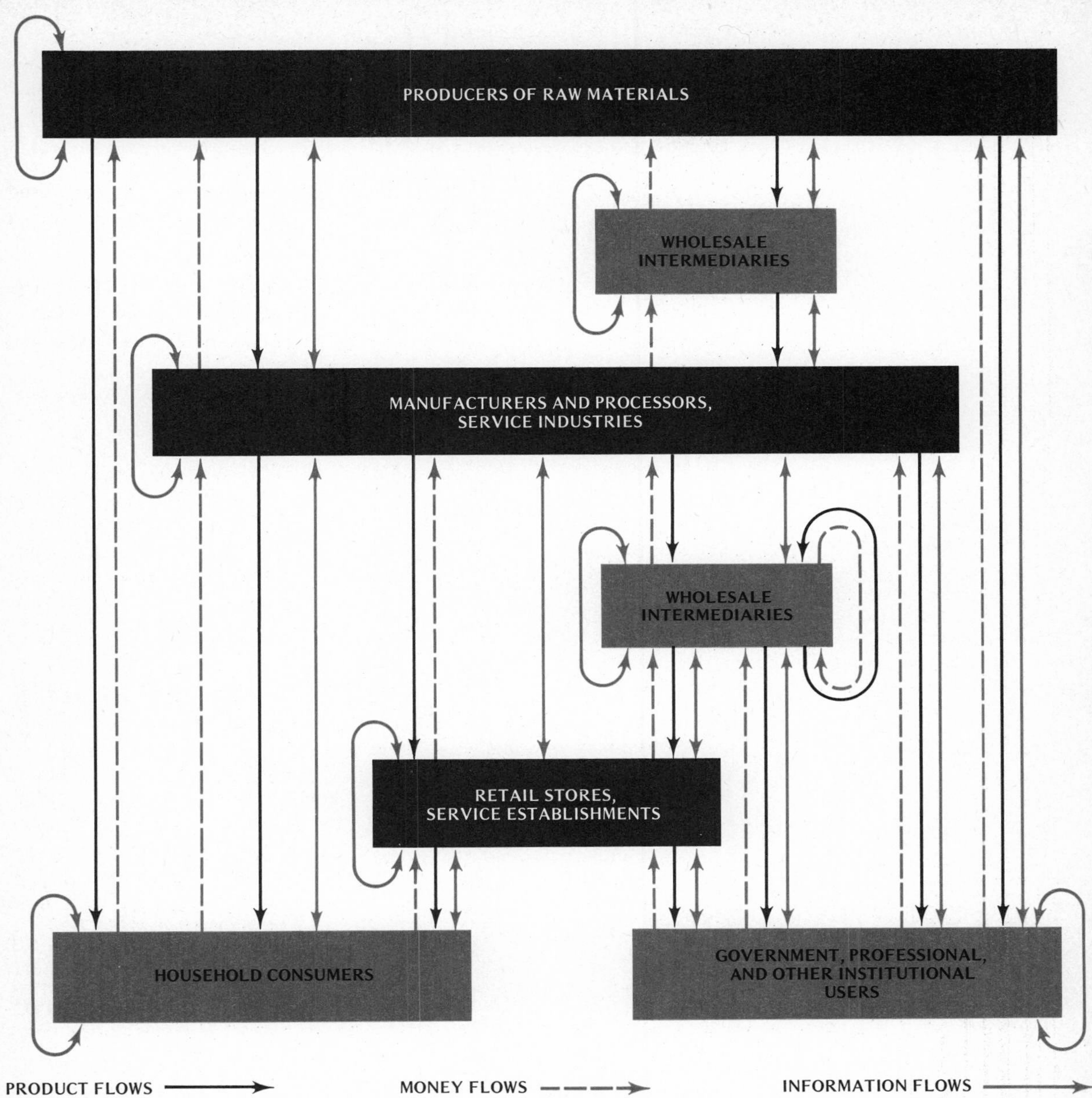
PRODUCERS OF RAW MATERIALS
WHOLESALE INTERMEDIARIES
MANUFACTURERS AND PROCESSORS, SERVICE INDUSTRIES
WHOLESALE INTERMEDIARIES
RETAIL STORES, SERVICE ESTABLISHMENTS
HOUSEHOLD CONSUMERS
GOVERNMENT, PROFESSIONAL, AND OTHER INSTITUTIONAL USERS
PRODUCT FLOWS
MONEY FLOWS
INFORMATION FLOWS

FIGURE 2-1
The marketing system

sequence of production-distribution-consumption for bread. The principal raw material, wheat, is grown by farmers and sold by them, perhaps through cooperative marketing associations, to millers. The millers process the wheat into flour and sell it to baking companies. The latter, in turn, use the flour and other raw and processed materials—such as yeast, packaging materials—to produce bread and other baked goods, which they sell to retail stores. Finally, housewives purchase the bread for their families' consumption. Because bread is a perishable product, it is not feasible to utilize wholesale middlemen in distributing the finished product to retailers. But wholesale intermediaries may participate in the sale of wheat to millers, and in the sale of flour to bakers.

□

MARKETING CHANNELS AND MIDDLEMEN

The businesses involved in the marketing of a product, up to the point at which its form is changed by manufacturing or processing activities or at which it is finally consumed, constitute a marketing channel.□

□ *The marketing channel for a product or service is the course through which title to and control over the product or service pass from original producers to end users. It comprises all the business institutions and individuals who participate in the purchase and/or sale of the product or service, up to the point at which its form is changed or the point at which it is finally consumed. Synonymous terms are channel of distribution, distribution channel, and trade channel.*

To some extent, the marketing channel for a product or service constitutes a *sub*system of the overall marketing system. An executive in a firm is much more affected by, and concerned with, the institutions in his own channel(s) than with others outside it. For example, a marketing executive in a manufacturing firm must select wholesale and retail outlets to handle his firm's products and work with them to develop effective marketing policies. He is also directly concerned with other manufacturers in his channel(s), since they are more or less directly in competition with him. Similarly, an executive in a wholesale or retail firm is affected more by the manufacturers whose products he handles, by wholesale and retail firms handling similar product lines, and by the customers who finally use these products than he is by businesses or customers not included in his marketing channel(s).

A majority of marketing channels include one or more intermediaries or *middlemen*.□ For instance, the owner of a drugstore buys and resells drugs, proprietary medicines, and other items. A distinctly secondary activity (and one of declining importance in the post-World War II years) is that of compounding prescription drugs for customers. In contrast, a tire manufacturer may own and operate warehouses and retail stores, but this activity is subsidiary to the main business of manufacturing.

□ *An intermediary or middleman is an institution or agent that buys and/or sells products and services, but does not process, manufacture, or otherwise change the form of products except as an incidental activity.*

Note that the definitions of marketing channel and middleman stress the flow of *title and control* over goods and services, rather than physical distribution. Although transportation agencies such as trucking firms play a vital role in marketing, they are not included in marketing channels or classified as marketing institutions because in most instances such agencies play a passive role in the marketing process. The institutions involved in exchange, on the other hand, have much greater and more direct control over the process.

Middlemen are further classified as wholesale and retail. *Retail* middlemen are those which sell goods to household customers; thus, drugstores, food stores, and automobile dealers are all retail middlemen. Service establishments selling directly to household customers, such as barbershops, can also be regarded as essentially retail institutions. *Wholesale* middlemen are those which sell to business firms and to institutional customers such as the government. The distinguishing feature of a wholesale transaction is that the goods or services are used by the buyer in the production of other goods and services, or are resold.

□ CUSTOMERS AND MARKETS

The marketing channel for a product or service may be long, including many distinct levels or steps; or it may be short, including only one or a few. In either case, the end result is that goods and services are sold to customers who consume or use them.

Customers may be classified into two groups: ultimate or household consumers□ and business and institutional users.□ For example, when a housewife purchases toothpaste for her family's use, the various members of the family are ultimate consumers. They use the toothpaste to derive certain satisfactions arising from cleanliness, pleasant taste, etc. In contrast, when a bank purchases a bookkeeping machine, it is a business user and employs the machine in the performance of financial services for depositors and borrowers, including household consumers and business firms.

□*Ultimate or household consumers are those who use (consume) products and services in order to enjoy the satisfactions embodied in them.*

□*Business and institutional users are those which utilize goods and services in the conduct of their operations, in order to produce goods or render services to ultimate consumers and/or to other businesses and institutions.*

The various types of customers who purchase a product or service constitute the *markets* for that product or service. Markets may be categorized in several ways on the basis of customer characteristics. For example, manufacturers of electronic components (such as transistors and tubes) make a distinction between the original equipment manufacturers (OEM) market, who buy their products for assembly into such finished products as television sets, and the "replacement" market, consisting of household consumers and business users who purchase the products to replace worn-out parts.

A market is simply a group of customers with certain characteristics. Customers may be grouped in terms of how they use a product or service (original equipment manufacturers versus replacement); location (the United States market versus the Canadian market); type of business (banks versus insurance companies for bookkeeping machines); and in any other ways that seem useful for analysis and decision making. A market can be defined and described both *qualitatively,* in terms of characteristics such as those just cited, and *quantitatively,* in terms of its expected size.

To a great extent, the relative success or failure of a marketing manager depends on how well he knows the markets he serves, and on his capacity to design marketing programs tailored to those markets. Knowledge of a market, as used here, implies some specific requirements. The manager must be able to identify groups of customers who comprise a potential market. He must be able to detect important demographic, economic, psychological, and social influences among these customers. He must also be able to predict and measure the factors having a significant impact on those making up the market.

Sizing up groups of customers in this fashion is commonly referred to as *market analysis*. Some of the more important questions that might be involved in a typical market analysis can be illustrated by an example. A few years ago, Honor Products Company of Cambridge, Massachusetts, developed an inexpensive battery-powered teaching machine. Small and readily portable, the machine enabled its user to learn programmed instructional material on an individual basis, in his own time, at his own pace. The company had no previous experience with teaching machines, and thus was starting almost "from scratch" in planning a marketing program. In this situation, a market analysis might well have been highlighted by questions much like the following:

1. *Does a market exist?* Is there a group of potential customers who need a machine of this kind and would be willing to buy it?
2. *If so, where is the market?* In homes? In schools? Business firms? Among members of professional societies or institutions? (Perhaps there is not one market, but several.)
3. *What are the characteristics of the potential markets?* What is their composition in terms of age, sex, geographic distribution, economic characteristics, educational levels, and so forth? What psychological or social factors significantly affect customer behavior in buying a product of this kind?

□ *Market potential is an estimate of the maximum volume of possible sales opportunities for all sellers of a good or service, during a given future period in a given area.*

Answers to these and similar questions would enable Honor to define its potential market (or markets)□ in qualitative terms. To design effective marketing programs, the company would also find it important to measure the market(s) in quantitative terms. For this purpose, several types of estimates would be useful. The first, and perhaps most basic, type of estimate is that of market potential. Under this estimate, the emphasis is on the *total* sales of *all* firms which compete in a given industry or product class. Thus, the automobile industry may predict that new-car demand will reach 10 million units next year. Similarly, Honor Products might well estimate that total sales in one of its several teaching-machine markets will be x units in a given annual period.

Market potential provides a useful starting point for planning marketing programs, but most companies would want to know much more about the market's expected response to their *own* products in an upcoming time period. In the language of forecasting and sales management, this estimate is defined as a sales forecast.

□ *A sales forecast is an estimate of the sales of a company's products that are expected to be achieved during a given future period in a given area.*

Most companies make some attempt to make sales forecasts□ for their products. In fact, a sales forecast may involve several estimates relating to a given market. These might include estimates of how sales would vary with price, what customer preferences are likely to be in styles of clothing, colors of floor tile, and so forth. Whatever their form or degree of detail, sales forecasts provide the basis for planning a great deal of corporate organizational activity: budgeting, raw material and manpower planning, estimating plant size and equipment needs, planning the nature and size of the physical distribution system, projecting the size and nature of the sales force, product planning and pricing policy, to name but a few.

If we return to our previous example, it is not difficult to see how important a sales forecast would be to Honor Products in planning an introductory program for the teaching machine. In this particular case, depending on how Honor defined its "market" qualitatively, it is possible that the company might be the only firm selling to it. At the time of its development, there were no other comparable, low-priced teaching machines known to be available (the Honor machine eventually retailed for less than $20). Under such circumstances, the estimate of market potential and the sales forecast would be identical.

There are numerous methods that can be employed in forecasting—all have both strengths and shortcomings in their capacity to measure the "true" demand that will occur in future time periods. These will be examined in greater detail in Chapter 26.

Relationships among business institutions and customers

Flows of product, information, and money in the system are governed by the *decisions* of the active members of the system. A jeweler cannot sell a Bulova watch (product) to a customer in his store unless he has at some time made a decision to stock the Bulova line. Nor can the sale be completed until the customer decides that he is willing to part with his money. The aggregate of many decisions like these determines the flows of product, information, and money and, ultimately, the overall performance of the system.

Within a given class, flows may assume many different forms. Products may be raw materials or finished goods. Information may be advertising, sales promotion, or word-of-mouth communication. Money may be cash, checks, or various forms of credit. Products may also be described in terms of who buys them, how customers go about purchasing them, or how the product is consumed by its user. Marketers make distinctions of this kind for one principal reason: they are valuable in improving decisions. The fact that a product is intended for a household or business buyer is important in formulating marketing strategy because the habits, motives, and skills of these two buyers tend to be different. Marketing strategy is affected, because customers tend to shop around when buying some types of products, while they buy others largely on a convenience basis.

PRODUCTS

Consumer goods and services are those purchased and used by household consumers.

Business goods are those used by business firms either as material or components of other goods or in the performance of services.[2]

In our earlier discussion of customers and markets, we made a distinction between (household) consumers and business users. Products, including both goods and services, may be similarly distinguished.

The distinction between consumer and business goods and services is not always a hard and fast one. Many products and services are sold in both markets. For example, an automobile sold to a household is a consumer good, while the same automobile sold to a taxicab operator is a business product. Similarly, life insurance on John Doe, husband and father, is a consumer service, while "keyman" insurance on John Doe, business executive, is a business service.[3]

The distinction between buyers of consumer and business goods is useful to marketers because of the differences in the habits, motives, and skills of these types of buyers. These differences usually dictate that separate marketing programs are appropriate for each group. In general, consumer goods are advertised more heavily than business goods. A popular cigarette, for example, undoubtedly has more advertising dollars devoted to it than to all the kinds of pumps that are available to business firms. The cigarette market in the United States may include nearly 60 million people, whereas the industrial pump market is far smaller. Demand for this type of consumer product is stable, while pump demand is more volatile. Different methods of distribution are usually involved. The cigarette reaches its ultimate market through thousands of drugstores, variety, grocery, and other kinds of stores, while the pumps reach their market through a comparatively small number of direct salesmen and distributors.

Convenience goods are goods which the customer usually purchases frequently, immediately, and with the minimum of effort in comparison and buying.

Shopping goods are goods which the customer characteristically selects and purchases after comparing alternatives on such bases as suitability, quality, price, and style.

Specialty goods are goods with unique characteristics and/or brand identification for which a significant group of buyers are habitually willing to make a special purchasing effort.

For marketing decision making, consumer products may also be distinguished in terms of how buyers go about purchasing them. This classification defines goods and services as convenience goods, shopping goods, or specialty goods.[4] Examples of merchandise customarily bought as convenience goods are: tobacco products, soap, newspapers, small packaged confections, and many food products. Goods that most consumers buy as shopping goods are products such as millinery, furniture, dresses, and major appliances. Specific brands and types of fancy foods, stereo components, photographic equipment, and men's suits are often bought as specialty goods.

These definitions have useful marketing applications. Producers of conve-

[2] The term *industrial goods* is often used synonymously with *business goods*. However, it is partially misleading because not all business users are "industrial." Doctors, dentists, and lawyers (professional) all purchase goods and services for use in their business, as do hospitals (institutional) and government agencies. For this reason, we prefer the more embracing term *business goods* to describe products used by business customers.

[3] *Keyman insurance* is life insurance carried by business firms on key executives, to compensate firms for losses associated with the death of such executives.

[4] These three definitions are adapted from *Marketing Definitions,* American Marketing Association, Chicago, 1960, pp. 10, 21, 22.

nience goods, such as cigarettes or sugar, must have their products easily available in as many appropriate outlets as feasible. On the other hand, manufacturers of such shopping goods as major appliances know that most customers will go to several stores to compare prices, appearance, and other factors; this makes it less essential to have wide distribution. Finally, the importer of a specialty good such as Norwegian smoked salmon can assume that those who prefer his brand because of its special characteristics will make an extra effort to purchase it from one of the limited number of outlets that carry it. He may also assume that price will not be a major factor in the purchase decision because the special quality of the salmon is the primary factor in creating the demand for it.

These classifications also affect promotional policies. The marketer of chewing gum, a frequently purchased convenience item, wants his advertising to serve as a constant reminder of his brand. With this in mind, he will use frequent advertisements in media designed to reach large numbers of people. At the other extreme, perhaps, the seller of expensive hunting rifles knows that his customers and their buying processes permit infrequent advertising in highly selective media directed at hunters and lovers of fine guns.

Though useful, these classifications are general. They cannot be applied rigidly either to product types or to all types of customers. Promotion may make a difference. Candy bars are usually considered as a convenience good, but a manufacturer's advertising might be so effective that his brand becomes a specialty good to many customers. Product characteristics can also be an important variable. Newspapers are generally convenience items, but often people are willing to make a special effort to purchase a particular paper. Customer income may also affect the relevance of these classifications in many situations. Low-income groups, for example, may be so attentive to the prices of staple food items that the latter become shopping goods.

□ *Durable goods are tangible goods which normally survive many repeated uses and have a relatively long serviceable life.*

□ *Nondurable goods are tangible goods which normally are consumed in one or a few uses, therefore having a relatively short life.*

□ *Services are activities, benefits, or satisfactions which are offered for sale, or are provided in connection with the sale of goods.*[5]

A further classification of goods and services is that of durable goods, nondurable goods, and services.□ Automobiles, furniture, and electrical appliances all are considered to be durable goods, while foods, fuels, and cosmetics are examples of nondurables. Services might include amusements, hotels, transportation, and barbershops. As with previous classifications, these definitions are somewhat arbitrary and subject to areas of ambiguity. For example, it is not altogether clear how long a product's useful life need be before it becomes a durable good. Three years is often used arbitrarily as a minimum serviceable life for a durable good. Yet clothing, which may frequently have a life longer than three years, is generally not defined as a durable good. Electricity is classified as a service, probably because most people do not conceive of electricity as tangible.

[5] *Marketing Definitions, op. cit.*, p. 21.

The distinction between durables, nondurables, and services is based both on the tangibility of a product and on its rate of consumption. It is a useful distinction because both factors have implications for marketing strategy and decisions. Because a nondurable is purchased frequently and consumed quickly, it is usually available in many locations and commands a low unit margin for its seller. A nondurable is often susceptible to the development of strong brand loyalty on the part of its users. Similar marketing patterns prevail for many services, but the "intangible" aspects of some services can play havoc with a generalization of this kind. Within reasonable limits, membership in a golf course is more likely to be purchased on the basis of prestige and social factors than convenience of location. On the other hand, durables present the need for quite different marketing strategies. Purchased infrequently and required to survive many uses, durables generally require more personal selling, must be explained and sometimes installed, require after-sale services, and are more often sold on a credit basis.

INFORMATION

The movement of products from manufacturers to customers would not be possible without concurrent flows of *information* within the marketing system. Some types of information, such as advertising, hopefully serve to stimulate product movement. Others, such as derogatory comments about a product made by one user to another, may have the opposite effect.

Information flow, or communication, can assume a wide variety of content and form. But for our purposes, we can regard information movement within the marketing system as falling into one of three classifications.

1. To stimulate demand, manufacturers and distributive agencies direct persuasive communication to potential customers. These efforts are collectively referred to as *promotion*. The most important promotional activities are advertising, personal selling, and sales promotion.
2. To aid managers in recognizing, defining, and resolving the marketing problems and opportunities confronting a company, business firms collect data relevant to these purposes. Collectively, these data are referred to as *marketing information*.
3. Product-related communication among potential customers, for example, two housewives discussing a brand of coffee, is referred to as *word-of-mouth communication*. The aggregate effect of many such discussions can be a powerful determinant of demand.

Elements within the marketing system both transmit and receive product-related information, and the decisions of a marketing manager are frequently concerned with these information flows. He must decide what information the firm should *initiate* on its own behalf, and what it should *collect* to understand the markets it serves. It is fair to say that these decisions are among the most complex and demanding that the manager is called upon to make. They can be reviewed only superficially within the scope of this chapter. Decisions involving specific kinds of information flows will be examined in detail in later chapters.

In 1970, total advertising expenditures in the United States were estimated to be $20.8 billion.[6] As shown in Table 2-1, the magnitude of advertising spending in this country dwarfs that of any other nation. Only three other countries—West Germany, Great Britain, and Japan—had advertising expenditure levels in excess of $1 billion in 1968.

No comparable estimates of personal selling and sales promotion expenditures are available. The U.S. Department of Labor, however, has estimated that more than 4.7 million persons were employed in personal selling in the United States in 1968. The division of the workers among various classes of selling activities, illustrated in Figure 2-2, gives some indication of the magnitude of effort directed to selling at the retail level.

The most effective promotional programs are carefully integrated by marketing management. In general, the relative importance of advertising, personal selling, and sales promotion in a specific marketing program will vary with the nature of the product, the buying behavior of customers, the competitive prac-

[6] *Advertising Age*, Mar. 30, 1970, p. 47.

□
TABLE 2-1
Total 1968 advertising expenditures in selected countries
(Millions of U.S. dollars)

Country		Country	
Argentina	$ 247	Italy	$ 484
Australia	385	Japan	1,469
Belgium	159	Portugal	35
Canada	844	Spain	66
Ceylon	2	Sweden	402
Chile	34	Switzerland	416
Denmark	218	United Arab Republic	22
France	857	United States	18,016
Great Britain	1,178	West Germany	3,938
Israel	17		

Source: *World Advertising Expenditures* (1968), International Advertising Association, Inc., New York, 1970. Only parts of the data are reproduced here.

FIGURE 2-2

Sales employees in major United States sales organizations, 1968

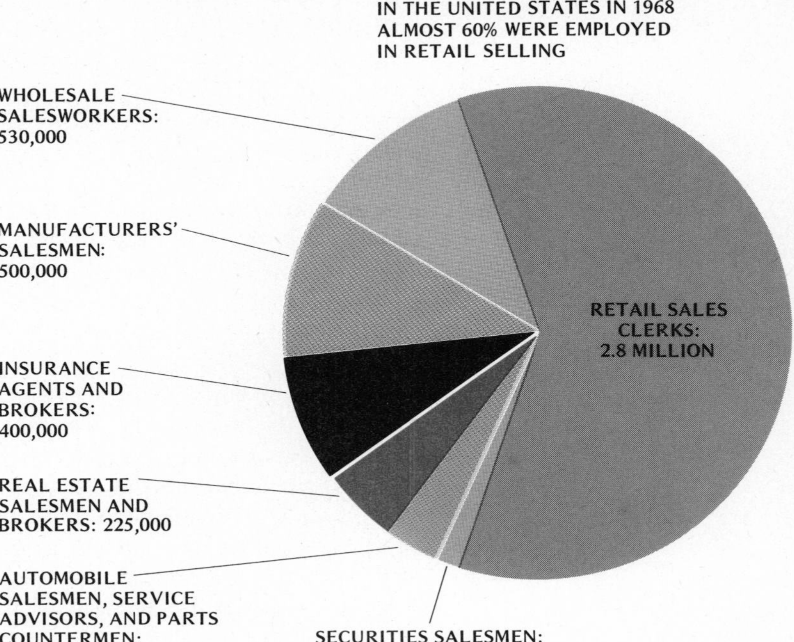

Source: U.S. Dept. of Labor, Bureau of Labor Statistics, *Occupational Outlook Handbook,* 1970–1971, pp. 295–318.

---

tices of the industry, and the manner in which marketing management chooses to employ its resources. Each type of promotional activity will attain maximum effectiveness, however, only if it is coordinated with the others.

Promotional decisions involve questions pertaining to the *dissemination* of information. Of equal importance are decisions the manager must make concerning the *collection* of marketing information. Broadly stated, the tasks of the marketing manager involve recognizing, defining, and resolving the problems and opportunities confronting his company. They also include implementing and controlling the strategies chosen to meet this challenge. For all these tasks, the manager requires information. For example, he needs information on the firm's customers and markets (characteristics, attitudes, purchasing behavior, knowledge), competitors (activities, strengths, plans), suppliers (price, capacity), marketing channels (capabilities and shortcomings), and the present and future effects of alternate marketing strategies (advertising effectiveness, effect of a price change).

The results achieved by marketing management depend in part on the quality of marketing information available to managers—its relevancy, accuracy, and timeliness. In some cases, needed information may be readily available by direct observations, or the manager's own previous experience may provide the necessary basis for making decisions. But direct observation and experience can often prove both inadequate and/or misleading. The manager may think he knows the source of a problem, but is his judgment necessarily correct? A Canadian manufacturer of a breakfast product felt certain that the poor performance of the item in the province of Quebec was due to the lack of a package on which both French and English were used. Later investigation revealed a quite different source of difficulty. French Canadians have a "sweet tooth" and were purchasing a competitor's product because it was sweeter.

Because direct observations and experience are incomplete guides to marketing decisions, well-managed companies also employ formal programs to obtain and interpret marketing information. Marketing research departments are assigned responsibility for gathering information relating to specific management problems. In some highly sophisticated companies, the more advanced concept of a "marketing information system" has been instituted. A system of this kind within a company provides a continuous *flow* of marketing information rather than a series of "one-shot" research projects initiated in response to problems as they arise.

Social scientists have long been aware that word-of-mouth communication can be an important determinant of opinion. In the 1940 United States presidential election, a study of the voters of Erie County, Pennsylvania, revealed that those who shifted voting intentions attributed their change more to word of mouth than to any influence by the mass media. But marketers, while acknowledging word of mouth as an influence on product demand, apparently ignored the phenomenon or were unable to see any way of employing it to advantage. William H. Whyte, Jr., studying the purchase of air conditioners in a Philadelphia suburb in 1954, stated, "There are manufacturers, wondering why their market is acting so strange, who should tune in on the (conversational) grapevine."[7] By the early 1960s, some marketers began to take note. The Wilkinson stainless-steel razor blade, in the absence of initial advertising support, apparently rose to success on the crest of word of mouth.[8] The Ford Mustang's spectacular acceptance was in part attributed to its position as "the most talked-about auto of the year."[9]

There now seems little doubt that word-of-mouth communication is a far more important determinant of marketing system performance than was initially realized. Many marketing managers now are explicitly trying to take the word-of-mouth factor into account in formulating marketing strategy. Their at-

[7] William H. Whyte, Jr., "The Web of Word of Mouth," *Fortune*, Nov., 1954, p. 140.
[8] *Business Week*, Dec. 22, 1962, p. 81.
[9] *Time*, Mar. 13, 1964, p. 91.

tempts are still greatly hampered by a lack of systematic knowledge as to the conditions under which word of mouth is important, or how it can be influenced to act as a catalyst for demand.

MONEY

In primitive societies, the exchange of goods and services was effected by means of barter—one kind of merchandise was traded directly for another. In advanced societies, the more specialized output of each man makes barter impossible. The worker at a nut-and-bolt factory would find it difficult to locate persons willing to take nuts and bolts in direct trade for food, housing, clothing, and his other needs. Instead, the worker's output is sold for money, and he uses *money* to buy the goods he wants.

The performance of a marketing system depends on the acceptance of money as a medium of exchange. Money flowing within the system generally offsets the flow of product. That is, as raw materials, semifinished and finished products move through successive producers and distributors to ultimate users, each transfer of title is offset by a corresponding money flow. The amount of money exchanged covers the seller's costs, plus a margin of profit. Nor is it necessary that exchange within the system be effected with cash. Of great importance to the functioning of the marketing system is the role played by *credit*. Almost all exchanges between business institutions are on some kind of credit basis. For example, a wholesaler or retailer receiving goods from a manufacturer might be billed with an invoice indicating the gross amount due, plus a notation stating the terms to be "2/10 net 30." This can be interpreted as meaning that if the buyer pays within 10 days, he may deduct a 2 percent discount. If he does not pay within 10 days, he is expected to pay the full amount within 30 days. After 30 days, interest may be charged.

One of the most dramatic changes in the post-World War II period has been the expanded use of consumer credit. In effect, credit serves as a source of purchasing power for consumers above and beyond their current incomes. Banks and finance companies, the traditional sources of consumer credit, have been supplemented in recent years by credit cards and a wide variety of credit plans and devices. Some of these will be examined further in Chapter 5.

The management of money is an important part of the marketer's job. It is hardly necessary to point out the relationship between money flows and prices, cost control and budget decisions. Consumer credit decisions can prove particularly difficult to assess. The marketing manager who seeks to minimize credit losses may well be setting a shortsighted objective detrimental to maximizing overall profitability of the firm. If the company's product is one particularly sensitive to consumer income levels, a car, for example, a more liberal credit policy might result in substantially increased sales. Even though credit losses may rise under a liberal policy, profits from increased sales may more than offset these losses.

Marketing systems in other countries

The institutions and flows described in the preceding sections are characteristic of a highly advanced marketing system. It is one which has evolved over time as American society became more industrialized, urbanized, and sophisticated. Approximately similar marketing systems are to be found in Canada, most of the countries of Western Europe, and in Australia. The dramatic growth of Japan in the past two decades has also led to the evolution of an advanced marketing system.

How do other marketing systems differ? The most dramatic contrasts are to be found in the crude marketing activities of primitive lands. In a subsistence economy, there is very little marketing. Each person grows the food he consumes and probably makes the tools he uses and the clothes he wears. The individual is largely self-sufficient, albeit at a very meager level of subsistence. Societies of this kind are rare in the twentieth century, but can be found among some isolated tribal groups in South America, Africa, and parts of Asia.

Apart from primitive societies, the marketing systems which differ most from that of the United States are those of *underdeveloped* nations and *controlled* economies.

□

MARKETING IN UNDERDEVELOPED NATIONS

In underdeveloped economies, the present state of the art in marketing is largely a consequence of many socioeconomic factors such as national income, availability of labor, education, social customs, and traditions. It is useful to examine how these factors have contributed to the evolution of marketing patterns.

The appallingly low income levels of underdeveloped countries manifests itself in customer buying behavior quite distinct from that of more prosperous societies. Lacking funds or storage facilities, buyers' irregular and unsystematic shopping trips for extremely small quantities result in waste and diseconomy throughout the system. Small retailers are forced to offer almost universal credit, and are usually overextended in this regard. Heavily indebted farmers must dispose of their crops even before harvesttime to gain much-needed cash. Often, their buyers are unscrupulous middlemen who, taking advantage of the farmer's dilemma, effectively deprive him of competitive market prices.

Since most underdeveloped countries are burdened with enormous labor surpluses, methods of production and distribution tend to be labor *absorbing* rather than labor*saving*. In marketing, this leads to a predominance of middlemen operating on a very small scale. Street hawkers are common, and retail stores are usually staffed with an overabundance of clerks. Lengthy price haggling is common—the idea of a fixed price is almost unknown. For those few who can afford durables, planning and shopping for an article is an extremely long, drawn-out affair. This is hardly surprising when one considers that a middle-class Indian needs the equivalent of one month's wages to purchase a radio or an electric fan.

A near-universal lack of education gives rise to a considerable degree of consumer exploitation, misrepresentation, and other unfair trade practices. Perhaps more important is the resultant attitude of apathy which provides little impetus for any change in inefficient and unfair practices.

The effects of tradition, social customs, and religion on a country's marketing system are usually profound. In Ceylon, social class distinctions have led to the establishment of specific retail food outlets for each social class. In many parts of India, buying is mostly done at times of religious celebrations and marriages. Often these occasions coincide with harvesttime. The resultant seasonal purchasing patterns affect wholesalers and retailers. A prevalent philosophical outlook is that of prejudice against the trading community, which is regarded as performing no useful service for society. Only the traders of rare spices and herbs somehow escape this condemnation.

Thus, the marketing systems of most underdeveloped lands reflect prevailing social and economic conditions. They are inefficient, archaic, and crude. For many years, it was regarded as inevitable that there could be no real change in underdeveloped marketing systems until further measures of basic social and economic growth were first achieved. But more recently, it has been suggested by some economists that improvements in the marketing system might well *precede* economic growth, that is, marketing improvements can be a cause of economic growth rather than a result of it.

THE ROLE OF MARKETING IN ECONOMIC GROWTH

After centuries of near stagnation, recent decades have seen the beginning of deliberate efforts to bring about economic growth in the world's underdeveloped countries. In Latin America, industrialization began just before or during World War II. In most areas of Africa and Asia, serious efforts did not get started until after 1945. In some countries, attempts to bring about economic growth have yet to get under way in earnest.

With few exceptions, the developing nations have concentrated their initial efforts in two areas: the production of industrial goods at the expense of consumer goods and the building of a basic "infrastructure"—including roads, electric power, and education. There is a basic rationale for this approach. Economic growth depends on the utilization of modern science and technology. Nowhere are the benefits of modern technology more apparent than in heavy industry, and the development of a basic infrastructure is a direct prerequisite to industrialization. At the same time, in both capitalist and socialist economies, there was a systematic neglect of modernization in the agricultural and rural sectors of underdeveloped economies. Agriculture seemed to be associated with colonialism and, as such, was clearly not in fashion.

The combination of these factors has led many underdeveloped countries to a particular phase of economic development. It is exemplified by the existence of a few large cities surrounding a small number of industrial enterprises, with rural areas largely in isolation. At this point, efforts directed toward economic growth in many instances began to falter. In the opinion of many economists, most notably Walt Rostow, a leading American foreign-policy planner, the improvement of marketing systems is the next requisite to continued growth in these economies.[10]

How can marketing contribute to economic growth? At least part of the answer lies in the enlargement of existing fragmented markets into more unified *national* or regional markets. If marketing institutions in underdeveloped countries can reach out to rural areas, and if the entire marketing system can be better organized, several improvements could be made. For example, the enlargement of markets can lead to greater efficiencies in mass production and mass distribution, thereby resulting in lower costs and a higher standard of living. Better organization can result in the elimination of costly middlemen. Reduction in inventories can free much-needed capital resources. At the same time, bringing modern marketing institutions to rural areas can contribute to monetizing the economy. In India, for example, more than one-third of agricultural output is still exchanged by barter.

The need for a self-sufficient agricultural sector in an economy is now being recognized by most underdeveloped countries. Few are yet self-sufficient, however, and the majority must therefore use up valuable foreign-exchange resources to feed their populace. Here again, the improvement of marketing functions is a necessary adjunct to growth. Storage, efficient transportation of farm products, stabilization of prices, and dissemination of market information are all needed.

These benefits are but a few of many that might well be achieved by a more efficient marketing system in an underdeveloped country. The marketing system need not be just the consequence of a country's social and economic growth, it can also be a prime mover in *achieving* growth.

MARKETING IN HIGHLY CONTROLLED ECONOMIES

A fundamental tenet distinguishes the free-enterprise system of most Western nations from the controlled economies of the Soviet Union and its allies—private ownership of the means of production and distribution. In free-enterprise, or capitalistic, systems, ownership is entrusted to the private sector with belief in the principle that the "market is the master." It is assumed that business enterprises will regulate their activities in such a way as to provide the goods and services demanded by their customers. The motivator that encourages private

[10] Walt W. Rostow, "The Concept of a National Market and Its Economic Growth Implications," *Marketing and Economic Development,* Proceedings of the Fall Conference of the American Marketing Association, American Marketing Association, Chicago, 1965, pp. 11–20.

enterprise to adjust to the needs of the market is profit. Only when a firm satisfies the needs of its customers can its profit be maximized.

Controlled economies like the Soviet Union were founded on a Marxist philosophy that rejects these basic tenets of capitalism. Instead, ownership of productive and distributive resources is claimed by the state. Production is not directly geared to the demands of the market, but rather is dictated by a central planning agency of the state. Production goals established by the central planning agency are based on national priorities determined by the government. Under this system, there is no need for the profit regulator. In fact, profit is regarded as an anachronism of capitalistic systems.

Initially, centrally planned economies appeared to work with at least moderate success. But as the economies of the Soviet Union and Eastern Europe became more complex and sophisticated, substantial inefficiencies in the use of resources began to appear. Nowhere were the failures more serious than those which arose at the level of individual enterprise. The director of an enterprise was required to meet numerous goals assigned to him from above: average wage, productivity of labor, amount of production cost per unit, amount of bank credit, and, not least of all, a quota for gross production. The directors bargained for low, easily achievable goals, and as a result, plants frequently produced well under capacity. Raw materials were overpurchased to ensure their supply. Product innovation was avoided, because goals could be achieved without it. Quality was often shoddy because goals were usually stated only in quantitative terms. Some products were produced in abundance, while others remained in short supply. For example, if a goal were stated in terms of producing a certain number of nails, small ones were made to achieve the goal more easily. If the quota were expressed in weight, large nails were produced.

□

MODIFICATIONS OF THE PLANNED ECONOMY SYSTEM

The first renegade from the planned economy system was Yugoslavia. Between 1947 and 1951, Yugoslavia had operated under a planned system that set production targets for 16,000 to 20,000 commodities. The results were so dismal that a new system of a "planned market economy" was introduced. The enterprise was given freedom to determine what to produce, how many workers to hire, where to purchase inputs, to whom to sell, and what to import and export. But constraints on investment policy were imposed from above, and ownership remained public. The result was a system midway between a controlled and a free-enterprise economy. Such reforms were nonetheless heretical to the concept of a planned economy, and subsequently contributed to Yugoslavia's expulsion from the Cominform.

Within the Soviet Union, discussion of the failures of a planned economy began in the 1950s, and culminated with the proposals of Prof. Yev Liberman between 1962 and 1964. Based on Professor Liberman's proposals, a new set of statutes governing enterprises was introduced on January 1, 1966. Liberman sharply criticized existing practices of enterprise planning on two fronts. He asserted that the manager had a better knowledge of his plant's capabilities than any central planning authority, and that the manager would respond best to financial incentives, including profit. Under the new system, centrally planned goals were reduced, but not eliminated. For some important goods they included physical production, but the categories were broad and afforded considerable latitude of action to the enterprise. Perhaps the most important addition was a requirement for profitability as a goal and as a key index on which worker and manager bonuses were based. Greater independence was given the enterprise in order that it could influence profitability. For example, contracts were to be made directly between an enterprise and its customers. These changes were timid by Western standards or even by those of Yugoslavia. Major decisions over investment, wages, and prices are still made by the central planners, and not the enterprise.

By the end of 1967, a total of 7,000 enterprises, accounting for 40 percent of industrial production and one-third of the Soviet labor force, had been switched to the new system.[11] Similar reforms were under way in several East European nations.

UNIVERSALITY OF MARKETING FUNCTIONS

Despite the philosophical differences between free-enterprise and controlled systems, the marketing tasks and problems facing the two systems are strikingly similar. On the basis of his on-the-spot studies in the early 1960s, Prof. Marshall I. Goldman stated flatly, "The basic structure of the marketing operation in the Soviet Union is essentially the same as in the United States."[12] He points out that installment credit has been used to expand Russian sales of television sets, cameras, and watches in certain areas when they became "overproduced."[13] Advertising is used in the Soviet Union, including television, radio, billboards, newspapers, and handbills. There are state-owned advertising agencies, and an advertising journal, *Informatsionnyi Reklamnyi Bulletin,* is published. To date, few expenditures have been incurred for competitive advertising, but this might well change under the reformed system.[14] Brand names have also been used, in some cases to distinguish the output of different factories. In this way, customers are able to reject those goods produced in factories with a record of shoddy quality.

[11] *The Economist,* Feb. 3, 1968, p. 31.

[12] Marshall I. Goldman, "The Marketing Structure in the Soviet Union," *Journal of Marketing,* July, 1961, p. 7.

[13] Marshall I. Goldman, "Retailing in the Soviet Union," *Journal of Marketing,* April, 1960, p. 15.

[14] Reed Moyer, "Marketing in the Iron Curtain Countries," *Journal of Marketing,* October, 1966, p. 9.

Questions

1. What specific tasks must a manufacturer of men's suits perform to ensure his clothes are available to customers in the right places, at the right times, and in the desired forms?

2. How might management of the Creswell Toy Company use (a) estimates of market potential, (b) sales forecasts, and (c) market share estimates to perform its marketing functions more effectively?

3. The Thomas Motor Company was one of the world's largest manufacturers of trucks, buses, and motor coaches. Its product line included trucks ranging from ¾ ton to over 10 tons. Both cab-over-engine and models of simpler design were available. The motor buses and coaches accommodated from 15 to 100 passengers and sold at prices ranging from $8,000 to $65,000. Smaller models were generally gasoline powered, while larger trucks and buses were usually driven by diesel engines.

In preparing the company's plans for the 1970s, the president asked the coach sales manager to study market conditions and present a report dealing with two key problems. First, he was concerned about the types of bus that would afford the largest potential market for Thomas in the ensuing five to ten years. Several types of bus could be manufactured, including trackless trolley, gasoline electric, gasoline mechanical, diesel electric, diesel mechanical, or some hybrid combination of these that was yet to be developed. The president was anxious to learn which type would presumably be most in demand. Second, the president requested an estimate of the approximate size of the market for each major type of bus and, for each type, the probable passenger capacities most likely to be in demand.

What specific kinds of information would the coach sales manager need to prepare the report?

4. For centuries philosophers and economists have condemned middlemen as unproductive members of society. It has been argued that middlemen extract a toll on the products they handle without contributing anything to their value. How would you appraise such criticisms?

5. In determining the extent of competition for purposes of investigating and prosecuting antitrust cases, the Federal Trade Commission and the Department of Justice place considerable stress on the concept of a "relevant market." For example, in one major case, it was argued that the relevant market for automobile finishes sold by a chemical concern consisted of those automobile manufacturers using a certain type of finish. In general, how should a market be defined for purposes of analyzing the nature and extent of competition?

6. The text suggests that consumer goods may be distinguished by how consumers go about buying them. Three classifications are suggested: conve-

nience goods, shopping goods, and specialty goods. How would you classify each of the following products?

a. Furniture
b. Automobiles
c. Greeting cards
d. Headache remedies
e. Prescription drugs

How, if at all, would differences in the way you classify these products affect your selection of a marketing strategy?

7. In August 1968, the Royal Crown Cola Company was in the process of planning the market introduction of a new carbonated beverage to be known as Gatorade. The name of the product was derived from the University of Florida football team, the Gators. A noncarbonated version of the beverage had originally been developed at the University for use by its football team.

Gatorade differed from conventional soft drinks in that it could be absorbed by the body about 12 times more quickly than water, and it rapidly replenished body salts lost during exertion. The company planned to make Gatorade available in several common soft drink flavors including cola, lemon-lime, and orange.

a. Using your best judgment, prepare a market analysis for Gatorade.
b. What implications does your analysis have for the marketing strategy for this new beverage?

8. The Soviet automobile industry, like its American counterpart, produces a variety of automobile sizes, designs, and brands. By and large, buyers of Soviet cars are self-selective, as in the United States. People who can afford cars buy them according to their taste and pocketbooks. The Soviet auto industry is expected not only to cover its costs with the revenue produced by its auto sales, but also to produce a surplus (profit) which helps finance expansion and improvements. As minister of the Soviet auto industry required to work within the framework of state control, how would you organize and operate the automobile marketing system? How would it differ from what you know the system to be in the United States?

9. In Great Britain, as in the United States, critics are often heard to call for greater government regulation of advertising in what is asserted to be the interest of the consumer. Unlike the United States, however, government in Great Britain has taken substantial steps toward regulating advertising. An example is the detergent industry, which came under investigation by the Monopolies Commission in Great Britain in the mid 1960s. The industry was regarded as prone to investigation because of its high concentration (two companies—Procter and Gamble and Unilever—accounted for 90 percent of all

detergent sales) and high profits (one of these companies earned more than 50 percent on invested capital in 1965).

Noting that physical differentiation between competing detergent products was minor, a 1966 report of the Monopolies Commission stated in part, "Advertising and promotion has tended to reduce price competition. The effects of this are to increase prices to the extent that additional expenditures in this field are wasteful. . . ."

On the basis of its investigation, the Monopolies Commission recommended that the two leading companies voluntarily undertake to reduce their promotional expenditures by 40 percent, together with an immediate 20 percent reduction in detergent prices.

a. What effect would this action have on each of the elements involved in the marketing system for detergents?

b. To what extent would the performance of the marketing functions by the system be facilitated or hindered?

The recommendations of the Monopolies Commission proved highly controversial. Typical of detergent industry reactions was the remark of Lord Cole, chairman of Unilever: "We could not agree with these recommendations, or with the reasoning that led up to them, and we will not agree to implement them voluntarily."

c. What arguments might Lord Cole have used in rejecting the proposals?

At the same time, representatives of the detergent and advertising industries requested that the Board of Trade (to whom the Monopolies Commission reports) reassess the situation, and offered to work together with the government to bring about a compromise solution. In April 1967, the Board of Trade announced that an agreement had been reached. In lieu of the original proposals of the Monopolies Commission, each of the detergent companies agreed to market a high-quality detergent priced to sell for 20 percent less than other highly promoted brands. At the same time, the Board of Trade, in conjunction with the advertising and detergent industries, would undertake a series of studies designed to learn more about the economic role of advertising in the marketing system.

d. How do you think household consumers would respond to the lower-priced products?

e. Recommend some specific studies that the Board of Trade should undertake as part of its program.

Customer and market behavior

PART TWO

The first two chapters have served as a general introduction to marketing. We have shown that in any nation—advanced or underdeveloped, free enterprise or highly controlled—there are essential marketing functions to be performed. These functions are carried out by a marketing system, a collection of interdependent business firms, institutions, and customers engaged in arketing activities.

roughout the remainder of the book,
focal point of our attention is not
narketing system per se, but the
dual marketing manager and the
s by which managers make de-
Our objective, broadly stated,
provement of these decision-
ocesses. But to make deci-
tively, the manager must
ing aware of the environ-
h he operates. He must
e dynamics of its per-
to the best of his ability,
t its responses to
nd influences. One
should bear in mind that the total marketing system, its elements and their interactions, constitutes the environment of the marketing manager's decision-making activities.

In Part 2 we begin our study of marketing management with a detailed examination of a firm's customers and the markets that they comprise. While customers are by no means the sole participants in a marketing system, they are nonetheless the most important from a manager's point of view. It is customers who make the final and most crucial marketing decisions—those of buying choice. A firm cannot passively place its wares before the public in anticipation of sales. To ensure sales, it must aggressively seek to satisfy the needs and desires of those who purchase and consume. All marketing activity, whatever its form, must have the customer as its ultimate point of origin.

The Consumer Is King

The importance of a customer orientation for marketing managers is reflected in the axiom, "The consumer is king." This brief and simple statement outlines nothing less than an entire philosophy of business conduct in which the needs, desires, and buying responses of the customer are viewed as the major determinants of a firm's success. In the final analysis, a company's marketing programs must satisfy its customers. Those which fail to do so will meet with rejection and failure. The most famous case of customer rejection of marketing policy in modern times is the Edsel automobile. The Edsel was introduced to the American public in the middle 1950s. Like Mr. Woolworth's mousetrap, it was preceded by much thought and research. Like his product, it was a dismal failure, for it failed to satisfy the then current needs of automobile buyers. Conversely, the later introduction of the Mustang and Maverick automobiles by Ford Motor Company were outstand-

ing examples of customer acceptance of a marketing program. In a vibrant economy, examples of both customer rejection and acceptance of new products and marketing ideas are legion.

The concept of customer satisfaction as the basis for marketing activity is often referred to as the "modern" marketing concept. We can digress briefly to point out that this concept has not always prevailed as a philosophy of business conduct, nor is it universally applied today. The most common alternative, sometimes called the "old" marketing concept, views the product as the focal point of business activity. Marketing is looked upon solely as a means of distributing the output of production to buyers. In the early part of this century, most firms operated either implicitly or explicitly under the "old" marketing concept. At one point, a widespread problem of unsold inventories of finished goods developed, and for a brief period, businessmen looked to advertising as a hoped-for panacea for their difficulties. Advertising did not prove to be the answer, however, for no amount of promotional effort could substantially induce customers to purchase products not suited to their needs.

In Chapter 3, we will begin our study of customers with an examination of household customers. The role of various participants in a household buying decision, and the kinds of influences that each brings to bear on a purchasing decision, will be explored. Subsequent chapters will deal with demographic, economic, social, and psychological factors affecting household buying decisions. The concluding chapters of Part 2 describe business, professional, and government customers and markets.

Some words of caution regarding terminology are in order before proceeding further. In marketing, the term consumer is commonly used to refer to a household customer. Similar groups of household customers are not usually described as "household customer markets," even though the latter phrase would be entirely correct. Instead, they are referred to as consumer markets. In one sense, our heritage of this terminology is unfortunate, since the word "consumer" implies usage of a product. A household customer may buy a product but not use it himself. An infant eats baby food, but its mother buys it. A coed uses luggage in traveling home from college, but her parents may have been the people who bought it. In both cases, common terminology would describe the infant's mother and the coed's parents as consumers. The reader should bear in mind that, as used in marketing, the term consumer is synonymous with household customer, but does not necessarily imply personal usage of the product or service purchased.

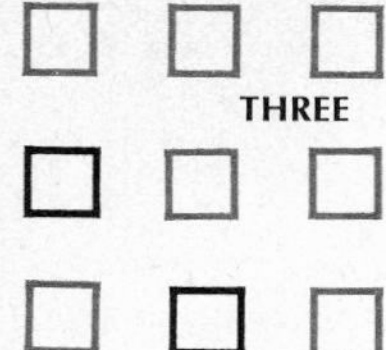

Consumer markets

It is useful to think about consumers in two ways. One is in terms of the *individual consumer,* say Mrs. Smith, who makes purchase decisions about products that she purchases. The marketing manager's job begins with an understanding of who she is, what her wishes or needs are, and her possible reactions to different marketing programs. The second is in terms of aggregates, the thousands and millions of Mrs. Smiths and their husbands and their families. The aggregates are, in short, all the people who constitute the potential *consumer markets* for products and the targets for marketing strategies.

Each day, millions of Americans like Mrs. Smith make purchases for their own personal or household use. A housewife in San Francisco buys facial tissue, a systems analyst in Providence buys an automobile, and an elderly matron in Kalamazoo buys a new spring coat—these are typical of the multitude of consumer purchasing transactions that occur daily in commonplace fashion. They reflect the very nature of consumer markets. Individually, each purchase is relatively small, ranging from 19 cents for the facial tissue to, say, $3,000 for the automobile. But there are over 205 million people in the United States, or over 60 million households. Each engages in some measure of spending activity. In 1970, the aggregate of all expenditures made by household consumers amounted to $617 billion. It is from this vast collective quantity of spending that consumer markets are ascribed.

For the purposes of the marketing manager, it is scarcely sufficient to speak of a single $617 billion consumer market in the United States. For example, a franchised Coca-Cola bottler in the Pacific Northwest might find this information interesting, but hardly relevant to the marketing decisions that he is faced with. More probably, the Coca-Cola bottler would want information pertaining to the market for soft drinks (the kind of products he sells) in the Pacific Northwest (the area in which he sells them). In other words, markets must be defined in specific terms that are relevant to the kind of business decisions that have to be made.

We introduced some of the criteria by which markets are commonly defined in the previous chapter. One criterion is the *type* of consumer involved. The youth market, the Negro market, and the college-educated market are examples of markets defined in terms of consumer characteristics. A market can also be defined in terms of the product or service involved, such as automobiles and life insurance. It can be defined by geographic variables: the New England market, the urban market, or the temperate-climate market. For decision making, it is significant that a market also be described as existing in some discrete *time interval*. For example, in planning a marketing budget for 1972, the manager would speak of the potential market available in that year.

To be useful to a firm's specific marketing situation, some combination of two or more of the above criteria is usually desirable for market definition. A cereal manufacturer considering the introduction of a new product would probably speak of the consumer market for ready-to-eat cereals in the United States over, say, the next five years. In devising an annual marketing plan, the publisher of the *Denver Post* might think in terms of the market for daily newspapers in the metropolitan Denver area in, say, 1972.

Market segmentation

However defined, a market is always made up of a group of consumers. As an individual, each consumer who is part of a market is likely, to some extent, to demonstrate his own unique pattern of needs, wants, desires, and other buying characteristics. Whenever such differences between individual consumers become significant in magnitude, further refinement of market definition may be desirable. For example, the Maxwell House Division of General Foods Corporation is engaged in marketing coffee products throughout most of the United States. But variations in the patterns of buying and consumption by coffee drinkers have led General Foods executives to further subdivide the total coffee market. The divisions are illustrated in Figure 3-1. Their usefulness stems from the different patterns of coffee drinking displayed in the East and West. Traditionally, Westerners drink more coffee per day than Easterners. But light coffee drinkers, relatively more abundant in the East, tend to prefer instant coffee to fresh coffee. Thus, even though the East is more pop-

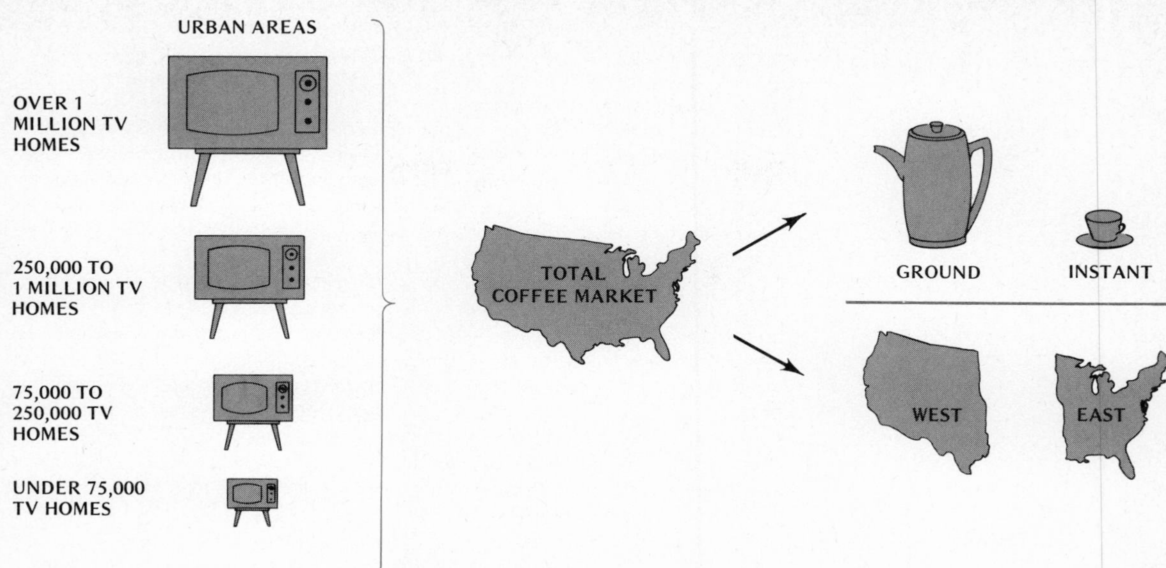

Source: Based on information in the case study, "General Foods Corporation—Maxim A," Stanford University, 1968.

FIGURE 3-1

Representation of coffee market segments by Maxwell House Division, General Foods Corporation

ulous than the West by half, it accounts for half again as many units of instant coffee sales. The East also contains more densely settled areas—cities with over 250,000 TV homes account for 75 percent of its population as compared with only 64 percent in the West. This distinction is of significance to General Foods since the company feels that high-quality food innovations are more readily adopted by consumers in large urban areas, and frequently makes use of extensive television advertising in its introductory marketing programs.

The process by which General Foods has subdivided the coffee markets, and by which other firms may similarly choose to divide their markets, is referred to as market segmentation.□ Because consumer markets are mass markets comprising large numbers of people, they are often capable of being segmented. Here are some further cases in which market segmentation has been utilized:

□ Market segmentation is the process of identifying significant differences in buyer characteristics in order to divide a market into two or more groups of consumers for the purpose of (1) selecting those portions of a market which a firm will serve, and/or (2) designing products and marketing programs to satisfy the distinctive buyer characteristics of each group.

In 1968, the Sicks Rainier Brewing Company of Seattle, Washington, introduced three varieties of beer under a common brand name, *Rainier:* "Light-light, the lightest a beer can be and still be beer"; light, which was the Rainier beer that had been sold for many years; and "not-so-light, a traditional beer for those who prefer beer as it used to be." The company's television advertising campaign accompanying the introduction made this attempt to segment the beer market quite clear to consumers through the slogan, "You're not supposed to like all three."[1]

Regional differences in smoking habits result in most Canadian cigarette manufacturers segmenting their market geographically, either explicitly or implicitly. Residents of Quebec, in particular, demonstrate quite different cigarette smoking habits from those of other Canadians. They are heavier smokers, prefer regular-length cigarettes to king-size or 100-millimeter brands, and have an overall low acceptance of menthol brands. Quebeckers also like a little added incentive to purchase cigarettes—35 percent of all cigarettes sold in the province are brands having bonus coupons or some other promotional incentive.[2]

In order to permit their advertisers to "zero in" on specific market segments, many magazines publish a number of different editions of each issue, which are in turn directed to specific customer types on their subscriber list. In 1968, *Time* magazine was reported to have published 187 editions of each issue in the United States alone, including regional editions (such as New England), metropolitan market area editions (such as metropolitan Chicago), and occupational editions (such as for college students and medical doctors). In the same year, *Look* magazine separated those zip-code areas having median incomes in the top 10 percent of the total income range and offered advertisers the opportunity to reach the "high-income" market segment resulting from this process.

In studies conducted in the mid-1960s, Clark L. Wilson attempted to describe the purchasing behavior and homemaking attitudes of housewives according to a number of socioeconomic variables. His findings resulted in the identification of a number of different "homemaking types," including "the careful shopper," "the happy housekeeper," "the child-oriented mother," "the community and club woman," "the religious woman," and others. While these dimensions may not yet have been utilized in designing any marketing programs, they are nonetheless indicative of directions that market segmentation could take at some future time.[3]

□

HOW USEFUL IS MARKET SEGMENTATION?

Market segmentation, as exemplified by the above cases, offers the marketing decision maker a number of potential benefits. By seeking to discover important buying characteristics of consumers, he may be able to identify opportunities in a market that have hitherto been ignored or overlooked by competitors. Marketing programs tailored to individual market segments, if economically feasible and practical, may result in greater efficiency in the utilization of a firm's marketing budget. In highly competitive consumer markets, the exploitation of one or two small segments may be the only feasible strategy for survival for a small company with limited human and financial resources.

Nonetheless, there is a limit to how far segmentation can be carried. At the extreme, each consumer in a market could be thought of as constituting a "segment." For firms selling products of very high unit value to a limited number of industrial or institutional users, such as commercial aircraft manu-

[1] *Advertising Age,* Apr. 22, 1968, p. 2.

[2] *Marketing,* Oct. 18, 1968, p. 67.

[3] Clark L. Wilson, *The Homemaker Studies,* unpublished research paper, Graduate School of Business Administration, Harvard University, Boston, 1967.

facturers, this treatment may be justified. But for consumer markets with their vast numbers, the strategy is clearly absurd. To favor segmentation, it follows that a market segment defined on the basis of a consumer characteristic must be sufficiently large in size to justify separate treatment. The segmentation variable(s) should also be measurable. It is all well and good to hypothesize that a proportion of wristwatch buyers purchase in order to satisfy a motivation for acquisitiveness,[4] but it is extremely difficult to measure the extent to which this factor actually exists among potential customers. Finally, a market segment should also be of such a nature that special marketing programs can be designed to service it. The "acquisitive wristwatch buyer" may exist in substantial numbers, but it is nearly impossible to construct a marketing program tailored to this market segment. Acquisitiveness suggests no special product features, little in the way of unique promotional appeals, and no promotional media by which potential consumers possessing this characteristic could be efficiently reached.

It is interesting to note that successful marketing programs are sometimes created by *reversing* traditional ideas about segmented markets. For many years, personal deodorants were distinctively designed and promoted as either men's *or* women's deodorants. Then, in the mid-1960s, the Gillette Company introduced Right Guard as a product for the whole family to use. By effectively "unsegmenting" a market that had always been viewed as segmented, Gillette created a product that quickly rose to sales leadership in the industry.

In the final analysis, the identification of market segments and the tailoring of marketing programs suited to them are based on the same principle that applies in dealing with total markets. The principle, which cannot be overemphasized, is the marketing manager's need to identify the consumers he is dealing with, and to thoroughly understand the processes by which they make buying decisions.

Buying decisions

□ *A buying decision is the total process by which people or groups of people make and carry out the decisions whether, where, when, and how to buy and use the goods and services made available by the marketing activities of business firms.*

Our definition of buying decisions is one stressing decision making in the *fullest* sense of the phrase.□ A buying decision is not looked upon solely as the events of a momentary instant when the consumer commits himself to purchase, "places his money on the counter," and receives goods or services in return. The crucial aspect of the definition is its emphasis on decision making as a *total process.* It is a process that begins at the time a consumer starts to recognize a need or desire for a product—perhaps hours, days, or years prior to the actual exchange transaction. The buying decision may not be

[4] Acquisitiveness is defined by psychologists as a learned motive manifesting itself in a tendency to acquire, possess, and defend whatever is found useful or otherwise attractive.

complete until the consumer has made use of his purchase and reassured himself of its utility, perhaps long after the act of purchase itself.

In this broad context of decision making, analysis of buying decisions involves determinations as to who consumers are, where they are located, how and when they buy, what their wants and desires are, and why they behave as they do. All this information is highly relevant to the manager who has to develop marketing programs. A manufacturer of women's luggage must know who (the kinds of people buying the product line, including parents, husbands, and women buying for their own use), where (the kinds of stores in which they purchase, such as department, jewelry, and specialty luggage stores), how and when (whether the purchase is planned or impulsive, prompted by special gift occasions, and more likely to be made at some times of the year than others), what (the needs women have for luggage, or others may have in giving a gift of luggage), and why (the reasons behind both the needs and the buying behavior of consumers purchasing luggage).

A detailed illustration of a consumer buyer decision, that of "Mr. and Mrs. Wilson buying a car," will be discussed in this chapter. The illustration serves three purposes. First, it indicates the nature of a buying decision process, the role of various participants in the process, and the kinds of factors that marketing decision makers must consider as they try to understand the consumers that make up their potential markets. Second, it helps to enrich the next several chapters, which discuss factors affecting the buying decisions of consumers in more detail. Third, because Part 3 deals with marketing policy, the example presented here may help to give insight into the questions that confront marketing decision makers in such policy areas as promotion, pricing, and the like.

Remember that the Wilsons' experience in buying a car is only an *illustration*. The factors that are described are conjectural, and only by chance would they reflect all the factors that might actually be involved. Remember also that the process described here is not intended as descriptive of the process that all consumers go through, even for the specific product discussed. The nature of buying decisions varies from individual to individual and from group to group.

Mr. and Mrs. Wilson buy a car

Mr. and Mrs. Charles Wilson, both between forty-five and fifty, live in a fairly prosperous suburban neighborhood adjacent to a large city. Mr. Wilson was recently appointed vice-president of a small manufacturing concern. Mrs. Wilson is a housewife, gregarious and active in women's organizations and many civic affairs. Their one son Bill is twenty-four, married and working as a purchasing agent in a small city about 100 miles away. The Wilsons live well but without ostentation, and consider themselves a typical American upper-middle-class family, although their income is in a higher category.

"DO WE NEED A NEW CAR?"

A new medium-sized Buick sits in the Wilsons' two-car garage, next to Mr. Wilson's commuting car. The idea of a new car had been discussed for almost a year. It had first arisen when the old family car, a 1966 Chevrolet, had to have new shock absorbers and a front transmission seal within a 30-day period. Mr. Wilson pointed out that more repair bills could be expected shortly because the car had run over 50,000 miles, and he said that his experiences with run-down machinery at his company's plant had convinced him that in the long run it would be wiser to get a new car than to keep repairing the old one.

Mrs. Wilson was lukewarm at first. She rather liked the old car. She also said she could put a new refrigerator to much better use and mentioned that they had never been to Hawaii. Her friend Mrs. Huff had given the bridge club a lecture about Hawaii and had shown some colored slides, and Mrs. Wilson had been a bit envious. She suggested that they put off buying a new car until they had done some of the things they had talked about doing for so many years.

Mr. Wilson dropped the subject for a while, although he was surprised to learn that his wife harbored ideas about travel. He was also somewhat resentful of the implication that he might not be able to afford a new car in addition to other things. On one occasion, he discussed the subject privately with his son Bill, who was visiting with his wife for the weekend. Bill agreed on the need for a new car, but said his father ought to switch brands because the old car had not run too well. He also felt that "a car with a little more class than a Chevy" would be more fitting to Mr. Wilson's position as a company vice-president. Bill also spoke enthusiastically of ordering a stereo tape player for the new car, but Mr. Wilson did not seem too impressed with that suggestion.

The more Mr. Wilson thought about it, the better he liked the idea of a new car. But several months passed before both he and Mrs. Wilson could agree that one was desirable. On one occasion, Mr. and Mrs. Wilson went to a potluck supper at their church and parked the old car near those of several friends. The nearest car belonged to the Beckwiths. It was a white convertible, and during the evening the Beckwiths mentioned many of the car's advantages to the Wilsons. The Wertheims also had a new car that they had brought back from a European trip. Mr. Wilson mentioned to his wife that he did not like European cars, and that he had a lot more faith in American manufacturers. When the evening ended, Mr. Wilson had difficulty starting the family car, and Mrs. Wilson was noticeably silent during the ride home.

At dinner two weeks later, Mrs. Wilson said that she had been thinking it over. She had decided that she would go along, but she still hoped that any car they bought would not be flashy and showy.

□

"WHAT CAR DO WE WANT?"

The next decision was what type of car and what brand to buy. The Wilsons knew that many of their friends had been loyal for many years to certain manufacturers and had always bought the same makes of cars or chosen a different make by the same manufacturer. Mr. Wilson said that he had a lot of faith in all the big Detroit companies. After considerable discussion, Mr. and Mrs. Wilson decided that the new car would be a four-door type like the old one. Although Mr. Wilson did not say so, he thought that a two-door car might look strange to some of their friends.

The Wilsons had trouble deciding how much to spend on a new car. Mr. Wilson said they could afford anything "within reason." Mrs. Wilson was unable to understand what that phrase meant, except that it had something to do with the trade-in price of the old car and the future trade-in value of the new car. Mr. Wilson also talked about depreciation and operation costs, and had figures on sheets of paper. Mrs. Wilson looked at them and decided to leave the figuring to her husband.

After getting nowhere on what they should pay, the Wilsons decided to look at some cars. At this point, both admitted that they had been looking at advertisements on television and in magazines. Mrs. Wilson wanted to look at a Torino. She had seen a yellow one advertised in a magazine and had an idea that she had seen something about free savings bonds if enough people bought Torinos. Her husband asked if a yellow car would not be too flashy, and Mrs. Wilson said that a nice yellow was not flashy at all. Mr. Wilson said he wanted to look at cars made by the Chrysler company because their cars had always been well engineered. The Wilsons looked at Torinos and at Plymouths and Dodges, but they were not very enthusiastic about anything the dealers showed them.

One evening the Wilsons had a visit from a car salesman whose company's showroom was near the supermarket where Mrs. Wilson did her shopping. At the door, the salesman said he had heard the Wilsons were thinking about a new car. He wanted them to see some brochures. Mrs. Wilson thought the salesman was a pleasant young man; so she invited him in. Mr. Wilson was watching a baseball game on TV, and although he was polite to the young salesman, he paid very little attention. Mrs. Wilson was embarrassed. When the young man went, he left his card and suggested that the Wilsons drop into the showroom at their convenience. After he had gone, Mrs. Wilson said they ought to visit the showroom because the salesman had taken his time to call on them, but her husband said the salesman had been a pest and he did not like being bothered at home—it was bad enough to have to see salesmen around the plant.

For the next several weeks, the Wilsons continued to look at advertisements. The old car was running well, however, and Mr. Wilson seemed to be losing some of his interest. On one occasion, he said that as far as he could see there was not much real difference between the various kinds of cars and that all manufacturers were just interested in gadgets and fancy accessories. Besides, the time did not seem right to buy a car—the stock market had been tumbling in recent weeks.

Several months after they had first talked about a new car, the Wilsons went on a Sunday drive. While passing a large billboard advertising the medium-sized Buick, Mr. Wilson announced that he expected to receive a fairly substantial bonus from his company in the near future. The bonus would be large enough to cover the cost of a new car and still leave "something extra toward a trip." Mrs. Wilson reacted happily, but then paused to ask her husband whether he was not still worried by current problems in the stock market. Mr. Wilson said that the market would go back up as soon as things picked up a bit and added that he was not really that worried anyhow; as he put it, "Blue chips are blue chips, and the economy is basically sound."

The next morning, Mrs. Wilson called the owner of the Buick agency, who said that he would have the sales manager take care of them as soon as they arrived.

When the Wilsons got to the Buick agency, the sales manager was waiting. He showed them several floor models and a number of brochures and offered to let them test drive any car the agency had. He answered Mr. Wilson's questions about prices, trade-ins, delivery dates, and guarantees and helped Mrs. Wilson on questions of color and fabric. During these conversations, he also called in the service manager to talk to Mr. Wilson about the operating features of various models.

□

"LET'S BUY THE BUICK."

After an hour or so, the Wilsons retired to the family car for a conference. It became quickly apparent that both preferred the medium Buick. The decision was made in 10 minutes, and the couple returned to the sales manager's office, where Mr. Wilson arranged the delivery date and payment. He was obviously in an expansive mood and left for his office after telling his wife that she could choose the colors, but to remember they had agreed that flashy colors were out.

That night, as the Wilsons talked about the new car, both were surprised that they had been able to make the decision so quickly and with so little disagreement.

□

"WAS OURS A GOOD DECISION?"

When the new car was delivered, the Wilsons' first step was to take it out for a drive immediately. Mr. Wilson seemed elated as he sat at the wheel, and noted that the new car handled with much greater ease than the old Chevrolet. He also offered that he felt very much "at home" in the Buick—its clean lines and sophisticated styling were particularly appealing to him. Mrs. Wilson spotted another new Buick passing in the road in the opposite direction. It was red, and she commented that it looked ghastly. Color made all the difference in the world to a car, she thought, and the dark blue they had chosen was ideal for the medium-sized Buick. Mr. Wilson nodded in agreement.

About two weeks after receiving delivery of the new car, Mr. Wilson noticed a fairly large advertisement on the sports page of the newspaper. Another Buick dealer in the city was offering a car, similar to the one the Wilsons had purchased, for $100 less than Mr. Wilson had paid. This disturbed Mr. Wilson, and he finally telephoned the dealer who was sponsoring the advertisement. He was quite pleased to learn that the car pictured was a demonstrator with 7,500 miles on it. The salesman on the telephone was quite ambiguous as to what a similar new car would cost, but Mr. Wilson implied from the man's remarks that it would be at least $150 more than he had paid.

Decision-making units

A marketing manager needs information about consumers to reduce the uncertainty in estimating their responses to alternative marketing policies. In order to get such information, he first needs to identify the people who are involved in buying decisions concerning his product. Considering the example of the Wilsons buying a car, a manufacturer would be concerned with gathering information about the behavior of Mr. *and* Mrs. Wilson, because *both* were involved in the buying decision. This would not be necessary for a manufacturer of frozen orange concentrate (where Mrs. Wilson alone would be sufficient) or pipe tobacco (where Mr. Wilson would make the buying decision on his own).

By comparing buying situations for automobiles, frozen orange concentrate, and pipe tobacco, we can see that the kinds of people involved in different buying situations depend substantially on the nature of the product being purchased. A manufacturer's initial concern is in identifying and learning the nature of what we shall call the decision-making unit (DMU)□ for his product.

□ A decision-making unit is an individual or group of individuals in a decision-making process, who share a common goal or goals (such as family welfare) which the decision will hopefully help them to achieve, and who share the risks arising from the decision.

Decision-making units play an important part in the analysis of consumer behavior for at least three reasons.

1. Incorrect specification of decision-making units can lead to a reduction in the effectiveness of a firm's marketing program.
2. Published data concerning various aspects of consumer behavior frequently concern people, or groups of people, who are close approximations to a product's decision-making unit. When this situation exists, the marketing

manager has information available to him that may be useful in analyzing his decision-making units.

3. Members of decision-making units affect each other's behavior. Therefore, it is important to look at them as a single unit of behavior instead of reviewing each individual member as a separate entity.

INCORRECT SPECIFICATION OF DECISION-MAKING UNITS

To illustrate the consequences of incorrect DMU specification, consider the example of the sales manager of one of the nation's leading encyclopedia publishers. His product consists of a 32-volume set of encyclopedias that sells for $349.95. Return coupons or cards are placed in the firm's advertisements and direct mail pieces. The coupons and cards are a principal source of prospects. The salesmen typically call and/or write prior to visiting a home to arrange an appointment. Recently one of the sales manager's assistants suggested that this practice be dropped, and that instead the salesmen make unannounced calls from 9 to 11 A.M. and from 12 to 2 P.M. He said that during these times there appeared to be a good chance that at least one member of any given family would be home.

What would probably happen as a result of such a policy? Only on rare occasions would a salesman find the entire family present. Usually he would find only the wife and preschool children. Will a sales story presented to these members of the family be as effective as one presented to the husband, or to both the husband and wife, or to the entire family? The decision-making unit for the purchase of an encyclopedia is apt to involve at least the father and mother, and possibly even the children. It is typically a joint decision. The mother is not apt to act without consulting the father. The sales manager's knowledge of the joint roles of the various members of the family would probably lead him to reject this proposal in favor of one that has a substantially greater chance of finding at least the husband and wife present, and perhaps also the children.

RELEVANCE OF EXISTING INFORMATION

The usefulness of published data about decision-making units is best illustrated by recalling the experience of Mr. and Mrs. Wilson when buying a car. The Wilsons' purchase is typical in the sense that the relevant decision-making unit was the *family*. For automobile manufacturers, think of the potential value of these kinds of published data about families:

> The Bureau of Labor Statistics of the U.S. Department of Labor publishes average annual family expenditures for a number of commodities, including several durables. Data are broken out by urban/rural and white/Negro families.[5]

[5] U.S. Department of Labor, Bureau of Labor Statistics, *Consumer Expenditures and Income, Total United States, Urban and Rural* and *Monthly Labor Review.*

Similar data, but in much greater detail, are found in two publications of the National Industrial Conference Board.[6]

The Survey Research Center of the University of Michigan publishes annual data on family automobile ownership. Included are statistics on number of automobiles owned, age of automobiles owned, number purchased new and used, prices paid, and methods of financing used—all on a family basis.[7]

The Census Bureau of the U.S. Department of Commerce provides statistics on family income in the United States.[8]

The Census Bureau also publishes quarterly information on consumer buying expectations for automobiles. The Bureau estimates the average probabilities of a family buying an automobile within the next 12 months, depending on family income, changes in family income over the past year, and prospects of a substantial increase in family income within the coming year.[9]

The Federal Reserve System publishes data on the propensity of different types of families to save.[10]

All the foregoing sources use similar definitions of "family." The definition of the Michigan Survey Research Center is typical, "a family unit is two or more people living in the same dwelling unit and related to each other by blood, marriage or adoption."

□ INTERACTION AMONG DMU MEMBERS

In order to illustrate the notion of interaction among DMU members, consider the brand preferences for automobiles in a market where the only two available brands were being studied. Suppose that husbands and wives in 200 families were asked what brand (A or B) they preferred, and results were as follows:

	Prefer brand A	*Prefer brand B*
Husbands	64%	36%
Wives	30	70

From these data, could the percentage of decision-making units (in this case husband-wife families) that account for each of the four possible combinations of husband-wife brand preferences be predicted? The answer is that the prediction could be made only if we assume husbands' and wives' preferences to be independent, that is, that husbands in no way influence their wives' pref-

[6] *Expenditure Patterns of the American Family,* National Industrial Conference Board, New York, 1965; and *Market Profiles of Consumer Products,* National Industrial Conference Board, New York, 1967.

[7] The University of Michigan, Survey Research Center, *Survey of Consumer Finances.*

[8] U.S. Department of Commerce, Bureau of the Census, *Current Population Reports,* Series P-60.

[9] U.S. Department of Commerce, Bureau of the Census, *Survey of Consumer Buying Expectations.*

[10] Board of Governors of the Federal Reserve System, *Report on the Survey of Financial Characteristics of Consumers and Federal Reserve Bulletin.*

erences, and vice versa. Under these conditions, it is reasonable to assume that the preference distribution among decision-making units would be as follows:

Preference combination of DMU	*Percent of families*	
Husband prefers A, wife A	19.2%	(30% of 64%)
Husband prefers A, wife B	44.8	(70% of 64%)
Husband prefers B, wife A	10.8	(30% of 36%)
Husband prefers B, wife B	25.2	(70% of 36%)
	100.0%	

Because we have assumed husbands' and wives' preferences to be independent, there is no need to collect data on decision-making units. All that is needed are data on husbands and wives taken separately, that is, information about the individual participants within the decision-making units.

Unfortunately for many marketing problems, the manager is quite uncertain about (1) whether the members of a decision-making unit have no effect on each other, or (2) whether it seems reasonable to suppose that they do interact and influence one another. In the case of automobile purchases, interaction is nearly always present. Not surprisingly a study of family decision making by *Time* magazine revealed that 96 percent of couples *always* discuss an automobile buying decision; the remaining 4 percent sometimes discuss it. The same report found similar high levels of husband-wife interaction for other major household purchases, as illustrated by the data shown in Table 3-1.

The only way to obtain data on combinations of preferences is to collect information about decision-making *units* as such. Mr. and Mrs. Wilson are an

□ TABLE 3-1

Degree to which husbands and wives discuss products before purchasing

Product	Always	Sometimes	Never
Automobiles	96%	4%	0%
Refrigerators	98	0	2
Rugs	96	0	4
Sofas	96	2	2
Television sets	89	7	4
Toasters	45	47	8
Washers	96	2	2

Source: *A Pilot Study Concerning the Relative Influence of Husbands and Wives in Consumer Purchasing,* Marketing Information Research Report 1428, *Time* magazine, New York, 1968.

FIGURE 3-2
Relative influence of husbands and wives in selected dimensions of an automobile purchase

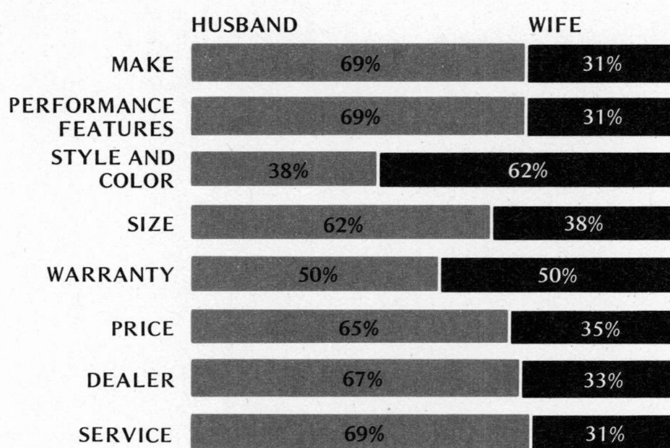

Source: *A Pilot Study Concerning the Relative Influence of Husbands and Wives in Consumer Purchasing,* Marketing Information Research Report 1428, *Time* magazine, New York, 1968.

---

automobile decision-making unit. Mr. Wilson handled financial matters independently while Mrs. Wilson chose the color of the car alone, but they participated *jointly* in all other aspects of the buying decision.

We would not expect all automobile decision-making units to behave in the same manner as the Wilsons. There are, however, general patterns of DMU behavior that we can expect will occur in the majority of automobile purchases. The research data illustrated in Figure 3-2, for example, show us that husbands tend to exert greater influence over most dimensions of automobile purchases, except for questions of style and color where wives usually predominate. Wives, however, are more likely to be influential in decisions to purchase home furnishings, while the decision of where to go for a vacation is apt to be determined equally by both.

□

PURCHASING UNITS, CONSUMING UNITS, AND DECISION-MAKING UNITS

Frequently, the membership of purchasing units and consuming units is different from that of the units which make decisions as to what or where to buy. Consider the case of a family of three in which the birthday of the child is coming up. Aware of the need for a gift, the husband and wife discuss alternatives such as a toy, some clothing, or a set of children's books. Their decision is influenced by seeing and admiring a newly published set of children's books while visiting some neighbors. The husband and wife agree on the books as a suitable gift, and because there is a large bookstore adjacent to the husband's office, he offers to buy the gift on his way home from work.

Because he alone made the eventual purchase at the bookstore, the husband constitutes the *purchasing unit* for this decision. But he shares membership in the *decision-making unit* with his wife. Both husband and wife participated in the process leading to the decision to buy a book, both shared the common goal of finding a suitable gift for their child, and both shared the risk that the child might not be happy with their choice. The child did not participate in the decision, and is not a member of the decision-making unit—he is instead the *consuming unit* who will use the product. Neighbors had an indirect role in the decision, but the extent of their involvement was limited to one of influence. They are not members of the purchasing unit, the consuming unit, or the decision-making unit.

The distinction among consuming units, purchasing units, and decision-making units is not always so obvious in household buying decisions. When the Wilsons bought a car, no differences existed in membership of all three units—each was comprised of Mr. and Mrs. Wilson. The distinction is usually of far greater importance in industrial buying situations, as will be discussed in Chapter 9. There, specialization of functions among individuals is often of far greater importance.

Despite the fact that there is less specialization of function in a household, the distinctions are nonetheless useful. The late Wroe Alderson, a prominent marketing practitioner, made the following distinction in the context of household analysis[11]:

> Consuming habits are part of the pattern of living, but buying habits (purchasing habits and consumer habits) are only derived from this pattern. Buying habits, in the sense of repetitive purchase of a given brand or customary trading at a given store, can be broken overnight with no real disruption in the pattern of living. Buying habits, in fact, can more safely be regarded as deliberately chosen routines designed to save time and energy for rational consideration of more important matters.

This distinction is important to marketing management because it implies that the marketing manager's ability to manipulate the determinants of buying habits is apt to be greater than his ability to manipulate the determinants of consumption habits. For example, it is more likely that the content of a household's dinner can be influenced than the time of day at which the meal is served. Mealtimes are determined by living habits such as working hours, which a marketer can seldom modify.

In essence, therefore, the distinction among decision-making, purchasing, and consuming units is important for two reasons:

1. The membership of the respective units may not overlap and may thus imply different marketing strategies depending on the unit with which the policy maker is primarily concerned.

[11] Wroe Alderson, *Marketing Behavior and Executive Action,* Richard D. Irwin, Inc., Homewood, Ill., 1957, p. 166.

2. Even though the membership of the groups may overlap, the variables that determine the particular type of behavior involved may be somewhat different and may imply different marketing policies depending, once more, on the concern of the policy maker.

Stages in consumer buying decisions

To some, the Wilsons' behavior in purchasing a new car may seem disjointed and even illogical. Why did it take almost a year to decide on a car? What was the significance of some events that took place, such as seeing friends' cars at the church potluck dinner? Why did Mr. Wilson telephone a dealer to ask about an advertised Buick when he had just bought a Buick? These and other issues are typical of the kinds of questions that have to be asked if we are going to develop a coherent framework for describing, explaining, and predicting the buying decisions of consumers like the Wilsons. They are not always easy questions to answer, nor can they always be answered without ambiguity.

In this section, we continue our quest to understand consumer buying decisions by examining the chronology of events that transpired in the Wilsons' purchase. While numerous, these events can be viewed as making up a relatively small number of *stages* in a consumer buying decision. Depicted in Figure 3-3, these stages are arbitrarily referred to as *need arousal, search and evaluation, purchase,* and *postpurchase feedback*. Together, they comprise an entire process of consumer decision making. The process is by no means unique to the Wilsons: it is one that marketers have observed over and over again in studying a myriad of buying situations.

□ NEED AROUSAL

For the Wilsons, buying behavior was initiated when their old car required two major repairs within a 30-day period. An event of this kind is sometimes called a *triggering cue*[12] because it serves to *arouse a need* for potential purchasing action. In the Wilsons' case, the stimulant to need arousal was external—repairs to the old car. Other buying decisions may originate without external stimuli, arising as the result of an individual becoming independently alert and responsive to a need or drive.

Because need arousal is the first stage in all buying behavior, it is particularly crucial to marketers. Mrs. Wilson's reaction to the idea of a new car was one of reluctance as she conjured visions of a refrigerator or a trip to Hawaii as alternatives. Her resistance resulted in *postponement* of the car purchase, a course of behavior that is common when people are considering buying durable goods. Many sellers of durables, such as furniture, appliance, and au-

[12] John A. Howard, *Marketing Management Analysis and Planning,* rev. ed., Richard D. Irwin, Inc., Homewood, Ill., 1963.

FIGURE 3-3
Major steps in the new car purchase

PURCHASING STAGE	MAJOR STEPS INVOLVED
NEED AROUSAL	☐ Old car needs repairs. ☐ Mr. Wilson talks to wife, relates to experience with plant equipment. ☐ Mrs. Wilson hesitant—raises alternatives of refrigerator and trip to Hawaii. ☐ Subject dropped—Mr. Wilson contemplates causes of wife's resistance. ☐ Son Bill supports his father's idea of buying a new car. ☐ See new cars of friends at church supper. Wilson's car hard to start, and Mrs. Wilson is disturbed. ☐ Mrs. Wilson concedes to buying a new car.
SEARCH AND EVALUATION	☐ Discuss alternative brands and types. No decision on brand, but agree on 4-door car. ☐ Mr. Wilson works out cost data, but Mrs. Wilson confused and leaves decision on what to pay to her husband. ☐ Mrs. Wilson impressed by yellow Torino in advertisement. Mr. Wilson questions yellow color, says he likes Chrysler cars for their engineering. ☐ Look at Torinos, Plymouths, and Dodges, but not impressed. ☐ Young salesman calls at house. Mrs. Wilson impressed, but husband views as intrusion. ☐ Both continue to look at advertisements, but Mr. Wilson losing interest. ☐ Bonus from company raises Mr. Wilson's interest again. Sees Buick billboard advertisement. ☐ Phone Buick agency, arrange meeting. ☐ Meet with sales manager. Mr. Wilson discusses prices, trade-in, delivery, guarantee, and operating features. Mrs. Wilson interested in colors.
PURCHASE	☐ "Family conference" and decision to buy. ☐ Mr. Wilson completes deal, leaves wife to select colors.
POSTPURCHASE FEEDBACK	☐ New car delivered, taken on drive. ☐ Mr. Wilson thinks car handles well, feels "at home" in it. ☐ Mrs. Wilson sees red Buick on road, but prefers the blue she chose. ☐ Mr. Wilson sees newspaper advertisement offering an apparent lower price than he paid. Phone call reveals car is a demonstrator, a new car would be more.

tomobile retailers, attempt to overcome postponement by offering frequent "sales" that create a sense of purchase urgency.

Several further stimuli were necessary before the Wilsons both felt sufficiently motivated to begin looking for a car in earnest. Bill's visit, seeing friends' new cars, and difficulty in starting the old car all contributed to need arousal.

SEARCH AND EVALUATION

Once the Wilsons had agreed that they would buy a new car, their next step was to search for and evaluate alternative brands and models. The significance of identifying search and evaluation activities as a discrete stage in consumer buying decisions rests in the predominance of *information gathering* at this stage. Consumers are often very active and aggressive in seeking out the information they require to make a purchase. Their sources include not only friends and opinion leaders, but also advertisements and salesmen. It is in the search and evaluation stage, more than any other, that a firm's marketing communications are important in influencing buying decisions.

The Wilsons' behavior highlights the information-gathering aspect of search and evaluation. Mrs. Wilson's early infatuation with a yellow Torino was the result of an advertisement. Mr. Wilson's prejudice for Chrysler products was based on a belief in their superior engineering. (Where did he acquire that information?) Yet in neither case was the information sufficiently persuasive to create a disposition to buy. A passing glance at the Buick billboard was apparently connected with Mr. Wilson's decision to visit the Buick dealer, where further information from the sales manager eventually brought the couple to the point of purchase.

While marketers find it useful to identify stages in buying decisions, the case of Mr. and Mrs. Wilson also illustrates that the stages are not always discretely defined. At the onset of searching for a new car, the Wilsons both admitted that they had been looking at advertisements *for some time;* probably beginning well *before* Mrs. Wilson conceded to the idea of buying one. It is also difficult to ascertain exactly when the couple stopped evaluating and decided on a specific purchase. Nominally, the trip to the Buick dealer was the act leading directly to purchase, but the decision itself was not made until that point when Mr. and Mrs. Wilson held a "family conference" in their old car.

PURCHASE

The Wilsons were surprised at how quickly, and with how little disagreement, they decided on the Buick. No marketer, however, would agree with the couple's viewpoint of what constitutes a purchase decision. The act of purchase itself took less than an hour, consisting of a short family conference and some concluding arrangements between Mr. Wilson and the sales manager. But if *none* of the previous events in the Wilsons' case history had occurred, it is highly unlikely that they could have decided on the Buick so quickly. The "seeds of purchase" were planted long before by the information-seeking and evaluative activities the Wilsons undertook. Buying the Buick was conditioned on the outcome of these prior activities. The purchase was what one group of authors has described as "the *final result* when sufficient *information* is gathered to permit a selection with some confidence."[13]

[13] James F. Engel, David T. Kollat, and Roger D. Blackwell, *Consumer Behavior,* Holt, Rinehart and Winston, Inc., New York, 1968, p. 36 (italics added).

It is only by looking at the act of purchase as one stage in the total process of a consumer buying decision that marketers can begin to fully understand what has occurred. How often do people describe something as an *impulse purchase?* True impulse purchases are very rare. More often than not, they are the result of many prior events encompassing arousal of a need, and both conscious and semiconscious activities relating to search and evaluation.

POSTPURCHASE FEEDBACK

The marketer's view of a buying decision does not end with a purchase transaction because, as exemplified by Mr. and Mrs. Wilson, additional events can occur which are of significance to the design of marketing programs. The buyer may have doubts as to whether the *product* he bought was a good one, and seek information to justify his decision. In test driving the new car, Mr. Wilson sought his wife's approval as to the car's handling abilities, while Mrs. Wilson sought her husband's approval of blue as a better color choice than red. Doubts may also arise as to whether the *purchase* was a good one. Mr. Wilson seemed quite upset at the thought that he may have been able to get a better deal at another Buick dealer. His telephone call to the dealer was an attempt to reestablish his somewhat shaken confidence in the wisdom of his purchase. Mr. Wilson coupled the additional information he obtained (the advertised car was a demonstrator) with a slight distortion of that information (he *implied* a new Buick would cost more than he had paid) to achieve this end.

Coined by Prof. Leon Festinger, the term *cognitive dissonance* is used to describe confidence-seeking behavior occurring after a purchase transaction. This *postpurchase feedback* is important to marketers because it affects the possibility of eventual future purchases. Studies of automobile buying, for example, have established that consumer satisfaction after the purchase is a key factor in brand loyalty.[14] The handling ease of the new Buick impressed Mr. Wilson and, in a small way, increased the probability of his buying another at some time. The telephone information on prices left him satisfied with his present dealer. At the same time, informal word-of-mouth communication between Mr. Wilson and his acquaintances is likely to be favorable to the Buick in the light of his postpurchase experiences.

PROBLEM SOLVING IN CONSUMER DECISION MAKING

Not all buying decisions involve as many activities as the purchase of an automobile. A housewife may discover she needs facial tissues (she is out of them), search and evaluate alternatives (she compares prices on the supermarket shelf), and purchase tissue on her weekly shopping trip. Postpurchase feedback may arise only if the facial tissue proves inferior in some way. While the same stages of consumer decision making can exist for both automobiles

[14] Gerald D. Bell, "The Automobile Buyer after the Purchase," *Journal of Marketing,* July, 1967, pp. 12–16.

and facial tissue, there are also enough differences between the two to warrant distinguishing between them.

Professor John Howard has provided a useful way of thinking about distinctions in the intensity of activities surrounding buying decisions.[15] Howard views consumer decision making as *problem-solving behavior.* The Wilsons' purchase of an automobile is typical of *extensive* problem solving, and closely approximates the model of rational behavior posited by microeconomists. In extensive problem solving, the buyer identifies as many alternatives as he can, and collects information pertaining to each. The buyer is ready to purchase only when he has "complete" information about each alternative. This information and that obtained following the purchase provide inputs for future purchase decisions.

In *limited* problem-solving behavior, a buyer still identifies alternatives, but collects only partial information about each. Limited problem solving is more likely to occur in purchases of smaller unit values. The housewife who compares facial-tissue prices at the supermarket is exemplifying limited problem-solving behavior. Eventually, her experience in buying tissue may lead her to *automatic response behavior.* In this instance, she does not bother to identify alternatives at all. Past experience with, say, Scotties has been satisfactory, and her disposition is to consider only this one alternative.

A useful way to analyze consumer problem-solving behavior is by diagramming the *decisions* involved at each stage of a purchase process, as in Figure 3–4.

Determinants of consumer buying decisions

So far, we have come part of the way in our attempt to understand the buying behavior of household customers. We have reviewed the nature of a consumer buying decision, examined the importance of identifying the decision-making unit making a decision, and discussed the value of viewing buying activities as a series of stages in a total decision-making process. These steps are important in helping to *describe* consumer buying decisions, but provide only a starting point for *explaining* and *predicting* consumer behavior. To gain a full understanding of the structure of buying decisions, we must address the question of why consumers behave as they do. Necessarily, this involves (1) identifying the variables that impinge on a consumer in a decision-making role and (2) defining how these variables act as determinants of buying decisions.

□ DISCIPLINARY APPROACHES TO UNDERSTANDING CONSUMER DECISIONS

Suppose that we asked a group of experts, each from a different field of study, to examine the case history of Mr. and Mrs. Wilson buying a car. For this task, we are able to recruit a demographer (one who studies the vital statistics of

[15] Howard, *op. cit.,* Chaps. 3 and 4.

populations), an economist, a psychologist, and a sociologist. What insights could each provide to a marketing manager concerning the determinants of the Wilsons' buying decision?

The demographer might lead off by saying that many of the Wilsons' activities were exactly as he would have predicted. As a *suburban family,* they are members of a population group that is most likely to buy a new car. Suburban families make up 29 percent of the population in the United States, but account for 37 percent of expenditures on automobiles. Just by observing that Mr. Wilson is a company vice-president, the demographer would also point out an increased likelihood of purchasing a new car. Furthermore, the selection of a Buick over a Torino, Plymouth, or Dodge was quite congruent with Mr. Wilson's *occupational status.* Finally, identifying the *life-cycle stage* of the Wilson decision-making unit provides the demographer with further explanatory ammunition. He describes the couple as an "empty nest" in which the family head is still employed in the labor force. Families in this category are most likely to have money saved and to be in a secure financial position. Thus, financial issues presented no true obstacle to the Wilsons. Mrs. Wilson's concern with a refrigerator and a Hawaiian trip could almost have been expected; for people in this couple's life-cycle stage are most inclined to spend money on travel, luxuries, and home improvements. The rejection of Bill's suggestion for a stereo tape player was natural, for empty-nest families are generally not interested in new products.

Our remaining experts would find no difficulty in agreeing with the demographer's analysis, but they might comment that he was really using socioeconomic variables to explain behavior. It is true, in fact, that demographic variables are socioeconomic in character. But because they are distinguishable by the relative ease with which they can be measured, and because published sources of demographic information are readily available, demographic data are the variables most widely used by marketers in explaining consumer buying decisions. Despite limitations in use, it is for these reasons that demographic variables frequently warrant separate and distinct consideration.

The economist would probably step forward to add some insights that he felt the demographer overlooked. The Wilsons were by no means immune to economic influences. *General economic conditions* were uncertain at one point during the buying decision, as reflected in the temporary downturn of the stock market, and this no doubt contributed to Mr. Wilson postponing his purchase for a while. Further, Mr. Wilson's postpurchase concern about having paid $100 too much for his Buick indicates that he was not entirely oblivious to financial considerations. More important in explaining his decision to buy was the fact that his bonus provided a substantial quantity of *discretionary income* with which to buy a car and still have money available for other purchases.

At this point, the psychologist might comment that his associates have

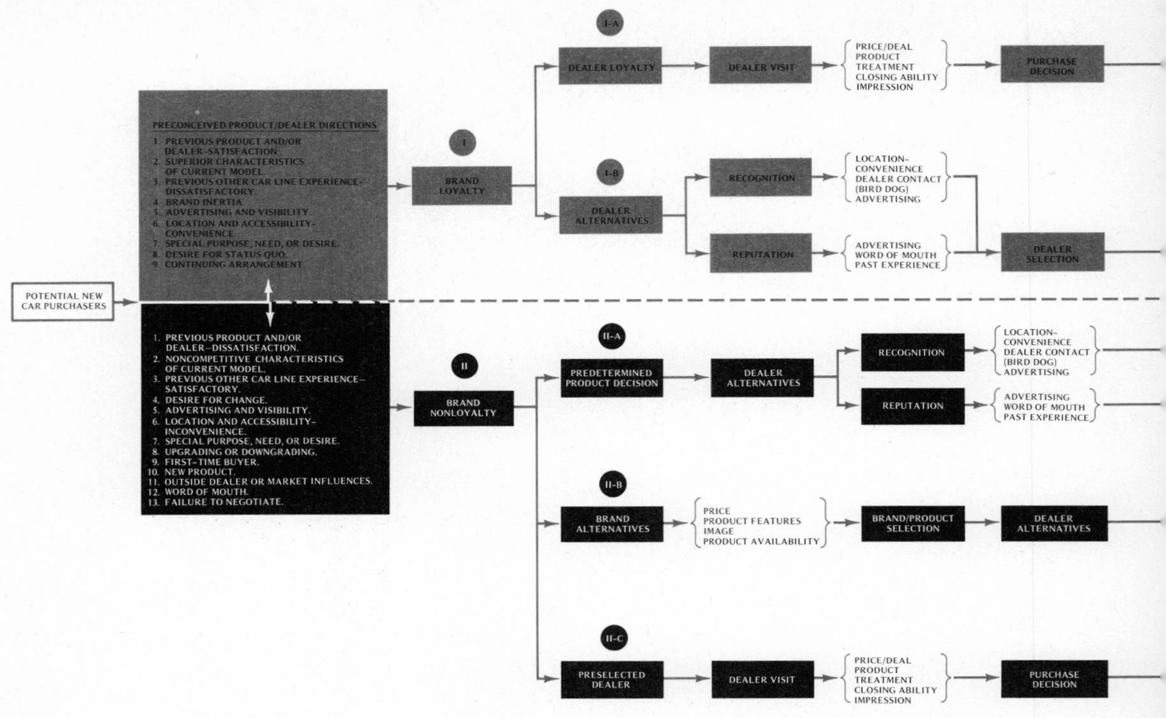

Source: "Fuller Ford, Inc.," case study, Harvard Business School, 1968. Reproduced with permission.

FIGURE 3-4
New car purchase decision process

neglected to offer adequate explanation of the brand and color of car chosen by the Wilsons. Typical of the psychologist's remarks would be those surrounding the concept of *reinforcement*. The old Chevrolet, with its frequent need of repairs, had obviously resulted in such negative reinforcement of the brand that the couple did not ever consider another. Also, the individual influences of Mr. and Mrs. Wilson within the decision-making unit are explainable by their *role dispositions* — it is a characteristic mode of behavior for women to be concerned about color, men about financial matters, in a situation of this kind.

Meanwhile, the sociologist would be eager to point up the many and varied influences of the Wilsons' *reference groups* on their buying decision. There are friends and acquaintances with whom the Wilsons identify and use as standards of behavior. One concern of Mrs. Wilson is her status in the bridge club. Mrs. Huff's address to the bridge club about her trip to Hawaii had such an im-

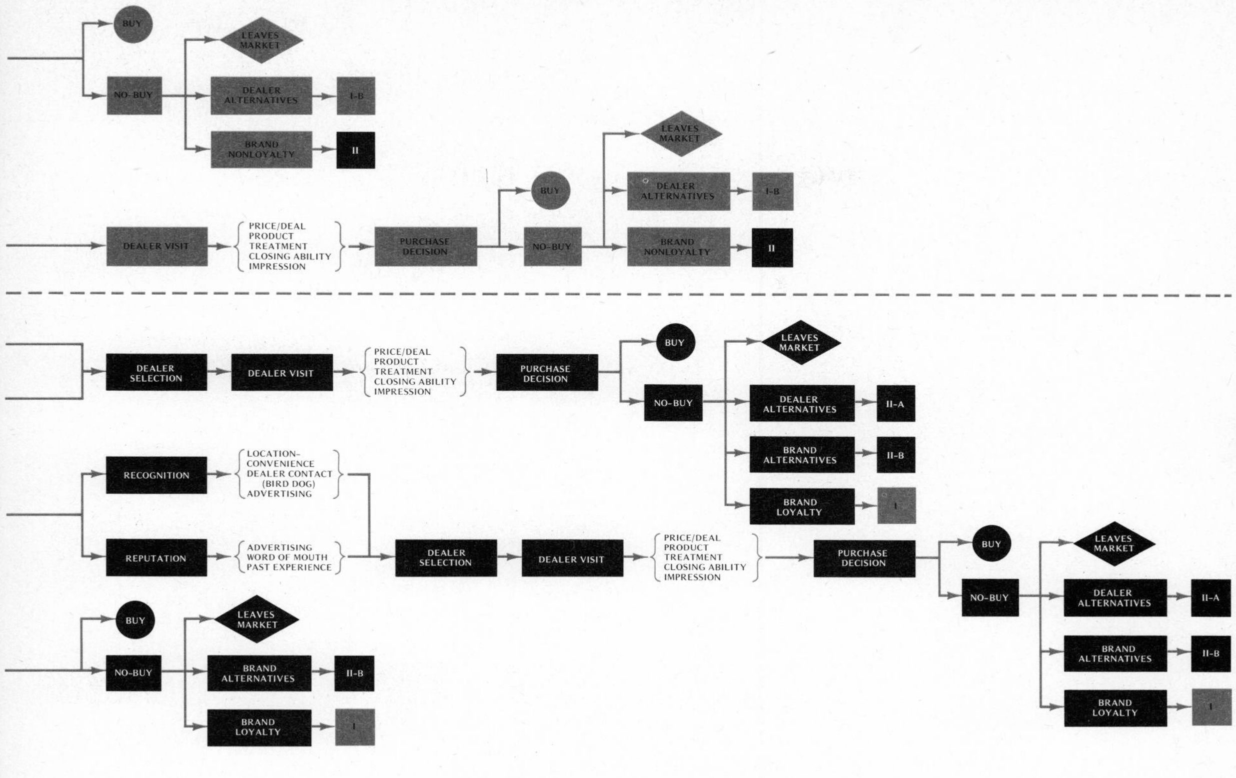

pact on Mrs. Wilson that she remained resistant to the idea of a new car for some time thereafter. It was not until Mrs. Wilson saw members of another reference group, her church, with new cars that she became favorably disposed to buying a new automobile.

THE MARKETER'S PERSPECTIVE

Each of the four so-called experts put forth a different interpretation of the important variables influencing the Wilsons' decisions. Which is correct? The answer is that each has contributed partially to our understanding, but none has provided a comprehensive explanation. The demographer, economist, psychologist, and sociologist have all viewed the decision from their own perspectives, each giving particular prominence to variables from his own field of experience that he regards as causal.

The difficult task of the marketing manager is reflected in the above situation. He must understand the nature of his consumers' buying decisions if he is to be able to influence these decisions favorably. To do so, the manager must apply the concepts and research findings of a number of related disciplines, at the same time integrating different perspectives into a single unified explanation of behavior. In this sense, the marketer's perspective is an *interdisciplinary* one. He is in much the same position as an urban planner who is asked to design a new town—demographic, economic, psychological, sociological, political, and cultural factors must all be taken into account.

The next four chapters are devoted to gaining further understanding of the determinants of consumer buying decisions. Each chapter deals with one of the major "external disciplines," exploring the contributions it has made to the understanding of consumer decisions and, ultimately, to the advancement of marketing management.

Questions

1. A study of the male after-shave lotion market revealed the following information:

   a. 76 percent of all men use after-shave lotion.
   b. 52 percent of users are heavy users (seven or more times per week).
   c. Heavy users consume 74 percent of all after-shave lotion, regular users 18 percent, and light users 8 percent.
   d. Use of after-shave lotion increases with education—25 percent of light users, 36 percent of regular users, and 42 percent of heavy users have at least some college education.

If your company marketed after-shave lotion, would you recommend that they view this as a segmented market? On what basis should the market be segmented? State the specific benefits you would hope to derive from segmentation in this instance.

2. How might the marketing mix for a breakfast cereal differ if it were aimed at each of the following?

   a. Housewives
   b. Husbands
   c. Children
   d. Housewives and children
   e. Housewives and husbands
   f. Entire families

3. The Jones family includes Mr. and Mrs. Jones, Mrs. Jones' mother, their three children (Susan, 13; Dick, 10; and Jimmy, 8) as well as their dog Trixie.

For each of the following purchases, identify the likely decision-making unit and, where you would expect a joint decision, identify the likely role of each participant:

a. Purchase of a portable typewriter

b. Purchase of a new overcoat for Mr. Jones; for Mrs. Jones; for Susan; for Jimmy

c. Rental of a summer vacation cottage

d. Purchase of a new brand of dog food

4. The Jones family discussed above is considering the purchase of a new house. What specific decisions will have to be made? What role would you expect each member of the family to play in making these decisions?

5. Describe a buying decision you have recently made for a product or service whose cost was in excess of $10. What was the membership of the DMU, consuming unit, and purchasing unit in this case? Identify the activities in various stages of your decision-making process.

How, if at all, might the manufacturer or marketer of the product you purchased use his understanding of your purchase behavior to improve his marketing policies?

6. If you were developing an advertising campaign for an automobile, in what way might the campaign differ if it stressed the following attributes?

a. The color of the car

b. Its mileage

c. The texture and pattern of the upholstery

d. The size of the trunk

e. Its safety on the road

f. The design of the engine

7. What needs do you think would be important to DMU's of the following products?

a. Dining-room set

b. Sports car

c. Birthday cards

d. Headache remedies

e. Insulin

8. In an attempt to improve their marketing programs, some companies have developed logical-flow models of consumer buying decisions. Such models attempt to identify the essential activities in a buying decision and the sequence in which these activities occur.

An example of a logical-flow model of a new automobile purchase decision, developed by Ford Motor Company, is illustrated in Figure 3-4 on pages 74–75. In this figure the blocks, diamonds, and circles are used to identify questions asked and actions taken by the buyer. Arrows are used to indicate the flow or sequence of questions and actions.

a. To what extent does the logical-flow model in Figure 3-4 conform to the purchase decision of Mr. and Mrs. Wilson described earlier in this chapter?

b. What are the potential uses for this model for either an automobile manufacturer or for one of its franchised dealers?

c. How well do you think this model would describe the approach followed by new car buyers other than the Wilsons?

d. How could the model be modified to make it more generally applicable?

e. How would such changes improve its value to marketing managers in the automobile industry?

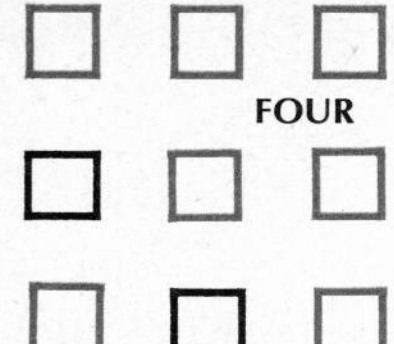

FOUR

Demographic foundations of consumer decisions

In this chapter, we will begin the development of a general understanding of consumer behavior. Our starting point is consumer demography, the "vital statistics" of populations. We will be concerned with how a person's location, sex, occupation, education, life-cycle stage, and racial or ethnic origin affect his decisions as a buyer. To be sure, these factors represent only a partial picture of behavior determinants. It is hard to imagine an instance of behavior that is not also influenced by numerous other economic, psychological, or social factors. But for reasons that will be explained shortly, demography often represents a marketer's first attempt at understanding consumer behavior.

A DRINK AFTER WORK

Both the value and shortcomings of demographic information can be illustrated by examining a brief instance of behavior in the lives of three hypothetical, but not atypical, Americans.

In Waterville, Maine, Paul Lesage stopped off at Pierre's Bar on his way home from work. He ordered a beer and talked with some of his many friends who were there. Paul stayed long enough to have two more beers before continuing home.
In Dallas, Texas, Mario Favelli returned to his hotel after completing a day's work. Mario was away from home. After a fast shower, he proceeded to the hotel cocktail lounge. Here he drank a bourbon with water, then moved on to the dining room for supper.

In Seattle, Washington, Bill Adams drove directly home from work. On arrival, he mixed martinis for himself and his wife, then poured soft drinks for his two boys. Together, the family group talked and sipped their drinks, then proceeded to the dinner table.

In each of these three cases, there is a common thread of behavior. Having completed a day's work, all the individuals depicted decided to relax with a drink before dinner. But there are also marked differences in behavior. One man drank with his friends, another drank alone, while the third drank with his wife. One man went to a bar, another went to a cocktail lounge, while the third went home. Finally, one man chose beer, the second chose a highball, while the third had a cocktail.

To the marketing manager of a brewing company or distillery, these differences could be significant. They might also be important to an entrepreneurial businessman who is considering investing in a new bar, cocktail lounge, or other drinking establishment. If behavioral decisions similar to those cited in the three cases are made by a significant number of individuals, then the resultant aggregrate behavior patterns represent important cues for marketing strategy. For the brewing and distilling companies, promotional programs might be tailored to suit the needs of the market segments represented by our three examples. For the entrepreneur, decisions about the nature of a new drinking establishment, its decor, location, and so forth, are likewise influenced. For these reasons, it is important that the business decision maker be able to explain the differences in behavior. But where to begin?

As a first step, most marketers would turn to demographic information. That is, they would look to see if there are any demographic factors that are *causal* in determining each individual's behavior, or some aspect of it. Let us therefore reveal some brief demographic information pertaining to each of the three after-work drinkers.

Paul Lesage, fifty-nine, is a self-employed plumber. He is of French-Canadian stock, as are many other residents of his rural Maine community. Paul has lived in Waterville all his life and attended the local high school there. However, he left school after the tenth grade to become an apprentice plumber. He is married and has four children, but all have now grown up and left home.

Mario Favelli, twenty-six, is a sales representative for an electronic components manufacturer in Houston. Mario's parents were immigrants from Italy, and he was born and raised in Boston. He has an engineering degree, and moved to Houston one year ago to take up his present job. Mario has been married for two years, has no children, and lives in an apartment centrally located in the city.

Bill Adams, forty-three, is a financial executive with a Seattle-based food chain. He is proud to say that his ancestors have lived in America for many generations. Bill, who has a master of business administration degree, lives in the suburbs with his wife and two sons, ages sixteen and fourteen. He has been in Seattle since joining his present firm seven years ago.

On the basis of these demographic data, we begin to see some possible explanations of the differences in behavior. Consider *where* and *with whom* the three men chose to drink. Mario Favelli's occupation as a salesman required that he travel away from home. Since he was staying in a hotel, it is not surprising that he went to the hotel cocktail lounge. As a stranger in Dallas, it is again not unexpected that he drank alone. Paul Lesage's choice of Pierre's Bar may have been the result of regional and ethnic factors. He lived in Maine, an area where there are many Americans of French-Canadian stock. His selection of Pierre's Bar suggests that he was seeking the companionship of others who were also of French-Canadian ethnic background. We cannot be sure why Bill Adams chose to go home, but plausible explanations may lie in the influence of life-cycle or occupational factors. As the only one of our three cases having children living at home, Bill may have been anxious to spend time with his family. As a business executive, he would often entertain customers or associates at lunch. He may have been more anxious to go home after work, since he often frequents restaurants on business during the noon hour.

Demographic factors also provide some rationale for differences in what each man drank. For example, we know from previous studies that, on the average, families headed by foremen and craftsmen purchase about 55 percent more beer than average American families. Also, families headed by men with college degrees purchase about 51 percent more distilled alcoholic beverages than average American families.[1] The choices of Paul Lesage (a plumber), Mario Favelli, and Bill Adams (both college graduates) seem to conform to the overall behavior patterns. However, we must be careful in our interpretation of these data. We might well have *predicted* the beverage choice of each man on the basis of his demographic profile, but it is stretching a point to assert demographic factors were *causal* in this instance. More likely, the demographic data are merely reflecting underlying economic and social factors causing each man to choose as he did.

Demographic factors offer no basis for understanding some elements of observed behavior. Why did Paul Lesage stay for two additional beers before continuing home? Why did Mario Favelli return directly to his hotel instead of stopping off at a cocktail lounge on the way? Why did Bill Adams and his wife both have martinis? To these and other questions, we must turn to additional sources of explanation.

□

THE USE OF DEMOGRAPHIC INFORMATION

As we have seen in the foregoing example, some aspects of consumer decisions cannot be explained in terms of demographic factors. Even those elements of behavior which we *can* attribute to demographic influences are at best described as tentative hypotheses. Whether a marketing problem involves

[1] Based on home consumption data cited in *Expenditure Patterns of the American Family*, National Industrial Conference Board, New York, 1965.

liquor or beer, furs, flooring, or fishing rods, it could be better analyzed with additional information on such topics as how much money customers have and how they spend it, what they think and how they think, and how they are influenced by other people. In building an understanding of consumer decision-making units, the marketing man's job is to develop an amalgam of demographic, economic, psychological, and sociological information and concepts. Only in this way can he really begin to know his customers.

Yet in practice, economic, psychological, and social factors are often considered only superficially in studies of consumer behavior, or even not at all. Despite limitations, demography frequently becomes the principal focal point of analysis. This should not be interpreted as indicating that demography is necessarily more useful in explaining behavior than any other kinds of influencing factors. The significant advantages of using demographic factors lie in their relative ease of measurement, and in the availability of relevant demographic data from secondary sources of information.

It is not a particularly difficult task to determine a person's age, occupation, education, place of residence, or family size. If asked, an individual can respond in unambiguous terms and is usually willing to do so. With some limitations, such as a woman asked her age, he is also inclined to be truthful in responding to questions of demography. This ease of measurement is not always present in assessing nondemographic influences on decisions. One can readily imagine the problems in measuring social approval, prestige, status, ego gratification, self-image, or security. Further, to the question of *how* to measure, there is also the problem of knowing *what* to measure. An individual is not always able, or willing, to delineate the true factors that are important in influencing his behavior. For example, a dinner host may claim to serve Beaujolais wine because he admires its flavor and bouquet. In fact, his choice of the French wine may be influenced more by a desire to gain the esteem of his guests as a connoisseur of fine imported wines.

In the United States, a tradition for collecting demographic statistics began on the day the nation was founded. Article I, Section 2, of the Constitution provided that "enumeration shall be made within three years after the first meeting of the Congress of the United States, and within every subsequent term of ten years." Through legislative interpretation, this constitutional mandate (which required only a population count) was extended over the years to provide the demographic facts present in today's modern census. This same tradition of information gathering has also been reflected in a plethora of privately published studies relating demographic factors to all varieties of behavior, buying and otherwise.

Measurement and prediction By looking at current conditions, the marketer can develop knowledge about the consumers that are available to him at the present time. But the widespread and consistent use of demographic statistics has also resulted in the availability of similar data over several time periods. This means that an astute observer can detect *trends,* thus implying something about conditions that may exist in the future. Levittown is a profitable real estate venture. It was started because its developers recognized (before their competitors did) that there was a trend to suburban living and an attendant rise in the desire for suburban homes. Book publishing has been transformed from a staid to a dynamic business because Americans, with better educations and broader interests than ever before, are buying more books.

Trend data, while valuable in identifying market opportunities, nonetheless require careful interpretation. A good example is the trend seen in recent data indicating an increase in the occurrence of mental illness, which Prof. Raymond Bauer of Harvard University suggests greatly exaggerate the true incidence of the disease.[2] The inflation seen in the data begins with the fact that some disorders previously considered to be physical disease are now classified as mental illness. Further, what once was merely regarded as unusual behavior is now recognized as a manifestation of disease. Also, as mental illness has become more socially acceptable, doctors are disposed to record it as such instead of disguising it under more polite labels.

On account of these changes in record keeping, mental illness statistics give the impression of an upward trend, whether or not there has actually been any change in occurrence of the natural phenomenon. Without close examination and interpretation, there is no way of knowing the true incidence of mental illness. All we can say for sure is that the measurement definition has changed.

Keeping in mind their potential fallibility, we will begin our study of demographic factors with an examination of how a person's *location* can affect his buying decisions.

Location

The physical location of consumers has a major influence on their buying behavior. Where a buyer lives, how long he has lived there, and how long he expects to remain living there are all determinants of the kinds of goods and services he chooses to buy, and the ways in which he goes about buying them.

Our discussion of location will be divided into three parts: regional differences, urban-rural distribution, and the mobility of the population. It is not difficult to imagine some of the more obvious ways in which these three factors serve as moving forces in determining the influence of location on buying decisions. A resident of Vermont might consider the purchase of a snowmobile, while the thought of a similar purchase would hardly enter the

[2] Raymond A. Bauer (ed.), *Social Indicators,* The M.I.T. Press, Cambridge, Mass., 1966, pp. 27–28.

mind of a Texan. Many residents of Manhattan apartment buildings shun the idea of buying a car. Congested traffic conditions and the availability of other modes of transportation make the automobile an asset of questionable value. The family of a young executive who has just been transferred by his company is quite likely to be looking for drapes, furniture, and appliances to outfit a new apartment or home.

REGIONAL DIFFERENCES

Within the United States, there are often marked differences in consumer spending behavior among geographic regions. These variations can be the result of climate or other physical factors, or of cultural and social patterns of the region involved. Some regional differences in consumer spending patterns are illustrated by the data shown in Table 4-1. People in the Northeast, for example, spend more on heavy clothing than those in the South. They also spend more on reading and education than their counterparts in other parts of the country. The relative lack of prosperity in the South is reflected in lower expenditures for more basic family needs: food, housing, and shelter. People on the West Coast spend more on recreation than do people in most other parts of the country.

In an age when the concept of multinational markets is becoming increasingly important, regional differences within a single country's borders are not always sufficient for market analysis. Companies selling in the European Common Market, for example, must consider regional differences among its

TABLE 4-1
Average annual expenditures per household for goods and services, 1961–1962

	North-east	North Central	South	West
Total expenditures for current consumption	*$5,761*	*$5,028*	*$4,410*	*$5,677*
Food	$1,464	$1,221	$1,058	$1,345
Alcoholic beverages	110	61	43	102
Housing and household operations	1,435	1,219	1,017	1,327
Clothing and accessories	599	504	462	548
Transportation	775	783	703	924
Recreation and equipment	221	199	166	260
Reading and education	122	98	81	100

Source: *Expenditure Patterns of the American Family,* National Industrial Conference Board, New York, 1965, p. 20. Only portions of the data are presented here.

member nations. A food processor should know that Belgians generally prefer a high-starch diet: Belgian households consume more potatoes and bread than those of any other Common Market country. Italians eat only small quantities of potatoes, but their bread consumption is very high.[3]

Regional differences provide a useful basis for predicting consumer behavior. But because the underlying causes of regional variations are frequently cultural, social, or economic, there is danger in designing marketing programs without understanding the forces that determine these differences.

Fireside Dining, Inc., was established to provide home-delivered, high-quality meals on a regular basis (that is, three, four, or five days a week to each customer) in the Boston area. Because a service of this kind is relatively expensive, the company began operations in prosperous suburbs of Boston where there were sufficient numbers of relatively high-income families to provide a potential clientele. Fireside was patterned after a similar firm in Miami, Florida, which had proved highly successful. But Fireside was not successful. While the Boston suburbs had families with average per capita incomes at least equal to those in Miami, the Florida firm's customers were largely Cuban immigrants highly receptive to the idea of home-delivered meals. Bostonians proved to be much more conservative in their dining habits, and largely rejected the concept of home-delivered meals.

URBAN–RURAL DISTRIBUTION

In 1970, there were approximately 149 million urbanites in the United States as opposed to 54 million people who lived in rural areas.[4] There has been a marked trend toward urbanization of the population, and this trend is expected to continue. By the year 2000, it is anticipated that over 80 percent of the population will reside in urban areas. The burgeoning "urban sprawl" is expected to result in vast unbroken stretches of urban civilization, or "megalopolises," stretching from Boston to below Washington, from Chicago to Detroit, from Cleveland to Buffalo, and from Santa Barbara to the Mexican border.

Urban areas do not comprise a single, homogeneous market, nor do rural areas. There are obvious differences between Elgin, Texas (population about 4,000), and metropolitan New York City (15 million people), although both areas are considered to be "urban." Large cities themselves are not homogeneous, typically consisting of a concentrated core area and sprawling suburbia and exurbia.[5] Nor are they static in composition. By 1980, almost 60 percent of the urban population will live in suburbs, compared with less than

[3] *Le Monde*, weekly overseas edition, Feb. 15–21, 1968.

[4] Urban areas, according to the Bureau of the Census, are places, incorporated or unincorporated, having 2,500 or more persons.

[5] Suburbia is the area within 5 miles of a city limit or urban fringe boundary; exurbia is the area considered part of the metropolitan area which does not lie within 5 miles of the city limit.

50 percent in 1962 and little more than one-third in 1900. At the same time, most experts predict that the decline of core areas will give way eventually to a revival of the central cities. Decaying structures due for destruction will be replaced by vertical "cities within cities," immense complexes housing tens of thousands of families along with offices, shops, and recreational facilities. Century City in Los Angeles is considered a forerunner of this trend. Located on a former movie lot, it now consists of two major office buildings, a hotel, two luxury apartment towers, and a shopping center. By the time of its completion in the late 1970s, Century City will accommodate some 12,000 residents and provide 20,000 jobs.

Beyond differences in size, composition, and concentration, there has historically been a cultural distinction in the *ways of life* associated with rural and urban living. Dwellers in rural areas tend to be relatively conservative, quiet, slow to change, and cling longer to traditions and established patterns of behavior. The "city mentality" is a freer one characterized by greater innovation, self-expression, and sophistication. In all nations, cities have been centers of the great achievements of modern civilization — learning, invention, art, and culture. They have also been the focal point of social and personal disorganization, as exemplified by the diminishing influence of the family, the church, and the community in urban life.

Such contrasts in urban and rural environment, and even within the urban environment, inevitably produce greatly different influences on buying behavior. The cities are mass markets where there are stores and services close at hand to serve the needs and whims of almost any buyer. Theaters, delicatessens, boutiques, and ethnic restaurants provide opportunities for spending that simply do not exist in rural areas. Cities introduce people to new cultures; so the city dweller wants exotic foods and new fashions. In the rush of urban activities, conserving time is important. Precooked foods and timesaving appliances therefore find favor with urban housewives. So do clothes driers, because cities are congested and the air is generally polluted. In a large city, residential areas and industrial or office areas may be separated by substantial distances; the urbanite must therefore spend more time on commuting, either by automobile or public transit systems. Modern city congestion has resulted in a revival of catalog shopping; 70 to 80 percent of catalog sales in 1969 were estimated to be derived from metropolitan areas, as opposed to only 50 percent in the early 1950s.[6] The buying patterns of rural dwellers, on the other hand, reflect a more conservative and quieter approach to living. They normally spend more money on such items as raw materials for building, cotton piece goods, and basic commodity foods.

[6] Peter L. Gillett, "A Profile of Urban In-home Shoppers," *Journal of Marketing*, October, 1970. p. 40.

Urbanization is by no means solely a Western phenomenon. The most startling recent changes have occurred in underdeveloped countries. Between 1900 and 1950, the population living in cities of 100,000 or more in Asia mounted from an estimated 19.4 million to 105.6 million (a gain of 444 percent), and in Africa from 1.4 million to 10.2 million (a gain of 629 percent).[7] In underdeveloped areas, cities have usually grown at a rate surpassing both the expansion of employment opportunities and the expansion of urban public services. The structure of American and some European cities, consisting of a declining core area and a growing circle of relatively affluent suburbs, is not at all the pattern in the cities of Asia, Africa, and Latin America.[8] Cities in the underdeveloped nations are characterized by suburban slums, where dirt, health hazards, and crowding often are greater than in the poverty-stricken rural villages. New York City, with its towering Manhattan skyscrapers, is regarded as a densely populated area. Population density is 24,697 per square mile. Although lacking skyscrapers, Lagos, Nigeria, has a population density of 87,000 per square mile.[9]

The influence of an urban environment on buying decisions is well documented. But the growth in urban population has occurred only because some persons chose to migrate from rural areas. Mobility refers to the tendency of people to move from one area to another, and itself has an influence on buying decisions.

MOBILITY

Americans are a mobile people. Each year, about 20 percent of the population changes residence. Of these, about two-thirds move within the same county (locally) and about one-third between counties (long distance). Generally speaking, the most mobile segment of the population is the young group, aged eighteen to thirty-four.

What makes Americans so prone to relocation? With particular reference to long-distance movers, Prof. Alan Andreasen has suggested that the causes of mobility are related to two principal factors: opportunity and willingness.[10] New employment opportunities and scholastic ambitions represent a stimulus to a household to consider a move. Most often, these kinds of opportunities present themselves to individuals with proven or potential managerial compe-

[7] United Nations Secretariat, Bureau of Social Affairs, *Report on the World Situation including Studies of Urbanization in Underdeveloped Areas,* United Nations, New York, 1957, p. 114.

[8] Gerald Breese, *Urbanization in Newly Developing Countries,* Prentice-Hall, Inc., Englewood Cliffs, N.J., 1966.

[9] William Bascom, "Some Aspects of Yoruba Urbanism," *American Anthropologist,* August, 1962, p. 699.

[10] Alan R. Andreasen, "Geographic Mobility and Market Segmentation," *Journal of Marketing Research,* November, 1966, pp. 341–348.

□
TABLE 4-2

Average time required for relocating families to select suppliers of various products and services

Product or service	*Number of weeks*
Supermarkets:	
First	1.0
Favorite	3.4
Beauty parlors:	
First	5.0
Favorite	7.0
Banks	1.7
Automobile insurance	5.2
Property insurance	2.7
Life insurance	7.6
Appliance stores:	
First	5.3
Second	3.9
Clothing:	
Women's better dresses	8.6
Men's suits	8.3
Medical services:	
General practitioner	7.3
Specialist	6.9
Dentist	9.2

Source: James E. Bell, "Mobiles—A Neglected Segment," *Journal of Marketing,* April, 1969, pp. 41–43.

tence or scarce technical and intellectual skills. The willingness of a household to accept the challenge of new opportunity is a function of several complex factors: the extent to which a household is embedded socially or psychologically in the old community, and the attitudes of its members toward the risks associated with moving to a new environment. Obstacles to moving, real or imagined, tend to be lowest among young people.

The mobility of the population affords opportunities to marketers. Not only do "mobiles" represent a large population segment, but also they have unique product and service wants. Their distinguishable buying needs arise on one hand because mobiles typically differ from stay-at-homes in several respects. Mobile consumers are relatively young, well educated, in higher status occupations, have above-average incomes, and tend to be socially active. Independent of socioeconomic and demographic differences, the fact of relocation itself gives rise to environmental pressures for unique purchasing patterns. There is a need to revise household inventories to suit new living quarters and retail availabilities, the need to conform to new regional norms of attitude and behavior, and the stimulus to adjust to new income, occupational, or social class levels attained in the move. As such, mobiles represent a superior market for furniture, clothing, drapes, and other dry goods and consumer durables such as appliances and automobiles.

Mobiles have also been found to exhibit distinguishable behavior in the way they go about making buying decisions.[11] These differences in buying behavior arise primarily because a new resident is unfamiliar with the local shopping environment. For example, there are new local brands and retail establishments, together with an absence of many items and institutions to which the new resident was accustomed in his previous community. Thus, there may be an initial preference for national brands (such as Maxwell House) or retail chains (such as Sears) until such time as the mobile learns more of the local environment and adapts to it. Mobiles, however, tend to establish new sources of supply with surprising rapidity. The results of one survey of recently moved families, shown in Table 4-2, indicate that the majority established an initial shopping pattern (contact, but not necessarily purchase) with suppliers of a wide variety of products and services within a few weeks of relocation.

Sex

The fact that men and women frequently see things in a different light should come as no surprise. This axiom certainly extends to buying decisions and the relevant criteria that each sex applies in making purchase choices. An example in point is the purchase of hand luggage, as revealed in a study conducted for the Samsonite Corporation. To women, the important factors to be assessed in selecting hand luggage are style, color, and weight. To men, it is the functional value and durability of the luggage piece that are most important. Similarly, as reflected in their relative influence in the purchase of a family automobile, women are most interested in color, while men are most concerned with the brand of car selected.[12]

[11] Alan R. Andreasen and Peter G. Durkson, "Market Learning of New Residents," *Journal of Marketing Research*, May, 1968, pp. 166–176.

[12] Daniel Starch and Staff, *Male vs. Female Influence on the Purchase of Selected Products*, Fawcett Publications Inc., Greenwich, Conn., 1958.

In part, the significance of sex to marketers rests on the fact that some products are purchased almost exclusively by one sex or the other. Women buy most of the food, children's clothing, and household supplies for their families. Men buy most of the life insurance and automobile repair services. But such clear-cut distinctions in the sex of buyers are more the exception than the rule. As pointed out in the discussion of family decision making in Chapter 3, many purchases are made jointly by *both* husband and wife. This is particularly true of major items such as furniture, appliances, and housing. At the same time, purchases once thought to be the exclusive domain of a single sex today often involve both sexes. With the advent of the two-car family, many women own and operate their own automobiles. Their importance as gasoline consumers is sufficient so that several oil companies have developed advertising campaigns directed specifically to women. With the advent of supermarkets, discount houses, suburban shopping centers, late hours, and the shorter workweek, men often help their wives buy groceries, clothing, and household items.

Women in particular buy many products that they do not use themselves. Wives purchase most of the deodorants for their husbands, buy beer with the family groceries, and even purchase significant quantities of lawn fertilizer. Workshop equipment, cameras, and electric razors are frequently given as gifts by women. Before marriage, single girls buy many clothing accessories such as leather goods and sports shirts for men. There is even evidence to suggest that women would prefer to spend their money on others. *Printer's Ink* asked about 800 married women how they would spend a 50-dollar bill if given one. Virtually all said they would spend it on their children or grandchildren.[13]

As with any demographic variables, the influence of sex on buying decisions is best understood when combined with other information. For example, there are marked differences in the buying behavior of young and older women, and in their relative influence on family purchase decisions. The *Printer's Ink* study found that most older (over forty-five) women claimed to control all the family budget, while 65 percent of young (twenty-four to thirty-six) women stated they shared control of the family budget with the husbands.

The influence of sex on buying decisions also varies greatly among countries. The English housewife is said to be vitally concerned with health, anxious to buy vitamins for her children and large quantities of disinfectants.[14] In contrast to their American counterparts, the women of Continental Europe are said by psychologist Ernest Dichter to be in a state of "reluctant emancipation."[15] Although their feeling of subservience to men is fading away, enough

[13] *Printer's Ink,* June 24, 1966, pp. 51–52.

[14] *Business Week,* Sept. 6, 1966.

[15] *Business Abroad,* Dec. 12, 1966, p. 10.

of it lingers to influence buying decisions. Consequently, Dichter recommends advertising a convenience food to European housewives as "making you a better cook" or "helping to please your husband" rather than as "a time-saver."

Occupation

An individual's occupation is a highly significant determinant of many aspects of his behavior. It has a great deal to do with his income and, therefore, with the money he has to spend. Beyond this, occupation determines how a large part of an individual's waking hours are spent and has much to do with social status, dwelling area, and intellectual outlook. These factors make it necessary to understand something about occupational influence on the buying decisions of consumers.

The number of employed Americans has grown from approximately 60 million in 1950 to over 78 million in 1970. More important, the trends illustrated in Figure 4-1 reflect the increasing number of persons finding work in white-collar and service jobs. In looking to the future, it seems reasonably clear that technological change and educational improvement will continue to

FIGURE 4-1

Growth and change in division of the United States Work Force, 1950 to 1970.

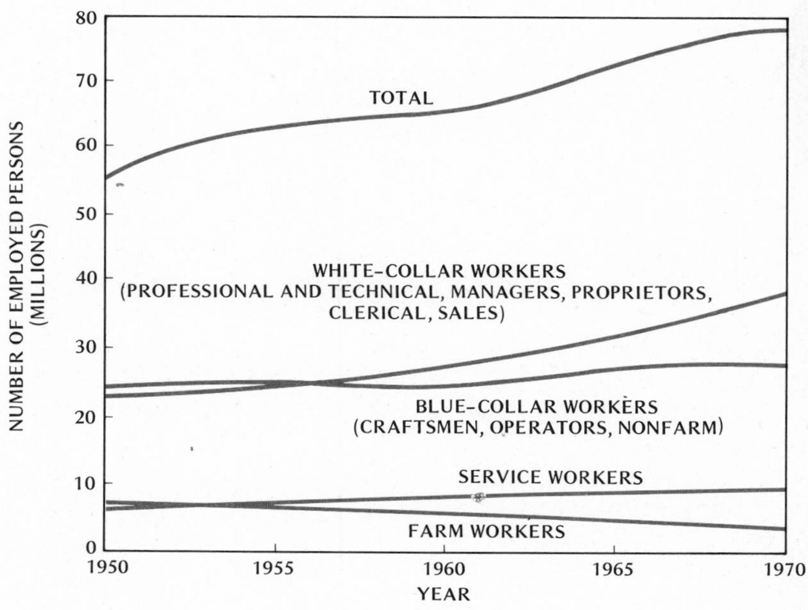

have a decided effect on the occupational status of the American people. Thus, the percentages of individuals at work in professional, technical, and skilled activities will probably continue to rise. Similarly, mechanization and automation should continue to cause a relative decrease in the proportion of individuals doing unskilled manual labor.

The relationship of occupation to income, and its effect on family budgets, will be discussed in the next chapter. In the sections that follow here, we will discuss the manner in which occupation influences an individual's life style, and consequently his buying decisions. The role of workingwomen is also singled out for special attention; the presence of a working wife has a decided influence on the spending behavior of a family.

□

INFLUENCE OF OCCUPATION ON LIFE STYLE

The kind of job an individual holds has a marked effect on the way in which he spends the majority of his time. How many hours he must spend at work, how much time is taken up by travel, how much is available for leisure, and how leisure hours are spent are all subject to occupational influences. In the aggregate, these factors go far toward determining a person's life style and, in turn, the kinds of goods and services he is most likely to require.

A study conducted in 1965 and 1966 compared the average daily "time budgets" for men in three occupational groups in the United States: executives and professionals, white-collar workers, and blue-collar workers. Some of the results of this study, shown in Table 4-3, reflect the influence of occupation on life style and bear closer examination. All three of the occupational groups have approximately equal amounts of time available for leisure, even though blue-collar workers spend almost three-quarters of an hour more time at work each day than executives. The difference is apparently compensated for by necessary nonwork activities. Executives spend more time on travel (they probably live farther from work), in sleeping (they are not required to be at work at an early hour), on shopping, and in helping around the house. In fact, the executive may actually spend *more* time working than other groups, since his leisure activities of reading, entertaining, and visiting often represent combinations of business and pleasure. Particularly noticeable is the way in which both executives and white-collar workers tend to distribute their leisure over a broad range of activities. Blue-collar workers, on the other hand, spend over half their leisure time, or two and one-half hours per average day, watching television.

The implications of these differences for marketers can only be touched upon here. The leisure-time activities of executives, professionals, and white-collar workers clearly mark these groups as preferred markets for such products and services as liquor, boating and fishing equipment, theaters, restaurants, and books. Moreover, their relative aversion to watching television

□

TABLE 4-3

Comparison of average daily time budgets for men in various occupational groups

Activity	Executives and professionals	Other white-collar workers	Blue-collar workers
Total hours	24.0	24.0	24.0
Work for pay	6.8	7.2	7.5
(Available nonwork time)	17.2	16.8	16.5
Necessary nonwork:			
Eating	1.3	1.2	1.3
Sleeping	7.7	7.6	7.4
Personal care	0.9	1.0	1.3
Household chores	0.7	0.6	0.3
Shopping	0.4	0.3	0.2
Other	1.6	1.5	1.3
	12.6	12.2	11.8
(Available free time)	4.6	4.6	4.7
Leisure (minutes):			
Visiting	68	74	39
Reading	50	36	24
Entertainment	11	13	13
Sports	10	12	5
Radio	5	4	10
Motoring	2	2	1
Clubs	5	8	5
Television	80	75	159
Miscellaneous	51	51	24
	282	275	290

Source: Adapted from John P. Robinson, "Social Change as Measured by Time Budgets," paper presented at the Annual Meeting of the American Sociological Society, August, 1967.

suggests that advertisers of these products might consider turning to newspapers, magazines, or other media. Looking to the future, the expected "upward mobility" of the labor force points to broadening markets for products associated with leisure. It also suggests a relative reduction in television watching as a leisure activity and possible revision in content of the television medium itself.

□

THE ROLE OF WORKING WOMEN

Women have always worked, but the modern industrial society is the first in which they have had the right to enter the labor market on their own, and to obtain jobs and promotions without the permission of men. In 1970, women comprised over 36 percent of the United States work force. Of these, nearly two-thirds were married women. In most of the countries of Western Europe, women make up 30 to 40 percent of the nonagricultural work force.

The percentage of women employed in the labor force has not changed greatly in recent years, but the nature of work undertaken has changed. Women are now able to move to the top of many professions, and a significant number find themselves in jobs once held exclusively by men. For many, work supplements income, but is not necessary to avoid poverty. The satisfactions of gainful employment, achievement, and social contact also serve as strong motivators for women to work.

The consequences of having a working wife in a family unit are varied and complex, but no doubt alter traditional patterns of family behavior. Husbands and older children become more involved in household maintenance activities, often at the expense of leisure activities. The working wife has less time to take care of the children; so she needs nursery schools and other kinds of help. Her available time to launder, clean, and sew is curtailed; so she must hire others or use dishwashers, frostless refrigerators, and other laborsaving devices. Because of her employment, she may require a second car and different kinds of clothing. At the same time, the working wife's income often contributes to the family's ability to afford many discretionary purchases: a better home, new furniture, and deluxe appliances.

Education

In 1940, only 18 million Americans held high school diplomas; they represented about one-quarter of the adult (age over twenty-five) population. By 1969, over one-half of all adults, or 58 million people, were high school graduates. It is predicted that, by 1985, the number of persons completing high school will have risen to 87 million, or 63 percent of the adult population. Of these, 37 million will have attended college or a university. College enrollment in 1985 will exceed 11 million, double the 1966 level.

The statistics tell in part of the tremendous growth that has occurred in American educational levels, and will continue to occur in the years ahead. To an increasing extent, we also find learning activities going on outside the formal educational institutions. The Job Corps, corporate training and retraining programs, and the Armed Forces (by far the largest "educational institution") are a few of many institutions of education not reflected in ordinary statistics. Reached by television, once-isolated residents of urban and rural "ghettoes" are able to see and learn what life is like beyond the ghetto; their aspirations for a better way of life are aroused accordingly. In recent years, there has been a marked growth in continuing adult education through university extension courses, educational television, and self-study programs. Never in history have so many terminally educated people continued their education in one way or another.

Education, formal or informal, invariably results in a change of attitudes, beliefs, values, and behavior on the part of those who experience it. Established traditions and time-honored patterns for living that earlier generations endured without protest become opened to question and even discard. New ambitions, aspirations, and life styles replace them. When changes of this nature occur on a large scale for a nation as a whole, there are naturally sweeping implications for marketers.

Educational attainment is associated with higher income levels and, consequently, the opportunity to purchase goods and services that previously could not be afforded. More remarkable than absolute income level are the differing *ways* in which income is spent by better educated people. Books, travel, and other cultural activities inherently become more popular. College-educated people spend only slightly more on furniture than less-educated persons having comparable incomes, but they exhibit distinct preferences for occasional pieces and have little interest in buying furniture in matched sets. America's rising level of education has other, more subtle marketing implications. For example, in planning advertising messages, it may be better to present both the pros and cons of the product in question. Better educated people, on the average, respond more favorably to two-sided arguments. They know things are complicated and are likely to be suspicious or bored if an advertiser pretends there is only one side to an argument. Conversely, people who are not well educated tend to be more influenced by one-sided arguments.[16]

The life-cycle concept

The age of a person or head of a family is a traditional demographic variable used to explain behavior. It has several advantages, including uniformity and ease of measurement, as well as obvious causal effects on an individual's actions and decisions. But in its capacity to explain some types of behavior, particularly *spending* behavior, age has serious shortcomings. It is generally thought that attitudes and behavior change as a person grows older. However, the chronological sequence of birthdays may not be as crucial a determinant of buying decisions as are the days when important changes occur in family status, for example, marriage or the addition of children to the family.

[16] Raymond A. Bauer and Robert D. Buzzell, "Mating Behavioral Science and Simulation," *Harvard Business Review*, September–October, 1964, pp. 116–124.

The idealized notion of *life cycle* is one which combines both age and family status in an attempt to explain spending behavior more fully. Over a lifetime, the vast majority of households pass through a series of life-cycle stages. There are many possible ways of classifying these stages. The one presented here consists of six basic categories:

1. The bachelor stage: young, single individuals not living at home
2. Newly married couples: young married couples with no children
3. The full nest I: young married couples with dependent children
4. The full nest II: older married couples with dependent children
5. The empty nest: older married couples with no children living at home, (*a*) head in labor force or (*b*) head retired
6. The solitary survivors: older single people, (*a*) in labor force or (*b*) retired

While the classification of life-cycle stages is an arbitrary one, at least two points regarding category definition are worth noting. First, this series of stages

FIGURE 4-2

Spending behavior over the life cycle

Bachelor stage; young single people not living at home	Newly married couples; young, no children	Full nest I; youngest child under six	Full nest II; youngest child six or over
Few financial burdens Fashion opinion leaders Recreation oriented Buy: basic kitchen equipment, basic furniture, cars, equipment for the mating game, vacations	Better off financially than they will be in near future Highest purchase rate and highest average purchase of durables Buy: cars, refrigerators, stoves, sensible and durable furniture, vacations	Home purchasing at peak Liquid assets low Dissatisfied with financial position and amount of money saved Interested in new products Like advertised products Buy: washers, dryers, TV, baby food, chest rubs and cough medicine, vitamins, dolls, wagons, sleds, skates	Financial position better Some wives work Less influenced by advertising Buy larger sized packages, multiple-unit deals Buy: many foods, cleaning materials, bicycles, music lessons, pianos

Source: Reprinted by permission from William D. Wells and George Gubar, "The Life Cycle Concept in Marketing Research," *Journal of Marketing Research*, November, 1966, p. 362.

represents a pattern followed by most, but not all, families. No consideration is given, for example, to middle-aged bachelors. Second, the stage of family formation is implicitly considered more important than chronological age in defining a life-cycle stage. Two young men might both be twenty-five years old, but the fact that one is married with children, the other single implies that their spending behavior will differ. Consequently, they are considered as belonging to separate life-cycle stages.

Some of the major elements of spending behavior commonly found in each life-cycle stage are summarized in Figure 4-2. The stages are so clearly related to changes in purchasing behavior that they are of vital importance to most consumer goods marketers. For example, each stage represents a change in *purchasing power status*. The average household's total income typically increases until the head is in his late forties, then declines. But there are deviations from this pattern. The arrival of a first child may result in a working wife ceasing employment, and a consequent decline in income. At later life-cycle

Full nest III; older married couples with dependent children	Empty nest I; older married couples, no children living with them, head in labor force	Empty nest II; older married couples, no children living at home, head retired	Solitary survivor, in labor force	Solitary survivor, retired
Financial position still better More wives work Some children get jobs Hard to influence with advertising High average purchase of durables Buy: new, more tasteful furniture, auto travel, nonnecessary appliances, boats, dental services, magazines	Home ownership at peak Most satisfied with financial position and money saved Interested in travel, recreation, self-education Make gifts and contributions Not interested in new products Buy: vacations, luxuries, home improvements	Drastic cut in income Keep home Buy: medical appliances, medical care, products which aid health, sleep, and digestion	Income still good but likely to sell home	Same medical and product needs as other retired group; drastic cut in income Special need for attention, affection, and security

stages, wives may return to work. Spending units in later stages may also have accumulated savings, and their purchasing power may exceed that apparent by their current income levels.

Life-cycle stages also reflect changes in *purchasing experience*. Single and young married women are more likely to try new products, and to be influenced by advertising, than are their older counterparts. Finally the life-cycle categories reflect differences in *product needs*. Durables such as furniture and appliances are apt to be bought at the time of family formation and not replaced until children have left home. Families with children require infants' clothing, toys, medicine, and educational services. Older couples are inclined to travel more widely, partake of luxuries, and purchase medicine. Some other distinctions are not so obvious. It has been found, for example, that first-born babies are likely to be fed 50 percent more processed baby foods than subsequent children of the same age.[17]

Ethnic factors

In 1970, there were 178 million whites, 23 million blacks, and 2.9 million people of other races in the United States. Of the whites, almost 77 percent have ancestral roots in Great Britain or Northern Ireland. Other major countries of ancestral origin include East and West Germany (7 percent), the Irish Free State (4 percent), the Netherlands (3 percent), and France (2 percent).

For the vast majority of these people, ethnic origin is not a major factor influencing decisions in the ongoing affairs of day-to-day living. The United States is perhaps the greatest "melting pot" the world has ever known. With some exceptions, ethnic heritages dissipate quickly and, for second-generation Americans, exert only minimal influence on behavior. It is true that the Irish parade on St. Patrick's day, that people of Italian origin consume a greater proportion of Italian foods and wines than those of other ancestries, and that Americans of Chinese background retain some of the habits of their ancestors. But even in these cases the majority of decisions are influenced primarily by nonethnic factors.

For marketers, ethnic factors are probably more significant for the way in which some national tastes have been embraced by wider segments of the population. The pizza palace has become an American institution. Chinese foods are popular, while the sitar and Nehru suits enjoyed moderate, if only passing, popularity. In many instances, the broader markets represented by such products were originally served by marketers intending to reach only a limited ethnic group.

[17] S. G. Barton, "The Life Cycle and Buying Patterns," in Lincoln H. Clark (ed.), *Consumer Behavior*, vol. 2, New York University Press, New York, 1955.

There are, of course, ethnic markets to be served among foreign nationals (residents of a country who were born in another country). This is particularly true when most immigrants from one country settle in a single city or concentrated region of their new country. Since World War II, a large number of Italians have emigrated to Canada, and most have settled in the city of Toronto. By 1970, over 10 percent of the people living in Toronto were born in Italy. Naturally, these new immigrants tend to continue reading newspapers in their native tongue and eating the foods they have always eaten.

□

THE BLACK MARKET[18]

The notable exception to the melting-pot phenomenon in America is the black. As put by John Johnson, publisher of *Ebony,* "Not only is the Negro not melting—he has not been permitted to get into the pot." Whatever the root causes, skin color or otherwise, it is a fact that the life of the black in America differs in many important respects from that of his white counterpart. The status of the black is concurrently a great social issue and a matter of practical business concern.

The black market is large in size: in 1967, blacks in the United States were estimated to have cash incomes in excess of $30 billion.[19] The black population is both younger than the white population and reproducing at a faster rate. This means that its significance as a market segment will increase. More important, the ways in which blacks spend their income and buy and use goods and services differ substantially from those of whites.

In part, differences in black market behavior can be attributed to a chronic condition of relative poverty. While the black market is large, it is nonetheless composed of a proportionately larger number of economically underprivileged people. The distributions of family incomes among black and whites in the United States is shown in Figure 4-3. For whites, the distribution is shaped like an inverted pyramid, with the largest number of families falling in the upper income (over $10,000) bracket. For blacks, the distribution resembles an upright pyramid, with the largest single group falling in the lowest income (under $6,000) bracket. In 1969, median white family income was $9,794, but for blacks only $6,059. The purchasing power of the black is substantially less than that of whites, and his spending patterns as a consumer consequently differ.

If differences in black and white buying behavior could be explained solely by differences in income levels, there would be no apparent need to examine blacks as a discrete market. But this is not the case; even after allowing for

[18] Material in this section, unless otherwise noted, is based on information contained in Raymond A. Bauer and Scott M. Cunningham, *Studies in the Negro Market,* Marketing Science Institute, Cambridge, Mass., 1970.
[19] "Why the Negro Market Counts," *Business Week,* Sept. 2, 1967, p. 64.

FIGURE 4-3

Percentage of white and black families in selected family income brackets, 1969

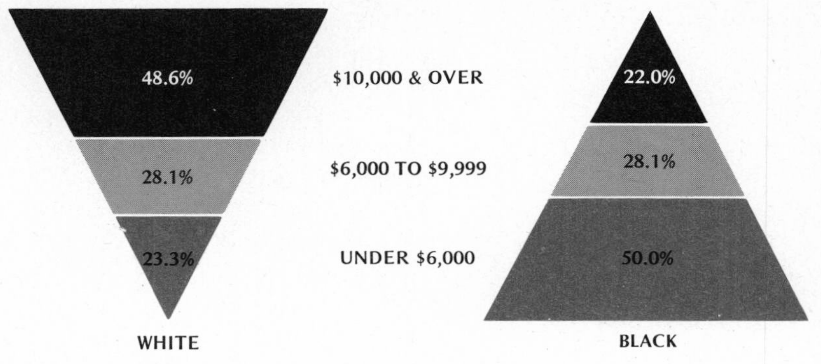

income differences, blacks exhibit distinct purchase preferences. For example, when compared with whites having similar income levels, blacks tend to spend:

Proportionately *less* on housing, automobile transportation, food, and medical care (excluding certain categories of proprietary medicines)
Proportionately *more* on clothing, furniture, and alcoholic beverages

In other words, blacks as consumers *are* different from whites for reasons besides economic ones. The differences do not stem from any biological attributes of blacks and whites. Instead, black buying behavior reflects the broader and interrelated conditions of lack of education, discrimination, and occupational and social deprivation. Ghetto schools have traditionally been of inferior quality, and opportunities for advanced education limited. Because the Negro is discriminated against, he is almost forced to spend less on travel, food outside the home, and good housing.

The typical life situation of the black is one of deprivation, but his reaction to this condition is both varied and complex. For example, are high black expenditures on clothing associated with a striving for respectability (as defined by white middle-class values), or do they merely reflect a desire for display and immediate gratification? Similarly, are high expenditures on liquor (especially Scotch whisky) associated with striving for social status, or a retreat from the present world? Questions such as these are representative of what has been called the *marketing dilemma* of Negroes. A black may accept the values of the majority white middle-class society. But being at a disadvantage in attaining those values, he must decide whether to make an extra effort to attain them, or to give in and do without most of them. Studies have indicated that Negroes react in both ways, sometimes taking and sometimes rejecting cues from the white community on what to buy. They will probably continue to do so as long as conditions of social and economic deprivation remain.

Interrelationships among demographic characteristics

This chapter has described many of the basic characteristics of consumers that are significant to the marketing manager in his attempt to identify and learn something about the people who make up the market for his goods and services. The information is concerned with how a person's location, sex, occupation, education, life-cycle stage, and racial or ethnic origin affect his buying behavior. In later chapters, attention will be paid to other factors that affect the buying decisions of consumers.

As pointed out earlier, demographic information is essentially raw material. It is useful in many ways and, in most instances, fairly easy to secure from governmental and trade sources in the United States and Canada. The fact that it is so abundant both lessens its cost and makes it sometimes more convenient to use than other kinds of information that are more difficult to obtain.

Nevertheless, we have repeatedly stressed throughout this chapter that differences in buying behavior are rarely the result of differences in any single demographic factor. Inevitably, consumers' decisions reflect the *joint effects* of several variables, some of which may be demographic and some of which may be economic, sociological, or psychological. Such variables may, themselves, be related. There is, for example, a relationship between life-cycle stage (a demographic variable) and income (an economic variable). An individual's income increases on the average from his early working years until near the end of his working career and then reaches a plateau or, in most cases, tapers off. Such a relationship was illustrated in the information presented in Figure 4-2. Similarly, there is frequently a relationship between education and occupation as well as between type of occupation and income.

In thinking about consumer buying behavior, it is important to recognize these relationships—what may seem to be caused by one factor may in reality be due to another related factor, or to a combination of factors. Compare, for example, the buying decisions of two consumers—Consumer A, who buys a plastic container of 12 Bufferin tablets for 29 cents in a drugstore, and Consumer B, who pays $1.17 for a bottle of 100 Anacin tablets in a discount department store:

Consumer A		*Consumer B*
16 years old		45 years old
Female		Male
Negro		White
Unmarried	*versus*	Married, three children
Small town		Suburb of large city
Deep South		Northeast
Income $1,500		Income $27,000
8th grade education		Master's degree
Domestic worker		Executive

Clearly, a comparison of the buying decisions of Consumer A and Consumer B based only on any *one* of the above characteristics tends to hide the possible effects of other variables. Consumer A may have purchased a relatively smaller package size than Consumer B because, being single, she did not need a large quantity. But her single status is a reflection of her age, which in turn may partly explain her low income level. Indeed, monetary factors may have been very important in Consumer A's buying decision, but her low income also reflects her education, regional location, and occupation. Similarly, the purchase of a 100-tablet bottle by Consumer B may have suited the needs of his larger family, but we cannot be sure that several other factors might not also have influenced his decision. In this instance, differences in buying behavior between the two consumers are apparently the result of many variables, demographic and otherwise, acting in combination. To attempt to explain the differences in terms of a single variable is virtually meaningless.

Questions

1. Table 4-1 shows average annual expenditures per household for goods and services in 1961–1962 by regions of the country. According to this table, households located in the Northeast spend $1,464 per year on food compared with $1,345 in the West, $1,221 in the North Central, and $1,058 in the South. How do you explain these differences? Do you think these relative differences would still be found today?

2. The incidence of mobility in the United States is higher among blacks than among whites. However, Negroes are less likely to move long distances than white segments of the population.
   a. What factors would cause the high rate of short-distance mobility among blacks?
   b. How might this mobility affect the behavior of blacks as consumers?

3. It has been estimated that, in 1970, college students spent only half as much on clothing as did their counterparts ten years earlier. How do you account for this change? What implications does this change have, if any, for each of the following?
   a. A manufacturer of made-to-measure men's suits
   b. A manufacturer of women's formal gowns
   c. A manufacturer of jeans or similar types of casual trousers

4. Which of the demographic factors discussed in the text would be most important in determining the market for each of the following products?
   a. Dining-room set
   b. Sports car
   c. Birthday cards
   d. Headache remedies
   e. Insulin

5. For many products, there are significant variations in consumption patterns among different demographic groups. How would you expect demography would vary among segments of consumers who

a. Spend different total annual amounts of money on alcoholic beverages?
b. Consume varying quantities of vodka?
c. Consume varying quantities of beer?

6. One answer to the problems associated with rapid growth of urban areas is the New Town concept. The idea envisions the creation of new self-contained communities in open countryside that would have their own employment opportunities, stores, and recreational facilities.

One of the New Towns in the United States is Reston, Virginia. Located on an 11-square-mile site 17 miles northwest of Washington, it eventually plans to have a population of 75,000. But in its early years, Reston has encountered difficulty in becoming a truly self-contained community. Only 25 percent of the town's residents actually work in Reston, and 75 percent of Reston's jobholders do not live in the town.

a. Why do you think Reston is experiencing difficulty in remaining self-contained?
b. If the New Town movement were to flourish in the future, what special factors would marketers have to consider in order to serve residents of these communities?

7. In what ways can children influence parental buying behavior? Should marketing programs be developed to appeal specifically to children? If so, for what kinds of products? Are child-directed marketing appeals more likely to be successful among some kinds of families than among others?

8. At an annual trade convention of sporting and recreational equipment manufacturers, a plenary session was held to discuss the future of the industry over the next two decades. Several members spoke with great optimism, citing a continuing decline in the number of hours Americans would be spending at work in the years ahead. One speaker cautioned, however, that future gains in nonwork time were not likely to take the form of a shorter workday. He said that three-day weekends, extended summer vacations, and similar "bunches of leisure time" were the more likely devices by which the amount of time spent at work would be reduced. He openly wondered what effect these trends would have on the industry, and if the optimism of his fellow members was not grossly exaggerated.

9. The Eurovolt Corporation, a subsidiary of an American electrical goods manufacturer, marketed a broad range of small and large electric appliances in the European Common Market. In early 1969, the company was particularly concerned about its relatively poor sales performance in southern Italy. Com-

pany executives concluded that special promotional efforts would be required in that region. While thinking about this problem, Eurovolt's marketing manager noticed a comment made by Giovanni Bianco, a staff member of the Milan-based consulting firm, Management Methods, Inc. "The northern [Italian] woman is emancipated," said Mr. Bianco, "but the southern housewife rates with the dog asleep under the porch." The marketing manager wondered how Eurovolt might take this remark into account in designing its special promotional programs.

10. In 1967, the *International Herald Tribune* combined with the *New York Times International* to form a single daily newspaper for distribution in Continental Europe. To determine a profile of readers of the new daily, which continued to be known as the *International Herald Tribune,* a survey was conducted in early 1968. In the survey, questionnaires were mailed to all subscribers of the newspaper, and were inserted in all newstand copies. Results of the survey showed that subscribers of the paper could be described in part by the following characteristics.

Sex	
Male	88%
Female	12%

Age	
Under 30	20%
30–50	56
Over 50	24

Nationality	
U.S. citizens	67%
French	6
British	5
Other countries of Western Europe (none over 3%)	15
Other	8

Country of residence	
France	21%
Germany	15
British Isles	10
Switzerland	10
Belgium	6
Italy	6
Other countries of Western Europe	16

Level of education reached	
Secondary schools or less	5%
Some university	16
University graduate	29
Postgraduate study	40
Other post-secondary training	10

Length of residence in present country	
Average	10.9 years

Number of income earners per household	
One	80%
Two	18
Three or more	2

Job title or position	
Owner, partner	16%
Executive	60
Professional, technical	10
Employee	6
Other	8

a. What use could a prospective advertiser in the *International Herald Tribune* make of these data?
b. As a prospective advertiser what further demographic breakdowns would you like to have available? Why?
c. What would you predict about this group with respect to (1) home ownership, (2) automobile ownership, and (3) cigarette and beverage consumption?
d. What kinds of products would be likely to find the *International Herald Tribune* an appropriate advertising vehicle?
e. What risks do you see in using these survey data as a basis for marketing planning?

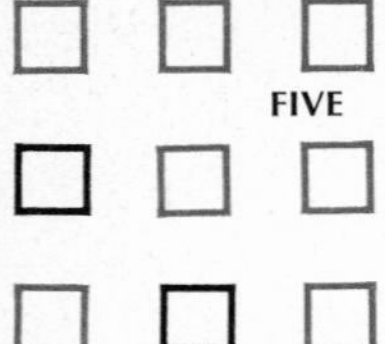

FIVE

Economic factors and consumer decisions

Suppose we are considering the marketing vice-president of the Cole Boat Company, a manufacturer of outboard motorboats. The company's president has asked him to make an estimate of total sales in 1985 by the outboard motorboat industry. How would he approach the assignment?

There are many things to be taken into account. His forecast would certainly involve estimates of the population in 1985, growth in recreational water facilities, and anticipated technological changes in the motorboat industry itself. In addition, he would need to consider other products that would compete with boats for consumers' dollars, such as automobiles, electric appliances, possibly private airplanes, and various other recreational and sporting devices. Expected social and political conditions in 1985, as they relate to protection of the environment, would have to be taken into account.

A major influence on his forecast would be an assessment of consumer purchasing power in 1985. Purchasing power refers to the ability of people to buy and is naturally dependent on income. Other sources of purchasing power include credit and the possession of financial assets. These enabling factors—income, credit, and assets—are representative of the *economic* determinants of consumer buying decisions we will discuss in this chapter. Later, in Chapter 9, we will explore some economic aspects of decision making by business, professional, and institutional customers.

Economic information can be looked upon from two perspectives. On one hand, economic data and trends for the nation as a whole can be useful to marketing in judging the overall purchasing power of the population. Because the United States is a prosperous nation, for example, a bricklayer in this country can earn $12,000, while his counterpart in a less-developed country earns only a fraction of that amount for equivalent work. Similarly, Cole Boat Company's forecast of motorboat demand would be dependent on the nation's economic growth to 1985. A projected "boom" economy would imply greatly expanded levels of purchasing power, while more sluggish growth would suggest a lesser enhancement of consumers' ability to buy.

On the other hand, marketers often find economic data pertaining to individuals or family decision-making units to be of more immediate concern. That is, given a stated overall economic climate, how does a bricklayer's income differ from that of other occupational groups in the country? Are some people more likely to use credit than others, and if so, how? How does propensity to save or spend vary among population segments? Knowing that everyone is not equally likely to purchase a boat, the Cole Boat Company would need information of this kind to develop its marketing programs efficiently.

Throughout this chapter, we will be looking at economic factors from both an aggregate and an individual perspective. As we progress, this distinction should be kept in mind, remembering that both kinds of data can be useful in marketing decisions.

General economic conditions

In every daily newspaper, there is a section devoted to financial matters. Apart from the latest stock-market quotations, its pages contain an assortment of articles dealing with such topics as taxation, inflation, unemployment, international monetary conditions, inventory levels, and weekly production statistics for key industries such as steel, crude oil, automobiles, housing, and pulp and paper. The articles are not widely read, appealing mostly to businessmen and active personal investors. A majority of people not only skip over the financial section, but probably would not fully understand the topics under discussion if they did stop to read them.

What *is* being discussed, of course, is the general economic prosperity of the nation. It is somewhat ironical that, while many people do not fully understand these matters, changes in the economy can affect their propensity to purchase and consume. In the extreme, the virtual collapse during the Great Depression sharply curtailed everyone's buying power. In less calamitous times, economic fluctuations can still influence buying decisions in significant, if not so dramatic, ways.

To witness one example of the effects of changing economic conditions on consumer buying behavior, we shall consider the following case study describing the frustrations of a young Canadian family in purchasing their first home.

THE CRANES'S DILEMMA

The Cranes were married in 1965 and, like many young newlyweds, soon began to think of the prospect of owning a house of their own. They were not alone in aspiring along these lines. In 1965, after a decade of stability, Canada was experiencing a sudden surge in new household formation and, with it, a substantial increase in the *demand* for housing. While more houses were needed, the *supply* of new houses being built was declining. As a result of lessened availability, the price of houses increased in most areas of the country. This price *inflation* put the cost of a house beyond the means of many Canadians, including the Cranes, who were forced to postpone buying a home.

The decline in the number of new houses being built in Canada continued in 1966. Housing starts, of which there were 166,000 in 1965, dropped to 134,000 in 1966. One major reason was the scarcity and high cost of *credit,* on which the housing industry depends heavily. Because Canada was enjoying a period of rapid economic expansion, there were strong demands for borrowed funds, particularly for business capital investment. Business, in a time of economic prosperity, was willing to pay increased interest rates for credit, and, as a result, major institutional lenders sharply curtailed their lending of mortgage money in favor of the higher interest rates in business capital investment. Gross mortgage loan approvals dropped from $1.2 billion in 1965 to $765 million in 1966. Meanwhile, economic prosperity added another kind of pressure. Immigration levels, which historically fluctuate with general economic conditions, rapidly increased during the mid-1960s. Families of new Canadians also needed housing, thereby adding significantly to demand. The total effect was to widen the gap between supply and demand even further in 1966, and housing prices spiraled upward accordingly.

Neither of the Cranes understood why prices were increasing so rapidly, but they *did* comprehend that they still could not afford a new house in 1966. A new baby had added to expenses during the year, and the couple had been able to save only a small additional amount toward a down payment. If prices had not gone up, they might possibly have had enough.

The slump in Canadian home building was reversed in 1967 and 1968, with the apparent causes of the change being attributable to *government action* on several fronts. Significant new amounts of public money were made available for mortgage lending through a government agency, Central Mortgage and Housing Corporation. Legislation that had previously held interest rates on many mortgages to artifically low levels was amended; rates moved upward to a more competitive level and began to attract institutional lenders back to supplying funds for mortgages. New legislation also enabled chartered banks, which had effectively been precluded from mortgage lending since 1959, to reenter the field. With more mortgage money now available, housing starts correspondingly increased to over 160,000 units in both 1967 and 1968, but this was not sufficient to alleviate the situation. It was estimated that Canada needed 195,000 new houses in each year between 1966 and 1971. Annual construction had yet to attain that level, let alone begin to make up for the backlog in demand from previous years. Prices therefore continued to rise.

The Cranes finally bought their house early in 1969, but it was not easy for them to do so. They could only shake their heads as the real estate agent admitted that their $29,000 house could have been bought for about $25,000 four years earlier. Both preferred not to think about the $20,000 mortgage—at a rate of 9½ percent, interest was currently costing the Cranes about $700 a year more than if a comparable mortgage had been taken out at the time of their marriage in 1965.

FLUCTUATIONS IN THE ECONOMY

The issues that plagued the Cranes's house-buying decision—disequilibrium in supply and demand, price inflation, and spiraling interest rates—are all typical of influences on consumer buying decisions that arise from fluctuating economic conditions. While the example illustrating these influences could easily have been an American one, we have chosen to describe a Canadian setting to emphasize the universality of fluctuating economic conditions as a determinant of buying behavior. It is useful to review briefly how these fluctuations arise, and how governments intervene to alter and adjust economic performance.

A basic goal of economic performance is to maintain the capacity of a nation's productive resources (supply) in approximate balance with consumption (demand) by household, business, government, and foreign buyers. If demand falls short of supply capability, part of the nation's productive potential is not realized. Excessive demand, on the other hand, results in inflationary pressures on costs and prices.

In the United States, the task of regulating the economy falls to the federal government. Generally, government is charged with a responsibility for maintaining balance between supply and demand, while at the same utilizing and expanding the nation's resources to the fullest possible extent. In more specific terms[1]:

> The Congress hereby declares that it is the continuing policy and responsibility of the federal government to use all practicable means consistent with its needs and obligations and other essential considerations of national policy . . . to promote maximum employment, production, and purchasing power.

[1] U.S. President, *Economic Report of the President,* 1969, p. 61.

The task is not an easy one because economic output is constantly expanding as the result of additions to the labor force and increases in productivity. In a sense, the economy is a "moving target" that must constantly be checked and balanced if the goals established by Congress are to be met. The principal tools for achieving these ends are fiscal and monetary policies.

Both fiscal policy and monetary policy operate primarily by affecting the demand side of the balance. Fiscal measures are those involving changes in the level of government spending or in the rates of taxation imposed by government. In 1970, federal government purchases of goods and services amounted to over 10 percent of gross national product. As the nation's largest spender, the federal government can, within reasonable limits, adjust its own spending up or down to help alleviate imbalances in supply and demand. By raising or lowering tax rates, the government can hold down or increase the flow of private spending.

Monetary policies affect private spending by changing the cost and availability of money. Monetary measures have a particularly marked effect on consumer purchases of housing, automobiles, and other "high-ticket" durable goods, as evidenced in the Crane case study cited above.

We find, then, that an economy is constantly in motion, with its natural tendency toward cyclical fluctuation being partially or wholly offset by the effect of government fiscal and monetary measures. As the economy flows and ebbs, so also is the buying ability of consumers enhanced or detracted. Yet being *able* to buy something is not necessarily synonymous with being *willing* to do so.

□ WILLINGNESS TO BUY

Many products and services are subject to short-term changes in consumption patterns that far exceed the effect of any comparable fluctuations in economic climate. These variations can usually be traced to changes in the "buying mood" of consumers. As George Katona has pointed out[2]:

> It goes without saying that nobody can buy if he has no income, assets, or credit. It does not follow, as some would seem to believe, that if people have sufficient income, assets, or credit they will necessarily buy. Ours is a complex economy in which the situation of different consumer and business groups varies greatly. Looking at the entire economy, rather than at individuals, in the short run only minor upward or downward shifts in ability to buy occur, and they may be preceded or followed by similar shifts in willingness to buy.

Katona's remarks emphasize the psychological aspects of buying decisions and serve to illustrate that, for many goods and services, willingness to buy can be equally or more important than purchasing power in its effect on consumer buying decisions. Businessmen are aware of the importance of buying mood

[2] George Katona, *The Powerful Consumer*, McGraw-Hill Book Company, New York, 1960, pp. 3–4.

and, in their assessment of business conditions, pay close attention to survey measures of consumer buying intentions. We will discuss the significance of these measures in the next chapter.

GROSS NATIONAL PRODUCT

The most widely accepted measure of how the economy is performing is the gross national product. GNP, (defined on p. 112), has particular significance to marketers of consumer goods because substantial proportions of it are made up of purchases by household consumers. In recent years, for example, personal consumption expenditures have averaged just over 60 percent of the GNP, or, in 1970, over $3,000 per person. The data in Figure 5-1 show that the

FIGURE 5-1

Gross national product and personal consumption expenditures per capita in selected countries, 1969

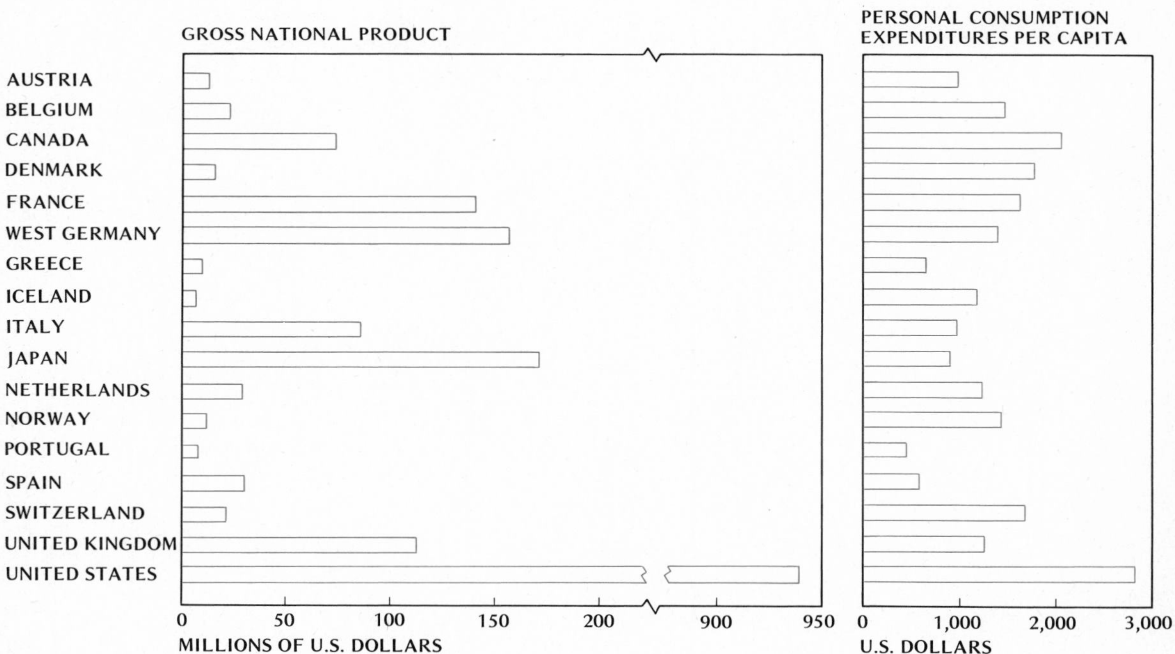

Source: *The OEC Observer,* February, 1971, pp. 22–23.

☐ *The gross national product (GNP) is the aggregate total of consumer purchases of goods and services, government purchases of goods and services, and gross private investment during a given time period. In short, it is the market value of the nation's production of goods and services.*

per capita level of consumer spending in the United States is almost 50 percent higher than in any other advanced nation, and over four times as great as comparable spending in less developed nations such as Portugal, Greece, or Spain.

In 1970, the GNP of the United States amounted to $977 billion, or almost $4,800 per person. By late 1971, the GNP had passed the $1 trillion mark. Comparable figures in 1929 and 1950 were $104 billion and $285 billion, respectively. Some economists have estimated that the 1975 GNP may reach $1.3 trillion, which would represent an average of $5,800 per person if the population rises to 225 million by that year. The attainment of a GNP of this level is dependent on many factors, most of which will not be discussed here. The willingness of consumers to buy, however, is one major factor.

While the GNP has risen substantially from a level of $104 million in 1929, prices have also risen. The U.S. Department of Commerce has converted the GNP into "constant dollars" by adjusting it with an index of price inflation. On this basis, while the dollar amount of the GNP was over eight times greater in 1970 than in 1929, the real (or purchasing power) GNP was only about three and one-half times greater. Further, since the nation's population grew from 120 million to 206 million during this period, the real growth in GNP *per person* was less than double.

The rate of growth in GNP in the United States has been exceeded recently by several other countries. This is particularly true in the case of Japan and some countries in Western Europe during the period since World War II. Table 5-1 shows the GNP growth rates (adjusted for price changes) in several countries for selected time intervals since 1929. There is little doubt that dramatic economic growth in other countries has given rise to an increased interest in international marketing by many American firms, and some ramifications of this development will be discussed in Chapter 24.

☐

TABLE 5-1

Average annual growth rates of gross national product, selected countries, 1929–1967

Country	1929–1950	1950–1960	1960–1967
United States	2.9%	3.2%	4.8%
Canada	3.2	4.0	5.3
France	—	4.6	5.1
West Germany	1.9	8.5	3.9
Italy	1.0	5.8	5.4
United Kingdom	1.6	2.7	3.0
Japan	0.6	9.4	10.2

Source: U.S. Department of Commerce, Bureau of the Census, *Long Term Economic Growth.*

Income

While the GNP is a useful measure of total annual economic activity, marketing managers have greater interest in economic data that more closely relate to the incomes of decision-making units. In the sections that follow, income is discussed for the nation as a whole and at the level of individual consumer decision-making units.

□

PERSONAL INCOME, DISPOSABLE INCOME, AND DISCRETIONARY INCOME

□ *Personal income is the total money income received by all individuals during a given period of time.*[3]

The level of personal income□ rose from $86 billion in 1929 to $801 billion in 1970. Table 5-2 shows the total amount and sources of personal income for selected years. Sellers in particular industries are often interested primarily in the specific components of personal income sources. For example, sellers of farm equipment and supplies might note that proprietors' incomes from farms, although rising from $6 billion to $16.1 billion between 1929 and 1970, grew far less rapidly than any other source of personal income. This would imply that sales of farm equipment and supplies might, in turn, lag behind sales of many other industries as farm income fails to keep pace with other sources of income.

□ *Disposable income is personal income after the payment of income taxes. In 1970, for example, such taxes amounted to $116 billion, leaving disposable income of $685 billion. This total represents the dollars available for expenditure by household consumers.*

All personal income is not available for spending. To get at the amounts that consumers can spend, economists turn to disposable income.□ A substantial proportion of disposable income must be used to meet fixed commitments and essential outlays for living. Although there is no precise way of defining what is "essential," it is generally agreed that expenditures of this nature include home ownership or tenant rent, food, clothing, transportation, medical expenses, payments to life insurance and pension equities, and health and accident insurance. In 1970, payments of this kind accounted for approximately $407 billion of the available disposable income of $685 billion.[4] The residual was available for expenditures of a "discretionary" nature.

□ *Discretionary income is that portion of personal income, in excess of the amount necessary to maintain a defined or historical standard of living, which may be saved with no impairment of immediate living standards.*[5]

On this basis, discretionary income□ in 1970 amounted to $278 million. By the very nature of its definition, the magnitude of discretionary income is particularly relevant to marketers of such products and services as home furnishings, recreation, education, foreign travel, liquor, and personal care accessories. The fact that these items have all experienced substantial growth in recent years is a reflection of the fact that discretionary income has grown more rapidly than either personal or disposable income. The data in Table 5-3,

[3] In stricter terms, but without definition of components, personal income is alternatively defined as (1) the GNP *plus* transfer payments (e.g., income from social security) minus depreciation, indirect business taxes, undistributed profits, corporate taxes, and social security tax contributions; or (2) the national total of wage receipts, unincorporated net income, rents, interest, dividends, and transfer payments.

[4] Based on estimated discretionary purchasing power of $278.0 million, as published in *The Conference Board Statistical Bulletin,* June, 1971, p. 7.

[5] *Marketing Definitions,* American Marketing Association, Chicago, 1960, p. 12.

□

TABLE 5-2

Personal income and major sources, selected years, 1929–1970

(In billions of dollars)

Source of personal income	1929	1950	1960	1970
Total personal income	$85.8	$227.6	$401.0	$801.0
Wages, salaries, and other labor income	51.0	150.5	282.8	570.5
Proprietors' income:				
Business and professions	8.8	24.0	34.2	51.4
Farm	6.0	13.5	12.0	16.2
Rents, dividends, and interest	18.6	27.4	52.6	114.1
Transfer payments (net)*	1.4	12.2	19.2	49.8

*Total income from old-age and survivors' insurance benefits (social security), state unemployment benefits, veterans' benefits, and similar sources, *less* personal contributions for social insurance.

Source: U.S. Department of Commerce, Office of Business Economics, *The National Income and Product Accounts of the United States,* 1929–65, and *Survey of Current Business,* June, 1971.

summarizing national income aggregates in 1960 and 1970, show that discretionary income increased by 228 percent in the 10-year interval. Comparable increases in personal and disposable income were 195 percent and 199 percent, respectively.

Thus far, this section has discussed a number of economic variables that can be used to relate aggregate income to consumption. While these are of some use as *general indicators* of the behavior of both individuals and families as decision-making units, each unit is most immediately and importantly influenced by its *own* current and prospective income.

□

TABLE 5-3

National income aggregates, 1960 and 1970

(In billions of dollars)

	1960	1970
Personal income	$402	$801
Disposable income	352	685
Fixed commitments and essential outlays	230	407
Discretionary income	122	278

MASS PURCHASING POWER

The American economy is conspicuous for mass purchasing power. This has been brought about to an increasing degree by what has often been called the *income revolution*. In brief, this means that total income has increasingly been distributed more widely among the American population. In 1947, for example, 27 percent of American families had incomes below $2,000, only 20 percent earned $5,000 or more, and less than 3 percent earned more than $10,000. In 1969, on the other hand, only 7 percent earned below $2,500, 81 percent earned $5,000 or more, and 46 percent earned more than $10,000. Even when these figures are adjusted to allow for price changes, as illustrated in Figure 5-2, the shift has been dramatic. Thus, not only has total income risen, but its distribution has been more nearly equal. Nor is there any reason to suspect that the trend toward greater equalization of income will cease, although its pace will probably slacken.

The growth in mass purchasing power that has taken place and is still occurring has vital implications for marketing men. Two major ones will be mentioned here. First, changes in overall expenditure patterns will continue to occur rapidly. As more individuals and families attain higher-income levels, the amount of total funds available for discretionary (as opposed to essential)

FIGURE 5-2

Distribution of United States families by income class, 1947–1969 (based on 1969 dollars)

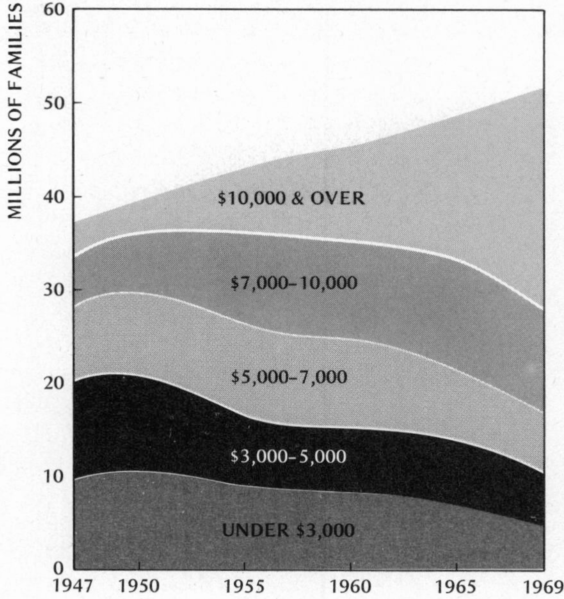

Source: U.S. Dept. of Commerce, Bureau of the Census, *Income in 1969 of Families and Persons in the United States*, p. 24.

spending will increase. This, in conjunction with other trends such as population increases and growth in leisure time, will greatly expand the markets for many goods and services. New or improved products, whether essential or nonessential, will find larger markets on which the skills of marketers can be brought to bear.

Second, equalizing changes in the pattern of income distribution will increasingly facilitate the development of the segmented markets discussed at the beginning of Chapter 4. Population growth plus wide distribution of income will make it possible for increasing numbers of business firms to develop product lines, price ranges, and promotional programs that are directed at specific income segments of consumer decision-making units. Thus, even though income will be more evenly spread, the wider degrees of consumer choice afforded by increased incomes will make it easier for marketers to aim their strategies at specific groups of people.

INCOME AND EXPENDITURE PATTERNS

A family's income, as a key determinant of its buying power, naturally affects the selection of the goods and services it purchases. Low-income families do not usually buy original art, while families of higher income are not as likely to purchase beer for home consumption. Often, by examining the expenditure patterns of different income groups, marketers can derive significant implications for their marketing programs.

Illustrated in Figure 5-3 are data concerning the purchase of major appliances by various family income groups. What implications do these figures have for those who develop marketing programs for the three appliances shown: nonautomatic washing machines, gas cooking stoves, and dehumidifiers? Most obvious is the fact that families with incomes below $5,000 represent a fertile market for nonautomatic washing machines. Although only one-third of all families have incomes in this range, they account for over one-half of the total expenditures on this kind of appliance. Conversely, families with incomes in excess of $7,500 are not a particularly receptive market—as might be expected, these families generally prefer automatic washing machines. Even though almost half of American families are in the two highest income brackets shown, their demand for nonautomatic washing machines is so low that the costs of marketing programs directed at them could probably not be justified.

The gas-cooking-stove market, on the other hand, is more evenly distributed among income groups. This implies that marketing policy and action can be profitably directed at families in practically all income brackets. For example, a company's product line could be developed so that its price range would appeal to consumers in each income bracket.

For dehumidifiers, demand is almost nonexistent among families having incomes below $5,000. There seems little question that a manufacturer of this

FIGURE 5-3

Distribution of expenditures on major appliances, by family personal income

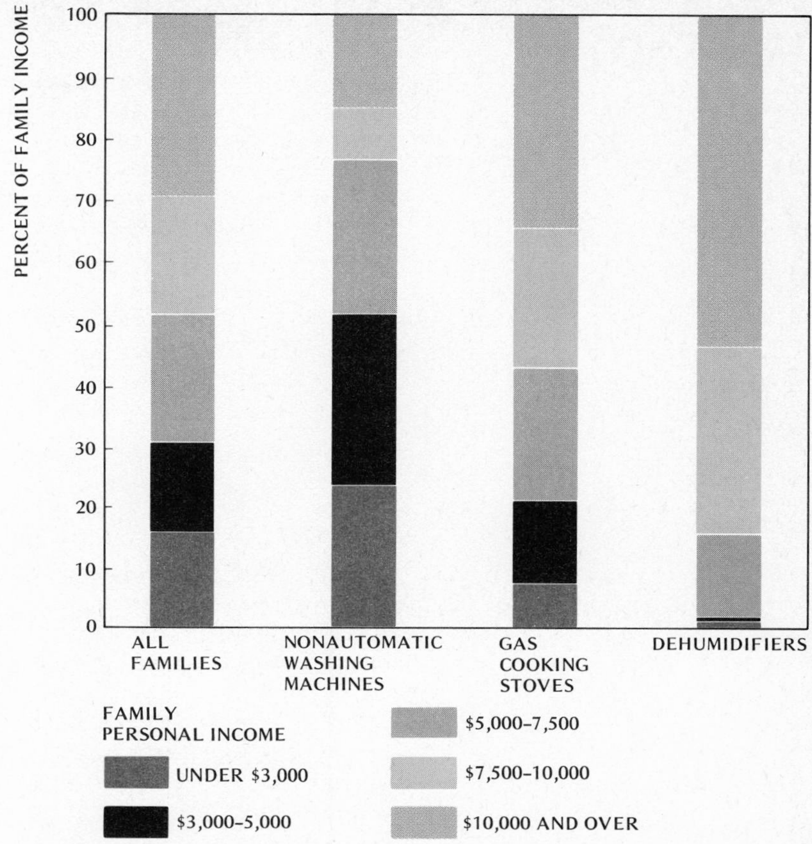

Source: *Market Profiles of Consumer Products* (New York: National Industrial Conference Board, 1967), p. 78.

kind of appliance must tailor his marketing program exclusively to the needs of families in higher-income brackets.

The foregoing example reflects the importance of income and income distribution as economic determinants of consumer behavior. It supports the notion that marketers must understand how total income is distributed among individuals and groups of individuals and what the future distribution of income is likely to be.

DISTRIBUTION OF INCOME WITHIN GROUPS

Many classes of marketing problems require that the decision maker have information on how incomes vary within a particular segment of the population.

For example, in deciding on a supermarket location, it is useful to have some idea of the income levels of predominant occupational groups in the neighborhood under study. Urban-rural differences in income levels could be an important factor in determining the allocation of a newspaper advertising

FIGURE 5-4

Median family incomes by age, education, and occupation of household head, 1969

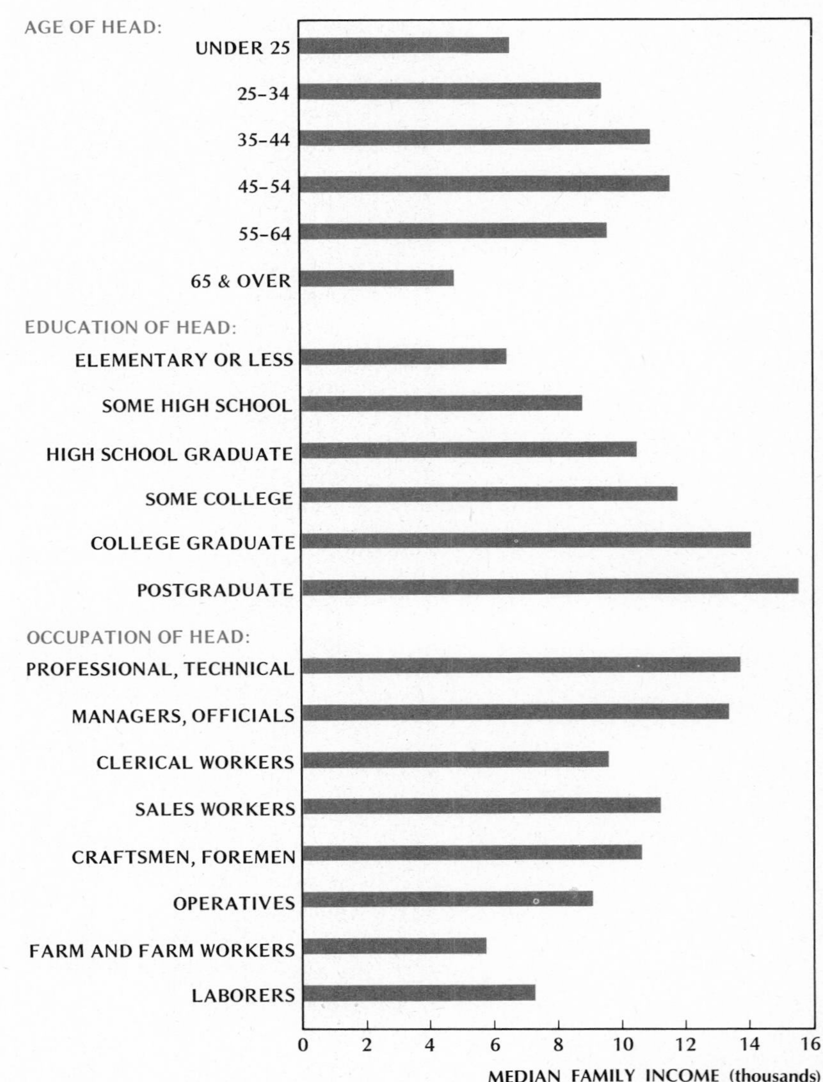

Source: U.S. Dept. of Commerce, Bureau of the Census, *Income in 1969 of Families and Persons in the United States.*

budget among a group of daily and weekly newspapers. There are many other possible ways of looking at income and income distribution. The "best way," however, can be defined only in terms of a specific marketing problem, the product involved, and the kinds of consumer decision-making units involved.

In Figure 5-4, three of the most commonly employed breakdowns of income distribution are illustrated. The three shown—age, education, and occupation of household head—are merely examples of the many possible ways in which income distribution can be viewed. They serve to demonstrate, however, that there are substantial variations in income within segments of the population and, as a consequence, considerable differences in buying power. Other bases on which income distributions are often meaningful to marketing decisions include geographic location, sex, size of family, and race.

It should be emphasized that no single class of income distribution data is likely to provide more than part of the information necessary for marketing decisions. Usually, it is desirable to combine various classes of data to shed adequate light on a problem. To a clothing manufacturer, for example, it is relevant that the disparity in income between black and white families is not uniform across all age brackets. Among younger families (head in twenty-five to thirty-four age bracket), white incomes are approximately 30 percent higher than those of blacks, while in older families (head in fifty-five to sixty-four age bracket), white family incomes are 62 percent higher. In dollar terms, the same young white families earn $769 per year more than their black counterparts, while the comparable income gap for the fifty-five to sixty-four age group is $4,316 per year.

□

EFFECT OF CHANGES IN INCOME

Thus far this section has dealt with aggregate measures of income and with various ways of considering the distribution of income. Implicit in the data presented is the fact that individual and family incomes in the United States have been increasing from year to year. It is useful to consider, therefore, the effects that rising income can be expected to have on actual spending and saving behavior.

There are several theories in economics that attempt to explain how consumers react to changes in income. The *absolute-income hypothesis* suggests that consumers' expenditures will vary in approximate proportion to the absolute amount of income change. The *relative-income hypothesis* holds that the willingness of people to increase expenditures as their income rises is also dependent on the ratio of their expenditures to those of the people with whom they associate in some fashion, for example, friends or some persons in comparable income and/or age groups. Variations of a third theory, known generally as the *permanent-income hypothesis,* suggest that spending is based on people's perception of their "permanent" income over future years rather than on income actually received in a given year. Considerable controversy surrounds each of these theories, however, because serious practical dif-

FIGURE 5-5

Median family income, by age and race of household head, 1969

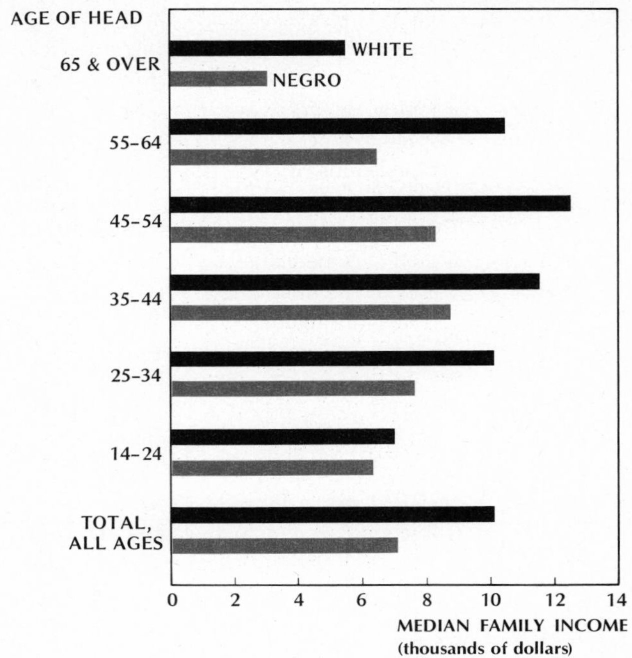

Source: U.S. Dept. of Commerce, Bureau of the Census, *Income in 1969 of Families and Persons in the United States.*

---

ficulties arise in attempting to test their validity with empirical data. It is difficult, for example, to isolate the effect of income on expenditure from the effect of other influencing variables such as price and promotion. Hence, there is no single theory to explain the effect of income change, and research has yet to establish which of several posited hypotheses most closely approximates actual behavior.

One measure of the responsiveness of various types of expenditures to changes in income is the coefficient of income sensitivity.□ By examining aggregate United States data over a period of several years, coefficients of income sensitivity for several products have been approximated in research studies. Data from the most recent of these studies, covering the period 1948–1965, are shown in Table 5-4. During the period, for example, a 1 percent increase in personal disposable income was found to be associated with an increase of 1.34 percent in expenditures on household appliances.

□ *The coefficient of income sensitivity expresses the average percent by which expenditures on a product have varied, over a period of years, corresponding to a 1 percent change in personal disposable income.*

The coefficient of income sensitivity reflects aggregrate response to *long-term* changes in income. Evidence regarding *short-term* changes in income can be found in a major study of income change conducted in the 17 months immediately following the income tax cut of 1964, the largest tax reduction in the history of the United States.[6] Not only did the tax cut provide an immediate increase in personal disposable income, but by its impetus on the general level of economic activity, it resulted in increases in wages, salaries, profits, and other forms of personal income that were approximately three times greater than the estimated gain from the reduction in tax rates. Hence, the tax cut provided an unusually rich opportunity to study the effect of substantial short-term income changes on household spending behavior.

The tax cut study, which involved a survey of approximately 1,000 households, distinguished among different types of income changes. *Sustainable* increases were defined as being of a relatively permanent nature, for example,

[6] George Katona and Eva Mueller, *Consumer Response to Income Change,* The Brookings Institution, Washington, 1968.

TABLE 5-4

Income sensitivity ratios, based on the years 1948–1965

Item	Income elasticity	Item	Income elasticity
Total personal consumption expenditures	1.00	Semidurable housefurnishings	.83
Food at home	.86	Household supplies	1.36
Restaurant meals	.32	Personal care services	1.25
Alcoholic beverages	.49	Toilet articles, preparations	1.84
Tobacco	.60	Medical care services	1.29
Women's, children's apparel	.92	Drugs, supplies	1.63
Men's, boys' apparel	.57	Automobile purchases	1.40
Footwear	.31	Tires, tubes, accessories	1.51
Jewelry, watches	1.46	Gasoline and oil	1.52
Shelter	1.44	Transportation services	.38
Household operation services	1.34	Sporting goods, toys	2.01
Furniture	.95	Foreign travel	2.11
Household appliances	1.34	Higher education	1.52
Radio, TV, etc.	2.13	Personal business	.98
China, glassware, utensils	.59		

Source: *A Graphic Guide to Consumer Markets, 1970,* The Conference Board, New York, 1970, p. 130.

pay raises. In response to a sustainable increase, people were found to undertake substantial and concurrent increases in discretionary expenditures (especially durable goods), to incur more short-term debt, and to add to both liquid saving and their rate of contractual saving. If increases were *very large* (more than 20 percent over 17 months), there was a tendency toward disproportionately higher discretionary expenditures. *Transitory* increases (such as overtime or temporary second jobs), on the other hand, were generally placed in some form of liquid saving such as a bank account and not spent immediately.

The effect of increased income on "everyday" expenditures (food, clothing, incidentals) differed markedly from that on durables and similar discretionary items. Generally, an increase in income had no immediate effect on the level of everyday spending. Apparently, people wait for about three months before making any upward adjustment in everyday spending, perhaps in order to divert all their newly acquired income to a durable or discretionary purchase they have been wanting for some time.

Reductions in income were found to have the exact opposite effect from increases. That is, people generally reduced their level of discretionary spending, incurred less short-term debt, and saved less. Again, there was a lag of about three months before everyday expenditures were adjusted to new income levels.

Consumer credit

When a consumer's savings and current income are insufficient sources of the funds needed to satisfy his purchasing desires, there exists the alternative means of facilitating purchase through the use of consumer credit.□ Despite rising incomes, the propensity of consumers to utilize credit as a means of purchasing has increased substantially in recent years. In 1970, for example, a total of $126.8 billion was outstanding in consumer credit. This represents more than double the outstanding amount of $56.9 billion just eight years earlier in 1961, and over ten times the $11.6 billion in consumer credit outstanding in the post-World War II year of 1947.

□ *Consumer credit, as used here, refers to funds borrowed or financial obligations incurred for periods of time of generally three years or less. It does not include longer term obligations such as home mortgages.*

To understand the nature of the growth in credit usage by consumers, it is useful to distinguish between two basic types of consumer credit. *Installment credit* is repaid in periodic installments over a period of time. This form of credit includes obligations incurred in the purchase of automobiles, furniture, electric appliances, and other "big-ticket" items as well as installment loans from banks or finance companies. *Noninstallment credit* is paid off in full at the end of a specified period such as 30 days or 60 days. Charge accounts at retail stores, single payment loans, and service credit (amounts owed to doctors, lawyers, and other service establishments) are included here.

THE USE OF INSTALLMENT CREDIT

Installment credit represents the largest single source of outstanding consumer credit. As shown in Table 5-5, a total of $101.2 billion in this type of credit was outstanding at the end of 1970—this compares with a total of $33.6 outstanding at the end of 1958.

It should be noted that the amount of credit *outstanding* at any given point in time is not synonymous with the amount of purchases made on credit (credit extensions). Because a large proportion of installment credit is utilized to purchase durable goods, the amount of credit extended is partly affected by the overall economic conditions cited in an earlier section of this chapter. For example, in the recession year of 1958, the amount of installment credit extended was even lower than credit repayments. In 1966, a "prosperous" year, new installment credit extended exceeded repayments by a substantial margin. By 1970, a downturn in economy had again reduced extensions to a level almost equal to credit repayments.

While the amount of outstanding installment credit has grown over the years, there have not been marked changes in the overall purposes for which credit is extended. Approximately 40 percent of installment credit is used for automobile loans, 30 percent for other consumer goods purchases, and 30 percent for personal loans.

You should not conclude that installment credit is used *only* for durable goods purchases. Credit extended by department stores, and the growth of bank credit plans such as Mastercharge and BankAmericard, have led to an increased propensity to purchase nondurables and services on an installment basis.

The growth in installment credit is attributable to numerous factors. In part, the cost of merchandise purchased on credit has been increasing. The National Consumer Finance Association reported that the average size of loan made by consumer finance companies increased from $238 in 1958 to $717

TABLE 5-5

Consumer installment credit, selected years, 1958–1970

(In billions of dollars)

	1958	1964	1966	1968	1970
Installment credit outstanding at year end	$33.6	$62.7	$77.5	$89.9	$101.2
Installment credit extensions during year	40.1	70.7	82.3	97.1	104.1
Installment credit repayments during year	40.3	63.5	76.1	88.1	101.1

Source: Adapted from selected issues of Board of Governors of the Federal Reserve System, *Federal Reserve Bulletin*.

in 1969.[7] Further, new forms of credit, such as revolving credit plans at department stores, have made credit usage more attractive and convenient. Finally, the use of credit as a source of purchasing power has been more widely accepted by consumers in America as a way of life.

What kinds of consumers are most prone to using installment credit? Data collected by the Survey Research Center of the University of Michigan, as illustrated in Figures 5-6 and 5-7, give some insights into this question. The most important users are families in the middle-income brackets. For example, only 35 percent of families with incomes of $7,500 to $9,999 owed no installment credit in 1969. Families with incomes of less than $3,000 apparently could not afford to buy on credit (78 percent owed no installment credit), while families with incomes in excess of $15,000 showed less need for credit (52 percent had no installment credit outstanding). Only 35 percent of families whose head was under twenty-five owed no installment credit in 1969. With increasing age of the family head, usage of installment credit gradually diminished.

[7] National Consumer Finance Association, *Finance Facts Yearbook, 1971,* p. 62.

FIGURE 5-6

Percent of families with outstanding installment credit, by family income, 1969

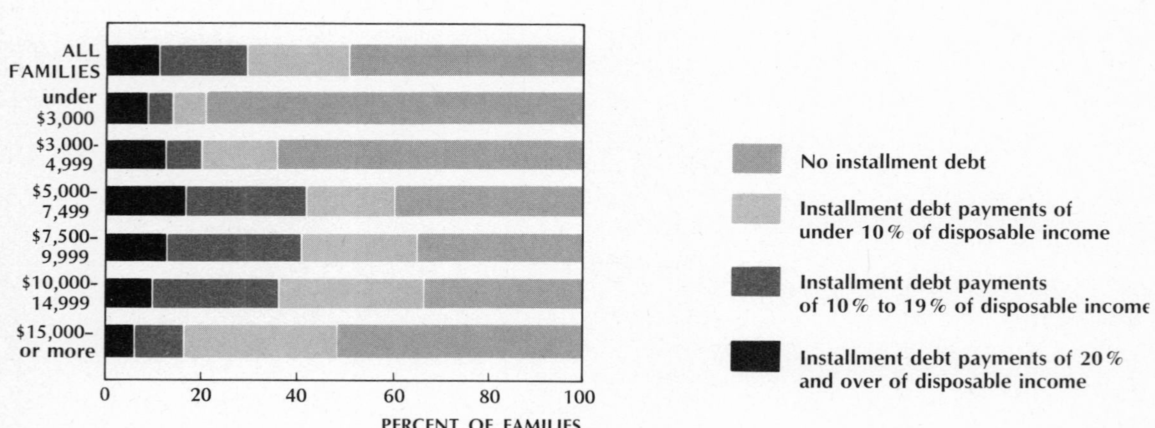

Source: Survey Research Center, University of Michigan, *1969 Survey of Consumer Finances,* p. 25.

FIGURE 5-7

Percent of families with outstanding installment credit, by age of family head, 1969

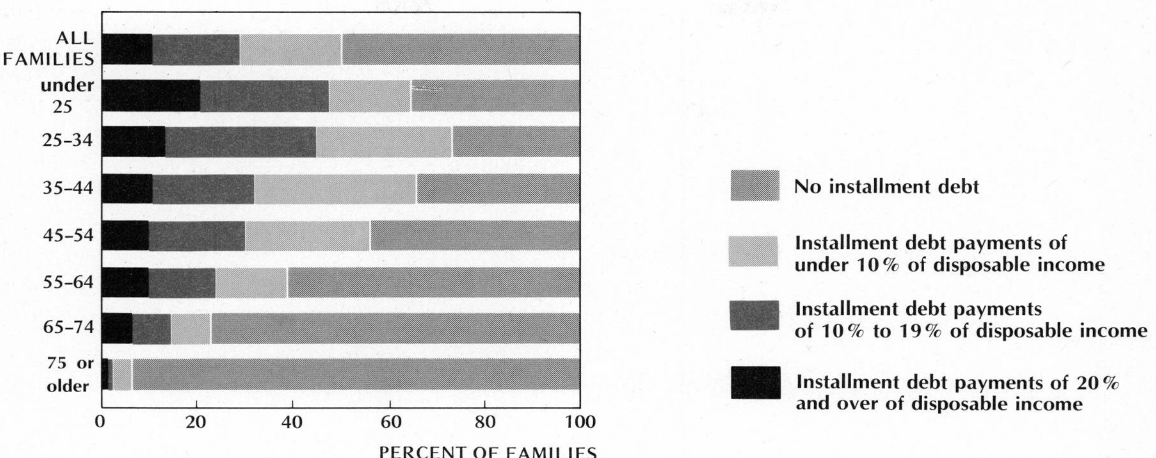

Source: Survey Research Center, University of Michigan, *1969 Survey of Consumer Finances*, p. 25.

THE USE OF NONINSTALLMENT CREDIT

The magnitude of outstanding noninstallment credit, as shown in Figure 5-8, is about one-quarter that of installment credit outstanding. But, in part, this statistic tends to misrepresent the importance of this type of credit. By their very nature, single-payment loans, charge accounts, and service credit "turn over" rapidly, usually being repaid in 30 to 60 days. While $25.6 billion of noninstallment credit was outstanding at the end of 1970, transactions representing several times this amount were financed on a noninstallment basis during 1970.

The doubling of noninstallment credit outstanding in the period 1958–1970 is attributable to numerous factors. Growth in service credit, for example, partially reflects much higher costs for services (medical, in particular), and the growing propensity of an affluent society to spend a larger proportion of its income on services, as opposed to goods, is another factor. Also underlying the growth is our increasing drift toward what is often called "the cashless society." As a matter of convenience, many consumers are finding it preferable to pay by means of a credit card or check. Some observers have predicted that, by the year 2000, cash will be virtually obsolete.

FIGURE 5-8

Noninstallment credit outstanding, 1958–1970

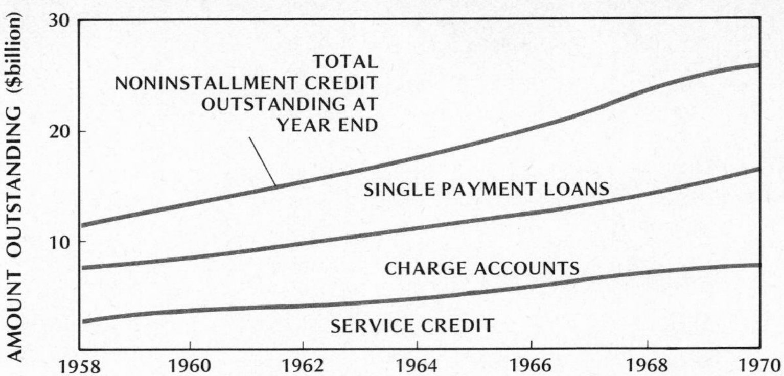

Source: U.S. Board of Governors of the Federal Reserve System, *Federal Reserve Bulletin,* selected issues.

Existing assets

If one thinks about the spending and buying behavior of a typical American housewife, it seems apparent that many economic factors will influence her. Two have already been discussed: the money that is coming in (income) and the money that she might borrow (credit). Her behavior will also be influenced by what she has on hand. If she already has a lot of money (financial assets) or an accumulation of goods (physical assets), these are apt to have some influence on what she does. In this section, these kinds of existing assets are discussed as additional economic determinants of consumer behavior.

In the first place, assets are not only a measure of existing wealth, but in many cases they reflect spending patterns. Most people do not have large amounts of inherited wealth, and the composition of their assets is normally a key to their tendencies to consume or save. Additionally, assets are typically highly correlated with income. It follows, therefore, that existing assets give some indication of a decision-making unit's ability and inclination to spend.

There are two additional reasons for considering existing assets as partial determinants of consumer behavior. The demand for many items that consumers purchase is a *derived demand.* The ownership of houses and automobiles creates related demands for furniture, appliances, gasoline, tires, and other automotive accessories. Heavy demand for such services as ocean trips or vacation flights will in turn enhance the demand for cruise clothes, sports equipment, and similar items. Thus, information on what consumers now have implies something about what they may later want or need.

In this same vein, existing asset data furnish information as to the possibility of *repeat sales* of many kinds of items. If 87 percent of all households own steam irons, manufacturers of steam irons may infer that their marketing strategies must be designed not only to attract new users of steam irons, but also to obtain the substantial replacement market represented by current owners of these products.

AMOUNT AND DISTRIBUTION OF ASSETS

Americans are a wealthy people. In 1970, the financial assets of families and individuals amounted to almost $1.8 trillion. Of this amount, $529 billion was in the form of currency and bank deposits; $922 billion in stocks, bonds, and similar instruments; and $361 billion in life insurance and pension reserves. Mortgages and other forms of household indebtedness amounted to $427 billion, leaving a net financial equity of almost $1.4 trillion. The extent of American wealth also reflects affluence when physical assets are considered. In the same year, individuals owned residences valued at $710 billion and durable goods valued at $276 billion.

Marketers, however, are interested in the *distribution* of assets as well as the total amount of assets. Liquid assets (defined as the sum of amounts in checking accounts, savings accounts, and bonds) give some indication of the potential spending power of different segments of the population. The data shown in Table 5-6, for example, drawn from an annual survey conducted by the University of Michigan Survey Research Center, illustrate liquid asset holdings of selected family income segments within the population.

TABLE 5-6

Liquid asset holdings by family income group, 1969

(Percentage distribution of families)

Total family income	No liquid assets	$1–$499	$500–$1,999	$2,000–$4,999	$5,000–$9,999	$10,000 or more	Total	Median liquid assets
Less than $3,000	47	19	13	10	5	6	100	$ 40
$ 3,000–$4,999	30	28	12	13	8	9	100	280
5,000–7,499	22	39	19	9	5	6	100	260
7,500–9,999	9	32	29	14	8	8	100	840
10,000–14,999	5	29	29	19	10	8	100	1,040
15,000 or more	1	7	27	22	15	28	100	4,100
All families	19	26	22	15	8	10	100	730

Source: Survey Research Center, University of Michigan, *1969 Survey of Consumer Finances*, pp. 100, 103.

As is true of income, the ownership of physical assets in the United States is relatively diffused, and becoming more so. Consider, for example, ownership of such major items as automobiles and homes, as shown in Table 5-7. In 1969, four out of five Americans owned at least one car, while three-fifths of all families owned their own home. Ownership of electric appliances is also widespread. The magazine *Merchandising Week* estimated that in 1970 the percentages of wired homes owning various appliances were as follows: refrigerators (99 percent); electric toasters (91 percent); room air conditioners (37 percent); electric and gas clothes dryers (40 percent); freezers (30 percent); dishwashers (24 percent); and food waste disposers (23 percent). Data such as these have many uses. They reflect the potential markets made up of existing homes without certain appliances. They might be combined with information about prospective housing to give a picture of the new market for appliances. Alternately, they could be combined with information on ages of existing appliances to show the potential replacement market. Further, by studying owner and nonowner characteristics, a marketer may develop general guides for product and promotional policies.

TABLE 5-7

Percent of nonfarm families owning automobiles and homes, by income group, 1969

Income of family	Owns at least one automobile	Owns home
Less than $1,000	32%	
$ 1,000 – 1,999	39	
2,000 – 2,999	46	52%*
3,000 – 3,999	54	
4,000 – 4,999	68	43†
5,000 – 5,999	78	
6,000 – 7,499	88	47‡
7,500 – 9,999	93	61
10,000 – 14,999	95	73
15,000 or more	97	91
All families	79	61

*Less than $3,000
†$3,000–4,999
‡5,000–7,499

Source: Survey Research Center, University of Michigan, *1969 Survey of Consumer Finances*, pp. 43, 68.

Consumer expenditure patterns

Income, credit, and asset ownership are of interest to marketers primarily as determinants of expenditures. Attention can now be turned to how these and other factors are reflected in the *expenditure patterns* of consumers. These patterns are of interest not only for the insights they provide into current consumer needs and wants, but also because they may give some indication of what may happen in the future.

□

OVERALL EXPENDITURE PATTERNS

Some of the more important trends in consumer expenditure patterns are reflected in Table 5-8, which shows total amounts of expenditures on major classes of goods and services for selected years since 1929. Between 1929 and 1969, total personal consumption expenditures increased by almost 750 percent. Certain categories of spending grew much more rapidly than others; ex-

□

TABLE 5-8

Personal consumption expenditures by major categories, United States, selected years, 1929–1969

(In billions of dollars)

Expenditure category	1929	1949	1959	1969
Total personal consumption expenditures	$77.2	$176.8	$311.2	$577.5
Food, beverages, and tobacco	21.2	56.6	85.2	131.9
Clothing and accessories	11.2	23.3	31.9	59.4
Personal care	1.1	2.3	5.0	9.7
Housing	11.5	19.3	43.7	84.0
Household operation	10.7	25.9	45.3	81.5
Medical care expenses	2.9	8.1	17.9	42.6
Personal business	4.2	6.2	13.9	31.9
Transportation	7.6	20.8	41.2	78.0
Recreation	4.3	10.0	17.4	36.3
Private education and research	0.7	1.5	3.4	9.7
Religious and welfare activities	1.2	2.2	4.4	8.1
Foreign travel and other	0.5	0.4	1.1	4.3
Total durables	9.2	24.6	44.3	90.0
Total nondurables	37.7	94.6	146.6	245.8
Total services	30.3	54.6	120.3	241.6

Source: U.S. Department of Commerce, Office of Business Economics, *The National Income and Product Accounts of the United States, 1929–1965*, and *Survey of Current Business*, July, 1970.

penditures on personal care, for example, increased by 880 percent, compared with 530 percent for clothing and 620 percent for food.

During the post-World War II period, very dramatic gains occurred in expenditures for various personal services. Between 1949 and 1969, for instance, higher education expenditures increased by 675 percent, while brokerage charges and investment counseling expenditures increased almost tenfold. A notable exception to the growth in services is found in admissions to motion picture theaters, where expenditures declined almost 20 percent during this period.

Changes in aggregate expenditure patterns result from a variety of socioeconomic factors. Many of the shifts that were shown in Table 5-8 reflect the substantial increase in total personal income that took place during this period.

□
TABLE 5-9
Share of annual U.S. household expenditures by household personal income, 1961–1962

	All households	Under $3,000	$3,000–$5,000	$5,000–$7,500	$7,500–$10,000	$10,000–$15,000	$15,000 and over
All goods and services: Total dollars	$5,152	$2,043	$3,859	$5,315	$6,788	$8,679	$12,687
Percent	100%	100%	100%	100%	100%	100%	100%
Food, beverages, and tobacco	28	32	30	28	27	26	23
Clothing	10	7	9	10	11	12	12
Housing and household operations	24	30	25	24	23	22	24
Housefurnishings and equipment	5	4	5	5	6	5	5
Personal and medical care	10	11	10	10	9	9	9
Transportation	15	9	14	16	16	17	15
Education and recreation	6	4	5	5	6	7	8
Other expenditures	2	2	2	2	2	2	4

Source: *Expenditure Patterns of the American Family,* National Industrial Conference Board, Inc., New York, 1965, p. 18.

FIGURE 5-9
*Expenditure patterns for manual and white-collar workers' households in selected European countries**

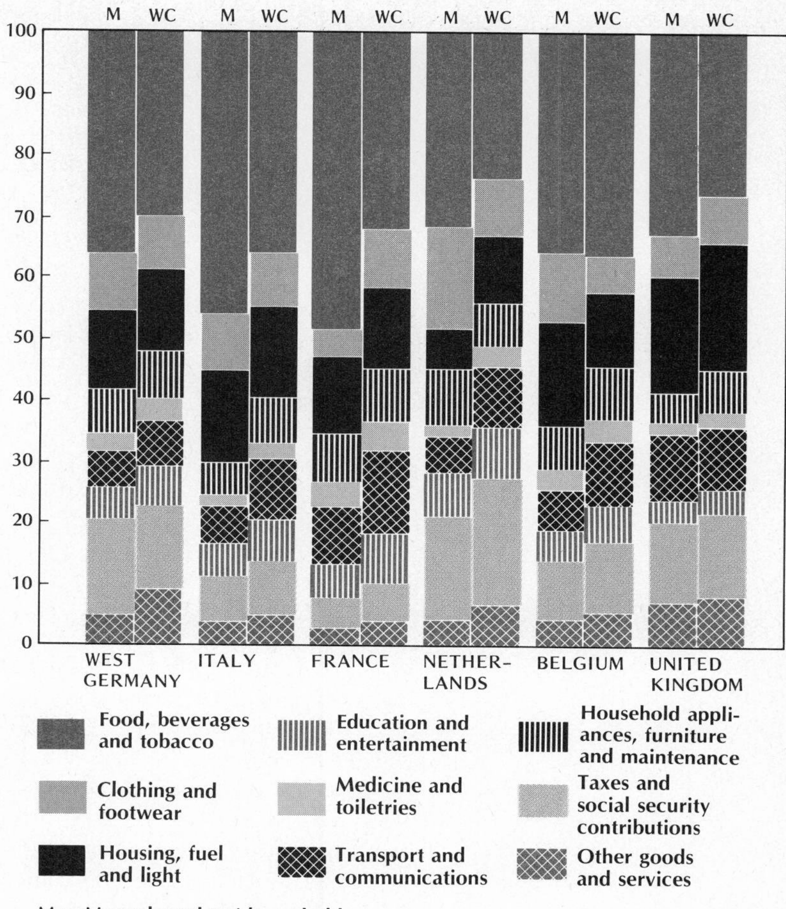

* Based on a survey of 43,000 families carried out by the European Economic Community in 1963–1964, except for Great Britian, where data are based on a 1966–1967 survey conducted by the British Department of Employment and Productivity.
Source: *A Survey of Europe Today,* The Reader's Digest Association, Ltd., London, 1970, p. 31.

As people have had more money available to spend, the fraction required for basic necessities such as most foods has declined. Another factor underlying changes in expenditures is that of consumers' tastes and preferences. Higher levels of education, increased leisure time, and more informal manners have all contributed to sharp gains in spending on various forms of recreation.

Operators of bowling alleys, color television manufacturers and repairmen, and phonograph record companies, to name a few, have shared in these gains. The Cole Boat Company, used as an example earlier, would also stand to benefit from the same trends. Hence, in predicting sales for 1985, the company would have to consider whether the same trends are likely to continue or whether some shift away from recreational activities might occur.

HOUSEHOLD EXPENDITURE PATTERNS

Another way of looking at consumer expenditures is to examine the disposition of income by individual consumer decision-making units. The data in Table 5-9 are based on a national survey of household expenditure patterns made by the National Industrial Conference Board. In looking at these data, it is interesting to think about the conclusions reached by Engel, who studied consumption expenditures in Germany during the middle of the nineteenth century. Engel's statistical analysis led ultimately to the formulation of what are called "Engel's laws." In general, Engel's laws held that as a *family's* income increased, the *percentage* spent on food would decrease; the percentage spent on clothing, rent, and home operation would remain substantially unchanged; and the percentage spent on other kinds of items would increase. Note that the expenditure patterns in Table 5-9 generally conform to the laws Engel formulated over a century ago.

Household expenditure patterns for selected European countries, illustrated in Figure 5-9, also confirm Engel's assertion. In all countries, manual workers (lower income) spend a higher proportion of total expenditures on food than white-collar workers (higher income). But even between British and French office workers (who have similar levels of income), we can see that there are marked differences in the way Europeans spend. The British office worker spends one-quarter of his income on food, while the Frenchman, consistent with popular lore, devotes nearly a third. In comparison with American families, Europeans generally spend a higher proportion of income on food, but relatively less on transportation and personal and medical care.

Questions

1. Snowmobiles were first introduced to the consumer market in 1959 by the firm of Bombardier Limited. In the winter of 1959–1960, 250 units were sold. A decade later, North American sales were expected to exceed 300,000 units a year, and over 60 companies were engaged in manufacturing these vehicles.

A snowmobile is a relatively simple mechanism—a bench that rests on a tank-type track powered by an engine similar to that of a lawnmower. Steering is aided by the attachment of two skis at the front of the machine.

Growth in snowmobile sales fostered demand for other new products. By the early 1970s, special suits of clothing for snowmobiling (at about $60 each) were a popular item, as were boots, goggles, gloves, and hats for the same purpose. Sleds to be towed by snowmobiles were quite common. Most manufacturers also sold car trailers for transporting snowmobiles—a very "hot item" in a leading manufacturer's line was a car trailer that carried *two* snowmobiles.

The increased popularity of snowmobiles can be linked in part to growth in an entire *system* of winter recreation. In the early 1970s skiing had never been more popular, and snowshoe sales were rapidly ascending. The cottage, once a summer habitat, was being built or modified for year-round use.

a. How have economic factors contributed to the growth of snowmobile sales, and of winter recreation products in general?

b. What other factors underlie this trend?

c. Is the trend likely to continue at its present growth rate in the future? Why or why not?

2. Economists generally believe that changes in the amount of installment credit outstanding are closely related to general business fluctuations. Why should such a relationship exist?

3. If only a small fraction of some group of consumers (such as those earning incomes between $3,000 and $5,000) own a specific product, is the opportunity to sell this product to members of the group relatively good or relatively bad? What factors might have a bearing on the answer?

4. A 1967–1968 market study of mobile housing in the United States revealed that the median age of a mobile home buyer was thirty-five, thirteen years less than the median age of household heads in the general population. Median income for the mobile-home buyer was $6,000 compared with $7,400 for all United States families in 1966. The mobile-home buyer moved once every four years. The median price for a recently purchased mobile home was $5,600 versus $21,400 for the median selling price of a new single-family home. Of those who financed mobile homes, 54 percent made a down payment of less than $1,000; 68 percent had a loan of less than $5,000; 64 percent made a loan payment of $54 to $89 monthly; 53 percent borrowed from commercial banks; and 62 percent borrowed the money for a period of seven years.

The main reasons given by owners for choosing mobile homes were that they suited family needs, could be lived in for less than other dwellings, and required less housekeeping and maintenance. The cost per square foot of a mobile home, including furnishings, was approximately $8, whereas the average price of other types of housing was approximately $14 per square foot unfurnished.

a. What possible uses could a manufacturer and/or marketer of mobile homes make of this information?

b. Is this information of value to a marketer of single-family or multiple-family dwellings? If so, in what way?

5. Product ownership often creates a *derived demand* for other products.

a. Identify several products for which ownership of a mobile home is likely to create a derived demand.

b. How might marketers of these products use the information presented in Question 4?

6. Do you think the income sensitivity ratio of each of the following products would be high or low? Why?

a. Electric razors

b. Art books

c. Golf shoes

7. Consumer finance companies are generally defined as firms engaged in the business of making direct cash loans to consumers (as opposed to sales finance companies who, in cooperation with retail establishments, extend credit for the purchase of items like furniture and automobiles). Selected data concerning loans extended by consumer finance companies are shown in Tables 5-10 and 5-11.

a. What changes do these data reflect in the nature and use of personal loans from consumer finance companies between 1950 and 1970?

b. Why do you think these changes took place?

c. What relationship would you expect to find between the monthly income of borrowers and the purpose of the loan? Why? What purpose might this comparison serve?

d. How might the statistics shown in Tables 5-10 and 5-11 differ in the case of personal loans made by other financial institutions, such as sales finance companies and commercial banks?

□

TABLE 5-10

Percentage distribution of monthly income of borrowers from consumer finance companies, selected years, 1950–1967

Monthly income of borrowers	Percent of number of loans extended		
	1950	1960	1967
$ 0.00–$ 100.00	0.9	0.3	0.6
100.01– 200.00	18.9	3.7	2.9
200.01– 300.00	46.0	13.1	6.6
300.01– 400.00	20.6	23.8	12.6
400.01– 500.00	8.7	25.0	18.7
500.01– 750.00	4.9*	26.6	36.1
750.01– 1,000.00	—	6.0	15.2
Over $1,000.00	—	1.5	7.3

*Over $500.

Source: *Finance Facts Yearbook, 1969,* National Consumer Finance Association, Washington, 1969, pp. 57–58.

TABLE 5-11

Distribution of number of loans extended, by purpose, selected years, 1950–1966

Purpose	Percent of number of loans		
	1950	1960	1966
To consolidate existing bills	30	40	44
Travel, vacation, education	7	10	8
Automobile purchase or repair	5	7	12
Home furnishings and appliances	5	8	3
Household repairs	7	4	3
All other purposes	46	31	30
Total	100	100	100

Source: *Finance Facts Yearbook, 1969,* National Consumer Finance Association, Washington, 1969, pp. 57–58.

8.a. Explain why "Engel's laws," formulated over one hundred years ago, still appear to describe some major consumption patterns.

b. Do the expenditure patterns presented in Table 5-9 reveal any contradictions to "Engel's laws"? Explain.

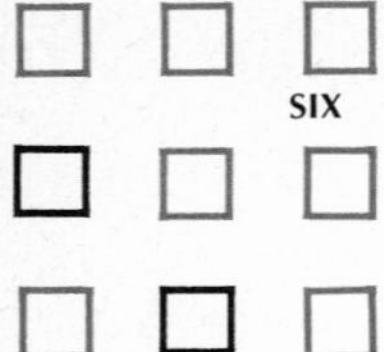

SIX

The psychology of consumer decisions

In some instances, the economic variables described in the previous chapter provide a significant source of understanding of consumer buying decisions. A man purchasing a new car battery, for example, may do so largely on the basis of economic and technical factors. In most purchasing situations, however, *psychological* and *sociological* factors also enter into buying decision processes with varying degrees of significance. Certainly, few people would buy new clothes without considering, explicitly or implicitly, how attractive they looked to others in them, and whether the styling was congruent with the kind of personality they saw themselves to be. As a help to understanding these dimensions of purchasing behavior we will, in this chapter and the next, review the basic theoretical foundations of psychology and sociology.

The collective efforts of psychologists and sociologists to understand human behavior have a great deal in common. At the root of all psychological and sociological theories, there is a basic conceptual model of human behavior. Illustrated in Figure 6-1, the model views individual behavior as being evoked by a stimulus—in other words, the stimulus is an input to the individual that serves as a trigger for action. The output is some form of *behavior,* such as buying or not buying. Standing between the input and output are the mental processes of the individual.

A great dilemma in understanding human behavior is that mental processes can never be observed directly. They can be inferred only by postulating the

FIGURE 6-1
Intervening variables and behavior

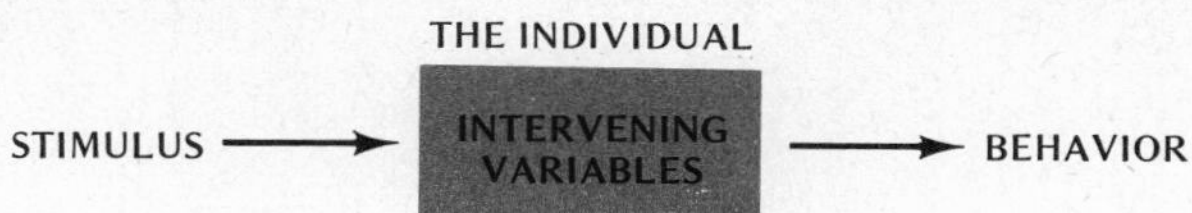

existence of hidden *intervening variables* within the individual that cause a specific mode of behavior. Many schools of psychological and sociological thought have arisen to explain the causality of behavior, each viewing the same phenomenon and inferring a different set of intervening variables. In general, psychological theories are built on intervening variables that are thought to exist within the individual, apart from the social environment in which he lives. Sociological theories, on the other hand, are constructed on variables derived from the support and constraint rendered by other people in the individual's environment. Within the disciplines of psychology and sociology, there is widespread disagreement and ferment as to which of the many postulated theories is "best," or most important. The disagreement persists because it is impossible to prove that any one theory is correct—each is predicated on variables that must be inferred, cannot be observed, and therefore cannot be measured directly.

The existence of many theories of individual behavior presents a difficult challenge to the marketing manager. His search to understand consumer decision making is complicated by the question of which theory is likely to provide the most fruitful insight into a specific buying situation. It implies that, as the manager moves from one problem to another, different theoretical schemes may prove useful in analyzing consumer buying decisions. There are no hard-and-fast rules to make this task an easier one. One should remember, however, that no one psychological or sociological theory is likely, in itself, to provide a complete understanding of purchasing behavior. It is wise, therefore, not to look on different schools of thought as conflicting, but instead as complementary, with each theory contributing an additional perspective to an overall understanding of the complexity of buying behavior.

The remainder of this chapter is devoted to a review of psychological theories and concepts that have found most widespread use among marketers. Chapter 7 follows with a parallel review of sociological theories and concepts.

Consumer behavior as a learning process

Almost everything a man does is learned. Through experience, he learns to talk, walk, perform arithmetic, hold political opinions, vent his anger, and purchase and consume. It is not surprising, therefore, that the psychological process of learning is one of the fundamental topics in an understanding of human behavior. Among all fields of psychological study, learning is the most discussed, researched, and controversial. The result is a multitude of different psychological theories of learning, each made plausible by evidence drawn from literally thousands of research studies in the field.

□ *Learning is a change in behavior, observable or unobservable, due to the effects of experience.*

Because there are so many different viewpoints as to how learning occurs, the term can be defined only in a very general sense.□ Most learning theorists agree that experience is a necessary requisite to learning, although there are many conflicting opinions as to the mechanisms by which experience brings about learning. Similarly, some theories of learning place considerable emphasis on observed changes in behavior as evidence of learning, while others point out that attitudes, preferences, and motives are also learned, but not necessarily observable.

Prevailing theories of learning can be classified into two schools of thought, depending on an underlying belief as to the process by which learning occurs. *Stimulus-response* theorists (sometimes called *connectionists*) believe that learning occurs as the result of associations between stimuli and responses, and in the strengthening of this association as a result of reinforcement. *Cognitive* theorists prefer to view learning as a restructuring of the individual's cognitions about his environment, that is, the way in which he perceives his environment and the attitudes he holds toward it.

□

STIMULUS-RESPONSE LEARNING

As the name implies, the central components of this viewpoint of learning are a stimulus, a response, and what goes on in between them. *Stimuli* may take the form of drives which initiate tendencies to general activity, or cues, which are internal or external stimuli that direct specific drive-reducing responses. *Responses* are, of course, the individual behavior evoked by stimuli.

The stimulus-response learning model places emphasis on the *experience* of stimulus and response as the mechanism by which learning occurs. Learning is viewed as the development of associations between stimuli and responses—what is important is how these associations came about and how they are changed. Development of associations in this manner is regarded as the only necessary explanation of behavior. The stimulus-response theorist does not attempt to postulate the existence of intervening variables, other than "learning" itself.

If a particular response to a stimulus proves rewarding, reinforcement is said to occur. Many psychologists consider reinforcement as a necessary requisite for learning to continue. When a response is frequently and continuously reinforced, the response becomes automatic and a *habit* is formed.

Among the earliest to recognize the importance of habit formation to marketing was John B. Watson, who proposed an approach to advertising strategy for which he coined the term "behaviorism."[1] Watson deduced that repetition of advertising would reinforce a response and lead to firm purchasing habits. The behaviorist viewpoint endorsing repetition found widespread appeal among many advertisers, and is still adhered to by some today. It is probably an oversimplified concept, however, neglecting more recent evidence clearly establishing that attitudes, perceptions, and other factors influence consumer responses to repetitive advertising.

It is not difficult to imagine that housewives, making regular shopping trips to a supermarket, can develop habits of purchasing the same products or brands repeatedly. The stimulus-response learning model has accordingly served as a foundation for many marketing studies of brand loyalty, as well as the effect of changes in price, advertising, and promotion (which are stimuli) on brand choice.[2] By studying the effects of a series of past purchases over a period of time, predictive models of brand share have also been developed for marketing analysis.

□ COGNITIVE LEARNING

Cognitive theories of learning differ from stimulus-response theories by rejecting the idea that an individual's behavior can be the result only of his previous experiences. Most cognitive theorists accept the importance of a stimulus-response experience in learning, but add that stimulus-response links must be organized around some purpose. The organizing influence, referred to as cognition, is regarded as the crucial intervening variable in an explanatory model of learning. *Cognition,* in the sense that it is used here, refers to how an individual perceives his environment and the attitudes he holds toward it.

The concepts of perceptions and attitudes are both extremely important for their marketing implications. The effects of advertising, for example, are determined by the way in which consumers perceive advertising messages. At the same time, most advertising is intended to create some measure of attitude change in its target audience. Because perception and attitudes are fundamental concepts whose marketing implications extend far beyond cognitive learning theory, they will be dealt with in separate sections later in this chapter.

Motivation in buying decisions

Motivated behavior refers to a sequence of steps that an individual is thought to go through in initiating and carrying out behavior. To illustrate, picture a man watching a Sunday afternoon football game on television. During a break

[1] John B. Watson, *Behaviorism,* The People's Institute Publishing Company, New York, 1925.
[2] See, for example, Alfred A. Kuehn, "Consumer Brand Choice as a Learning Process," *Journal of Advertising Research,* December, 1962, pp. 10–17.

in the play, he feels thirsty and goes to the refrigerator for a can of beer. His behavior can be said to have been initiated when he felt thirsty or, in precise terms, when there was activation of a *drive*□ for thirst.

□ *A drive is a bodily state that initiates tendencies toward general activity.*

□ *A motive is a predisposition that directs behavior toward a specific drive-reducing goal.*

The football fan has probably learned from previous experience that a specific kind of behavior, in this instance drinking beer, is drive reducing. Drinking beer is accordingly referred to as the man's *motive*□ for accomplishing thirst satisfaction.

Motives are thought to be learned and, once learned, stable over a period of time and difficult to change. Each individual is thought to possess an enormous number of motives stored in his memory; though all are not called upon in a specific situation. For example, the football fan was probably aware that he could have satisfied his thirst by going to the tap for a glass of water. As one psychologist has commented, "The first and most important thing to be learned about motives is that everybody has a lot of them and nobody has quite the same mixture as anybody else."[3]

Each individual's complex organization of a wide variety of motives, acting singly or in combination, serves as a powerful determinant of behavior. In the process of behaving, each individual also develops more generalized patterns of action that are referred to as *response traits*. The trait approach to motivation holds that an effective theory can be built by finding patterns in behavior that are broader than a single, specific motive, but less complex than the individual's total behavior. Competitiveness, aggressiveness, self-consciousness, and exhibitionism are examples of a few response traits that have been identified by psychologists.

□

THE USE OF MOTIVES IN MARKETING ANALYSIS

The identification of motives in consumer buying decisions has traditionally received widespread, if not oversimplified, attention among marketers. As early as the 1920s, Melvin T. Copeland, a pioneer in the development of marketing thought, spoke of *patronage motives* that influence industrial firms to trade with one source of supply over another.[4] Among patronage motives identified by Copeland were reliability of the seller, promptness of delivery, ability to secure exact specifications, and dependability of repair service. Subsequently, other marketers developed lengthy lists of motives thought to exist in different buying situations. *Primary buying motives* (leading to the purchase of a class of good, such as breakfast cereal) were distinguished from *selective buying motives* (leading to the purchase of a particular type, such as corn flakes). *Rational motives* were suggested to be observable and measurable

[3] Saul W. Gellerman, *Motivation and Productivity*, American Management Association, New York, 1963, p. 175.

[4] Melvin T. Copeland, *Principles of Merchandising*, McGraw-Hill Book Company, New York, 1924.

(such as economy, efficiency, durability, and convenience), as distinct from *emotional motives* involving personal feelings and opinions (such as status, pride, conformity, and ambition). Numerous other lists and classifications of motives, too abundant to mention, have embellished the marketing literature of recent decades.

While marketers have borrowed liberally from motivation theory, serious questions can be raised about the value of these efforts in gaining a true understanding of consumer decision making. There has been a widespread, though not universal, tendency to treat motives as *generalized, all-encompassing* explanatory variables. The great danger of this approach is the ease with which one can slip into "seat-of-the-pants judgments," incorrectly describing almost any plausible explanation of behavior as a "motive." To say that a housewife purchases a supermarket's private brand of peas because of an "economy motive" not only is superficial, but may be wrong. Some private brands, such as those of Kroger and A & P, are highly esteemed and generally synonymous with quality for many housewives.

□

EMOTIONAL APPEALS IN ADVERTISING

Motive and *emotion* stem from the same Latin root (*movere,* to move), and are closely associated in psychological thought. In general, motives are thought to be accompanied often by a stirred-up condition of the organism that is called an emotion. Examples of emotions are joy, love, fear, or anxiety. Because the release of emotion is a pleasurable experience for individuals, many products are advertised using emotional appeals. The makers of Shalimar perfume, for example, associate their product with a release from the mundane by featuring exotic scenes of Far Eastern cultures in advertisements. In 1968, a civil group lobbying for more effective gun control legislation in the United States used an emotional appeal of fear to enlist public support. One advertisement showed four expended revolver cartridges with the names of John F. Kennedy, Medgar Evers, Martin Luther King, and Robert Kennedy appearing beside them—a fifth unexpended cartridge was labeled "Next?" Emotional release was provided by the simple copy of the advertisement, "Write your senator—while you still have a senator."

Personality characteristics as predictors of buying behavior

The study of personality is concerned with the causality of *general patterns* of behavior that persist in an individual across a broad spectrum of different situations. For example, one might observe an individual's behavior in a number of situations (purchasing in a store, working in an office, at home with the family, at church, etc.), and through these observations it might be possible to characterize certain elements of his behavior that seem reasonably consistent from

□ *Personality refers to the configuration of characteristics that determine the general pattern of behavior in an individual, particularly insofar as it makes the individual unique or distinctive from others.*

one situation to another. The individual might be referred to as very dominant, as having a great desire to achieve, or as being quite aggressive.

Because it is concerned with the broadest possible patterns of behavior, personality encompasses both motives and response traits.□ The latter two explanatory variables, it will be recalled, are concerned with explaining behavior in specific situations or groups of similar situations. As one might expect, the field of personality theory is both complex and controversial. One review of theories of personality listed those of 17 individuals, each of whom is a leading proponent of a particular school of thought.[5]

□

IS "PERSONALITY" IMPORTANT TO THE MARKETER?

For some years, marketers have been attracted by the potential promise of personality as a predictor of consumer buying behavior. The best-known study in this field is probably Franklin B. Evans's examination of personality differences between Chevrolet and Ford owners.[6] Evans found that, using test measures of personality, he could correctly predict whether an individual owned a Chevrolet or Ford automobile in 63 percent of the cases he studied. But since he could correctly classify 70 percent of his sample using only demographic data, Evans concluded that personality was not a powerful predictor of automobile brand choice. Since Evans's work, numerous other studies have attempted to correlate personality with such dimensions of buying behavior as persuasibility, product choice, brand choice, durables purchases, convenience item purchases, and propensity to save. These studies have produced only meagre results. After reviewing 120 studies of this nature, for example, Harold Kassarjian concluded that "a few studies indicate a strong relationship between personality and consumer behavior, a few indicate no relationship, and the great majority indicate that if correlations do exist they are so weak as to be questionable or perhaps meaningless."[7]

Why has personality failed to provide a reasonable explanation of buying behavior? The principal problem would appear to rest not in the concept of personality itself, but in the way in which researchers in marketing have chosen to measure it. Most personality tests were designed for measuring social or antisocial behavioral tendencies, particularly those of an abnormal nature. There is serious doubt that measures derived for this purpose have particular relevance to purchasing behavior. As Kassarjian concludes[8]:

instruments originally intended to measure gross personality characteristics such as sociability, emotional stability, introversion, or neuroticism have been used to make

[5] Calvin S. Hall and Gardner Lindzey, *Theories of Personality*, John Wiley & Sons, Inc., New York, 1957, p. 548.

[6] Franklin B. Evans, "Psychological and Objective Factors in the Prediction of Brand Choice: Ford versus Chevrolet," *Journal of Business*, October, 1959, pp. 340–369.

[7] Harold H. Kassarjian, *Personality and Consumer Behavior: A Review*, unpublished address given to the 1970 Fall Conference of the American Marketing Association, Boston, August, 1970.

[8] *Ibid.*

predictions as to the brand of toothpaste subjects purchase or their preference of Salem cigarettes over Camels. The variables that lead to the assassination of a president, intake into a mental hospital, or suicide may not be identical with those that lead to the purchase of a dryer, a pair of shoes, or chewing gum.

Thus, while personality would ostensibly seem *related* to buying behavior, we should probably await the development of more relevant test instruments before assessing its power as a *predictor* of consumer actions.

Perception

☐ *Perception is the process by which an individual receives, interprets, and responds to stimuli in his environment.*

In earlier discussions in this chapter, we made reference to the human capacity for *perception.*☐ The concept of perception is not a difficult one, but its simplicity belies its overwhelming importance and centrality to a number of psychological theories of behavior. Cognitive learning theory, for example, differs from stimulus-response theory in its assertion that man's perception of his environment is more important than unqualified stimulus-response experience. Perception is a crucial ingredient in the makeup of man's psychology, for it is in the process of perception that an individual attaches *meaning* to stimuli in his environment.

Three generalized factors are thought to influence the process of perceiving stimuli: (1) characteristics of the stimulus itself; (2) its gestalt or, in other words, how the stimulus relates to its background; and (3) mediating personal variables in the individual receiving the stimulus. Each of these factors is significant for its marketing implications, where virtually every element of a marketing program represents a stimulus that is perceived in some fashion by potential consumers.

Although a human possesses the largest brain of all living creatures, its capacity is grossly inadequate for taking note of *all* stimuli that the body senses. One expert has estimated, for example, that a brain the size of a cubic light-year would be required to process information received by the eyes alone.[9] The human must therefore ignore the majority of stimuli he senses, and in turn, these stimuli must vie for his attention.

We know, however, that man is more apt to notice certain kinds of stimuli than others, and this knowledge is used extensively by marketers in product design, advertising, sales promotional material, store layout, package design, and an entire host of other ingenious applications too numerous to cite in detail. For example, an individual focuses attention on *novelty;* so it is not surprising to find marketers in a constant battle to be the first with a new product, a new package, or almost anything else they can associate with a "New, New, New" slogan. *Color* is the most versatile of stimulus components—it can alarm (red), soothe (pastels), create moods (blue), and even stimulate sensations

[9] Wilbert J. McKeachie and Charlotte L. Doyle, *Psychology,* Addison-Wesley Publishing Company, Inc., Reading, Mass., 1966, p. 171.

(green, as in magazine advertisements for the coolness of menthol cigarettes). *Contrast, position,* and *size* are all important determinants of the effectiveness of advertisements as stimuli to behavior.

Most objects are comprised of many different stimuli, the aggregate of which may take on a broader pattern of meaning than the simple sum of the individual parts. The resultant gestalt can profoundly influence the way in which an object is perceived. An outstanding example of applying the gestalt concept to marketing can be found in the design of a commuter train for metropolitan Toronto in 1966. Because no commuter train had previously served the area, new equipment for the GO (Government of Ontario) train was designed from scratch. In particular, the interior designer was asked to create something that did not project the dull, impersonal atmosphere normally associated with commuter travel. The result was a train car with vinyl bucket seats separated by a console panel. When coupled with other design features, the total result was unmistakable in its meaning—Mr. Commuter was wheeling home in a sports car.

Motives, traits, and attitudes are all mediating personal variables that can influence perceptions. In the early 1960s, Dow Brewery Limited introduced a new Kebec brand of beer to the Quebec market. Kebec (the original spelling of Quebec) was intended to appeal to French-Canadian patriotism, and its advertising and label incorporated the fleur-de-lis and other symbols of French Canada extensively. But the time of introduction was one of great social upheaval in Quebec, and many French Canadians were developing new attitudes of hostility toward French dominance by the English-speaking minority in the province. Kebec, the product of a company owned by English Canadians, was perceived as a hostile attempt by an "English" company to exploit French-Canadian culture for a profit. Political and social organizations in the province reacted so violently to the new product that it became a front-page issue in newspapers, and Dow was forced to withdraw the new beer from the market a few weeks after its introduction.

IMAGES

Marketing managers are often heard to express concern over the *image* of their company, store, product, or brand. The term is actually a misnomer whose colloquial use refers more correctly to consumers' *perceptions* of their purchases and suppliers. Because images represent a set of consumer perceptions of a product or firm, they can affect buying behavior. Frequently, the marketing program for a product is tailored so that all its elements project a consistent, specific image. Certain brands of furniture, for example, are priced high, sold only through selected reputable retailers, and advertised with a conservative theme in order to project a "quality" image. The Cadillac automobile is reported to have used a consistent advertising theme since 1934, one that associated an image of success with Cadillac ownership. The creator of the Cadillac advertising theme has been quoted as saying, "I don't sell a mechanism, I sell a state of mind."[10]

PERCEIVED RISK

A recently emerging explanatory concept of behavior focuses attention on the fact that individuals usually perceive some elements of risk in decision-making activities. Because risk is a characteristically uncomfortable state, people develop decision strategies and ways of behaving that serve to reduce risk, thereby enabling them to act with relative confidence and ease in a situation. It is not necessary that risk be "real" in an objective sense in order to elicit behavior—that which the individual perceives is the relevant determinant of what action he will take. For example, a woman may be concerned that the fabric of a dress she is thinking of buying is of poor quality. Even if the fabric is actually of very high quality, the woman's subjective perception of poor quality may be sufficient to discourage her from buying the dress.

In purchasing situations, we can distinguish between two forms of perceived risk. *Performance risk* relates to whether the product will function as it should. Will a new raincoat, for example, keep water out? *Psychosocial risk* is addressed to questions of whether the purchase will enhance one's sense of well-being or self-concept. Will the buyer think himself well dressed if he buys the coat, and will others think likewise? In any given buying situation, varying amounts of both types of risk may be present. One study, for example, found headache remedies to be higher in perceived performance risk than fabric softeners or dry spaghetti.[11] Thomas Robertson found that a new telephone product was low in performance risk, but high in psychosocial risk. Apparently, consumers were not worried about the telephone not working, but they were concerned about what others would say about the product.[12] The automobile buying behavior of Mr. and Mrs. Wilson, discussed in Chapter 3, reflected high levels of both performance *and* psychosocial risk.

CONSUMER RISK REDUCTION

A consumer who perceives either performance or psychosocial risk is likely to undertake some form of risk-reducing behavior. Because perceived risk is a function of both the consequences of an action and the uncertainty associated with these consequences, risk reduction can be achieved in two ways: reducing the consequences or increasing the certainty of the purchase out-

[10] "A Cadillac Is a Cadillac Is a Cadillac," *Fortune,* April, 1968, p. 118.
[11] Scott M. Cunningham, "The Major Dimensions of Perceived Risk," in Donald F. Cox (ed.), *Risk Taking and Information Handling in Consumer Behavior,* Division of Research, Harvard Business School, Boston, 1967, pp. 82–108.
[12] Thomas S. Robertson, *An Analysis of Innovative Behavior and Its Determinants,* unpublished Ph.D. dissertation, Northwestern University, 1966.

come. Consequences of a purchase might be reduced, for example, by buying lesser quantities. More frequently, however, consumers choose to increase purchase certainty, and to do so by their use of *information*.

The propensity of consumers to employ information to reduce risk has been documented by research. Studies reported by Cox, for example, show at least three patterns of risk-reducing behavior that depend on how consumers handle information.[13] One pattern is the *acquisition* of additional information. A consumer exhibiting this kind of behavior might be likely to pay close attention to advertisements, to compare prices at different stores, or to seek out informal sources of purchase information. How consumers *process* information has been found to depend on the form of perceived risk, performance or psychosocial, they are trying to reduce. According to Cox, consumers perceiving high psychosocial risk are most likely to turn to other people for assistance, while those perceiving high performance risk will most often refer to advertisements or use the product on a trial basis. Information *retention* is, in effect, a way of describing brand loyalty. By always buying a known brand, the consumer avoids the relatively higher risk of unknown and untried alternatives.

In our discussion in Chapter 2, we mentioned the central importance of information flows in the functioning of a marketing system. Here, with perceived risk, we discover a concept of individual behavior that points out the significance of information to the behavior of individual consumers. We still have a great deal to learn about perceived risk and, more importantly, about why consumers react to risk in differing ways. Notwithstanding, it seems likely that marketers' ability to influence advertising, personal selling, and various other information flows in the marketing system will lead them to refer to this concept with increasing propensity in the future.

Attitudes and attitude change

☐ *An attitude is an evaluative organization of beliefs, motives, and response traits associated with a particular object, event, or phenomenon.*

In the process of coping in daily life with events, people, and other elements in his social environment, man develops attitudes☐ toward his surroundings. The basis of attitude formation lies in the motives, traits, and patterns of behavior that are repeatedly evoked in the course of day-to-day life. These response patterns are stored in an individual's memory and, in time, gradually become organized in some overall, consistent fashion. The result of this process of mental organization is a set of attitudes that guide an individual to act in a reasonably consistent and predictable manner.

The factor that distinguishes attitudes from other types of predispositions to behave, such as motives or traits, is the organization of these elements in an

[13] Donald F. Cox (ed.), *Risk Taking and Information Handling in Consumer Behavior*, Division of Research, Harvard Business School, Boston, 1967.

evaluative way toward persons or objects in the environment. Thus, a man may come to like outdoor sports, to prefer liberal politicians to conservatives, or to be disgusted with hippies, yippies, or the youth generation. It is the evaluative component that makes attitudes so powerful a determinant of behavior. They affect a man's judgments and perceptions, his efficiency in learning, his reactions to others, and even his basic philosophy of life. Naturally, they also affect his purchasing behavior.

Marketers have shown extreme interest in attitude formation and change, perhaps more than in any other psychological and sociological concept. This interest stems mainly from a desire to find a measurable intervening variable that can be used to predict purchasing behavior. A person's attitudes can be measured, but, as we shall see shortly, there is considerable controversy about the ability of attitudinal measures to predict purchasing behavior.

The marketer's interest in attitudes is also not surprising when one considers that most marketing programs, and marketing communications in particular, are intended to influence consumer attitudes in order to create more favorable predispositions to buy. We mentioned in Chapter 2, for example, that over $20 billion was spent on advertising in the United States in 1969, and that equal or greater amounts were spent on other forms of promotional effort. A sizable proportion of these efforts in persuasive communication had the immediate objective of confirming some existing attitudes, changing attitudes, or creating new attitudes among potential buyers.

Marketers, too, have begun to use attitude measures as a basis for segmenting consumer markets, much in the same manner as demographic variables are used for the same purpose. The use of attitudes as a basis of segmentation is sometimes referred to as *psychographics*. One study of this kind, for example, classified automobile buyers according to their attitudes on travel, social activities, mobility, highway safety, liberalism-conservatism, self-image, car buying and maintenance, and driving habits. Data emanating from the resulting clusters of buyers with similar attitudes were put to use in new product concept tests, advertising tests, and media selection and automobile line extension decisions.[14]

THE INFORMATION-PROCESSING APPROACH TO ATTITUDES

There are several different schools of thought about attitudes and how they are formed and changed, but the approach marketers have found most relevant to their decision making is that called *information processing*. In this approach, an individual is looked upon as an "information-processing machine" who, when presented with new information, tries to deal with it as effectively as pos-

[14] Harry E. Heller, "Defining Target Markets by Their Attitude Profiles," in Lee Adler and Irving Crespi (ed.), *Attitude Research on the Rocks*, American Marketing Association, 1968, Chicago, pp. 45–57.

sible and alter his behavior accordingly. By looking on attitude formation and change in this way, marketers can begin to posit conditions under which persuasive communication is likely to be most effective.

To illustrate the information-processing approach to attitudes, we can examine the scheme suggested by William McGuire, shown in Figure 6-2, as a means of viewing the effectiveness of advertising in changing purchasing

FIGURE 6-2

*Indexes of advertising effectiveness related to the behavioral steps in being persuaded**

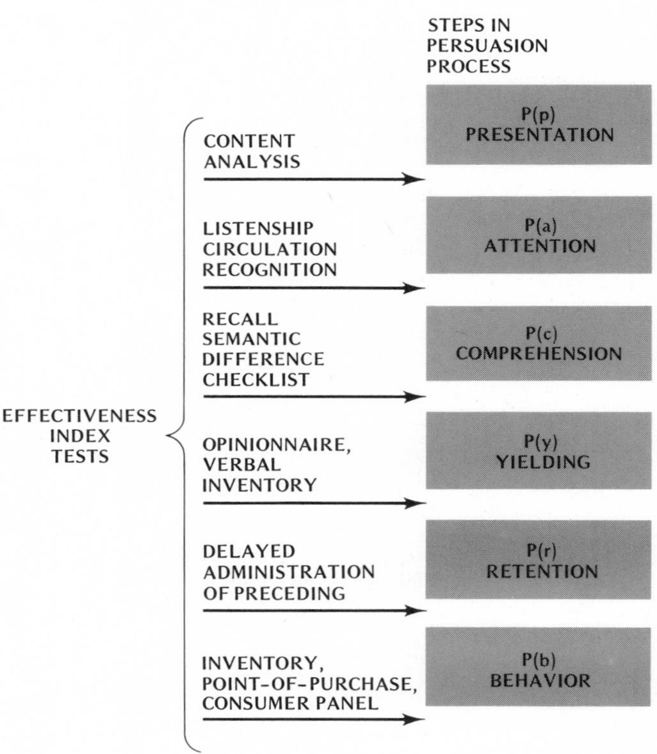

* In this scheme, the probability of attitude change is indicated by $P(p)$, $P(a)$, $P(c)$, $P(y)$. The probability of change in purchase behavior is given by $P(p)$, $P(a)$, $P(c)$, $P(y)$, $P(r)$, $P(b)$.

Source: William J. McGuire, "An Information-processing Model of Advertising Effectiveness," paper presented at the Symposium on Behavioral and Management Science in Marketing, Center for Continuing Education, University of Chicago, July, 1969.

behavior.[15] McGuire suggests a series of six sequential steps, each probabilistically linked to the previous one, through which the individual must pass to be effectively persuaded. To affect a consumer, a message must first succeed in being *presented* to him. He may or may not pay *attention* to this message. If he does, he not only must *comprehend* it, but must *yield* and *retain* its suggestion if there is to be a chance of a change in his behavior. If these five steps are successfully completed, then the remaining question is whether he will *behave* in the manner suggested by the message.

Among many possible implications of looking on attitude change as information processing is the inherent suggestion of ways to measure advertising effectiveness. Content analysis, for example, can determine if a message succeeded in being presented to an individual, while tests of advertisement recognition can assess if the individual paid attention to the advertisements. Other tests, suggested by McGuire as appropriate at successive behavioral stages, are indicated in Figure 6-2.

The foregoing scheme gives no indication of the conditions under which persuasive communication is likely to succeed in "moving" an individual through successive stages toward attitude and behavior change. Marketing managers and researchers have devoted considerable effort to addressing this question, however. The results of their efforts can be summarized only briefly.

Certain conditions fostering attitude change relate to the source of a persuasive communication. *Source effect* refers to the fact that, all other things being equal, a message from a source which is believed to be trustworthy and credible, such as a friend, is more likely to produce attitude change than one from another kind of source.

The content of a message also bears on its ability to alter attitudes. An example of *message effect* can be found in the propensities of different individuals to accept communication in which one side of a controversial topic is presented, as opposed to communications delineating both sides of the topic. In general, it has been found that (1) giving both sides is most effective in producing attitude change in individuals initially opposed to a point of view; (2) for those already convinced of a main argument, one-sided messages are most effective; and (3) attitudes of people with higher education are most likely to be affected if both sides are presented.

Channel effect refers to the capacity of communication channels to change attitudes. It has been found, for example, that not all channels are equally persuasive at successive stages of a purchase decision process. In general,

[15] William J. McGuire, "An Information-processing Model of Advertising Effectiveness," paper presented at the Symposium on Behavioral and Management Science in Marketing, Center for Continuing Education, University of Chicago, July, 1969.

marketer-controlled channels (advertising, personal selling, and sales promotion) are most often mentioned by consumers as original sources of information about products, while interpersonal channels not controlled by the marketer are most often mentioned as having greatest influence on events immediately preceding purchase.

Audience effect illustrates that the state of an individual receiving communication can effect his propensity to adopt new attitudes or change existing ones. In general, it has been found that attitude change is most likely to occur when (1) the topic under consideration is not of central importance to the individual, (2) the relevant attitudes are independent of other attitudes held, (3) prior information on the topic is small, and (4) the individual is not dogmatic.

ATTITUDES AND BUYING BEHAVIOR

Marketers express considerable interest in the relationship of attitudes to behavior because, if a buyer's attitudes can be accurately gauged, it may be possible to predict his buying behavior. The *predictive* capacity of attitude measures, however, is one of marketing's most controversial issues.

There is no question that attitudes are directly related to an individual's behavior. In the introduction to this chapter, we stated that most psychological thought is founded on the concept of intervening variables that explain behavioral responses to internal stimuli. Attitudes are an example of one class of intervening variables. They are hypothetical constructs which, by virtue of the framework of their definition, must be related to behavior.

The ability of attitude measures to predict buying behavior is complicated, however, because other factors (in addition to attitudes) may also influence a purchase decision, particularly those related to the purchase situation. A buyer may not like a certain brand, but will he go to another store if no other is available?

A limited number of studies have shown attitudes to be reasonable predictors of purchase behavior. Alvin Achenbaum, for example, found a high degree of correlation between brand attitudes (favorable-unfavorable) and product usage among buyers of cigarettes, deodorants, laxatives, and gasoline.[16] George Day studied a sample of 220 convenience food buyers and found that he could explain 24 percent of the variability in purchase probability by brand attitude measures. By looking only at those buyers whose brand attitudes were most stable, he could explain 54 percent of the variability in purchase probability by brand attitude measures.[17] Yet despite these findings, there is an equal or greater number of contrary studies raising skepticism. After reviewing 32 studies of attitude-behavior relationships, for example, Allan

[16] Alvin A. Achenbaum, "Knowledge Is a Thing Called Measurement," in Lee Adler and Irving Crespi (eds.), *Attitude Research at Sea,* American Marketing Association, Chicago, 1966, pp. 111–126.
[17] George S. Day, *Buyer Attitudes and Brand Choice Behavior,* The Free Press, New York, 1970.

Wicker concluded "that it is considerably more likely that attitudes will be unrelated or only slightly related to overt behaviors."[18] It would appear that, until more evidence is available to demonstrate the relative importance of attitude and situational factors in purchase decisions, the predictive capacity of attitudes will remain in its currently controversial status.

COGNITIVE DISSONANCE

Repeated studies have shown that it is the nature of man to develop attitudes—social, political, and cultural—that are *consistent* with one another. This consistency usually extends to his behavior—a man who firmly believes that Japanese cameras are of higher quality than American ones is unlikely to buy an American camera. The word "usually" is stressed, however, because there are many exceptions to this rule. Many people who believe smoking is harmful continue to smoke.

What happens in these exceptional cases where a man's attitudes are inconsistent with his behavior? It has been found that few individuals can "live with" inconsistency or, as it is generally called, *cognitive dissonance*. Instead, they seek new forms of behavior to rationalize the inconsistency. The smoker, for example, may try to convince himself that stopping smoking would make him very nervous or overweight, and that this would be worse for his health than the unrealized threat of lung cancer or heart disease. In this way, he tries to reduce dissonance and achieve consonance; the relative success of his attempts determines how long the state of cognitive dissonance persists.

Cognitive dissonance is thought to be present in the postpurchase stage of many buying decisions. Its significance to marketing strategy is twofold. On one hand, if the potential exists for future repeat purchases (as in insurance, automobiles, or appliances), reduction of consumer dissonance may increase future predispositions to buy. One study found, for example, that poor dealer service on new automobiles created a state of cognitive dissonance in owners, thereby greatly diminishing the likelihood of repeat purchases of the same make.[19] At the same time, the dissonant buyer is likely to attempt rationalization through the medium of conversation with friends and acquaintances, themselves potential buyers. The resultant word-of-mouth messages may influence these other potential buyers substantially, quite possibly in an unfavorable direction.

Cognitive dissonance is particularly important in marketing products that require postpurchase service or contact with the buyer. Some major household-appliance manufacturers operate their own repair depots in major

[18] Allan W. Wicker, "Attitudes versus Actions: The Relationship of Verbal and Overt Behavioral Responses to Attitude Objects," *The Journal of Social Issues,* Autumn, 1969, pp. 41–78.
[19] Gerald D. Bell, "Self-Confidence and Persuasion in Car Buying," *Journal of Marketing Research,* February, 1967, pp. 46–52.

centers to ensure a high quality of service. Many insurance agents personally deliver renewal policies instead of mailing them to clients. While there may be other reasons justifying these activities, they nonetheless serve the purpose of reducing or preventing dissonant states in consumers.

Intentions

One approach to marketing analysis involves asking potential consumers a series of questions aimed at determining if they plan to purchase a given product in the foreseeable future. In its simplest form, for example, a question of this kind might be, "Do you plan to buy a new automobile within the next 12 months?" The individual's reply is usually referred to as a measure of his *buying intentions*. In a sense, intentions measures can be viewed as an extension of the attitude measures discussed in the previous section. They combine a consumer's regard for an item with a statement of its likelihood of purchase.

In the United States, surveys of household buying intentions have been conducted since 1946 by the Survey Research Center of the University of Michigan. Similar surveys are also conducted by the National Industrial Conference Board, the Bureau of the Census, and numerous private survey research firms. Among European countries, France, West Germany, and the United Kingdom have all compiled survey data on consumer buying intentions.

The basic idea behind surveys of consumer intentions was first suggested in Chapter 5. Consumer purchases, particularly of cars, major appliances, and housing, are subject to variations not directly correlated with changes in income, credit, and financial assets. In addition to changes in purchasing power, fluctuations in consumer purchases are apparently also a function of willingness to buy, and are thought to be foreshadowed by changes in anticipatory variables that reflect degrees of consumer optimism or pessimism. Hence, by obtaining survey measures of buyer intentions, it is hoped that future purchase behavior can be predicted.

□ INTENTIONS DATA AND PURCHASE PREDICTION

Used alone, intentions data have proved only moderately useful in predicting durable goods purchases. The data reflect combinations of household attitudes regarding many different aspects of personal and economic conditions, both present and future. They also encompass judgments by the householder on how he anticipates spending money among various available alternatives. These assessments by an individual can easily change over a period of time. As a result, many of those indicating intentions of buying do not actually do so. There is usually an even larger group who do not indicate an intention of buying, but end up making a purchase in the time period under consideration in the survey. Consequently, predictive accuracy is impaired to the point that other types of variables usually provide greater predictive accuracy. One study, for example, found that change in disposable income was a better predictor of house purchases than intentions data. By combining income and intentions data, however, the resultant predictive ability was better than when either variable was used alone.[20]

In lieu of intentions, Thomas Juster has suggested that improved predictive capacity can be obtained from survey measures of consumer purchase *probability*.[21] After classifying a sample of consumers as "intenders" or "nonintenders" by traditional survey techniques, Juster asked the same people if there was any probability of their making a purchase during the time period under consideration. He found that a substantial number of nonintenders reported purchase probabilities higher than zero and that, of the 10 percent of the sample who reported "don't know" when asked about their buying intentions, every one provided an estimate of purchase probability. By obtaining subsequent information on actual purchases of automobiles and household durables from the same sample of consumers, Juster found the probability data to yield better predictions than that given by any of the information on buying intentions.

Questions

1. What circumstances would have to prevail in a marketing situation before psychological variables could provide a useful basis for designing marketing programs on a segmented basis?

2. What purchase motives do you think would be important for each of the following products?
   a. Toothpaste
   b. Sports car
   c. Honey
   d. Breakfast cereal

3. What psychological considerations would lead a marketer to rely on the extensive use of product sampling rather than higher levels of consumer advertising?

4. In a study of the price images of 27 supermarkets in five different cities, it was found that consumers were substantially incorrect in their perception of the relative prices charged by nine of the stores. That is: (1) consumers perceived that a store offered relatively low prices, when in reality its prices were

[20] J. Alex Murray, "Canadian Consumer Expectational Data: An Evaluation," *Journal of Marketing Research*, February, 1969, pp. 54–61.

[21] F. Thomas Juster, *Consumer Buying Intentions and Purchasing Probability*, National Bureau of Economic Research, New York, 1966.

high in comparison to other supermarkets in the area; or (2) consumers perceived that a store's offerings were relatively high priced, when in reality prices were low when compared to other supermarkets in the area.

a. What factors might lead consumers to perceive a store's prices as being either relatively higher or lower than they actually are?

b. What are the possible implications of an inaccurate price image to a retail store?

c. What possible actions could you suggest to a retailer who discovered that his real prices were substantially lower than perceived by his customers?

5. Castrol Limited, a British firm, was one of the leading sellers of motor oils in the world. The company held an estimated 30 percent of the British market, and its subsidiaries operated in over 40 different countries.

In 1969, in an attempt to improve on its relatively small share of the Canadian market, Castrol launched an extensive consumer advertising campaign. In the opinion of the firm's marketing director, the campaign had been successful in creating a high level of customer awareness of the Castrol name and of its latest new product, GTX Motor Oil.

Having established awareness, the marketing director reasoned that the next step called for a change in advertising theme to one stressing the scope of the worldwide Castrol organization. As he contemplated possible advertising messages to communicate the new theme, the marketing director jotted down the following notes to pass along to Castrol's advertising agency.

Are you using Castrol Motor Oil? If not, why not? Air Canada keep their turbo-prop fleet flying on Castrol. Cunard keep the most modern passenger liner in the world, the QE II, cruising on Castrol. British Motor Corporation uses it for their racing team and recommend Castrol in their specification books. Ford uses it in their 1969 Trans-Am Mustang winning team. The Queen used it!

So if Castrol Motor Oil is good enough for all these people, it should be good enough for you. For cruising, flying, racing—even riding like the Queen of England—rely on Castrol, the world's best motor oil!

a. How would knowledge that Castrol is a worldwide organization be likely to affect a consumer's buying behavior? Given the company's situation in Canada, do you think the proposed theme was an appropriate one?

b. How do you think Canadian motorists might perceive the advertising message proposed by the marketing director? Is this what the marketing director intended?

c. What effects, if any, do you think the proposed campaign might have on motorists' attitudes toward Castrol?

6. A group of people were asked to choose between two raincoats. One was a prestigious brand selling at a high price. The other bore an unknown label and a low price. The two coats were physically identical, but the customers were

not told this. What percentage do you think would choose the higher-priced coat? Why?

7. Each individual is unique in his motives, attitudes, and personality. How then is it possible for marketers to avoid dealing with individuals separately in designing marketing strategies?

8. When purchasing gasoline, it has been suggested, most consumers perceive a low level of both psychosocial and performance risk. If this is true, it could be expected that consumers' information needs with respect to gasoline would not be high, since there is no apparent need for risk-reducing information. "Gas is gas, and one brand is about the same as the next," stated one typical motorist.

Despite the logic of the above argument, the Shell Oil Company based several years of corporate advertising on a theme stressing the good-mileage properties of its product. Early advertisements extolled the mileage-producing properties of "Platformate," the company's trade name for an additive contained in some form in all major gasoline brands. Later advertisements described Shell simply as the "good-mileage gasoline."

Utilizing the concept of perceived risk, and/or any others you consider relevant, explain why you would judge Shell's advertising campaign to be appropriate or inappropriate in a highly competitive United States market for gasoline.

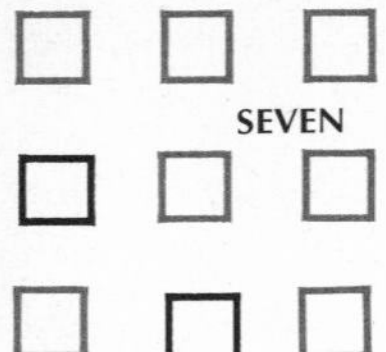

SEVEN

Social influences on consumer decisions

Zoologist Desmond Morris, in his book *The Naked Ape,* outlined man's evolutionary history from the early primates through to modern times.[1] In a revealing fashion, he demonstrated that many of man's patterns of behavior can be traced to inheritances from his arboreal forefathers. Not least of these is a propensity for *social* organization. Like chimpanzees and Old World monkeys, man shares spatial territories with other men, has friends and enemies, leaders and followers. The successes or failures of others serve as standards for his own performance, and, before making decisions, he thinks first about how others will judge him, or would act themselves in a similar situation. It is, in other words, an evolutionary and historical fact that a man's behavior is influenced by others in his environment.

The sociologist, like the psychologist described in the previous chapter, searches to discover why humans behave as they do. His approach differs only in the kinds of variables he uses to explain the hidden link between stimuli and action. The psychologist employs intervening variables that in some way relate to properties of the individual—his drives, motives, perceptions, and so forth. The sociologist, on the other hand, confines himself to studying the ways in which *other people* affect the behavior of an individual.

[1] Desmond Morris, *The Naked Ape,* McGraw-Hill Book Company, New York, 1967.

In this chapter, we will explore some of the principal findings of sociology and, in particular, examine how social variables influence consumer buying decisions. We will begin by looking at *reference groups,* the social entities with which an individual identifies and which he uses as performance standards. Later sections will examine how specific kinds of reference groups affect consumer decisions. When the Columbia Stereo Tape Club offered two free tapes to any member who persuaded a friend to join, it was merely capitalizing on the fact that *friends and associates* are a reference group that can influence individual buying decisions. The *family,* with its role structures and interactions, is another example of a reference group, as are the *social classes* that exist within the fabric of all societies. Concluding sections of the chapter will deal with *culture* as a determinant of buying decisions and with the underlying contribution of reference groups to the *diffusion of innovations*—the process by which new ideas and new products spread throughout social groupings.

Reference group influence

□ *A reference group is an aggregation of persons interacting with an individual, directly or indirectly, to influence his behavior in some manner.*

A central concept of sociological study is the reference group.□ There are many possible types of reference groups, with great variations in size, composition, and structure. They may be *membership groups* to which an individual actually belongs, such as a church, a family, a men's service club, or a consumers' union. An *aspirational* (or *anticipatory*) group is one to which an individual does not belong, but to which he aspires. Small boys dream of playing on a big-league baseball team, while young girls aspire to be models, actresses, or to travel in high society. There are also negative, dissociative groups in which an individual wishes to avoid membership; a person may steer clear of certain kinds of action because they are associated with the "wrong" group. A man, for example, may avoid buying a black leather jacket with metal studs lest he be mistaken as a member of a motorcycle gang. The term *primary group* is applied to reference groups that are small enough in size for members to communicate and interact with one another on a regular face-to-face basis: the family is an outstanding example of a primary group.

Of course, a customer can be a member of, or be influenced by, more than one reference group. For example, a housewife may be at the same time a member of a family, a church, a neighborhood lady's bridge club, and the Republican party. Each of these groups, and probably many others, can have some influence on her behavior.

□ THE NATURE OF REFERENCE GROUP INFLUENCE

Reference groups influence the behavior of individuals in a variety of ways. In general, an individual's reference groups can serve as a basis of *comparison,* as a source of *sanction,* or as a means of reducing perceived *risk.*

Remembering that an individual may be or may aspire to be a member of several reference groups, consider how each of these functions can be performed by a different group. A housewife, for example, may be considering the purchase of an electric toothbrush for herself and her family. She does not know much about the product or about the brands that are available. She may learn that several of her friends in the church circle (one reference group) have electric toothbrushes; this gives her a basis for comparing her opinions with someone else's. Her family (a second reference group) discusses the purchase and likes the idea; the purchase is thus sanctioned. Finally, she discovers that many of her husband's associates who are trained engineers have electric toothbrushes in their homes and are satisfied with them; this reference group reduces the potential performance risks that may be involved in the actual operation of the brushing mechanism. She might also be afraid that there would be a psychosocial risk in having an electric toothbrush in the sense that people would think her family lazy or "gadget crazy." This kind of perceived risk would be reduced by the knowledge that many of her church friends (the first reference group) had electric toothbrushes.

Note again that an individual can be a member of more than one reference group, and that different groups can play different roles or more than one role in their influence on individual behavior. It is also important to recognize that the reference group concept can work negatively as well as positively and, in addition, can work in terms of aspirations as well as current status. Thus, had the housewife discovered that some group toward which she had a negative attitude, perhaps some neighbors whom she disliked, had several electric toothbrushes among its members, this fact might be a negative influence on her decision. On the other hand, if she aspired to membership in the local garden club, knowledge of a high incidence of electric toothbrush ownership in that group might be a positive influence.

SUSCEPTIBILITY OF BUYING DECISIONS TO REFERENCE GROUP INFLUENCE

Reference groups have considerable influence on consumer buying decisions. Studies of purchasing behavior have demonstrated the importance of reference groups in changing consumer attitudes, in modifying perceptions, and in actually motivating and directing buying decisions.[2]

Whether or not reference groups are likely to come into play in influencing a buying decision depends on many complex and interrelated factors. In simplified terms, these factors can be classified into two principal groups:

1. Factors pertaining to an individual's relationship to a reference group, and the norms of behavior of the group. Members of a women's civic committee,

[2] See, for example, M. D. Beckman, "Are Your Messages Getting Through?" *Journal of Marketing,* July, 1967, pp. 34–38; and James E. Stafford, "Group Influences on Consumer Brand Preferences," *Journal of Marketing Research,* February, 1966, pp. 68–75.

for example, may regard it as desirable for housewives to combat pollution by using phosphate-free detergents. A woman who highly values her membership in the committee will probably feel compelled to follow the norm of using phosphate-free detergents; while a peripheral member to whom membership is relatively unimportant may choose to ignore this group norm.

2. Factors relating to the matter to be decided, such as the individual's previous experience with a buying decision and the attributes of the product under consideration. A new bride, inexperienced in shopping, is likely to accept the recommendation of friends or relatives regarding types or brands of grocery products to buy. As she becomes more experienced as a shopper, she is likely to rely increasingly on her own judgment.

In formulating marketing strategy, it is sometimes practical to utilize factors relating to unique attributes of individual reference groups (the first classification). Market segments may be defined in terms of reference groups, and products differentiated to fit the needs and wants of a segment defined in this manner. The *Journal of Marketing Research,* for example, is a magazine (a product) directed principally to marketing educators (a market segment delineated in terms of a particular reference group).

Product-related factors (the second classification) also present practical marketing implications. For example, where consumers have little previous experience to guide them in a buying decision, reference group influence has been found to be particularly strong. During the early months after the introduction of a new drug, it was found that a doctor's colleagues had an important effect on his decision to try the product. After the product had been on the market for a while and the risk and uncertainty surrounding its use had been substantially reduced, the decisions of the remaining doctors to try the product no longer depended on their direct professional associations. Instead, their decisions to adopt the product depended largely on their exposure to pharmaceutical salesmen, articles in medical journals, advertising from drug houses, etc.[3] Thus a drug company trying to get doctors to try a drug for the first time shortly after its introduction might try to secure its adoption by direct personal solicitation of influential doctors with the hope that they would influence their colleagues. At a later stage in the drug's introduction, advertisements with the same objective might stress appeals relating to the drug's chemical characteristics and to research findings about its effects in use.

The influence of a consumer's reference groups on his decision-making behavior toward a product also depends, in part, on the product's conspicuousness. This, in turn, depends on both the extent to which a product can be seen and identified by others and on the ability of the product itself to make its

[3] Raymond A. Bauer and Lawrence H. Wortzel, "Doctor's Choice: The Physician and His Sources of Information about Drugs," *Journal of Marketing Research,* February, 1966, p. 40.

possessor "different" and more "visible" socially. For example, a consumer's decision to buy a refrigerator, as opposed to a specific brand of refrigerator, is not apt to be affected by his reference groups because virtually all Americans own refrigerators. Therefore, ownership cannot serve as a basis for differentiating one individual or family from another. A consumer's decision to purchase gasoline is not apt to be greatly influenced by reference groups because the product cannot be easily seen or identified by others. In contrast, automobiles are quite visible, and makes may imply something about the income, tastes, or habits of their owners.

Friends and associates as reference groups

A person's friends, neighbors, and associates often have important effects on his buying decisions. They may serve as sources of information about products or certify that a product is socially acceptable and/or that its possession increases the owner's prestige. With the possible exception of his own family, an individual's friends and associates are, by definition, the reference groups with whom he comes into direct contact most frequently. It is not surprising that these contacts play an extremely important role in shaping his attitudes, consumption habits, and other characteristics as a buyer.

A number of companies have taken advantage of the importance of personal acquaintances in determining the purchasing behavior of an individual. For example, diaper services frequently ask mothers who are present customers for names of *other prospects*. By offering free books to new members and their recruiters, Basic Books, Inc., encourages its current members to recommend the service to friends. King-Size, Inc., a firm specializing in the mail-order sale of clothing to big and tall men, offers free merchandise to customers who introduce other outsized men to the company's products.

A few companies have gone so far as to build total marketing and selling strategies based on interpersonal relationships among friends and acquaintances. A good example is Schwab, a German mail-order firm with annual sales of almost $100 million. Schwab sells primarily through a system of more than 100,000 part-time agents under the direction of district supervisors. Each agent circulates the Schwab catalog among her friends and neighbors, takes orders from them, and personally delivers merchandise to customers. The catalog items include men's, women's, and children's clothing; home furnishings such as towels, blankets, and bed linens; chinaware; sporting goods; toys; giftwares; and furniture.

□ WORD-OF-MOUTH COMMUNICATION

In marketing, informal product-related conversation between an individual and his friends and associates is usually referred to as *word-of-mouth com-*

munication. The importance of word of mouth as an influence on buying decisions has long been known to marketers, although only recently has the topic become a subject of systematic study and prominence. In Chapter 2, for example, the role of word of mouth in influencing the purchase of air conditioners was mentioned. Some other studies demonstrating the impact of word-of-mouth communication on buying behavior are as follows:

As early as the 1930s, a study of a sample of children revealed that 42 percent discovered their favorite radio programs through the recommendation of other children.[4]

Among a group of Iowa housewives, word of mouth was found to be more important than any other information source in convincing the women to purchase the then-new fabrics of orlon, dacron, and nylon.[5]

An investigation of the sources of product-related information of department store customers in New York and Cleveland indicated that 41 to 48 percent mentioned store advertisements, while 57 to 62 percent mentioned word of mouth.[6]

A study of 415 families in Wichita, Kansas, showed that 58 percent were found to rely on advice from friends and relatives in selecting a physician, while only 20 percent requested information from professional sources.[7]

A study of the prepurchase behavior of buyers of small electrical appliances revealed that word of mouth was more frequently mentioned than any other source of information.[8]

Not only is word of mouth a frequently used source of information for buying decisions, it is also a powerful one. In studies conducted by *Progressive Grocer* magazine, food shoppers were asked to indicate which sources of information about new products most often led them to actual purchase of a new item. The shoppers' replies, shown in Table 7-1, indicated that recommendations of friends or relatives were most influential in bringing about purchase.

What makes word of mouth such a powerful influence on buying decisions? Given the current state of knowledge on word-of-mouth communication, only a tentative answer can be given to this question. However, on the basis of a review of the collective evidence of many fragmented research studies, one author has suggested three principal reasons for the substantial impact of word of mouth on purchasing behavior.[9]

[4] L. W. Doob, *Public Opinion and Propaganda,* Henry Holt and Company, Inc., New York, 1938, p. 486.

[5] G. M. Beal and E. M. Rogers, "Informational Sources in the Adoption Process of New Fabrics," *Journal of Home Economics,* vol. 49 (1957), pp. 630–634.

[6] S. U. Rich, *Shopping Behavior of Department Store Customers,* Division of Research, Graduate School of Business Administration, Harvard University, Boston, 1963.

[7] S. P. Feldman, "Some Dyadic Relationships Associated with Consumer Choice," in R. M. Haas (ed.), *Science, Technology, and Marketing,* Proceedings of the 1966 Fall Conference of the American Marketing Association, American Marketing Association, Chicago, 1966, pp. 758–775.

[8] J. G. Udell, "Prepurchase Behavior of Buyers of Small Electrical Appliances," *Journal of Marketing,* October, 1966, pp. 50–52.

[9] Johan Arndt, *Word of Mouth Advertising: A Review of the Literature,* Advertising Research Foundation, Inc., New York, 1967, p. 25.

TABLE 7-1

Likelihood of buying a new food product by various means of introduction

Source of information	Percentage of shoppers who almost always or frequently bought
Recommendation of friend or relative	60%
Received coupons in mail	42
Saw product on display in store (with special price offer)	41
Saw product advertised:	
On television	30
In magazine	19
In newspaper	18
Saw product on display in store (with no offer)	16
Heard product advertised on radio	9

Source: *Progressive Grocer,* October, 1967, p. 71.

1. Word of mouth is thought to give reliable, trustworthy information, and hence it can help people to make better buying decisions.
2. In contrast to the mass media, personal contacts offer social support.
3. The information provided is often backed up by social pressure and surveillance.

OPINION LEADERS

It is tempting to ask if there are particular *types* of individuals within reference groups who systematically influence the purchasing decisions of others. If such a class of "influentials" could be found and identified by some measurable characteristics (such as reading habits, for example), then it would be appropriate to direct special promotional efforts to them. The hope, of course, would be that the influentials would relay purchasing appeals to their friends and acquaintances.

It would appear, however, that there is no *general* type of influential. Instead, people tend to select *different* individuals as sources of purchase information depending on the nature of the information required. Those selected are referred to as *opinion leaders,* but it is important to recognize that the influential role of an opinion leader is restricted to his particular areas of expertise.

An opinion leader in fashion, for example, is not apt to serve as an influential source of information in another area, such as food purchasing.

Within a particular sphere (fashion), opinion leaders *are* often systematically different from other customers. For example, fashion leadership is known to be concentrated among younger women who tend to be outgoing in their social relationships, whereas influentials for food products tend to be married women with relatively large families. Knowledge that opinion leaders in fashion tend to be younger women may lead a dress manufacturer to choose a different promotional approach than if fashion leadership were fairly evenly distributed across all age groups.

The use of "expert" testimonials in advertising programs for some products is related to the concept of opinion leadership. When Andy Granitelli and Mario Andretti, racing drivers, endorsed STP automobile engine additives, it was obvious that two men with substantial expertise in the performance of automobile engines were recommending the products. A similar approach was used in Canada when RCA Victor based an advertising campaign on the theme, "What kind of set does a television repairman watch when he goes home at night?" By strict definition, neither example represented true application of the opinion leader concept since those endorsing the products were communicating through mass media; they were not interpersonal sources from whom reference group members could seek whatever information they required. Instead, the advertisers in question did the next best thing—they simulated the existence of an opinion leader in the form of an accepted expert on the product in question.

The family

In all societies, almost everyone lives his life in a network of family interactions, rights, and obligations. Apart from religion, the family is the most persuasive and formally developed of all social institutions. There are over 50 million families in the United States,[10] the extent and nature of whose behavior influence and shape the essential fabric of the nation. Among its many activities, it would be folly not to recognize the family's significance as a buying unit, and as an influence on the purchasing decisions of its members as individuals.

The importance of family behavior to marketing managers stems from its twofold role in the buying process. On one hand, the family may serve as a *decision-making unit* in the purchase of some products. This was the case in the example of Mr. and Mrs. Wilson buying an automobile, as discussed in Chapter 3. Where the family acts as a decision-making unit, it is inappropriate

[10] We shall use the term family in the sense of the *nuclear* family, the immediate group of father, mother, and children living together in the same household.

for the marketing manager to examine the needs and aspirations of its members individually; for here family members are acting together to achieve common buying goals. In a social context, however, the family's influence also extends to situations where a member makes a purchase that is seemingly for his individual consumption and benefit. Here, the family members serve as a *reference group* who, because of the unique characteristics of the family as a social entity, are free to criticize, suggest, cajole, order, praise, or establish standards of behavior. Thus, if the father in a family chooses to smoke, he does so only in the face of possible criticism from his wife (who fears the consequences of his early demise) and children (who have learned through broadcasts and school programs that smoking is unhealthy).

□

CHARACTERISTICS OF THE FAMILY

In many ways, the family differs from other social institutions, and its unique aspects are important in understanding its role as an influence on buying decisions. It is a *primary* group characterized by the ultimate in face-to-face contact and intimacy, and, as a result, a powerful determinant of the motives, traits, attitudes, and personalities of its members. The family differs from other reference groups in that it is both *an earning and a consuming unit.* The needs of its members, individually and collectively, must be met from a common pool of assets and income. Consequently, there is frequent need for compromise. It is also a *formational group* in which a child first learns about broader societal and cultural values which, in large part, he carries forward with him for the remainder of his life.

Despite its familiarity, the family is a complex institution about which we know relatively little in a formal sense. Much of our supposed knowledge is, in fact, predicated on popular misconceptions. Some examples of misconceptions have been cited by a prominent sociologist[11]:

1. The present divorce rate in the United States is much higher than rates in primitive societies, and higher than any other nation has ever experienced.
2. Because of the importance of the extended family in China and India, the average size of a household is very high, with many generations living under one roof.
3. In Western nations, the age at marriage among lower classes was always low, because early marriage meant that children would soon be produced and these were useful in farming. The age at marriage among higher classes was generally greater.

All these statements are false. A majority of primitive nations have higher rates of marriage dissolution than the United States—Japan in the late 1800s experienced 300 divorces per 1,000 marriages. Chinese and Indian house-

[11] William J. Goode, *The Family,* Prentice-Hall, Inc., Englewood Cliffs, N. J., 1964, p. 3.

holds are small, varying from 3.5 to 5.5 persons in different regions. Historically, upper classes have almost invariably married earlier than the lower classes, who lacked land or other resources to facilitate marriage.

□

FAMILY INFLUENCES ON BUYING DECISIONS

Despite misconceptions regarding the family, we have, particularly in the last decade, began to collect an inventory of factual knowledge concerning family influences on buying decisions. If anything, recent findings have served to highlight the complexity of the field of family decision making.

It is possible, for example, to characterize families by their *general* patterns of decision making. Such classifications could include (1) autonomic (equal number of decisions made by each spouse), (2) husband dominant, (3) wife dominant, or (4) syncratic (most decisions made by both spouses).[12] But these general classifications are totally misleading in the case of specific *buying* decisions, where evidence suggests that the influence of family members varies widely from product to product.[13] In buying lawn fertilizer, the husband may dominate, while in the purchase of towels and linens, choice is likely to be left to the wife. Even a generalization of this nature can be misleading, however. One study of 97 families examined marital roles in automobile and furniture purchase decisions. The results, illustrated in Table 7-2, indicated that relative influence of husband and wife depended on which aspect of the overall decision was under consideration—where and when to buy, how much to buy, and so forth. The same study also revealed substantial variability in influence patterns among different families in the sample.

In 1969, over half of American families had varying numbers of *children* living at home. These families are significant to marketers because of their proportionately higher expenditures on commodities such as food, clothing, shelter, and certain kinds of recreation. Yet we know very little about the roles played by children in family buying decisions. One study set out to confirm the seemingly plausible hypothesis that a child-centered mother would be more likely to purchase her child's favorite brands of breakfast cereal. The hypothesis was rejected. Apparently, child-centered mothers show a greater tendency to purchase cereals following their own views of what is right and healthful, overriding any preference that the child may have.[14]

Further studies have shown that many variables intervene to affect the behavior of a family as a decision-making unit and as a reference group influencing individual purchases by its members. Stage of family life cycle,

[12] P. G. Herbst, "Conceptual Framework for Studying the Family," in O. A. Oeser and S. B. Hammond (eds.), *Social Structure and Personality in a City*, Routledge and Kegan Paul, London, 1954.

[13] David M. Heer, "The Measurement and Basis of Family Power: An Overview," *Marriage and Family Living*, vol. 25, pp. 133–139, 1963.

[14] Louis A. Berey and Richard W. Pollay, "The Influencing Role of the Child in Family Decision Making," *Journal of Marketing Research*, February, 1968, pp. 70–72.

□

TABLE 7-2

*Marital roles in selected aspects of automobile and furniture purchase decisions**

(Based on a sample of 97 families)

Who decided	Percentage of families indicating		
	Husband has more influence than wife	Husband and wife have equal influence	Wife has more influence than husband
When to buy the automobile?	68%	29%	3%
Where to buy the automobile?	62	35	3
How much to spend for the automobile?	62	37	1
What make of automobile to buy?	60	32	8
What model of automobile to buy?	41	50	9
What color of automobile to buy?	25	50	25
How much to spend for furniture?	22	47	31
When to buy furniture?	16	45	39
Where to buy furniture?	7	53	40
What furniture to buy?	3	33	64
What style of furniture to buy?	2	26	72
What color and fabric to select?	2	16	82

*As perceived by husbands. Patterns of influence, as perceived by wives, did not differ greatly.

Source: Harry L. Davis, "Dimensions of Marital Roles in Consumer Decision-Making," *Journal of Marketing Research,* May, 1970, p. 169. Reproduced with permission.

social class, employment status of the wife, and location (urban versus rural) of the family unit are all significant in this regard. If any one lesson is to be learned, it is that the family is a complex social entity about which it is dangerous to generalize. Each marketing situation—the product and its potential markets—must be examined separately and carefully to determine specific patterns of family influence.

Social class

In every society, there is some basis by which friends, families, and other small groups combine into larger divisions within the social system. Groups that are

☐ *Social classes are divisions in a society, each consisting of individuals or groups of individuals who are alike in terms of characteristics valued in their society, and whose possession of those characteristics differentiates them from others.*

similar in nature tend to interact and associate with each other, thereby forming distinct strata commonly referred to as "social class."☐

Some of the characteristics that are valued in contemporary American society, and many others as well, are *occupation, wealth,* and *power.* These form the principal bases for determining a family's membership in a particular social class.

People tend to associate occupational titles or professions with varying degrees of prestige, irrespective of the individual who fills a position. These rankings of occupational prestige are of fundamental, though not exclusive, importance in determining social class membership. They also tend to be generally consistent over long time periods, as indicated by the data in Table 7-3 comparing rankings of occupational prestige in the United States in 1947 and 1963.

Income and ownership of tangible assets, as discussed in Chapter 5, are perhaps the most obvious components of a household's wealth. But wealth, as a symbol of social class membership, also implies a more subtle appraisal of the nature of one's choice of possessions. In America, the most powerful single symbol of wealth is one's home, including both its location and type. A conservatively styled home of moderate size, situated in an older "exclusive" district of the city, may constitute a greater symbol of wealth than a much larger and more ostentatious residence in suburbia. Choices in furniture and clothing, patronage of the arts, and the college attended (by both parents and children) are also reflections of wealth.

Some individuals have political, economic, military, and/or religious advantages to an extent that they can more easily make their desires prevail. Such people are perceived as having power, and the possession of power tends to elevate an individual's social status. Doctors, lawyers, and judges, for example, are attributed relatively high status because their activities can impinge so directly on the welfare and future of others.

In addition to occupation, wealth, and power, social class is frequently defined by other criteria such as education, outstanding personal performance, the class to which a household *says* it belongs, the class to which *others* say a particular household belongs, or the degree to which different families associate with each other.

☐

SOCIAL CLASSES AND BUYING BEHAVIOR

The most accepted system for determining social class was developed by a sociologist, Lloyd Warner. He defines a *class structure* as "two or more orders of people who are believed to be, and are accordingly ranked by the members of the community, in socially superior and inferior positions."[15] Warner also

[15] Lloyd Warner and Paul S. Lunt, *The Social Life of a Modern Community,* Yankee City Series, vol. I, Yale University Press, New Haven, Conn., 1941, p. 82.

□
TABLE 7-3

Rankings of occupational prestige in the United States, 1947 and 1963

Occupation	1947 rank	1963 rank
U.S. Supreme Court justice	1	1
Physician	2.5	2
Nuclear physicist	18	3.5
Scientist	8	3.5
Government scientist	10.5	5.5
State governor	2.5	5.5
Cabinet member in the federal government	4.5	8
College professor	8	8
U.S. representative in Congress	8	8
Restaurant waiter	79.5	80.5
Taxi driver	77.5	80.5
Farmhand	76	83
Janitor	85.5	83
Bartender	85.5	83
Clothes presser in a laundry	83	85
Soda-fountain clerk	84	86
Sharecropper	87	87
Garbage collector	88	88
Street sweeper	89	89
Shoe shiner	90	90

Source: Robert W. Hodge, Paul M. Siegel, and Peter H. Rossi, "Occupational Prestige in the United States: 1925–1963," in Rinehard Bendix and Seymour Martin Lipset (eds.), *Class, Status, and Power*, 2d ed. The Free Press, New York, 1966, pp. 322–334. Only part of the data is reproduced here.

places emphasis on the pattern of social relations between people and groups of people, that is, their interaction patterns. His classification used the following six categories[16]:

1. Upper-upper (UU). The old-family elite, with enough wealth to maintain large houses in the best neighborhood; the wealth has to have been possessed for more than one generation.

[16] This summary of Warner's system is presented by Joseph A. Kahl, *The American Class Structure*, Holt, Rinehart and Winston, Inc., New York, 1957, p. 26.

2. Lower-upper (LU). Slightly richer than the upper-uppers, but with newer money, manners somewhat less polished, and a sense of lineage and security that was less pronounced.
3. Upper-middle (UM). Moderately successful business and professional men and their families, but less wealthy than the LUs. The group had some education and polish, but lineage was unimportant as a criterion for UM membership.
4. Lower-middle (LM). Small businessmen, the school teachers, and foremen. People in this group tended to have morals that were close to Puritan fundamentalism, and were churchgoers and lodge joiners.
5. Upper-lower (UL). The solid, respectable laboring people.
6. Lower-lower (LL). People in this group were described by fellow citizens as disrespectable and often slovenly people.

A great many studies have been conducted to reveal differences in consumption patterns among social classes. Studies by Pierre Martineau in the late 1950s identified significant differences among social classes in attitudes toward, and consumption of, many products such as cigarettes, soups, detergents, automobiles, appliances, and beer.[17] Differences in choices of store patronage, receptivity to advertising appeals, spending and saving habits, and psychological orientations were also noted. In one of many more recent studies, holders of commercial bank credit cards were found to exhibit different card-use patterns related to class membership. Results of this study, shown in Table 7-4, revealed that lower social classes tended to use their cards

[17] Pierre Martineau, "Social Classes and Spending Behavior," *Journal of Marketing,* October, 1958, pp. 121–130.

□
TABLE 7-4
Use of commercial bank credit cards by social class

Social class	Percentage of social class respondents: Using card as a convenience	Using card for installment credit
Upper class	48%	52%
Upper-middle class	38	62
Middle class	29	71
Lower-middle class	24	76
Lower class	18	82

Source: H. Lee Mathews and John W. Slocum, Jr., "Social Class and Commercial Bank Credit Card Usage," *Journal of Marketing,* January, 1969, p. 73.

for installment credit rather than as a convenience device. Upper classes, on the other hand, divided their card usage almost equally between installment credit and convenience. Lower classes of credit card holders were more likely to seek out stores honoring their cards, a practice thought to reflect the generally favorable attitude of these classes toward use of installment credit. Upper classes, more prone to using the card for convenience, stated that they did not seek out stores accepting the bank charge plan.

The significance to marketers of findings of motivation and consumption differences among social classes is that they imply that marketing programs can be designed to suit the values and aspirations of various social classes. This approach must, however, be applied with caution. Though class differences in consumer attitudes and behavior have been observed for a number of products, what these imply for marketing programs is not always obvious. For example, a manufacturer may observe that his product is purchased mainly by members of the lower-middle class. Should he use words and pictures which are part of their everyday experience? Not necessarily. If the product is bought mainly by those families which aspire to a higher social position, in anticipation of their new position, it might be better to choose advertising content consistent with the lower-middle class *impression* of what the upper-middle class is like, rather than emphasize present everyday experiences. The class attitude and experiences reflected in a particular campaign depend not only on the class to which a customer belongs, but also on the meaning of the product to the consumer.

Culture

The term *Bantu* is used to describe a population group of approximately eleven million blacks living in urban areas of South Africa.[18] Although town dwellers, Bantus trace their ancestry to rural villages of the Xhosa, Zulu, and several other South Africa tribes. Their contemporary way of life, after generations of migration, reflects a curious mixture of traditional tribal heritage and modern urbanism. What has emerged is a distinctive Bantu *culture,* and a powerful example of how cultural phenomena can influence the consuming behavior of members in a society.

On one hand, Bantu culture reflects the anxiety and insecurity of relatively recent urbanization. Witchcraft is heavily relied upon, and plays an important psychiatric role. The Bantu personality is characterized by intent aggression and insufficient moderation and control. He is highly responsive to emotional advertising appeals and to marketing approaches that reduce personal tension or offer some form of security. The Bantu is a discriminating consumer, and

[18] *The Bantu Consumer Group in South Africa,* l'Institut pour l'Etude des Méthodes de Direction de L'Entreprise, Lausanne, Switzerland, 1968.

generally prefers products of high quality and workmanship. At the same time, the quest for more money has become the Bantu's basic motivation. As a consequence, he tends to be thrifty and to buy in very small quantities. Wherever possible, he is prone to save—the idea that one's money is able to work for him by earning interest is a wonderful concept to the Bantu.

□ *Culture is the aggregation of "historically created designs for living, explicit and implicit, rational, irrational, and nonrational, which exist at any given time as potential guides for the behavior of men."*[19]

It is possible, of course, to draw similar inferences about the importance of cultural phenomena to the buying behavior of any population, including American. In this context, it is relevant to recognize those factors which render culture□ distinct from other forms of sociological influence. Culture is a set of learned responses to recurring situations. Most important, it is a kind of learning that is passed from one generation to another. Friends, acquaintances, and social classes all participate in acculturation, but the family is undoubtedly the crucial vehicle for most cultural learning. Cultural values and attitudes learned early in one's life are more resistant to change than those learned in later years. But cultures are not static and rigid. On the contrary, cultural formation is an adaptive process continuously responding to changes in the economic, social, political, and technological environment. Historically, cultural change has been extremely slow, but there is ample evidence to suggest that rapid technological developments are speeding up the process considerably.

Cultural habits, as sociological phenomena, are limited to those shared by large aggregates of people living in organized societies. It is appropriate, for example, to speak of the American culture, the Italian culture, and so forth. Yet in any society or nation sharing many common cultural habits or elements, there may be some characteristic traits that distinguish one group from another. A *subculture* refers to a distinguishable entity within a larger culture. The "hippie" and "yippie" movements of the late 1960s are examples of subcultures in the United States. These particular examples are also indicative of "cultural rebellion," and serve to remind us that not everyone is guided in his behavior by the dominant societal culture.

□

CHARACTERISTICS OF AMERICAN CULTURE

What characterizes American culture? It is obviously a multifaceted phenomenon; yet there would appear to be a set of cultural values that are particularly significant in influence and close to universal in acceptance. America is a nation, for example, in which the Judaic-Christian perceptions of religion exercise substantial influence. Implicit in these religions are beliefs that emphasize the value of the individual, and condone the attainment of wealth as an extension of individual enterprise. The culturally accepted route to obtaining wealth is through hard work and entrepreneurship. Such beliefs have contributed

[19] Clyde Kluckhohn and William Kelby, "The Concept of Culture," in Ralph Linton (ed.), *The Science of Man in World Crisis*, Columbia University Press, New York, 1945, p. 97.

greatly to the establishment of the nation as a mass-consumption society with unparalleled technological and economic growth.

Another fiber of American culture is the value placed on achievement, and on the virtue of competition as a catalyst to achievement. Further, American life is a sociable life in which relationships and interactions with others are highly valued. Products and services that enhance one's social capacities are in abundance. Unlike many societies in which wisdom and experience are of vital importance, America pays homage to youthfulness. The young set the pace in innovation, advertising themes are designed "for those who think young," and cosmetics bestow a youthful appearance on those who have lost it.

Awareness of cultural similarities and differences among countries and regions is highly relevant to multinational corporations. In advertising, for example, there is evidence to suggest that, during the 1960s, American firms expanded their advertising activities to cover more areas of the world and a wider variety of cultures. In 1963, only 26 percent of the international billings of United States advertising agencies were in areas other than Europe. By 1967, non-European expenditures made up 45 percent of international billings.[20] These data are not fully conclusive, of course, because many American corporations employ local advertising agencies in foreign countries. One survey of 68 large multinational American corporations indicated that 37 percent of the companies used a foreign-based agency when placing advertising in foreign areas, while 41 percent used an American agency with overseas branches in the country concerned.[21]

Diffusion of innovations

In an age of changing technology and rapid obsolescence, the growth, profitability, and stability of many companies are increasingly dependent on consumer acceptance or rejection of their new product offerings. The toy-making firm of Mattel, Inc., for example, owes a great deal of its success to the Barbie Doll and Hot Wheels, both new products introduced in the 1960s. For a marketer, it would obviously be beneficial to have an understanding of the process by which people learn about new products, try them, and eventually accept or reject them. *Diffusion theory,* a body of knowledge that has evolved from sociology, provides this kind of understanding.

The foundations of diffusion theory were established in the 1930s by rural sociologists interested in learning how farmers adopted new agricultural techniques and products. A quarter of a century later, marketers began to realize

[20] Dan Smith, "The Mixed-up World of Advertising," *International Management,* July, 1967, p. 46.
[21] James H. Donnelly, Jr., "Attitudes toward Culture and Approaches to International Advertising," *Journal of Marketing,* July, 1970, p. 61.

the significance of this work and to apply diffusion theory to a broader scale of products and societal groups. Central to the theory is the concept that there is a *process of diffusion* by which an innovation spreads from its source of invention or creation to its ultimate users or adopters. Four elements are required for this process to take place:

1. An innovation, which is an idea or product that is perceived as new—the innovation need only be new in the eyes of its beholder, and may actually be quite well known to others.
2. Its communication from one individual to another.
3. Its permeation in a social system.
4. Its use over a period of time.

Ultimately, the extent to which an innovation permeates a social system depends upon the number of people who adopt it. *Adoption* refers to the decision by an individual to accept or use an innovation; in a sense, it is merely a particular kind of consumer buying decision.

THE ADOPTION PROCESS

Fortunately, from the findings of hundreds of research studies, we have been able to draw a number of significant generalizations concerning the adoption process. It is thought, for example, that the individual consumer passes through a series of stages of acceptance of a new product before finally adopting it. The presence or absence of a number of personal characteristics in an individual affects his relative propensity to adopt innovations. Propensity to adopt is also affected by interpersonal influences, and by characteristics of the innovation itself. Each of these generalizations merits further exposition since, from a marketer's perspective, each implicitly suggests ways in which the rate and extent of new product adoption can be influenced.

Individuals have been found to move through a series of stages of acceptance of a new product before finally adopting it. Rogers[22] identifies five such stages: *awareness, interest, evaluation, trial,* and *adoption*. A woman, for example, is likely to hear about a new hair-conditioning product through an advertisement or a casual conversation. Some event, perhaps seeing a friend who has used the product, may serve to heighten her interest and, in time, to seek an explicit evaluation of the product's merits. This assessment leads to trying the hair conditioner once and, if satisfied, to using it on a continuing basis. For a marketer, the usefulness of viewing the adoption process in this manner comes largely in identifying potential "bottlenecks" in the stages leading to adoption. Housewives, for example, may know that a new brand of low-phosphate detergent is on the market and be quite aware of its advan-

[22] Everett M. Rogers, *Diffusion of Innovations,* Free Press of Glencoe, Inc., New York, 1962, pp. 81ff.

tages. Yet, they may be unwilling to give up using their favorite detergents. In this case, a free sample or a price inducement to trial use may be the necessary catalyst to widespread adoption.

ADOPTER CATEGORIES

Not all people are equally prone to adopting innovations. Rogers[23] categorized people into five *adopter categories* according to the time at which they first accepted new products or ideas: *innovators,* the first 2½ percent of those ultimately adopting; *early adopters,* the next 16½ percent; *early majority,* the next 34 percent; *late majority,* the next 34 percent; and *laggards,* the last 16 percent.[24] Members of each adopter category have been found to possess a number of distinguishing personal characteristics. In comparison with others, for example, innovators have usually been found to be:

More venturesome in their consumption behavior than noninnovators
More socially mobile
Relatively more financially privileged
More socially integrated
Interested in a wider range of consumption areas
More status concerned
More cosmopolitan in outlook

While these characteristics *generally* prevail among innovators, the findings should be applied with caution. Innovators are not always the same people for every new product that comes along, and the relative importance of each characteristic in distinguishing innovators from noninnovators varies for different products. In the case of new home appliances, for example, venturesomeness and social mobility have been found to account for almost all the differences between innovators and noninnovators.[25]

CHARACTERISTICS INFLUENCING ADOPTION RATE

Many of the concepts presented in earlier sections of this chapter deal with how interpersonal influences affect the adoption process. Word-of-mouth communication, for example, is the principal mode by which information about an innovation is passed from one individual to another. The likelihood of an individual participating in this network of communication is dependent upon his membership in various kinds of reference groups, and on the presence of opinion leaders in these social groupings.

[23] *Ibid.,* p. 162.
[24] Rogers's choice of a normal distribution to distinguish among adopter categories is arbitrary, but is supported by many research findings. A number of marketers, however, consider innovators as the first 10 percent of those eventually adopting a new product.
[25] Thomas S. Robertson and James N. Kennedy, "Prediction of Consumer Innovators: Application of Multiple Discriminant Analysis," *Journal of Marketing Research,* February, 1968, pp. 64–69.

Five characteristics of an innovation have been identified as influencing the rate of its adoption.

1. Relative advantage. Oil and gas quickly replaced coal for home heating, because the newer fuels were much cleaner and easier to handle and control. Electric heating's relative advantage over oil and gas is not nearly as great, however, and its penetration has been slower and less extensive.
2. Compatibility. Introduction of self-cleaning ovens required no changes in the way a housewife went about baking. Electronic ovens, however, cook much more rapidly and do not "brown" food to the same extent. Because they require a change in the way cooking has traditionally been done, electronic ovens are likely to encounter a slower rate of adoption.
3. Complexity. Equity-based life insurance policies[26] were slow to gain initial acceptance because of the difficulty that many potential buyers had in understanding the intricacies of these policies.
4. Divisibility. A new cereal product can be tried by first buying a small box, but there is no way to divide a $3,000 car with a radical new engine design into small pieces of low unit purchase price.
5. Communicability. Fashion trends move rapidly through social groups because they are readily observed and described. Preemergent weed killers, on the other hand, were very slow to be accepted because weeds were killed before they started to grow—a farmer had no dead weeds to see or show his neighbor.

In developing marketing programs for new products, opportunities frequently arise to apply knowledge of the adoption process. It may be possible, for example, to derive a profile of the new item's innovator group and develop advertising strategies appealing to these innovators—as penetration of the new product proceeds, a different advertising strategy may become appropriate when later adopters consider trying the new product. In some cases, it is possible to select the social system in which diffusion is most likely to be successful as a target market segment. Promotion, pricing, and distribution systems can be combined to reach a particular social system most effectively. Emphasis on relevant product attributes may serve to hasten consumer adoption. In these and other ways, some of the most difficult obstacles to achieving new product acceptance may be diminished and overcome.

Questions

1. Identify the major reference groups likely to influence a college student about to purchase a car with funds inherited from a recently deceased uncle.

[26] In an equity-based life insurance policy, the cash surrender value is largely determined by the market value of a portfolio of common stocks held by the insuring company.

What aspects of the purchase decision would each group be likely to influence? Why?

2. Under what conditions are a consumer's reference groups apt to retard rather than accelerate the acceptance of a new product?

3. In the majority of families, what pattern of purchase decision influence (wife predominant, husband predominant, children predominant, joint husband-wife, husband–wife–children) is likely to predominate in buying the following products or services?

a. Fishing equipment
b. Cooking utensils
c. Electric stove
d. Furniture for the living room
e. Golf lessons for the wife
f. Toys for the children
g. Wrist watch for the husband
h. Furniture for the children

4. The use of "expert" testimonials in advertising is very common. Under what circumstances can celebrity testimonials (by well-known athletes, movie stars, etc.) be effective outside their areas of professional expertise?

5. In discussing car buyers, the sales manager of a large automobile retailer in a major city observed that "a rich man is simply a poor man with money—given the same income, a poor man would behave in exactly the same way as the rich man."

Do you agree or disagree? Explain, and comment on whether your comments would apply to other products or services.

6. A study conducted in the mid-1950s examined the extent to which various social classes accepted innovations. Among its findings were the following: (1) The upper classes were conservative in accepting television; (2) the lower classes were conservative in adopting a new type of card game; (3) both upper and lower strata reacted conservatively to new supermarkets, with the greatest number of acceptors found in groups between the extreme ends of the class scale; and (4) there were no significant differences among classes in responding to two innovations in health insurance.

a. How do you explain these findings?
b. What social classes, if any, might respond most favorably to:
(1) The introduction of high-fashion men's clothing?
(2) A new golf course in the city?
(3) High-speed, intercity rail travel?
(4) Milk packaged in plastic bags?

c. What other factors might affect the acceptance of each of the four products listed above?

7. In early 1970, a leading manufacturer of lawnmowers was asked to consider installing Japanese engines in the firm's 1971 models. Many lawnmower manufacturers did not produce their own engines, but purchased them from outside suppliers. In recent years, the company in question had purchased its engines from the American distributor of a German engine producer.

The new Japanese line of engines had been subjected to a number of technical tests and field trials, and was at least equal in performance characteristics to any line of engines presently on the market. On a model-for-model basis, it would cost about 20 percent less than the German line. Since engines represented a major proportion of the cost of manufacturing lawnmowers, the potential saving was significant. Notwithstanding, the manufacturer was reluctant. His company's products had a reputation of high quality and durability. The firm was very concerned about how consumers would react to learning that the lawnmowers were now powered by a Japanese engine. Even though quality and durability might actually be improved by using the Japanese engine, the company was worried that potential buyers would *perceive* it as being inferior.

a. Do Americans perceive Japanese products, *in general,* to be of inferior quality? If so, why?

b. Are the manufacturer's concerns about consumer attitudes toward the Japanese *engine* well-founded?

c. If the new engine line were adopted, should the manufacturer emphasize or de-emphasize this feature in its advertising and promotional literature (assuming some identification of country of origin on the engine itself is required by law)?

8. The initial users of a new automotive "diagnostic center," the first of its kind in a large American city, were studied by a group of researchers in an attempt to learn more about their decision-making processes. It was found that the initial users, or *innovators,* were more likely than the general population to disseminate information about the new service. Ninety percent told at least one other person about it, and over 40 percent told two or more people.

Compared to the general population, the innovators were found to have a greater willingness to experiment with new ideas; be more prone to buy new products earlier; have a greater tendency to be rational and logical; be less likely to switch brands for reasons of price; and not be interested in low prices per se.

The innovators' own automobiles averaged 3.7 years in age compared to 4.7 years for the population as a whole; 51 percent owned two cars compared to 33 percent for the population.

A majority of the innovators also perceived themselves as opinion leaders. Almost 60 percent stated that they were asked for their opinion about new things more often than average, and only 8 percent thought that their opinions were asked less often than average.

The innovators used considerable initiative in seeking information before patronizing the center. Most of them first learned about the center through articles appearing in the mass media, and a large proportion even visited the center before making their decision to use it. Nearly 60 percent, however, reported word-of-mouth communication to be the single most effective source of influence in their decision. Less than one in five were disappointed in the service after having used it.

a. What factors might have caused the innovators to tell others about the new diagnostic center so readily?

b. Why did the innovators see themselves as opinion leaders? Are innovators always opinion leaders? Are opinion leaders always innovators?

c. If you were the general manager of the first diagnostic center to open in your community, what use could you make of these findings in developing your marketing program?

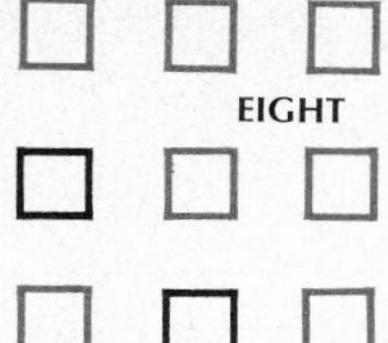

Business, institutional, and government markets

In the preceding chapters, we discussed the characteristics of markets comprised of household customers or, as they are commonly called, consumer markets. The nature of consumer buying decisions was examined, together with a review of the factors that influence these decisions. This chapter discusses other classes of customers in the marketing system—businesses, institutions, and governments.

In terms of relative magnitude, business, institutional, and government markets are substantially more important than the consumer markets we have been discussing up to this point. Most industries in the United States sell less than half of their output in consumer markets or, conversely, more than half of their output to business, institutional, and government users. U.S. Department of Commerce data indicate that, for 82 major classifications of industries comprising the United States economy, 68 sold a majority of their output *outside* consumer markets in 1963. For a selected number of these industries, the proportion of output sold outside consumer markets is illustrated in Figure 8-1. It is interesting to note that only four of the 82 industries did not sell at least one-quarter of their output in nonconsumer markets.

The shoe industry provides a good example of business purchasing power. In *selling* its own finished products, this industry looks primarily to consumer

FIGURE 8-1
*Selected producing industries in the United States ranked by percent of output not sold in consumer markets, 1963**

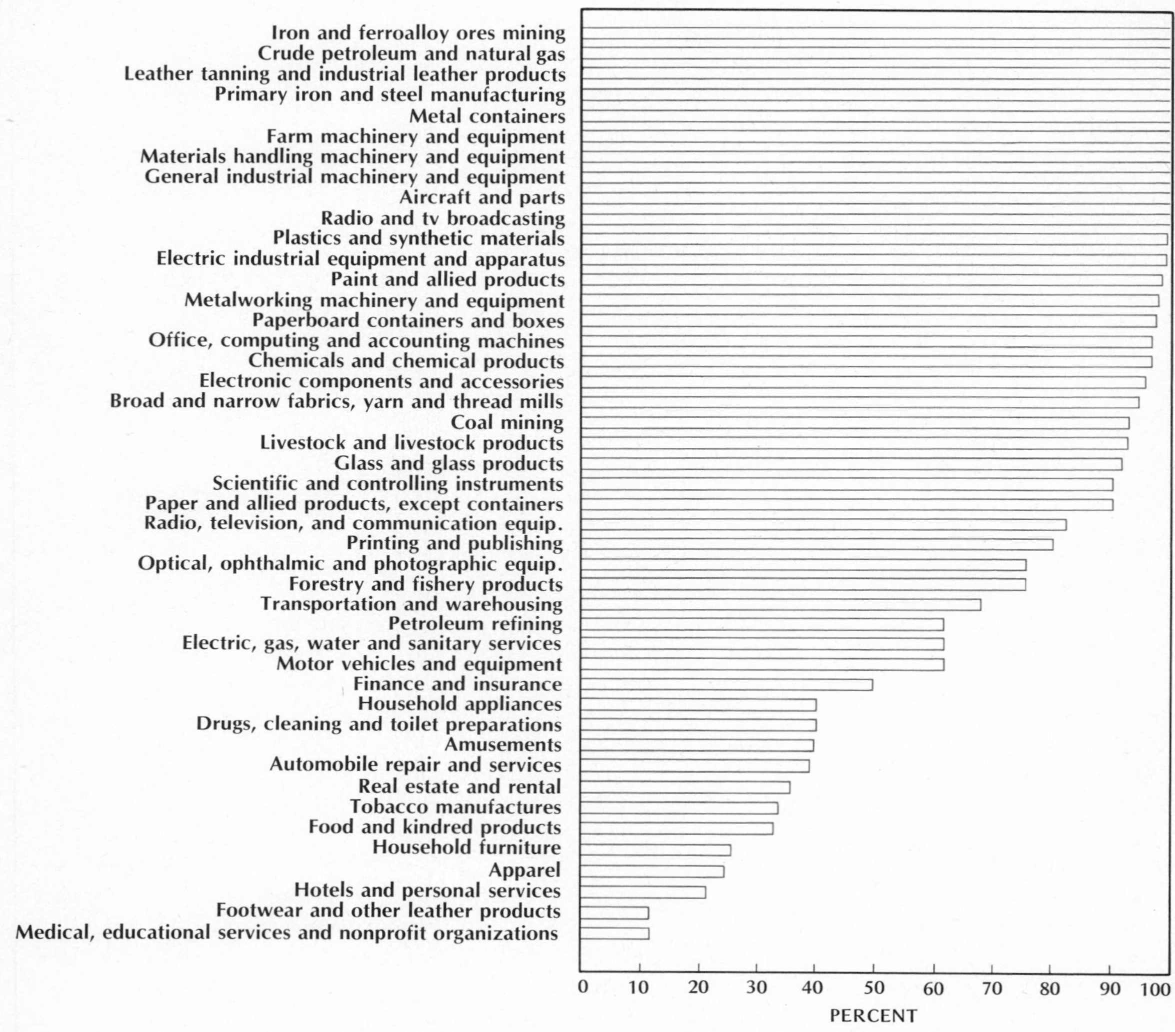

* In exact terms, these percentage figures indicate the share of each industry's output that is consumed as intermediate inputs, gross private fixed capital formation, net inventory change, federal government purchases, and state and local government purchases.

Source: Derived from data published in "Input-Output Structure of the U.S. Economy," *Survey of Current Business*, November, 1969, pp. 34–35.

markets. Over 80 percent of its 1963 output of $3.5 billion was sold to household customers. But to produce this footwear, shoe manufacturers *spent* $607 million on industrial leather products, $315 million on rubber and plastics, $226 million on textiles, $55 million on paperboard containers, and $86 million on business services. To marketers of these goods, the shoe industry represented an important source of potential revenue.

In the remainder of this chapter, each of the three major classes of nonhousehold customers—businesses, institutions, and governments—will be reviewed. Among business markets, which will be dealt with first, there are distinguishing characteristics that make it useful to segment this group further. Most significant in magnitude are the *manufacturing* industries. Manufacturers buy more goods and services than any other class of business enterprise. Their productive function naturally leads these firms to purchase large quantities of such items as metals, chemicals, stampings, and assembly components. *Service* industries, on the other hand, require very few commodities of this kind, but the intangibility of services adds some unique dimensions to the task of selling to service firms. Doctors, dentists, and architects are examples of *professionals* who, in reality, are also members of the service industries. We will devote a separate section of the chapter to professionals, however, since these specialists are in a position to exert unusually high influence on the purchasing behavior of those they serve. *Agricultural* industries perhaps are changing more rapidly than any other class of business. For many years now, the number of farms in the United States has been declining. The 2.9 million farms remaining in 1970 were, on the average, larger, more mechanized, and better managed than those of even a decade earlier. A final class of business enterprise, wholesaling and retailing institutions, will be examined in Chapters 10 to 12.

Hospitals, universities, charities, and other institutional organizations do not generally pursue profit as a primary objective. The social or charitable goals of customers in institutional markets place special constraints and influences on their buying behavior.

Historically, a large proportion of federal government purchases has fallen into the category of defense. State and local governments spend most heavily on education and road construction and maintenance. Because they involve expenditure of public funds, the purchasing decisions of governments are usually characterized by highly formalized and systematic procedures.

Business markets in general

In discussing the major characteristics of business markets, we shall first look in various ways at the entire complex of business firms. Our approach will begin to develop general answers to several of the broad questions that are important to marketers of goods and services to business firms. For example:

How many business firms are there? Are they increasing in number? What do they do? How big are they? What do they spend money on?

NUMBER AND SIZE OF BUSINESS FIRMS

In 1967, there were over 11 million business firms in the United States. Their distribution among major industry groups is shown in Table 8-1. The total number of firms increased only slightly between 1960 and 1967, even though the volume of industrial output grew substantially. Unlike earlier periods when the number of firms grew almost constantly from year to year, a trend toward business mergers and acquisitions has been largely responsible for stabilizing the total number of firms in operation.

The data in Table 8-1 refer only to number of firms in industry sectors and imply nothing about size. In fact, the majority are quite small. Approximately 10 million of the firms shown had annual receipts of less than $100,000.

IMPORTANCE OF MAJOR INDUSTRY GROUPS

Another way of looking at business firms in the aggregate is to consider the numbers of people employed by major industry groups. In 1970, manufacturing establishments constituted the largest source of employment (almost 20

TABLE 8-1

Number of business firms in the United States, by major industry group, and national income arising from major industry groups, 1967

	Number of business firms* (thousands)	National income† (billion dollars)
Agriculture, forestry, and fisheries	3,353	$ 23.8
Mining and construction	929	48
Manufacturing	402	229.1
Transportation, communications, electricity, and gas	359	59.1
Wholesale and retail trade	2,528	112.6
Finance, insurance, and real estate	1,223	85.2
Services	2,714	94.4
Total	11,560	$771.2

*Total number of proprietorships, active partnerships, and active corporations.

†National income is composed of wages and salaries, interest, corporate income and excess profit tax, corporate profits after taxes, and income of unincorporated enterprises.

Source: U.S. Treasury Department, Internal Revenue Service, *Statistics of Income, 1967, Business Income Tax Returns;* and U.S. Department of Commerce, Office of Business Economics, *Survey of Current Business,* February, 1970.

million) while approximately 14 million were employed in wholesale and retail trade. Other industry classifications, when measured in terms of employment, were government (12.8 million); services (11.4 million); finance, insurance, and real estate (3.7 million); and contract construction (3.3 million).

The comparative importance of manufacturing is also reflected in the amount of national income that arises in selected industry groups. Table 8-1 shows that the manufacturing sector is more than twice as important as any other sector in terms of national income generated.

PLANT AND EQUIPMENT EXPENDITURES

It is also useful to look at business expenditures on new plant and equipment. Capital expenditures are an important barometer of national economic activity. In the context of marketing, they also reflect the manner in which billions of dollars of business funds are spent. Marketers of machinery, construction equipment, industrial supplies, and machine tools, for example, study trends and fluctuations in the plant and equipment expenditures of the industries to whom they sell. In 1969, manufacturing industries spent almost $32 billion on new plant and equipment, or 42 percent of the national total of almost $76 billion. Commercial firms, defined to include trade, service, finance, and construction, spent $16.0 billion and public utilities $11.6 billion.

INVENTORIES

Another important investment area for business firms is inventory. Most businesses try to maintain some approximately constant relationship between sales and inventory, and this practice can lead to great fluctuations in their purchases. The phenomenon is known as the *acceleration* principle. Since it applies to all kinds of business buying, it is important enough to merit explanation.

Suppose a manufacturer tries to keep on hand a supply of raw material equal to three months sales. His sales this month are 200 units, and his raw material stocks are therefore 600 units. Suppose that the next month his sales rise to 300 units. If he wants to maintain the 3 to 1 ratio, he will be forced to purchase 400 units of raw material (the extra 100 sales reduced his inventory to 500 units, and 300 additional units are needed to bring his inventory to a new level of 900). In this fashion, a sales increase of only 100 units will increase his buying from 200 units to 400 units.

The acceleration principle is one major factor behind what is generally accepted as the great *volatility* in business buying. Note that in general this volatility is brought about by two factors: (1) the fact that the demand is *derived* in that it begins with someone else (in the example cited, the manufacturer's customers) and works its way back up the pipeline and (2) the fact that there are several levels in the distributive chain, each of which has some accelerating impact on the one next to it in the chain.

INPUT-OUTPUT: THE ANALYSIS OF INTERINDUSTRY FLOWS

An increasingly important method of examining business markets is to employ what is called an input-output approach.[1] Input-output data show the dollar value of transactions among the various sectors of the business economy during a period of time. In that sense they are analogous to information on the flow of incomes into and out of the sectors of the consuming public.

Input-output data are usually expressed in tabular form as shown in Table 8-2. The principal significance of this approach is the information it reveals about *interrelationships* among sectors of an economy. The table shows the value of each industry's sales to every other industry, as well as to consumers, government, and foreign users (the outputs). Conversely, it also shows each industry's purchases from every other industry (the inputs). The data cited earlier in this chapter on purchases made by the United States shoe industry, for example, were drawn from an input-output table for 1963 compiled by the U.S. Department of Commerce.

The input-output approach was first developed by an economist, Wassily Leontief. Leontief constructed historical input-output tables of the United States economy for 1919, 1939, and 1947. Most of the recent work with the input-output technique has centered on developing tables for national and regional economies. For example, tables have been constructed for at least 40 countries as well as for regional areas such as the European Common Market, the states of Washington and Oregon, and the Canadian province of Ontario. Studies have also been undertaken to project the expected interrelationships of industries in the future.

[1] For a description of the input-output technique and its potential applications, see William H. Miernyk, *The Elements of Input-Output Analysis*, Random House, Inc., New York, 1965.

TABLE 8-2
Simplified, hypothetical input-output table
*(In millions of dollars)**

	Purchasing industry					
Producing industry	Industry A	Industry B	Industry C	Industry D	All other buying units	Total sales (output)
Industry A	6	3	19	2	56	86
Industry B	0	5	12	4	32	53
Industry C	14	8	8	1	19	50
Industry D	23	16	4	16	4	63
All other producing units	43	21	7	40	264	375
Total purchases (input)	86	53	50	63	375	627

*Each horizontal row shows sales of an industry to other sectors. Each vertical column shows purchases by an industry from other sectors.

Unfortunately, all this work has so far been of limited value to marketing managers because of the highly aggregated nature of input-output data. The most detailed study of the United States economy, for example, divides the economy into 370 basic industries. To a manufacturer of phonograph records, it is difficult to find direct utility in data that combine his product into an industry figure that includes radios, TV sets, telephone and telegraph apparatus, and other communication equipment.

To overcome these problems, a number of firms have constructed their own detailed input-output tables more suited to specific company situations. Celanese Corporation, National Steel Corporation, Union Carbide, and Ford Motor Company were among the earliest firms reported to have taken this approach. The potential uses of such data include sales forecasting, identifying new product opportunities, assessing market and technological trends, designing sales territories, and constructing logistical systems of supply and delivery. It must be realized, however, that constructing a set of input-output tables is an enormous, costly undertaking. The resulting data must contribute significantly to improving management decision making if the cost of the endeavor is to be justified.

Manufacturing industries

In 1968, there were almost 300,000 manufacturing establishments in the United States. They are often collectively referred to as the *industrial market,* and the process of marketing to them is frequently called *industrial marketing.*

□ MARKET POTENTIAL OF MANUFACTURING INDUSTRIES

The industrial market can be understood by looking at it from several perspectives. Table 8-3 begins by dividing manufacturing establishments into industry groups, thus illustrating the diversity of industry types and the variations within each. Manufacturing establishments vary greatly in size, however, and data on establishments provide only a crude measure of an industry's *market potential.*

A closer approximation of market potential in industrial markets can be gained by examining the *shipments* of each industry, also shown in Table 8-3. Barring major technological change, the value of raw materials and other inputs used by a manufacturing industry tends to remain at an approximately constant proportion of the total value of shipments. Trends in shipments data are thus indicative of changes in the market potential for manufacturing inputs.

Shipments data can nevertheless be deceiving. To illustrate, consider that the shipments of a manufacturing company are actually comprised of two parts: (1) the value of goods and services purchased from other companies and (2) the value that the company has added to these goods and services through its own manufacturing and marketing activities. The latter quantity, called

□

TABLE 8-3

Establishments, shipments, and value added in manufacturing, by industry group, 1968

Industry group	Number of establishments	Shipments (million dollars)	Value added (million dollars)
Food and kindred products	30,864	$88,059	$28,225
Tobacco products	361	5,062	2,150
Textile mill products	7,171	21,926	9,227
Apparel and related products	24,979	22,807	11,161
Lumber and wood products	31,358	12,850	5,832
Furniture and fixtures	9,332	8,488	4,581
Paper and allied products	5,922	22,969	10,491
Printing and publishing	35,930	23,438	15,413
Chemicals and allied products	11,317	46,371	26,118
Petroleum and coal products	1,816	23,262	5,538
Rubber and plastics products	6,192	14,553	6,853
Leather products	3,622	5,480	2,913
Stone, clay, and glass products	14,461	15,915	9,231
Primary metal industries	6,730	49,839	21,037
Fabricated metal products	26,199	37,384	19,544
Machinery, except industrial	36,351	50,373	28,702
Electrical equipment and supplies	10,488	46,734	26,635
Transportation equipment	7,273	79,857	33,267
Instruments and related products	4,255	10,705	6,878
Miscellaneous manufacturing industries	3,166	9,024	5,006
Ordinance and accessories	464	11,177	6,433
All industries, Total	298,460	$605,714	$285,293

Source: U.S. Bureau of the Census, *County Business Patterns, 1968,* Part I, p. 4; and U.S. Bureau of the Census, *1968 Annual Survey of Manufactures.*

value added, is a more precise measure than shipments of the scope of a firm's activities and purchases.

In assessing the market potential of an industry, the importance of examining value added data can be seen clearly in the case of the meat-packing industry. On 1968 shipments of $16.5 billion, the meat-packing industry contributed only $2.4 billion in value added, in other words, about 15 percent of the value of its shipments. *Within* a given industry, there may also be wide variations in value added among firms producing identical commodities. The value added by an integrated oil company with its own refineries, for example, will far exceed that of a firm that buys and distributes previously refined oil, even though shipments of the two firms may be approximately equal.

DISTRIBUTION OF INDUSTRIAL MARKET POTENTIAL

Beyond the question of absolute market potential, industrial marketers are also interested in the distribution of purchasing power. One relevant factor is the *size of firms* that comprise each market. The 50 largest manufacturers in the United States account for one-quarter of the country's total value added in manufacturing. The presence of large firms is significant not only because of their substantial purchasing power, but also because large companies tend to do their buying in a more formalized manner.

Naturally, the relative importance of large firms varies among industry groups or product classes. Figure 8-2 shows the percentage of 1966 shipments accounted for by the largest firms in selected product classes. These data are commonly referred to as *concentration ratios*. Concentration is relatively high in motor vehicles, aircraft, and cigarettes. Firms of smaller size predominate in metal stampings, lithographic printing equipment, and wood furniture.

Most large manufacturing firms operate several plants. General Foods Corporation, for example, has over 30 separate manufacturing establishments. Since large companies typically give a degree of autonomy to purchasing agents in individual plants, industrial marketers are interested in *establishment size* as a further dimension of the distribution of purchasing power. A measure of the difficulty in selling in industrial markets can be realized when it is seen that over half of the country's manufacturing establishments have fewer than 10 employees. Less than 1 percent of manufacturing establishments have as many as 1,000 employees.

A final dimension of the distribution of industrial market potential is the *geographic concentration* of manufacturing establishments. For the entire manufacturing industry, the dispersion of manufacturing establishments and value of the shipments through various regions of the country is illustrated in Figure 8-3. Leading industrial areas in the country are found in New York, Pennsylvania, Massachusetts, New Jersey, Ohio, Illinois, Michigan, Texas, and California. Within each state, the degree of concentration may be further intensified. Urban complexes such as Chicago, New York, Cleveland, and Los Angeles contain substantial shares of the manufacturing industries in their states. Within individual industry groups, geographic concentration may be even more pronounced. Virtually all the garment industry is located in New York, while a large proportion of the aerospace industry is in Texas and California.

FIGURE 8-2

Percentage of shipments accounted for by four largest manufacturing companies, selected industries, 1966

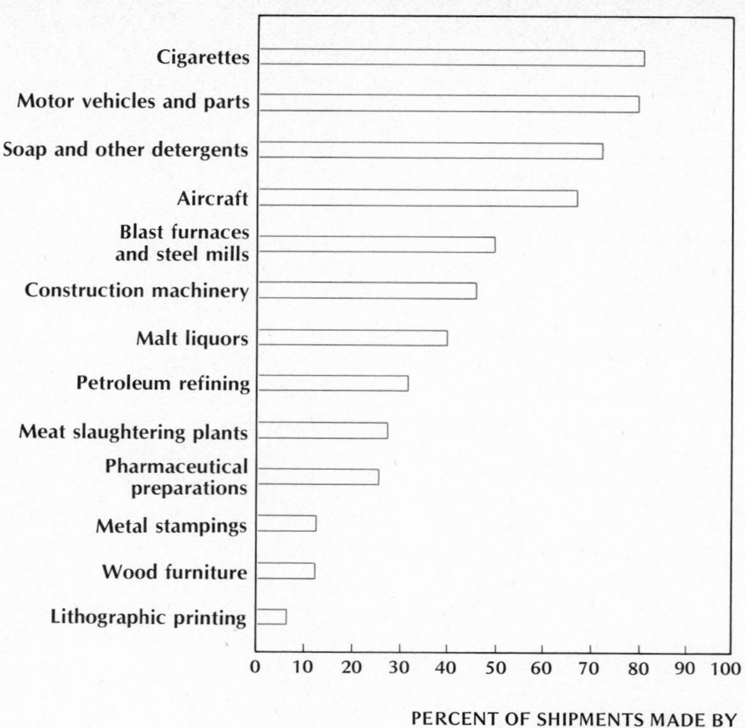

Source: U.S. Bureau of the Census, *1966 Annual Survey of Manufactures,* pp. 411–441.

Similar patterns of geographic concentration exist in other countries, sometimes even more pronounced than in the United States. Over half of the shipments of Canadian manufacturers, for example, emanate from two very small geographic regions: the area within a 75-mile radius of the city of Montreal, and the "Golden Triangle," a thin belt extending approximately 100 miles to the east and west of the city of Toronto.

Geographic concentration of customers particularly affects sales deployment and distribution decisions. It may be feasible, for example, to employ one's own sales force to call on firms in areas of high customer concentration, while the use of agents or distributors may be necessary in areas of greater customer dispersion.

FIGURE 8-3
Geographic concentration of manufacturing establishments and value of shipments, 1967

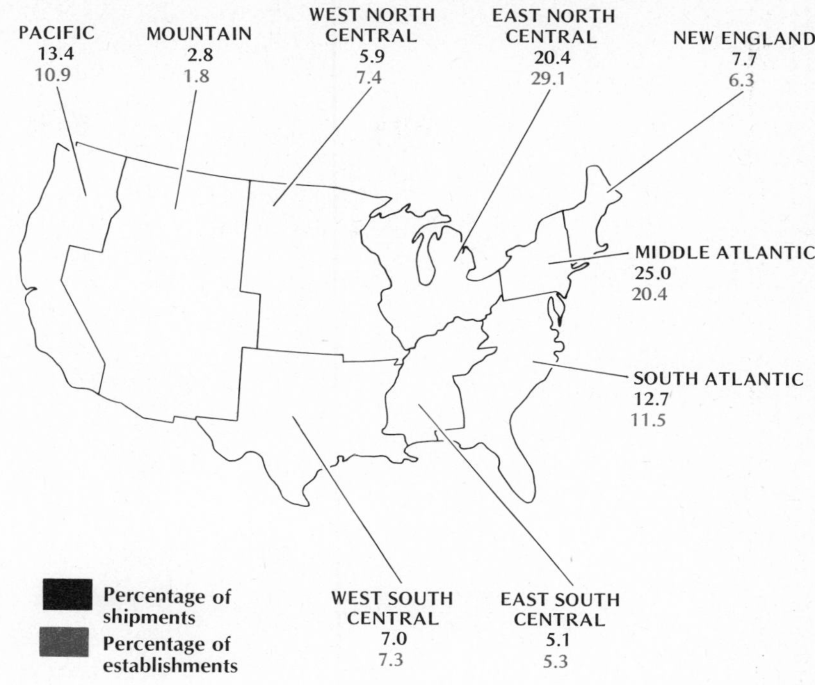

Source: Adapted from U.S. Bureau of the Census, *1967 Census Manufacturers* and *County Business Patterns, 1967, Part I.*

Service industries

Services, as defined in Chapter 2, are activities, benefits, or satisfactions offered for sale. A *service business* is what the name implies: an individual or firm that sells these intangibles to someone else. As the most rapidly growing segment of American business enterprise, the service industries cannot be ignored as potential customers.

Among the first services were domestic servants and the professions—doctors, lawyers, and engineers—all of whom existed in early historical times. Other services such as innkeeping, accounting, and banking were added gradually. In a modern, complex, and affluent society, thousands more have come into existence. They include insurance, business consulting, termite extermination, car rental, vocational training, telephone answering, income tax preparation, bowling alleys, and data processing—to name but a few.

There is no such thing as a "typical" service firm. Some of the largest firms in these industries are found in finance and insurance, where aggregate business receipts in 1969 exceeded $150 billion. In 1969, there were 13,662 commercial banks in the United States, but the 50 largest held 47 percent of all deposits. Among 1,820 life insurance firms, the 50 largest accounted for 74 percent of the insurance in force.

To imply that service industries are made up predominantly of large firms, however, would be misleading. The converse is generally true. Figure 8-4 illustrates the number of establishments and business receipts for a selected group of service industries in the United States and hints at the diversity within them. In 1967, the service industries shown comprised almost 1.2 million establishments with total business receipts of $60.5 billion—an average of about $50,000 per establishment. Total employment in this group was about 3.3 million persons, or less than three per establishment. We can see, therefore,

FIGURE 8-4

Number of establishments and business receipts in selected United States service industries, 1967

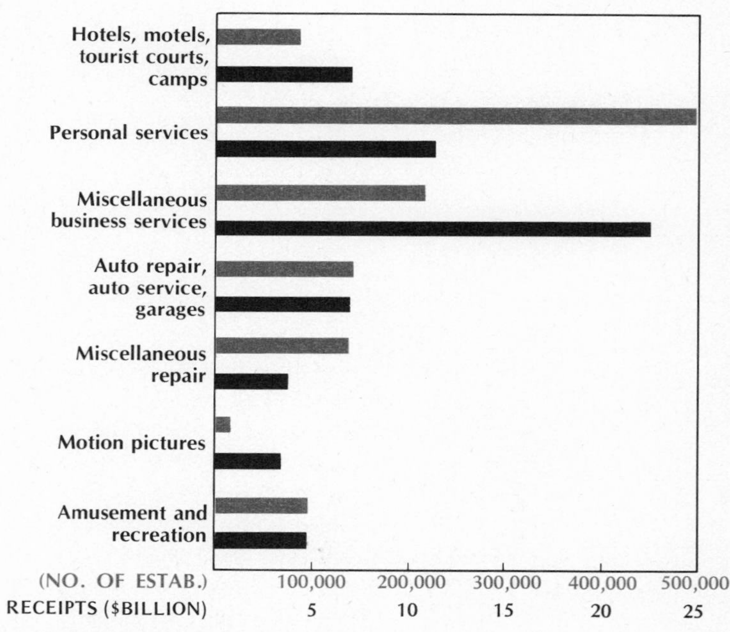

TOTAL ESTABLISHMENTS: 1,187,814
TOTAL BUSINESS RECEIPTS: $60.5 BILLION

Source: U.S. Dept. of Commerce, Bureau of the Census, *U.S. Census of Business*, 1967, vol. 8.

that *small* firms are the prevailing rule in most service industries. Yet here again, it is important not to overgeneralize. Holiday Inns, Inc., is of sufficient size to own a carpet mill and a furniture factory, both operated solely to provide for the needs of hotels and motels in the chain.

Not included in any of these statistics are the professions, which generally include the services of such specialists as doctors, dentists, and lawyers. While professionals are members of the service industries, their position of influence on the choice of products and services purchased by their customers makes it appropriate to examine professional markets separately.

The professions

The term *professional,* as used here, refers to a class of service businesses conducted by highly educated specialists operating as individuals or in partnerships of a few people. The most familiar examples are physicians, dentists, lawyers, architects, and consulting engineers. The magnitude of activities encompassed by professionals can be seen from a few brief statistics. In 1968, for example, $11.6 billion was spent for the services of approximately 330,000 physicians in the United States, while another $3.6 billion was spent on the services of 90,000 dentists. Data for 1967 indicate that 143,000 law firms had gross receipts of $6.4 billion. There were 2,831 architectural firms (employing about 10,000 architects) with gross receipts of $865 million and 3,971 consulting engineering firms (employing about 21,000 engineers) with receipts in excess of $1.7 billion.

Of course, much of what is spent on the services of professionals is attributable to the high inherent costs of specialized labor. Hence, as customers, the purchases of professionals represent only a small fraction of the amounts just cited. These purchases are, nonetheless, significant in amount. The data shown in Table 8-4, for example, indicate that annual operating expenses of an average dentist amounted to over $16,500 in 1964. Roughly 3,000 new dentists enter private practice each year and spend, on the average, almost $14,000 for the basic equipment and supplies necessary to open a new practice.

It is not primarily on the basis of their own purchases, however, that professionals merit the special attention of marketers. By virtue of their position as specialists, professionals exert an overwhelming influence on the buying behavior of those they serve. In 1968, for example, $6.1 billion was spent on drugs and drug sundries, a large proportion of which was prescribed or recommended by physicians. Another $1.7 billion was spent on eyeglasses and medical appliances. Though not the buyer, or user, the doctor clearly played a role of decider in many of these purchase decisions. A drug firm marketing a new antibiotic would consider adoption by physicians as its primary marketing

□
TABLE 8-4
The professional expenses of a dentist

Average annual operating expenses	
Office rent and utilities	$ 2,411
Salaries and fringe benefits	4,807
Insurance related to dental practice	281
Depreciation on equipment	974
Travel to dental meetings, society dues, journals, license fees	479
Commercial dental laboratory charges	3,469
Dental supplies, drugs	2,098
All other	1,998
Total	$16,517
Basic equipment and supplies for a new practice	
Dental equipment and instruments	$10,487
Dental supplies	1,186
Reception room furnishings	415
Business equipment	357
Wiring, plumbing, partitioning, air conditioning, etc.	1,033
Other	143
Total	$13,621

Source: *Facts about the Dental Market,* American Dental Association, Chicago, 1967.

goal, even though doctors themselves would be purchasing only small quantities of the product. There are similar, though not so pronounced, professional influences on other purchase decisions. In 1969, the United States market for dentrifices, toothbrushes, mouthwashes, and related oral hygiene products amounted to $663 million. The successful introduction of Crest toothpaste, endorsed by the American Dental Association, attests to the existence of professional influence on the purchase of these products. Likewise, architects and consulting engineers, in designing new facilities for their clients, can exercise great discretion in the selection of materials and equipment used in these facilities.

Agricultural industries

In one sense, agricultural industries are similar to markets comprised of manufacturing establishments. To produce agricultural commodities, farmers must purchase machinery, feed, seed, and other essential inputs to production.

Thus, as the owner of a business enterprise intended to generate profits, the farmer, as we will see in Chapter 9, utilizes many of the same criteria as industrial buyers in making purchase decisions.

In other respects, however, agriculture is a unique class of business enterprise. Situated in a rural environment, the farmer is strongly influenced by the entrenched values of rural society. Generally, the farm is a family institution in which the farmer eats, sleeps, and raises children at his place of work. These elements combine to produce strong sociological influences on buying behavior.

The combined importance of business and sociological criteria in agricultural buying is reflected in a survey of Canadian farmers' machinery purchases.[2] When asked what influenced their choice of a dealer from whom to buy machinery, farmers cited dealer reputation, good repair and service facilities, and a good price deal as the most important factors. As we shall see in Chapter 9, these criteria closely parallel those we would expect of a manufacturer—they are business-oriented. When asked about the most useful sources of information regarding farm machinery, farmers most frequently cited watching neighbors' equipment in operation and talking with friends, neighbors, and relatives. In seeking product-related information, farmers apparently opted for informal sources as opposed to formal business sources such as implement company dealers, salesmen, and machinery company literature.

Recent years have seen a decline in the relative importance of small family farms, many of which are inefficient. The number of farms in the United States declined from about 4 million in 1960 to 2.9 million in 1969, while average farm size increased from 297 acres to 387 acres. Nonetheless, the majority of farms existing in 1969 were still relatively small, and farm income—an average net income per farm of $5,468 in 1969—was among the lowest of any business sector.

Collectively, the purchases made by American farms amount to a substantial sum. In 1969, aggregate farm operating expenses included $6.8 billion on feed, $4.3 billion on livestock, $1.9 billion on fertilizer, $4.8 billion on equipment operation and repair, and $5.4 billion on miscellaneous other purchases. In addition, farmers spent $4.9 billion for new farm machinery, vehicles, and equipment.

Among the unique aspects of agricultural markets, two are particularly worthy of mention: *store patronage* and *use of credit.* By virtue of their rural location, farmers naturally tend to patronize stores in small local communities. Many of these communities came into existence to provide for the needs of a surrounding agricultural region. As a result, there arose a number of retail institutions that specialize in selling goods and services to farmers. In 1967, for ex-

[2] Alexander Segall, *Farmers' Attitudes to Farm Machinery Purchases,* Royal Commission on Farm Machinery, Study no. 4, Queen's Printer, Ottawa, 1969.

ample, there were nearly 17,000 farm equipment dealers in the United States, with total sales of over $4.8 billion. Feed mills and farm supply houses are also common. Farm supply and service cooperatives, in which a group of local farmers organize together to buy goods and services in bulk quantities, are prominent. In 1967, there were almost 2,900 farm supply cooperatives in the United States, with sales in excess of $3.3 billion. In recent years, however, these specialized institutions have gradually declined in importance as improved highways and larger farms with more demanding buying criteria have resulted in an increased propensity for farmers to travel to the city to buy.

Agricultural purchasing is also characterized by an extensive use of credit. The farmer's need for credit is a function of the nature of his business. Farming is a seasonal occupation, the cash income from which is realized in one or two concentrated periods each year when commodities ripen and are sold. Weather, disease, and crop yield variations can produce a highly cyclical income from year to year. These seasonal and cyclical variations in cash flows dictate the use of credit.

To help farmers finance their crops, Congress established the Commodity Credit Corporation in 1933. In 1969, this government organization extended loans of almost $3 billion to farmers, and had outstanding loans totaling $3.5 billion. In the same year, farmers borrowed $14.5 billion from banks, credit associations, agricultural credit corporations, and livestock loan associations. A further $10.3 billion was estimated to have been lent to farmers by farm equipment dealers, merchants, and finance companies.

Institutional markets

There is no widely accepted definition of the word "institution." Generally, the term connotes an organization that provides a service to the public, or to a particular segment of the public. Within the scope of this meaning, many different classes of enterprise have at one time or another been considered as institutions. A hospital is one obvious example. Hotels, usually considered as service establishments, are sometimes classified as institutions, presumably because of their "public" nature. Marketing literature frequently refers to restaurants as members of "institutional markets," although they are actually retail establishments (and are treated as such here, see Chapter 10).

When interpreted in its broadest sense, the term institution lacks the precision necessary for meaningful marketing analysis.□ Hence for our purposes here, we adopt a more specific definition. Establishments falling within the scope of this definition include the majority of hospitals, nursing homes, clinics, colleges and universities, elementary and secondary schools, and prepared food outlets operated as commercial or industrial employee services.

□ *Institutions are organizations that provide a service to the public, or to a particular segment of the public, whose principal goals are expressed in terms of nonprofit criteria.*

The markets comprised of these establishments are collectively referred to as *institutional markets*.

The distinguishing characteristic that renders institutions worthy of consideration as separate markets is their public, nonprofit orientation. The cost of medical care, for example, is one of uppermost concern to a majority of Americans. As a result, hospitals are under intense public pressure to maintain costs at a minimum level. A further ramification of public scrutiny is widespread participation in institutional purchase decisions and, as a consequence, extensive and complex decision-making units. To serve institutional markets effectively, a seller must thoroughly understand who is involved in his customers' decision-making units, and the role played by each member therein.

The magnitude of institutional markets can be illustrated by several examples. In 1968, there were 7,172 hospitals in the United States. The wide variety of items needed to operate a hospital includes food, linen, furniture, patient care material such as syringes, needles, catheters, bandages, and instruments, complex equipment such as auto-analyzers for laboratories, monitoring equipment for intensive care units, diagnostic equipment for radioactive isotope treatment, and new improvements in X-ray equipment. In 1968, total hospital nonpayroll expenditures in the United States amounted to $6 billion, including commodity purchases of $2.5 billion and equipment purchases of $1.5 billion. In addition, about $2.3 billion was spent on new hospital construction. Not included in any of these data are the expenditures of 18,185 nursing homes and approximately 1,400 institutions for treatment of mental illness.

Government data indicate that there were over 116,000 elementary and secondary schools in the United States in 1968. Their aggregate expenditures included $8.2 billion in capital outlays and $54.9 billion in current expenditures (a majority of which was attributable to payroll). Unlike the 2,400 institutions of higher education, however, individual elementary and secondary schools do not themselves constitute buying units. Purchasing is usually carried out by a central authority, the public school board (or system), of which there were approximately 24,000 in 1968. The size of a school system naturally influences its buying decisions. Large systems typically employ more specialized personnel such as those listed in Figure 8-5, a summary of the results of a survey of decision-making unit composition in school instructional materials purchases. Smaller school districts cannot afford experts of this kind, and their decision-making units are correspondingly less complex.

Almost 40 percent of estimated expenditures on prepared food away from home is spent in noncommercial establishments. The data in Table 8-5 indicate, for example, that 1966 expenditures on food in hospitals, schools, and other institutions totaled almost $11 billion. Purchases made by these institutions probably represented at least half of this amount.

FIGURE 8-5

School system buying decision patterns for purchase of instructional materials

Purchasing activity	Most important	Second most important
Originates the need	Curriculum Director	Teachers and Instructional Materials Director
Gathers information	Curriculum Director	Instructional Materials Director
Evaluates brands and supplies	Chief Administrator	Instructional Materials Director
Recommends brand	Chief Administrator	Instructional Materials Director
Approves purchase	Chief Administrator	Board of Education and Business Manager
Places order	Chief Administrator	Business Manager

Source: "School Purchasing Decision Patterns: Instructional Material," research report published by *School Product News*, 1968, p. 41.

Government markets

While government markets have existed for many years, it is only in recent times that they have reached huge proportions. Historically, peacetime government expenditures have been limited to housekeeping supplies, except for special, complex items such as aircraft. Prior to the Korean war, for example, military establishments manufactured their own armaments, constructed their own warships, and limited expenditures in the business sector to items that

□

TABLE 8-5

Estimated sales volume of noncommercial food service establishments, 1966

(Millions of dollars)

Hospitals, nursing homes, and other health and welfare	$ 2,142
Colleges and universities	1,144
Schools and school systems	2,600
Commercial or industrial employee services	875
Military	2,811
Other (including "Ys," religious, fraternities, clubs, etc.)	1,287
Total	$10,859

Source: John C. Hofer and Russell L. Jones, "Forecasting Institutional Market Potential through Socioeconomic Analysis of the Patron/Customer," in Keith Cox and Ben M. Enis, (eds.), *A New Measure of Responsibility for Marketing*, Proceedings of the 1968 June Conference of the American Marketing Association, pp. 329–334.

they could not produce themselves. In the two decades since that time, the historical pattern has been reversed dramatically. With rapid changes in the technology of defense, medicine, education, transportation, and law enforcement, all levels of government have turned increasingly to purchasing needed goods and services.

The assortment of government purchases is enormous, ranging from stationery supplies and food to nuclear reactors and spacecraft, from janitorial services to complete systems of advanced educational programs. As shown in Table 8-6, the 1969 purchases of all levels of government in the United States exceeded $200 billion. A substantial additional amount was sold by American industry to governments in foreign countries. The largest single category of expenditure is defense which, in 1969, accounted for almost 80 percent of total federal government expenditures. State and local government expenditures, despite the Vietnam war, exceeded those of the federal government for the first time in 1968.

The relative importance of government markets varies, of course, with the nature of the goods and services that each seller produces. The ordnance and aircraft industries are heavily dependent on government markets, each selling

TABLE 8-6

Government purchases of goods and services, 1969

(Millions of dollars)

	Federal government	State and local government
National defense	$ 78,763	$ 566
Space research and technology	3,905	
Central government administration and management	2,896	10,138
International affairs and finance	575	
Education	1,014	47,363
Health, labor, and welfare	3,935	26,466
Veterans benefit and services	1,793	24
Commerce, transportation, and housing	3,541	22,146
Agriculture and agriculture resources	2,384	1,172
Natural resources	2,533	2,963
Total	$101,339	$110,838

Source: U.S. Department of Commerce, *Survey of Current Business*, July, 1970.

over 80 percent of its output in government markets, including direct sales and those made through subcontractors. Among other industry groups, electronic components (38 percent) and transportation equipment (27 percent) are only moderately dependent on government purchases, while food and apparel sell only 2 percent of their output to all levels of government.

UNIQUE ASPECTS OF GOVERNMENT MARKETS

The feature that serves to distinguish government purchases from those of private business is the extensive network of legal requirements that have been established to protect the public interest by assuring competition on price, quality, and performance. While there are many differences between government and private markets, the three principal ones we will discuss here all emanate from the public character of government markets, that is, precise specifications, competitive bidding, and bidders' lists.

Precise specifications Because of the immense volume of commodities purchased by government agencies, it has been possible to develop standards covering complete details of classes, sizes, materials, workmanship requirements, and inspection and testing requirements for a majority of the items purchased. Often, these standards are designed to avoid restrictive specifications that would favor the product or service of a single supplier, thereby inhibiting competition. Not only must products sold to government meet specifications, but a supplier may even have to submit his product for laboratory testing before being included on a list of firms eligible to bid.

Competitive bidding Competitive bids are required for the purchase of most goods and services by federal and state governments in the United States. While competitive bidding is used extensively in private business, the requirements of bidding are adhered to much more rigorously in government markets.

Distinctions can be made among various types of government bidding situations. Some bids are solicited through public notice, for example, advertised in public media, while others are solicited by invitation to a list of qualified bidders. The second approach may be used, for example, where purchases are below some minimum amount and the additional competition created by public notice is not judged sufficient to justify its cost. The Armed Services Procurement Regulation considers both these approaches as "procurement by formal advertisement," since the details of all submitted bids are fully disclosed and the winning bid is publicly announced. In "procurement by negotiation," direct negotiation with potential bidders is used instead. Negotiated procurements are generally employed in cases of extreme urgency or in experimental work that cannot be precisely defined.

In selecting winning bids, government agencies use many of the same performance and economic criteria as industrial buyers. Often, however, there are additional considerations unique to government. State and local governments frequently give preference to bidders located in their state, while the "Buy American" Act requires the federal government to give similar preference to domestic suppliers. Prison inmates, handicapped workers, small businesses, or concerns located in high unemployment areas may also be granted preference. Thus, social or political goals may affect the criteria used in making purchases.

Bidders' lists The use of bidders' lists in government buying makes it crucial for a prospective supplier to be included on the appropriate list. Requirements for inclusion vary substantially from the completion of a simple form to extensive inspection by government personnel. There is no common bidders' list maintained by the federal government, so a supplier must be on the list of all relevant agencies. In the myriad of buying agencies within all levels of government, the mere task of finding the buyer can be a job of not insignificant magnitude.

THE STRUCTURE OF GOVERNMENT MARKETS

Government as a customer is not a monolithic organization. It has been estimated, for example, that there are over 100,000 units of government that either make or influence buying decisions.[3] The federal government consists of a multitude of agencies, commissions, and committees that purchase goods and services. State governments have undergone a similar proliferation. Maryland, for example, has over 200 money-spending components. The greatest diversity exists at the local government level where there are an estimated 91,000 different units, some of which have several money-spending components.

In markets so huge and diverse, it is not surprising that market segmentation has evolved as an appropriate approach for analyzing and developing programs for marketing to governments. While there are many different ways of classifying government markets on a segmented basis, two dimensions commonly used include the kinds of goods and services sold and the level at which a contract is being negotiated.

Kinds of goods and services From a marketing standpoint, government markets can be divided into three basic categories: (1) products representing an extension of normal industrial and consumer markets, (2) traditional and commonly used products where government needs dominate demand, and (3) special markets peculiar to government.

For products representing an extension of normal markets, the needs and motivations of government buyers are essentially similar to those of business

[3] Blair A. Simon, "Analyzing Government Markets," in Victor P. Buell (ed.), *Handbook of Modern Marketing*, McGraw-Hill Book Company, New York, 1970, p. 2-54.

customers. A buyer of food or uniforms for the Army places similar demands on the seller as a buyer for Sears, although product specifications may not be the same. There are differences, however, in that government has open procurement requirements and bid invitations may be sent to all qualified suppliers. Minimal selling and advertising are required, but more attention must be given to procedures, technical data, and legal documentation.

Highway construction, aircraft, and education are examples of markets where there are some private purchases, but where government procurement and standards dominate and establish industry patterns. These markets are characterized by tight specifications established by government, with contracts usually awarded to the lowest bidders. They are also subject to public pressures, as in the case of citizen objections to a new highway, disapproval of a bond issue, or, as in the early 1970s, national controversy over the benefits of the supersonic transport aircraft.

Specialized government markets call for highly advanced technology and systems capability to manage a complex of components, technology, and innovation. These markets, historically dominated by the Department of Defense, the National Aeronautics and Space Administration, and the Atomic Energy Commission, typically involve heavy expenditures on research and development. The federal government pays for about 70 percent of all research and development in the United States. (We shall explore the peculiar nature of research and development purchases further in Chapter 9.)

Contract levels Another useful basis of segmentation is contract level, as depicted in Figure 8-6. This classification scheme serves to point out the risks and opportunities present at various levels of selling to government. For prime contractors, government business opportunities are few in number, high in unit value. At the subcontracting levels, a greater number of business opportunities exist, each with correspondingly less value. The subcontractor's prosperity depends heavily on the success of prime contractors. With the decline of defense expenditures in 1970, for example, many prime contractors began to assume work they had previously passed on to others. In the first half of 1970, about 1,200 defense subcontractors were reported to have filed for bankruptcy, as many as in all of 1969. Lockheed Aircraft Corporation had dropped 1,818 subcontractors in comparison to the same period in 1969.[4]

Summary

The common thread that links the various markets described in this chapter is, in a sense, the attribute that none possesses. We have described markets that

[4] "Subcontractors Suffer as Big Defense Firms Cancel Their Orders," *Wall Street Journal*, Mar. 1, 1971.

FIGURE 8-6
Government markets segmented by contract levels

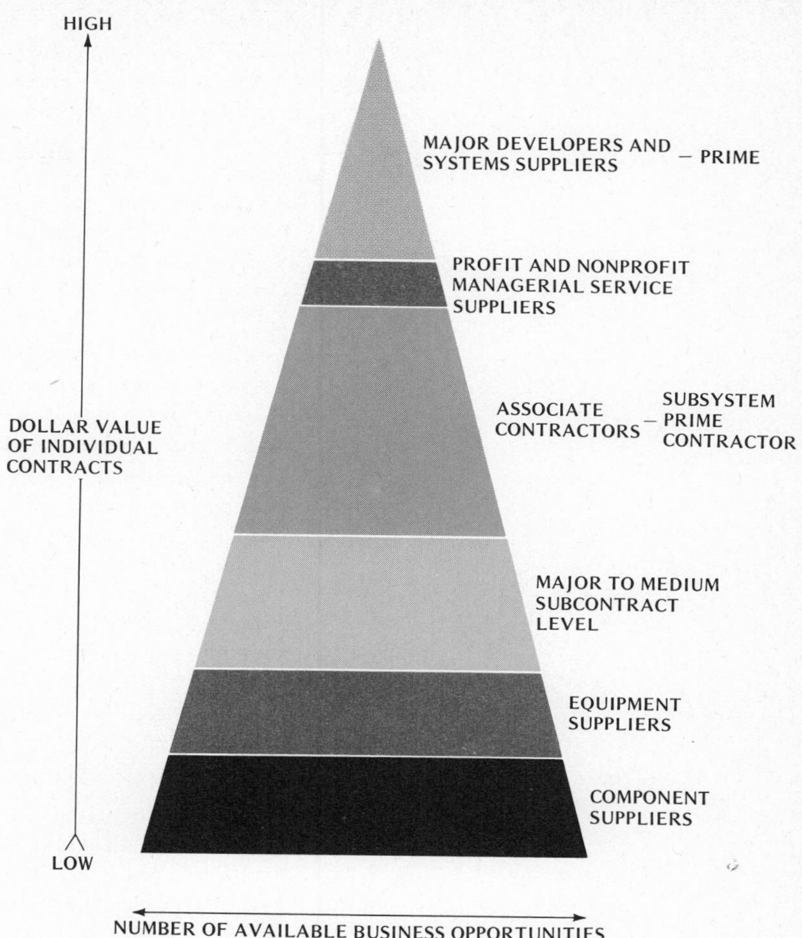

Source: Blain A. Simon, "Analyzing Government Markets," in Victor P. Buell (ed.), *Handbook of Modern Marketing,* New York, McGraw-Hill Book Company, 1970, p. 2-57.

are *not* comprised of household customers. Otherwise, the most notable characteristic of business, institutional, and government markets is their tremendous *diversity*. Petroleum refineries, automobile repair shops, architects, farmers, and the federal government are as heterogeneous a group as any firm could hope to deal with.

Because of the diversity of different markets in our economy, most companies attempt to specialize their expertise in one or two particular areas. Even in examining *Fortune* magazine's list of the 500 largest American corporations, one can discern notable patterns of specialization. Raytheon Company is engaged heavily in government contract work, while Ralston Purina focuses most of its attention on providing feed supplies to agricultural markets. Eli Lily markets ethical drugs, but does not sell proprietary medicines to household customers. General Foods Corporation is well known for marketing grocery products to consumers. Food service and institutional sales, which accounted for 12 percent of General Foods 1970 sales, are handled by a separate division of the company.

A major reason for specialization, either by company or by divisions within a company, is the necessity of developing different marketing programs to serve the needs of different groups of customers. To build a marketing program, one must begin with an understanding of buyer behavior. Hence, before proceeding to discuss marketing programs in Part 4, we must first look more closely in the next chapter at the buying behavior of different classes of customers who make up the markets we have identified in this chapter.

Questions

1. Figure 8-2 shows the concentration ratios for several industries. According to this figure, the four largest companies account for 81 percent of cigarette shipments but only 5 percent of lithographic printing shipments. As a manufacturer of chemicals used by both cigarette manufacturers and lithographers, how do you think the differences in industry concentration would affect the marketing mix you would employ in serving each of these industries?

2. The U.S. Bureau of the Census collects and publishes data showing the geographic concentration of manufacturing establishments as well as the value of shipments by region (see Figure 8-3).

   a. In what specific ways could the marketing research department of a packaging materials manufacturer use these data? Would it make any difference if the firm had more than one plant? More than one product line? Why?

   b. How might the same information be used by:

   (1) A property insurance company
   (2) A national janitorial source
   (3) A local janitorial service
   (4) A firm of consulting pollution engineers
   (5) A dentist

3. Many firms assign territories to salesmen on the basis of the geographic concentration and the value of shipments of potential customers. What disadvantages or problems might be caused by this method of assignment?

4. How would you expect the importance of different elements of the marketing mix (product, price, channels, promotion) to vary when each of the following products is sold in the defense market as opposed to commercial or industrial markets?
   a. Milling machines
   b. Trucks
   c. Prescription drugs
   d. Educational film strips

5. What impact, if any, does the decline in the number and relative importance of small family farms have on the marketing mix of a large manufacturer of farm implements? Why?

6. The Signal Wax Company sold a line of cleaning and waxing products. The line was sold through hardware jobbers to retail hardware outlets. The company also sold several of its high-volume products to discount and food-chain stores under distributors' labels. Looking for ways to build sales, management concluded that the institutional market might provide an opportunity for sales growth. What kinds of marketing problems would the Signal Wax Company face selling its line to schools, hospitals, and other institutions?

7. Identify, compare, and contrast the major decision influences likely to be involved in the following purchases of a major metropolitan hospital.
   a. Bed sheets
   b. Laboratory auto-analyzers
   c. A new design of motorized hospital bed
   d. Disposable syringes

8. The Rollins Company manufactured and sold a wide variety of business forms (invoices, inventory record forms, credit records, and so forth) throughout New England. As a result of recent capital equipment purchases, the company had considerable excess capacity and was attempting to identify new market opportunities.
   a. One opportunity for growth was to sell forms to public schools and municipalities. What kinds of information would the Rollins Company need to evaluate this alternative? If the company decided to solicit business from state governments, what further information would Rollins management need to collect? Why?
   b. Another possibility was to expand to new geographic areas not presently served by the firm. What specific information would Rollins need to evaluate this alternative? Why?
   c. Rollins' sales manager suggested that the company should enter the government market and solicit orders from both state governments and the federal government. What questions should management ask and answer before making this decision?

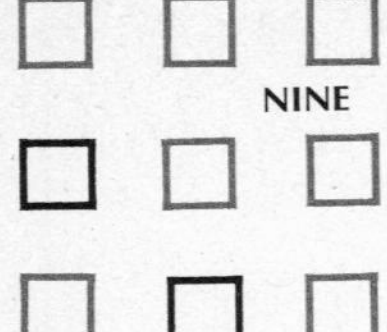

Business, institutional, and government buying decisions

Every marketing decision is based on some assumptions or estimates about how buyers behave and how they will respond to marketing stimuli. We have already demonstrated the importance of understanding buying decisions in consumer markets in earlier chapters. For firms selling to businesses, institutions, and government, it is no less important to know and understand buyer decision making.

This chapter parallels the sequence of topics introduced in Chapter 8. For each of the markets discussed in Chapter 8, we will examine the nature of customer purchasing behavior. We have neither sufficient space nor need, however, to explore all that is known about buying decisions in business, institutions, and government. Instead, a major portion of this chapter will be devoted to detailed examination of buying behavior in the most important class of business—manufacturing industries. Other types of business customers—services, professionals, and agriculture—will be treated more briefly. A similar treatment is afforded to buying decisions in institutional and government markets.

Buying decisions in manufacturing industries

There are both similarities and differences between consumer and industrial buying. Consumers generally purchase to satisfy personal needs, but industrial buyers seek to satisfy the needs of an organization. The industrial buyer is therefore constrained by the goals of the organization, which usually involve substantial emphasis on profits. Note that household customers rarely buy with a profit criterion, at least as the term is used in a monetary sense.

In industrial buying, the concept of a *decision-making unit* comes into its sharpest perspective. As mentioned earlier, in consumer marketing, the decision-making unit was often a single individual. Ordinarily, a consumer decision-making unit involves a small number of people, a family, for example. Industrial decision-making units, on the other hand, can involve far larger numbers with correspondingly greater complexity in who influences, decides, buys, and uses. In buying a computer, for example, 40 to 50 people in an organization may become involved in the purchase decision. They include purchasing agents, data processing experts, senior corporate personnel, financial managers, and representatives of all the company departments that will eventually use the facility.

Not all these people are so-called "rational buyers"—dispassionate, fully informed experts making hard-nosed decisions on narrowly defined technical and economic bases. It is true that many manufacturers employ purchasing agents who are professionals in buying, and equally true that performance and economic factors rank relatively high as decision criteria in industrial markets. But industrial buyers remain human when on the job and, as we shall see, susceptible to a full gamut of psychosocial influences on their purchasing behavior.

□

INDUSTRIAL DECISION-MAKING UNITS: A CASE ILLUSTRATION

Reporting an actual case history, *Modern Manufacturing* magazine described the sequence of events that transpired when a packaging materials manufacturer purchased a new $3,500 air compressor. The buying process, which is depicted in Figure 9-1, began when the plant manager suggested that a new compressor was required. Responding to this suggestion, the plant facility manager brought the matter to the attention of the vice-president of engineering. He agreed that a new compressor was required.

Working with his assistant, the vice-president of engineering established cost specifications for a new compressor. He also consulted the vice-president of purchasing to confirm his cost estimates. On the basis of these estimates, the expenditure was authorized by the vice-president of engineering, the vice-president of purchasing, the director of manufacturing, and the president.

A list of three possible vendors was established by the vice-president of engineering, the vice-president of purchasing, and the purchasing agent. Bids were solicited from these vendors. After reviewing the bids, the purchasing agent

FIGURE 9-1

The decision-making unit in an actual purchase of an air compressor by a packaging materials manufacturer

	DIR. OF MFG.	PLANT MGR.	PRES.	RECEIVING MGR.	V.P. ENG.	PLANT FAC. MGR.	ASST. TO V.P. ENG.	MAINT. SUPV.	CHIEF ELEC.	PURCH. AGENT	V.P. PURCH.	INVOLVEMENT PEOPLE: OPER.	INVOLVEMENT PEOPLE: ENG.	INVOLVEMENT PEOPLE: PURCH.	EST. TIME BETW. STAGES
NEED DETERMINED BY:		●			◉	◉						1	2	0	1 WEEK
SPECIFICATIONS ESTABLISHED BY:					◉		◉					0	2	0	
COST ESTIMATE PREPARED BY:					◉						○	0	1	1	
EXPENDITURES AUTHORIZED BY:	●		●		◉						○	2	1	1	
SUPPLIERS' LIST PREPARED BY:					◉					○	○	0	1	2	1 WEEK
SUPPLIERS CONTACTED BY:					◉					○	○	0	1	2	
BIDS OBTAINED BY:					◉		◉			○	○	0	2	2	
SUPPLIER SELECTED BY:					◉					○	○	0	1	2	
ORDER PLACED BY:										○	○	0	0	2	
RECEIVED AND TEMPORARILY STORED BY:				●							○	1	0	1	1 WEEK
INSTALLED BY:					◉			◉				0	2	0	1 WEEK
PRODUCT EVALUATED BY:								◉	◉			0	1	1	
												4	14	14	

● OPERATIONS MANAGERS
◉ ENGINEERS
○ PURCHASING AGENTS

Source: Reproduced with permission from "Who Gets Involved in the Purchase of an Air Compressor in a Typical Manufacturing Plant," a research paper published by *Modern Manufacturing* magazine.

concluded that the lowest bid met the specifications and recommended that it be accepted. The other two men agreed.

The order was placed by the purchasing agent and the vice-president of purchasing. The compressor was received about a week later by the receiving manager. It was subsequently installed by the vendor, under the general supervision of the maintenance supervisor and the chief electrician. The product was evaluated in use by the vice-president of engineering and the maintenance supervisor.

While the description is representative of a typical industrial buying decision, it should not be concluded that all air compressors are bought in this manner. We can imagine, too, that a great deal of the human interplay in this decision has been omitted from the case history. Nevertheless, what we can see is the complexity of *membership* in the decision-making unit responsible for this purchase.

Eleven people were involved. Four were from operations management, five from engineering, and two from purchasing. The role each man played reflected his job responsibilities. Management was primarily concerned with establishing that a real need existed, and in having the final say on whether funds were being well spent. The technical nature of the purchase dictated engineering involvement throughout the buying decision. Note that the purchasing staff, although very active once specifications were established, constantly worked with others in the organization. Only in placing the order did purchasing act independently.

□ FACTORS AFFECTING DECISION-MAKING UNIT MEMBERSHIP

If the same firm that bought the air compressor were to consider buying new office furniture, a different set of people might participate in the buying decision. It is characteristic of industrial buying that membership in decision-making units varies with the nature of the product or service being acquired. Who will use it, who is competent to judge technical specifications, and who is familiar with available sources of supply will all affect the nature and extent of purchase involvement.

Other factors that determine the membership of decision-making units include the size of the purchase and the customer's previous experience in buying similar items. Generally, large dollar transactions require careful scrutiny and high-level managerial approval, but this is not always the case. If a company regularly uses large quantities of a standardized commodity, such as grain for a flour mill, its purchasing agent may have authority to spend $100,000 or more without consulting others in his organization.

To illustrate how previous purchasing experience can affect the nature of an industrial buying decision, consider the classification scheme illustrated in Figure 9-2. The scheme describes purchasing situations as *new tasks, modified*

FIGURE 9-2
Distinguishing characteristics among three classes of industrial buying decisions

☐ NEW TASK

A requirement or problem that has not arisen before
Little or no relevant past buying experience to draw upon
A great deal of information is needed
Must seek out alternative ways of solving the problem and alternative suppliers
Occurs infrequently—but very important to marketers because it sets the pattern for the more routine purchases that will follow
May be anticipated and developed by creative marketing

☐ STRAIGHT REBUY

Continuing or recurring requirement, handled on a routine basis
Usually the decision on each separate transaction is made in the purchasing department
Formally or informally, a "list" of acceptable suppliers exists
No supplier not on the "list" is considered
Buyers have much relevant buying experience, and hence little new information is needed
Appears to represent the bulk of the individual purchases within companies
Item purchased, price paid, delivery time, etc., may vary from transaction to transaction, so long as these variations do not cause a new source of supply to be considered

☐ MODIFIED REBUY

May develop from either new task or straight rebuy situations
The requirement is continuing or recurring or it may be expanded to a significantly larger level of operations
The buying alternatives are known, but they are CHANGED
Some additional information is needed before the decisions are made
May arise because of outside events, such as an emergency or by the actions of a marketer
May arise internally because of new buying influences, or for potential cost reductions, potential quality improvements, or potential service benefits
Marketers who are not active suppliers try to convert the customer's straight rebuys into modified rebuys

Source: Patrick J. Robinson and Charles W. Faris, *Industrial Buying and Creative Marketing*, Marketing Science Institute Series, Boston: Allyn & Bacon, Inc., 1967, p. 28. Reproduced with permission.

rebuys, or *straight rebuys*. New tasks are those situations least familiar to the buyer. Lacking a foundation of prior experience, the buyer is likely to seek out a great deal of information and to consider several alternatives before buying. The opposite kind of situation, a straight rebuy, is one involving a continuing or recurrent requirement. Having made similar purchases before, the buyer is unlikely to seek further information or consider alternatives very seriously. Modified rebuys represent a midpoint on the spectrum between situations of new tasks and straight rebuys.

For industrial marketers, several benefits can be derived by examining purchasing situations in this way. It is helpful in identifying those opportunities where a seller has a reasonable chance of gaining a sale. It points out the informational needs of the customer when a salesman is calling on him. There is also a clear implication that the size and complexity of the customer's decision-making unit will be at a minimum in situations of straight rebuy, but will increase as the same customer moves to situations less familiar to him.

STAGES IN INDUSTRIAL BUYING DECISIONS

If we recall the air compressor purchase illustrated in Figure 9-1, it is apparent that none of the eleven people in the decision-making unit were involved throughout the entire buying process. The different stages in the process, and the activities encompassed by each stage, governed who was active at various points in time. Just as it was useful to view consumer buying decisions in discrete stages, so it is helpful to look on industrial purchases in the same manner.

The classification of stages for consumer buying decisions suggested in Chapter 3 is equally applicable in industrial marketing. There should be no difficulty, for example, in grouping the activities encompassed by the air compressor purchase (Figure 9-1) into respective stages of *need arousal, search and evaluation, purchase,* and *postpurchase feedback*. As in consumer marketing, many other systems of classifying buying stages have been suggested and may be equally as useful as those we have described here.

One purpose in viewing a buying decision as a series of stages is to provide clues for marketers on how they should approach prospective customers. In an industrial marketing setting, where decision-making units tend to be large and complex, different individuals tend to be most influential in successive stages of a purchase decision. In the air compressor example, there would be small gain for a compressor salesman who focused his attention on the purchasing agent during the initial stages of the decision. At this early point, the manufacturer was mainly concerned with establishing specifications, an engineering responsibility. If the salesman fails to communicate with the engineers during this initial stage, he may find that the specifications established are incompatible with the product he has to offer.

The stage of a purchase decision also affects the kind of information relevant to a customer. For example, it would be inappropriate for the salesman to have emphasized price considerations at the outset of the air compressor purchase. The customer eventually became very interested in assessing price, but it was not first in his mind when the buying decision was getting under way. The initial requirement was for technical information. Only when a decision was made on what technical specifications were required to meet his needs did the customer turn to calling for price bids.

Of course, the kind of information that is relevant to a buyer depends on more than the stage of a decision-making process. What is of greatest importance to a marketer is to identify the criteria that the customer uses in arriving at his purchase decision. In earlier chapters, we discussed at length how economic, demographic, social, and psychological variables bear on the buying decisions of household customers. It is equally important to identify and explain the factors that are likely to influence buying decisions of industrial customers.

DECISION CRITERIA IN INDUSTRIAL BUYING

Experience has shown that there are common threads, or *decision criteria*, underlying the buying decisions of most manufacturing firms. Although these criteria may vary from company to company, or from decision to decision within a company, they reflect a prevalent mode of business thinking that characterizes most industrial purchasing. Underlying a majority of buying decisions, for example, are considerations of performance, economics, seller reputation, and extent of reliance on suppliers. Reciprocity may also play a significant role.

Performance *Performance* evaluation begins with an assessment of the physical and technical properties of a product, and the use to which the product will be put. Naturally, an industrial buyer is unlikely to purchase a product that fails to meet his minimum technical standards. He may be equally unwilling, on the other hand, to pay extra for technical properties that are not required. Many industrial products have failed because they were "overengineered," and hence too costly relative to the needs of most customers in their intended target market.

A manufacturer's concept of performance extends beyond the question of physical and technical properties alone. Service provided by the seller is a crucial dimension of most purchase decisions. There must be assurance of on-time delivery, prompt and competent repair facilities, and where materials are involved, continuity of supply. In the case of complex products, the seller will probably have to provide production, engineering, and systems assistance to ensure satisfactory performance.

Economics Closely related to performance criteria are the *economics* of an industrial buying decision. Price is an obvious and important economic consideration. In situations where competing products are equal in all other respects, price will be a determining factor. All other things are seldom equal, however, and direct price comparison is frequently impossible. In designing a piece of heavy industrial machinery, for example, a steel gear that costs $65, an aluminum gear costing $85, and a fiberglas gear costing $15 may all merit consideration by the manufacturer. The steel gear will last the longest, but may outlive the useful life of other components in the machinery. The aluminum gear is light and also long wearing, but unless low weight is needed, its high cost may be unwarranted. Fiberglas could not endure heavy wear conditions, but its low cost renders this gear ideal for limited-wear applications. Clearly, the optimal choice involves a tradeoff between cost and the performance requirements of the application in question.

In the example just cited, the only monetary cost considered was the purchase price of the three different gears. Often, there are additional costs relevant to a purchase decision. In choosing between drilling equipment driven by compressed air and similar equipment driven by electric power, for example, a manufacturer would want to assess comparative operating costs over a period of time.

□ *Value analysis refers to "an organized effort directed at analyzing the function of a product with the purpose of achieving the required function at the lowest overall cost."*[1]

Because competing products may offer differing economic and performance benefits, the industrial buyer is often placed in the difficult position of finding a common standard for evaluating the alternative purchases available to him. This need has given rise to the technique of value analysis.□ In essence, a manufacturer using value analysis seeks to study the dollars-and-cents effects of purchasing a given product, *including* effects on other products that it may be used in association with. In considering the purchase of a new lathe, for example, value analysis would help him to examine the impact of the lathe on the items it will turn out. The task can be a difficult one. Many industrial products are not intended to function autonomously, but are integral parts of larger subsystems or total systems of production. A numerical control system, for example, is a complex electronic device designed to control the operation of lathes, pumps, drives, or other kinds of industrial machinery. By itself, a numerical control system produces nothing—its value rests in its effect on the machinery or equipment it controls.

We see, then, that the concept of value in industrial buying is a broad one. As well as the direct savings associated with the price of alternative products, the relative merit of different items may also depend on savings in time, labor, materials, transportation, inventory, safety, and management attention. It would be wrong, of course, to assume that all purchases are made on the basis of optimal value. Only a minority of manufacturers possess the capability of carrying out formal value analyses, and even in these firms not all purchases can be treated with such thoroughness.

Seller reputation Frequently, a buyer will also take into account the established *reputation of the seller*. If a seller is known among trade sources as one who has always provided a high level of value in the past, it is not unnatural for a buyer to assume that he will continue to do so in the future. A seller's reputation is therefore a valuable marketing asset, and many sellers go to considerable lengths to enhance their reputation through trade advertising and careful training and scrutiny of their sales representatives.

[1] Robert L. McGarrah and Donald L. Wallace, "A Context for Value Engineering," *The Journal of Industrial Engineering*, September–October, 1965, p. 318.

While a well-known reputation is undoubtedly an asset to a company selling in industrial markets, its value may vary under different conditions. A study conducted by one of the authors showed, for example, that purchasing agents are relatively less susceptible than technically trained personnel, such as engineers and chemists, to the influence of a company's good reputation.[2] In general, as the risk of the action the customer is expected to take rises, the likelihood of the customer being influenced by the seller's good reputation declines.

Multiple sources Industrial buyers often establish a policy of purchasing similar goods and services from several suppliers. By the *use of multiple buying sources* as a decision criterion, overreliance on one source of supply is avoided. Thus the risk of supplier dominance in the buyer-seller relationship is diminished and the consequences of a single supplier failing to deliver as promised are reduced.

Not all firms rely on using multiple buying sources, of course, and even those who do use multiple sources may still demonstrate pronounced loyalty to a particular favorite supplier. One study of industrial purchasing behavior in Great Britain, for example, showed that, for an equivalent product, half of the persons involved in purchasing would not change from their best supplier for a price reduction of less than 5 percent; one-fifth would not change for a reduction of less than 10 percent.[3]

Reciprocity The term *reciprocity* refers to the practice of a firm selling to its suppliers or buying from its customers. A distinction is sometimes made between "coercive reciprocity," connoting the overt threat of withdrawn purchases to secure sales, and "friendly reciprocity," representing the natural tendency to return a favor. Whatever its form, reciprocity is known to marketing and purchasing personnel as a "fact of life" in influencing purchase decisions. Naturally, the practice of reciprocity is discouraged by government regulatory agencies on the basis that it distorts the competitive process. Several large manufacturers have been successfully prosecuted for engaging in reciprocal buying practices. Notwithstanding, one study of this practice concluded that reciprocity had probably increased in prevalence during the 1960s.[4] The same study also concluded that, while reciprocity may be practiced by a small industrial firm, it is more apt to reach significant proportions and to be practiced in a systematic, organized manner in larger corporations.

The decision criteria we have described here are probably those most

[2] Theodore Levitt, *Industrial Purchasing Behavior,* Harvard Business School Division of Research, Boston, 1965.

[3] Hugh P. Bucker, *How British Industry Buys,* Hutchinson & Co. (Publishers), Ltd., London, 1966.

[4] F. R. Finney, *We Like to Do Business with Our Friends—A Special Report on Reciprocity,* Marketing Science Institute, Cambridge, Mass., 1969, pp. 7–8.

frequently relied upon by industrial buyers. If these were the *only* purchasing criteria used, the task of developing industrial marketing programs would be a relatively simple one. In reality, many additional variables enter the buying decisions of manufacturers, and, as a result, the process of industrial buying is an extremely complex one. This complexity stems in part from the diversity of manufacturing firms. Each organization is unique in its combination of objectives, resources, technology, activities, and people. The result is a milieu of buying situations and buying practices that differs markedly from one customer to the next.

To comprehend the complexity of buying in manufacturing organizations, marketers have drawn from their knowledge of the behavioral sciences, most notably from sociology and psychology. There have been numerous studies of this nature, though not nearly as many as comparable studies in consumer marketing. To illustrate how the behavioral sciences can help to understand industrial buying, we shall describe a number of psychosocial determinants of purchasing behavior in the following section.

□ PSYCHOSOCIAL DETERMINANTS OF PURCHASING STRATEGY

In dismissing the notion that decision criteria similar to those we have described are the sole basis of industrial buying decisions, Richard Cardozo introduces the concept of purchasing strategies.□ The significance of this concept is illustrated in Figure 9-3, beginning with the central observation that, despite complexity in industrial buying, purchasers are likely to adopt regular patterns of decision making, that is, purchasing strategies. The type of purchasing strategy adopted determines the manner in which the characteristics of suppliers, such as technical quality, service, delivery, cost, and reputation, are perceived and evaluated and, on this basis, a supplier is chosen. The factors determining purchasing strategy choice are *environmental forces,* their influence on the *buying situation and risk perceived,* and the *characteristics of the individual.*

□ *Purchasing strategies are regular patterns of decisions and actions whose objective is to identify and cope with purchasing problems within acceptable limits of risk and resource expenditure.*[5]

Types of purchasing strategies Cardozo identifies two types of purchasing strategies: sequential-evaluation and array-and-review.

The *sequential-evaluation strategy* involves contact with, and evaluation of, suppliers one at a time. Once the procurement manager and the using department have agreed on preliminary specifications, the procurement manager contacts a current supplier to determine if that supplier can provide the needed item on an acceptable basis. If he can, the purchase is made. If the first supplier cannot do so, the procurement manager goes to a second supplier, and so forth until a satisfactory source is located.

[5] Richard N. Cardozo, "Segmenting the Industrial Market," in Robert L. King (ed.), *Marketing and the New Science of Planning,* Proceedings of the Fall Conference of the American Marketing Association, 1968, p. 33.

FIGURE 9-3
Factors influencing purchasing strategies and supplier choice

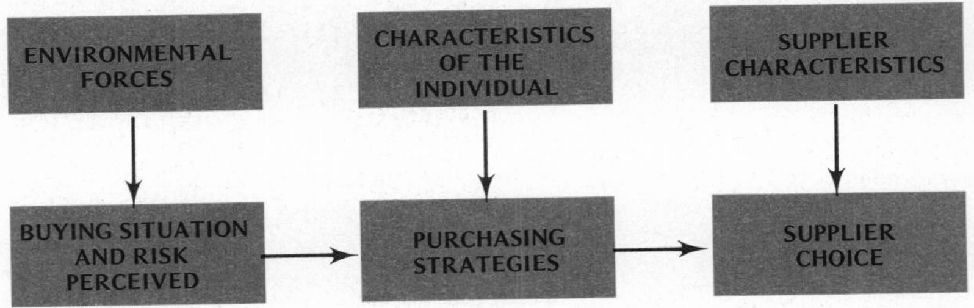

Source: Adapted from Richard N. Cardozo, "Segmenting the Industrial Market," in Robert N. King (ed.), *Marketing and the New Science of Planning,* Proceedings of the Fall Conference of the American Marketing Association, 1968, p. 434.

The marketing program appropriate for buyers using a sequential-evaluation strategy includes heavy selling and promotional efforts, design assistance, and prompt delivery. These activities are all intended to enable the supplier to "get in," that is, to become a current supplier since existing suppliers get first opportunity to bid on purchases. The nature of sequential-evaluation strategies suggests that having the lowest price is not a primary requisite.

In an *array-and-review strategy,* the procurement manager sends out requests for bids to both present and prospective suppliers, considers all bids received, and chooses the one that offers the lowest cost to the firm. Typically, bids are not sent out until specifications are tightly drawn.

The marketing strategy appropriate for buyers using an array-and-review strategy includes low price and strict adherence to specifications. Relatively less effort to "get in" is necessary, since both current and potential suppliers are given an opportunity to bid. Purchasers employing an array-and-review strategy are likely to rely extensively on the multiple-source decision criterion discussed in the previous section.

From the foregoing, we can see that different kinds of marketing programs are appropriate for a seller when dealing with customers using sequential-evaluation or array-and-review purchasing strategies. Therefore, it is important to understand the factors that influence the type of strategy a given customer is likely to employ. Significantly, many of these factors are psychosocial in nature.

Buying situation and risk perceived The nature of the purchase situation, and the inherent risk perceived therein by the purchaser, will affect his choice of a purchasing strategy. In general, sequential-evaluation strategies are most appropriate when the need is immediate, total dollar expenditures are low, and the major risk perceived is interruption of supply. This strategy is also more likely to prevail when management resources available to make the purchase decision are limited. Array-and-review strategies are appropriate when the need is less urgent, dollar expenditures are high, and the major risk perceived is overpayment. An array-and-review strategy also requires sufficient managerial resources to prepare specifications, seek out potential suppliers, and evaluate alternative bids.

Environmental forces We can distinguish between internal and external environmental forces influencing the buying situation and purchasing strategy choice. Internal factors include the relationship of the procurement manager to others in his organization, and his work load. External factors include the competitive environment of the market for the firm's end products and the value added to purchase inputs by the firm's activities.

The procurement manager's *relationship to others* is affected to the extent that he perceives a risk in failing to meet objectives for the purchase that are established by others. When production or line personnel require a new item for the first time (a new task), for example, they are most likely to want technical assistance in developing specifications, satisfactory performance, and guaranteed service and delivery. The procurement manager faces the risk of criticism if he fails to attain these attributes in his choice of supplier, but the risk of criticism for overpayment is minimal. Therefore, he will probably choose a sequential-evaluation strategy. A procurement manager employing an array-and-review strategy, on the other hand, probably seeks to follow what he considers good procurement practices and to avoid criticism for overpayment. There is also a risk of failing to meet established specifications in a purchase. These conditions are likely to exist when the product being acquired is a standardized one, or at least one with which line personnel in the company are thoroughly familiar (straight rebuy).

Procurement managers who face heavy *work loads* are most likely to use a sequential-evaluation strategy. Heavy work loads force greater reliance on routine activities, loyalty to existing suppliers, greater emphasis on avoiding mistakes, and resistance to suggestions from other departments for change in products or suppliers. New suppliers have a relatively low probability of gaining acceptance by a procurement manager under a heavy work load.

Among external environmental forces, the *competitive environment* for the firm's end product affects the nature of a buying situation. In industries characterized by a high rate of innovation and technical change, for example, speed of competitive response may be of crucial importance. Under such conditions, a sequential-evaluation strategy is likely to be appropriate since it places greatest priority on proven and established sources of supply. In industries characterized by low *value added,* cost considerations are likely to be crucial for the buyer to maintain his profitability. Here, an array-and-review strategy would be preferred.

Individual characteristics Individual characteristics bearing on purchase strategy choice include individual risk tolerance and preference and the degree of role commitment on the part of a procurement manager.

Buyers who have relatively low tolerance for *risk* are likely to prefer a sequential-evaluation strategy over array-and-review. Of course, not all buyers perceive similar risks in a given situation—their propensity for information (to reduce risk) is therefore affected by the type of risk each perceives.[6] The implication for marketers is clear. Buyers should be given information congruent with the prevalent type of risk, psychosocial or performance, that each perceives. This may imply, for example, that a salesman delivers a different selling appeal to technical line personnel and to purchasing agents within the same company. Among buyers who perceive a particular type of risk as high or low, there are also varying degrees of confidence in the ability to handle risk. Inexperienced or less capable buyers, for example, are not as likely to handle risk as effectively as those who are experienced and/or competent.

Among industrial buyers, there are differing perceptions of the *role* of a purchasing agent. In conservative organizations, for example, the role of the purchasing agent is likely to be restricted to buying in the strictest sense of the word. Individuals or groups strongly committed to a strict interpretation of the purchasing agent's job should be sold on the basis that the product offered is consistent with the established roles of the individual and the organization. Less formal organizations may be characterized by purchasing agents committed to a broader role of recommending new products, processes, and suppliers. The appropriate seller appeal for these buyers is one emphasizing benefits in a product that will help the company as a whole to do its job more effectively.

Service industry buying decisions

In selling to any business customer, *derived* demand is an important consideration. Take the case of a company that sells hair driers to beauty salons. It is obvious that the company has a chance of making a profit only if it sells its hair driers. But it can sell them *only* if its customers are successful in selling their beauty salon services. In a nutshell, the firm's success depends on its customers' success.

An alert marketer must therefore know his customer's business as well as the customer himself (and in some cases, better). Herein lies the difficulty of marketing to service firms, for, as we demonstrated in Chapter 8, service industries are pronounced in their *heterogeneity*. They are a highly fragmented group providing a diverse array of intangible benefits to their customers.

There are several characteristics, nonetheless, that distinguish service in-

[6] For a thorough examination of perceived risk and information handling in industrial buying, see Levitt, *op. cit.*

dustry firms from those marketing tangible goods. We will devote the remainder of this section to examining these characteristics since, by understanding the nature of a service customer's business, a marketer will have taken the most important step in selling to him.

DISTINGUISHING CHARACTERISTICS OF SERVICE COMPANIES

Many of the unique aspects of service industry firms are due to the intangible nature of services. Since a service firm often sells an idea, not a product, it must *tell* the buyer what the service will do. The need for personal contact between buyer and seller may dictate the use of direct channels of distribution.[7]

In services such as business consulting, the service cannot be separated from the person of the seller. Under these conditions, the buyer is more a client than a customer. He places himself in the "hands of the seller," being not altogether free to use the service as he wishes, as he would be in the purchase of a good.

Being intangible, a service's value is difficult to assess. Price levels and pricing practices therefore vary greatly. Prices are often expressed as rates, fees, admissions, charges, tuitions, or contributions.

Many services are created and marketed simultaneously. A barber, for example, produces the service of a haircut and markets it at the same time. In such instances, a major dimension of competition is in providing time (hours of operation) and place (convenient location) utility. This dimension of competition is also important in banking.

Since services are consumed as they are produced, they cannot be inventoried. The "perishability" of services is a further influence dictating direct channels of distribution. This same factor creates highly localized markets for many services.

In summary, we find that services possess certain unique characteristics, resulting in distinguishing features among service firms and their marketing programs. Recognition of the nature of these distinctions is an imperative step in understanding service industry buying decisions and in building effective programs to market to service industry customers.

The physician: an example of professional buying behavior[8]

Like the industrial buyer who is sometimes depicted as coldly rational, the physician has often been stereotyped in his role of deciding on the prescription

[7] See, for example, John M. Rathmell, "What Is Meant by Services," *Journal of Marketing,* October, 1966, pp. 32–36.

[8] This section is based on material contained in Raymond A. Bauer and Lawrence H. Wortzel, "Doctor's Choice: The Physician and His Sources of Information about Drugs," *Journal of Marketing Research,* February, 1966, pp. 40–47. For brevity, other studies of physician buying behavior cited in this article are not footnoted here.

of drugs. On one hand, the physician is sometimes seen as a servant of the pharmaceutical industry and, on the other, as a dedicated and independent man of science who has little to do with commercial sources of information. Neither stereotype is accurate, as we can learn from a number of studies of physician decision making conducted in the 1950s and 1960s. To illustrate professional buying decisions by an example, we will focus attention in this section on a specific aspect of the doctor's decision-making process—his sources of information about drugs.

□

THE PHYSICIAN AND HIS INFORMATION SOURCES

Several communication channels bring drug-related information to the physician. Some are commercial, such as detail men, direct mail, and journal advertisements. Others are professional, including colleagues, journal articles, conventions, and conferences. All represent potential influences on a doctor's decision to prescribe a certain drug.

Early studies of physicians confirmed that the decision to prescribe certain drugs is a result of the combined stimulus of several forms of advertising and communication. Nevertheless, when surveyed, doctors tended to cite a greater number of commercial than professional sources as affecting their drug choices. It became apparent from later research that there are causal factors determining the relative importance of these two source types.

The *stage of decision making* is one factor found to influence information sources. Doctors were found to cite commercial sources as important in leading to awareness of new drugs, but professional sources as important in inducing trial. A noteworthy study by Menzel and Katz found that selection of information sources varies with the *personal position* of individual physicians. Doctors frequently asked for advice by colleagues, that is, opinion leaders, are prone to choosing professional sources, while physicians not frequently consulted by colleagues make relatively greater use of commercial sources. *Situational factors* are also important. Doctors are increasingly likely to select professional sources as the severity of a disease increases, during the early years of a drug's history, or when the physiology of the illness is not well understood.

Even within the domain of commercial sources, doctors have preferences. Doctors apparently distinguish between their *attitudes* toward detail men and their attitudes toward the drug companies these men represent. Bauer found attitudes toward detail men, a function of personal characteristics, to be related to drug choice in situations of "low-risk" illness. Attitudes toward drug companies, a function of satisfactory experience with each company's products, becomes more important in situations of appreciable risk.

As an individual decision maker, the doctor, or any professional, is in many ways similar to a household consumer in his buying decisions. From the brief examples cited, one should realize that many of the other concepts described in earlier chapters can be helpful to marketers in understanding professional decision making.

The farmer as a buyer

There are two important dimensions that characterize the farmer as a buyer: his role as a businessman and his place as a member of a rural community. As a businessmen, the farmer relies on many of the same considerations in his buying decisions as industrial customers. Because we have discussed industrial buying at length earlier in this chapter, it is appropriate to focus our attention here on the second dimension: the sociology of rural living and the influence of sociological factors on farmer decision making.

□ DIFFUSION OF INNOVATIONS AMONG FARMERS

The discipline of rural sociology is noted for its contribution to the theory of diffusion of innovations, which was introduced in Chapter 7 in the context of household customer buying behavior. Much of our knowledge pertaining to consumer response to innovations was originally derived from studies of farmer behavior. For example, in a comprehensive review of 506 research studies on the diffusion of innovations, Rogers identified 286 that had been conducted by rural sociologists.[9] Some of these studies were conducted as early as the 1920s, although the majority have taken place in the period since World War II.

What we have learned about diffusion from the work of rural sociologists can be identified here only in brief terms. In general, we can define six distinct areas of investigation, as depicted in Figure 9-4, each of which deals with some aspect of how farmers respond to new ideas, concepts, and products. The scope of topics reflected in Figure 9-4 gives some indication of the remarkable amount of study that has been carried out in this field. In effect, Figure 9-4 is merely a "catalog" of major areas of investigation in studies of farmers' response to innovation. Many of the specific findings emanating from these studies have been described earlier within the general framework of social influences on customer behavior in Chapter 7.

□ FARMER RESPONSE TO COMMERCIAL CHANGE AGENTS

To illustrate how these studies can be of value in the development of marketing programs, consider some specific findings related to "commercial change agents," that is, salesmen. It has been established that:

Farmers rely most heavily on salesmen for information when they are in the early stages of a purchase decision, while friends and neighbors are the predominant information source in later stages of decision.

[9] Everett M. Rogers, *Diffusion of Innovations,* The Free Press of Glencoe, Inc., New York, 1962.

FIGURE 9-4
Six principal types of diffusion research conducted by rural sociologists

Type of research	Major topics of investigation
Social system norms on innovativeness	Importance of cultural values to the diffusion process Traditional and modern social system norms Influence of norms on individual innovativeness
The adoption process	Adoption as a form of decision making Stages in the adoption process Personal versus impersonal information sources in adoption Factors influencing length of adoption period
Characteristics of an innovation	Attributes of an innovation that affect its rate of adoption
Correlates of innovativeness	Classification of individuals on the basis of their propensity to adopt innovations (adopter categories) Characteristics of individuals in different adopter categories
Opinion leadership	Characteristics of opinion leaders Personal influence and its role in the adoption process
Change agents	Efforts by salesmen, government agents, and other professionals to bring about changes in farmer behavior

Salesmen are more important to those who adopt an innovation relatively early than to those who are late in adopting.

Farmers perceive salesmen as low credibility sources of information, while other farmers are seen as high credibility sources.

Among the implications of these findings, it is apparent that a salesman must "reach" prospective farmer customers early in their purchase deliberations. Farm equipment manufacturers and their representatives often do this by making regular sales calls on farmers, rather than waiting for the farmer to come into a retail outlet. To the extent that farmers receptive to early adoption of innovation can be identified, greater selling effort to these individuals is appropriate. Service after a sale is of utmost importance, if only because a dissatisfied customer is in a strong position to deter his friends and neighbors from buying. To overcome the low credibility of salesmen, some manufacturers employ practicing farmers as part-time salesmen or dealers. Research has shown that these "farmer-dealers" are generally perceived as high credibility sources of information.

Buying decisions in institutional markets

In Chapter 8 we mentioned that the predominant influence on institutional buying decisions is the public, nonprofit characteristic of these establishments. The effective result is close public scrutiny of institutional expenditures and operating costs, together with extended and complex decision-making units. To illustrate institutional buying decisions, we will focus our attention in this section on a specific, but representative, class of institution: the hospital.[10]

THE HOSPITAL DECISION-MAKING UNIT

In most modern hospitals, varying degrees of authority and responsibility are typically vested in three separate organizational units: (1) a governing body, usually a board of trustees; (2) the physicians who practice within its walls; and (3) the hospital administrator and his staff of clerical and administrative personnel, nurses, dietitians, therapists, and technicians. To a degree, representatives of each group may become involved in hospital purchase decisions. Ease of manipulation of a new piece of X-ray equipment, for example, is of direct concern to the X-ray technicians on a hospital's staff. There may be a hundred or more doctors and nurses who are equally concerned with the quality of the photographic image produced by the new machine, and with the speed of getting results for certain types of situations. Financial considerations are of primary interest to the hospital administrator and, ultimately, the board of trustees. The result is a decision-making unit of no small potential magnitude.

The central figure in hospital purchasing is the hospital administrator. It is the administrator who holds overall responsibility for the purchasing function, although in large, modern hospitals, he may have one or more professional purchasing agents to assist him. The role of the administrator is typically that of a "man in the middle." On one hand, he is subjected to pressures from users within the hospital to buy according to their assessment of need and specification. Since the technology of medicine is rapidly changing, the impetus to buy new equipment and supplies arises frequently. Doctors, nurses, and technicians are usually patient oriented in their judgment, granting highest priority to improved performance and technical efficiency. These criteria must be traded off against economic considerations, for the administrator is under constant pressure from the public in general, and his board of trustees directly, to run the hospital efficiently.

DECISION CRITERIA IN HOSPITAL BUYING

In common with the industrial buyer, the hospital buyer seeks to maximize value by combining performance and economic criteria. Unlike most industrial purchases, however, it is frequently difficult to express the value of medical items in monetary terms. A good example is the decision to adopt disposable medical supplies, such as disposable hypodermic syringes. Doctors

[10] The material in this section is based on Joseph H. McNinch, "The Hospital Buying Decision and How It Is Made," in Bernard A. Morin (ed.), *Marketing in a Changing World,* Proceedings of the 1969 June Conference of the American Marketing Association, pp. 36–39.

and paramedical personnel might argue that disposable items reduce the risks of patient infection and simplify work procedures—difficult benefits to express in monetary terms. Even straightforward economic considerations can become complex. The cost of the nondisposable item and its processing for reuse must be weighed against the cost of the disposable item which involves not only price, but increased storage requirements as well as problems of disposal.

In other respects, hospital buying decisions bear close similarity to those of industrial customers. Commonly invoked decision criteria include vendor reliability and assured delivery. Being literally a matter of life and death, technical service and maintenance assume a position of crucial importance in most hospital equipment purchases. Similarly, use of multiple buying sources is a frequent practice to assure continued supply of needed commodities.

Buying decisions of government agencies and departments

Government buying tends to be a highly formalized process characterized by competitive bidding as the principal mechanism by which supply sources are chosen. For developing marketing programs in this relatively formal purchasing environment, Prof. William Rudelius of the University of Minnesota has suggested that government buying decisions can be examined in four distinct phases.[11] These phases—prospecting, sales, production and delivery, and postdelivery—are analogous to the stages in industrial buying explored earlier in this chapter. They are depicted in Figure 9-5.

The *prospecting* phase is that in which the need for a commodity is first recognized. The significance of this phase to a contractor's marketing program depends on how need has been established. Where a government agency has recognized its own need, it will usually proceed to issue an "invitation to bid," in cases of procurement by formal advertising, or a "request for proposals," in the case of procurement by negotiation. In both instances, the prospective contractor bids for government business in a highly competitive environment. Where a seller recognizes an opportunity in which his goods or services may be of value to the government agency, he may submit an unsolicited proposal to the agency. Unsolicited proposals are most frequently used in seeking research and development contracts. Although unsolicited proposals have the advantage of not being in direct competition with other contractors for the same work, they often require extensive documentation to justify a unique expenditure by the agency concerned.

The *sales* phase typically involves the preparation and submission of a competitive bid. The mechanisms by which government bidding is conducted, together with the criteria commonly used in selecting winning bids, were dis-

[11] William Rudelius, "Selling to the Government," in Victor P. Buell (ed.), *Handbook of Modern Marketing*, McGraw-Hill Book Company, New York, 1970, pp. 12-122 to 12-135.

FIGURE 9-5

Principal steps in government buying decisions

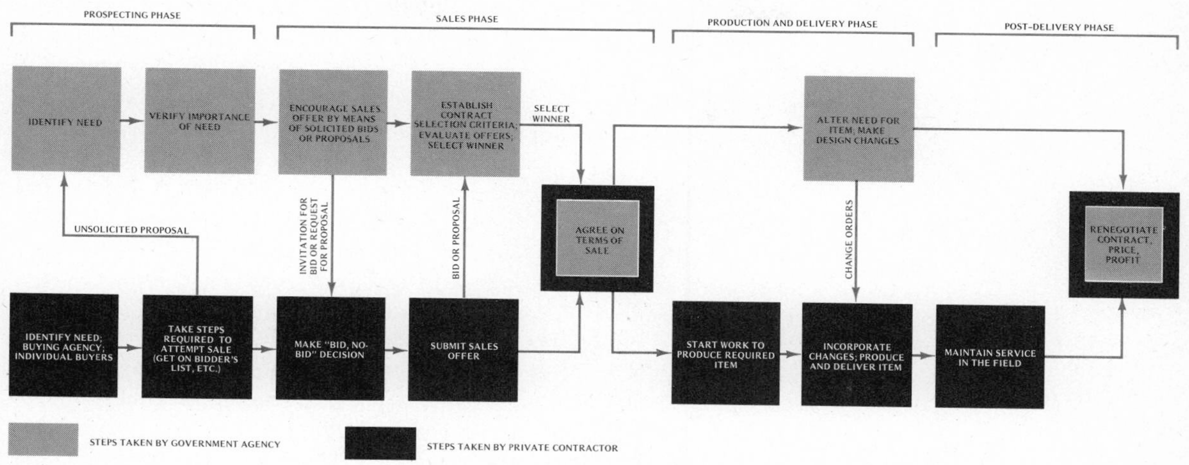

Source: Reproduced with permission from William Rudelius, "Selling to the Government," in Victor P. Buell (ed.), *Handbook of Modern Marketing*, New York, McGraw-Hill Book Company, 1970, p. 12-126.

---

cussed in the previous chapter. Different criteria may be used to judge bids for research and development work, however, and these will be discussed later in this section.

Where complex technological products are involved, the *production and delivery* and *postdelivery* phases frequently involve subsequent renegotiation of an original contract. This is particularly true of contracts for high-technology weapons and defense equipment where contract renegotiation is more often the rule than the exception. As a result of design changes, for example, the first Polaris submarines had to be cut in half to insert the missile silos in them. Contract renegotiation is much less frequent where standardized items, such as Army uniforms, are being purchased.

GOVERNMENT BUYING OF RESEARCH AND DEVELOPMENT SYSTEMS

When the government buys a research and development contract, it is essentially purchasing an approach or technology that does not exist at the time the contract is awarded. By definition, the research and development purchase involves a situation of high uncertainty. As a result, there are several unique aspects to this particular kind of buying decision that merit examination.

Competing for a government research and development contract can be both *complex* and *costly*. Government agencies typically require a seller to demonstrate his understanding of the technical problems involved and his ability to solve them. This sometimes requires a proposal team comprised of hundreds of engineers, scientists, and other specialists. It is estimated that the total expenditure of aerospace firms competing in the TFX aircraft competition in the mid-1960s was $75 million; Boeing (a loser) spent $10 million. Douglas Aircraft submitted a proposal of 60,000 pages in 625 volumes in competition for the C-5 cargo aircraft (and lost).

Since the early 1960s, most government requests for research and development proposals have been governed by the concept of *program budgeting* first introduced by Secretary of Defense McNamara and later extended to other government departments and agencies, Program budgeting forces government agencies to justify their expenditures by defining and substantiating the task or "mission" that an object or system performs. By considering "strategic retaliatory forces" as a single mission, for example, program budgeting forced Air Force B-52 bombers, intercontinental missiles, and Navy Polaris submarines to compete for the same pool of available funds. Program budgeting also requires use of an extended time horizon, usually five years, in substantiating expenditures. As a result, government agencies and departments have increasingly required sellers' research and development proposals to demonstrate their contribution to mission accomplishment, and to do so over a relatively long-term time horizon.

The criteria used in *selecting winning research and development bids* reflect the uncertainty associated with this kind of purchase. The technical content of a proposal, realism of its programming, cost estimates, availability of facilities and qualified personnel, past performance, and management capability are all assessed. Some research and development contracts, such as that for the C-5 aircraft, are let on a "total package procurement" basis in which the contractor must submit a proposal for developing *and* producing required quantities of a commodity.

Most research and development contracts are awarded on a *cost-reimbursement basis*. Instead of bidding a fixed price, the winning contractor is reimbursed for all his costs, even if they exceed original estimates and, in addition, is paid a fee for his services. In a cost-plus-fixed-fee contract, it has been argued that contractors have no incentive for efficiency because the government pays all costs, and the seller's fee is fixed. To combat cost overruns, government agencies in the 1960s shifted increasingly to incentive contracts. Under an incentive contract, the fee earned by a seller is related to his efficiency in factors of cost, delivery, and/or performance.

Research and development contracts are subject to frequent change and *renegotiation* after they are signed. The tragic Apollo fire in 1967, for example, brought about a major restructuring of many of the principal contracts associated with that project.

Summary

This chapter has provided an overview of the complexities of buying behavior in business, institutional, and government markets. In most instances, buying in these markets is an organizational, not an individual, process. Whether in a manufacturing plant or a hospital, the result may be a decision-making unit of substantial size, one whose purchase decision must rationalize the personal and organizational goals of its members.

We have seen that the buyer in any of these diverse markets does not cease to be a human being in his work situation. Performance, economic, and other business-related decision criteria are supplemented and modified by the psychological drives, desires, ambitions, urges, and social position of participants in the decision-making process. Thus, we have found that many concepts and techniques of analysis applicable to household customers are equally useful in understanding the classes of customers identified in this chapter.

Modern marketing, no matter what its situational setting, has the customer as its core and foundation. In this book, we have attempted to stress the importance of the customer by emphasizing differences among the major classes of markets, and by examining the buying decisions of customers within each class thoroughly. At this point, our formal examination of customer behavior ends. As we move forward, however, one would be wise to bear in mind the important concepts and ideas about customers that have been introduced throughout the past seven chapters.

Questions

1. For each of the following situations, attempt to identify the likely membership of the decision-making unit and the probable role of each member at various stages of the purchase decision.
   a. Toy manufacturer purchasing automatic machine tools
   b. Hardware supply distributor buying steel storage racks
   c. Insurance company buying paper clips
   d. Department of the federal government buying paper clips
   e. Major automobile manufacturer purchasing stainless steel sheets
   f. Retail food chain hiring a consultant on inventory control

2. What factors would be important to a taxi company in selecting the make

and model of new taxis being purchased? What factors would influence the cab company's selection of an automobile dealer?

3. A large corporation has decided to replace 200 electric typewriters in its head office.

a. What variables would you consider influential in determining the make or brand of typewriters purchased? Why?

b. Prepare a diagram showing the sources of information likely to affect the purchasing agent of this company in deciding to place the order with a specific typewriter manufacturer. Specify the kinds of information likely to be received from each source.

c. Based on your analysis, identify and list the marketing mix *elements* you think would be most important to a typewriter manufacturer selling to this company. Why do you think each would be important?

4. Compare and contrast the decision criteria likely to be employed by a pickle manufacturer buying salt for pickling brine with those of a housewife buying table salt.

a. What decision criteria might be used by each? Why?

b. Which of the decision criteria used by each do you think would be least important? Most important? Why?

5. In examining peaceful uses for atomic energy, the Atomic Energy Commission discovered a means of treating chemically impregnated wood with gamma rays to produce a new material. WPC (wood-plastic combination), as it was called, had the physical appearance of wood and the durability of steel.

When used as a flooring material, WPC was reputed to maintain a high gloss without waning for as long as 10 to 20 years. It required little maintenance other than sweeping and occasional washing with tap water. Convinced that it had the flooring material of the future, the AEC demonstrated its product to linoleum and tile manufacturers, carpet manufacturers, and hardwood floor producers. None were interested in testing the WPC flooring, nor were they interested in manufacturing or selling it.

a. Why do you think there was so little commercial interest in WPC?

b. How, if at all, might the AEC have obtained a more positive market response for WPC?

6. Science Supplies Inc. was a national distributor of scientific equipment for use in schools. The company's product line consisted of over 50,000 different pieces of scientific equipment and supplies including microscopes, photomicrographic equipment, physics demonstration equipment, and laboratory equipment chemicals and supplies. Virtually all the company's products were purchased from manufacturers for resale, although Science Supplies often packaged or repackaged products in more convenient form.

To reach the market, Science Supplies employed approximately 60 independent sales representatives, each of whom was granted an exclusive territory ranging in size from a large city to three or four states.

Sales representatives sold primarily to the 26,000 school systems in the United States, although a small number of sales were made to scientific equipment and supply dealers for resale. Sales representatives received a 15 percent commission on sales made at list prices and a 5 percent commission when orders were received on competitive bids. Sales representatives received commissions on all orders in their territory whether or not they actually solicited the order.

Science Supplies published an illustrated catalog listing all its products which was circulated to about 75,000 potential buying influences. Historically, the majority of sales had been made at catalog prices. During the 1960s, however, the accelerating movement of population to urban areas and a sharp trend toward school consolidation had resulted in a substantial reduction in the number of autonomous school systems. Accompanying these shifts had been a growing movement to consolidation of purchases within individual school systems and a growing emphasis on competitive price quotations. For example, after World War II, an estimated 20 percent of Science Supplies' sales were made on a competitive bidding basis. By the early 1970s over 75 percent of the company's sales resulted from competitive bids.

While the traditional role of the sales representative had been to obtain orders, in recent years this role had become less clear. Regular customers usually submitted repeat or fill-in orders directly to Science Supplies using order forms included in the catalog. Requests for quotations were usually submitted directly to the company's head office. Precise figures were not maintained, but management estimated that 75 to 85 percent of all orders came directly to the company's head office in this manner.

Because a large portion of its $8 million sales revenue seemed to be obtained on the basis of price and because a large and growing proportion of orders came directly to the company, management wondered whether it would be possible to eliminate the sales representatives entirely. Instead the company would sell only by direct mail through catalogs. Elimination of the sales representative would save $365,000. Even with a considerable increase in catalog distribution and an extensive direct-mail program, total selling costs seemed likely to drop considerably.

a. What specific information does Science Supplies need in order to evaluate the desirability of changing its distribution system?

b. Describe the likely decision-making units for school systems (see Figure 8-5) and indicate the information decision criteria you think each would use.

c. Based on your analysis in (a) or (b), what problems do you think Science

Supplies might encounter if it attempted to eliminate its sales representatives?

7. After studying the recent purchasing decisions of the public works department in a state government, the marketing director of the Dundas Paint Company concluded that the department was apparently following an *array-and-review* purchase strategy, as described earlier in this chapter. The marketing director was hoping to develop an effective program for marketing road paint (for center strips and markings on highways) to the department.

What marketing mix would you recommend as most appropriate for Dundas Paint Company in this situation? Why?

8. National Chemical was a large producer of industrial chemicals, including sulphates used in the manufacture of pulp and paper. Early in 1972, David Thieme, market manager of National's Pulp and Paper Products Division, received a phone call from John Jopson, purchasing agent of Quality Papers Inc., a large paper products manufacturer and one of Thieme's major customers.

In the course of their conversation, Jopson implied strongly to Thieme that Quality would not renew any of its contracts for the purchase of processing chemicals unless National agreed to purchase 35 percent of its paper bag and container requirements for the coming year from Quality Papers.

Thieme was not certain how to react. Quality Paper was a $1.6 million per year account. Moreover, National had considerable excess capacity and the order was expected to produce a 30 percent contribution to fixed costs and profits. On the other hand, National's traditional policy was to avoid reciprocal arrangements. Further, although Quality Paper's products and prices were comparable to those of competitors, its credit terms were not as good as available elsewhere.

What action should Thieme take? Why?

Retail and wholesale distribution

PART THREE

The three chapters in this part deal with the role of retailing and wholesaling institutions in the marketing system. These institutions play an important part in marketing. One indication of their importance is that in the United States, in the mid-1960s, they employed over 14 million persons—over 20 percent of the total civilian labor force. Another measure of their contribution is that 35 to 40 percent of the total value of goods and services produced (gross national product) consists of values created by retail and wholesale businesses. (See Harold Barger, Distribution's Place in the Economy since 1869, National Bureau of Economic Research, Princeton University Press, Princeton, N.J., 1955, p. 92.)

Understanding the nature and operation of the retailing and wholesaling "subsystems" is essential to the manager. Managers of retail and wholesale firms must, of course, deal directly with the problems of their respective stages in the marketing process. Managers of manufacturing firms, too, must often make decisions in which retail and wholesale institutions play a part. Selection of channels of distribution, which in most cases include retail and/or wholesale institutions, is one of the major tasks of marketing management in manufacturing companies. Beyond this, the motives, practices, and problems of distributive institutions affect, and are affected by, manufacturers' product, pricing, advertising, selling, and other marketing policies.

In this section, we shall first look at the overall institutional system of retailing, in terms of the number and types of stores and other retailing institutions through which products are sold to household consumers (Chapter 10). In Chapter 11, we consider how retailing institutions adapt to their environment and how the system evolves through this process of adaptation. The third and last chapter in Part 3 deals with wholesaling institutions and their role in the marketing system.

A note on statistical information

Most of the statistical information regarding retailing and wholesaling in the United States presented in Chapters 10, 11, and 12 is taken from the Census of Business conducted approximately every five years by the Bureau of the Census. Many of the comparative figures given for other countries come from similar government statistical agencies.

Because Census of Business data are so extensively used, a word is in order about the methods employed to collect the data. In the most recent (1967) Census, questionnaires were sent by mail to all retail and wholesale establishments with one or more paid *employees. Half of all establishments with no paid employees were selected from a list compiled from tax returns, and their reports were used to estimate total sales, employment, etc.*

Without doubt, Census data provide the best available information about the operations of retail and wholesale institutions. But these data are not perfect—coverage is not complete. Some establishments are incorrectly classified, and some figures are not properly reported. One example, from William Cox's article "The 'Census' of Business: Some Contrary Evidence" in the Journal of Marketing *(vol. 31, pp. 47–51), will illustrate the limitations of Census data.*

The City of Cleveland maintains a "Real Property Inventory" of all commercial establishments. This inventory showed 9,737 retail establishments in the city in October, 1963, while the *Census of Retail Trade* showed only 7,895—19% fewer—in December, 1963.

The discrepancy between the Census data and those compiled by the city of Cleveland reflects the difficulty (indeed, impossibility) of covering all *establishments in retailing and wholesaling. The Census deliberately excludes those with annual sales of under $2,500 and apparently misses many other small stores. In one sense, this is not very important, because these very small establishments account for only a small fraction of total sales and employment. But, in some cases, the lack of complete coverage may be significant. Some examples are mentioned in Chapter 10.*

It should also be recognized that Census data are based on definitions and classifications which do not always correspond to those used by trade associations and publications. Some terms, such as "supermarket" and "discount store," cannot be defined precisely, and the Census does not use them at all. Others, such as "chain," can be and have been defined in a great variety of ways. All this means that the Census data must be interpreted with care, and for some purposes they are of limited usefulness. We have tried to exercise due caution in our use of these figures in the next three chapters.

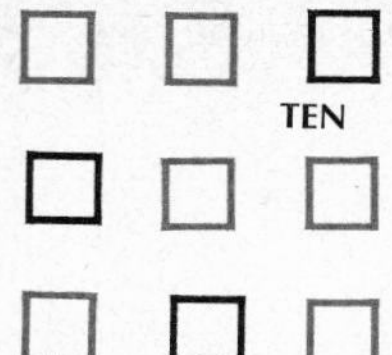

TEN

The retailing system

As we have seen in Chapter 2, the marketing process involves the performance of economic functions at each of several distinct stages, from original producers to ultimate consumers. The final stage of this process is that of *retailing*. This chapter and the next one provide a brief description of the institutional system through which the tasks of retailing are carried out. In this chapter, the major types of institutions and methods of operation in retailing are discussed. Chapter 11 deals with the adjustment of the retailing system to changes in market conditions through competition among institutions and methods. Our discussion deals primarily with the retailing system of the United States, but comparisons with other countries are also included where relevant and possible.

FUNCTIONS OF THE RETAILING SYSTEM

Everyday experience illustrates the great variety which characterizes retailing methods and institutions. A sidewalk vendor of roasted peanuts is a retailer. So is Sears, Roebuck and Company, with sales of $9.3 billion and over 350,000 employees in 1970.

In small villages of India, consumers place orders with merchants who make periodic bicycle trips to the nearest town to obtain the goods. This system, however cumbersome and costly, serves a legitimate economic need. In the vastly different conditions of downtown New York City, the exclusive dress salon also serves a need for its small but wealthy clientele.

Despite their diversity, all the many methods of retailing and types of retailing institutions perform essentially the same basic functions. These functions are most easily understood by considering what would happen if there were no retailing system at all. This would mean that consumers would have to obtain all their products directly from manufacturers, farmers, and other producers. Superficially, this might seem desirable. Indeed, the slogan "buy direct and save the middleman's profit" has always had considerable appeal. But suppose that a present-day consumer in any industrialized economy had to buy everything directly from producers.

First, he would find that most producers are not located nearby. Differences in climate and the economic advantages of large-scale manufacturing lead to a concentration of production in areas far removed from most consumers. Even if a sufficient variety of goods were available locally, the direct-buying consumer would find it necessary to:

Locate sources of supply
Evaluate their offerings and select among them
Obtain information about products and their proper use
Transport merchandise to his home, or arrange for its delivery

All this would obviously require enormous amounts of time, especially since changes in the products, services, and sources of supply available would require continuous revisions. In many cases, the consumer would also find it necessary to arrange for credit and to obtain product-related services such as installation and repairs.

From the consumer's viewpoint, the basic role of the retailing system is to perform the functions suggested above: to locate and evaluate sources of supply, to offer an *assortment* of goods and services at a convenient location, to store merchandise until needed, to provide credit facilities, and to provide product-related services as required. Most of these functions are well summarized in the statement: "The retailer is the consumer's purchasing agent."

From the manufacturer's viewpoint, the functions of the retailing system are essentially the opposite of those performed for consumers. Retailing institutions serve as *outlets* for the manufacturer, and provide him with a means of contacting potential customers and persuading them to buy. Moreover, retailing institutions perform various functions, such as storage, credit arrangements, and product-related services, which most consumers could not undertake themselves. These tasks would otherwise have to be carried out by the manufacturers.

Whatever methods and institutional arrangements are employed, certain basic jobs must be done in the retailing stage of the marketing process. Under certain conditions, some manufacturers and/or consumers can undertake to perform retailing functions themselves. When products are wholly or partly custom-made, it may be necessary for producers to deal directly with consumers. For example, custom tailors, boat builders, and producers of venetian blinds often sell directly to householders. But, as we shall see in a later section of this chapter, efficient performance of retailing functions usually requires the establishment of specialized facilities and specialized management. Regardless of who owns or controls retailing facilities, specialized institutions are almost always required.

RETAILING COSTS AND MARGINS

Retailing institutions buy merchandise from manufacturers and other suppliers and resell to ultimate consumers. The difference between the purchase and resale prices is called *gross margin* or *gross profit.* (In the case of a manufacturer-owned retail outlet, a "transfer price," equivalent to a purchase price, may be used.) Gross margin figures are normally expressed as a percentage of *selling price,* for a specific product, or of *net sales,* for an entire store or a merchandise category. For example, if a retailer purchases an automatic washing machine from the General Electric Company for $160 and resells it for $200, the gross profit is ($40 ÷ $200) or 20 percent. Further details of gross margin calculations are given in the Appendix.

On the average, for all types of retailing institutions and all types of consumer products in the United States, gross margins amount to around 30 percent of retail sales. As shown in Table 10-1, gross margins vary considerably among different lines of business and individual products. The overall figure has, however, been practically constant since around 1900.[1]

From its gross margin, the retail institution must pay *operating expenses.* Some of these are essentially fixed in amount for a given type of operation, while others vary more or less directly with its sales volume. The *net profits* remaining after payment of operating costs are typically small in relation to sales. On the average, net profits for retailers in the United States in the late 1960s amounted to around 2 to 3 percent of sales.

Retail gross margins represent the total "price" to the economy of performing retailing functions. As long as the retailing system is reasonably competitive, the price of retailing will tend to be set at a level equal to its cost, plus a normal rate of return on the capital invested in the system. On the whole, retailing in the United States and Canada has been quite competitive. To be sure, there have been and are instances of excessive profits and of inefficiency. But these cases are exceptions to a general rule of active competition and rapid adoption of new methods. In some other countries, legal restrictions have been

[1] See Harold Barger, *Distribution's Place in the American Economy since 1869,* National Bureau of Economic Research, Princeton University Press, Princeton, N.J., 1955, pp. 57, 60.

□
TABLE 10-1

Number and sales volume of retail stores by kind of business and estimated typical gross margins, United States, 1967

Kind of business	Number of stores (thousands)	Sales (million dollars)	Average sales per store (thousand dollars)	Typical gross margin (percent of sales)
Total: retail stores	1,668	$302,951	$ 181	
Food stores:				
Grocery stores	218	65,073	298	20%
Specialty food stores	76	5,277	69	
Eating and drinking places	348	23,843	69	50
General merchandise stores:				
Department stores	6	32,344	5,390	35
Variety stores	21	5,407	226	36
Apparel and accessory stores:				
Women's apparel and accessories	42	6,288	149	37
Men's and boys' wear	20	3,500	175	35
Shoe stores*	25	3,000	120	36
Furniture, furnishings, appliances:				
Furniture stores	33	6,564	199	40
Household appliances	21	3,014	144	28
Radio, television, and music	23	3,003	130	
Automotive:				
Motor vehicle dealers	62	48,635	784	15
Tire, battery, and accessory	29	4,235	146	
Gasoline service stations	216	22,709	105	25
Lumber, building, and hardware:				
Building materials and supplies	42	9,555	227	31
Hardware stores	27	2,812	104	32
Drug and proprietary stores	54	10,930	202	35
Liquor stores	40	6,662	166	23
Jewelry stores	24	2,207	96	48
Sporting goods and bicycles	16	1,173	73	30

* Estimates by the authors based on Census data for broader kind-of-business categories.

Sources: Establishments and sales data from 1967 Census of Business; not all individual lines of business are shown here. Estimates of typical gross margins based on various trade associations and financial reporting services, as compiled in *Expenses in Retail Businesses*, National Cash Register Company, Merchants' Service, Dayton, Ohio.

more extensively used to limit changes, with the result that retail gross margins have sometimes been maintained at artificially high levels.

Basic methods of operation

The most familiar and by far most important method of operation in retailing is the retail store. But there are at least three other basically different ways of selling goods at the retail level: house-to-house sales, mail-order and telephone sales, and machine vending. These nonstore retailing methods are discussed briefly in this section, while the rest of the chapter deals primarily with retail stores.

□ HOUSE-TO-HOUSE RETAILING

The house-to-house salesman is a familiar figure in history and folklore in the United States.

> It was scarcely possible to step out along a traveled highway from spring to fall in the first half of the last [nineteenth] century without running into a man carrying a tin trunk, or perhaps a pack wrapped in black oilcloth. . . . This was the Yankee peddler, so called. . . . The peddler had a knack of seeming to be everywhere, and always at the right time.[2]

In nineteenth century America, the traveling peddler played a far more important role than he does in a modern industrial society. However, his role in underdeveloped nations is still important today, and even in present-day America, house-to-house selling is still an important form of retailing. In 1967, the United States Census of Business indicated that 78,000 "direct selling" retail establishments accounted for sales of $2.5 billion—around $^{8}/_{10}$ of 1 percent of total retail sales. (The category "direct selling" includes retailers selling via in-home "party plans," and truck vendors as well as door-to-door salesmen.)

Census data do not indicate the true magnitude of house-to-house selling as a retailing method, because they do not include direct sales by manufacturers and other processors, or by salesmen from retail stores. In the mid-1960s, for example, dairies made approximately 30 percent of their total milk sales via house-to-house ("retail") routes.[3] Other products and services frequently sold by this method include baked goods, books and magazines, housewares, and insurance.[4]

[2] Gerald Carson, *The Old Country Store,* Oxford University Press, New York, 1954, p. 37.

[3] *Organization and Competition in the Dairy Industry,* Technical Study no. 3, National Commission on Food Marketing, Government Printing Office, Washington, 1966, p. 156.

[4] In many cases, house-to-house salesmen handling a manufacturer's line, such as Fuller household supplies and Avon cosmetics, are actually independent merchants who buy and resell their goods. Each such salesperson, with annual sales over $2,500, is counted as an "establishment" by the Census Bureau.

House-to-house selling is usually more expensive than distribution through retail stores, because of the high costs of personal sales calls and the typically small average value of at-home transactions. For example, studies by the National Commission on Food Marketing indicated that in 1965, total retail distribution costs for milk were 2.5 to 4 cents higher per half-gallon on home routes than on sales through food stores. As a result, average prices for home-delivered milk were around 10 percent higher than for milk purchased in food stores.[5] Door-to-door salesmen are almost always compensated by a commission on sales, and the commission percentage must be substantial to offset the high frequency of unsuccessful calls and the small size of the average sale.

□

ADVANTAGES OF HOUSE-TO-HOUSE RETAILING

If house-to-house retailing is so costly, why do manufacturers ever use this method? Perishable products—milk, bread, produce—have traditionally been distributed to the home to ensure freshness. When ownership of refrigeration facilities and of automobiles is limited, this system of distribution serves a basic need.

Nonperishable products may be sold door-to-door either because the manufacturer cannot obtain adequate distribution through stores, or as a means of providing specialized and intensive sales effort at the consumer level. This kind of selling is especially valuable for relatively new, complex, and expensive products, and for products which can best be demonstrated in the home. In the early twentieth century, the vacuum cleaner qualified by all these tests as an "ideal" house-to-house product. The success of the Hoover Company, both in the United States and elsewhere, was founded in part on H. W. Hoover's pioneering use of door-to-door selling. Singer sewing machines also were, and, in some countries, still are sold in the home. Even in the late 1950s, it was estimated that in France 50 percent of all automobiles were sold by salesmen calling at customers' homes.

As a product becomes more familiar, the need for specialized selling diminishes. More generally, the greater mobility of consumers and the feasibility of intensive promotion via advertising, especially through television, have reduced the relative advantage of house-to-house selling for introducing new products. These changes are reflected in the history of the Hoover Company. In the 1950s, Hoover discontinued door-to-door sales in the United States, and in 1964, Hoover Ltd. (U.K.) abandoned the method in Great Britain. According to *Fortune* magazine, Hoover improved its profits "by abandoning the expensive and no longer competitive door-to-door sales force in favor of a regular net of dealers."[6]

House-to-house retailing is not *always* more expensive than store distribu-

[5] *Organization and Competition in the Dairy Industry, op. cit.*, pp. 158, 200–201.
[6] *Fortune*, June, 1964, p. 146.

tion. One of the most successful companies using this method is Avon Products, Inc., with 1969 sales of $657 million. According to one published account, Avon cosmetics were sold by some 200,000 independent representatives, who received a 40 percent margin on sales. With the promotional support provided by these women, Avon spent much less on advertising than the 15 to 20 percent of sales typical of major cosmetic producers. Since retail store margins on cosmetics were 35 to 50 percent, Avon's total marketing cost apparently compared favorably with that of firms distributing through conventional channels.

House-to-house selling has been widely criticized, for several reasons. Many people feel that it is an invasion of privacy. At the same time, conventional retailers have often initiated attempts to restrict door-to-door sales, which represent one form of competition for their stores. In the United States, many cities and towns have followed the early (1933) example of Green River, Wyoming, in prohibiting at-home selling except with the prior consent of the customer. Similar laws have been enacted in other countries, for instance, in Paris.

Criticism of house-to-house selling has also arisen because of the prevalence of misrepresentation. Some unscrupulous persons sell appliances and other "big ticket" items to poorly educated, low-income consumers on an installment basis, charging excessive prices and rates of "interest" for inferior products. This kind of swindling also occurs in stores, of course, but the opportunity for high-pressure tactics seems especially great in the home, and it is difficult to provide effective legal protection against it.

□

MAIL-ORDER AND TELEPHONE SELLING

In 1967, Census figures showed 5,948 establishments in the United States primarily engaged in mail-order retailing, with sales of $3.1 billion—about 1 percent of total retail sales. As in the case of house-to-house sales, these figures do not tell the whole story. Some manufacturers sell directly via mail order, and many conventional retail stores make a portion of their sales in this way.

History Mail-order retailing first developed in the United States in the late nineteenth century. At that time, residents of small towns and of rural areas bought at rural general stores and other small, unspecialized establishments. These stores did not offer wide assortments of merchandise, and their margins and prices were high. They were not well equipped to handle the rapidly increasing quantity and variety of manufacturing output. Mail-order houses, taking advantage of the expanding railroad system and, later, the new government parcel post service, offered a better selection of goods at lower prices. Thus, the mail-order catalog became a nearly universal possession (and the subject of a thousand jokes) in rural America.

During the twentieth century, mail-order retailing came to be dominated by a few very large firms. Sears, Roebuck was the largest retailer in the world in 1969 with sales of nearly $9 billion, while Montgomery Ward was the sixth largest in the United States with sales of $2.2 billion. Both of these companies were originally exclusively mail-order sellers. But by the 1960s, both derived the majority of their revenues from chains of retail stores.

A traditional system of mail-order retailing is to distribute catalogs to prospective customers, to receive orders and payments, and to deliver merchandise, all by mail. The major American firms have supplemented this system in recent years by establishing catalog order offices, as departments within regular stores or as separate establishments, especially in suburban shopping areas. Customers usually place orders, make payments, and accept delivery of merchandise via some combination of telephone communication and personal visits to catalog order offices. This system offers convenience to the consumer primarily in terms of avoiding traffic congestion, and thus serves a very different purpose than did the original mail-only method. In the 1960s, Sears and Ward obtained considerably more business through their "nonmail-mail-order" offices and desks than they did via traditional mail orders.

Present-day use The costs of producing and distributing catalogs and of developing and maintaining mailing lists are very great for mail-order retailers. In the mid-1960s, for example, the average cost of Montgomery Ward's large general catalog was around $2. For a customer receiving all catalogs issued in a year—two general "books" and various smaller seasonal and special catalogs—the total cost might amount to $7 to $8. Since Ward's customer list included some 6 million names, the total costs were very substantial. To make this expenditure profitable, the mail-order firms attempt to restrict distribution of catalogs to customers who "qualify" in terms of past purchases and/or other characteristics thought to be indicative of future purchases.

Partly because of the high cost of catalogs and mailing lists, some firms use other methods to contact customers. As mentioned in Chapter 7, Schwab, a major German mail-order seller, uses a network of housewives as part-time agents. Each agent has a catalog which she shows to neighbors and friends. Orders, payments, and deliveries are all made through the agents. This system is similar to the "club plan" operations of several firms in the United States, and is, in effect, a hybrid of mail-order and house-to-house retailing.

In Western Europe, mail-order retailing grew rapidly in the 1950s and 1960s. According to trade estimates, by 1965 mail-order sales represented 5 percent of total retail sales in Germany and 4 percent in Great Britain. In France, less than 1 percent of all retail sales were made by mail in 1965, but mail-order volume had increased by an estimated 80 percent since 1960.

There are no reliable statistics available on the magnitude of telephone selling. Few, if any, establishments specialize in this method of retailing. But many retail stores sell in part by telephone, and in some cases the sales volume involved is substantial. One study of department stores in metropolitan areas indicated that telephone sales represented 4 percent of the stores' total sales. For many women, especially those with small children at home or without access to automobiles, this method of buying is a real convenience.[7]

AUTOMATIC VENDING

To some, vending through machines represents the "automation" of retailing, equivalent to mechanical and electronic control of manufacturing operations. Over the years, many inventors have sought to develop and improve mechanical devices for selling goods. According to the Greek mathematician Hero, a coin-operated device was used for dispensing sacrificial water in Egyptian temples as early as 200 B.C.[8] Not until the 1890s, however, did large-scale automatic vending become practical. Since that time it has become an important method of retailing, at least for a limited range of products.

By 1967, sales of establishments classified in the Census as "merchandising machine operators" reached $2 billion. Total merchandise sales through vending machines, many of which were operated as sidelines by other types of businesses, were estimated to be as much as $5.5 billion in 1969.[9]

Traditionally, automatic vending has been confined to sales of standardized, low-priced products such as candy, cigarettes, and soft drinks. In the late 1960s, these products still accounted for around three-fourths of total vending machine sales. But the vending method was also being extended to other types of merchandise: prepared foods, especially for large-scale feeding in factories and offices, accounted for an estimated 6 percent of total vending machine sales. The development of practical devices for accepting or changing paper money has opened up the possibility of automatic vending of more expensive items. Still another recent application for vending machines is that of after-hours selling for emergency needs, in conjunction with regular retail stores. For example, some food stores offer milk, bread, and similar items, through machines, on a 24-hour basis.

Although many improvements have been introduced to make automatic vending more widely applicable, it is still an inherently limited method of retailing. Operating costs tend to be high, because of the need for machine servicing and repairs and the frequency of accidental damage and vandalism. Machine vending, at least in its present form, does not really eliminate much

[7] See Stuart U. Rich, *Shopping Behavior of Department Store Customers,* Division of Research, Harvard Business School, Boston, 1963.

[8] Cited by G. R. Schreiber, "A Concise History of Vending in the U.S.A.," *Vend Magazine, Chicago,* 1961.

[9] "Census of the Industry: 1970," *Vend Magazine,* May 1, 1970. This does *not* include receipts of coin-operated record players, amusement devices, etc.

labor. Rather, it substitutes machine servicing for personal selling and other store labor. In most cases, this substitution has not resulted in any net reduction in total costs.

Merchandise lines

One of the most important characteristics of any retail outlet is the kind of merchandise which it carries. Retailers compete in terms of selling specific products or groups of products, and selection of merchandise lines is a fundamental aspect of a retailer's strategy. From the standpoint of the consumer, shopping decisions are made primarily in relation to specific product needs, although these needs may not be fully determined prior to entering a store. The manufacturer, too, is principally interested in patterns of retail distribution for his products.

□ KIND-OF-BUSINESS CLASSIFICATIONS

In the Census of Business and other published sources of information, retail establishments are classified by "kind of business." A summary of statistical data for retail stores in the United States, for selected kind-of-business groupings, was given in Table 10-1. These data are taken from the most recent Census of Retail Trade, conducted in 1967.

The figures in Table 10-1 reflect the vast differences among different lines of trade in number of stores, average size, and gross margins. Note, for instance, the contrast between "Eating and drinking places" and "Department stores." There were 348,000 establishments in the former group, with average sales of only $69,000 per establishment; but only 6,000 department stores, with average sales of over $5 million. Again, passenger car dealers operated with an average gross margin of only 15 percent of sales, while furniture stores typically had a margin of 40 percent.

These variations in numbers, size, and gross margins reflect basic differences in the *functions performed* by retail stores in the various lines of business, and they have important implications for manufacturers and consumers as well as for the retailers themselves. For example, a manufacturer selling to restaurants must somehow make contact with, and distribute to, a large number of small widely scattered outlets. Department stores, on the other hand, are few in number, large, and relatively concentrated.

The extent of the merchandise lines carried by different types of retail stores varies from extremely broad assortments of goods, for example, department stores, down to very narrow, highly specialized product categories such as shoe stores. In this connection, the term "merchandise line" must be defined specifically.□

□ *A line consists of a set of products, related in manufacture, in methods of storage, display, and sale, and/or in use, which are customarily stocked and sold by the same outlets.*

For instance, "men's apparel" is a line which customarily includes suits, coats, hats, sportswear, and furnishings. A store handling all these items, and not handling significant amounts of other products, is called a *single-line* apparel store. A store carrying only part of such a line, say only men's hats, is a "specialty" apparel store. The opposite extreme is represented in Table 10-1 by the *general merchandise* stores which carry several distinct and unrelated lines: men's apparel, women's apparel, furniture, appliances, and other lines.

General merchandise stores, while relatively few in number, are of considerable importance from a competitive standpoint. Two types of stores within this classification are of special interest.

Department stores are stores carrying several different lines, usually including women's apparel, piece goods, men's and boys' apparel, and home furnishings, and organized into several departments which are separate organizational units in terms of accounting, control, and merchandising. The Bureau of the Census further restricts the term to establishments employing 25 or more persons. (The history and competitive position of the department store are discussed in Chapter 11.)

Variety stores handle many different types of goods, usually concentrating on low-priced items and selling almost entirely on a self-service basis.

As shown in Table 10-1, these two types of stores accounted for almost $38 billion, or more than 12 percent of total retail store sales in 1963.

MARKETING USE OF KIND-OF-BUSINESS CLASSIFICATIONS

The distinctions and boundaries among various kinds of retail stores have a very practical significance to manufacturers and wholesalers who deal with them, and to consumers. First, while the exact boundaries have never been well defined, the customary "kind-of-business" groupings do reflect the result of a long process of trial and error in determining what kinds of merchandise combinations can effectively be sold together in terms of consumer convenience, common sources of supply, common merchandising requirements, similar storage, handling, and display characteristics, and (to some extent) specialization in merchandising and servicing skills. Second, because the groupings are customary, they serve as useful indicators of the expectations of both consumers and retailers. Consumers tend to associate specific products with certain types of stores where they would expect to find such products. Similarly, retailers in a given line tend to think of themselves as a group; as such, they form trade associations, exchange operating information, and sometimes band together to combat what they regard as unfair competition from "outsiders." Thus, for example, in several states retail druggists have supported proposed legislation which would prohibit the sale of drugs, even such "proprietary" items as cough remedies, by any store which does not have a registered pharmacist on duty at all times. These efforts are aimed largely at food supermarkets which have become important outlets for drug products in recent years.

Finally, the kind-of-business classification of retail stores is relevant in that the combination of goods handled by a store may affect the store's value as an outlet for an individual product or product grouping. Stores carrying a wide range of merchandise usually cannot, for that very reason, stock numerous brands, models, sizes, etc., of any one item. Consequently, if it is important that a manufacturer's line be represented at the retail level by adequate stocks of all models, sizes, and other variations, specialty stores may be more effective channels than single-line stores or general merchandise outlets. Stores carrying a wide range of merchandise are also seldom able to provide intensive selling effort or specialized product services for any one item.

□

OVERLAPS IN MERCHANDISE LINES

The classifications used in Table 10-1 are based on the primary merchandise lines handled by each store. Thus, a store selling both drugs and liquor is classified as a drugstore as long as "drugs" represents over half the total sales volume. This implies, obviously, that "sales of drugstores" is not equivalent to "retail sales of drug products." Not only do drugstore sales include other product lines, but some sales of drugs are made by stores in other kinds of business, such as variety stores, grocery stores, and department stores.

The diversity of products sold by stores in a kind-of-business group is illustrated in Figure 10-1. This chart shows the composition of total sales reported by stores classified as "drugstores" in the 1967 census. While approximately 70 percent of these stores' sales might be regarded as falling within the ambiguous category of "drugs," drugstores also sold substantial amounts of tobacco products, meals, alcoholic beverages, and other products.

The other side of the coin is illustrated in Figure 10-2, which shows the reported breakdown of total retail sales of automobile tires, batteries, and accessories by stores in different kind-of-business groupings. Tire, battery, and accessory stores specializing in these products accounted for less than 30 percent of the total sales by all types of outlets.

Not only do the merchandise lines of different store classes overlap, but the relative importance of different classes is subject to change. The hardware store serves as a good example. Sales of stores in this group increased by only 8 percent between 1948 and 1960, compared with 68 percent for retail trade as a whole. During approximately the same period, hardware stores' average return on investment declined by half. According to one observer, this erosion was due primarily to increased competition from food supermarkets, drugstores, automotive supply stores, and other "outside" competition.[10]

[10] Clarence E. Vincent, "The Retail Hardware Decline," *Journal of Marketing,* vol. 28 (January, 1964), pp. 26–29.

FIGURE 10-1

Sales of drugstores: percent distribution by merchandise lines, United States, 1967

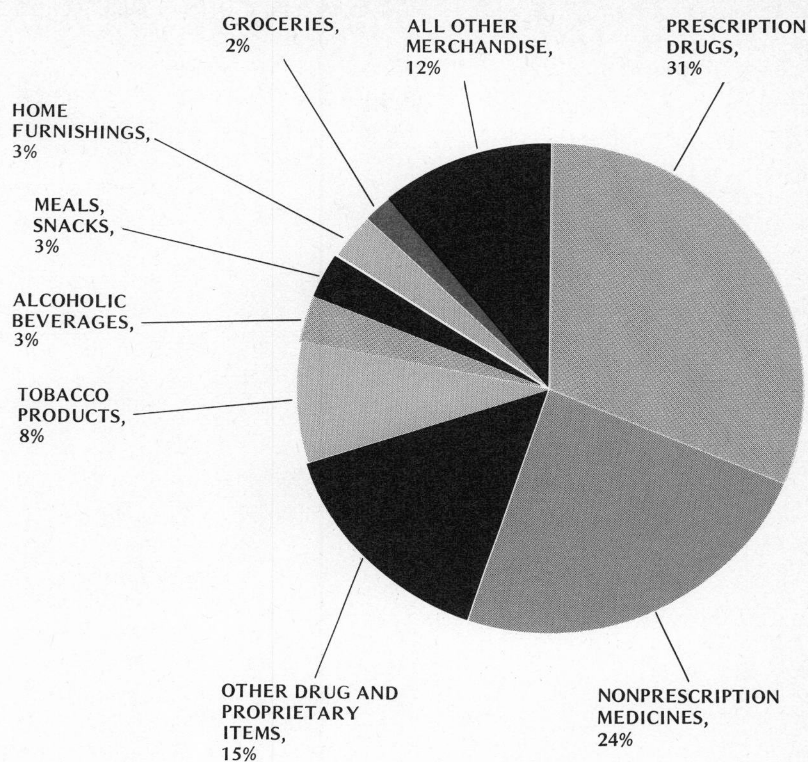

Source: U.S. Bureau of the Census, Census of Business, 1967, *Retail Trade:* Merchandise Line Sales, United States, BC67-MLS-1, Government Printing Office, Washington, 1970, p. 1-12.

□

MERCHANDISE LINE DECISIONS

To some extent, decisions on basic merchandise lines to be carried by a wholesale or retail enterprise are predetermined by the character of the enterprise. Thus, for example, drugstores are expected to carry prescription drugs and proprietaries; grocery stores must carry bread and milk. At the periphery of a given merchandise line, however, the decisions are not so clear cut. Should a drugstore carry cosmetics? Toys? Stationery? In many trades, such decisions as these have been greatly complicated in recent years by the tendency toward "scrambled merchandising," which has in some cases led to a virtual breakdown of traditional boundaries between lines.

It is not possible to give general answers to questions such as those posed in the preceding paragraph. A retail outlet's ability to carry a given merchandise line profitably depends on many factors peculiar to its individual situation.

FIGURE 10-2

Sales of automobile tires, batteries, and accessories of different types of retail outlets—United States, 1967

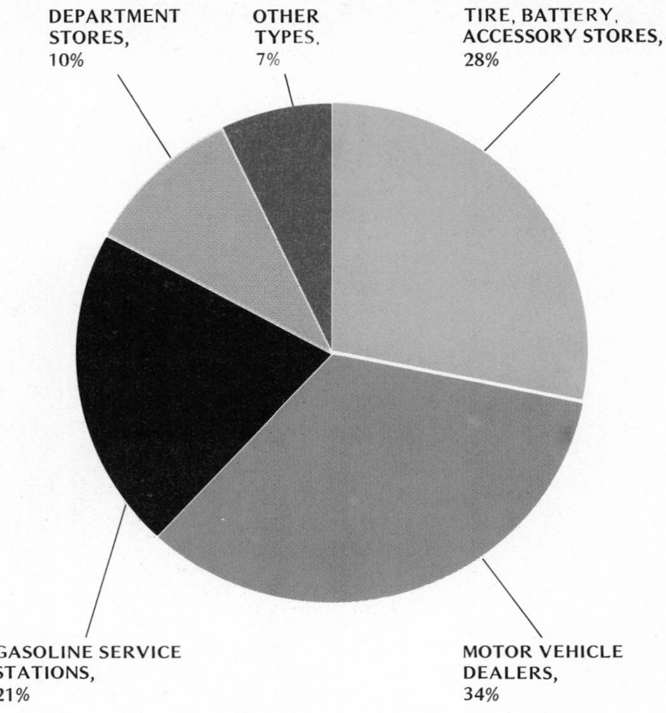

Source: U.S. Bureau of the Census, Census of Business, 1967, Retail Trade: Merchandise Line Sales, United States, BC67-MLS-1, Government Printing Office, Washington, 1970.

These include the nature and extent of competition in each line; the availability of capital, floor space, and other facilities; and management capabilities. In the final analysis, the most important consideration is the pattern of customer purchasing behavior for the merchandise lines in question. Some products are naturally related in use (gasoline and oil, shirts and ties, pipe and valves), while others are so clearly unrelated as to be incompatible (automobiles and fresh produce, fine paper and coal). In the "undistributed middle" between these extremes, no hard-and-fast rules can be made.

□

BRANDS AND TYPES OF MERCHANDISE

Within each of the lines carried, retailers must determine the specific brands, models, sizes, and other varieties to be included. These decisions are essentially predetermined for concerns participating in franchise programs or exclusive agency arrangements, since such agreements usually, explicitly or in effect, limit the number of brands and specify minimum standards regarding the models, sizes, etc., of the manufacturer's line that must be stocked and promoted. In the absence of contractual commitments, the merchant is free to set his own policies on merchandise assortments, and competing manufacturers or distributors attempt to influence him by means of promotional activities.

The basic criterion for handling a specific brand or type of merchandise is, of course, profitability. Ideally, managers of retail outlets seek to judge merchandise offerings on the basis of their impact on net profits, both in the short run and in the long run. As more items are added to the outlets' assortment, their "drawing power" to customers increases. Costs also increase with greater product variety, however, since investments must be made in inventory, purchasing and control functions must be performed, and so on. Thus, it seems plausible that increasing the number of brands and types will increase total profit up to a point, beyond which the added costs will outweigh the gains.

In the absence of accurate net profit information for specific merchandise items, retail concerns often use indirect measures which are thought to reflect net profits, more or less. Because floor space, or shelf space, is usually the scarcest resource in a retail store, it is customary for retailers to judge merchandise items on the basis of sales per square foot, or linear foot, of space or gross margin per unit of space, per unit of time. For example, "space productivity" ratios for several types of products carried in food stores were determined in a recent study, as shown in Table 10-2. These figures are based on the experience of just one major food chain, but they illustrate the variation among different products that is characteristic of retailing in general.

□

TABLE 10-2

An illustration of "space productivity" figures: gross margin per foot of shelf space per week, food store product lines

Product	Gross margin per shelf foot per week
Baby foods	$0.32
Cigarettes	1.16
Paper products	1.25
Soft drinks, beer	2.90
Health and beauty aids	2.19
Magazines	0.34

Source: "The Dillon Study," *Progressive Grocer*, November, 1960, p. D-102.

Another indicator of profitability for product lines or items commonly used by retail concerns is *inventory turnover.* The importance of turnover rests on the fact that capital for investment in inventory is usually almost as scarce as space. Assuming that gross margins and expenses for various items are about the same, sales per square foot and sales per dollar of inventory investment jointly reflect return on investment, and thus provide a good basis for judging products. To the extent that margins and expenses differ, however, these criteria are rather imperfect measures. A more sophisticated approach to measuring item profitability is the *merchandise management accounting* system developed for department stores.[11]

Under this system, operating expenses are classified into two groups: those which are fixed with respect to the stocking of a particular merchandise item and those which are directly affected by carrying that item. Standard cost allocations are developed, either in terms of dollars or as percentages, for various categories of items, since the number of items carried by a large store is so great as to prohibit the allocation of costs literally to individual items. Each item can then be evaluated in terms of its *controllable item profit,* that is, the difference between gross margin and item variable costs. This approach reflects both space requirement and inventory turnover, since these factors enter into item variable costs.

An approach similar to merchandise management accounting has been developed for food stores, and experimental applications indicate that use of the approach can improve the stores' overall profits.[12] But systems for estimating profitability of individual products were not yet widely used in retailing in the late 1960s. The main obstacle was the difficulty and cost of obtaining the required information on a regular basis.

Even if very precise accounting systems were available, wholesalers and retailers should not judge items in their lines solely on the basis of net profit in a given time period. First, this criterion is not a fair one for new items. It may take considerable time for new products to attain a satisfactory level of sales, while in the long run they may well be desirable additions. Second, decisions to accept or reject a given item have some impact on sales and profits of other items, since breadth of assortment in itself tends to attract customers. Some well-known and heavily advertised items are, in fact, widely believed to be unprofitable by the retail concerns selling them. They are regarded as essential items in spite of this, because customers expect to be able to buy certain products, and failure to stock them might result in losing some customers' business altogether.

[11] Malcolm P. McNair and Eleanor G. May, "A Practical Approach to Merchandise Management Accounting," *Stores,* May, 1958, pp. 29–50.

[12] Robert D. Buzzell, Walter J. Salmon, and Richard F. Vancil, *Product Profitability Measurement and Merchandising Decisions,* Harvard Business School Division of Research, Boston, 1965.

It should be clear from the preceding discussion that the evaluation of specific merchandise items by channel outlets is a very complex problem, going far beyond the direct profitability of an item. To illustrate how the various factors involved are considered and weighed, consider the procedure followed by buying committees in retail grocery chains. These committees represent a much more formal mechanism for evaluating products than that used by most wholesale and retail concerns. The need for a systematic procedure is imposed by the great number of new products developed annually in the grocery field. Among the factors considered by a buying committee are the following[13]:

1. Product characteristics, especially "newness"
2. Packaging: size, shape, and appearance
3. Advertising devoted to the product
4. Merchandising support: displays, demonstrations
5. Anticipated profit based on markup, estimated costs, allowances, free goods, sales volume, etc.

In a sense, all these factors are relevant only insofar as they affect anticipated long-run profit. It seems clear, however, that buying committees do not operate by formula, and that other factors often override explicit cost and profit estimates.

Ownership of retailing facilities

As explained earlier, retailing institutions serve as connecting links between producers and household consumers. Although there is a clear economic case for the existence of specialized retailing facilities, there is no *prima facie* reason why these facilities cannot be owned by either producers or consumers. Manufacturer-owned stores and consumer-owned "cooperatives" are examined briefly in this section.

□ MANUFACTURERS' STORES

Stores owned by manufacturers account for less than 2 percent of total retail sales. The reason for this lies in what the late Wroe Alderson termed the "discrepancy of assortments."[14] He points out that the most convenient assortment of goods at one stage in the production-to-consumption sequence is not usually the most convenient at another stage. Thus, an assortment of goods may be manufactured by the same enterprise because of common raw materi-

[13] Adapted from Donald G. Hileman and Leonard A. Rosenstein, "Deliberation of a Chain Grocery Buying Committee," *Journal of Marketing,* National Quarterly Publication of the American Marketing Association, vol. 25 (January, 1961), pp. 52–55.

[14] Wroe Alderson, "The Development of Marketing Channels," in Richard M. Clewett (ed.), *Marketing Channels,* Richard D. Irwin, Inc., Homewood, Ill., 1954, pp. 11–12.

als or processing facilities, while at the consumer level an entirely different assortment is appropriate because of common end uses or purchasing patterns. Tires are sold in the same outlets as gasoline because these products are related in use; but industrial lubricants (produced by oil refineries) are sold through entirely different channels because they are used by a separate group of consumers. Since few manufacturers produce a line of products that corresponds with consumers' desired assortments, few are able to operate their own retail outlets.

Manufacturer-owned stores are of some importance in certain industries. In the United States, some major producers of men's clothing, shoes, tires, sewing machines, and candy operate chains of stores. A distinction should be made between these fully owned stores and others which appear to be manufacturer-owned but are actually independent merchants franchised by suppliers. The most familiar example of this latter type is the gasoline service station handling the products of a major oil company. (The development of retail franchising is discussed in Chapter 11.)

□ CONSUMER COOPERATIVES

Consumer cooperatives are stores owned by groups of consumers and operated on a nonprofit basis. In a cooperative, any excess of income over costs not needed for investment in the business is returned to the members as a "patronage dividend" proportional to each member's purchases.

In some countries, especially in Scandinavia, consumer cooperatives are important elements of the retailing system. But in the United States, they have never attained any real significance despite numerous attempts to encourage their formation. Cooperative feed and farm supply enterprises, which are not really retail businesses, are of considerable importance.

The limited role of consumer cooperatives in the United States is apparently due primarily to the dynamic and competitive nature of the retailing system in this country. As explained in the next chapter, chains, supermarkets, and other "mass distributors" have had considerable freedom to introduce new methods of operation, with resulting improvements in efficiency. Elsewhere, the inability or unwillingness of retailers to compete in this way has been a major stimulus to consumers to develop their own stores.

Store size

Retail stores in a given line of business differ from one another in many ways; one of the most significant is that of store size. It is obvious that a very small store, operated usually by its owner with no employees, is a very different sort of enterprise from a huge downtown department store with sales of $100 million or more and hundreds of employees. Nor are the differences confined to size per se. Methods of operation, cost structure, and competitive strengths vary along with size. Consequently, small and large stores tend to have characteristically different management problems. From the viewpoint of the manufacturer, there are also distinctions in the problems of dealing with large versus small outlets.

There are two aspects of "size" in retailing: the size of an individual *establishment,* and the size of a *company,* which may operate many establishments. This section deals with store size; company size is discussed in Chapter 11.

□ PREDOMINANCE OF SMALL STORES

Retailing is, and always has been, predominantly a field of small-scale businesses. As shown in Table 10-1, the average sales volume per store in the United States in 1967 was only $181,000. Another indication of size is that the average number of employees per store, including owner-proprietors, was just over six; about a third of all stores had no employees at all.

There are marked differences in average store size, and in the relative importance of large versus small outlets, among the various kind-of-business classifications. Figure 10-3 gives a distribution of stores by sales size groups, for several lines of trade. The contrasts between such groups as department stores and drugstores are striking. Over 90 percent of all department stores had sales of $1 million or more, compared with around 2 percent for all drugstores. Although it is accurate to say that retail trade in general is dominated by small stores, there are certainly exceptions, such as department stores and passenger car dealers.

Many stores are so small that they provide only subsistence level incomes for their owners. To illustrate, consider a store with annual sales of $25,000. Depending on the kind of business, such a store might have an annual gross margin of $7,500 to $10,000. After payment of rent and other operating expenses, and after allowance for some minimal return on the owner's invested capital, the net income left to him would probably be $3,000 to $4,000 – not far above the "poverty" level as defined by governmental agencies in the late 1960s. These figures are only rough approximations, but they give a realistic picture of the marginal character of many stores – and not just the extreme cases, since about 30 percent of all stores in the United States had sales of less than $25,000 in 1967. In other countries, especially the underdeveloped nations, retail stores are typically even smaller.

How can such small stores survive? In many cases, they are part-time enterprises. Housewives operating gift shops, retired men indulging their hobbies, and many others engaged in retailing as a sideline. But most small stores are simply unsuccessful. Every year, numerous stores are closed. Many of these are outright failures. The high rate of discontinuance among retailers is

FIGURE 10-3
Percent distribution of retail stores by sales size, United States, 1967

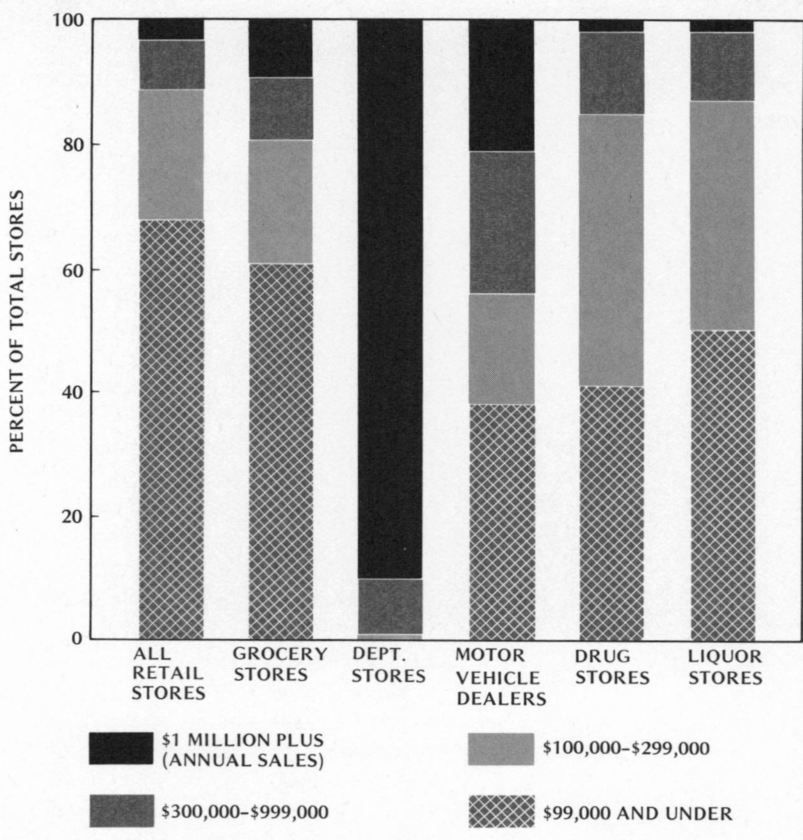

Source: U.S. Bureau of the Census, Census of Business, 1967, *Retail Trade: Sales Size*, BC67-R52, Government Printing Office, Washington, 1971.

offset, however, by an approximately equal rate of new entries. As a result, the number of retail stores has changed very little over the period 1929–1967.

□

TREND TO LARGER STORES

Although the typical retail store is still quite small, the average size has increased considerably since 1929. Average sales per establishment for the various Census of Business years are shown in Table 10-3. These figures reveal a sharp upward trend in average store size. After allowance for price changes, the average sales per store in 1967 was 2.7 times as great as in 1929. During the depression, average store size declined, as many unemployed persons

TABLE 10-3

*Average sales per establishment retail trade, 1929–1967**

Year	Average sales per establishment	
	In current dollars	In 1967 dollars
1929	$ 32,400	$ 67,500
1939	23,500	60,000
1948	77,200	98,000
1958	111,600	126,000
1967	181,000	181,000

* Figures include nonstore establishments as well as stores. Sales adjusted to equivalents at 1967 price levels by means of the Index of Retail Prices compiled by the U.S. Department of Commerce.

Source: U.S. Bureau of the Census, Census of Business, *Retail Trade: United States Summary*, BC 67-RA1, Government Printing Office, Washington, 1970.

were attracted to the field. But since 1939, the average has climbed steadily.

Large stores are still relatively few in number, but in most lines of business they account for a substantial proportion of total sales, as shown in Figure 10-4. These figures, together with those in Figure 10-3, reveal the concentration of business among the larger stores. Overall, stores with sales of $1 million or more, representing slightly over 3 percent of all stores in number, account for 44 percent of total sales.

The importance of large stores, in terms of sales relative to numbers, accounts in large part for the so-called "pork-chop" distribution of an individual manufacturer's or wholesaler's sales. Most companies that sell to retailers find that a small proportion of all stores account for a very great proportion of total sales. In most cases, this simply reflects the skewed overall distribution of sales among stores. (Depending on a particular manufacturer's policies, his distribution may be more or less skewed than the average.)

ECONOMIES OF SCALE IN RETAILING

One reason for the trend toward larger stores is that there are some economies of scale in most kinds of retailing. These economies result in lower "average unit costs" for large stores, and enable them to sell at lower prices and/or earn higher net profits than small stores.

Cost advantages related to store size, as distinct from company size, are far less significant in retailing than in most manufacturing industries. This is true primarily because there are fewer opportunities for mechanization in the performance of retailing functions. Nevertheless, the large store typically has some cost advantages:

FIGURE 10-4

Percent distribution of total retail store sales, by size of store, United States, 1967

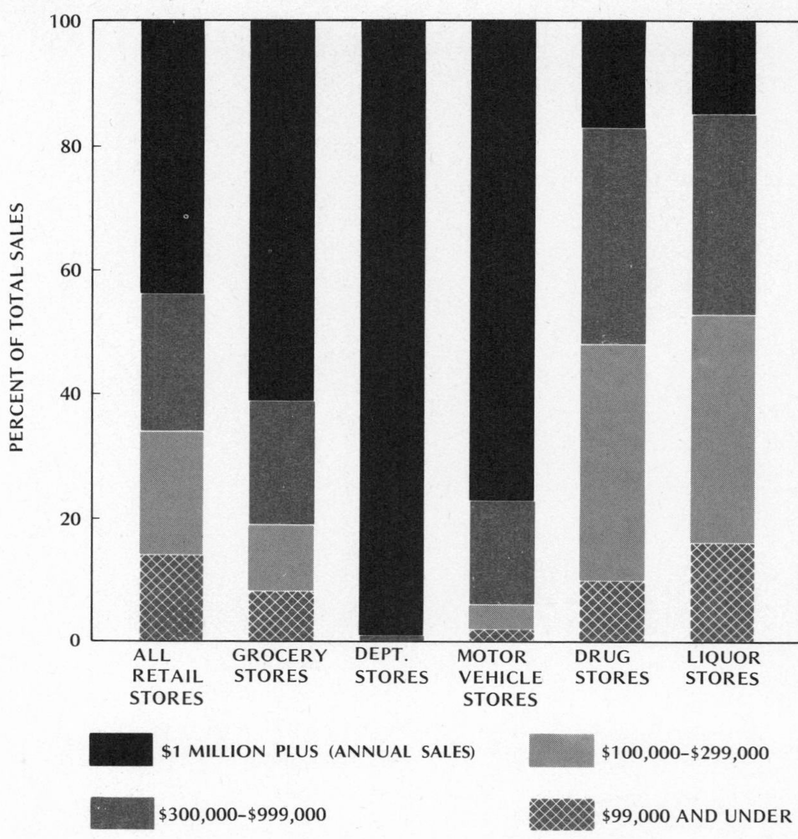

Source: U.S. Bureau of the Census, Census of Business, 1967, *Retail Trade: Sales Size,* BC67-RS2, Government Printing Office, Washington, 1971.

Labor can be more specialized. For example, a large grocery store can support specialized managers in its produce, dairy, and meat departments. Each of these specialists can be more efficient in his sphere of operation than the one-man management of a small store.

Some mechanization can be introduced, especially in physical handling of merchandise.

Management and supervision costs can be spread over a larger total volume. Up to a point at least, this implies lower cost per dollar of sales.

There have been numerous studies of retail operating costs in relation to store size. The results of these studies have usually been somewhat ambiguous, primarily because of the difficulty of isolating the effects on costs of size per se from the effects of numerous other factors including store location, merchandise lines, and quality of management. The studies do indicate, however, that large stores tend to have somewhat lower costs in relation to sales volume.

For example, as part of an extensive investigation of marketing practices in the food industries conducted in the mid-1960s, the National Commission on Food Marketing analyzed operating expense data for several thousand food stores.[15] This analysis showed that on the average, operating costs were about one-tenth of one cent lower (per dollar of sales) for each 1,000 square feet of selling area. (The stores studied ranged in size from 4,000 to 16,000 square feet.) Since the larger stores also tend to have broader assortments of merchandise and more customer services, these figures no doubt understate the cost advantages of larger stores.

SURVIVAL OF THE SMALL STORE

If economies of scale exist in retailing, however slight they may be, how can small stores compete successfully? Part of the answer lies in the inherent conflict between large store size and customer convenience. The large store, by definition, must draw its customers from a larger trading area, and the average time required to visit it is, therefore, greater. Unless this penalty is somehow offset by lower prices and/or better services, most customers are unwilling to incur it. Even if prices are slightly higher in the more convenient nearby outlet, many consumers will prefer to avoid the loss of time and possible difficulties in parking, etc.

Apart from an inherent locational advantage, the smaller retailer has other potential advantages. He can be more flexible in the services he provides to customers, and can benefit from personal relationships with them. Whether these potential strengths are utilized depends, of course, on the ability and energy of the individual merchant.

Questions

1. To what extent would either house-to-house selling or telephone selling be desirable or feasible for each of the following products and services? Explain your reasoning in each instance.
   a. Mutual funds (shares of ownership in a portfolio of common stocks and other securities selected by the fund's advisers)
   b. Fire extinguishers
   c. Typewriters
   d. Home study courses

[15] National Commission on Food Marketing, *Organization and Competition in Food Retailing*, Technical Study no. 7, Government Printing Office, Washington, 1966, chap. 7.

e. Children's clothing
f. Electric housewares (e.g., toasters, electric mixers)

2. A manufacturer of a headache remedy wanted to determine the relative importance of various types of retail outlets in the marketing of his product. How should he proceed to obtain this information? Why would such information be important to the manufacturer?

3. What factors might induce a large appliance manufacturer, such as General Electric, to open its own retail outlets to sell appliances to the public? What factors might dissuade it from such action?

4. A supermarket store manager who wanted to buy a small diamond bracelet for his wife criticized a jeweller friend for his high prices. The jeweller insisted that he required a 50 percent markup because of his high operating expenses. The supermarket operator noted that his operating costs were high too, but that he operated on a 22 percent gross margin. Do you think the jeweller deserved criticism for his high margins? Explain.

5. For many years the major tire and rubber manufacturers in the United States have operated company-owned retail stores. By the early 1950s, there were around 2,000 such stores in operation; they accounted for an estimated 10 percent of total replacement tire sales. Most of these stores carried diversified lines of merchandise in addition to tires, including such products as bicycles, toys, and automotive supplies. During the 1950s and early 1960s, the share of the market accounted for by tire company-owned stores declined to about 7 percent. Other types of outlets, especially discount stores of various kinds and automotive centers operated by large general merchandise retailers (including Sears, Roebuck) gained significantly in importance. Several changes in the tire market were thought to be related to the shift in retail distribution patterns.

(1) According to some observers, brand names were no longer of great importance to most consumers. Consumers took it for granted, it was claimed, that all tires are safe. This belief was strengthened by the aggressive promotion of discount retailers, featuring longer and longer guarantee periods for their tires.

(2) The tire company stores were located in older, downtown areas and were often unattractive. In contrast, discounters and suburban branch department stores were more conveniently located for most buyers, and had ample parking and modern facilities. These features were thought to be especially important to women, who played an increasing role in tire buying, partly because of the growing ownership of second cars.

(3) In most areas, other outlets offered lower prices than those charged by tire company stores. (Direct price comparisons were difficult because of the

lack of clear-cut quality designations for tires. But it seemed clear that for a *given* quality, the tire company store prices were usually higher.)

a. Why do you think tire companies have experienced difficulties in operating their own retail stores?

b. What steps might the companies take to correct or avoid the competitive weaknesses of their stores?

c. What does this example suggest about the *general* advantages and drawbacks of manufacturer-owned retail stores?

6. George Thompson was vice-president for merchandising of a chain of food stores. His son, a student majoring in economics at a Western university, told him that the company's decisions about whether to handle various products should be resolved by applying a *marginalist approach.* For each item, estimates should be made of the effect of adding or dropping it (a) on operating costs and (b) on sales revenue. How should Mr. Thompson proceed to apply this approach?

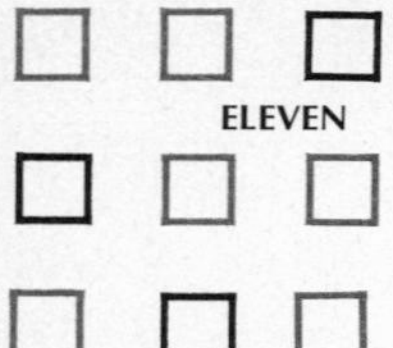

Competition and change in retailing

This chapter deals with five major classes of retailing institutions: department stores, chains and quasi-chains, supermarkets, planned shopping centers, and discount stores. These institutions are singled out for special attention partly because of their importance in the retailing system. Stores included in these groups or classes account for a major proportion of total retail trade in the United States and Canada, and a substantial, growing fraction of total sales in Western Europe. Furthermore, each of these five types of institutions represents a distinctive strategy or method of operation in retailing. When first developed, each was a major innovation in the retailing system. A review of these innovations and their effects on existing institutions illustrates the process by which the system adapts to changes in the market environment. Understanding the process of adaptation, in turn, provides a foundation for anticipating and dealing with future changes.

Department stores

In most of the world's cities and towns, the largest single store is a department store. Leading department stores are, in many ways, the "showcases" of urban shopping areas. Examples include Macy's and Gimbels in New York, Galeries

Lafayette and Au Printemps in Paris, and GUM in Moscow. These stores and their counterparts elsewhere symbolize broad selections of merchandise and leadership in merchandising techniques.

Most consumers are familiar with one or more department stores, but would be hard put to define exactly what constitutes such a store. The Bureau of the Census defines a department store as one which employs at least 25 people, and which sells some items in each of three broad merchandise categories: furniture, furnishings, and appliances; apparel; and household linen and dry goods. As implied by the name "department store," such stores are virtually always organized by merchandise departments for purposes of management and control. Thus, the distinguishing features are size, variety of merchandise, and organization. In addition, most department stores are characterized by relatively full customer service and by location in major shopping districts.

□

HISTORICAL DEVELOPMENT

There is some debate as to which was the first "true" department store. The operating methods and policies which distinguish department stores from other types of stores were apparently introduced piecemeal by several merchants in the United States, France, and Great Britain between 1840 and 1880. Each of these methods and policies was, to some extent, a departure from the prevailing retailing practices of the times.

Perhaps the most important of the several innovations which made up the department store's strategy was the "one-price" policy. According to John Wanamaker, one of the pioneers in the field, in the typical retail store of the 1860s, "There was no selling price for goods—there was an asking price, and the most persistent haggler bought the goods far below the unwary."[1] The policy of selling for a fixed price, with no bargaining, was adopted by a number of stores as early as the 1850s. This feature of the department store has since become nearly universal in retailing in the United States and other industrialized nations. But at the time it was a real departure from prevailing practice.

A second innovation was that of merchandise line diversification. In the 1850s, retail stores in large cities were extremely specialized. Separate stores sold only such items as china and glassware, laces and embroideries, or silks and ribbons. Moreover, throughout the first half of the nineteenth century the trend was toward narrower and more strictly defined product specialization. To some extent, the evolution of the department store represented a *reaction* to this trend toward increased specialization.[2] Most of the early department

[1] Quoted in *Golden Book of the Wanamaker Stores, Jubilee Year, 1861–1911*, as reprinted in N. S. B. Gras and H. M. Larson, *Casebook in American Business History*, Appleton-Century-Crofts, New York, 1939, p. 483.

[2] Ralph Hower, "Urban Retailing 100 Years Ago," *Bulletin of the Business Historical Society*, vol. XII (December, 1938), pp. 91–95.

stores—such as Macy's, Wanamakers, and Lord & Taylor—evolved from stores which originally specialized in clothing or dry goods, but later added other types of merchandise to these lines.

A third new feature of the department store was customer service, especially with respect to merchandise returns. In the 1850s, Macy's advertised "satisfaction guaranteed or money refunded," and by the 1870s this policy had become standard with leading urban retailers.

The early department stores attracted customers partly through price appeals. Their prices were lower than those of traditional stores, partly because they were able to buy in large quantities directly from manufacturers.

No reliable statistics are available for the early period of department store development. By 1929, stores classified in this group by the Census Bureau (including mail-order houses) accounted for sales of $4.3 billion. This figure represented 27 percent of total retail sales of general merchandise, apparel, and furniture and furnishings—the so-called "GAF" group of merchandise lines. In 1967, as shown in Table 10-1, 6,000 department stores had total sales of $32.3 billion or over 40 percent of GAF sales.

TYPES OF DEPARTMENT STORES

A key distinguishing feature of the early department stores was the provision or customer services. One pioneer in the field, Marshall Field of Chicago, summarized his policy in the slogan "Give the lady what she wants." Over the years, a variety of specific services were developed in line with the general philosophy of full-service retailing, and have come to be associated with the *conventional* type of department store. These typically include:

1. Liberal return and adjustment policies. On the average, customer returns and allowances amount to around 7 or 8 percent of sales.
2. Various forms of credit, including regular charge accounts, installment credit, revolving credit.
3. Free delivery.
4. Customer facilities such as lounges, restaurants, nurseries, rest rooms, and telephones.

Although full service is a hallmark of conventional department stores, there are also many *limited-service* department stores. Most of the outlets operated by Sears, Roebuck and Montgomery Ward qualify as department stores in terms of merchandise lines and size. So do many of the larger general merchandise *discount stores* which were built in the United States and in Western Europe during the 1950s and 1960s. Generally speaking, these stores offer fewer "free" services, and emphasize lower-priced lines of merchandise, than do conventional department stores. Chain stores and discount stores are discussed below.

In terms of ownership, there are several distinct types of department stores. Some are single-unit or independent stores. Most, however, are members of multiunit companies, including:

1. Regular chains. Sears, Roebuck and most of the discount stores fall into this classification.
2. Ownership groups. These are groups of conventional department stores under central ownership, but usually managed on a decentralized basis. Many of the leading urban stores belong to one or another of the major ownership groups. Among these are Federated Department Stores (1970 sales $2,097 million), Allied Stores Corporation ($1,225 million), and May Department Stores ($1,170 million).
3. Branch stores. Many conventional downtown stores, which may themselves belong to ownership groups, own branches in suburban areas, or even in other cities. These branches are typically controlled by their parent stores in terms of management, buying, and promotional activities.

COMPETITIVE POSITION

For several years following World War II, department stores' share of total GAF sales declined steadily. Although this share, as measured by Census data, increased from 1958 to 1967, the improvement was due in part to the reclassification of some stores, including discount stores, into the department store category. If allowance is made for this, the "market share" of conventional department stores was probably somewhat lower in the mid-1960s than in the 1930s and 1940s.

In competing with other types of stores, the conventional department store has some characteristic strengths and weaknesses. Among the competitive strengths of the department store are its wide customer appeal, arising from size, merchandise variety, and services; the general advantages of large size, as discussed in Chapter 10; a strong bargaining position in dealing with suppliers; and financial resources. In the better managed department store organizations, these strengths have been effectively used as the basis for substantial growth in sales and profits. Sales of Federated Department Stores, for example, increased from $636 million in 1957 to $1,685 million in 1967—a gain of 165 percent. This impressive growth was achieved through a combination of branch store expansion, modernization of downtown stores, and diversification into nontraditional lines such as automotive supplies and services.

The weaknesses of the department store, like its strengths, arise from its distinctive operating methods and policies. Primarily because it does provide extensive customer services, the conventional department store typically has relatively high gross margin and operating expenses. Typical figures for stores reporting to the National Retail Merchants' Association in 1965 were[3]:

	Percent of sales
Gross margin	35.6
Gross operating expense	31.2

Department stores' high operating costs reflect the high rate of merchandise returns associated with liberal return policies, the costs of other customer services for which no separate charges are made, and the high overhead costs of a large, complex organization.

During the late 1940s and 1950s, department stores also suffered to some extent from inflexibility in adjusting to changed conditions. In New York City, for example, six major conventional department stores closed during the 1950s. A major reason, according to one observer, was the stores' "conservative decisions to stand pat and not change with the times."[4] Some stores waited too long to establish surburban branches; others failed to compete effectively with discount stores' prices. At the same time, the more progressive department stores adapted quite successfully to the same challenges.

□

LEASED DEPARTMENTS

One feature of department stores deserves special mention: the use of leased departments. These are merchandise departments operated by companies independent of the store itself. The lessee pays a fee to the store in return for space and central services such as charge accounts and delivery. In the late 1960s, leased departments accounted for around 6 percent of total sales for conventional department stores. They are also widely used by general merchandise discount stores, as discussed in the last section of this chapter.

Department stores often lease certain departments to outside operators when the merchandise or services involved require specialized skills which the store itself cannot provide as effectively. For this reason, departments selling optical goods, photographic products, furs, and specialty goods such as Oriental rugs are widely operated by lessees. In the case of discount stores, another important reason for the use of leased departments has been their lack of capital relative to needs for expansion. A leased department's inventory and other working capital are provided by the lessee.

Chains and quasi-chains

Like the term "department store," the word "chain" is familiar but somewhat ambiguous. The basic idea is clear enough: a chain is a group of stores

[3] Controllers' Congress, National Retail Merchants Association, *Financial and Operating Results of Department and Specialty Stores in 1965,* New York, 1966. The "typical figures" are averages of the interquartile range of figures reported by 211 companies with combined 1965 sales of $5.3 billion.

[4] *New York Retailer,* April, 1957, p. 5.

operated by some kind of central organization. But there are many variations on this theme. Some chains are centrally owned, while others are not; some have only two or three stores, while others have thousands. Thus it is necessary to introduce some more specific terms and definitions. □

□

DEVELOPMENT OF REGULAR CHAINS

□ *A regular chain is a group of two or more retail establishments in the same general kind of business, owned and operated by the same firm. (This corresponds to the term "multiunit organization" as employed in the Census of Business.)*

□ *A quasi-chain is a group of separately owned retail establishments which are affiliated with some kind of central organization. Such stores may use a common name, and cooperate with the central organization for purposes of achieving economies in buying, promotion, and management.*

The key operating methods associated with chain store systems were first developed by regular chain companies, commencing in the late nineteenth century. At about the same time that the early department stores were evolving from clothing and dry goods stores, pioneer merchants in other lines of business were experimenting with the chain concept. In 1859, George Gilman and George Huntington Hartford opened a store in New York City, with the strategy of importing tea direct from the Orient and selling it at lower than prevailing retail prices. By 1865, they had 25 such stores in operation, and in 1869 they adopted the name Great Atlantic and Pacific Tea Company.[5] Some of the other major grocery chains also had their beginnings prior to 1900, for example, Kroger in 1882 and Grand Union in 1872. Similarly, most of the leading variety store chains—Woolworth, Kresge, Kress, and McCrory—were all established prior to 1900.

The basic principle of all the early chains was the same: to achieve a large volume of operations, and thus be able to buy and sell merchandise at lower prices. For example, Frank W. Woolworth initiated the idea of selling a variety of merchandise at prices of 5 cents and 10 cents. After two or three years of experimentation, he concluded that "real success would require a number of such stores. Only in that way would purchases be big enough to command the most favorable prices, and thus extend the range of items which could be sold profitably at 5 cents or 10 cents."[6]

While some of the early chain companies were quite successful, total sales of regular chains grew relatively slowly up to around 1920. A study by the Federal Trade Commission showed that in 1918, the 645 companies that operated some 29,000 chain stores accounted for only about 4 percent of total retail sales.[7] During the 1920s, however, the number of chain stores and their sales volume increased very rapidly. By 1929, there were over 200,000 chain stores, and they accounted for 30 percent of total retail sales.

Several factors apparently contributed to the expansion of the chains during the 1920s.[8] One was the sharp rise in retail prices following World War I,

[5] Godfrey M. Lebhar, *Chain Stores in America*, 3d ed., Chain Store Publishing Co., New York, 1963, pp. 24–27.

[6] *Ibid.*, p. 37.

[7] Federal Trade Commission, *Chain Stores: Growth and Development of Chain Stores*, Government Printing Office, Washington, 1932.

[8] See Charles F. Phillips and Delbert J. Duncan, *Marketing: Principles and Methods*, 5th ed., Richard D. Irwin, Inc., Homewood, Ill., 1964, pp. 210–214.

which made consumers more price conscious. Another was the trend toward urbanization. Chain store methods are especially effective in urban areas, because (1) stores can be efficiently serviced from central warehouses and offices and (2) advertising media, especially newspapers, can be used most efficiently.

Following their "golden era" of growth in the 1920s, chain stores' share of total retail sales was stable at about 30 percent up to the mid-1950s. During the post-World War II period, it increased substantially, as indicated by Census of Business figures:

Year	*Multiunits, share of total retail sales*
1954	30.1%
1958	33.7
1963	36.6
1967	39.9

□

ECONOMIES OF SCALE

As pointed out in Chapter 10, there are two potential kinds of economies of scale in retailing: those associated with store size and those associated with company size. Clearly, the most important economic and competitive advantage of the chain is its ability to achieve economies based on company size. The early chains did not, for the most part, operate significantly larger store units than those of independent retailers. For example, the great growth of A&P after 1912 was based on the establishment of numerous "economy stores," each operated by one man.[9]

The nature of the chains' scale economies has already been suggested: the ability to buy in large quantities, at lower prices; central warehousing and delivery systems; centralized advertising and other promotion; and specialization of labor generally. How important are these advantages in terms of costs? Published evidence is not plentiful, and determination of the relationships between size and individual elements of total cost is a complex task because of the difficulty of isolating the effects of size from those of other factors. Nevertheless it is clear that chains do have significant cost advantages over independent retailers and that large chains have similar advantages over small chains. In food retailing, studies by the staff of the National Commission on Food Marketing indicated that "warehousing costs decline as volume increases up to an operation of $75–$100 million annual retail sales . . . economies accruing from combining several warehouses in a single firm arise primarily from manu-

[9] Lebhar, *op. cit.*, p. 31.

facturing operations, the procurement of private label merchandise, and field buying of perishables."[10]

In considering the economic aspects of chains, the effect of their size on other firms must also be taken into account. The early chains were able to sell at lower prices than their competitors mostly because they bought at lower prices. Then, and especially later when some chains evolved into very large companies, their buying advantages were no doubt based in part on pure bargaining power. But the chains' ability to buy for less also reflects "real" economies accruing to their suppliers, such as lower manufacturing costs associated with sales in large quantities and with stabilization of output rates and lower costs of sale and delivery.

□

LARGE AND SMALL CHAINS

The definition of a "regular chain" given above encompasses all firms operating two or more stores. Obviously there are important differences between a 2-store chain and a 1,000-store company, especially with respect to economies of scale. The Bureau of the Census and other agencies have made repeated attempts over the years to decide where the "true" dividing line is between chains and independents. Sometimes chains have been defined as groups of 4 or more stores, and sometimes as groups of 11 or more. No universally acceptable boundary is likely to be found, however, and it is more meaningful simply to distinguish different size groups within the general chain category.

The relative importance of large and small chains in the 1960s is indicated by the accompanying Census data.

Company size	Number of stores	Sales (millions)
2–3 stores	58,764	$18,097
4–10 stores	30,178	14,601
11–50 stores	33,471	20,039
51–100 stores	15,518	13,035
101 or more stores	82,200	57,731

During the 1950s and 1960s, there was a general trend toward increasing size among chains. Between 1948 and 1967, the share of total retail sales made by chains of between 2 and 10 stores remained constant at about 11 percent, while chains of 101 or more units increased their share from 12 to 18 percent. This trend was partly due to mergers and acquisitions among chain organizations. Between 1951 and 1961, the 40 largest retailing firms acquired

[10] National Commission on Food Marketing, *Organization and Competition in Food Retailing*, Technical Study no. 7 Government Printing Office, Washington, 1966, p. 140.

more than 250 other companies.[11] Safeway Stores for example, acquired 26 companies during this period.

The trend toward larger chains has led to concern in some quarters regarding the issue of concentration in retailing. The federal antitrust laws are based on the premise that "excessive" concentration in any industry is undesirable. (See Chapter 27 for further discussion of the antitrust laws.) If a small number of retail chains dominate their respective lines of business and market areas, then, it is feared, socially undesirable market behavior may result.

Generally speaking, retail trade is considerably less concentrated than most manufacturing industries. For example, in 1963, the four largest food chain companies accounted for 20 percent of total grocery store sales on a national basis. In individual metropolitan areas, the four largest companies typically accounted for around 50 percent of total area sales, and this figure was approximately the same in 1963 as in 1958.[12]

COMPETITIVE POSITION OF REGULAR CHAINS

As explained above, the competitive advantages of regular chains have always been based primarily on certain inherent economies of scale. Beyond these basic cost advantages, chains have typically employed competitive strategies based on limited customer services and limited merchandise assortments. These policies imply lower operating expenses, quite apart from efficiencies related to size itself, and contribute to the chains' ability to sell at lower prices. Limited service and assortment policies are neither universal among chains nor exclusive to them, however.

The competitive position of regular chains varies considerably among the various lines of retail trade. Census of Business figures for 1967 reflect this situation, as shown in the accompanying table.

	Percent of sales made by	
Kind of business	All multiunits	Companies with 101 or more units
Department stores	94%	46%
Grocery stores	61	36
Drugstores and proprietary stores	35	15
Gasoline service stations	17	7
Automotive dealers	11	4

[11] *Mergers and Superconcentration,* staff Report of the Select Committee on Small Business, 87th Congress, Government Printing Office, Washington, 1962, pp. 39–40.
[12] *Organization and Competition in Food Retailing, op. cit.,* pp. 41, 51.

Differences in the competitive position of chains among lines of trade arise from variations in the degree to which cost savings can be achieved, as well as special conditions. For instance, cost savings in large-scale warehousing and transportation are important in the food trade, but not in the automotive business. On the basis of cost economies alone, the chains' share of retail food sales would probably be much higher than it is. But independent stores and wholesalers supplying them have responded to chain competition especially effectively in this line of business, as described in a subsequent section of this chapter.

LEGAL RESTRICTIONS ON CHAINS

The big gains made by chain stores during the 1920s came largely at the expense of traditional independent retailers. Moreover, the chains' direct-buying methods struck at the very existence of the wholesalers who supplied the independents. Both of these groups naturally resisted the new competition in a variety of ways. One form of resistance was to put pressure on manufacturers (1) not to sell to chains at all and/or (2) to establish minimum resale prices under so-called "fair-trade" laws, so that chains could not sell at lower prices than independents. (Fair-trade laws are discussed in Chapter 16.) For example, an association of wholesale grocers in one state advised its members to "look over their list of manufacturers . . . and see the ones that are selling the chain stores at the same price they are selling the wholesale grocer . . . give them the club that they are pounding you with."[13]

When the independent retailers and wholesalers were unsuccessful in preventing the chains' growth via pressure on manufacturers, they sought relief through legislation. Beginning in the early 1920s, bills were filed in practically every state legislature in the United States to impose special taxes on chain stores. Ultimately more than 1,300 such bills were introduced through 1965, and 60-odd laws were enacted in 28 different states. In the mid-1960s, only 11 states still had special chain store taxes in effect.[14]

Chain store tax laws provide for graduated license fees, based on the number of stores operated by a company either in the state or in total. The most costly such tax is that of Texas, which requires an annual fee of over $800 per store for each company operating more than 50 stores in that state.

The state chain store taxes appear to have had little effect on chains' growth. Some laws which imposed heavy penalties on chains were declared unconstitutional. Those which are in effect do not represent significant economic barriers. A significant barrier would have been imposed, however, if the so-called "Death Sentence" bill, a *national* chain store tax proposed in 1938, had been

[13] Lebhar, *op. cit.*, p. 120.

[14] *Ibid.*, chap. VII; and *1967 Statistical Supplement*, Chain Store Age Books, New York, 1967.

enacted. This bill called for a fee of $1,000 per store for all units in excess of 500 operated by a company. If a bill had become law, A & P would have been liable for a tax of $472 million, 50 percent of its 1938 sales.

The most important result of the anti-chain store legislative efforts of the 1920s and 1930s was the passage in 1936 of the Robinson-Patman Act, which restricted the chains' ability to obtain preferential treatment from suppliers. This law is discussed in Chapter 27.

Outside the legislative sphere, independent retailers and wholesalers responded to the competition of chains by adapting the methods of the chains to their own use. This was the main impetus for the development of several types of *quasi-chains*.

QUASI–CHAINS

"If you can't beat them, join them." Acting on this premise, independent retailers in some lines of business have competed successfully with chains by affiliating with one or another of the quasi-chain types of organizations. The most important of these are retailer cooperatives, wholesaler-sponsored "voluntary" chains, and franchise systems.

Retailer cooperatives These are groups of independent retailers who jointly own and operate central facilities for buying, warehousing, and other services. The retailer members, some of which may be small "chains," own shares of stock in a wholesaling enterprise, and any profits earned in this enterprise are refunded in proportion to purchases. The members agree to purchase the bulk of their merchandise from the cooperative. The central organization, in turn, provides members with various services which may include advertising, supplying private brand merchandise, and managerial assistance.

Wholesaler-sponsored voluntary chains "Voluntaries" operate in much the same way as retailer cooperatives, except that the central organization is an independent wholesaler. Both cooperatives and voluntaries have been extremely successful in the food trade; between them they accounted for more than 40 percent of total grocery store sales in the mid-1960s.

Many cooperatives and voluntaries are associated with federations of such groups. These include such nationally known organizations as the Independent Grocers' Alliance (IGA) and Red and White in the food trade.

Franchise systems Franchising was a "boom" industry in the late 1960s. Numerous franchise systems were established and expanded rapidly in such diverse fields as restaurants, employment agencies, hotels, and automotive supplies. In a franchise system, independently owned outlets are affiliated with a sponsoring firm which may be a manufacturer, a "wholesaler" who supplies the outlets, or simply a central service organization. In any of these types of systems, the sponsor provides services to the members such as advertising, location and planning of the outlet itself, and management assistance.

In all three types of quasi-chains, the guiding principle is to obtain as many as possible of the chain's advantages in terms of centralized buying, promotion, and management, while still maintaining substantial autonomy for the individual member. To the extent that this autonomy and the financial commitment of the member provide greater incentives for performance than salaried employment, the quasi-chains have a distinctive advantage of their own. Their success in matching the chains' efficiency is limited, however, by the degree to which members actually cooperate in the organization. The manager of a regular chain store can be ordered to comply with company decisions regarding such areas as merchandise assortment and frequency of deliveries. The owner of a store affiliated with a voluntary group can only be asked and persuaded. As a result, quasi-chains have a constant problem of balancing autonomy with the cost advantages of standardization.

Supermarkets

Perhaps the most distinctively American retailing institution is the supermarket. The operating methods of the supermarket epitomize "mass distribution," and have been widely adopted throughout the world. Although supermarket methods have been extensively discussed and applied, there is no clear-cut definition of a supermarket. For present purposes, we can define it as a *large, departmentized food store selling primarily on a self-service basis.*[15]

□ ORIGINS OF THE SUPERMARKET

Some of the key methods of the supermarket have been used by various types of stores in the past. The combination of these methods can, however, be traced to a small group of innovators in the retail food business in the early 1930s. One man, Michael "King" Kullen, stands out as a special leader in this group.[16] In 1930, Kullen was an employee of the Kroger Company, one of the largest food chains. He wrote a memorandum to a vice-president of the company, outlining his idea for a new type of food store. Kullen envisioned a "large" store—6,000 square feet versus a typical size of perhaps 800 square feet for conventional stores—selling groceries on a self-service, cash-and-carry basis at substantially lower prices than those of conventional outlets. He

[15] Cf. T. N. Beckman and W. R. Davidson, *Marketing,* 8th ed., The Ronald Press Co., New York, 1967, p. 298. Some trade sources define "large" stores as those with annual sales of $500,000 or more, while others draw the line at $1,000,000.

[16] See M. M. Zimmerman, *The Supermarket,* Mass Distribution Publications, Inc., New York, 1955.

believed that such a store would achieve sufficiently high sales volume to operate profitably with a gross margin of 9 to 10 percent of sales—about half that of the traditional food stores.

Kullen's proposal was not accepted by Kroger management. As a result, he left the company and opened his own store in Jamaica, New York, in August 1930. It was an immediate success. Within two years an estimated 300 supermarkets, as they were quickly designated, were in operation. Their low-cost, low-price approach was ideally suited to the needs of consumers in the depth of the economic depression of the 1930s. By 1939, approximately 5,000 supermarkets attained a combined annual sales volume of $1.5 billion—around 20 percent of total grocery store sales.

The early supermarkets were mostly independent stores. The successful operators soon branched out, however, and thus became chains. Moreover, the established chain companies also began opening supermarkets. During the ensuing years, these new units supplanted the chains' older, small stores. For example, between 1931 and 1957, the number of stores operated by Kroger declined from 5,138 to 1,450, while the company's total sales increased almost sevenfold from $244 million to $1.64 billion.[17] In this fashion, the major food chains were transformed from operators of small, clerk-service groceries to groups of large, self-service supermarkets.

The pioneer supermarkets had simple, inexpensive facilities. Most of them were set up in converted garages, theaters, or other vacant buildings, often in out-of-the-way locations. They had crude fixtures and offered a minimum of service to customers. "Self-service," the hallmark of the supermarket, required the housewife to locate and select her groceries and bring them to a check-out cashier. No delivery service was provided, and there were no "frills."

□ DEVELOPMENT SINCE 1945

The growth of supermarkets was interrupted by World War II. After 1945, there was a period of rapid expansion. Between 1960 and 1969, an average of 2,400 new supermarkets were opened each year, even though the *total* number of food stores continued to decline. By 1970 there were an estimated 37,000 supermarkets in operation, and their share of total retail grocery sales was over 75 percent.

The supermarkets built in the 1950s and 1960s differed considerably from those of the 1930s. Perhaps the most striking change was in store *size*. The typical supermarket opened in the late 1960s had an overall floor area of around 20,000 square feet.[18] This increase in size was due, in large part, to the tremendous expansion in products handled by supermarkets. In 1946, it was

[17] "Bigger Store, Bigger Profits for the Kroger Co.," *Business Week,* Aug. 10, 1957.
[18] "Facts About New Super Markets Opened in 1969," Super Market Institute, Inc., Chicago, 1970.

estimated that a typical food store handled 3,000 items; by 1967, this had increased to 7,500.[19] Much of the growth in product lines resulted from the outpouring of new food products—convenience foods, dietary foods, and many others.

Supermarkets also expanded their *nonfood* product lines during the 1950s and 1960s. According to trade estimates, nonfoods, apart from paper goods and laundry and cleaning supplies, represented 8 percent of total food store sales in the late 1960s. Important nonfood lines include health and beauty aids, housewares, magazines, books, toys, and in some cases, clothing.

In contrast to the early supermarkets, modern stores have expensive, attractive facilities and offer a wide variety of customer services such as check cashing, restrooms, and music while shopping. Most of them are also open evenings and, in some areas, on Sundays.

As might be expected, the progressive "upgrading" of supermarket facilities and services has led to higher operating costs and gross margins. In 1966, the typical "store door margin," that is, company gross profit minus warehouse, delivery, and administrative expenses, was 18.1 percent for firms reporting to the annual Super Market Institute figure exchange.[20] These higher gross margins reflect the costs of *trading stamps,* in addition to the expenses associated with store facilities and services. In 1967, some 55 percent of supermarkets gave their customers trading stamps, which can be redeemed for merchandise premiums.[21] The cost of stamps to the stores is approximately 2 percent of sales. There has been considerable controversy over the net effect of trading stamps on a store's total operating costs. According to the trading stamp companies, the use of stamps does not necessarily increase total expenses, and thus retail prices, because their promotional appeal may generate sufficient additional sales volume to yield offsetting cost reductions. No doubt this was true for some individual stores which adopted trading stamps before their competitors did. But by the early 1960s, in many metropolitan areas virtually all the major supermarket operators were offering stamps. Unless the stamps produced increases in *total* consumer food purchases, which seems highly unlikely, they eventually came to represent some net addition to total operating costs.

The rising costs of supermarkets and their extensive adoption of trading stamps contributed to the emergence in the 1960s of a modified type of food store, the "food discounter." These stores are "supermarkets which have lower prices and do not give trading stamps, often carry fewer items . . . and

[19] *Progressive Grocer,* April, 1968, p. 82.
[20] *The Super Market Industry Speaks—1967,* 19th Annual Report, Super Market Institute, Chicago, 1968, p. 9.
[21] *Ibid.,* p. 16.

may give reduced customer services."[22] One study of a sample of comparable discount and conventional supermarkets showed that discounters' operating expenses were 2½ to 3½ percent of sales lower. The greatest source of expense reduction, in each case studied, was the elimination of trading stamps.[23]

Many of the discount food stores opened in the 1960s were connected with general merchandise discount stores, which are discussed in a later section of this chapter.

□ IMPACT OF SUPERMARKET METHODS

The operating methods pioneered by food supermarkets have had considerable impact in retailing generally. *Self-service,* one of the distinguishing features of the supermarket, has been widely adopted, to varying degrees, by stores selling general merchandise, drugs, hardware, and other types of products. In most lines of retail trade, too, the trend toward larger stores has reflected a movement toward "mass merchandising"—larger store buildings, more diverse product assortments, lower gross margins, and higher rates of capital turnover. All this was facilitated, of course, by the growth of population and consumer income in the United States during the 1950s and 1960s.

Supermarket methods have also been adopted to some extent in other countries. One of the first food supermarkets in Europe was opened in 1951 by Migros, a major Swiss chain. By the early 1960s, it was estimated that there were some 2,000 supermarkets in Western Europe, about half of them in the United Kingdom. Supermarket-type stores have also been opened in Japan, Latin America, and elsewhere.

Stores designated as "supermarkets" in other countries are typically smaller than those in the United States. In France, for example, trade groups define a supermarket as a self-service food store with more than 400 square meters (4,300 square feet) of selling area. On the basis of this definition, there were around 500 supermarkets in France in the mid-1960s, accounting for perhaps 5 percent of total food sales. Because automobile ownership is less common and refrigerators are smaller in other countries, their supermarkets typically have smaller transactions and less parking space than those in the United States.

Planned shopping centers

Most of the new branch department stores, chain stores, and supermarkets which have been opened in the United States since 1945 are located in or near

[22] *Ibid.,* p. 15.

[23] Robert J. Minichiello, "An Exploratory Study of Selected Discount Food Stores," unpublished doctoral thesis, Harvard Business School, 1965.

planned shopping centers. The shopping center is not a type of store, but a planned grouping of stores and related facilities, especially parking space. The growth of shopping centers has had a significant impact on the retailing system. Its effects cut across virtually all major lines of business and operating methods, and thus represent another dimension of competition and change.

DEVELOPMENT OF SHOPPING CENTERS

During the depression and war years of the 1930s and 1940s, relatively few new retail stores were built. At the same time, the population of the United States grew substantially—by 14 percent between 1930 and 1945. Population not only increased, but it shifted to the suburban areas surrounding major cities, especially during the "boom" of new household formation and home construction of the immediate postwar years.

These developments set the scene for the emergence of the planned shopping center, commencing in the late 1940s. Unlike downtown and city neighborhood districts which have simply grown up over the years, shopping centers are planned as integrated units by their developers. Integrated planning includes architecture, the composition of stores within the center, access roads and parking, and in some cases services such as cooperative promotional activities.

By 1965, it was estimated that there were more than 8,000 shopping centers in the United States, including some 158,000 stores. These stores accounted for total sales of $54 billion or around 20 percent of total retail sales.[24]

TYPES OF SHOPPING CENTERS

Planned shopping centers vary greatly in size, number, and types of stores, and other facilities. At one extreme, there were (in 1965) some 75 large "super-regional" centers with more than 800,000 square feet of store area each. These centers typically include one or more branch department stores, several apparel stores, and other shopping goods outlets. At the other extreme, there were nearly 5,000 neighborhood shopping centers with an average of 56,000 square feet of space each. A neighborhood center typically includes a supermarket, a drugstore, and other convenience goods and service outlets.

IMPACT ON RETAILING

Although shopping centers vary, there is no doubt that they have generally tended to "homogenize" retailing. Most stores in a given line of business operating in planned shopping centers, even in different parts of the country, are similar in appearance and general operating methods. This similarity is in

[24] These and other statistics cited for shopping centers are estimates by *Chain Store Age*, Executive Edition, May, 1966.

part a reflection of the fact that a higher than average proportion of shopping center stores are chain or quasi-chain outlets. Shopping center developers tend to prefer chain store tenants because lease commitments by these large companies facilitate the initial financing of the centers. As a result, the growth of shopping centers contributed to the improved competitive position of chains during the 1950s and 1960s (see above).

A direct effect of shopping centers has been a loss of business by downtown retailers. In some cities, retail trade has actually declined in absolute terms. For example, the Central Business District of Detroit experienced a decline of 8 percent in number of stores, and of 21 percent in sales, between 1953 and 1963.[25] As noted earlier, conventional department stores have been handicapped during the postwar period by their commitment to downtown locations. In some major cities, downtown retailers have responded to the challenge of shopping centers by active participation in programs of urban renewal and improvement. The problems of downtown areas extend far beyond retailing, of course, to such areas as education and housing. But retail trade has always been one of the primary activities of "downtown," and retailers will no doubt play a major role in future programs to deal with the social and economic problems of the central city.

Shopping centers have been developed in other countries as well as the United States, but in smaller numbers because of lower rates of increase in population and income. In many cases, European shopping centers are incorporated into large apartment developments and designed primarily to serve their immediate neighborhoods. Regional centers relying on customers who travel by automobile from relatively distant points are rare outside North America.

Discount stores

The most recent major development in the American retailing system is the evolution of discount stores. A discount store is even harder to define, as a type of institution, than a supermarket. But discounting as a basic method of operation, involving reductions from customary prices, reduced customer services, and low operating expenses, is familiar to most consumers, retailers, and manufacturers.

□ EVOLUTION OF DISCOUNT STORES

The term "discount" implies some notion of a normal or customary price (or pricing structure) for a specific product or product category. Prior to the adoption of the one-price policy by most major retailers in the late nineteenth

[25] William Applebaum, "Consumption and the Geography of Retail Distribution in the United States," *MSU Business Topics*, Michigan State University, Summer, 1967, p. 37.

century, the term would have been meaningless. By the 1920s, however, customary prices and markups had become reasonably well established in many lines of business. As described in preceding sections of this chapter, both the chains and the supermarkets initially attracted business from established retailers by means of lower prices, that is, by "discounting."

The adoption of so-called fair-trade laws in many states during the 1930s provided a widely recognized, legally supported definition of "normal prices" for many products. These laws permit manufacturers to establish minimum or absolute *resale* prices for their products through contractual agreements with retailers and/or wholesalers. Prices established in this way came to be recognized by retailers and consumers alike as the "regular" prices of the products involved. (The history and effects of fair-trade legislation are discussed further in Chapter 17.)

Especially during the 1930s, fair-trade retail prices, and other, less formal "regular" prices, were set so as to allow for retail gross margins characteristic of relatively small, full-service, "conventional" retail stores. In the drug trade, for example, a gross margin of 33½ percent has been regarded as normal, and attempts to reduce it have been resisted for many years. Similarly, in most other lines of business, traditional rates of gross margin had become widely recognized by the late 1930s.

In the years immediately following World War II, there was a tremendous increase in the demand for durable goods. Consumers had accumulated savings during the war when automobiles and appliances were not available. This "pent-up demand," together with the introduction of new products such as automatic washing machines and television, led to a boom era for appliance retailers.

It was in this atmosphere that the early postwar discount houses emerged. Initially, they concentrated on "hard goods," especially electrical appliances. One of the first discounters, for example, was E. J. Korvette, which opened in 1948 in the loft of a building in midtown New York City. Korvette sold nationally advertised brands of luggage and small appliances at prices from 35 to 40 percent below regular list prices. Merchandise samples were displayed, and customers received their selections at a check-out counter. The store operated at a total expense ratio of between 10 and 15 percent of sales.

Korvette and other similar stores enjoyed rapid success, and soon began expanding in terms of both store locations and merchandise lines. By 1954, Korvette had seven stores and sold photographic equipment, major appliances, toys, records, and other products. Nearly all the early discount stores employed the same basic operating methods: limited services (separate charges were typically made for delivery if required), relatively crude facilities, and heavy emphasis on discounts from list prices for well-known products. In effect, they applied supermarket methods to appliances and similar lines of merchandise.

□

COMPETITIVE POSITION

By the 1960s, the discount store concept had been extended and modified in several ways. Korvette and other major companies in the field evolved into general merchandise store operators, featuring "soft goods" (apparel and household goods) as well as the original hard goods lines. A survey of self-service discount department stores' operations in 1965 showed the following partial distribution of total sales[26]:

Apparel	43.0%
Hard goods	34.0
Drugs and cosmetics	8.5
Books, stationery	2.5
Photographic	2.0

Most of the discount store firms also expanded their customer services and their store facilities. A visible symbol of this trend was the opening of a Korvette store on Fifth Avenue in New York City, traditionally the location of "prestige" department and apparel stores. At the same time, many conventional retailers, especially department stores and variety store chains, emulated the discount stores' methods. The F. W. Woolworth Company, for example, established a new division in the early 1960s to operate "Woolco" general merchandise discount stores.

The net result of the competition between discounters and conventional retailers during the 1950s and 1960s was a substantial reduction in the differences between these two classes of stores. Discount stores' operating expenses and margins have increased. Typical figures for stores reporting in a 1965 survey were[27]:

Gross margin	27.2% of sales
Income from leased departments	4.5
Gross income	31.7%
Total expense	27.5

Although these figures are still lower than those of conventional department stores, they are markedly higher than the costs and margins of the discount houses of the late 1940s.

Although discount stores may have "disappeared as a distinctive form of enterprise," as one authority has suggested,[28] the companies which gained their foothold through discounting have certainly achieved an important position

[26] *Operating Results of Self Service Discount Department Stores in 1965,* Center for Business and Economic Research, University of Massachusetts, Amherst, Mass., 1967.

[27] *Ibid.*

[28] William R. Davidson, "The End of the Discount House," *Department Store Economist,* reprint series on Discounting, 1961.

in the retailing system. According to trade estimates, in 1969 there were over 4,600 discount stores with total sales of $22.2 billion, more than 6 percent of total retail sales.[29] (These figures are based on a definition of a discount store as one with minimum sales of $500,000 and a minimum store area of 10,000 square feet.) Over 1,500 of these stores were operated by the 10 largest firms in the field, and these large chains accounted for about 30 percent total discount store sales volume. Nearly half of the discount stores included food departments.

General patterns of change

As suggested in preceding sections of this chapter, the American retailing system has experienced major upheavals at intervals during the past century. There have been similar periods of change, albeit less rapid, in most other industrialized countries. No doubt there will be further changes in retailing in the future, and these changes will have important consequences for existing retailers, for manufacturers, and for consumers. It is, therefore, useful to draw whatever lessons are possible from history.

Each of the changes in the retailing system has been, in some respects, unique. but there are also some common threads running through these changes.

□ THE "WHEEL OF RETAILING"

One basic common pattern of change is what Prof. Malcolm P. McNair has termed the "wheel of retailing." According to this thesis, new retailing institutions gain a competitive foothold by offering a price advantage to customers, made possible largely by reducing or eliminating customer services. Once an institution becomes established, however, there is a tendency to improve customer services gradually, and operating costs increase correspondingly. Eventually this reaches a point which affords some new type of institution an opportunity to do unto the innovator as he did unto his predecessors, whereupon the cycle is repeated.[30] According to this viewpoint, institutional changes represent dynamic adjustments to a "moving equilibrium" between customer services and prices.

Most of the major changes previously described seem to fit the "wheel" pattern reasonably well. Certainly department stores, chains, supermarkets, and discount stores all utilized price appeals in their early stages, and it is also

[29] "The True Look of the Discount Industry," Tenth Annual Study, *Discount Merchandiser,* June, 1970.

[30] Malcolm P. McNair, "Significant Trends and Developments in the Postwar Period," in A. B. Smith (ed.), *Competitive Distribution in a Free, High-level Economy and Its Implications for the University,* The University of Pittsburgh Press, Pittsburgh, 1958, pp. 1–25.

true that in each case, costs and margins increased as the institution grew and matured. Professor Stanley Hollander has pointed out, however, that not all new retailing institutions have followed the same path.[31] Some, including automatic vending and suburban shopping centers, did not enter the market on a low-price basis; others have apparently escaped the long-run trend toward higher costs. But these exceptions do not necessarily discredit the wheel theory; they may simply indicate that it is an incomplete model of change in retailing. The pattern has been sufficiently common to suggest that at least some future developments will follow a similar route.

□

RESPONSES OF ESTABLISHED RETAILERS TO CHANGE

In addition to the wheel theory, another repeating pattern may be discerned in the history of institutional changes in marketing. When a new institution emerges, existing firms tend to resist it by attempts to discredit the innovator and secure the passage of restrictive legislation. One example of this has already been mentioned in Chapter 10: the proposed law prohibiting the sale of proprietary drugs by stores without pharmacists on duty. Besides this, druggists in one city also conducted an advertising campaign to show that discounters' claims of price savings were, in fact, fraudulent.[32] Similar efforts to use propaganda and lobbying were made in opposition to mail-order houses (prior to World War I), chain stores, and other innovators. In the case of retail chains, these efforts led to the passage of chain store tax laws in many states and were largely responsible for the passage of the Robinson-Patman Act in 1936. Such laws and the accompanying publicity have seldom, if ever, had any real effect in modifying the direction or rate of change.

Once this lack of effectiveness becomes apparent, conventional marketing institutions are forced to adapt to new forms of competition by meeting the innovators directly. Usually this takes the form of adopting some of the innovators' methods, at least in modified form. Thus, independent food wholesalers and retailers met the challenge of the corporate chains by forming quasi-chains of their own. Similarly, food chains imitated the early supermarkets, which were operated by independents; and small-town business districts have attempted to provide parking space to compete with planned shopping centers. In the meantime, as suggested by the wheel theory, the innovator is gradually adding services and becoming more like his older competitors. Ultimately, this process leads to the emergence of a new equilibrium, combining features of both the old and new. A close analogy can be drawn with the

[31] Stanley C. Hollander, "The Wheel of Retailing," *Journal of Marketing,* vol. 25 (July, 1960), pp. 37–42.

[32] "Cleveland Drug Men's Ads Blast Drug Discounters," *Advertising Age,* Feb. 19, 1962, p. 10. The League of Independent Pharmacies was also quoted as planning to emphasize druggists' services in subsequent advertisements.

Hegelian concept, employed by Karl Marx, of thesis, antithesis, and synthesis in the history of social and economic systems.

THE PENDULUM EFFECT

Finally, past changes in the retailing system seem to indicate that there is a general tendency for changes to be carried too far, leading to corrective reactions of one kind or another in the system. It has already been suggested that the emergence of the department store was at least in part a reaction to the trend toward merchandise specialization which characterized the first half of the nineteenth century. Similar apparent counteracting "swings of the pendulum" include:

1. The progressive increases in size and merchandise lines by supermarkets in the 1950s. One result of this was increased shopping time for customers. This was one of the major factors underlying the emergence and success of "convenience food stores"—small stores handling very limited lines of groceries, located on highways in suburban areas, and open during late evening hours. These stores offer greater convenience for customers who want only a few items.
2. The development of discount food stores. In a sense, this was a reaction to the trend toward increased services and costs, especially those of trading stamps, on the part of regular supermarkets.
3. The emerging trend toward renewing and improving downtown shopping areas. This can be viewed as a reaction to excessive concentration on suburban shopping centers.

CONCLUSION

As should be apparent from this brief discussion of general patterns of change, there is not yet any general theory which will enable future managers and public officials to predict the direction and magnitude of changes with certainty and precision. Nevertheless, the past probably does provide some clues to the future. It is to be hoped that further research will improve our ability to predict change and adapt to it.

Questions

1. The policy of selling products for a fixed price with no bargaining, a feature of early department stores, has become nearly universal in retailing in industrial countries. Why has this practice not become established in automobile retailing? Is it likely to become common in this area in the future? Why or why not?

2. Chains and quasi-chains appear to offer many benefits to the individual retail outlet. This being so, why do so many retail outlets remain independent?

3. What factors might lead an independent retailer to join a retailer cooperative or a wholesaler-sponsored voluntary chain?

4. Why are furniture stores so seldom chain-store operations? Do you see any factors which are likely to cause this situation to change in the future? Discuss.

5. Leased departments are often utilized by discount stores because of their own inventory and working capital needs. What problems do you think might be created for the management of a discount retailing firm by the use of leased departments?

6. The importance of nonfood products in supermarkets has increased sharply in the 1950s and 1960s and, by 1970, these products accounted for close to 10 percent of total supermarket sales.

a. Why has the importance of nonfood products increased?

b. Is the importance of such products likely to continue to grow in the future? Why or why not?

c. What factors would you consider in evaluating the potential sales and profits of each of the following nonfood items from the viewpoint of a supermarket operator: (1) high-priced children's toys ($10 and up), (2) power lawnmowers, (3) garden furniture, (4) watches, and (5) small appliances (irons, toasters, etc.)?

7. One major brand of photographic film is sold in drugstores, supermarkets, specialty photographic stores, and discount stores. The price of this film, however, varies substantially among these different types of outlets. How do you explain this phenomenon?

8. In recent years, shoe stores have faced increased competition from discount stores and variety stores which have added limited lines of footwear. Does it make sense for shoe stores to broaden their lines in response? Why or why not?

9. The "wheel of retailing" hypothesis holds that new types of retailers enter the market as low-status, low-margin, low-price operators. Gradually, they acquire more elaborate establishments and facilities. Finally, they mature as high-cost, high-price merchants vulnerable to newer types of retailers who in turn go through the same pattern.

Discussing this phenomenon, one observer noted that the early discounters operated in cramped, low-cost quarters. They sold major appliances, carried very limited inventories, offered a minimum of customer services, and invested little in advertising and display. By the early 1970s, however, the typical discounter bore little resemblance to this early prototype. Many discounters had become department store chains. These firms carried soft goods, hardware, drugs, photo supplies, notions, housewares, small appliances, furniture, and even food. They operated spacious, attractive stores; some provided ample free parking, offered a variety of customer services including credit and delivery, accepted returns, and advertised extensively.

a. Why have these changes taken place?

b. What impact do you think these changes have had on the growth rate and profitability of the discount stores? Why?

c. What impact have these changes had on the product lines and pricing policies of traditional stores whose business has been hurt by the broadening of discount store product lines? Why?

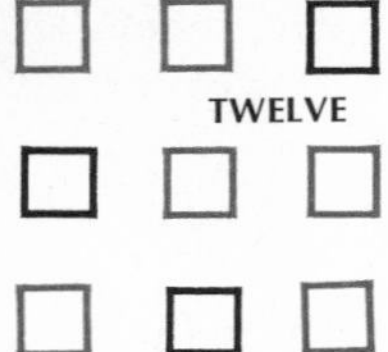

The wholesaling system

In the two preceding chapters we have described the institutional system for retailing. Now, we turn our attention to a second major category of institutions specializing in marketing activities: those engaged in wholesale trade. The fundamental distinction between wholesale and retail transactions was explained in Chapter 2: retail transactions are those in which the buyer is an ultimate consumer purchasing for personal or household use. All other transactions are, by definition, "wholesale." Note that in terms of this definition virtually all sales made by farmers, manufacturers, mines, and other producers of goods, and many services, too, are wholesale sales, and the management tasks related to these sales might be called "wholesale marketing." But our concern in this chapter is with sales handled by specialized institutions, separate from the activities of producers themselves. The total sales of these specialized wholesaling institutions, which amounted to $477 billion in 1967, represent about a third of the total of all "wholesale sales" in the broader sense.

In this chapter, we describe briefly each of the major types of wholesaling institutions and discuss the role of each in the marketing of various types of products. Then, we give a brief account of the dimensions of competition and change among different forms of wholesale distribution. As in our discussion of retailing, the facts and figures cited deal primarily with the United States, but the types of institutions described have counterparts in other industrial countries.

Types of wholesaling institutions

Wholesale trade, as conceived for purposes of the United States Census of Business, includes the operations of all establishments *primarily* engaged in the purchase and/or sale of products to retailers and to business and/or institutional users. Defined in these terms, the wholesaling system in 1967 consisted of more than 311,000 places of business with sales of $477.2 billion, employing 3.5 million persons.

Wholesaling institutions display enormous variety in methods of operation, products handled, and customers served, even more than in the case of retailing. They range, for example, from huge gasoline bulk terminals operated by major refining companies to small brokerage firms representing sellers of iron and steel scrap. Some, such as drug wholesalers, sell almost entirely to retailers; others, such as dentists' supply houses or school supply distributors, sell only to narrowly defined institutional markets.

□

MAJOR CATEGORIES OF INSTITUTIONS

In terms of ownership and functions performed, wholesaling institutions can be grouped into four basic categories: merchant wholesalers, agents and brokers, manufacturers' sales branches and offices, and retail chain warehouses. Some key facts and figures for each of these classes of institutions are given in Table 12-1.

As shown in the table, more than two-thirds of all wholesale establishments and over half of total sales volume are accounted for by merchant wholesalers. As suggested by the term "merchant," these institutions *buy and resell* goods, rather than representing other firms. Depending on the types of products and customers involved, they may also provide extensive services to their customers, including financing, technical services, and managerial assistance.

We include in the merchant wholesaler category not only so-called regular or "full-function" wholesalers and special-function wholesalers, but also assemblers of farm products, terminal grain elevators, importers, exporters, and petroleum bulk stations operated by independent firms. Each of these types is discussed in subsequent sections of this chapter.

Terms used more or less synonymously with "merchant wholesaler" include "distributor" and "jobber," among others. Other terms are used in various industries to distinguish among different types of wholesalers; for example, in the automotive parts and supplies business, some wholesalers are

□
TABLE 12-1

Basic dimensions of the wholesaling system, United States, 1967

	Type of institution			
Basic statistics	Merchant wholesalers	Manufacturers' sales branches and offices	Agents and brokers	Retail chain warehouses
Number of establishments	238,000	47,300	26,000	5,000
Sales volume (billions)	$223.8	$174.3	$61.3	$17.7
Buy from or represent	Manufacturers, other whole-salers agents, and brokers	(Owned by manufacturer)	Manufacturers, farmers	Manufacturers, wholesalers, agents, and brokers
Percent of total sales made to:				
Retailers	40%	30%	20%	97%
Business and institutional users	40	45	45	
Other wholesale establishments	15	20	30	3
Other types of customers	5	5	5	
(Export, farmers, households, etc.)				

Source: Based on data reported in the Census of Business, *Wholesale Trade,* 1967. "Assemblers" and petroleum bulk stations operated by independent firms are included in the merchant wholesalers category. Petroleum bulk stations operated by refiners are included in manufacturers' sales branches and offices.

called "direct jobbers" and others "indirect jobbers." We do not attempt to catalog all these terms, but shall mention some of them in the discussion that follows.

The second most important type of wholesaling institution is manufacturers' sales branches and offices. These are places of business owned and operated by manufacturing firms for the distribution of their own products. Over half of these, the sales *branches*, carry inventories and operate in a manner similar to that of wholesalers. Sales *offices,* on the other hand, generally do not carry any goods in stock but limit their activities to selling and product-related services such as installation and repairs.

Agents and brokers, who account for just under 15 percent of total whole-sale sales, act on behalf of sellers or buyers, usually the former, in carrying out sales and purchases of goods. They work on a commission basis, usually do not physically handle the products they sell, and provide only limited services beyond those of negotiation and transmitting orders.

Chain store warehouses are establishments owned by retailing firms, through which they buy, store, and redistribute goods for their stores. These operations are not included in the Census of Wholesale Trade, although they once were. We classify them as wholesaling institutions, however, because their functions are clearly wholesale in nature just as are those of manufacturers' branches.

□

WHOLESALING: LINK BETWEEN SUPPLIERS AND CUSTOMERS

The entire wholesaling system serves as a network of linkages between manufacturers and other producers, on the one hand, and retailers and business and/or institutional users, on the other. In Table 12-1 we show the approximate distribution of sales by type of customer for each of the four major categories of wholesaling institutions. Note that sales to retailers constitute less than half of the total in each case, except, of course, for retail chain warehouses. For all three other types of institutions, sales to business and institutional users represent a bigger share of total sales than do sales to retailers.

Another important part of wholesaling activity is sales to "other wholesale establishments." For example, a manufacturer's sales branch may sell to a wholesaler, who in turn sells to another wholesaler, who finally sells to a retailer. This implies that there is considerable double-counting in the figures for wholesale trade. In fact, of the $477 billion total sales made by wholesale establishments, nearly 20 percent (almost $90 billion) represents sales within the wholesaling system.

Wholesalers

As suggested in the preceding section, the most important category of wholesaling institutions is that of merchant wholesalers. Although all merchant wholesalers, by definition, share certain basic characteristics, there are many variations in their services, product lines, and methods of operation. Some of the major classes and types of wholesalers are described in this section.

□

TYPES OF WHOLESALERS

Probably the most common concept of a wholesaler is that corresponding to the regular or "full-service" wholesaler, who operates a warehouse, solicits orders from customers through a sales force, extends credit, and provides other services in conjunction with selling merchandise. Regular wholesalers are, indeed, the most numerous type within the merchant wholesaler category, and account for the bulk of all sales by this group of institutions.

Besides regular wholesalers, there are also various types of "special-function" wholesalers, some of which provide a limited range of services, while others perform additional functions above and beyond those normally associated with wholesaling. Some of the main types of special-function wholesalers are described in later parts of this chapter.

Overall, wholesalers have accounted for between 46 and 48 percent of total wholesale trade throughout the period between 1939 and 1967. The stability of wholesalers' aggregate "share of market" conceals great variations and shifts in their competitive position in individual industries, however. In some lines of business, wholesalers have never been of much importance; in others, they were once dominant but have lost in position. In still other cases, wholesalers have gained significantly in relation to other forms of distribution. Because there have been such great differences in wholesalers' performance, we shall relate our discussion of them to specific industries wherever possible.

FUNCTIONS OF THE REGULAR WHOLESALER

The "regular" wholesaler is one who provides the full range of services to his customers and suppliers that are traditionally associated with the wholesaling role in the channel of distribution. Regular wholesalers perform market contact functions of merchandising and selling as well as warehousing, delivery, credit, and managerial and/or technical service functions. Any and all of these functions can also be performed by manufacturers and/or by retailers and industrial users; thus, the wholesaler's position in the channel of distribution depends on his performing the functions more efficiently or more effectively than his customers or suppliers can. In those cases where the wholesaler cannot meet this competitive test, he has declined in importance.

Market contact The single most important function of the regular wholesaler, and of other types of wholesalers, too, is that of making and maintaining contacts between suppliers and customers. The basic concept of the market contact function is illustrated in Figure 12-1. As shown there, the presence of a wholesaler in a channel of distribution reduces the number of contacts that must be made, and thus the total cost of contact activity, between sources of supply and users or resellers. The difference between direct contact and contact via wholesalers can be expressed in general terms:

If each of M suppliers sells his products directly to each of N customers, the total number of market contacts required will be $M \times N$; if the M suppliers all sell to a single wholesaler, the total number of contacts required will be reduced to $M + N$. For example, if 100 suppliers all sell directly to each of 500 customers, 50,000 contacts will be required; if all these suppliers and customers deal through a single wholesaler, the number will be reduced to $100 + 500 = 600$, or 1.2 percent of the number involved in direct dealing.

FIGURE 12-1

How the use of wholesalers reduces the cost of market contacts between suppliers and customers

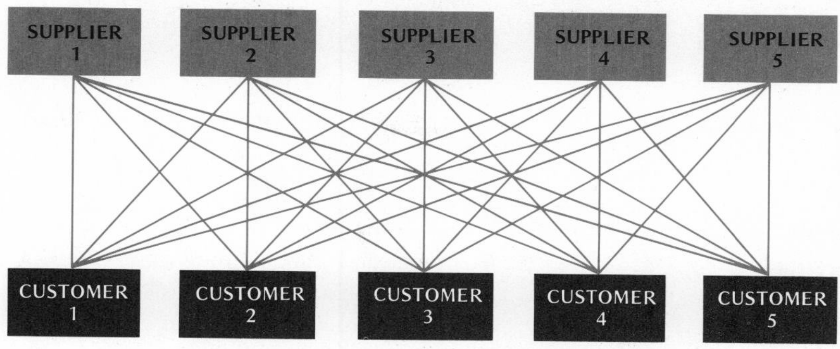

(5 Suppliers, each contacting 5 customers = 25 contacts.)

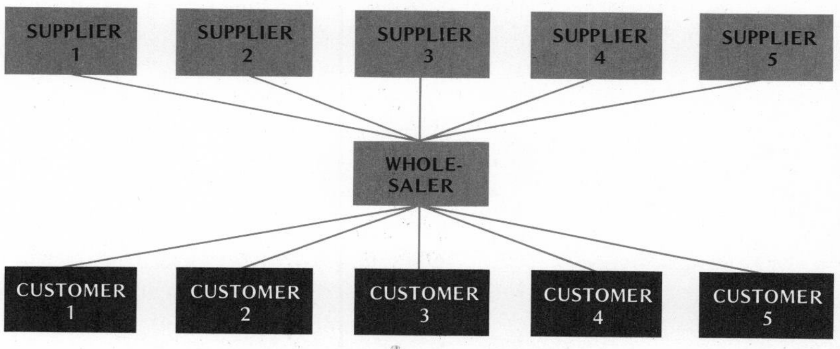

(5 Suppliers, each contacting the wholesaler, who contacts each of 5 customers = 10 contacts.)

Each contact between a supplier and a customer gives rise to certain costs, associated with (1) sales contact, (2) purchasing activities, (3) order handling and accounting, and (4) shipping of orders. Although the wholesaler's cost per contact is higher, because, for example, a sales call representing 100 suppliers requires more time than one by a single supplier, the cost per contact is *not* increased in proportion to the number of suppliers and/or customers involved. (In the numerical example presented above, the cost per contact would be almost 100 times as great before the wholesaler would lose his cost advantage. In practice, it is unlikely that the cost of contact would be increased by more than three or four times, at most.)

Thus, market contact via wholesalers is inherently less costly than direct contact between suppliers and customers. However, because the operation of a wholesale enterprise involves certain fixed costs, the net advantage of the wholesaler is positive only if the number of contacts to be made exceeds some minimum number, which depends on the specific costs involved, and his relative advantage increases with the total number of suppliers and/or customers involved in a market.

The significance of the wholesaler's "market contact" function depends on the viewpoint of the institution that benefits from it—supplier or customer. From the supplier's viewpoint, the wholesaler provides a service of *sales contact* at a generally lower cost than that required for direct selling. The regular wholesaler employs a field sales force and usually also a telephone and/or mail-order sales staff, solicits orders from customers at regular intervals, takes orders and handles the necessary bookkeeping, and provides information about products and services to the customers. All these activities would, in the absence of the wholesaler, have to be provided by the supplier himself.

From the viewpoint of the wholesaler's customer, an industrial user or a retailer, the wholesaler's "market contact" function involves a *merchandising* service. The wholesaler identifies sources of products, selects an appropriate assortment from them, provides information about the items he sells, and offers advice to the customer about purchase amounts and timing. Again, if there were no wholesaler present in a channel, the customer would have to perform these functions for himself. He would have to identify and screen sources of supply, deal with each one via personal contact or otherwise, and order needed items from each supplier individually.

One may wonder at this point why products are ever sold by manufacturers directly to retailers and industrial users, in view of the inherent economies of selling through wholesalers. This question is considered at length in Chapter 18, in the context of marketing channel decisions and policies. At this point, we can mention a few reasons briefly. For one thing, as suggested above, the wholesaler has an absolute cost advantage only if the reduction in (variable) costs of market contact is great enough to offset the (fixed) cost of adding a separate enterprise to a marketing channel. Moreover, the relative cost advantage of the wholesaler depends on the number of contacts that are required for direct supplier-customer contact and the average value of transactions made between them. For example, the use of a wholesaler might afford a reduction of $5 per contact; this is a significant amount if the average amount purchased by a customer from a single supplier is, say, $50. But if the supplier is selling machine tools with an average value of $10,000, then a saving of $5 is insignificant.

The significance of a given reduction in the cost of market contact depends, not just on the amounts involved, but also on the importance of offsetting factors. In general, for reasons explained in Chapter 18, wholesalers cannot provide as aggressive a form of selling for any one manufacturer's line as the manufacturer can through direct selling. If there is significant value in aggressive selling, either because a market can thus be expanded or because competition among competing manufacturers is intensive, then the net benefit of direct selling may be sufficient to offset the greater costs associated with it. Furthermore, contact with customers via wholesalers usually requires more time than direct contact. If a product is perishable, or if there is need for an extensive interchange of information before a sale can be made, then the delays associated with selling through wholesalers may cost more than any savings involved.

In brief then, the wholesaler virtually always has a net advantage in terms of reducing the total cost of market contacts; but this advantage may or may not be offset by other factors, so that the overall economics of channel choice are more complex than might be inferred from Figure 12-1. We defer further discussion of the subject until Chapter 18.

Breaking bulk A basic economic function of the wholesaler, closely related to that of market contact, is to buy in large quantities and resell in smaller lots, that is, to "break bulk." The wholesaler almost always buys from manufacturers in quantities many times larger than the average amounts bought by his retailer and industrial user customers. This results in economic benefits for the total distribution channel. First, transportation costs are reduced because goods can be shipped greater distances in rail carload or truckload lots than would be possible if small orders were shipped directly to retailers and industrial users. Second, costs of selling and of handling orders are reduced, for reasons explained in the preceding section.

Warehousing Another major function of the regular wholesaler is to store the products that he sells, at a location much closer to the customer than that of the typical supplier. In 1967, merchant wholesalers' inventories amounted to over $21 billion, or about 1½ months' supply. Storage and maintenance of these stocks, and provision of the capital required to finance them, are among the most important services performed by wholesalers in the channel of distribution.

The warehousing function, like that of market contact, can be performed by suppliers and/or customers rather than by wholesalers. As discussed later in this chapter, retail chain warehouses and manufacturers' sales branches are specialized places of business, owned by customers and suppliers, and operated in part for the purpose of storing inventories at locations near the point of demand. In general, however, integrated wholesaling facilities do not enjoy any significant cost advantage in warehousing costs when compared with well-managed independent wholesalers. Often, a wholesaler is able to operate on a larger scale because his merchandise line is more extensive than that of a single supplier or customer, and this larger scale may permit operating economies through the use of such facilities as more efficient materials-handling equipment and larger computer systems for inventory control.

In some cases, wholesalers carry almost the entire burden of maintaining inventories at locations from which customer demand can be supplied quickly. For example, furniture wholesalers in large metropolitan areas carry extensive assortments of styles, colors, etc., which only the largest retailers attempt to do. Frequently, a retailer or an interior decorator takes a customer to the wholesaler's showroom and the buyer selects what he wants directly from the wholesaler's stock. The efficiency of this arrangement has been cited as a principal reason for the growth in furniture wholesalers' sales.

A similar inventory-carrying function is performed by wholesalers of automotive parts, plumbing, heating, and air-conditioning equipment, and parts for various types of machinery. An automotive service garage, for instance, could not possibly carry inventories of all the thousands of parts which might be needed for repair jobs. Instead, these are obtained from automobile parts distributors as needed.

Delivery Regular wholesalers deliver merchandise to their customers. Because the wholesaler's inventories are usually located closer to the customer than a manufacturer's, delivery can be made more rapidly. For many industrial users, the wholesaler's ability to provide rapid replacements for parts and supplies needed to keep a manufacturing facility in operation is an essential service.

Credit Practically all regular wholesalers extend credit to their customers, usually on an "open account" basis with bills settled monthly. Estimates by Dun & Bradstreet indicate that wholesalers' accounts receivable from customers in the late 1960s typically represented around 1½ months' sales, ranging from as low as 17 days' sales for tobacco and confectionery distributors to more than 60 days' sales for commercial machinery and equipment wholesalers.[1]

The provision of credit by the wholesaler means that, in effect, he finances part of his customers' inventories. The financing function can be, and frequently is, performed by other types of institutions too, especially by commercial banks. Often, however, the wholesaler has a closer relationship with his customers than a bank does, because he is in regular, frequent contact with the customer and is in a good position to evaluate the risks involved in extending credit.

Managerial and technical services Many regular wholesalers, especially those selling primarily to small retailers, have developed extensive programs of

[1] "The Ratios of Wholesalers," *Dun's Review*, October, 1970, pp. 72–73.

managerial assistance for their customers. These may include such services as:

Merchandising programs, in which inventory quantities and reordering systems are designed for different types and sizes of stores
Promotional programs, including displays, circulars, and periodic price specials
Accounting and control systems
Store facilities planning, including store layout and fixtures

The scope of the services provided and the degree of cooperation between the wholesaler and his customers depend on the nature of the relationship between them. In voluntary chains, the wholesaler has a continuing, close relationship with participating retailers, and may also have part ownership in some or all of the stores he supplies (see Chapter 11). This kind of relationship leads to a cooperative form of management almost as closely integrated as that employed in corporate chains. Even in the absence of contractual obligations between wholesalers and retailers, there is a trend toward closer coordination among them, as described later in this chapter.

Wholesalers also provide technical advice and services for the products they sell. Their salesmen are trained in the operation and maintenance of their product lines, although they seldom have the same degree of specialized technical competence as the manufacturer's own sales force. In some cases wholesalers have separate technical advisory services; for example, many drug wholesalers have prescription information departments, staffed by pharmacists, to assist retail druggists in keeping informed about new products and other developments.

SPECIAL-FUNCTION WHOLESALERS

In the preceding section we described the range of services which regular wholesalers may offer to their customers and suppliers. When all these services are combined, a "typical" transaction might take place somewhat as follows:

The wholesaler's salesman calls on a customer, say a retail hardware store, and reviews the customer's needs with him. The salesman examines the store's inventory; he presents some new products for consideration by the store manager; and he describes some special promotions that his company has planned for the following month. The retailer places an order for approximately $200 worth of merchandise, consisting of 16 different products manufactured by 11 different producers. The salesman transmits the order to the wholesaler's office, where the customer's credit standing is checked and the extension of credit is approved. Then, the order is passed on to the warehouse where the items ordered are selected from stock and assembled. The next day, the order is placed on a truck which delivers it to the customer.[2]

Although the regular wholesaler is organized to provide all these services,

[2] This is, of course, a description of the system operating as it is supposed to. In some cases, the customer does *not* qualify for credit; items ordered may not be in stock; there may be delays in processing the order, so that it does not get delivered the next day.

there are considerable variations in those actually provided from one line of business to another and for a given wholesaler, among different individual customers. If an air-conditioning contractor needs a new V-belt to make repairs on a machine he has installed, he will probably go to a wholesaler's sales counter himself in order to get faster service, thus eliminating the need for delivery in this particular transaction. Some customers do not qualify for credit, and must buy on a cash-only basis; some products are not carried in stock by the wholesaler, but are ordered only when a customer has specifically requested them. Thus, the regular wholesaler typically offers a flexible range of services, depending on circumstances.

Some wholesalers, however, have methods of operation basically different from those of the regular wholesaler: they normally provide a special combination of services, often more limited than those of the regular wholesaler but sometimes more extensive. The most important of these "special-function" types of wholesalers are cash-and-carry wholesalers, drop shippers, truck distributors, and rack merchandisers.

Cash-and-carry wholesalers Cash-and-carry wholesalers, as one might suspect, do not offer either credit or delivery services. Their customers come to the wholesaler's warehouse, select their own goods, and pay for them on the spot. This method of operation first came into prominence in the United States in the 1920s and 1930s, when the growing competition of corporate chains and, later, supermarkets made it increasingly difficult for small, unaffiliated grocery stores to remain competitive in price. The regular wholesalers serving these stores could not handle their small orders profitably on a full-service basis; so they offered the cash-and-carry arrangements as an alternative.

In some other countries, where chains and supermarkets are in an earlier stage of development than in America, cash-and-carry wholesalers grew rapidly during the late 1960s. In Great Britain, for example, the number of cash-and-carry outlets grew to over 600 in 1970, with an estimated sales volume of over $1 billion. One large food processor, Crosse and Blackwell, was reported to have eliminated its direct sales to some 80,000 small retail direct accounts by serving them through 400 cash-and-carries.[3]

The cash-and-carry method is inherently limited as a method of wholesale distribution. Although it meets the immediate needs of small retailers under certain competitive conditions, it is not really an efficient way to supply the bulk of a modern store's needs. Retailers cannot buy large quantities of merchandise in this way, for instance, unless each operates a sufficiently large truck. Even more important, going to and from the wholesaler's warehouse and selecting orders requires substantial amounts of time on the part of the re-

[3] "Growth of Cash and Carry," *Marketing*, November, 1970, pp. 54–56.

tailer or his employees (or relatives). These activities can almost always be performed more efficiently, that is, at a higher rate of output per man-hour, by the wholesaler's own employees. Thus, the method is suited primarily to supplying small orders to customers whose personnel have low opportunity costs, and these are, by definition, not likely to be viable retail enterprises in the long run.

Because of these inherent limitations, cash-and-carry wholesalers account for only a small share of total wholesale trade, primarily in groceries, in the United States.

Drop shippers Drop shippers, called "desk jobbers" in some lines of business, are wholesalers who do not handle or store the goods they sell. They take customer orders and then arrange for manufacturers to ship directly to the buyers. In many respects, drop shippers' operations are more similar to those of manufacturers' agents (see below) than to regular wholesale merchants. The key difference is that drop shippers *do* take title to the products and assume the corresponding risks, especially those associated with customer payment.

Drop shippers are of some importance in the distribution of products for which costs of physical distribution represent a major element of total marketing expense, such as lumber and other building materials, coal, and some types of industrial machinery.

Truck distributors Truck distributors, once called "wagon distributors" in pre-internal combustion days, deliver and sell merchandise to customers on regularly scheduled calls, carrying their inventories right on their trucks. This method of distribution is widely used for perishable products, including most of the "store-delivered" merchandise handled in retail food stores. A typical early morning scene in an American supermarket finds a dozen or more trucks delivering such goods as bread, milk, cookies and crackers, soft drinks, and refrigerated products. Most of these products are bought directly from processors such as dairies, wholesale bakeries, and soft drink bottlers. But some are handled by independent wholesale distributors.

Since the truck distributor makes deliveries directly to stores and usually puts his products onto the shelves or into refrigerated displays, he provides an element of service above that of regular wholesalers. But truck distributors usually sell on a cash basis, and do not offer extensive services beyond those of merchandising and delivery. Their operating expenses are typically higher than those of regular wholesalers, primarily because their average orders are so small.

Rack merchandisers The rack merchandiser, also known as the "rack jobber" or "service merchandiser," employs a method of operation generally similar to that of the truck distributor. Rack merchandisers came into prominence during the 1950s, when supermarkets first started handling "nonfood" lines on a large scale. The food chains had little experience in the buying, display, and promotion of these nontraditional product lines, and the rack merchandiser evolved as a specialist in providing the required skills. They sold, and have continued to sell, such products as health and beauty aids, housewares, toys, and other types of merchandise handled as "supplementary" lines by food stores and other retail outlets. They have also become an important form of distribution for phonograph records, which, like the other product classes mentioned, are sold as sidelines in many types of stores.

The difference between the rack merchandiser and the traditional truck distributor is that the rack merchandiser provides a much more complete merchandising service to retailers. He selects the lines and individual items to be stocked, arranges the displays (often providing the fixtures, too, hence the term "rack"), often marks the products, and sometimes sells on a consignment basis, collecting for goods only as they are sold by the retailer.

Farm products assemblers Another special-function type of wholesaler is the assembler of farm products. The assembler's method of operation is, in a sense, the reverse of that used by wholesalers of manufactured products. Whereas the latter buy from manufacturers in large quantities and "break bulk," reselling in much smaller average amounts, the assembler buys in small quantities and assembles goods into large lots. Assemblers handle such agricultural products as grain, milk, and fruits. Similar wholesale enterprises buy fresh seafoods and resell them to processors and institutional buyers. In 1967, there were about 11,000 establishments operated by assemblers, with aggregate sales volume of over $10 billion. Although this is a substantial volume of business, the relative position of assemblers in the distribution of farm products has declined since the early 1900s because improvements in transportation and communication have made direct contact between producers and buyers more practical.

SPECIALIZATION BY MERCHANDISE LINES

Like retailers, wholesalers specialize in terms of the product lines they handle. In many cases, the traditional "kind-of-business" groupings of wholesalers correspond closely to those of retail lines of trade, for example:

Wholesale	*Retail*
Drug wholesalers	Drugstores
Hardware wholesalers	Hardware stores
Sporting goods distributors	Sporting goods stores

Statistical data for wholesalers in selected lines of business, together with comparative figures for other types of wholesale business, are given in Table 12-2. These figures give some indication of the product lines in which wholesalers are relatively strong or weak, and also tell something about the characteristics of the "typical" wholesaler in each kind of business. Consider, for example:

Of the 238,000 merchant wholesaler establishments in all lines of business combined (Table 12-2), nearly 10 percent are in the food business. Almost 10 percent sell automotive equipment and parts. Less than ½ of 1 percent, on the other hand, specialize in paints.

The average size of a wholesaler's establishment varies greatly from one line of trade to another. For all lines of business combined (see Table 12-2), sales per establishment amounted to just under $1 million. But in the "general line groceries" classification, the average sales per establishment was $6.2 million, compared with only $336,000 in the automotive equipment business.

Wholesalers' operating expenses also vary greatly among different lines of trade. Distributors of commercial machinery and equipment, for instance, had average operating expenses of 25.6 percent of sales, compared with less than 1 percent of sales for independently owned petroleum bulk terminals. These variations reflect differences in functions performed, merchandise lines, and average size of establishments in the different classifications.

General-line and specialty wholesalers Within a given kind-of-business classification, there is often considerable variation in the breadth of merchandise lines carried by wholesalers. In several of the fields where wholesalers have traditionally played a major role, a distinction is made between *general-line* distributors and *specialty* distributors. (Separate figures are shown for these two categories in the food group in Table 12-2.) The general-line wholesaler is one who carries a broad assortment of products corresponding to the "total requirements" of customers in his line of business. A specialty distributor, on the other hand, carries a much narrower assortment of goods within the traditional general line. For example, specialty food wholesalers include those who handle only produce, or only frozen foods, or only dairy products.

The distinction between general-line and specialty distributors, and the significance of competition between the two types, is generally recognized in the food, drug, hardware, and industrial supply lines of trade. Of course, what constitutes a "general line" cannot be specified precisely at any given time, and it also changes over time because of the continuing emergence of new products and new patterns of customer needs in a particular line of business. In one study of industrial distributors, for example, self-designated general-line distributors were asked which individual product lines they carried.[4] There

[4] Robert D. Buzzell, *Value Added by Industrial Distributors and Their Productivity,* Bureau of Business Research Monograph no. 96, College of Commerce and Administration, The Ohio State University, Columbus, Ohio, 1959, pp. 31–35.

□
TABLE 12-2

Wholesale establishments, by type of operation, in selected kinds of business, 1967

Kind of business	Wholesalers			Manufacturers' sales branches		
	Number of establishments	Sales (millions)	Operating expenses	Number of establishments	Sales (millions)	Operating expenses
Total, all kinds of business	237,712	$223,808	13.1%	33,320	$84,400	9.1%
Food products:						
Groceries, general line	2,543	15,548	6.4			
Specialized food lines	20,029	19,882	11.7	2,814	9,458	11.3
Beer, wine and liquor	6,862	10,444	11.9	124	1,448	6.9
Tobacco products	2,515	5,315	5.9	47	663	14.2
Apparel, textiles:						
Piece goods, dry goods	4,075	4,578	13.1	135	1,115	9.9
Clothing and footwear	4,771	4,283	15.4	202	1,128	14.5
Furniture and home furnishings	6,047	4,329	19.1	502	963	12.7
Home appliances, TV, radio	2,299	5,718	12.9	143	1,512	9.8
Automotive:						
Motor vehicles	3,858	5,345	11.2	510	11,687	4.8
Automotive equipment	21,855	7,389	23.2	635	2,011	20.4
Tires and tubes	2,800	1,359	21.7	202	1,138	7.1
Petroleum bulk terminals	13,618	7,597	0.8	16,611	17,225	0.1
Lumber and construction materials	10,877	9,074	15.6	1,079	2,238	12.2
Drugs	3,053	4,748	14.3	311	2,450	15.0
Hardware	3,513	3,197	19.7	278	453	14.1
Industrial supplies	7,658	5,198	20.2	677	1,721	9.7
Industrial machinery and equipment	8,795	6,104	30.1	1,139	2,431	15.1
Commercial machinery and supply	5,931	1,929	25.6	2,253	5,170	24.8
Professional equipment and supply	4,633	2,893	22.7	703	418	22.3
Farm machinery and equipment	1,498	1,110	18.1	222	2,625	5.2
Paper products	7,663	6,422	17.4	367	1,123	13.6
Paints	1,268	424	25.5	935	623	18.4
Chemicals	3,380	2,636	16.0	614	3,856	11.0
Metals	4,937	11,273	12.1	. . .	. . .	. . .

Source: U.S. Bureau of the Census, Census of Business, 1967, *Wholesale Trade, United States Summary,* BC-67 WA-1, Government Printing Office, Washington, 1970.

Manufacturers' sales offices			Agents and brokers'		
Number of establishments	Sales (millions)	Operating expenses	Number of establishments	Sales (millions)	Operating expenses
13,970	$89,922	4.1%	26,462	$61,347	4.0%
1,481	5,586	7.7	4,440	15,948	3.5
192	1,977	4.1	131	295	6.1
. . .	. . .	. . .	35	69	5.0
225	4,022	3.7	567	2,337	3.4
262	1,577	8.5	1,163	2,240	5.5
406	1,183	6.2	1,068	1,249	6.4
241	411	7.5	252	490	5.7
214	13,581	1.4	201	716	4.3
139	1,109	2.7	688	1,106	5.5
77	640	5.7	35	41	6.5
872	3,965	4.5	794	1,113	5.2
176	1,531	10.2	220	504	5.6
211	327	7.4	436	462	6.1
712	2,778	4.0	1,122	1,037	8.0
1,129	2,522	7.1	2,193	2,482	8.3
825	1,023	17.2	610	288	9.4
140	251	9.8	283	223	8.5
28	258	4.2	106	114	6.2
1,018	4,231	4.5	538	1,007	4.9
73	347	17.7	101	100	6.0
942	9,818	4.1	470	757	5.0
1,395	17,847	2.1	824	2,576	3.0

was no product line carried by every one of the distributors studied, and only five (abrasive products, cutting tools, hand tools, power tools, and fasteners) were carried by 90 percent or more of the companies. It was concluded that there were 20 product lines generally recognized as ingredients of a general line, and that a general-line distributor was one who carried most of these lines, but not necessarily all.

Changes in product line assortments constitute a major dimension of competition in wholesaling. The impact of this kind of competition is discussed in a later section of this chapter.

□
SPECIALIZATION BY MARKETS SERVED

Another kind of specialization by wholesalers, which sometimes conflicts with specialization in terms of product lines, is in relation to markets or customer groups served. Several of the kind-of-business categories shown in Table 12-2 reflect the orientation of wholesalers toward the needs of particular customer groups. "Professional equipment and supply distributors," for instance, carry whatever product lines are needed by the particular professional groups to whom they sell, such as physicians or dentists. There are many other examples of this kind of specialization, including barbershop and beauty shop supply distributors and hospital supply distributors.

Often, wholesalers who serve specific types of customers have evolved as the industries or occupations to which they sell have emerged and grown. An outstanding example is the American Hospital Supply Company, which was formed in the 1920s. At that time, hospitals in their current institutional form were in their infancy. They typically had little or no professional "management," and the procurement of needed equipment and supplies was handled as a part-time responsibility by the doctors and nurses themselves. American Hospital Supply developed a systematic approach to the determination of a hospital's needs, a well-organized system of keeping inventory records, and a much broader line of products than had previously been available from a single source of supply. This combination of product lines and customer services evolved gradually during the period from the 1920s to the 1960s, as hospitals became larger, as professional hospital administrators came onto the scene, and as the technology of medicine advanced. By 1969, American Hospital Supply had become a company with 90 branches, total sales volume of $446 million, and extensive manufacturing operations as well as wholesale distribution activities.[5]

□
REDISTRIBUTION

The figures in Table 12-1 indicate that around 15 percent of wholesalers' sales are to "other wholesale establishments." Some of these sales represent oc-

[5] The history of American Hospital Supply Company is told in Frederick D. Sturdivant, *Growth through Service: The Story of American Hospital Supply Corporation,* Northwestern University Press, Evanston, Ill., 1970.

casional transactions, as when one wholesaler buys from another because he is out of stock on a particular item. But a more important type of product flow between wholesalers is that involved in "redistribution," the regular use of a multistage wholesale marketing channel. This kind of distribution is confined primarily to a few lines of trade in which special circumstances make it necessary, or more efficient, to utilize a multistage channel regularly.

One of the most important fields for redistribution is that of automotive parts and supplies. In this industry, the principal "consumers" are service stations and repair garages that provide services to automobile and truck owners. These users are numerous and widely scattered, and their needs for particular products are sporadic and hard to anticipate. As a result, there are many small wholesalers who carry stocks to supply the service outlets. These "indirect jobbers," as they are called, are too small and too numerous to be contacted on a direct basis by most manufacturers. Consequently, another level of wholesale distribution is usually employed: the "warehouse distributor," who buys from manufacturers and resells to indirect jobbers. Both direct and indirect jobbers are included in the figures for "automotive equipment wholesalers" in Table 12-2; hence the great number and small average size of establishments in this group.[6]

Redistribution is also fairly common in some other lines of business, including agricultural chemicals and fertilizers, tobacco products, and some types of paper products. Also, some product lines that are imported are frequently sold by the direct-importing wholesaler to other wholesalers.

Integrated wholesaling

As described in the preceding section, the independent wholesaler stands between the manufacturer and retailers and industrial users to whom he sells. In this position the wholesaler performs necessary marketing functions. But under some circumstances, these same functions can be performed more effectively or more economically by the manufacturers and/or by the customers for themselves.

In many industries, separate wholesale distribution facilities, either independent or owned, have never been utilized to any great extent. More than half of all industrial products are sold directly by manufacturers to users, and so is a substantial fraction of total consumer goods output. This direct selling may be necessary because the products are custom-made; because of a need for technical modifications, installation, or other services best provided by the manufacturer; because the number of customers is sufficiently small, and their size

[6] The structure of the automotive service industry in the 1950s has been documented in great detail by Charles N. Davisson, *The Marketing of Automotive Parts,* Bureau of Business Research, University of Michigan, Ann Arbor, Mich., 1955. Although the data in this study are now out of date, the structure of the industry is still basically the same.

sufficiently great, to permit economical direct contact; or because the products involved are perishable (for example, bread) and cannot be delayed in distribution.

A slightly different situation is that in which separate wholesaling facilities *are* employed, but these facilities are owned and operated by the manufacturer or by a retailer.

□ MANUFACTURERS' SALES BRANCHES

A manufacturer's sales branch is a wholesale establishment which, though owned by a manufacturer, performs functions essentially similar to those of an independent wholesaler.

As shown in Table 12-2, there were over 33,000 sales branches in operation in 1967, accounting for sales of $84 billion or 18 percent of total wholesale trade. Sales branches have increased in number and in overall share of wholesaling activity throughout the post-World War II period in the United States.

Sales branches carry inventories, sell through field sales forces, extend credit, and otherwise offer approximately the same services as independent wholesalers in the same lines of business. Often their merchandise lines are less extensive than those of wholesalers, because they limit their lines to those of their parent companies, although these may be supplemented by products of other noncompeting suppliers if necessary.

Statistical data for manufacturers' sales branches in selected lines of business are given in Table 12-2. Note that over a third of the total number of establishments, and about 10 percent of the total sales volume, consist of petroleum bulk terminals operated by oil refining companies. Other important lines of trade that use sales branches extensively include motor vehicles, commercial, industrial, and farm machinery, chemicals, and food products.

Comparison of the first two columns of figures in Table 12-2 gives some indication of the relative importance of wholesalers' versus manufacturers' sales branches in different industries. It should be kept in mind that the sales of these two types of wholesaling enterprises cannot be added to a meaningful total because comparable figures for direct factory-to-user and factory-to-retailer sales are not available. To complicate matters further, there is some ambiguity about the treatment given in the Census of Wholesale Trade to sales facilities located at, or adjacent to, manufacturing plants. How "separate" must a distribution activity be to qualify as a "separate establishment" and to be reported as such to the Bureau of the Census? Since the Census data are collected by mail, different firms probably follow different rules in deciding how to report. Not only does this give rise to some confusion, but the Census Bureau classifies "Sales locations of manufacturing companies which are engaged in the sale of electrical appliances, radio and TV primarily to retailers . . . as merchant wholesalers. All metals service centers of manufacturing companies are also classified as merchant wholesalers."[7]

Despite these difficulties, we can make a few cautious comparisons of the figures in Table 12-2. Independent wholesalers are clearly much more numerous than sales branches, and have substantially greater total sales volume, in certain lines of trade: food, apparel, alcoholic beverages, tobacco products, furniture, automotive equipment, lumber and construction materials, drugs, hardware, industrial supplies and equipment, professional equipment and supplies, and paper products. Sales branches are much stronger, relative to wholesalers, in the distribution of motor vehicles, petroleum products, commercial machinery and equipment, farm machinery, and chemicals.

The figures in Table 12-2 also permit comparisons of the operating expenses of independent wholesalers with those of sales branches. In general, sales branches have lower average expense ratios than wholesalers in the same line of business; but this is not always the case, as illustrated by the figures for tobacco products and drugs.

Although sales branches typically have lower operating costs than independent wholesalers, it should not be concluded that they are generally more efficient. Manufacturers often establish their own sales branches only in major markets, leaving smaller market areas to be covered by wholesalers. Moreover, the full costs of management may not be included in the figures reported for sales branches. Some of these costs may be incurred at the headquarters office level and not allocated to individual branch offices. When these factors are taken into account, it appears likely that costs of sales branches are about equal to those of independent wholesalers, under comparable conditions.

□

MANUFACTURERS' SALES OFFICES

Manufacturers' sales offices do not include warehousing facilities, but are locations from which salesmen operate. Apart from sales contact and possibly product service, these offices provide little in the way of services to customers; credit and other functions are typically provided by the manufacturer's factory or sales branch facilities.

Sales offices, which accounted for a total of $90 billion in sales or 19 percent of total wholesale trade in 1967, operate in a manner generally similar to that of manufacturers' agents, as described in a later section of this chapter.

□

RETAIL CHAIN WAREHOUSES

In 1967, there were some 5,000 establishments in operation under the ownership of retail chain organizations, providing warehousing and other services to the stores belonging to these companies.

[7] Louis Greenberg, "Some Problems Related to Census Statistics on Wholesale Trade," paper presented to the Fall Conference of the American Marketing Association, Boston, Mass., Sept. 1, 1970.

Chain warehouses operate in a manner similar to that of independent wholesalers, except that they do not, of course, "sell" their products—they simply transfer them to other components of their parent companies. These "distribution centers," as they are often called, maintain inventories in anticipation of demand from company stores, deliver orders, and frequently also serve as headquarters locations for management activities such as buying. Staff groups located at warehouse locations may provide various services to the stores such as assistance in store layout, allocation of shelf space, and planning and implementation of promotions.

In comparison with independent wholesalers, chain store warehouses have certain inherent advantages arising from closer coordination of merchandising and inventory policies with those of the stores they serve. Well-managed voluntary chains and retailer-owned cooperatives can achieve almost the same degree of coordination, however, so that the net economic advantage of the fully integrated system is probably not great.

Operating cost data for chain warehouses are not available, unfortunately, so that factual comparisons of their performance with that of independent wholesalers cannot be made.

Agents and brokers

Agents and brokers are independent middlemen who represent suppliers or customers, usually the former, in the sale or purchase of goods, working on a commission basis. In 1967 there were approximately 26,000 establishments operated by *merchandise* agents and brokers (Table 12-1). These figures do not include the numerous agents engaged in the sale of real estate and insurance. Moreover, because the Census figures include only those establishments with at least one paid employee, they omit many one-man enterprises and no doubt substantially understate the number of agents and brokers actually in business.[8]

As shown in Table 12-2, agents and brokers operate in virtually every line of business. They are especially numerous in the food, industrial machinery and supply, apparel, and furniture industries. Over one-fourth of their total sales volume is done in the food products category.

Within the broad classification of agents and brokers, there are several distinct types. The most important ones are manufacturers' agents, selling agents, and brokers.

[8] In 1948 and prior years, Census data were collected by field "enumerators" who obtained information from all recognizable places of business, whether or not they had any paid employees. Even this approach would not uncover many agents and brokers who operate out of their homes. But, of the total number of agents and brokers reporting to the 1948 Census, *35 percent* would not have been covered by the mail survey methods used in 1954 and subsequently. It is likely that the real total number of agents and brokers is as much as twice that reported in the Census. On the differences in coverage pre- and post-1948, see Greenberg, *op. cit.*

MANUFACTURERS' AGENTS

The most numerous of the various types of agents and brokers is the manufacturers' agent; in 1967, about 12,000 establishments in this group made sales of over $15 billion.

Manufacturers' agents operate on a local or regional scale, representing several manufacturers on a continuing basis. They often have exclusive rights to represent their suppliers in a given territory.

A manufacturer uses a system of agents essentially as a substitute for his own sales force. The functions of the agent are confined almost entirely to selling and to collecting and transmitting information related to the sale of products. Agents do not, except in rare cases, provide warehousing or delivery services.

As shown in Table 12-1, manufacturers' agents sell primarily to business and institutional users and to "other wholesale establishments," often wholesalers, rather than to retailers. For many smaller manufacturers, agents provide access to wholesaling channels which would otherwise be very costly.

Agents are compensated on a commission basis, with commission rates ranging from around 2 percent of sales up to 15 to 20 percent. In most lines of business, commissions are 5 to 6 percent. Because commissions are paid only on sales actually made, the cost of an agent is completely variable from the standpoint of the manufacturer. Often, the choice between utilization of agents and direct selling boils down to a tradeoff between the high initial fixed cost of a sales force as compared with its lower cost once a certain level of sales volume has been achieved. Many companies maintain their own sales offices in larger markets and supplement these with agent representation in areas with lower volume potential.

In the marketing of processed foods, manufacturers' agents are widely used and are traditionally called "food brokers." According to a survey conducted by the National Food Brokers Association, the "typical" food broker represents about 20 manufacturers, has 8 salesmen, calls on more than 30 wholesalers and 8 to 10 food chains, and makes visits to more than 500 food stores in his territory.[9]

SELLING AGENTS

The selling agent acts as a "contract marketing department" for the firms that he represents. He handles all the output of each supplier and provides a wide range of managerial services including product line planning, selling, and credit management. Like the manufacturers' agent, the selling agent is compensated by a commission, with rates ranging from 2 to 6 percent of sales.

Selling agents are concentrated in a few lines of business, primarily textiles, coal, and lumber. Traditionally, producers in these industries have been small companies located in producing areas, and lacking in effective management or staff services. The selling agent system evolved to meet these special needs.

[9] "Food Brokers Broadening Their Role in Food Distribution," *Progressive Grocer*, February, 1965.

Although the need for selling agents' services diminished by mergers and consolidations among producers during the 1950s and 1960s, there were still 1,900 such establishments operating in 1967 with combined sales of nearly $7 billion.

BROKERS

Brokers are functional middlemen who represent either sellers or buyers in completing transactions, generally on a noncontinuing basis. When the broker works on behalf of a seller, he locates a customer for a particular lot of merchandise, and is compensated by a commission paid by the seller. On other occasions the broker is paid by the buyer in return for locating a source of supply. In either case, his services are virtually always limited to negotiation. As a result, the broker's commission rates are typically lower than those of manufacturers' agents; for some standardized products they are as low as 1 percent of sales.

Because brokers provide limited services and work on a transaction-by-transaction basis, they do not constitute a practical channel of distribution for manufacturers who need regular, continuing marketing services. Brokers are widely used in industries in which supply and demand fluctuate in quantity and/or quality: fresh produce, livestock, and standardized raw materials.

OTHER TYPES OF FUNCTIONAL MIDDLEMEN

In addition to manufacturers' agents, selling agents, and brokers, there are several other types of institutions that make purchases and sales on a commission basis.

Commission merchants provide services similar to those of brokers but, in addition, store and display the products they handle. This method of operation was developed in the distribution of certain agricultural products which producers ship to a "central market" for inspection and purchase by processors and distributors. Livestock and grain are the principal categories of goods sold through commission merchants.

Auction companies operate in a manner similar to commission merchants, except that sales are made to the highest bidder among those offering bids on a specific item or lot of merchandise. The auction system is, of course, widely used at the retail level for such products as works of art, rare books, stamps, and coins. At the wholesale level, auction companies are important in the distribution of fresh fruits and vegetables, tobacco, and livestock. Auctions are also frequently used to sell used merchandise, including automobiles, machinery, and restaurant and store fixtures.

Competition and change in wholesaling

The institutional system for wholesale distribution, like that of retailing, is continuously evolving and being modified in response to changes in other components of the total marketing system. Changes in technology, mergers and acquisitions among manufacturers, new approaches to industrial procurement, the growth of large retailing enterprises—all these and many other trends are reflected in changing patterns of competition among wholesaling organizations. The dynamic aspect of wholesaling is less visible than that of retailing, and changes in wholesaling tend to be more gradual, but over a period of time significant shifts do occur. In this section, we discuss briefly a few of the more important changes in wholesaling that developed during the 1950s and 1960s.

□ DECLINING POSITION OF AGENTS AND BROKERS

The relative importance of agents and brokers in the wholesaling system has been declining since the 1920s. In 1929, agents and brokers accounted for over 20 percent of total wholesale trade; by 1948, their share had fallen to 17 percent; and in 1967 it was only 13 percent (see Table 12-1). As mentioned earlier, changes in the methods used to collect Census data may have had some effect on these figures; but even when this is taken into account, the downward trend is clear cut.

The reasons for a decline in the position of agents and brokers should also be clear from what has already been said about the conditions favoring their use. In the marketing of agricultural products, the need for representation in terminal markets by brokers, commission merchants, and auctions has been reduced by improved transportation and communication. In particular, more and better roads and trucks have increasingly made it possible to bypass terminal markets altogether. Thus, farmers whose fathers sent their crops via train to Chicago for sale through an auction may now ship directly to a processor or food chain in Indianapolis, eliminating the requirement for the old system of wholesaling.

Agents are also declining in importance in the distribution of many manufactured products. Here, the main reason is probably the increasing average size of manufacturers in most industries. As mentioned earlier, the use of agents in lieu of a sales force is an especially attractive alternative for the smaller manufacturer, because it avoids the risks inherent in making a commitment to the fixed costs of direct selling. But as manufacturers grow larger and as mergers and acquisitions reduce the number of small, specialized producers, the need for agents is diminished. A comparison of sales changes for agents and brokers with corresponding figures for wholesalers and sales branches will emphasize this point. The table on page 306 shows how this trend toward larger manufacturers has affected some industries between 1958 and 1967.

	Change in sales, 1958 to 1967		
	Wholesalers	Sales branches and offices	Agents and brokers
Air conditioning, refrigeration equipment and supplies	+84%	+126%	+21%
Electrical apparatus and supplies	+64	+113	+18
Lumber and construction materials	+44	+ 85	+19
Plumbing and heating equipment	+38	+ 59	+29

Of course, the use of agents and brokers is not confined to small manufacturers. Although their overall relative position is declining, they still play an important role and are by no means "doomed to extinction." Even some of the largest manufacturing companies use agents extensively, although typically as a supplement to their own sales organizations. For example, some of the largest food processors, with sales forces numbering in the hundreds, use food brokers to distribute certain products that need special handling, display, or promotion (such as refrigerated products and frozen foods).

INCREASING PRODUCT SPECIALIZATION

Among independent wholesalers, there has been a long-term trend toward increasing product line specialization. Although the traditional term "general line" still has meaning, fewer and fewer wholesalers find it possible to maintain anything approaching "full" coverage of all lines in a broad kind-of-business category. In the field of industrial supplies and equipment distribution, for example, a so-called "Census of Industrial Distributors" has been conducted several times by *Industrial Distribution* magazine. In the 1968 edition of this survey, only 18 percent of the distributors designated themselves as "general-line" wholesalers, a much lower proportion than in earlier years. Commenting on the survey, *Industrial Distribution* suggested that[10]

> Because of increased technical complexity in product lines, many suppliers weigh and select distributors by their in-depth product knowledge and engineering competence. Distributors' customers are also turning toward distributors offering the advantages of specialization. Thus, urged to specialize by their suppliers and customers, the overall character [of distributors] has changed greatly.

The same kinds of pressures that exist in industrial distribution affect wholesalers in other fields. In almost every industry, the number of products available tends to increase regularly and the complexity of products becomes ever greater. Although statistical data are not available to document the trend, it seems clear that the traditional general-line wholesaler is declining in importance in most fields.

[10] "Facts about Industrial Distribution," pamphlet, *Industrial Distribution*, New York, 1968.

□

EVOLUTION OF VERTICAL CHANNEL SYSTEMS

Perhaps the most important trend affecting wholesaling during the 1950s and 1960s was the continued growth of various kinds of integrated systems of distribution. As mentioned in Chapter 10, corporate retail chains, voluntary and cooperative organizations, and franchise systems all have common basic purposes and features. All of them achieve greater effectiveness and efficiency than do traditional distribution systems by some kind of centralization in management, through which operations at all levels, from manufacturing through final sales, can be coordinated. In view of their common properties, all such types of channel networks have been termed "vertical channel systems" by some authorities in the field.

In some cases, wholesalers have taken the lead in organizing and managing vertical channel systems. Midas International, for example, was originally a wholesale distributor of automotive supplies and equipment. Seeing an opportunity for more effective marketing of certain kinds of replacement parts, Midas developed a network of franchised muffler and brake repair shops in which standardized work methods are used, and which are heavily promoted to motorists. By 1970 Midas had over 500 outlets, and was engaged in manufacturing parts as well as in distributing them. Many other franchisers also operate in effect as wholesalers, deriving their principal income from the sale of products to members of the franchise system, although they may not be classified as wholesalers by the Census Bureau.

Although wholesalers have sometimes taken the lead in organizing channel systems, in most fields they have traditionally played a more passive role and, as a result, have more often been the victims rather than the beneficiaries of new forms of marketing. Because of continued competitive pressures, however, many wholesalers are now taking a more aggressive and imaginative posture. According to one observer, writing in 1969, wholesalers "[now] appear quite willing to develop marketing systems, some of which include manufacturing and retailing operations, using their wholesale houses as operational focal points."[11]

The approaches used by wholesalers to participate in emerging vertical channel systems will no doubt vary. But it seems certain that, in the future, the role of the wholesaler and of other wholesaling institutions will increasingly be that of a component in integrated, professionally managed systems.

Questions

1. What considerations might prompt a manufacturer of industrial chain saws to distribute his line through an industrial distributor of some type rather than directly through his own sales force?

[11] Richard S. Lopata, "Faster Pace in Wholesaling," *Harvard Business Review*, July–August, 1969, p. 143.

2. How do the characteristics of each of the following products, and their ultimate customers, influence the extent to which wholesalers are used in their distribution?

a. Plate glass
b. Stereo equipment
c. Greeting cards
d. Fresh peaches
e. Bread
f. Cement
g. Industrial sandpaper

3. The automotive "aftermarket" is defined as the market for all automotive parts and equipment except products and services that go into new cars and trucks. Typically its distribution channels are complex, involving several layers of wholesale distribution.

Prior to World War II, most automotive manufacturers sold directly to *automotive jobbers,* who in turn sold to retail outlets such as gasoline stations and independent repair outlets. Following the war, however, the number of automotive jobbers grew rapidly until, by the late 1960s, it was estimated that there were about 25,000 jobbers in the United States. Most were small, with average annual sales of about $150,000.

The majority of jobbers concentrated their efforts on selling to retail establishments. A number of larger jobbers, however, also engaged in selling automotive parts and equipment to small jobbers. On this basis, they came to be known as *redistributing wholesalers.* Due to the difficulties in defining what constituted a redistributing wholesaler, the number of jobbers who could be described in this manner was not known.

While redistributing wholesalers bought some of their merchandise from manufacturers, most relied heavily on another class of wholesaler, the *wholesale distributor.* Wholesale distributors, which emerged during the late 1940s and early 1950s, engaged solely in the redistribution of parts and equipment to other wholesalers. In the late 1960s, it was estimated that there were about 1,500 wholesale distributors in the United States.

a. Why has this channel structure developed in automotive aftermarket?
b. What effect, if any, does this channel network have on the cost of automotive replacement parts?
c. Are these channels likely to change significantly in the next ten to fifteen years? Why or why not?

4. According to Table 12-2, the average operating expenses of industrial machinery and equipment wholesalers was 30.1 percent in 1967. The average operating expenses of industrial machinery and equipment manufacturers' sales branches was only 15.1 percent. The sales volume of the wholesalers,

however, was well over double the sales volume of manufacturers' sales branches.

a. In view of this cost disparity, why have wholesalers in this field been so successful?

b. Why do you think the operating expenses of wholesalers distributing industrial machinery and supplies are higher (as a percent of sales) than for any other group of wholesalers included in Table 12-2?

5. Why have wholesaler-sponsored voluntary supermarket chains increased in importance in recent years?

6. Midas International, founded by Mr. Nate Thurmond in 1938, became known in its early history for dependable wholesale distribution in the automotive field. Functioning as a wholesaler, the firm grew to a sales volume of $3.5 million in 1950. In that year, Mr. Thurmond's son Gordon formed the organization and promoted the idea of establishing a franchised chain of retail outlets specializing in the installation of mufflers and exhaust systems.

Midas Muffler Shops, as the franchised retail outlets came to be known, enjoyed substantial success. By the late 1960s, Midas' sales approached $50 million, a majority of which emanated from the muffler shops.

a. What factors do you think contributed to the success of Midas Muffler Shops? To what extent might these factors be applied successfully in other industries or products?

b. What risks does a wholesaler incur in integrating forward into the operation or franchising of retail establishments?

7. How do you think changes in the nature of the market for phonograph records have affected the structure and practices of wholesaling activities in this industry? Similarily, how have changes in the market for frozen foods affected wholesaling of these items?

8. The wheel of retailing was discussed in the preceding chapter. What parallels can you see between the evaluation of retail channels and changes in the importance of different patterns of wholesale distribution?

9. What factors other than direct costs influence a specialty food manufacturer in deciding whether or not to use agents, brokers, and/or wholesalers? Why?

Marketing management

PART FOUR

In Part 1, we defined and described marketing, and looked at it as a system. Part 2 dealt with various types of customers. In it, we described different kinds of customers, analyzed their decision-making processes, and explored some of the basic factors that influence decision-making units. In Part 3, we looked at the wholesaling and retailing institutions through which most manufacturers reach their ultimate customers, and described the dynamics of change that characterize wholesaling and retailing.

In Part 4, we turn our attention to marketing management. We shall concern ourselves with the various activities of marketing managers as they define and solve the problems that confront them in identifying, stimulating, and meeting the demand for their goods and services. Broadly speaking, this part will deal with the components of marketing strategy, which itself is defined as the development of an effective response to market opportunities and problems.

More specifically, the chapters in Part 4 deal with the various elements of the marketing mix, which were defined briefly in Chapter 1. Thus, the marketing problems involved in product policy and the special problems of developing and introducing new products will be discussed in Chapters 14 and 15. The next two chapters, 16 and 17, will concern price; pricing concepts, policies, and methods will be presented. The role of place, which may also be called distribution or channels of distribution, in marketing management decisions will be the subject of Chapters 18 and 19. The next element of the marketing mix that Part 4 will deal with is promotion, or marketing communications. Chapter 20 will discuss the role of promotion in marketing decisions, and Chapters 21 and 22 will be devoted to personal selling and advertising sales promotion, respectively. Chapter 23 will deal with marketing organization, and Chapter

24 with the special problems of marketing management in the international marketplace.

Before moving to the specific elements of marketing management, we need to recognize that marketing is only one component of the total operation of a company, even though it is always important and often the most important component. Howard Morgens, president of Procter and Gamble (P & G), whose company is generally recognized as one of the best managed in the United States and is particularly noted for its marketing strength and success, has said, "There is no such thing as marketing skill by itself. For a company to be good at marketing, it must be good at everything else, from R & D [research and development] to manufacturing, from quality controls to financial controls" (as quoted in "The Ten Best-managed Companies," Dun's Review, *vol. 96, no. 6, December, 1970, p. 23*). A company may have an excellent product, excellent information as to who its existing and potential customers are, and excellent plans for promoting and selling the product, but these are of no use unless it has the facilities and materials to produce the product, competent people, an organization requisite to its needs, and the money to finance its operations. Thus, we shall begin Part 4 by looking in Chapter 13, at the totality of business management, and discuss the relationship between it and marketing management.

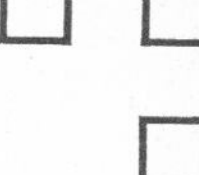

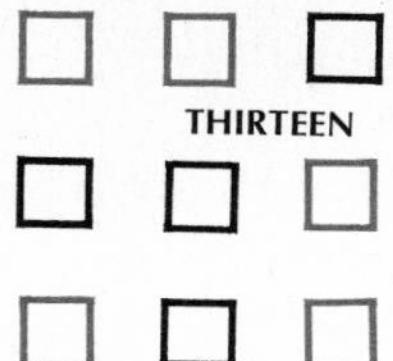

THIRTEEN

Marketing and business management

As indicated in the introduction to Part 4, marketing, although essential to business success, is only one component of the total operation of a business firm. In this chapter, we shall make that idea more explicit. We shall first discuss the overall activity of a business firm, centering on the concept of business strategy, and then relate marketing operations to total operations. Then, because this chapter serves also as an introduction to the various elements of the marketing mix, we shall emphasize the importance of integrating those elements in terms of marketing strategy and marketing planning. Finally, since profits and costs are key elements in both the overall activity of a firm and in its marketing operations, we shall turn our attention to some fundamental profit and cost concepts.

The concept of business strategy

Almost every business firm operates in an environment that changes rapidly and in major ways. In the American economy, as in the economies of other industrial nations and most of the developing nations, the changes that arise from competition and technology, from education, and from the expectations of the public are so well known as to require no elaboration. If a business firm

☐ *Strategy is the pattern of objectives, purposes, or goals and major policies for achieving these goals, stated in such a way as to define what business the company is in or is to be in and the kind of company it is or is to be.*[1]

is to be successful over a period of time, it must have a strategy☐ that makes it possible to react effectively to the dynamics of change.

It is useful to consider business strategy in terms of a specific company. The Xerox Corporation, whose sales rose from less than $40 million in 1960 to more than $1.5 billion 10 years later, achieved most of that growth from its copying and duplicating machines. By the early 1970s, Xerox spent more than $100 million a year on research and development so that it could stay ahead of competition in its traditional field and at the same time move into educational publishing, computers, and other fields—all related to information and information technology. Xerox management, over the years, succeeded in achieving its objectives of 20 percent annual growth rates in sales and profits.

To achieve these growth objectives, Xerox had to develop policies and programs that fit together and met adequately both the needs of its customers and the activities of its competitors. It had to develop new machines, do research on customer needs and information technologies, solve engineering and design problems, hire and train a rapidly expanding labor force, build and operate plants, develop distribution facilities, install accounting and control systems, find and train managers for various levels and for various kinds of jobs, keep an eye on its competition, finance operations and pay dividends, expand international activities, and, of course, develop the marketing program necessary to achieve the profitable sales of its product line.

Xerox is widely regarded as competitively preeminent in its original product field and as a major competitor in its newer fields. When one considers the multitude of decisions and actions implicit in the list just cited, it is apparent that, although marketing is important to Xerox, the extent of the company's success could have been achieved only through the effective coordination and integration of *all* segments of the Xerox enterprise. Xerox, then, has been successful because it has had an effective strategy. It has, over the years, been able to define *what* it wants to be, *where* it wants to go, and *how* it intends to get there. And it has done this in the face of rapid environmental change and aggressive competitive activity.

☐

DESIGNING A FIRM'S STRATEGY

A discussion of strategy design could easily be the subject of an entire book, but we can present here only a brief treatment of the topic.[2] Our objective is to

[1] The authors are indebted to their Business Policy colleagues at the Graduate School of Business Administration, Harvard University, for this definition and much of the conceptual framework of this section. For a more detailed discussion of corporate strategy, see the text portions of Edmund Learned, C. R. Christensen, Kenneth Andrews, and William Guth, *Business Policy: Text and Cases,* Richard D. Irwin, Inc., Homewood, Ill., 1969.

[2] In addition to *Business Policy: Text and Cases, op. cit.,* see Marvin Bower, *The Will to Manage,* McGraw-Hill Book Company, New York, 1966; and Ansoff, H. Igor, *Corporate Strategy,* McGraw-Hill Book Company, New York, 1965, for more detailed discussions of corporate strategy.

give a conceptual scheme for the process of designing a strategy, rather than an exhaustive description of the methods that managements employ. While reading, one may wish to think back to the Xerox example or to the activities of some other familiar company and visualize the specific steps the company might take in designing the strategic process described below. The process can be divided into three parts: information, analysis and definition, and decision.

Information A company must continuously collect information as the raw material upon which its strategy is based. Information inputs may come from internal sources such as executives, personnel responsible for studying competitive activity, or other employees, and from such external data sources as consultants, research firms, governmental agencies, and general information media. Those responsible for designing a strategy will try to find out as much as they can about economic, political, and social trends (see the detailed discussions of these areas in Part 2), about technological developments that affect the company and its products, about relevant national and international activities, and about competitive developments in their industry or other industries that may at some time have an impact on the affairs of their firm. The need, in brief, is to acquire as much information as necessary about the environment in which the firm operates.

Information of an internal nature is also necessary to the development of an effective strategy. Strategy formulation requires knowledge of the resources that currently exist or may become available, in order that management can assess properly the firm's strengths and weaknesses as decisions on where the company is going are made. Internal data must help management answer such questions as the following: What are our strengths and weaknesses in the areas of production, finance, marketing, and research? Do we have the financial and manpower resources to grow at rate x, rate y, or rate z? If we are currently weak in marketing or production, how much will it cost and how long will it take to correct the situation? In essence, an audit of internal resources, current and potential, is required.

Analysis and definition Internal and external information, once collected, must be analyzed. The internal data help to indicate what can be done by a company, and the external data help to shed light on what might be done. Combining the two sets of data is necessary to answer the ultimate question as to what the company will do, or at least will try to do.

Careful analysis of information, both external and internal, is essential in order that alternative courses of action can be defined. Each alternative must be analyzed in terms of the opportunities and the risks that it presents, both for the immediate future and in the long run. A small manufacturer of a line of women's dresses whose sales are almost entirely on the East Coast might, for example, be considering geographical expansion, the establishment of its own stores in major East Coast cities, or adding other apparel items to its line. Each alternative carries with it different opportunities and risks, requires different internal resources for accomplishment, and necessitates an understanding of a different competitive and external environment.

Decision Decisions among major strategic alternatives are normally made by senior company officials on the basis of analyses presented by persons at subordinate levels of an organization. The overall strategic decision says, in effect, "This is what we are going to do in response to the several opportunities presented by our environment, these are the resources we shall commit in order to achieve our objectives, and these are the policies that govern the way in which those resources will be used."

Remember that our definition of strategy refers to a pattern of objectives and major policies for achieving these goals. Both are important. Our small dress manufacturer, having analyzed the available information and defined the opportunities and risks of the strategic alternatives, may choose to expand geographically by selling on the West Coast. His objectives might be to raise his total sales and profits by 20 and 30 percent, respectively, within two years, or perhaps to achieve some specific total dollar amount of West Coast sales within a year. To achieve his objectives, he will need to adopt some policies that affect the character of his business. External borrowing may have to be used to finance the operation, part of the production may be carried out on the West Coast, the sales force will have to be reorganized to permit control from new regional offices, new financial controls will probably have to be installed, and the company may decide to triple its advertising budget to get as much impact as possible on the West Coast when its line is first introduced.

Designing a strategy is only part of the management job. Objectives and policies are of little use unless they are implemented. The carrying out of a firm's strategy is our next topic, and it, too, can be dealt with only briefly here.

□ IMPLEMENTING A FIRM'S STRATEGY

How does a company achieve its objectives and carry out its policies? If Ford Motor Company has decided to increase its share of the automobile market by 1.5 percent by 1975 and has made the policy decisions it hopes will achieve that objective, what does the company do then? Or if Paul Smith, the principal owner of Smith Construction, Inc., a $1 million construction firm, decides to increase profits 30 percent by operating in two more cities, what does his company do? Strategies have been decided upon, but the two companies are so different in size, scope, and other respects that we can talk only at a conceptual level if we are to find common threads in respect to the implementation of the strategies. We shall now consider such common threads, citing a few examples to illustrate differences that arise because of size or other reasons.

Let us state the obvious first. No single manager can do everything in a company, unless we are talking about a one-man operation, nor can he look constantly over the shoulders of all the people who are doing the work. The question then becomes one of defining the areas of influence through which managements try to ensure the successful implementation of a company's strategy. We suggest that at the conceptual level there are six such areas of influence: planning, organization, information systems, rewards and punishments, management development, and leadership.

Planning Planning is defined as "deciding in advance what is to be done, when it is to be done, how it is to be done, and who is to do it."[3] In our context, a plan is a detailed description of how objectives and major policies are to be implemented. Most companies use both short- and long-range plans, generally making the latter much less explicit than the former; many companies provide for the annual revision of both types of plans. Larger companies frequently have planning departments which serve top managements in a staff (advisory) capacity and are responsible for working with operating executives in marketing and production to ensure that plans are made and reviewed at appropriate times. As indicated, plans are specific statements, closely integrated and interdependent, of *how* objectives and policies are to be achieved, *when,* and *by whom.* An illustrative, and manifestly incomplete, list of topics that may require plans in medium-sized or large companies follows:

Capital equipment
Plant facilities
New stores or distribution facilities
Personnel expansion
New products or styles
Financial requirements
Acquisitions or mergers
Real estate developments
Plant and equipment renovation
Raw materials supplies
Geographic expansion
Organization changes
Management development
Cash requirements
Product line changes
Computer facilities
Dividend policies
Financial control systems

The detail and time span of planning vary according to company size, complexity of operation, and the subject matter of the plan itself. A small company may have a master plan that covers some of the topics in the list cited above, but the plan is apt to be fairly inexplicit and mostly in the owner's head—Paul Smith, our contractor of a few paragraphs ago, has probably only begun to plan more explicitly and to see the need for thinking about where he wants his company to be four or five years from now. But General Motors, with

[3] George Steiner, *Top Management Planning,* Collier–Macmillan Canada, Ltd., Toronto, 1969, p. 7. Chapters 18 and 19 of Professor Steiner's book deal with marketing planning and product planning.

sales of around $25 billion, is planning 25 or 30 years ahead in such areas as raw materials and plant facilities, and is fairly specific in terms of its 5-year plans.[4]

Organization Another major area for decision is organizational structure. This, too, is a topic of great complexity, and we can give it sketchy treatment at best. First, we can generalize by saying that organizational form depends on a company's strategy, its size, and the complexity of its operations. To illustrate this, let us consider the president of a company that manufactures and sells decorative ceramics for the home. Sales are in the neighborhood of $5 million, and retail customers are reached in some states with company salesmen and in others through wholesalers; some advertising is also done in regional magazines and newspapers. The company has some stock on the market and uses bank loans to augment its working capital. The employees are unionized, and health, hospitalization, and other types of employee benefit plans have been installed. Chances are that the structure of the organization will look somewhat as shown in Figure 13-1. This is known as a functional organization because the major organizational units reflect the primary business functions.

Now let us assume that several years have passed, and the company is on *Fortune* magazine's list of the country's 500 largest manufacturing companies. It has long since expanded beyond the decorative ceramics business, and has moved into machine tools, sporting goods, office furniture, earth-moving equipment, small appliances, and a few other products. The company's sales are reaching toward $1 billion, and it is a full-fledged conglomerate (a com-

[4] Five years is the normal long-range planning period for most large companies, so far as detailed plans are concerned.

FIGURE 13-1

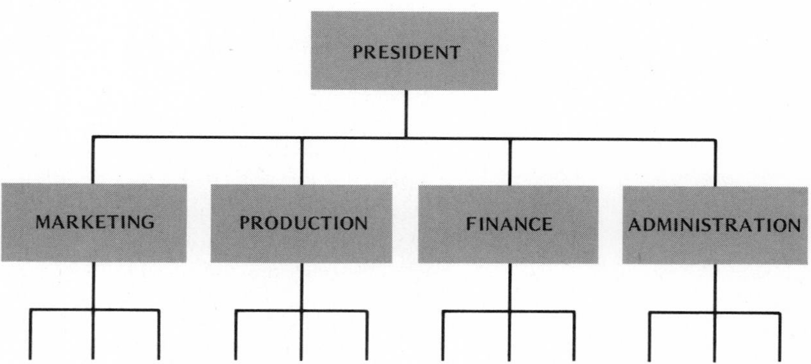

FIGURE 13-2

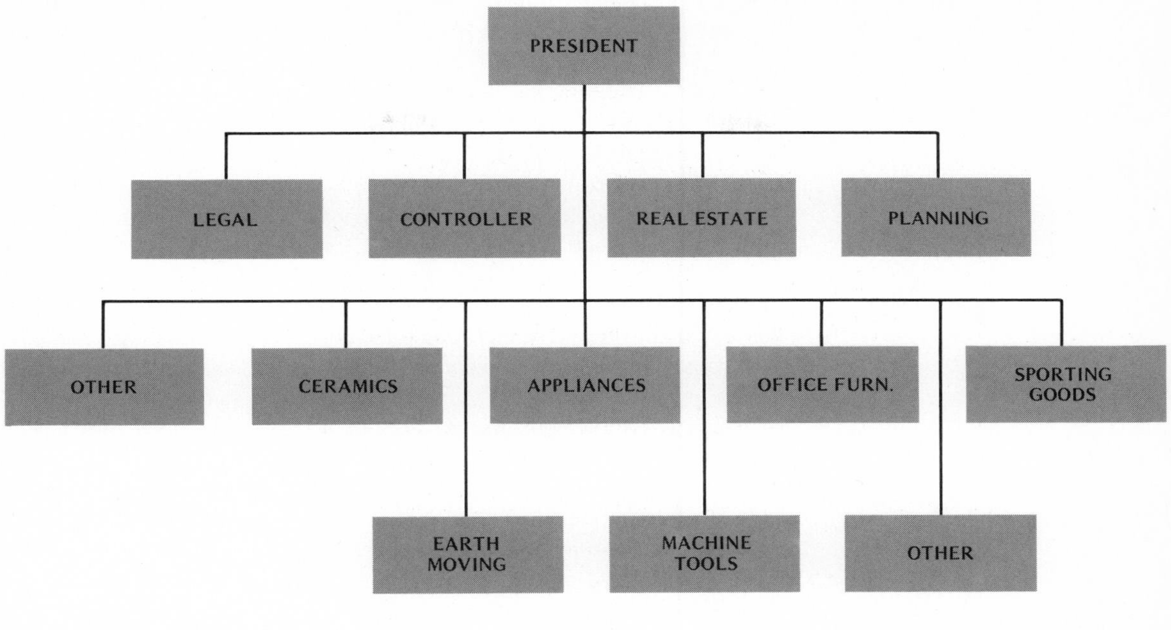

pany which operates in a variety of product markets that are completely or somewhat unrelated). By now it has almost certainly been found that the old functional organization does not work well, and has been replaced with a different type. The new organizational structure is apt to be departmental or divisional (experts use different terms in describing the components of large organizations), by products or product types, as shown in Figure 13-2. This chart is only a skeleton, and necessarily incomplete. The advisory staff services are on the line just below the president; other kinds of staff offices might have been included. Also, although we have omitted him for purposes of simplicity, there might be an executive vice-president to supervise the operations of the product divisions while the president concentrates on policy and planning. At the level of the product divisions (or departments), it should be emphasized that there will be subunits that might make each individual product organization resemble Figure 13-1. Finally, though no chart showing the possibility is presented, it should be mentioned that the president might have chosen to combine individual product divisions into *groups*. Litton Industries, for example, a company that in 1971 operated in perhaps 100 different product-market areas, has clustered what we have called product divisions into groups, each under an executive responsible for the achievement of whatever objectives Litton's senior executives have established for his group.

Even so brief a discussion of organization should highlight the fact that organizational form, except perhaps in small companies whose size remains relatively constant, is not static. As people, organizational theory, size of operations, and the nature of product and market relationships change, so too does organizational structure. This is as it should be, for the structure of a company has great impact on the attitude and behavior of the people who work for it, and hence on the achievement of company goals.

Information systems Operating as they do in environments that are conspicuous for complexity and change, companies need information that is accurate, timely, and as complete as is economically feasible. Data, both external and internal, are an essential input to management judgment for purposes of strategy design and implementation, particularly so as organizations grow in size and internal complexity. The last several years have witnessed explosive developments in computers, related software, and communications devices—these have helped immeasurably in making information available, but the process of designing information systems has become more complicated and more expensive.

In addition to problems of cost, there are two other major problems in designing information systems. The first is the nature of the data that are needed. The second is the levels of organization that make use of various data.

So far as the nature of needed information is concerned, we have already outlined the kinds of external data that can be useful to a company.[5] Internally the needs are equally great, the more so as the size and operational complexity of a firm increase. In 1971, International Telephone and Telegraph Corporation (ITT), with sales of over $6 billion, was a conglomerate with more than 200 operating units, that is, businesses, which ranged from insurance to car rentals. ITT's information systems were "so complicated and thorough that [their] match could only be imagined for a moon launching."[6] The operating units of ITT made forecasts of sales, earnings, plant and equipment needs, materials requirements, personnel, financial needs, and many other items. These, after review, were translated into plans and budgets. Information systems then provided periodic data so that performance could be measured and action taken to correct problems. ITT's systems were set up in such a way that problems and deviations from targets were highlighted in reports. Large

[5] See the section "Information" earlier in this chapter. For a detailed study of the nature of external information and processes by which it can be acquired, see Francis Aguilar, *Scanning the Business Environment,* The Macmillan Company, New York, 1967.

[6] "The Ten Best-managed Companies," *Dun's Review,* vol. 96, no. 6, December, 1970, p. 25.

companies, such as ITT, frequently have staff organizations that are responsible for planning and installing information systems, and for helping organizational subunits devise their own internal information systems. A marketing department in one of ITT's "businesses," for example, will have its own informational needs in such areas as sales forecasting, customer sales, lost business, and sales expense, and systems providing such data are normally designed with the help of the parent company's control staff.

Reflected in the above statement is the problem of the level of organization to which information should go. In the sales area, for example, salesmen often are required to submit detailed reports to their field supervisors regarding such items as calls, expenses, new customers, lost customers, competitive products, and orders. Field supervisors combine and consolidate such data for submission to the headquarters sales office, which in turn may report only such items as sales, expenses, and lost business to the chief marketing executive. In production, in accounting, and in other areas of business activity, information is normally similarly condensed for evaluation and comparative purposes as it travels upward in an organization.

To this point, our concern has been with the nature and upward flow patterns of the data conveyed by information systems. Some mention of downward flow is also necessary. One cardinal principle of organizational theory is that people work most effectively when they (1) know the objectives and functions of their organization units and (2) understand why and how their performances are evaluated. In addition, of course, people at all levels of organization need certain kinds of information to carry out their assigned responsibilities effectively. The furniture salesman in Spokane, for example, can more effectively sell the company's line if the home office in North Carolina keeps him informed when a competitor is introducing a new line or making a change in the prices it charges. It is essential, then, for reasons of both morale and performance, that the design of information systems take into account the downward flow of data.

Rewards and punishments Related to organizational structure and management information systems is the process by which a company rewards performance and punishes the lack thereof. The responsibilities of an individual employee typically are defined in relation to the objective(s) of his organizational unit, and the information needed to evaluate him is at least partially provided by information systems. Obviously, the problems that attend the implementation of an effective rewards and punishment system are multiplied as companies grow and their product lines and organizations become more complex.

The central mechanism of a rewards and punishment system is almost always financial. Most employees, including executives, derive a major portion of their company incomes from their basic salaries. A salary structure, therefore, must be equitable and understandable, taking into account the nature of the tasks, the level of responsibilities, and the scarcity of talent available to do the job in question. Salary systems are often expressed in terms of ranges, so that merit and years-of-service increases can be given.

Incentive compensation is often also used as a financial incentive. Just as production workers are often paid on some type of piece-rate system, salesmen in marketing organizations frequently receive a portion, sometimes a large one, of their compensation on an incentive basis. Commissions may be paid on total sales, on sales above quota, on gross margin dollars, on sales of selected products or groups of products, on new accounts opened, or on many other bases.[7] Company executives can be given incentive compensation in a variety of ways. They may be members of a profit-sharing plan, and receive a portion of the profits earned by the company, by their individual divisions, or by both. Or they may be rewarded, for example, as market share increases or as return on investment goes up. Finally, an additional avenue for incentive compensation exists through such devices as stock options or deferred compensation; the latter is a way of postponing the receipt of income for tax purposes. Not all incentive compensation, however, is tied to objective criteria based on data from a firm's information system; many companies pay bonuses to executives on the basis of evaluations that are somewhat or largely subjective.

Rewards and punishments are not confined to financial considerations, however. Important though the paycheck and the bonus are, a wise management recognizes that other kinds of satisfactions are important to most people.[8] Thus, an effective system of rewards and punishments will provide the potential for enlarging or decreasing responsibility, for good supervisor-subordinate relationships, and for clear and adequate statements regarding performance evaluation.

A final word should be said about rewards and punishment systems. Note the word "punishment" – it is used here deliberately. It is logical to state that if performance above expectation should be rewarded, then performance below expectation should be punished. But people are not always logical. In the field of business management, this is particularly true in regard to incentive compensation. Company after company complains that employees, including executives, look upon incentive compensation as a one-way street, one on which successes are to be rewarded but failures forgiven. They also say that there is a tendency to take profit sharing or bonuses "for granted" after these

[7] Sales compensation will be discussed in detail in Chapter 22.

[8] A classic study in this general area is F. J. Roethlisberger, *Management and Morale*, Harvard University Press, Cambridge, Mass., 1947.

have been in operation for a period of years. If rewards *and* punishments systems are to cope as effectively as possible with human frailty, it is imperative that objectives be fairly established, that information systems adequately reflect results by measurement criteria that are as objective as possible, and that actions and discussions concerning failure to perform are both timely and candid.

Management development A vital step in ensuring successful strategy implementation, particularly over the long run, is to provide a company with able managers. Selection, training, and motivation are integral features of the management development process. Talent needs are most dramatic when seasoned executives retire or as companies grow, but management development in any firm is a continuing need given the ever-changing nature of our competitive environment and the "knowledge explosion" that confronts all sectors of American and other societies. For the last several years, both businessmen and academicians have stated that skills become obsolete so rapidly that everyone should periodically "go back to school."[9]

For once, we cannot say that increases in size, organizational complexity, or the diversity of product-market relationships make management development more important or even necessarily more difficult. The General Electric Company runs its own management development institute, attended each year by hundreds of company executives, while our friend Paul Smith may have a very modest program, and the owner of the TV shop on the corner may train his son in his spare time. But the resources and skills available to all three firms match their needs, and the real question is whether they will devote a portion of those resources and skills to management development. We shall not comment here on the details of procedures and programs for the selection and training of managers; there are a wealth of them, which may be studied in other management courses. It is sufficient for our purposes to say that any firm that ignores management development and training will not easily survive.

Leadership The final area of influence that is important in implementing a strategy is leadership. The actions and attitudes of the people who head organizations and their subunits set a tone and create a climate for the people who work with and for them. The way a leader responds to challenge or crisis, or to success or defeat, has much to do with the way associates and subordinates will react. The fact that these statements are self-evident does not make them less important.

There is a multitude of theory and literature about leadership, leadership

[9] This is perhaps not a comforting statement, but it is nevertheless an accurate one. It applies just as much to professors and businessmen as it will one day to you as a manager.

style and quality, and the personalities of leaders.[10] Any detailed treatment of these complex subjects is inappropriate here. Let us, rather, return to the internal climate in which a company or any other organization tries to achieve its strategic objectives, and say simply that a leader should think and act so as to create a climate which is characterized by:

1. Absence of political maneuvering for position, with penalties for unfair personal competition and petty conspiracy.
2. Rejection of preferment on grounds other than approval of performance, that is, blood relationships, friendship, ethnic, educational, or social background.
3. High standards of excellence explicit in instructions for work as well as in its evaluation, expectations of continuous improvement in competence with increasing experience, disciplined attention to meeting detailed commitments.
4. High value assigned to interpersonal amity and tolerance of individual differences.
5. Willingness to take risks (and acceptance of the inevitability of occasional failure) in delegating responsibility to the relatively inexperienced.
6. Acceptance and encouragement of innovation with consequent freedom to act upon new ideas. Disapproval in cases of failure attached to results and causes rather than to departure from conventional practice as such.
7. High standards of moral integrity, including rejection of expediency even at the cost of windfall profits.[11]

In Chapter 23, which deals specifically with the organization of marketing activities, we shall point out several reasons why organizing for marketing is especially difficult. The reasons arise basically from such factors as the geographical dispersion of sales forces, frequent changes in products and in markets, and the need for coordination among advertising, selling, sales promotion, and physical distribution. Therefore, as we discuss these and other elements of marketing activity in subsequent chapters of Part 4, and in particular about marketing organization in Chapter 23, it will be useful to keep in mind the importance of leadership, internal climate, and the other factors that have been discussed here in regard to the implementation of overall corporate strategy.

□ ADDITIONAL COMMENTS ON BUSINESS STRATEGY

To this point, we have discussed the concept of strategy and its design and implementation. Many topics have been covered, some only briefly. It is useful

[10] See, for example, Philip Selznick, *Leadership in Administration*, Row, Peterson & Company, Evanston, Ill., 1957; and Abraham Zaleznik, *Human Dilemmas of Leadership*, Harper & Row, Publishers, Incorporated, New York, 1966.

[11] Kenneth Andrews, *The Effectiveness of University Management Development Programs*, Division of Research, Graduate School of Business Administration, Harvard University, Boston, 1966, p. 247.

to summarize them here in schematic form, as shown in Figure 13-3, and then to make some final observations. The strategic process, as summarized in this diagram, cannot fully reflect the complexities of formulating and carrying out strategy. A few additional comments may help to demonstrate why this is so.

Strategy design and implementation are in many ways a continuous activity. This does not mean that the formal processes that management uses are constantly in operation but, rather, that management must be continuously on the alert for developments that affect its strategic choices. Airline purchases of the Boeing 747 (the 365-seat passenger jet) are a case in point. Following the lead of Pan American Airways, many airlines in the United States placed orders for the big jets in the late 1960s, on the assumption that there would be a continuing rapid expansion of national and international air travel. But the growth did not materialize; to the contrary, the demand for air travel proved disastrously low in 1970 and 1971. As a result, the 1970s are seeing many airlines, which were planning major strategic changes in terminals, passenger handling procedures, and related services, drastically revising their strategic thinking. For many of them the 747 has been a highly unprofitable undertaking.

Another factor that complicates the strategic planning is the interacting effect of its components. Although Figure 13-3 does not reflect them, there are potential cause and effect relationships implicit among all segments of the diagram. An analysis of its environment, for example, might indicate to a firm

FIGURE 13-3

The strategic process

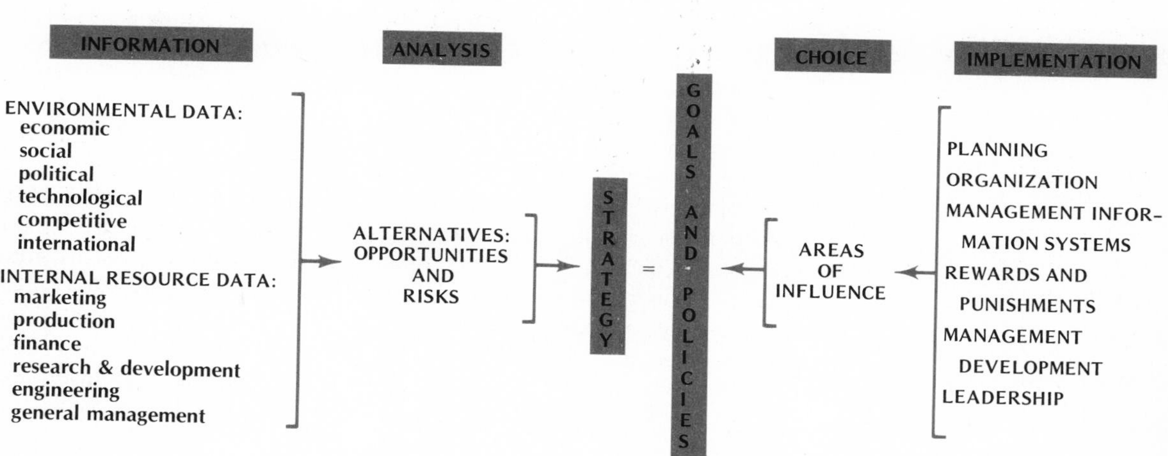

that competitors have failed to fill a niche with their product lines, but there is little the firm can do to jump into the gap unless it has the internal resources to do the job or can set them quickly. Several years ago Singer, then largely a sewing machine company, decided that it had major opportunities both for product diversification and increased international sales; the absence of effective control systems and trained management slowed the company's progress for several years. The potential for interaction among all the factors listed in Figure 13-3 demonstrates the old axiom that any weak link can break a chain.

Finally, we have said little about the timing of management action, which can be of crucial importance in effectively carrying out a strategy. Timing is important for reasons both external and internal. Externally, for example, the market must be "right." The unlamented midi-skirt of 1970 is a case in point. For whatever their reasons, the vast majority of women simply did not want to switch to the midi—the vagaries of fashion are such that it might have been a major success at an earlier, or perhaps a later, time. Timing is equally important in terms of internal considerations. The Singer example, cited above, is again appropriate: Singer had to time its overseas expansion to fit the development of skilled personnel and adequate information systems.

Marketing strategy and business strategy

Marketing strategy is the development of an effective response to a market opportunity. It is, of course, a component of the total strategy of a company. In some cases it can be the most important component. Many kinds of consumer packaged goods illustrate this. For the Avon Company, a large manufacturer of cosmetics and toiletries sold on a door-to-door basis, success comes from an ability to package, advertise, and sell effectively; more than 50 percent of Avon's sales revenue is used to meet marketing costs. As mentioned in Chapter 10, Avon's use of door-to-door selling is a very different marketing approach than those of its competitors, who normally rely on wholesale and retail establishments to reach customers.

In other kinds of situations, marketing skills, though still important, are matched in significance by other aspects of corporate strategy. The marketing expenditures of prescription drug companies, which have to market their products to doctors, hospitals, medical centers, and drugstores, are substantial. Yet they cannot be described as more important than the drug companies' continuing research efforts to develop and test new pharmaceuticals or to control the quality of products in the production stage. And there are, certainly, company situations in which marketing plays a role that is subordinate to other elements of business strategy. When the National Aeronautics and Space Administration (NASA) asks potential suppliers to develop and bid on guidance systems, there is surely a marketing job to be done. But the primary keys to success are research capability, engineering skills, and manufacturing know-how. These examples reflect the ever-present but varying importance of marketing strategy, and illustrate the validity of Mr. Morgens's statement, cited in the Introduction to Part 4, that marketing skill by itself is of little use.

Marketing strategy, like overall business strategy, is, or should be, a totality. It constitutes a definition of *who* customers are and *how* they are to be served effectively. A successful marketing strategy can be defined as one which correctly selects the customers who are to be the subject of marketing effort and then provides the right product, makes sure that it is offered in the right place, accompanies it with the right type of promotion, and establishes the right price—and does these things within the limits of a cost structure that permits the achievement of profit and other objectives.

INTEGRATING THE MARKETING STRATEGY

Subsequent chapters discuss how marketing management tries to assure the "rightness" of the various elements of the marketing mix. For now, we shall concentrate on the importance of making sure that the elements of a marketing strategy add up to an integrated and interrelated totality. An example serves to illustrate this.

Let us suppose that the XYZ Company, a large manufacturer of cereals and other food products, has studied trends in the marketplace and has decided that there may be an opportunity, given the public's increasing interest in health, weight-consciousness, and nutrition, for a new low-calorie cereal with a high nutritional content. The company's technical staff develops one that is in fact high in nutritional value and low in calorie content, and can be manufactured at a cost level that will permit the company to price the cereal at a level that provides funds for promotion, other marketing costs, and a satisfactory profit.

Research But who wants the product? It is different, but it is not unique. Researchers are assigned the task of defining possible users. Clearly the latter are not small children, whose interest in calories and nutrition is minimal at best. Besides, XYZ already produces Zippie Zaps for the children's market. The researchers must analyze the market and decide whether, for example, teenagers, young adults, older people, or perhaps entire families are the best potential targets for marketing activity. It is important to decide which group or groups are the best targets because other cereal brands produced by XYZ and competitors are directed at specific target groups, and because the choice of ultimate target(s) or market segment(s) will, as we shall see, have considerable impact on XYZ's mix of marketing policies.

Let us assume that marketing research indicates that the best market target is middle-aged people who have at least high-school educations and average incomes. Research data also indicate that there are large numbers of people who fit this description, and that they live in areas and buy in stores now reached by other XYZ products. Middle-aged people thus potentially constitute an economically valid market.

But the battle has only begun. An integrated and profitable marketing mix must be developed if the total marketing strategy is to be successful. In essence, XYZ must develop and tie together, for the new cereal, all the elements of marketing activity that will be discussed in the next nine chapters—and it must do all these things profitably if the new cereal is to achieve the objectives that corporate and marketing management set for it.

The product Our consideration of XYZ's activities might start with product characteristics. In addition to its nutritional and calorie characteristics (and the proper blend of these must be selected), XYZ's marketing specialists must decide on the taste and shape and size of the cereal, and perhaps test combinations with employees and customer panels established for the purpose. Package shape and size(s) must be chosen. How do the various possibilities match other XYZ cereals for purposes of shelf display, and does the middle-aged market have any specialized requirements that might affect package size? What should be the color scheme and printing style that will be put on the package, and what should the printing say about the cereal? What brand name should the new cereal carry? Zippie Zaps is a name clearly chosen to appeal to children, but what name will attract XYZ's middle-aged targets, and what appeals will it convey? The marketing staff and the company's advertising agency may discuss possibilities, and such names as Nutri-Flakes and Bites O'Health may come up.

Promotion Promotional decisions are also required. How much money is available for the introductory campaign and, if the cereal sells, on a continuing basis? The introductory campaign must be planned in terms of media (such as television, magazines, and newspapers) and messages (what shall be said about the product?), and in terms of shelf streamers and display bins for in-store promotion at the point of purchase. Perhaps some sort of consumer deals, such as two packages for the price of one or "6 cents off," will help get the product off to a good start. What information in the form of bulletins or announcements should be given to retailers and wholesalers, who are inundated with such materials by XYZ and other food marketers, to interest them in the new cereal? We know that the XYZ sales force can add the new item to its existing lines, but the company will probably want to consider ways of making the product "important" to the salesmen. All these decisions have to be made in regard to both the introductory campaign and the continuing sale of the cereal.

Distribution We have reduced the need for XYZ's marketing executives to make place decisions by assuming that current channels of distribution are appropriate. But this assumption should be questioned. Perhaps health spas, exercise studios, or food-fad stores might be interested in carrying a product that is designed to appeal to at least some of the people who patronize them. If so, XYZ will have to develop new channels of distribution at the retail level, find new wholesaling mechanisms to reach the new kinds of retail outlets, and hire some new salesmen to sell to the new outlets. In any case, plans must be made to service whatever wholesale and retail outlets are used.

Price XYZ also has price decisions to make. The price of the new cereal must be attractive to customers, related to prices of other cereals, furnish an incentive to wholesalers and retailers, cover XYZ's costs, and yield whatever profit margin has been established as a target. What is the right price to meet all these requirements? The company is already in the cereal business and has the knowledge and experience to make some reasoned judgments, but price possibilities will probably have to be tested. So may many other decisions that have tentatively been made.

XYZ's marketers will probably test various combinations of the factors that have been mentioned here by doing some *test marketing* in various parts of the country, as do most companies that market consumer packaged goods. If the test meets the objective set for it, then, and only then, can management assume it has an effective marketing mix. And then, and then only, is the new cereal ready for introduction.

But the battle is still not over. Nor will it be so long as XYZ offers the cereal for sale. The marketing manager responsible for the market performance of the cereal will have to keep abreast of competitive activity, changes in the tastes and habits of ultimate customers, and developments inside XYZ Company that can affect his product. His only certainty is change.

This example, simplified though it is, demonstrates that marketing strategy is comprised of interrelated elements, and it is easy to visualize that failure or weakness in one element may so damage the other elements that the total marketing effort may be endangered or fail.

It should also be stressed that we used as an example a company adding a product to its existing line. This endowed the company's marketing executives with knowledge and insights that enabled it to make reasoned judgments about customers and a marketing mix, whereas a new company or a company entering a new product or customer field would have had more unknowns to contend with. In either case, however, the best possible decisions can be made only through a blend of experience and knowledge (where available) and marketing research data. In our example, we cited only a few of the possible research projects or tests that the XYZ Company might have used. Part 5 will deal with marketing information and marketing research. But it should be evident that marketing research, though important, cannot economically provide the answers to all possible questions in the situation faced by the XYZ Company. The individual possible actions and decisions regarding each aspect of the marketing mix, and the permutations and combinations among them, are far too numerous to be tested. The wisdom of the marketing manager is fully challenged in deciding which things are important enough to be tested and in combining test results with his experience and judgment in making decisions.

In summary of our XYZ Company example, it should be noted that the company has had to develop a marketing strategy, using all the elements of the marketing mix, that permits it to take advantage of an opportunity presented by its environment. To do this successfully in the face of competition, it has had to use not only its marketing resources and skills but also its production, distribu-

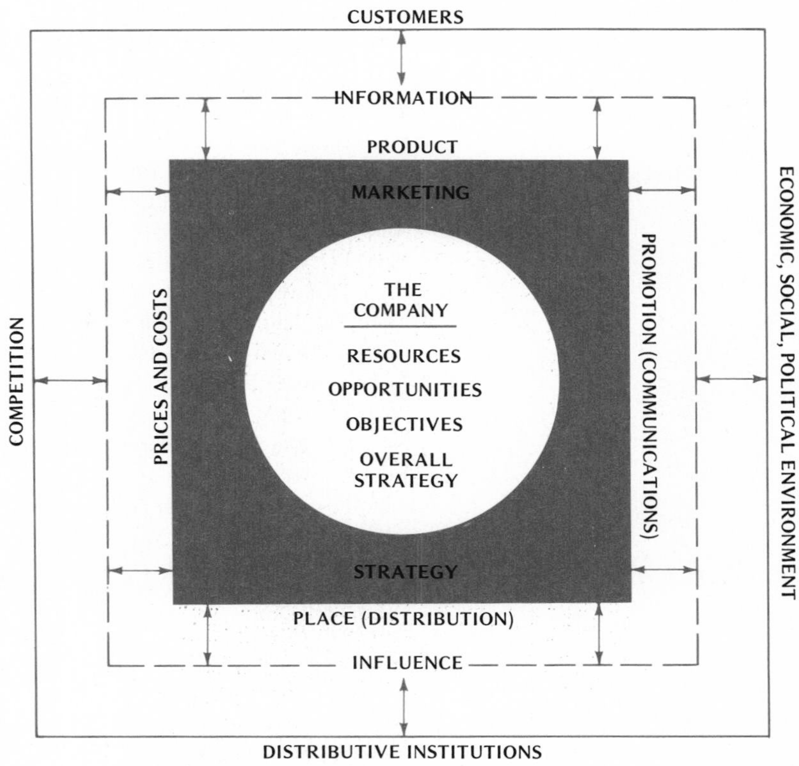

FIGURE 13-4
Synthesis of business and marketing strategies

tion, financial, and other resources. Only by combining marketing and other activities can the XYZ Company attain the profit, market share, and other objectives established for the new cereal. Thus business strategy and marketing strategy work in concert, as is reflected in the diagram shown in Figure 13-4.

MARKETING PLANNING

In discussing business planning, planning was defined as "deciding in advance what is to be done, when it is to be done, how it is to be done, and who is to do it." Planning in the marketing field is just as necessary as is corporate planning. Marketing management needs a planning mechanism that ties together, in a time framework, all the variables mentioned earlier in regard to both the choice of target customers and the elements of the marketing mix.

Later, in Chapter 26, we shall discuss in detail the process by which marketing performance is controlled and measured in terms of established plans. We present here, in Figure 13-5, a general framework for marketing planning, because it is important at this stage to see how marketing plans relate to overall business plans. Also, because subsequent chapters deal with individual aspects of marketing management activity, it is important to establish that effective marketing requires that all aspects of marketing activity relate to one another. Only thus does marketing become a system which enables the total firm to compete successfully, to adapt to the changes that confront it, and to meet its near-term and long-range objectives.

Figure 13-5 illustrates the flow and relationships of the marketing planning process. The diagram encompasses all the major kinds of marketing decision areas that are discussed in this book, as can be seen by the chapter titles in the contents. It is apparent, then, that the task of planning a marketing strategy, or marketing strategies, if more than one product or customer group is involved, is immensely complex and difficult. For most kinds of products, consumer or industrial, many potential customer groups exist, and analyses and choices must be made. In our XYZ Company cereal example, we simplified the company's task of choosing a customer group by a product type that had appeal for an easily defined class of customers. In reality, XYZ's marketers would almost surely have been analyzing a broad spectrum of possible customer groups as possible targets for many different kinds of cereals.

Substrategies Similarly, even after customer targets and product choices have tentatively been made, a variety of possible substrategies exists regarding other elements of the marketing mix. The variety can be made apparent by looking at only one additional mix component, even though others are obviously involved. Take promotion as an example. Promotional funds are limited, and how are they to be divided among advertising, personal selling, sales promotion, and attempts to get publicity? At what times of day or night do

FIGURE 13-5
The marketing planning process

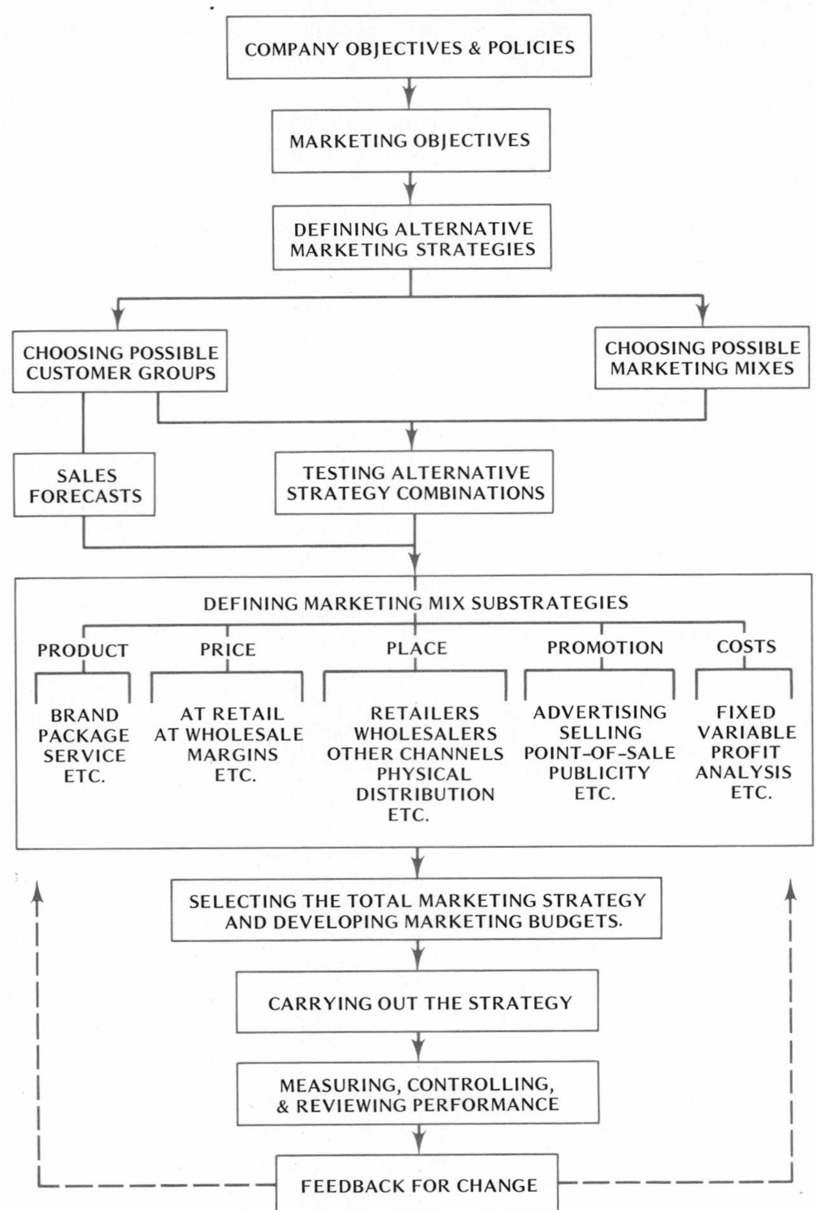

COMPANY OBJECTIVES & POLICIES
MARKETING OBJECTIVES
DEFINING ALTERNATIVE MARKETING STRATEGIES
CHOOSING POSSIBLE CUSTOMER GROUPS
CHOOSING POSSIBLE MARKETING MIXES
SALES FORECASTS
TESTING ALTERNATIVE STRATEGY COMBINATIONS
DEFINING MARKETING MIX SUBSTRATEGIES
PRODUCT
PRICE
PLACE
PROMOTION
COSTS
BRAND PACKAGE SERVICE ETC.
AT RETAIL AT WHOLESALE MARGINS ETC.
RETAILERS WHOLESALERS OTHER CHANNELS PHYSICAL DISTRIBUTION ETC.
ADVERTISING SELLING POINT-OF-SALE PUBLICITY ETC.
FIXED VARIABLE PROFIT ANALYSIS ETC.
SELECTING THE TOTAL MARKETING STRATEGY AND DEVELOPING MARKETING BUDGETS.
CARRYING OUT THE STRATEGY
MEASURING, CONTROLLING, & REVIEWING PERFORMANCE
FEEDBACK FOR CHANGE

target customers watch television or listen to radio? What kinds of programs attract them, and what kinds of appeals most advantageously and accurately describe the product? The list of questions to be asked and decisions to be made is seemingly endless, but the marketing planning process must highlight the need and provide for the opportunity for all the necessary questions to be asked and answered. It must also provide a framework in which marketing executives can coordinate the several substrategies or elements of the marketing mix.

Feedback and modification In view of the many facets and alternatives that are involved in each segment of the marketing planning process, we should note that Figure 13-5 can reflect only partially the complexity of the process. Note that only at the bottom does the figure provide for feedback. That is, the dotted lines imply that performance review may lead to change in any or all elements of the marketing plan. Though this is true, it is, of course, an oversimplification of what happens in reality. At any point in the process, competitive behavior, other external developments, market test results, or changes in some substrategy of the marketing mix may require that marketing management reevaluate and change its plans, possibly in major ways. When the government, for example, decides to stimulate the economy with expansionary monetary and fiscal policies, this may require changes in the overall corporate and marketing objective of business firms, and in the strategic components that flow from them. Or, less dramatically, an increase in television network advertising rates may force a change in a decision to advertise during the Super Bowl football game; as a result, entire advertising and sales promotion plans may have to change.

Funding The planning process chart mentions budgets.[12] A marketing budget, in brief, is a detailed statement of how and when the funds allocated for various marketing activities are to be spent. The marketing budget translates the marketing plan into dollars. Just as the marketing department has an overall budget, so do such subordinate activities as advertising, selling, product development, and physical distribution; each element of the marketing mix, in other words, has its own budget. Budgets, like other aspects of marketing planning, are subject to review and revision where necessary.

Marketing plans may cover different time spans.[13] Most companies, of course, have annual plans, which coincide with financial accounting periods,

[12] Under "cost," the chart also mentions "fixed" and "variable" costs. These terms are defined and discussed later in this chapter and in the Appendix.

[13] A more detailed discussion of marketing plans, including planning time periods, can be found in Mark Stern, *Marketing Planning: A Systems Approach,* McGraw-Hill Book Company, New York, 1966, paperback.

and many subdivide these into quarterly or monthly plans. An annual plan is typically referred to as an operating or short-range plan, though sometimes the same term covers a two-year plan. In addition, companies use long-range marketing plans, usually covering a period of five or more years; the differentiating features of long-range plans are the comparative generality of objectives and policies and the flexibility that surrounds the total plan because of the uncertainty created by the longer time span.

Profits and costs

□

PROFITS

Our treatment of company strategy and marketing strategy would be incomplete without some discussion of profits. Even though a company may define its responsibilities (see Chapter 1) and strategies in different ways, these cannot be carried out on a continuing basis unless the firm has the financial resources to achieve them. And profits are the key to financial resources. In a free-enterprise system, companies grow or perish as a result of their ability to compete with one another for customer acceptance, and competitive strength is assessed by investors in deciding whether they will or will not supply capital to a company seeking to sell its stocks or bonds. Profits are thus both a major measure of a company's strength and ability to compete and a source of money. Even though customers and investors may also concern themselves with other factors, such as efforts made by companies to alleviate racial and environmental problems, it is still true that only profitable firms will, over a period of time, have the resources to achieve these wider, socially oriented objectives. Profit, then, plays a central role in determining the success of a business, no matter how one defines success.

Profit, as a dollar measure of success or lack thereof, can be viewed and expressed in different ways. At the bottom of an income (or profit and loss) statement, profit is usually expressed in absolute dollar terms. The same profit dollars might also be defined as a percentage of sales, which permits management to evaluate profit in terms of the company's sales results. If sales go up but the profit as a percentage of sales stays the same or decreases, this may imply that the company is not controlling its costs effectively, or at least that the cost of expanding sales has been high during the period in question. If a company has a budget, actual profit is often compared with budgeted profit and expressed as a percentage. If the percentage exceeds 100, the company has done better than predicted.

Profits are also frequently measured by their relationship to investment, and expressed as a percentage thereof; the term most commonly used is *return on investment*. Thus, for example, a steel company's accountants will use the company's balance sheet to compute the investment that the stockholders have in the company, and cite its profit figure as a percentage of that investment. Comparable percentages, computed over the years, give an annual reflection of the return that the company has earned on the stockholders' invested funds.[14]

Marketing men, as well as other business executives, are often interested in another profit concept: incremental profit. This means, basically, that management's analysis of a proposed expenditure will relate, in dollars and in percentage form, the profit postulated for the investment against the costs of the investment. Suppose that the marketing vice-president of a chain of retail dress shops is considering the addition of a new store. He will estimate the dollar profitability of the store by preparing an income statement that subtracts the probable costs of operating the store from its probable sales revenue; the resulting figure is the incremental profit arising from the new store. The profit figure may also be computed as a percentage of the investment required to put the store in operation. This is also a return-on-investment calculation, but is different from the one cited in the preceding paragraph because the source of this investment is not necessarily restricted to stockholder funds. As we shall see below, the important aspect of incremental analyses in connection with possible investment is that they involve only those revenues and cost that arise from the decisions under consideration.

Should managers be primarily interested in long-range or short-run profits, or in a balance between the two? Intuition would seem to make balance the wisest choice, and rough logic seems to lend credence to intuitive choice. But a generalization of this type is too easy an answer. Though a company that intends to stay in business for a long time must have a balanced view of the importance of near-term and long-range profits, different circumstances require different emphases. A company capitalizing on what is likely to be a fad—to invent one, perhaps fluorescent tie-dyed sneakers—is likely to concern itself with profits in the short run, believing that the demand for such sneakers will be short lived. But if the same company were considering going into the business of making and selling the type of women's shorts known in 1971 as "hot pants," and if it assumes that they will be popular for several years, then considerations of profit (and production and marketing costs) will cover a longer time span. At the other end of the time spectrum, companies producing machine tools and other items with long lives, whose customer relations must be planned for periods of several years, will necessarily give relatively more emphasis to long-range profits unless short-range problems arise.[15]

[14] This calculation is not the same thing as the dividend payout. Stockholders' dividends are paid out of profits, but most companies retain a portion of profits to finance expansion, equipment replacement, and other internal needs.

[15] Our examples all have to do with products that presumably have differing market lives or life cycles. In Chapter 14, the product life-cycle concept and its impact on considerations other than profits are discussed.

COSTS AND COST CONCEPTS

If profits are to be made, the businessman must be able to do more than make and sell a product. He must also be able to measure his costs, control them, and estimate what they will be in the future. Costs affect every aspect of a firm's operation, and although we shall have more to say later about costs in the chapters on pricing and marketing performance, it is useful here, in this more general chapter, to take a brief look at some of the more important cost concepts. These are useful, as we shall show, in many of the decisions that marketing managers and other business executives have to make.

Fixed, variable, and discretionary costs[16] A cost is *fixed* when its amount does not change over a given period of time or over a specified (usually large) range of output. A *variable* cost is one that varies directly with the volume of output, that is, it is a constant amount per unit of output. *Discretionary* costs, unlike fixed or variable costs, arise largely by management choice. Let us see, briefly, what these three kinds of costs might be in a hypothetical situation.

The manager of a manufacturing plant will include among his *fixed* costs such items as maintenance, the salaries of foremen and supervisory personnel, and whatever his accountants tell him is the proper amount of depreciation on his plant and equipment; such costs, as a general rule, do not vary with the rate of output in the plant.[17] Other costs do vary, however. If production increases, for example, more raw materials and more packages in which to put finished products will be needed. The total amounts of such costs will rise as output rises, even though they do not change on a per unit basis—the fact that their total changes makes them *variable*. Suppose that the industrial relations department convinces the manager that employees work better with background music, and he decides to pipe some in. This is not required as are the plant, the equipment, and the maintenance, and we may therefore call it a *discretionary* expense; later, of course, if the music proves effective it may become, for all practical purposes, a fixed expense.

Why is it useful to think about costs in these ways? Certainly the plant manager will want to produce and sell enough products to cover at least all his fixed costs. Steel companies, with heavy investments in plant and equipment, must operate at or near capacity in order to cover their substantial fixed costs, and their marketing executives will have to work hard to ensure high sales volumes for that purpose and, of course, to cover variable costs and make a profit.

[16] A more detailed description of the nature of fixed and variable costs, together with detailed examples of their relevance to marketing problems, is presented in the Appendix.

[17] Depreciation is an amount charged against operations that represents the wearing out of the plant and equipment. Although not an actual out-of-pocket cost (because the company has already paid for the plant and equipment), both good management practice and the fact that depreciation can be deducted for tax purposes require that the financial statements reflect the gradual wearing out of physical items.

Variable costs, on the other hand, are more subject to control by the individual manager and require constant attention. They must be held in line, on a per unit basis, to make sure that price-cost relationships do not get out of line. In our example, if the packaging or material costs rise per unit, total profit will drop and a price change may be necessary. The same general comment applies to discretionary costs, and these too must be carefully watched. In sum, a plant manager has a plan and a budget that necessitate his close attention to his *total* cost, but his variable and discretionary costs are ones over which he has the greatest amount of control. Finally, while the concept of fixed, variable, and discretionary costs is continuously useful for management purposes, it is particularly so when a manager is making a *break-even* analysis, that is, when he is trying to decide a production level at which his costs and revenues are equal. The Appendix includes a detailed description of break-even analysis.

Controllable and noncontrollable costs Another way to think usefully about costs is to divide them in terms of their controllability. This approach is particularly useful for managers who are responsible for evaluating the performance of subordinate organizational units. A regional sales manager with a dozen field sales offices reporting to him would be more interested in the field office manager's ability to control such items as travel, costs per customer call, and clerical assistance than in the costs that might be applied to that field office as a result of the allocation of home office administration, corporate research and development, and related types of expenses. The latter are important, of course, but there is probably nothing that either the regional sales manager or the field office manager can do to control them. Similarly, those who evaluate his performance may look closely at his skill in managing his controllable costs, and less so at the costs that are allocated to his operation by higher authority.

Direct and indirect costs Closely allied to the foregoing is the concept of direct and indirect costs. When a manager evaluates the cost to revenue relationships of a particular product, for example, he may wish to divide the relevant costs into direct and indirect categories. The direct costs, obviously, are those which are created only in connection with the product itself, for example, packaging and raw materials. Indirect costs, on the other hand, are those associated with the product and with other products. If a salesman sells 30 additional items in addition to product X, some portion of the salesman's total salary and expenses represents an indirect cost to product X. The portion attributed to product X may be somewhat *controllable* from the sales manager's point of view, but it is an indirect, or *common,* cost so far as product X is concerned.

Incremental costs Managers frequently have to make decisions between alternative investment possibilities, and such decisions can be complex. The concept of incremental costs is vital to comparative analyses of alternative possibilities.

The concept of incremental costs is, in theory, simple. It means that, in analyzing the costs of alternative decisions, only those costs should be considered which are affected by the decision alternatives in question. If alternatives A and B are being analyzed, the cost aspects of each should deal only with the costs affected by each. For example, if a person were deciding whether to keep his old car or to buy a new one and junk the old (he paid cash for it just last year), the only relevant economic considerations are the costs connected with the alternatives that confront him now. That is, he must compare all the costs of buying and operating the new car against all the costs of operating the old one; it makes no difference, in terms of the economics of the decision, what he paid for the old one.[18] His concern is with the *incremental*, or extra, costs of his alternatives. He will have to be careful, however, to include all the incremental costs; if he knows that deciding against the new car will make him so unhappy that he will then go out and buy a tape recorder to soothe his emotions, economic analysis requires him to define the tape recorder cost as one of the incremental costs associated with the old car.

Though the concept that incremental cost analysis should include only those costs which are affected by one decision alternative as opposed to another is simple and straightforward, such analyses can be very complex in the business world. One must include all relevant incremental costs and exclude all irrelevant costs, and it is frequently difficult to think of all possible costs of both types and to decide upon their relevancy. Another complicating factor is that alternatives may have different lives; for example, alternative A may last for 5 years and alternative B for 10, and the incremental costs and revenues of each may have different outflow and inflow patterns within the 5- and 10-year periods. Fortunately, people skilled in financial analysis have developed a technique called *present value* analysis to deal with such problems. We shall not discuss it here, but the purpose (and result) of present value analysis is to define the present economic value of alternatives that carry different risks and have dissimilar lives and revenue and cost patterns.

THE MARKETING MANAGER AND COST ANALYSIS

Marketing managers often make use of incremental cost analyses. An advertising manager who is considering adding an increment of $50,000 to his pro-

[18] We are talking only about the *economics* of the decision. One may "kick" oneself for having spent as much as one did on the old car, but that cost, to use the harsh word of economists and business analysts, is a "sunk" cost—it is over and done with, and not affected by the current decision problem.

posal for next year's television time budget must compare that cost and any other incremental costs connected with it (such as, say, an extra copy specialist) against what he believes will be the incremental revenue generated by the $50,000 of television time. Or the advertising manager's supervisor, the marketing vice-president, may be deciding whether to use $350,000 of next year's promotional budget for either more salesmen or a point-of-sale promotion campaign. Difficult though it will be, he will have to make at least a rough, judgmental analysis that compares the incremental costs of each alternative against its incremental revenues so that he can make his decision between the two. If the alternatives have incremental revenues with different life expectancies, he may wish to use the present value technique referred to above.

Or he may choose to use what is called the *pay-out period* method of making his decision. The pay-out period is the amount of time necessary for an investment to pay for itself. This type of analysis is less complicated than present value analysis, but yields less effective decisions if different time spans exist between the alternatives. The pay-out period approach, briefly, computes the number of years (or months) that it takes for the incremental revenue from each alternative to cover the incremental costs of each alternative. Unless some other consideration is involved, the marketing vice-president may choose to reduce his risk by deciding on the alternative with the shorter pay-out period. We have used the words "less effective" in comparing pay-out period analysis to present value analysis. Let us see why. Alternative A, say, may cover all its incremental costs in one year while alternative B may require three years. But if alternative B continues to produce revenue for six more years, while the revenue from A ceases at the end of the year, then B is clearly more desirable in spite of the fact that its pay-out period is two years shorter than B's.

□ RISK

Early in this chapter, we mentioned risk as a factor to be considered in analyzing possible business strategies. More recently, in discussing cost analyses of alternative decision possibilities, risk was mentioned again. In a sense, then, we have come a full circle, for some degree of risk is implicit in any action to be taken in the future, whether the action is corporatewide, within the marketing department, or personal. Risks must be taken into account in analyzing the future costs and revenues of possible actions. Consider an example. If one could invest $100 for a guaranteed return of $500, would this be preferable to investing the same $100 for a return of $1,000 if one's best judgment were that there was only a 45 percent chance of actually getting the $1,000? The second alternative is riskier, and offers what decision-theory experts would call an "expected monetary value" of only $450 (45 percent × $1,000). But perhaps one's preference is to take a chance on $1,000 as opposed to the certainty of $500.

This example is a simplification of the risk problems that accompany business decisions. There are complex mathematical tools that permit business executives to relate their preferences concerning different degrees of risks to various cost/revenue possibilities in making decisions regarding investment opportunities. The use of such tools is usually confined to complicated, high-cost investment possibilities. In any case, regardless of the tools used to analyze them, the risks that a course of action carries should be always considered by an executive.

Questions

1. The U.S. Time Company has brought about drastic changes in the watch industry. Several years ago it took advantage of (and accentuated) changes in the public's conception of watches. Its strategy was to automate production, mass-produce quality watches inexpensively, and sell them at low prices in many kinds of traditional and nontraditional outlets. By 1968, the company's Timex watches accounted for about 25 percent of all the watches sold in the United States.
   a. What external factors contributed to the success of the company's total strategy?
   b. What countervailing strategy might have been adopted by a manufacturer of high-priced watches?

2. Identify four different strategies which American Motors might employ to improve its position in the United States automobile market. What information would you need to evaluate the relative desirability of each of these alternatives?

3. (a) Do educational institutions and governmental agencies have to have strategies? Why? (b) What is the strategy of the college or university you attend? How successful is it? (c) If you were the president of your university or college, how would you go about formulating or changing its strategy? What groups would you consult in formulating that strategy?

4. In what kinds of industry situations do companies need to rely most heavily on marketing executives in developing their total corporate strategies?

5. What factors determine the importance of product policy, personal selling, price, and advertising as parts of a company's total marketing strategy?

6. If you were the president of General Motors, what information would you want to have in order to evaluate the performance of the Chevrolet Division? If

you were in charge of Chevrolet's sales department, how would you evaluate the performance of field sales offices?

7. Are formal planning systems more important in big companies than in small ones? Why? What factors are important in marketing planning?

8. In general, what considerations affect the relative degrees of emphasis that a company should place on long-range and short-range profits? What circumstances might alter those emphases in either direction?

9. Define fixed, variable, and incremental costs. Why are these methods of classifying costs important to marketing managers?

10. Cite some specific marketing situations where incremental cost analysis is important. Do you see any problems in the use of incremental cost analysis? Explain.

11. Under what circumstances should a company conduct risk analysis in making marketing decisions? Why?

12. Until 1971, Dansk Designs followed a highly successful corporate strategy. Using Scandinavian designers and craftsmen to plan and produce its merchandise, it sold a line of table-top items (stainless steel flatware, copperware, bowls, candleholders, dishes, etc.) through carefully selected high-prestige outlets in many parts of the United States. Dansk products were priced high, and advertised so as to convey notions of elegance and informal good taste.

In 1971, Dansk was getting ready to implement a major change in corporate strategy; management had decided to add a new line, called Gourmet, to its product family. The Gourmet line, which also consisted of table-top items, was being planned to appeal to a market slightly below the existing line in quality and price.

a. What factors may have led to Dansk's new strategy?
b. What companywide problems do you foresee in its implementation?
c. If you were the marketing vice-president of Dansk, how would you go about developing and implementing a marketing strategy for the Gourmet line? What risks do you see?

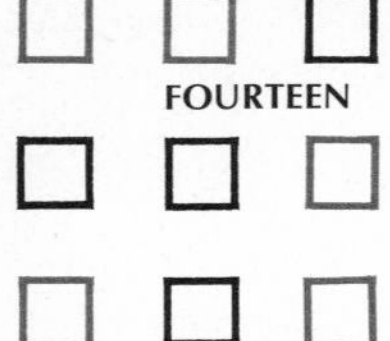

Product policies

What is a product? Consider an automobile. Is it a means of transportation? Is it an assembled package of pieces of metal, rubber, paint, and other materials? Is it a mass of molecules? Is it a symbol of economic and social status? Is it a convenience to the housewife and a source of bills to her husband? Is it a pathway to adventure? Is it the epitome of America's genius for mass production, or is it the epitome of planned and wasteful obsolescence?

The automobile is some of these things to some people and different things to others. From a marketing viewpoint an automobile, like any other product, is a combination of physical, economic, and psychosocial elements from which a customer expects to derive satisfactions or benefits. The importance of this definition is in its orientation: it is in terms of customers and the many different dimensions in which they perceive needs and desires. It is from this perspective—the product as the customer sees it—that the marketing manager approaches product decision making.

This chapter is concerned with the formulation and implementation of product policy. Here, we turn our attention to the essential considerations that guide a firm in its decisions to add new products, drop existing ones, and position products relative to their competition in the marketplace. Other important product policy issues we will examine include branding, packaging, and questions of product liability.

PRODUCT POLICY AND THE FIRM

A company's choice of products represents the foundation of its business. Through its product decisions, the firm affects all other elements of its marketing program, the nature and magnitude of its manufacturing facilities, its workforce, its capital requirements, and even its basic operating procedures.

To illustrate, consider the decision of American automobile manufacturers to introduce small cars to compete with European and Japanese imports. This decision, made in the late 1960s, affected all areas of operations. Engineering and production decisions had to be made about design, performance characteristics, and production schedules and facilities. General Motors constructed a new $100 million plant to assemble its Vega. Under pressure to price competitively with imports, manufacturers conducted extensive investigations of sources of supply for component parts. Only one small car, American Motors' Gremlin, consisted entirely of components manufactured in North America. Accounting studies of the costs of various alternative models had to be made. Financial questions involved the funds for new or existing facilities, as well as for advertising and selling programs. Top management had to evaluate the possible effects of the small cars on existing models and had to make final decisions on the introduction of the new lines.

Marketing executives were also involved in the development of the small car policies. Marketing researchers studied potential demand and the possible actions of competitors. Other marketing executives aided in design and in the development of plans for advertising, pricing, dealer relationships, and related marketing activities. In general, marketing personnel played a key role in product decisions because of their direct knowledge of customers, the market, and competition.

Formulating product policy

For many years, the Brunswick Corporation was widely known as the "kingpin of the bowling business." Bowling balls and equipment dominated the company's sales pattern. In the early 1960s, the market for bowling equipment declined precipitously, and Brunswick was forced to look for additional sources of corporate revenue. Its decision was to diversify into new and different product lines. By 1971, the firm's products included hospital supplies, golf clubs, outboard motors, fishing reels, metal fibers, and complex technical components for industrial and aerospace markets. Almost 60 percent of Brunswick's 1970 revenue of $450 million was reported to be derived from industrial markets the company had not served as recently as 1964.[1]

The example of Brunswick serves to illustrate how, to varying degrees, a company may be forced to make changes in the products it sells. Its traditional

[1] "Brunswick Mixes Up Its Marketing," *Industrial Marketing*, April, 1971, p. 26.

markets may decline because of changing consumption patterns, or because improved or substitute competitive products have made the firm's existing products less attractive. Alternately, a line of products may continue to generate substantial sales volume, but competitive pressures in the industry may depress profit margins to an unsatisfactory level. Whatever the reasons, it is evident that the majority of companies must, at some point, face questions of changing their product mix.

What products should a firm add? What ones should it drop? What effects will new products have on existing items the company markets? These questions are difficult to resolve; yet, as previously mentioned, they are of central importance to the growth and profitability of a business enterprise. To address them, a firm must have a policy to guide it in its product decision making.

Although our discussion deals primarily with product policy in the business firm, it should be noted that nonbusiness organizations often face similar problems of adapting their "products" to the needs of the market. For example, for many years the Tuberculosis Association focused its efforts on fund raising for research and for free X-ray clinics, all aimed at preventing and curing tuberculosis. During the 1950s and 1960s the incidence of tuberculosis declined, while other types of disease became relatively more important. Eventually the association's name was changed to Tuberculosis and Respiratory Disease Association, reflecting its expanded "product line" of public services.

In this section, we outline the essential considerations involved in the formulation of product policy. The four principal areas we will examine are the resources of the firm, its existing markets, competition, and the objectives of the corporation.

RESOURCES OF THE FIRM

Every company is, in some respects, unique. Its own combination of personnel, experience, and capabilities set it apart from others. By virtue of its uniqueness, a firm is inherently better equipped to do some things well while, at the same time, it lacks the resources to perform other kinds of tasks capably. Herein lies a key to successful product policy formulation. The optimal choice of products is one that enables the firm to utilize and trade upon its inherent strengths, while avoiding those areas in which it is weak. In this respect, the firm's resources are a prime determinant of its product policy.

The kinds of corporate resources that can affect product policy formulation are illustrated in Figure 14-1. Financial strength is perhaps the most important of the considerations shown. Many products require substantial investments in manufacturing facilities and raw material inventories. Others, aimed at high-volume mass markets, may necessitate extensive financial outlays for finished goods inventories, receivables, or advertising and promotion. Still other prod-

FIGURE 14-1

Inventory of company resources to be considered in appraising product suitability

Financial strength	Money available or obtainable for financing research and development, plant construction, inventory, receivables, working capital, and operating losses in the early stages of commercial operation
Raw material reserves	Ownership of, or preferential access to, natural resources such as minerals and ores, brine deposits, natural gas, forests
Physical plan	Manufacturing plant, research and testing facilities, warehouses, branch offices, trucks, tankers, etc.
Location	Situation of plant or other physical facilities with relation to markets, raw materials, or utilities
Patents	Ownership or control of a technical monopoly through patents
Public acceptance	Brand preference, market contracts, and other public support built up by successful performance in the past
Specialized experience	Unique or uncommon knowledge of manufacturing, distribution, scientific fields, or managerial techniques
Personnel	Payroll of skilled labor, salesmen, engineers, or other workers with definite specialized abilities
Management	Professional skill, experience, ambition, and will for growth of the company's leadership

Source: Charles H. Kline, "The Strategy of Product Policy," *Harvard Business Review*, July–August, 1955, p. 92.

ucts may require large expenditures on research and development. In general, products requiring heavy financial commitments are appropriate only for large corporations. Smaller companies must, of necessity, limit their product mix to lines demanding lesser financial outlays.

Small firms are not without their own strengths. Proximity to local markets and a familiarity with regional tastes and preferences may give the small company built-in advantages of location. Variation in regional preferences for beer, for example, enable many small regional breweries to coexist with large national concerns in the beer industry. Other small firms survive by developing specialized expertise in products that serve the needs of a limited market. A large food processor, for example, is not generally interested in marketing specialized gourmet foods such as *pâté de foie gras*. Instead, foods of this kind are usually sold by small companies who specialize in these lines.

Generally speaking, small firms are better able to handle products with relatively small potential markets. One reason is that a big firm's organization structure and control system are usually designed in such a way that some minimum commitment of personnel and other resources must be made to a product, regardless of its sales volume. This minimum commitment may represent a fixed cost that is excessive in relation to sales for some products. Thus, in the 1960s, one major producer of food and household products set a minimum of $10 million sales as a policy requirement for its new products.

There are, of course, many resource considerations that bear little relationship to size. The company that possesses preferential access to raw material reserves, efficient physical plant, qualified personnel, specialized management skills, or established public acceptance can select products that enable it to use these resources to greatest advantage.

The process of "taking an inventory" of corporate resources can often lead to the discovery of unexpected fields of potential profitability. During World War II, for example, the United States Army offered a lucrative supply contract to any firm that could develop a manufacturing process for large-scale production of orange juice concentrate. The contract was won by National Research Corporation of Boston. By modifying a production technique it had previously used in manufacturing blood plasma, National Research was able to produce a powdered orange concentrate. After the war, the company formed a subsidiary which subsequently gained market leadership in the frozen juice concentrate field with its now-familiar Minute Maid brand.

EXISTING MARKETS OF THE FIRM

A further consideration in product policy formulation is the extent to which a proposed product conforms to the existing markets served by the firm. Does it involve the same types of customers? Does it utilize the same distribution channels? Can it be sold by the company's present sales force? Does it involve the kinds of price, quality, and advertising appeals with which it is familiar?

In a sense, these questions represent an extension of those raised in the previous section, that is, familiarity with a class of customers. The marketing skill for serving them effectively is itself an intrinsic resource of a corporation. The possession of marketing skills and experience is sufficiently important, however, that we will give it separate consideration here.

Consider a manufacturer of industrial paints whose products are used by metal fabricating companies. The manufacturer sells direct to the fabricators, using his own technically trained sales force. A small advertising campaign in trade journals complements the salesmen's efforts. A suggestion is made that the manufacturer develop a line of metal paints for sale to household consumers. No technical problems are anticipated in developing and producing the new product.

It is easy to see, however, that an entirely different set of skills would be required to market the new line. New channels of distribution would be required to reach household consumers. The manufacturer's salesmen have no experience in calling on specialty paint stores, hardware stores, department stores, discount stores, or on the classes of wholesalers that serve these retail outlets. To advertise the product would involve new classes of media, and raise unfamiliar questions of designing an advertising campaign for a consumer market. Parts of the line might have to be marketed in aerosol cans, an unfamiliar packaging technique. In summary, the proposed product line, when appraised in terms of its fit with the paint manufacturer's existing markets, raises so many problems that the company should probably not add this new product unless it has such a strong technical advantage that it can overcome this lack of marketing skills.

It is by no means essential, of course, that a proposed product be a perfect fit with a firm's existing markets. For example, in September 1965, General Mills Corporation took a step that was to establish a pattern for itself and three other leading breakfast cereal manufacturers. By acquiring Parker Brothers, a firm producing family games such as Monopoly, General Mills entered the toy and hobbycraft market. Over the next five years, the company continued to expand its line of toys and games while Quaker Oats Company, General Foods Corporation, and National Biscuit Company all followed suit. By December 1970:

General Mills' toy, craft, and game division included Rainbow Crafts, Kenner Products Company, Craft Master Corporation, Parker Brothers, and the Lionel toy division of Model Products Corporation.

Quaker Oats had gained control of Fisher-Price Toys.

General Foods had acquired Kohner Brothers, a producer of infant, preschool, and educational toys and games.

National Biscuit was in the final stages of acquiring Aurora Products Corporation, a manufacturer of hobby and toy products.

The apparent basis for cereal manufacturers diversifying into toys and hobbycrafts was that the target customer was, for all intents and purposes, the same for both groups of products. Cereal manufacturers apparently believed that their vast experience and resources in marketing to families with children could be applied to advantage in marketing toys and hobbycrafts. Their highly sophisticated marketing knowledge was unmatched in the traditionally fractionized toy industries, particularly as it applied to techniques of advertising and promotion. With a common target market, there were even potential economies in promotion. A 30-second cereal commercial, for example, could be "piggybacked" with a similar toy commercial in a 1-minute television spot.

□ COMPETITION

Another factor in formulating product policy is the stance a firm chooses to adopt relative to the products of its competitors. Many large firms, for example, insist that any products they offer must be technological leaders in their field. Companies such as Du Pont, Monsanto, and IBM all seek to obtain competitive advantage through innovation. The implicit rationale for such a strategy is that the pioneer in a field will reap the rewards of a previously untapped market. The strategy possesses obvious risks. Du Pont's Corfam, for example, failed despite extensive expenditures on development and promotion. (See Chapter 25 for further discussion.) A synthetic material for shoes, it could not compete effectively with less expensive vinyls intended for the same purpose.

At the opposite extreme is a product strategy of "following the leader." Firms adopting this strategy rely on competitors to establish product markets, subsequently entering the established market on the basis of price or some different marketing appeal. Most food chains, for example, adopt this product strategy in their decisions on which items they will offer under their own distributor's brand name.

The decision to be a product leader, a follower, or to adopt some middle ground between these extremes depends in part on the resources and marketing skills of a firm in relationship to its competitors. Ultimately, the decision also reflects the firm's overall choice of corporate objectives.

CORPORATE OBJECTIVES

The resources of a firm, its existing marketing skills, and its competition generally reflect constraints on what a firm can do in its choice of products. To a greater extent, the corporation's objectives are discretionary. They reflect what a firm wants to do and, in turn, impinge upon its product policy.

As explained in Chapter 13, there are many different dimensions on which a firm can express its overall objectives. Three that we will discuss here are profitability, growth, and stability.

Virtually all business enterprises are committed to the generation of a reasonable level of *profits*. Their product mix is central to maintaining profitability. As many products grow older, for example, they tend to experience increasing price competition from similar items marketed by other companies.[2] As a result, unit profit margins decline. Unless unit sales volume increases sufficiently to offset the decline in unit margins, the result is lower total dollar profits. If the former profit levels of the firm are to be restored, new products bearing higher unit margins must be found.

Better managed companies, of course, do not wait for the profitability of a line to decline before seeking new products bearing higher margins. Instead, they *plan* their product mix to include a balance of products in varying stages of maturity. Slowly declining products, products currently earning high profits, and products it is hoped will be tomorrow's breadwinners all combine to ensure both current and future profitability.

The company committed to a high rate of corporate *growth* has four basic alternatives open to it. These alternatives, depicted in Figure 14-2, involve the option of working with existing products or developing new items, and the

[2] In Chapter 15, we will examine this tendency more fully in the context of a discussion of the product life cycle.

FIGURE 14-2

Product-market strategies for corporate growth

MARKETS

Increasing Newness →

PRODUCTS — Increasing Newness ↓

MARKET PENETRATION	MARKET DEVELOPMENT
An effort to increase company sales by increasing the volume of sales to present customers, or by finding new customers for present products	The adaption of present product lines to new classes of customers or users
PRODUCT DEVELOPMENT	**DIVERSIFICATION**
The development of products with new and different characteristics to serve the company's existing customers and use applications	A simultaneous departure from existing products and markets

Source: Adapted from H. Igor Ansoff, "Strategies for Diversification," *Harvard Business Review,* September–October, 1957, pp. 113–124.

similar option of serving existing markets or moving to entirely new types of customers or geographic markets. Accordingly, the four alternatives shown are sometimes referred to as *product-market strategies.*

Note that while new products represent one avenue to corporate growth, they are by no means the only available route. Consider the success of the William Wrigley, Jr. Company in applying a market penetration strategy. Since 1892, its sales have been derived almost entirely from four flavors of a single product, chewing gum. "It's not that we have a closed mind on diversifying," Wrigley's president once stated, "but you're better off doing what you know how to do best."[3]

Wrigley appears to know best how to market chewing gum. In 1971, its products were sold in virtually every country of the free world. The company's 1970 sales revenue of $176 million placed it among the 500 largest corporations in the United States.

The goal of attaining *stability* in patterns of sales and profits can also affect the product decisions of a firm. Consider a manufacturer of wood dining room and bedroom furniture. Because furniture is a durable good whose purchase can be postponed by consumers, the company's sales and profits fluctuate with general economic conditions. In "boom" economies, revenue is high;

[3] "Wrigley: A 7-cent Bonanza," *The New York Times,* May 9, 1971.

during recessions, it is depressed. Suppose the company now considers adding a line of upholstered living room furniture. The proposed new line, though complementary in many respects, is equally susceptible to the cyclical influence of economic climate. If added, it would accentuate the overall influence of economic conditions in the company. If stability is regarded as a key corporate goal, the firm would be better off to consider an entirely different product line that was not so susceptible to the same cyclical patterns.

Product decisions

Many firms commit themselves to written statements of product policy. In this way the policy, as a guide to decision making, can be disseminated to all levels of management throughout the organization. Typical examples would be the following hypothetical statements:

> The policy of the corporation is to market high-quality processed food products that provide the consumer with maximum ease of preparation and convenience in use. We endeavor to be among the first to discover and apply new developments in food technology and to make such products available to consumers. Products should be suitable for mass distribution to food chains, cooperatives, and independent grocery stores, throughout the United States. Any new product line should be capable of generating at least $10 million in sales revenue within one year of attaining national distribution (a large food processor).

> Products of the XYZ Company are intended to provide shoe retailers with a "second line" of children's footwear for consumers wishing to pay less than the price of advertised national brands. On the basis of normal retailer margins of 50 percent, any product offered by our company should be capable of retailing at a price 20 percent lower than its nearest national brand equivalent. Our shoes should stress functionality and durability rather than style leadership. Each line of shoes should be designed to provide the XYZ Company with a minimum margin of 60 percent on selling prices (a small shoe manufacturer).

Having formulated a product policy, it is equally important that this policy be properly *applied* to specific product decisions. In the remainder of this section, we will explore the principal kinds of product decisions typically encountered in a company. Our initial task will be to recognize the existence of different levels of product decision making, and their relationship to questions of breadth, depth, and consistency of product mix. Subsequently, we will single out new product decisions, decisions to drop weak products, and product positioning, for individual examination.

□ LEVELS OF PRODUCT DECISION MAKING

Some modern corporations produce hundreds or even thousands of different items. The General Electric Company, for example, manufactures television sets, turbines, light bulbs, transistors, nuclear reactors, and engines for military and executive jet aircraft, to name but a few. The only apparent connecting link among General Electric products is that they are all produced by General Electric. Within such a broad and heterogeneous assortment, it is clear that product decisions are made at several different levels.

First, decisions are made pertaining to individual *items*. An example would be a decision to develop and introduce a 100-watt, "long life" light bulb.

Other decisions may relate to an entire *product line,* such as light bulbs in general. Product lines are generally defined to include a group of products that are "related" in the sense that they possess common physical or technical characteristics, perform essentially the same function, are used together, are sold through the same channels, or are priced within the same range.

Finally, decisions must be made regarding a firm's overall *product mix,* meaning the entire assemblage of products that are marketed by the company.

The distinction is important for, while a firm's product policy guides its decision making at all levels, application of the policy may differ in specific decisions involving individual items, entire product lines, or the total product mix. The small shoe manufacturer cited earlier, for example, required that each line of shoes generate a specified profit. A particular style of shoe within the line, that is, an item, may nevertheless be unprofitable, but still be carried because retailers insist on presenting a range of styles for customers to consider.

BREADTH, DEPTH, AND CONSISTENCY OF PRODUCT MIX

Closely associated with different levels of product decisions are the concepts of breadth, depth, and consistency of product mix.

Breadth of product mix refers to the number of product lines marketed by a company. For many years, the Drexel Furniture Company produced only a single product line consisting of middle- to high-priced wood furniture. Later, a line of upholstered furniture was added. While precise measurement of breadth depends on how a company defines its product lines, Drexel's breadth of product mix was, by any standards, narrow. On the other hand, General Electric, described earlier, is an example of a firm with a very broad product mix.

Depth of produce mix refers to the average number of items in each product line. The depth of Volkswagen's product mix, with relatively few models of each car, for example, is substantially less than that of Ford or General Motors.

Consistency refers to the extent to which product lines are similar to each other in terms of technology, use, production requirements, or other characteristics. General Electric's products are consistent in the sense that almost all are related to electric or electronic technology. On the other hand, International Telephone and Telegraph Corporation's involvement in consumer finance, car rentals, commercial baking, residential building, life insurance, and hotels is not consistent with the firm's historic emphasis on industrial electronic products.

One should not conclude that, if a firm's product mix is not broad, deep, or consistent, it is necessarily a poor one. Instead, these dimensions merely reflect the basic product policy that a company has chosen to adopt. For example:

By maintaining a consistent product mix, a company may hope to acquire the highest reputation of excellence within its chosen field.

A small firm with a shallow product line may be concentrating its limited resources on appealing to a specific segment of consumers having a particular set of needs or wants.

A broad product mix may reflect the desire of a company to make itself less vulnerable to cyclical fluctuations in the demand for any one of its product lines.

NEW PRODUCT DECISIONS

In the 1960s and 1970s, new products played a major role in the growth and profitability of many American companies. Many products which today are considered commonplace were almost unknown in the 1940s or 1950s; in some cases, they did not exist at all. There is every indication that this revolution in innovation is far from over; an abundance of new materials and technology is awaiting commercialization.

Together with a potential for reward, the firm that undertakes the development and introduction of new products faces an enormous number of problems and risks. All these reach their greatest intensity, of course, when the firm undertakes the development of a product line previously unknown to the company or to the marketplace. Decisions involving the addition of a new *item* to an existing product line, on the other hand, typically involve risks and rewards of lesser magnitude.

We shall postpone further discussion of new product decisions until the next chapter. The complexity and importance of new product decisions are sufficient that we will devote Chapter 15 to this topic.

DROPPING WEAK PRODUCTS

In a modern, highly competitive market, firms understandably concentrate much of their attention on new product decisions. It is characteristic of many businesses that too little attention is often given to a review of the performance of existing products.

Sometimes, it can be surprisingly difficult to ascertain if existing products are still "earning their way." The nature of an accounting system can make it difficult to determine the true profitability of an item, especially where distribution or other marketing costs are hard to allocate. On occasion, a product may be someone's "pet," and the easy course may be to let it linger on in the hope that market conditions will change, deficiencies in its marketing program will be corrected, or that it will begin to earn a profit by some unspecified stroke of luck.

There *may* be valid reasons for the decline in sales and/or profitability of an item, of course, and a troubled product should be given a thorough review before it is discarded. There may be hidden costs, however, in retaining a product that is found genuinely weak. In particular,

The weak product tends to consume a disproportionate amount of management's time.
It often requires frequent price and inventory adjustments.
It generally involves short production runs and excessive setup times.
It requires both advertising and sales force attention that might better be diverted to making the healthy products more profitable.
Its very unfitness can cause customer misgivings and cast a shadow on the company's image.[4]

It is because of these hidden costs that a formal, periodic review of the firm's products is so important. They should, in effect, receive the same scrutiny as new products, as discussed in the following chapter.

PRODUCT POSITIONING

Positioning a product refers to the manner in which it is aimed at particular customer segments, either through intrinsic features in the product itself and/or the image that is created for the product through promotion. Hence, we can speak of most automobiles in terms of how they are positioned: a Cadillac as prestigious, a Mustang as sporty, a Volvo as durable, a Volkswagen as economical. Each of these cars, through its particular combination of style, design, peripheral features, and advertising and promotional messages, is designed to appeal differently to particular customer segments.

Some products are positioned to compete directly against others. Thus, the Pinto, Vega, and Cricket were all positioned to take direct aim at European and Japanese imports, particularly the Volkswagen. In other instances, a product may be positioned to find a niche in the marketplace not currently served by its competitors. The story of the Mustang, described in Chapter 1, is an outstanding example of successful positioning in a previously untapped segment of the market. Changing market and competitive conditions may necessitate eventual repositioning of an established product. Gillette's Right Guard deodorant was originally marketed as a product for males, but later repositioned as an all-family deodorant.

One type of deliberate repositioning is referred to as *trading up* or, in its opposite form, *trading down*. Trading up refers to improving a product's physical quality and/or improving its image in order to appeal to a more affluent and

[4] Philip Kotler, "Phasing Out Weak Products," *Harvard Business Review*, March–April, 1965, pp. 107–118.

quality-conscious customer segment. An interesting example of trading up can be found in the newspaper industry. *The National Enquirer* was, in the mid-1960s, a leading weekly tabloid specializing in bizarre stories of gore and mutilation. The newspaper's circulation had leveled off at about one million copies, and its owner, Generoso Pope, Jr., became concerned that the "market for gore" had become saturated. Starting in 1966, he began trading up *The National Enquirer's* market position by eliminating bizarre stories and moving the tabloid's editorial content closer to what Mr. Pope described as a "condensed *Reader's Digest.*" Circulation dropped 25 percent as many old readers were lost, but *The National Enquirer* gradually began acquiring a new class of readers. By early 1971, circulation had reached two million. To reach its new target customer, the middle-aged housewife, *The National Enquirer* had over spent $300,000 to gain distribution and favorable display in supermarkets.[5]

Brand policies

□ *A brand is "a name, term, sign, symbol, or design, or a combination of them which is intended to identify the goods or services of one seller or group of sellers and to differentiate them from those of competitors."*[6]

Among the important decisions that marketing managers make are whether to brand their products, and what brands to use.□ Once a brand is employed, it becomes an integral part of the product. For that reason, brand policy will be discussed as a portion of product policy, even though it is closely tied to advertising and other forms of promotion.

From the viewpoint of a manufacturer, middleman, or retailer who is considering using a brand, a brand might also be defined as a device designed to aid in the processes of creating, stimulating, strengthening, or maintaining demand. Brands are most commonly used with consumer goods, but are also used for industrial goods.

There is considerable confusion in the terminology of branding. Take, for example, the often-heard distinction between "private" and "national" brands. In everyday use, the term "private brand" refers to a brand owned by a distributor, usually a retailer, while a "national brand" is one owned by a manufacturer and sold throughout most of the country. Neither term is accurate or comprehensive. Nearly all brands are private, in the sense that they are the property of privately owned firms (including manufacturers). The brands of several retailers, Sears, for example, are sold nationally. Further, many manufacturers' brands are not sold nationally, but are sold locally, regionally, or internationally.

A more appropriate basis of distinguishing among brands, which we will use, is in terms of their ownership. In this regard, we can distinguish between *manufacturers' brands* and *distributors' brands*. Note that by focusing on own-

[5] "Going Straight: The National Enquirer Finds Gore Doesn't Pay, But Reassurance Does," *Wall Street Journal*, Apr. 12, 1971, pp. 1,10.

[6] *Definition of Terms*, American Marketing Association, Chicago, 1960, pp. 9–10.

ership, we not only avoid ambiguity in definition, but also direct our attention to who is responsible for the branding decision.

□

REASONS FOR BRANDING BY MANUFACTURERS

The manufacturer who puts a brand on his product hopes that it will play an important part in the demand-promotion process. In the first place, the use of a brand makes it easier for repeat sales to be secured with a minimum of effort by both the manufacturer and his channels of distribution. For example, the housewife who has been satisfied by her initial purchase of Green Giant peas will presumably buy the same brand the next time. The efforts of Green Giant's competitors are designed to make her switch brands, of course, but at least the Green Giant name is presumed to mean something to her about the quality or price or taste of the Green Giant peas. The manufacturer who stamps his brand on a grinding wheel or a lathe is hopeful that the brand will have some favorable impact on his industrial customers.

The use of a brand thus becomes important in pulling a product through channels of distribution. *Pulling* means the establishment of customer desires for a brand that are so strong that wholesalers and retailers will have to carry the brand in question. To go back to the illustration cited above, Green Giant management hopes that customer demand for the Green Giant brand is so strong that wholesalers and retailers throughout the country will have no alternative but to carry Green Giant peas. The manufacturer of industrial products *hopes* that his brand will yield the same result, but typically recognizes that the influence of the brand as such will be less than is the case with many consumer goods brands.

To the extent that brands create product loyalty, manufacturers gain sales stability. For example, customer loyalty makes it more difficult for wholesalers or retailers to exert effective pressure for advertising allowances (funds made available to channels for advertising purposes), for reduced shelf space, or for merchandising assistance. In essence, a strong brand becomes a device for enhancing the control that a manufacturer exerts over his middlemen and retailers and is tantamount to a reduction in the importance of their selling efforts.

From the manufacturer's viewpoint, a well-known brand facilitates the introduction of new products. Customers develop their own perceptions of the quality, price, and value aspects of a brand. Its subsequent use on a new product implies similar things about that product. When Campbell introduced its Man-Handler soups in 1969, the new line presumably profited from the brand image built by Campbell's other soups. There is another side to this situation, however. The new line had to meet the quality and value standards of the company's other products. If it did not, the new line's inferiority could hurt sales of the other items.

Brands also make it easier for manufacturers to differentiate products in terms of quality or features. The Bulova Watch Company, for example, sells a less expensive line of watches under the brand name Caravelle, its regular line under the Bulova name, and a line of electric timepieces under the Accutron brand.

Finally, so far as manufacturers are concerned, a brand enhances the likelihood of successful advertising and promotion. A catchy, pleasant brand name is typically easier for customers to recognize, remember, and talk about than the name of a manufacturing firm. Pepperidge Farm, for example, is better in all these respects as a brand for bakery products than Campbell Soup Company.

In summary, we see that manufacturers brand their products to *identify* them and to *differentiate* them from other products. Their brand names serve as guarantees of quality.[7] They invest money and effort in research and development to produce new or better products and to control quality. Leading manufacturers spend large sums of money to advertise their products and to build and maintain consumer acceptance and loyalty for these products.

□

BRANDING PROBLEMS CONFRONTING THE MANUFACTURER

A problem faced by many manufacturers concerns whether products should have a common family brand or individual brand names. All Heinz products, for instance, carry the Heinz name, but Procter and Gamble, for the most part, uses individual brand names for its products.

The use of a family brand has certain advantages. A new product can be helped by the "free ride" it gets from other items that carry the brand and have comparable package and design features. This is true even though the sharpness of the promotional effort may be reduced by the commonality of the brand. The new item may also benefit from the quality reputation of the established items.

Family branding is not without potential disadvantages. There are instances when a family brand is obviously undesirable. Where prices or quality vary considerably among the items in a line or where families of products serve different purposes, it is undesirable to have products appear closely related. For example, Helena Rubinstein would find it inexpedient to associate her name with a new varnish remover, excellent though the product might be. In other instances, companies would run substantial risks to existing products if a new product of unintended inferior quality were introduced under a family brand. There is also the risk that a new product may simply be a flop. When this

[7] In this connection, it is interesting to note that even state-owned factories in the USSR use "brand names" as a means of identifying the products of individual plants. This, it is claimed, serves as a mechanism for enforcing quality standards. See Marshall Goldman, *Soviet Marketing*, The Free Press, New York, 1963, pp. 145–146, 196–197.

happens, a stigma may be created with regard to the other products in the minds of both customers and trade channels.

The individuality of products is far more difficult to attain and maintain under a family brand policy. Procter and Gamble is again a case in point. That firm has extensive resources, and the anticipated sales volumes of its new products are large. It prefers to have individual brands managed by brand managers and to be able to pinpoint profitability and responsibility in this way. These factors, in conjunction with the fact that promotional and advertising campaigns can be pinpointed more easily for a unique name, make an impressive case for the use of a single brand where appropriate.

Among firms that employ a policy of individual branding, there appeared to be a growing trend in the early 1970s to find some alternate means of associating individual brands with the name or a symbol of the corporation. General Motors' "Mark of Excellence," for example, was used universally in association with Cadillac, Buick, Oldsmobile, Chevrolet, Frigidaire, Delco, AC, and other products of the corporation. Jello, Maxwell House, and Birds Eye products were all clearly marked with the seal of the General Foods Kitchen.

Another problem for the marketing manager is the choice of a brand name. Examples are useful in evolving some generalizations in this area. Bold and Punch are well-known brands in the household detergent field. Each is short, easy to pronounce and remember, and can handily be put on a package, a television screen, or a printed page. Note that each name also implies what the product will do. *Bold* implies that the contents of the package will attack dirt and grime with aggressive zeal, while its competitor *Punch* is presumed to do so with the speed and power of a pugilist.

Generalizations are probably as dangerous here as elsewhere. In multinational marketing, it may be wise to use a short, unique name that is easily recognizable in any language. Kodak is a classic example in this regard. Budweiser and Black & Decker are powerful brand names that fit none of the criteria outlined above.

BRANDING BY DISTRIBUTORS

There are many reasons why distributors use their own brands. Basically, they are trying to secure greater control over their markets and their marketing processes. Hence, many of the reasons advanced earlier on the usefulness of brands to manufacturers apply equally to retailers and other classes of distributors. Customer loyalty to a retailer's brand, for example, makes the retail organization far less susceptible to the influence of the manufacturer or to the vagaries of the manufacturer's competition.

Several other dimensions of the distributor's branding decision are unique to this class of marketing institution. For example, while retailers seek to attain differentiation through branding, they are frequently more interested in differentiating a *store,* as opposed to any single *product* it sells. By offering a line of merchandise under its own brand, the retailer hopes to create a *store image* that will draw customers. Frequently, the image associated with distributors' brands is one of low price.

The rise of discount stores, discussed in Chapter 11, provided an additional impetus to distributor branding. Many traditional retailers base their competitive appeal on providing delivery, credit, and other customer services that discounters do not provide. Burdened with the cost of these services, it is difficult for a traditional retailer to match the prices of discounters on manufacturers' brands. Instead, the retailer uses his own brands, selling at prices below those of manufacturers' brands, to compete with discounters.

It should not be forgotten that distributors' brands compete with each other, as well as with manufacturers' brands. Hence, many distributors feel that they must have their own brands if they are to compete with other distributors.

Economic factors are among the most crucial considerations in a distributor's branding decision. To realize attractive margins while selling at low prices, the distributor needs to obtain his merchandise at low product cost. Some distributors accomplish this by acquiring their own manufacturing establishments. Sears, for example, is reported to have equity interests in over half of its supplier companies. On the other hand, distributors can often obtain low product costs when purchasing from independently owned manufacturers. By offering the manufacturer a long-term contract to supply a product that will carry the distributor's brand, one that the manufacturer need not promote or advertise, the distributor may be able to negotiate low purchase prices. For manufacturers with excess capacity, a contract to supply distributors' brands may be particularly attractive.

The complexity of economic considerations in a distributor's branding decision can be seen by examining the data illustrated in Table 14-1. These data, drawn from a survey of food chains conducted by the National Commission on Food Marketing in 1966, indicate the relative prices, gross margins, and sales of distributors' and manufacturers' brands in a selected group of food product categories.

The relative profitability of a distributor's brand depends in part on its *retail price*. While distributors' brands are priced lower than a typical manufacturer's brand in all product categories shown in Table 14-1, the magnitude of price difference is not uniform. The manufacturer's brand of canned peaches, for example, is only 5 percent above the average price of distributors' brands, while for frozen orange concentrate the price difference is 36 percent. Differences in cost prices *paid* by a retailer, when combined with retail prices, result in percentage gross margins, as shown in Table 14-1. For all categories except frozen orange concentrate, distributors' brands earn slightly higher percentage gross margins. If you were to calculate dollar gross margin per case

□
TABLE 14-1

*Relative prices, gross margins, and scales of distributors' and manufacturers' brands, selected food product categories, 1966**

Product category	Average retail price per case		Average percentage gross margin		Percentage of category sales accounted for by	
	Distributors' brands	Advertised manufacturers' brands †	Distributors' brands	Advertised manufacturers' brands	Distributors' brands	Advertised manufacturers' brands
Frozen orange concentrate	$ 8.74	$11.57	22.0%	23.0%	79%	20%
Frozen green beans	4.94	6.42	37.2	30.5	77	21
Canned green peas	4.76	5.54	25.8	21.2	29	60
Canned peaches	6.24	6.54	18.5	18.1	47	53
Catsup	4.46	5.51	17.3	16.5	28	70
Tuna fish	12.72	15.46	23.8	19.2	31	63
Evaporated milk	6.52	7.49	12.6	11.2	45	54

* The data shown are averages based on a survey of 7 to 12 food chains (the number of chains reporting varies among product categories).
† These data are reported for a typical advertised manufacturer's brand. All other data are averages of *all* distributors' and advertised manufacturers' brands in the product categories shown.

Source: Adapted from National Commission on Food Marketing, *Special Studies in Food Marketing,* Technical Study no. 10, Superintendent of Documents, Washington, 1966, pp. 66, 70–71, 73.

(retail price times percentage gross margins), however, you would see that manufacturers' brands yield more than distributors' brands for all these categories except tuna fish. The total dollar gross margin earned by the retailer depends on the magnitude of his sales in each product category. As we can see from the last two columns of Table 14-1, the propensity of consumers to buy distributors' brands varies considerably among product categories—79 percent of frozen orange concentrate sales are accounted for by distributors' brands, as opposed to only 28 percent for catsup. It should be added that the retailer has some discretionary control over the sales performance of his own brands. He can, for example, allocate extra shelf facings to them, give them preferential shelf positions, and promote them heavily in newspaper advertising and end-aisle displays.

Beyond the direct economic considerations outlined above, the distributor who adopts his own brands must also cover several indirect costs. Building a distributor's brand name requires a substantial investment of time and money. There are problems of maintaining quality control and assuring reliable sources of supply. In the area of promotion, the funds and creative talent available to large manufacturers are difficult to combat, particularly when manufacturers' brands are already popular among customers. Finally, the distributor's chances of success will also be affected by his current reputation; in fact, a distributor can seldom hope to achieve much success with his brand unless his reputation among customers is already high.

THE BATTLE OF THE BRANDS

Throughout the twentieth century, distributors' brands have grown in importance in most product categories. Today, it is not uncommon to see distributors' brands and manufacturers' brands competing side by side in department stores, supermarkets, discount houses, drugstores, and numerous other retail outlets. Because of its intensity, this competition has come to be known colloquially as "the battle of the brands."

In the United States, up to around 1900, manufacturers typically did little advertising. They directed their selling efforts to wholesalers, who in turn sold to retailers, and retailers were expected to sell to end consumers. With the gradual evolution of mass media advertising, manufacturers began to direct more promotional effort to end consumers. The "pull" created by this advertising slowly eroded distributor control of the marketing channel and, in defense, distributors began to introduce their own brands. As early as World War I, distributors' brands of coffee, tea, and canned fruits were competing with manufacturers' brands. By 1967, it was estimated that distributors' brands accounted for 7 percent of all portable appliance sales, 13 percent of grocery products, 16 percent of gasoline, 33 percent of major appliances, 36 percent of tires, and 52 percent of all shoe sales.[8]

From the previous section, we have already seen why distributors are motivated to enter the battle of the brands and, by implication, what is at stake in this battle for manufacturers. At this point, it is appropriate to look briefly at how consumers perceive the two brand types.

A study conducted in 1965 by Opinion Research Corporation found that about one-quarter of American women clearly recognized the distinction between manufacturers' and private brands.[9] Another quarter had some understanding in that they could discuss well-known brands and less well-known

[8] Victor J. Cook and Thomas F. Shutte, *Brand Policy Determination,* Marketing Science Institute, Allyn and Bacon, Inc., Boston, 1967, p. 3.

[9] *Selected Findings from O.R.C. Caravan Survey on Attitudes toward Private versus National Brands,* Opinion Research Corporation, Princeton, N.J., 1965.

brands. The remaining half had no understanding of the distinction between the two brand types.

In general, there would appear to be a relationship between education and understanding of the brand distinctions. With increasing education, a higher proportion understood the distinction. The study did not report, however, on whether higher understanding necessarily meant higher usage of distributors' brands.

In determining why people buy distributors' or national brands, a study of food products conducted for the National Commission on Food Marketing is relevant.[10] As one might expect, "well-known" brands (which may include some distributors' as well as advertised manufacturers' brands) were found in the study to be bought because of their perceived high quality, while "less well-known" brands are bought for their lower price. About a third of the women surveyed in this study indicated they had a consistent preference for well-known brands in their shopping, while 14 percent stated a consistent preference for less well-known brands. The remaining half of the sample stated they bought both types, choosing in individual situations on the basis of past experience and other decision criteria.

PROTECTION OF BRANDS AND BRAND NAMES

There would be little reason to build a brand unless it could be protected against use by someone else. This section sets forth briefly some of the legal aspects of branding. However, this discussion serves only as an introduction. Many brand problems are exceedingly complex in their legal ramifications, and most marketing managers rely heavily on legal counsel for advice.

The Lanham Act of 1946 makes it possible for sellers to register their brands with the U.S. Patent Office. Registration is not compulsory, nor does it establish ownership of a brand. Ownership may be shown presumptively by demonstrating that the brand has been used exclusively and continuously for a period of five years. The brand must not have become a generic name, nor can there be any litigation against the brand in either the Patent Office or a court. If these conditions are met, the brand becomes the *incontestable* property of its owner. Even then, however, the owner, not the government, is responsible for bringing litigation against anyone who infringes on his brand.

Because it is a federal statute, the Lanham Act applies only to goods in interstate and foreign commerce. The act prohibits the registration of certain kinds of brands. Among those are portraits of people who have not given consent, flags or insignia of governments, and brands that are "immoral, deceptive, scandalous, or disparaging of persons, institutions, beliefs, or national symbols."

[10] National Commission on Food Marketing, *Special Studies in Food Marketing*, Technical Study no. 10, Government Printing Office, Washington, 1965, pp. 79–84.

It was pointed out above that a firm can lose ownership of a brand if the latter becomes a *generic* name, that is, a widely used descriptive name for the product with which it is used. "Cellophane," for example, was originally a Du Pont trade name for the film that bears that name. Over the years, the word *cellophane* became so widely and closely associated with the product that the film itself became known as cellophane. Once this happened, Du Pont lost its ownership of the brand, which became public property. A similar fate befell brands on such products as aspirin and shredded wheat.

Packaging

Gone are the days of the cracker barrel. Today's crackers are found in a wooden box, a tin, a plastic bag, a sheet of glassine or cellophane, a paper box with a cowboy on the cover or a tiger on the back, or any one of a hundred, or perhaps a thousand, things. The transformation of the cracker package reflects the revolution that has occurred in packaging. This revolution will continue as new materials, new processes, and new purposes for packages are found. Packaging has itself become an important industry, serving both the consumer and industrial goods fields. The uses of packaging for purposes other than protection, shipping, and storage are increasing in both fields. The growth in the importance of packaging has been enhanced by the rapid growth of the self-service process in the retailing of foods and many other consumer items. In a word, packaging is a vital part of product policy.

□ PACKAGING FUNCTIONS

Beyond the functional role of giving protection to a product, a package can provide convenience to customers, aid in selling the product, and help in achieving product differentiation and identification.

Protection and convenience A package protects a product during transportation, inventory processing, shelf life, and in the customer's home or place of business. Such protection yields obvious economic benefits to all parties by reducing damage in transit and diminishing perishability. Modern packaging techniques also provide convenience to customers by improving ease of handling, opening, and storage.

Selling The selling function can be appreciably aided by packaging. Packages are designed to educate customers and, to some extent, channels of distribution on the merits of products. Frequently, packages contain a visual tie-in to an advertising campaign through color choice, pictures, or message. At a more prosaic level, packages frequently carry directions for use or descriptions of contents.

Containers are often designed for display purposes at the retail level. There is a never-ending battle for shelf space and good location in retail stores. The manufacturer's problem is to design a package that will be easy for the retailer to put up, that will fit the available shelf space, and that will catch the customer's eye during the shopping trip. This is no easy task, in view of the thousands of items and great use of various types of point-of-purchase selling stimulants typically found in grocery, drug, and other kinds of retail stores.

Product differentiation and identification Packaging can help to achieve a greater degree of product differentiation. This is particularly true when intrinsic differences between the products of manufacturers are negligible or not easily apparent or very important to the customer. Consider Miller's High Life beer. Its advertising campaign and appeals are certainly different from those of most breweries. The company uses a clear glass bottle, and a label that is also quite different in shape. One may hypothesize that these differences were carefully planned to convey the message that Miller's High Life is "The Champagne of Bottled Beers."

Packaging is also used to achieve common identification of the various products in a line. Baby foods are a good example. When Gerber, a manufacturer of baby foods, brings out a new item, the familiar Gerber baby symbol on the package identifies the manufacturer and implies that the new product is as good as the rest of the Gerber line. Conversely, if a company wants to bring out a product in a lower quality or price bracket, a different package (or brand) will help to dissociate it from the remainder of the line.

Thus packaging is an important part of product policy. The problem for the marketing decision maker is to work out the most effective and economic manner of putting his product into a container representing a blend of utilitarian, promotional, and aesthetic objectives. His problems involve size, shape, material, finish, design, color, visual effect, printing, style, strength, weight, and the characteristics of the product itself. Starting in late 1966, however, the marketer in the United States was compelled to add a further consideration to his packaging decision: conformity to new legislation on fair packaging.

FAIR PACKAGING AND LABELING

Beginning in the early 1960s, advocates of so-called "fair packaging" legislation gained increasing attention for the assertion that there were persistent and widespread abuses in the packaging practices of many manufacturers. As a result, it was argued, consumers were unable to make reasonable comparisons of value among competing products. The principal complaint was undue package proliferation, in which similar products were sold in an excessively large number of different package sizes. The U.S. Department of Commerce reported, for example, that there were 57 different sizes of toothpaste available in 1966. Other practices under criticism included confusing and inconspicuous labeling, "slack fill" (placing a small quantity of product in the bottom of a package and filling the remainder with air), packaging to price (keeping the package size and price constant, but decreasing the costs by diminishing the amount of product the package contains), fractional-ounce package sizes, and cents-off labeling by manufacturers that could not be enforced at the retail level.

The federal Fair Packaging and Labeling Act was first introduced in 1965 and, after some revision, signed into law in November 1966. The act required that product labels show such information as net quantity of contents, that labels be legible and conspicuous, that "number of servings per package" be defined in terms of quantity per serving, and that qualifying terms, for example, "giant 12-ounce," not be used to distort content information. The act also suggested that voluntary packaging standards be adopted by industry wherever "undue proliferation of weights, measures, or quantities impairs the ability of consumers to make value comparisons." Areas for voluntary industry regulation included maximum slack fill limits and package size standardization.

In addition to adhering to the mandatory requirements of the act, about two dozen industries had, by early 1970, agreed to voluntary packaging standards. In many of these industries, the number of container sizes was dramatically reduced, for example, toothpaste (from 57 to 5 sizes), cereals (from 33 to 16), dry detergents (from 24 to 6), and paper towels (from 33 to 8).

In the early 1970s, however, many consumer groups remained adamant that more stringent packaging legislation was still required, and that further amendment to the act was necessary. Their most vocal demand was that value comparison be further facilitated by *unit pricing,* that is, that retailers be required to indicate prices of grocery and related items according to a standard unit of measure. Under this system all detergent products in a supermarket, for example, would be affixed with a label indicating their price per ounce. In 1970 and 1971, some grocery chains, including Safeway and Jewel Tea, had initiated unit pricing on a voluntary test basis. A Massachusetts state law requiring unit pricing for a wide range of food store products went into effect in May 1971, and other states were actively discussing similar laws in mid-1971.

Product liability

Fair packaging legislation was one of several issues in the 1960s and early 1970s that gained impetus from widespread public support for the consumerism movement. We will devote more attention to consumerism in Chapter 27, but, for the moment, it is important to recognize two key objectives of this movement. Advocates of consumerism seek to educate people to become more effective as consumers and, at the same time, to ensure that business firms adopt marketing practices facilitating value comparisons by shoppers. In the context of the latter objective, increasing pressure has been brought to bear on the question of products that do not perform as the consumer has been led to expect they will. It seems apparent that, in the 1970s, businesses will be required to pay increasing attention to their *liability* for product performance and related questions of product safety.

LEGAL CONCEPTS OF PRODUCT LIABILITY

The United States has, for many years, provided legal recourse for persons who have been sold faulty merchandise. Under contract law, for example, a manufacturer is required to honor his express warranty. In the absence of a contractual agreement between buyer and seller, legal action can still be taken under tort law (the law of personal injury) if the buyer can establish that he has suffered personal injury as a result of negligence on the part of the manufacturer. These laws have not changed appreciably in recent years, but the number of product liability suits has risen dramatically, and the interpretation of these suits by the courts has been increasingly in the consumer's favor.

Growth in product liability suits seems related, at least in part, to an increased public awareness of the consumer's right to safe and effective products. This awareness has been heightened, for example, by publicity surrounding government hearings on automobile, tire, and drug safety; by news releases on faulty product design, such as the emission of harmful X-rays from color television sets; by the publicity attendant to fair packaging, truth in lending, meat inspection and poultry inspection legislation; by product recalls in the automobile and appliance industries; and even by the public debate on cigarettes and lung cancer.

Recent interpretations of seller responsibility by courts of law have had the effect of expanding business liability. In addition to express warranties, for example, a manufacturer is likely to be bound legally to claims in advertisements, sales promotion materials, labels, instructions, and oral sales presentations, if the buyer establishes that he relied on these claims in making a purchase. The value of disclaimers written into sales agreements, whereby limits on seller liability are outlined, has been reduced by court decisions overriding them. The concept of seller negligence in tort law has been expanded greatly. As a result of these and other changes, it has become easier to recover damages from sellers through legal recourse.[11]

PRESSURES ON THE MANUFACTURER

The problems of product liability confronting a manufacturer are not always easy for him to resolve. In an age of increasing complexity in product design, it

[11] For a more complete description of these changes in legal interpretation of product liability, see David L. Rados, "Product Liability: Tougher Ground Rules," *Harvard Business Review*, July–August, 1969, pp. 144–152.

may be extremely difficult for consumers to discriminate between good and poor quality. How many consumers can evaluate the technical circuitry of a color television set, for example? For manufacturers who build quality into their products, market demand does not always respond to quality in the expected fashion. This is particularly true in instances where quality features are difficult to communicate. It is a simple task to state the protein and vitamin content of a nutritional cereal, but quite difficult to describe their *health benefits* in clear, unequivocal terms.

Intense price competition in some markets may add pressure to keep manufacturing costs to a minimum. In markets where new products are essential to competitive survival, these are further problems, for quality control may be unusually difficult during the development and early production of a new item. In the spring of 1971, every Ford Pinto built since the car's introduction in the previous year had to be recalled to correct a design defect.

Some believe that acceptable levels of product safety and effectiveness are beyond the control of an individual manufacturer. The National Commission on Product Safety, in its report released in 1970, proposed the creation of a new government agency with power to enjoin the marketing of unsafe products. In the commission's view, self-regulation by manufacturers would not work because "competitive forces may require management to subordinate safety factors to cost considerations, styling, and other marketing imperatives."[12]

Questions

1. Consider the following events that occurred in the 1960s or early 1970s:

General Electric Company sold its computer division to Honeywell, another major computer manufacturer.
RCA Corporation acquired Hertz, the leading automobile rental firm.
Sears, Roebuck began marketing mutual funds.
A major promotional campaign was launched describing the soft drink Seven-Up as the "Un-cola."

a. Why do you suppose each of these apparent changes in product policy was made?
b. What possible benefits and costs might be associated with these changes for each of the companies involved?
c. Do you think the changes should have been made? Why?

2. As described in the text, the product policy of the Brunswick Corporation is very different from that of the William Wrigley Jr. Company.

[12] *Advertising Age*, June 29, 1970, p. 78.

a. What risks or problems do you think these companies face because of their product policies?

b. Using whatever information may be available in your library or elsewhere, see what additional information you can find to help explain the differences between the product policies of the two companies.

c. Suppose Wrigley decided to broaden its product line. What major product alternatives can you identify? What are the pros and cons of each?

3. The two major rivals in the cola soft-drink market are the Coca-Cola Company and Pepsico, Inc., makers of Pepsi-Cola. Both firms also market low-calorie diet cola products: Coca-Cola's product is branded *Tab* while Pepsico's product is branded *Diet Pepsi*. Evaluate the branding decisions of these two companies for their diet cola products.

4. National Screw Company manufactured a wide line of brass and steel screws, nuts and bolts, and miscellaneous fasteners. These products were distributed to over 50,000 retail hardwares, lumber supply yards, and other retail outlets as well as to industrial distributors.

Concerned with low profit margins, management authorized the accounting department to conduct a product cost study. The study revealed that 150 of the company's 1,700 products accounted for 80 percent of total sales, but a much lower proportion of total costs. The reports noted that direct manufacturing costs were substantially lower for products manufactured in large quantity, that order handling costs were substantially lower for products ordered in large quantities, and that inventory stock turn was significantly higher for products with high sales volume. The major conclusion of the report was that a number of the company's slow-moving products were not profitable and should be dropped.

a. What factors would you want to consider in deciding what products, if any, should be dropped from the line?

b. What further information would you want? Why?

5. What factors would the Campbell Soup Company have to consider if faced with a request from a major national food chain to supply soups branded under the chain's own name?

6. The advertising agency for a large brewery suggested that the company should introduce two or three new brands of beer over a period of time, rather than concentrate on selling only one brand. The agency argued that this approach, followed by cigarette and detergent manufacturers, would help the company improve its sales, market share, and profit for more than would be possible through an intensification of the effort devoted to the one brand of beer currently being marketed. How would you evaluate this suggestion?

7. What kinds of changes could you suggest to the conventional packaging of each of the following products? Why?
   a. Frozen orange juice
   b. Cigarettes
   c. Fresh milk
   d. Eggs
   e. Automotive oil
   f. Portable typewriters

8. For each of the products listed above, what factors should be considered by a company in its decision on whether to adopt your recommendation?

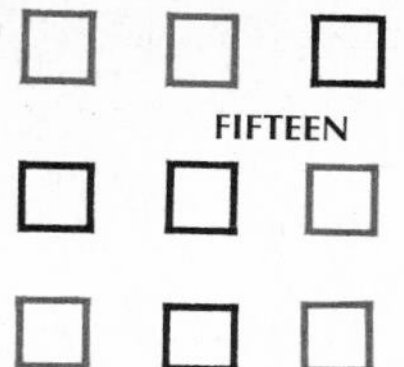

New product decisions

People throughout the developed countries of the world, and Americans in particular, have grown accustomed to the idea of newness in the last two decades. They have witnessed a cornucopia of ingenuity and innovation that has touched upon and altered every dimension of their life styles. It sometimes appears that, sooner or later, a product can be developed to do virtually anything. Science-fiction writer Arthur Clarke, in establishing what he called Clarke's law, put it succinctly: "When a distinguished but elderly scientist states that something is possible, he is almost certainly right—when he states that something is impossible, he is very probably wrong."[1]

Technology, it seems, presents little or no barrier to progress. Yet many new ideas, concepts, and product prototypes never reach the light of day in the marketplace, or if they do, quickly fail. For all its benefits, innovation can be a wasteful process to members of a society and, in particular, to those business enterprises which sponsor it. The crucial problems, it seems, are in the management of technological change and the innovative process.

THE MANAGEMENT OF INNOVATION

Today, almost every marketer is aware of the importance placed by top management on corporate new product activity. A company's record of new prod-

[1] "Putting the Prophets in Their Place," *Time*, Feb. 15, 1971.

uct successes is one of the major yardsticks by which managerial performance is measured. In this chapter, we turn our attention to the important issues underlying the quest for new products and the process of new product development and introduction.

We will begin by examining the *product life cycle* which is, in essence, a framework for understanding the sales pattern and competitive conditions surrounding a product category over its lifetime. Subsequently, we will explore how manufacturers, distributors, and customers each view new products from a different vantage point and how, in turn, their differing perspectives have implications for the process of developing and introducing new products. We will proceed to examine licensing, acquisition, and internal development—the alternative means by which a firm can obtain new products. The remainder of the chapter will be devoted to internal development, the most risky, but potentially most rewarding, of these alternatives. We will review the *economic considerations* confronting a firm that undertakes to develop and introduce new products, and consider the central issues in managing each stage of the new product process: idea generation, screening, economic analysis, product development and testing, test marketing, and commercialization.

The product life cycle

It is useful to begin thinking about products in terms of what is called the product life cycle. Briefly stated, the product life cycle is a general framework explaining long-term trends in a product class or category, and related changes in competitive behavior.

The "cycle" through which a product passes includes four stages: first, an *introductory* stage, in which sales increase slowly; second, a stage of *rapid growth;* third, *maturity,* a stage during which sales change only slightly; and fourth, a stage of *decline.*

The general form of such a cycle is shown in Figure 15-1. The curve in this exhibit represents total sales of a product over an extended period of time. The first or introductory stage of the cycle, commencing with the introduction of a product to the marketplace by an innovator, is characterized by slow growth in sales. This is attributed to some combination of four possible causes:

1. Delays in the expansion of production capacity
2. Technical problems, that is, "working out the bugs"
3. Delays in making the product available to customers, especially in obtaining adequate distribution through retail outlets
4. Customer inertia, arising primarily from reluctance to change established behavior patterns

A successful product eventually passes from the introductory stage into one

FIGURE 15-1

A generalized product life-cycle pattern

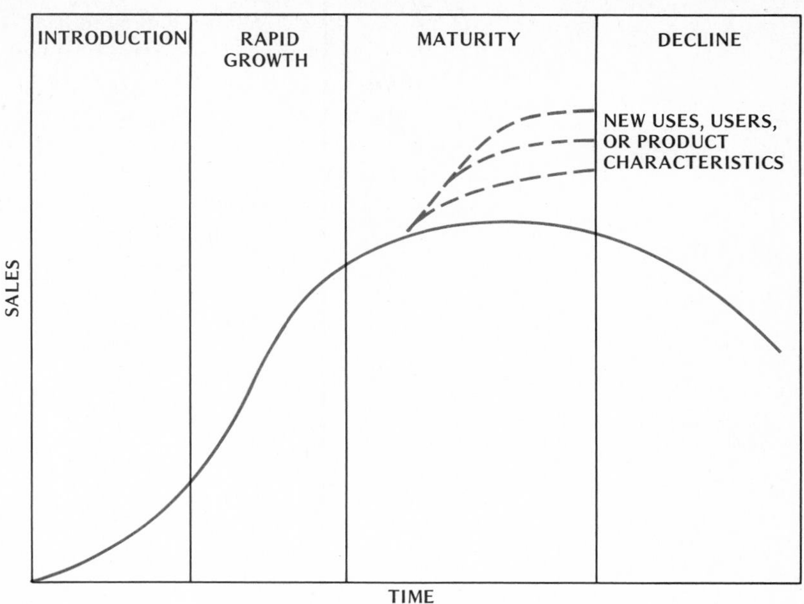

of rapid growth, during which sales volume expands rapidly. In the case of consumer products, the transition to rapid growth is explained partly in terms of an imitation process among consumers, and partly in terms of intensified promotion as competitors of the innovating company introduce "me-too" products.

The rapid growth stage of the life cycle is usually thought to be self-limiting because there is some natural "ceiling" or saturation rate of sales for any product. As the sales rate approaches this ceiling, both the rate of growth and the absolute amounts of growth from year to year decrease, and ultimately a plateau is reached. At this point the product is mature, and for some time, perhaps for a long period, subsequent changes in sales will be governed largely by changes in the size of the relevant total market.

An interesting phenomenon, indicated by the dotted lines in Figure 15-1, is that the length of the maturity stage for some product classes, and the height of its ceiling, can be extended by finding new uses and/or users, or by modification of product characteristics. The life cycle of nylon was lengthened for many years by successively extending its application to rope, sweaters, bearings, carpets, and other end products. Similarly, per capita consumption of "regular" ready-to-eat breakfast cereals remained virtually constant in the period 1948–1964, but the introduction of "presweetened" and "high-nutrition" cereal products increased total per capita cereal consumption by almost 40 percent in the same time period.

The maturity stage may last for many years, in some cases even centuries. With few exceptions, however, all products are thought ultimately to reach a stage of decline, during which sales will decrease more or less steadily. The passage from maturity to decline is usually explained primarily in terms of the development of substitute products. For example, canned vegetables have been replaced to some extent by frozen vegetables, and vacuum tubes have been replaced by transistors.

CHANGING PATTERNS OF COMPETITION THROUGH THE LIFE CYCLE

One obvious use of the product life cycle is as a tool in forecasting the sales trend of a product class or category. But the implications of life cycles extend far beyond forecasting. Life cycles also involve changes in patterns of competition.

A brief summary of how the competition in a product category changes from one phase of the cycle to another is shown in Figure 15-2. The introductory period is characterized by heavy promotion aimed at building up primary demand; price is relatively unimportant. During the growth phase, more competitors appear and there is an increasing pressure on price. Promotional expenditures decline in relation to sales; there is a shift to competition on the basis of brands and specific features. As the product enters maturity, there is increasing product brand competition, promotional expenditures and prices tend to stabilize, manufacturers begin efforts to extend life cycles, and new brands may appear. Finally, in the decline phase, further declines in price and promotional expenditures can be expected.

It is these changes in patterns of competition over the life cycle that render the concept most useful to marketers. Decisions relating to new product op-

FIGURE 15-2
Summary of changing competitive patterns at different stages of the product life cycle

Stage	Competitive situation
Introduction	Heavy promotion–aimed at building primary demand
Growth	More competitors Increasing pressure on prices Lower rate of promotional expenditures—shift to brands, specific features
Maturity	Increasing private brand competition Prices, promotional expenditures stable or declining Efforts to extend life cycles
Decline	Further declines in price, promotion

FIGURE 15-3
Instant coffee sales, prices, and advertising, 1946-1964

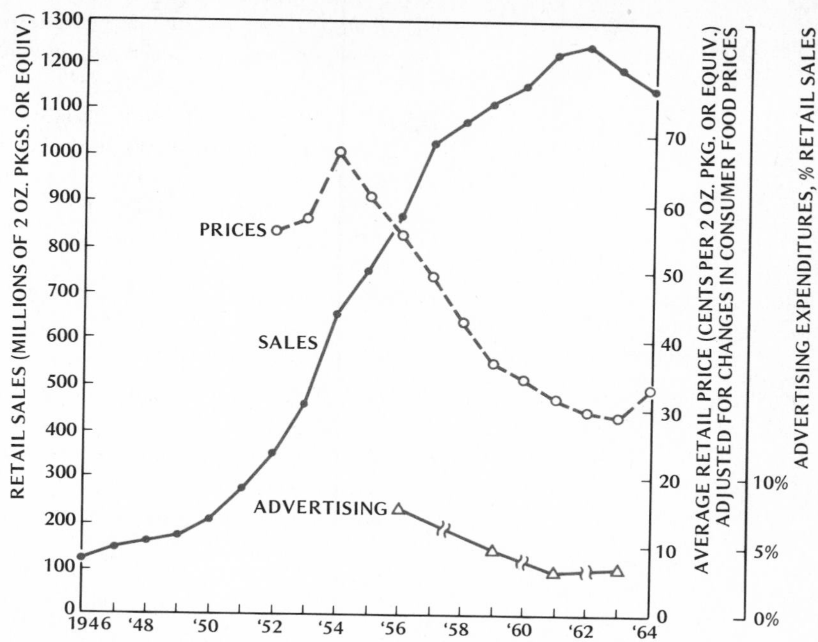

Source: Robert D. Buzzell, "Competitive Behavior and Product Life Cycle," in John S. Wright and Jack L. Goldstucker (eds.), *New Ideas for Successful Marketing,* Proceedings of the 1966 World Congress, American Marketing Association, Chicago, June, 1966, p. 50.

portunities, the generation and selection of marketing strategies, resource allocation, and responses to actions of competitors are all aided by a comprehension of competitive changes that can be provided by the product life cycle.

TESTING THE LIFE-CYCLE CONCEPT

Studies conducted in the 1960s have established the general validity of the life-cycle concept for categories of products. One of the authors studied 17 processed food categories and found that rates of market growth and patterns of competitive behavior generally conformed to those expected by the life-cycle model.[2] The history of instant coffee, for example, is illustrated in Figure 15-3. In another study, the concept was found to apply to color television sets.[3]

[2] Robert D. Buzzell, "Competitive Behavior and Product Life Cycles," in John S. Wright and Jack L. Goldstucker (eds.), *New Ideas for Successful Marketing,* Proceedings of the 1966 World Congress, American Marketing Association, Chicago, June, 1966, pp. 46–47.

[3] Hugh M. Beville, "The Product Life Cycle Theory Applied to Color Television," unpublished M.A. thesis, New York University, 1966.

There remains some doubt, however, about the applicability of the life-cycle concept to subclasses of categories, iced tea, for example, as opposed to tea, or to individual brands, such as Lipton or Tetley. It would appear that subclasses and brands do tend to follow, to varying degrees, the pattern of market growth predicted by the life cycle.[4] It does not seem likely, however, that changes in the promotion and price levels of subclasses or individual brands are necessarily as would be predicted by the life-cycle concept.

□

SOME IMPLICATIONS OF THE PRODUCT LIFE CYCLE

As a starting point in thinking about products, the product life cycle is valuable because it serves to remind us how conditions change over a period of time. Whole classes of products can become obsolete, or cease to be competitive. This can happen to even the most commonplace of items. Entering the 1970s, for example, the food industry faced imminent competition from synthetic coffee, sugar, and lemonade, while synthetic meat and dairy products had already been introduced to the market.[5] The original use for a product can disappear or decline, as in the case of horseshoes. Customer habits may change. It is estimated that more men's suits, 20 million, were sold in the depression year of 1935 than in 1970, when only 16 million were sold.[6]

For marketers, the implications of these trends are obvious. Eventually, a company's existing products may decline, die, or cease to be profitable. New products to replace them are a necessity.

What is a new product?

There is considerable confusion over the meaning of the term "new product." At one extreme, the phrase is sometimes used to include not only all products which differ in any way from those previously produced or sold by a given company, but even changes in advertising appeals for existing products. On this basis, one author has stated, "What is new depends on what the customer perceives, or can be brought to perceive. . . . Even the well-established [product] can be 'new' so far as the buyer is concerned."[7]

At the other extreme, some commentators would exclude everything except really fundamental innovations. Representative is the statement of E. B. Weiss

[4] For a study involving grocery products and brands, see Rolando Polli and Victor Cook, "Validity of the Product Life Cycle," *Journal of Business,* October, 1969, pp. 385–400. For ethical drug brands, see William E. Cox, Jr., "Product Life Cycles as Marketing Models," *Journal of Business,* October, 1967, pp. 375–384.

[5] Essences May Underlie Creation of Future Synthetic Foods, Beverages," *Advertising Age,* Mar. 18, 1968.

[6] "High Style Disrupts the Men's Wear Industry," *Fortune,* February, 1971, p. 70.

[7] Chester R. Wasson, "What Is 'New' about a New Product?" *Journal of Marketing,* July, 1960, pp. 52–56.

that "at least 80% of new products aren't new products at all. They are simply modifications—and minor modifications at that—of existing products."[8]

The definitional confusion apparently arises because both words, "new" and "product," are subject to varying interpretation. A product, on one hand, may mean a particular item (a 5-horsepower, variable-speed electric motor), a line of items (variable-speed electric motors of all horsepower sizes), or a particular brand of an item or line (General Electric variable-speed electric motors). The different viewpoints, of course, merely reflect what we have already discussed in Chapter 14. There are different *levels* of product decision making that must be addressed by businesses and their customers, and different concepts of "product" corresponding to each of these levels.

The word *new* is perhaps subject to even greater variations in meaning. For example:

New to whom? To a person who has never bought shares in a mutual fund, the idea of mutual funds is new. To an insurance company considering diversifying into the sales of mutual funds, it is also new. But to the ABC Company, which has been selling mutual funds for 10 years, it is not new.

New in what ways? Newness, on one hand, may refer to changes in design, materials, composition, or ingredients. At the same time, newness in a product also implies new activities and problems for those who produce, distribute, consume, or otherwise use a product. A consumer buying the identical product may have to adopt new behavior patterns if he is to use the new product effectively.

How new? Anderson Clayton Company's Chiffon margarine was the first "soft margarine" marketed in the United States. Almost universally, it was regarded as new. But what of the fifth or sixth brand subsequently introduced? Although new to the companies that sponsored them, these later brands were clearly of a lower order of newness to distributors and consumers. Furthermore, how long did Chiffon *remain* new? Six months? One year? Longer?

It should be apparent that newness is ultimately a matter to be decided "in the eye of the beholder." The answer to what is new depends on who is asking the question.

WHY DOES NEW PRODUCT DEFINITION MATTER?

Our purpose in discussing new product definition is not to find to a single, all-encompassing amalgam of words and phrases with universal application. Clearly, the foregoing discussion suggests that no such definition can exist. What is important is that definition is dependent on the decision situation under consideration.

To illustrate the significance of this concept, consider the case of a plastics fabricator who wants to develop and introduce a line of plastic pipes for use by plumbing and heating contractors. How much he must spend on research and

[8] E. B. Weiss, "That Malarky about 80% of New Products Failing," *Advertising Age*, Aug. 2, 1965, p. 101.

development, how much time is needed to bring the product to market, and the extent of product testing necessary are all affected by the fact that the line is new to the fabricator himself. As the fabricator thinks about establishing distribution channels to market the piping, however, he must consider the perspective of the plumbing wholesalers who will probably be asked to carry it. Their enthusiasm for the piping will depend on whether they already have similar lines and, if so, how the two compare in such areas as gross margin, inventory requirements, and selling support. The plumbing contractors' perspective, of course, will provide the basis of the fabricator's entire marketing program. For contractors already using another plastic piping, marketing appeals must emphasize the advantages of the new *brand* of plastic piping. For those now using copper or lead piping, appeals emphasizing the merits of plastic per se may be more appropriate.

□ THE PERSPECTIVE OF THIS CHAPTER

We see, therefore, that an appropriate definition of "new products" depends on *who* is addressing the new product decision, and what *level* of product decision is being considered. In examining new product decisions in the remainder of this chapter, it is clearly not feasible to review the multiplicity of decision situations that arise. Instead, we will focus our attention on the situation where the risks and rewards associated with new products are generally greatest. Therefore, we will explore new product decisions from the perspective of a manufacturer considering the addition of new products which, at minimum, represent the introduction of a line new and unfamiliar to the sponsoring company.

Sources of new products

There are three basic alternatives open to a company that seeks to obtain new products: licensing, acquisition, and internal development. In this section, we examine the benefits and pitfalls associated with each of these options.

□ LICENSING

Licensing is a contractual agreement under which one company, the licensor, grants access to its patents or technical know-how to one or more other companies, the licensees. Usually, the licensor receives financial compensation in return, although licenses are occasionally granted free of charge. The practice is a common one in both domestic and multinational marketing. For example, one study of domestic licensing among 119 manufacturing companies in the United States found that all but six had extended licenses to others; 102 of the companies had also sought or accepted licenses from other American firms.[9]

Companies of all sizes and from nearly all industries enter into license agreements, but the practice is particularly prevalent in high-technology, research-intensive industries such as aircraft, electrical and electronic equipment, industrial machinery, instruments, chemicals, metals processing, and petroleum refining. A considerable number of license agreements also exist in the food processing and textile industries.

There are many reasons why a company might grant a license to other firms. The most obvious benefit is royalty income. Income from licensing can help defray research and development costs, and is particularly attractive if the licensed technology is to be applied in noncompetitive fields. Licenses are sometimes granted to competitors, however, in the hope of gaining wider market acceptance of a new product or technology. In the 1950s, for example, RCA made its patented color television circuitry available to other manufacturers. By encouraging other companies to market color television, RCA hoped to enhance primary demand among American households. Granting a license may also help to establish the validity of a patent and reduce the potential number of patent infringers.

To a *licensee,* the most apparent benefit of this type of contractual agreement is in the ready access it provides to new products and technology. Cost savings in research and development can usually be realized by using the patents and know-how of another company. Of no less concern is the saving in time achieved by accepting a license in lieu of a company-sponsored research program. In situations where speed of competitive response is vital, licensing provides quicker entry into a market with new products or processes. In less crucial applications, licensing of one product may free corporate research facilities and personnel to work on other, more important projects.

Nonetheless, there are also pitfalls in licensing. Frequently, a license agreement results in two or more firms dividing a market area on a geographic or product basis, thereby limiting the market potential available to each. Many licenses stipulate fixed commitments, such as minimum annual payment guarantees. If the licensed product is a market failure, the licensee is burdened with a continuing fixed financial obligation. A license effectively "mortgages" a company's future freedom to develop similar products itself, particularly in instances where the contract extends over a long period of time. Many licenses also contain "grant-back" clauses stipulating that any further improvements the licensee makes to the original technology or product must be made available to the licensor.

[9] *Domestic Licensing Practices,* National Industrial Conference Board, New York, 1968. A comprehensive review of foreign licensing practices can be found in *Appraising Foreign Licensing Performance,* National Industrial Conference Board, New York, 1969.

Licensing is, in effect, the renting of technology. Companies often seek to avoid its pitfalls by turning to purchasing technology by acquiring another company, its technology, and its products.

□

ACQUISITIONS

The impetus to acquire other companies often stems from the same fundamental rationale as licensing: the desire to obtain new products and technology rapidly. The obvious advantage of acquisitions is that the acquiring company gains total control over the facilities and assets involved, as opposed to being restricted by a contractual agreement with another firm. Of course, many companies that are available to be purchased are not in a healthy state. Acquisition, therefore, can be a risky undertaking. Increasingly, there are legal problems in acquisition. Under amendments to the Clayton Act of 1914, acquisitions are prohibited if they result in a lessening of competiton. In a major, well-publicized case, for example, Procter and Gamble was forced to divest itself of its earlier acquisition of Clorox, a bleach manufacturer.

Tobacco manufacturers were among the most active firms engaging in acquisition during the 1960s and early 1970s. As large companies participating in a static, slowly declining market, it became apparent that most tobacco manufacturers would have to look to new products to attain growth. Consider the case of R. J. Reynolds Industries, Inc. About 35 percent of the company's 1969 revenue was derived from nontobacco products, the majority of which were acquired within the previous 10 years. Among Reynolds' acquisitions were several food companies, including Chun King (Chinese foods), Patio (Mexican foods), Hawaiian Punch (fruit juices), College Inn (chicken specialties), and Penick & Ford (prepared desserts). McLean Industries, acquired in 1969, specialized in containerized freight transportation systems. Other acquisitions included R. J. Archer (aluminum packaging products). Under a 1969 action by the U.S. Department of Justice, however, Reynolds was ordered to divest itself of its ownership of Penick & Ford within two years.

The ability to achieve rapid growth through acquisitions is reflected in a 1970 survey of 142 companies conducted by the National Industrial Conference Board.[10] Among companies in the sample whose sales had grown by 200 percent or more in the past five years, 71 percent cited mergers and acquisitions as their prime source of growth.

For large companies in particular, legal obstacles and other considerations may preclude acquisition as an attractive source of new products. Hence, many companies turn to their own internal development of the products they seek.

[10] *Sources of Corporate Growth,* National Industrial Conference Board, New York, 1970.

□

INTERNAL COMPANY DEVELOPMENT

The third major route to obtaining new products is internal company development. As opposed to "renting" (licensing) or "buying" (acquisition) new products and processes, this approach might appropriately be characterized as "do-it-yourself" innovation. Unlike the amateurism of a suburban husband with a hammer and pipe wrench, however, the development of new products is a task demanding the very highest of technical and managerial skills.

The advantages of having one's own new product development program are numerous. By directing its own efforts, a firm is able to produce and market the exact products that it wants, as opposed to licensing or acquiring a compromise version from another company. Legal difficulties of antitrust, as they apply to mergers and acquisitions, are avoided. Properly set up and managed, an internal product development program may be economically more attractive than the alternatives of licensing or acquisition. Finally, there is the crucial strategic question of leadership. For the firm that chooses to be a technological and market leader, it is impossible to rely on other companies to provide the ongoing basis for that leadership. New products and new technology must flow from the leader itself.[11]

New product development programs are nonetheless fraught with potential difficulties. Research and development can be extremely costly, time-comsuming, and frustrating. It can involve enormous commitments of manpower and money, with no assurance of reasonable payback.

We will devote the remainder of this chapter to the topic of new product development programs. Initially, we will examine the task of creating and maintaining an organizational climate conducive to new product development. Thereafter, we will explore the costs, risks, and economic benefits involved in new product programs. Finally, we will examine the central issues in managing a new product from the time of its germination as an idea through to its introduction to the market on a full-scale basis.

Organizing for new product development

An important ingredient of new product success is the corporate environment in which new products emerge. Consider, for example, how the following questions might typify the concerns of a corporation engaged in a new product program[12]:

How can we get our research people to be responsive to the needs of the market?
What can we do to get our salesmen more involved in selling new products and seeking new applications?

[11] There is also a case to be made for a strategy that directs new product development toward creating products imitating the successful innovations of competitors. See Theodore Levitt, "Innovative Imitation," *Harvard Business Review,* September–October, 1966, pp. 63–70.

[12] Jay W. Lorsch and Paul R. Lawrence, "Organizing for Product Innovation," *Harvard Business Review,* January–February, 1965, p. 109.

Why are our production people so conservative when it comes to introducing new products?

How can we get sales, research, and production people to pull in the same direction on product development?

THE COMPANY–MARKET INTERFACE

These questions illustrate the organizational dilemma of creating a "match" between the needs of the company and the needs of its market. It is not enough to have an organization in which research scientists and engineers can work creatively. Their skills must be addressed to market needs as well as to technological problems. Nor can it be assumed that sales and production people will become spontaneously enthused about a new commodity that is suddenly thrust upon them as a *fait accompli*. The transfer of product ideas and prototypes from the laboratory to market reality must be accomplished smoothly. To do so implies early involvement in a program by all those who will eventually be concerned and affected by it.

The accomplishment of these ends is a complex process whose resolution varies according to the particular characteristics of each company and the market environment in which it must operate. They can be considered only briefly here (the overall issues of marketing organization are discussed further in Chapter 23.)[13]

TOP MANAGEMENT INVOLVEMENT

Because of the importance attached to new product development, and the stakes involved, this activity typically requires the support and participation of top management. In some companies, the company president considers new products as one of his most important responsibilities. His activities might include stimulating company divisions to generate new product ideas, providing overall direction to new product programs, and promoting an awareness and interest in new products throughout the firm.

NEW PRODUCT DEPARTMENTS

Where new products are a central component of the firm's business, many companies establish a separate department to manage them. The responsibilities of this department might include recommending new product objectives and programs, planning activities for generating and screening new ideas, and coordinating the multitude of activities associated with developing and testing a product before it is handed over to other divisions of the company for commercial introduction. In virtually all cases, new product departments report directly to top management.

[13] For a more complete treatment, see *Organizing for New Product Development*, National Industrial Conference Board, New York, 1966.

The Monsanto Company's New Enterprise Division, employing over 2,000 persons, provides an interesting example of how this organizational approach can be extended in scope.[14] Organized in 1968, the division is responsible solely for developing and introducing products to markets in which Monsanto has not previously participated. The division is set up almost as an autonomous company reporting directly to the president. It is self-contained, and includes all the key people needed to carry a new product through research, production, and introductory marketing. The division is not required to earn a profit, but must meet other goals established for it. Once a product is established in the marketplace, described as meaning sales in the "hundreds of millions of dollars," it is handed over to an existing company division, or a new division of its own. Among the most successful of the division's achievements is Astro Turf, the artificial grass turf used in sports stadia.

As elsewhere, it is dangerous to overgeneralize about new product organization. The "best" organization for a given company varies, depending on size, product lines, and patterns of total company organization.

The economics of new product development programs

In examining new product development programs, we will turn first to questions of economics. What is the extent of corporate research and development efforts in the United States? What costs are involved in developing and introducing a new product? What are the inherent risks? What are the apparent benefits to be derived from such programs?

As we examine these questions, for illustrative purposes we draw extensively on data from the food processing industries. We rely on these examples solely because comparable information is not generally available for other industry groups. We are definitely not implying that food industries are the most important forum of new product activities.

□ RESEARCH AND DEVELOPMENT EXPENDITURES IN THE UNITED STATES

Research and development played a relatively unimportant role in the United States prior to World War II. War needs provided the impetus for a greatly enlarged research program, however, and after the war, research and development expenditures continued to expand. Growth was attributable not only to defense requirements, but also to the fact that business firms became more aware of the profit potential to be realized by a well-managed research program.

In 1968, research and development expenditures in the United States were

[14] "Far-out Monsanto Unit Ponders New Concepts," *Advertising Age,* June 23, 1969, p. 24.

$25 billion.[15] Over $17 billion of the amount represented the research efforts of business firms, about half of which was financed by the federal government. The remaining $8 billion was accounted for by institutions of higher learning, nonprofit organizations, and government.

Research and development expenditures by business grew steadily from $3.4 billion in 1953 to $17.4 billion in 1968, and an increasing proportion of these efforts has been funded by companies themselves, rather than the government. The data in Figure 15-4, for example, show that in 1968 over half of business expenditures on research and development was paid for from company funds. The trend reflects not only a slackening of government support for defense and aerospace, but also increased business involvement. Between 1966 and 1968, company-funded research and development increased by 23 percent; that sponsored by government grew by less than 3 percent.

As might be expected, the goal of most industrial research is the translation of technology into marketable products and processes. Of its total $17 billion expenditure, industry spent about $14 billion on product and process develop-

[15] National Science Foundation, *Research and Development in Industry, 1968,* Government Printing Office, Washington, 1970.

FIGURE 15-4

Company and federal share of industrial R&D spending, 1953–1968

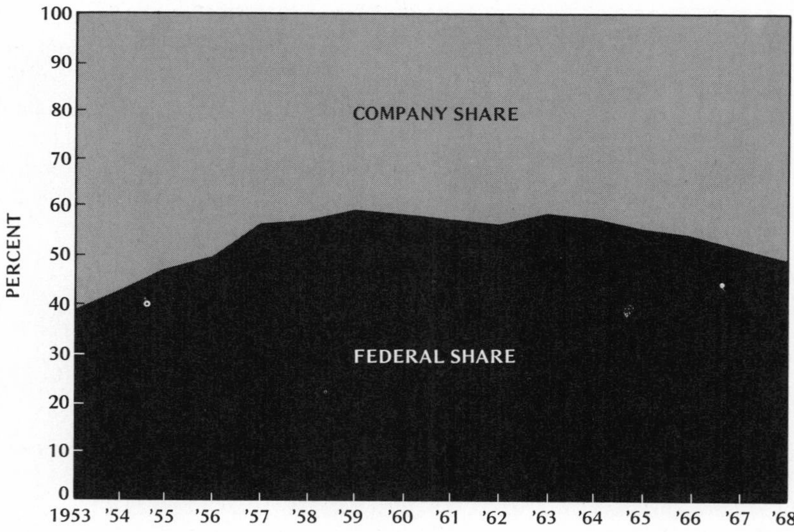

Source: National Science Foundation; *Research and Development in Industry, 1968,* Washington, Government Printing Office, 1970, p. 25.

ment. The remainder was spent in so-called "basic" and "applied" research centering on the discovery of new scientific knowledge.

Aggregate expenditure data are valuable in gaining an appreciation of character, direction, and total magnitude of research efforts. We can gain further insight, however, by examining the costs, risks, and rewards that confront an individual company undertaking a program of new product development and introduction.

THE COST OF DEVELOPING AND INTRODUCING NEW PRODUCTS

It is impossible to generalize about the amount of money required to develop and introduce a new product. The ill-fated supersonic transport aircraft would have involved expenditures running into the billions of dollars, but instances of this magnitude are obviously rare. Even less "exotic" new products, however, require substantial expenditures.

Take the case of a new ready-to-eat breakfast cereal. To a layman, developing such a product might seem to involve little more than reformulating the mix of basic grain ingredients used in all cereals and adjusting some highly automated production equipment to create a cereal of different shape or consistency. In fact, a study of 20 new breakfast cereals introduced by six different companies in the period 1954–1964 revealed that an average of $122,000 was spent on research and development for a single product.[16] This sum included only those expenses *directly* attributable to the product, without allowance for unallocated expenses such as research facilities, equipment, and administration. On the average, each cereal resulted in a further expenditure of $60,000 in marketing research. Eleven of the 20 products were test marketed at an average cost, including net losses on sales, of $921,000. Seventeen of the 20 cereals were subsequently introduced into regional and national distribution, each supported by average marketing expenditures of $3.4 million in their first year of distribution, or 51 percent of sales revenue in the same time period.

These figures are illustrated in Table 15-1, together with comparable data for new cake mixes, frozen dinners and specialty products, margarine, and pet food products. Summary data are provided for a total sample of 124 products introduced in 19 different food categories. They reveal average expenditures per product of $68,000 on research and development, $26,000 on marketing research, and $248,000 for those subjected to test marketing. Introductory marketing expenditures were equal, on the average, to 43 percent of first year sales.

[16] All data cited in the remainder of this section are taken from an extensive study of product innovation conducted by two of the authors of this text. See Robert D. Buzzell and Robert E. M. Nourse, *Product Innovation in Food Processing: 1954–1964,* Harvard Business School, Division of Research, Boston, 1967.

TABLE 15-1

Profiles of new food products introduced in period 1954–1964

Product category	Preintroduction: Number of products	Preintroduction: Cost of R & D	Preintroduction: Cost of marketing research	Preintroduction: Cost of test marketing	First year of regular distribution: Sales	First year of regular distribution: Marketing expenditures, percent of sales	First year of regular distribution: Total months elapsed between first development activity and achievement of full distribution
Ready-to-eat breakfast cereals	20	$122,000	$60,000	$921,000	$6,605,000	51%	55
Cake mixes	14	27,000	13,000	61,000	938,000	61	29
Frozen dinners and specialties	10	15,000	8,000	47,000	416,000	20	41
Margarine	10	65,000	17,000	N.A.	6,084,000	30	33
Pet foods	13	91,000	37,000	531,000	3,943,000	49	40
19 product categories (including those above)	124	$ 68,000	$26,000	$248,000	$3,249,000	43%	37

Source: Robert D. Buzzell and Robert E. M. Nourse, *Product Innovation in Food Processing: 1954–1964,* Harvard Business School, Division of Research, Boston, 1967, pp. 112, 132.

In addition to monetary cost, new product development also requires a cost of *time*. The last column of Table 15-1 indicates the time elapsed between first developmental activities and the introduction of new foods on a national basis. On the average, a food product required over 3 years to pass through this process, with the average time requirement exceeding 4½ years for breakfast cereals.

For a food processor who undertook the expenditures and time to develop and introduce a new product, market success was by no means a certainty. By virtue of their inherent newness, innovative products represent a risky venture.

RISKS IN DEVELOPING AND INTRODUCING NEW PRODUCTS

The inherent risk in a new product is the possibility that, having commited resources to its development, a company will be unable to recoup these resources successfully in the market. To understand risk fully, it is helpful to view it as consisting of two components: *consequences* and *uncertainty*. We can best illustrate these concepts by continuing with our earlier examples drawn from the food industry.

In part, level of risk depends on *how much is at stake*. Few people would get too worried about betting $2 on the Kentucky Derby, but a wager of $10,000 would leave most of us very concerned about the outcome of the race. In new consumer product programs, the "stakes" usually increase rapidly as a product moves from early stages of development toward market introduction. This tendency is corroborated by the data cited previously in Table 15-1. Average preintroductory expenditures per food product amounted to $68,000 for research and development, $26,000 for marketing research. Note that if the product were discontinued at this point, the maximum loss would be $94,000. Going to test market, however, raises the stakes by an average additional $248,000, and entering national distribution increases the amount even more.

The second component of risk is uncertainty—the chances that, having commited company resources to a new product program, the product will subsequently be withdrawn or discontinued. What are the odds, for example, that an idea for a product can be successful in the marketplace? On the average, the probabilities for food products are not high. Survey data have indicated that, for every 1,000 ideas for a new food product,[17]

810 are rejected at the idea stage, about half by informal means and half on the basis of formal consumer research.
135 are rejected on the basis of product tests, either formal or informal.
12 are discontinued after test marketing.
43 are introduced on a regular basis.

Even *after* introduction on a regular basis, not all products succeed. Many are withdrawn without recouping the amount invested in them. In the study previously cited, about four out of ten food products that remained in regular distribution for a period of three years had still not recouped their direct costs of development and introduction.

We see, then, that new product programs not only are costly, but also possess an inherently high risk of failure. At this point, there is cause to ask if a new product program is a worthwhile undertaking. What are the benefits?

□ BENEFITS OF NEW PRODUCT DEVELOPMENT PROGRAMS

The degree to which a company relies on new products depends, in part, on the *industries* in which it competes. Firms dealing in commodities, such as steel or petroleum, rely on product innovation only to a limited extent. In instruments, chemicals, and other high-technology fields, on the other hand, new products assume far greater significance. It is common for firms in high-technology industries to have 30 to 50 percent of their current sales volume accounted for by products introduced within the past five years.

The principal incentive to companies to undertake new product programs is the belief that new products will yield increased sales and profits. There is no doubt that some companies succeed in attaining these goals; it is equally clear

[17] *Ibid.*, p. 105.

that some other companies fail. Note, however, that a successful new product program does not imply that all new products are successful. Over a period of time, any given firm is likely to experience a "mix" of successful and unsuccessful products. Even the largest companies often depend on market acceptance of a relatively small number of their new products. Their hope, of course, is that the gains realized from successful market entries will more than offset the losses from unsuccessful items.

There is evidence to confirm that high rates of new product activity are associated with corresponding high rates of growth in total company sales. A group of 11 large food processors, for example, were categorized as having attained "high" growth (an average of 43 percent) or "low" growth (an average of 20 percent) in the period 1958–1964. Among high-growth companies, 22 percent of 1964 sales were accounted for by products introduced since 1958, and almost three-quarters of their 1958–1964 sales increase was accounted for by these new products. Among low-growth firms, new products accounted for only 8 percent of 1964 sales, and less than half of their 1958–1964 sales increase.[18]

There are no known data to illustrate the effect new products have on overall corporate profitability. Generally, it is expected that a new product has the highest rate of contribution of its entire history during the years just following its introduction, when the product still retains some degree of distinctiveness. Offsetting this expected flow of funds, however, is the need to recoup developmental and introductory marketing costs. Even the most successful products may take as much as two or three years to recoup these costs and begin contributing net profitability to the corporation.

Generating new product ideas

Earlier in this chapter we saw that, for every 1,000 ideas for a new food product, only 43 products eventually reach the marketplace. Across a broad spectrum of industries, there is indication that the "idea-to-product ratio" is even less favorable. A study by a management consulting firm, Booz-Allen and Hamilton, Inc., revealed that an average of 58 product ideas is required to yield one successful new product.[19] Even when a product is successful, its expected life may be short. Companies must therefore be continually searching for new product ideas, even though they expect only a small number of usable products to result.

□ THE SEARCH PROCESS

Anthony Jay has remarked: "Perhaps the most valuable of all qualities in the creative manager is the ability to locate hidden demand, to think of something

[18] *Ibid.*, p. 146.
[19] *Management of New Products,* 4th ed. Booz-Allen and Hamilton, Inc., New York, 1965, p. 9.

people have not got but would like, and which his firm could make at a price they would pay."[20]

A crucial task for the business firm is to tap the creative quality Jay describes from people within its organization. If any single lesson has been learned from experience in seeking new product ideas, it is that good ideas rarely come through chance. Businesses cannot afford to wait for a good idea simply to crop up. They must organize to discover ideas. Because the search for ideas involves a group of activities requiring the commitment of corporate resources, it is referred to here as the search *process*.

Well-managed companies often seek to formalize their search process through committees, employee incentive plans, and similar organizational arrangements. One typical method is the formation of a *new products planning committee*. Meeting on a regular basis, this kind of committee typically draws membership from throughout the company: the marketing department, officers of the corporation, the technical research staff, and the new products department, for example. Each participant shares the burden of bringing forward product ideas for consideration. Note that this arrangement avoids placing sole reliance on a single company department for the generation of new product ideas.

□ SOURCES OF IDEAS

The four principal sources of new product ideas are customers, the firm's industry and trade contacts, independent research organizations, and internal company sources.

Customers The most promising source of ideas for successful products is a firm's existing or potential customers. An increasing number of consumer goods companies, for example, invite customers to participate in "brainstorming" sessions in return for a small honorarium. Others go further by utilizing survey questionnaire techniques. Most firms receive unsolicited mail from customers, often containing product suggestions. Salesmen's reports and service records can be designed to allow space for suggestions and customer complaints on existing products. Magazines and trade shows also provide opportunities to monitor the ideas of customers and product users.

Ideas are sometimes discovered by observing how customers use one of the company's existing products. Ralston Purina, for example, is said to have discovered customers mixing its Chex cereals with peanuts and pretzels to create a party snack. The observation led to the development and to the introduction of a successful snack product using essentially these ingredients.

[20] Anthony Jay, *Management and Machiavelli,* Holt, Rinehart, and Winston, Inc., New York, 1968, p. 96.

The firm's industry and trade contacts Additional sources of new product ideas are the distributors, dealers, or retailers with which a company does business. Their catalog, sales records, and conversations with company salesmen can all provide clues to new opportunities. A firm's suppliers, advertising agencies, and marketing research firms may also prove helpful. Trade associations and trade journals, including those published in foreign countries, often suggest new products. The products and advertisements of competitors also represent a source of ideas to be monitored carefully.

Independent research organizations A number of marketing research firms will undertake a search for product ideas on behalf of a company. Two firms in the United States who do so are New Products Institute, Inc., and Product Development Corporation. Other organizations, such as The International New Products Center, publish monthly annotated reports of new product ideas.

Other potential sources falling within this category include state and federal government agencies, municipal industrial development commissions, universities, patent attorneys, venture capital firms, commercial banks, and nonprofit research organizations.[21]

Internal company sources Many product ideas can lie dormant within a company. A good search program takes the initiative in seeking out these ideas, training personnel in idea recognition, and rewarding the submission of promising concepts for new products.

The Andersons, a grain partnership with 1970 sales in excess of $150 million, is reported to have diversified into new products made from corncobs at the suggestion of a prospective employee.[22] Until 1957, corncobs were considered waste. They piled up in huge mounds all across the Midwest, emitted a noxious odor when wet, and often caught fire through spontaneous combustion. Urged by John Vander Hooven, The Andersons constructed a mill to dry, grind, and mill corncobs. The resulting raw material served as a basic ingredient for products used in cleaning fur coats, polishing ball bearings, poisoning insects, and manufacturing cosmetics. In 1970, the corncob, once considered waste, provided the basis for a $4 million industry.

Screening

The purpose of screening new product ideas is twofold. First, the process serves to dismiss from further consideration those ideas which are inconsistent

[21] A subject-indexed guide to nonprofit research activities and organizations is contained in *Research Centers Directory*, Gale Research Company, Detroit. The 1968 edition of this directory contains over 4,000 entries.

[22] "A Miraculous Product Arises from Corn Fields across the Midwest," *Wall Street Journal*, Jan. 26, 1971, p. 1.

with a firm's product policies. In this regard, screening is little more than a formalized system for comparing an idea with the basic factors that influence product policy: resources of the firm, its existing markets, its competition, and corporate objectives. A device such as a *rating scale* is usually employed to organize these judgments.

A subsequent purpose of screening is to rank remaining product ideas according to their attractiveness. The rating scale can also be designed to accomplish this screening objective. Many firms go further, however, by subjecting their most promising ideas to *concept testing* among potential users.

RATING SCALES

A typical rating scale for new products is illustrated in Figure 15-5. Note that the information it contains is of two basic types. On one hand, there is an approximate evaluation of the idea's sales potential and costs of market development, presumably as they would apply to any company. The scale also contains an evaluation of how well the product "fits" the company. This assessment presumably differs for each company, depending on the strengths and weaknesses of the firm conducting the evaluation.

An obvious prerequisite to rating is that the product idea be sufficiently well established to permit a meaningful description and a reasonably realistic assessment of its market opportunities. This requirement is particularly acute if the company decides to complement its own evaluation with an assessment obtained from customers through concept testing.

CONCEPT TESTING

Concept testing represents a first step toward gaining some indication of how potential customers assess a product idea. The techniques underlying this marketing research approach are relatively simple. By means of a verbal description, films, video tapes, a written description, or a physical prototype, customers are presented with a product concept and asked for their opinions of it. The majority of concept tests are conducted using personal or group interviews, but mail surveys and telephone interviews have also been employed for this purpose.

The advantages of a concept test lie in its cost, timing, and versatility. Simple and inexpensive, concept tests can sometimes be tied in to other ongoing marketing research studies. The most attractive feature of the technique, however, is that it can be conducted early in a new product program when the company has not yet committed itself to a substantial financial investment. Variations of a product concept, its physical features, price, and advertising appeals, can be tested inexpensively among different groups of customers.

In some instances, concept testing is the only feasible marketing research technique for a company. Consider, for example, these remarks by an executive of Continental Can Company[23]:

[23] *Market Testing Consumer Products,* National Industrial Conference Board, New York, 1967, p. 46.

FIGURE 15-5

Example of product idea/concepts rating scale

Project no. 10 Product Bituminous materials for spreading compositions

A Section	B Coding	C Factor	D Weighting	E Rating	F Score
Stability	a	Durability of the market	3	+1	+3
	b	Breadth of the market	2	−1	−2
	c	Possibility of captive market	1	−2	−2
	d	Difficulty in copying	1	−2	−2
	e	Stability in depressions	2	+1	+2
	f	Stability in war time	1	+1	+1
Growth	a	Unique character of product or process	2	−2	−4
	b	Demand-supply rate	3	0	0
	c	Rate of technical change	1	+2	+2
	d	Expert possibilities	1	−2	−2
	e	Improved opportunities for management personnel	2	+2	+4
Marketability	a	Relationship to existing markets	2	+1	+2
	b	Company's image in allied fields	1	+2	+2
	c	Ease of market penetration	1	−2	−2
	d	Company's ability to give technical service requirements	2	−1	−2
	e	Competition with customers' products	2	+2	+4
	f	User stratification	1	+1	+1
	g	Few variations required	1	+1	+1
	h	Freedom from seasonal fluctuations	2	−1	−2
Position	a	Ease of development of manufacturing process	2	+2	+4
	b	Value added by in-company processing	1	0	0
	c	Exclusive or favored purchasing position	1	+2	+2
	d	Effect on purchasing position	1	0	0
	e	Availability of raw materials within company	2	−2	−4
	f	Effect on negotiating position	1	+1	+1

Continental Can cannot test market a new aluminium beer can. We do not brew beer. Our customers do that. We must know a year or two before our customers go into test markets that the package will succeed. Since we can often test the proposed new container in the idea and model stage, we prefer not to waste two years and $200,000 to develop a beautiful dud.

Concept testing is also used extensively by industrial marketers. Here, the technique is particularly valuable because a concept can be readily presented

Project no.	10	Product	Bituminous materials for spreading compositions		
A Section	B Coding	C Factor	D Weighting	E Rating	F Score
R&D	a	Utilization of existing know-how	1	0	0
	b	Relationship to future development planning	2	−2	−4
	c	Utilization of existing laboratory or pilot plant equipment	1	+1	+1
	d	Availability of research and development personnel	1	+2	+2
Engineering	a	Reliability of process or know-how	2	−1	−2
	b	Utilization of standardized equipment	1	+2	+2
	c	Availability of engineering personnel	2	+2	+4
Production	a	Utilization of idle equipment	1	−2	−2
	b	Utilization of surplus steam, electricity and water capacities	1	+2	+2
	c	Utilization and upgrading of by-products	1	−2	−2
	d	Utilization of process familiar to company personnel	1	0	0
	e	Availability of production and maintenance workers	2	+2	+4
	f	Plant maintenance requirements	1	0	0
	g	Ability to cope with waste disposal problems	1	+2	+2
	h	Ability to cope with hazardous operating conditions	1	+2	+2
		Overall weighted rating (score) + 15			
		Maximum weighted rating (score) +116			
		Minimum weighted rating (score) −116			

Source: Aubrey Wilson, "Selecting New Products for Development," *Scientific Business* (*U.K.*), November, 1963, p. 261. Reproduced with permission.

to different membership groups, in a customer decision-making unit, such as engineers, purchasing agents, production personnel, or management. For a product that is costly to produce, a concept test has obvious merits.

There are dangers, however, in this technique. If the concept is not described accurately in terms of what it is, what it can do, and how it compares with known competitive products, the results of the test can be misleading. In markets characterized by a limited number of potential customers, there is also a danger of revealing a firm's product ideas to its competitors.

The product ideas that survive the screening stage represent a company's best assessment of its most promising candidates. Before proceeding to commit resources to product development, it must first be determined which of the candidates offers greatest potential for profit.

Economic analysis

The basic purpose of economic analysis is to make projections of financial results for a new product over a period of time. Invariably, an analysis of this kind involves combining judgments on a large number of variables, including demand factors, competitive conditions, cost factors, and the expected effect of company marketing programs.

The economic analyses of most companies have certain basic features in common:

1. They produce *pro forma* profit and loss statements, year by year, or even quarter by quarter, for a three- to five-year planning horizon period.
2. Sales are predicted under some given set of assumptions about size of the total market and some controllable factors such as price and advertising budgets.
3. Costs, usually involving some simple division into fixed, variable, and discretionary costs, are estimated at various levels of sales.
4. The revenue and cost figures, along with estimates of investment in "hard" assets, are used to derive a range of estimates of return on investment for the new product.[24]

Increasingly, a number of business firms are finding it valuable to program their economic analysis techniques on a computer. Employing a computer not only speeds up the analysis and permits rapid comparison of alternative products, but also enables "what if" analyses to be carried out. That is, wherever assumptions about market conditions, sales potential, costs, or other key factors are a subject of uncertainty, the computer can provide rapid assessment of how *changes* in these factors would affect return on investment.[25]

[24] The costs and investments associated with a new product are difficult to interpret. For example, are abnormally high marketing costs associated with introducing a new product an "investment"? For a thorough examination of this topic, see Philip A. Scheubel, Jr., "ROI for New Product Planning," *Harvard Business Review,* November–December, 1964, pp. 110–120.

[25] A variety of computer-based models of new product economic analysis have been developed by scholars, consulting firms, and individual companies. See, for example, John D. C. Little, "Models and Managers: The Concept of a Decision Calculus," *Management Science,* April, 1970, pp. 466–485; Glen L. Urban, *Evolutionary Modeling in the Analysis of New Products,* MIT Working Paper no. 424-69, September, 1969; and A. Charnes, W. W. Cooper, J. K. Devoe, and D. B. Learner, "DEMON: Mark II Extremal Equations Approach to New Product Marketing," *Management Science,* May, 1968, pp. 513–524. For a description of a model developed by The Pillsbury Company, see Gerald J. Eskin and Raymond Dabbah, "Toward a Planning-oriented Marketing Information System," in B. A. Morin (ed.), *Marketing in a Changing World,* Proceedings of the June 1969 Conference of the American Marketing Association.

Product development and testing

After a product proposal has successfully passed its initial evaluation, there comes the task of turning an idea or concept into a salable product. At this stage, management is concerned with two kinds of questions. On one hand, it must deal with problems of engineering, specifications, design, and product feasibility that together comprise product development. At the same time, careful attention must be given to measuring customer preferences and reactions to the emerging new product, that is, product testing.

□ PRODUCT DEVELOPMENT

A major question in product development is that of *specifications*. Decisions here involve size, weight, performance characteristics, quality, safety requirements, durability, engineering, and other requirements dictated by the technology of the product and by the markets for which it is intended.

Attention must also be paid to appearance, or, as it is more often called, *design*. Color, shape, aesthetic appearance, packaging, and display requirements are among the many relevant factors that may have to be incorporated and comprised in technical feasibility. Early versions of a product may be produced on a pilot basis, but decision making must nevertheless be geared to the technical and economic considerations that apply to eventual full-scale production.

The ultimate objective of product development, of course, is to create a product that, as closely as possible, is congruent with the needs and wants of its intended users. Hence, at various points in a product's development, it is not uncommon to submit the new item to testing among potential customers.

□ PRODUCT TESTING

The term *product testing* refers to evaluating customer preferences for different product characteristics to find the most appealing combination to the customer. Note that the emphasis of this definition is the "fit" between the product and the customer, not on technical and performance properties of the product as such.

Product testing is an essential step in uncovering shortcomings or deficiencies in a new commodity, in bringing out new uses or benefits, and in refining earlier estimates of eventual sales and profitability. Besides giving indications of overall customer reaction to a product, it can be used to probe specific qualities that are liked or disliked, to compare the new item's appeal to that of existing products, and to derive indications of the value of the product to the customer.

Among the most widely used product testing techniques is the *panel* test. A panel is a group of households or business firms who agree to use the new product over an extended period of time, and to respond to a series of questions about the product at the termination of the test. On occasion, panels are set up specifically to test a certain product, but, more often, members of a panel have a continuing relationship with a manufacturer or research firm and are used periodically for various types of research. Some companies maintain panels comprised of their employees.

The panel technique offers numerous advantages. It permits measurement of customer interest over an extended time. Usage patterns and habits can be studied, and, occasionally, additional uses may be discovered. Product features with the greatest appeal can be identified, as can variations in preferences among different members of a decision-making unit. For all this, however, panel tests can be expensive. It has been estimated, for example, that a panel test for a new grocery product costs $5,000 to $15,000.[26]

An alternative approach to product testing involves bringing the prospective customer to a laboratory or research facility. There, the customer views, consumes, or otherwise uses the new product, and is asked for his reaction to it. There are many different methods by which product tests can be designed and conducted, some of which may involve comparison with existing products or choice among alternative designs. Generally, these methods cannot provide as much information as a panel test, but, at the same time, they offer the advantage of being considerably less expensive.

In the kinds of testing we have discussed so far, the product is evaluated in isolation of competitive forces in the marketplace. As an executive of Beech-Nut Corporation has commented[27]:

> A concept test can show you that the concept motivates; a use test can verify that the product works or tastes good; a package test can indicate that the package appeals. But you have not yet seen how these factors—concept, product, package, etc.—work in combination.

Test marketing

Test marketing represents an attempt to evaluate the nature and degree of customer acceptance of a product by actually putting it on the market in selected areas. It may involve using a full-scale marketing program in those areas, or it may use different combinations of marketing factors, such as promotional appeals, prices, or types and intensity of distribution, in various areas in an attempt to determine the most effective way of marketing.

□ TEST MARKET ENVIRONMENT

Traditionally, test marketing of consumer products has been conducted under conditions that, as closely as possible, simulate a normal marketing environment. The product is presented to the trade by the company's regular sales force and brokers in the same manner that it would be on a national distribu-

[26] "The Management of New Product Development," *Grocery Manufacturer*, January, 1971, p. 12.
[27] *Market Testing Consumer Products, op. cit.*, p. 72.

tion basis. During the 1960s, however, an increasing number of firms turned to testing under a controlled marketing environment. This method usually involves the use of an independent research organization that undertakes the joint function of wholesaler and auditor. The product is quickly "forced" into optimum distribution conditions at a prearranged date and maintained under these conditions for the duration of the test.

The company that utilizes a controlled test marketing environment is not able to test for trade acceptance of its product. On the other hand, it gains speed in getting the test started, faster measurement of product movement because full distribution is achieved instantly, and cost savings because a shorter test period is required.

NUMBER AND CHARACTERISTICS OF TEST CITIES

There is considerable variation in the number of metropolitan areas used as consumer product test markets. A survey conducted in 1970 found that one out of five test markets was conducted in only one city, while a similar proportion was conducted in five or more market areas. The median number of cities used for test marketing was three.[28]

In general, marketers try to select areas that are representative of the population in the United States in terms of its characteristics and behavior. There are no exact miniatures of the national market, however, and this ideal can only be approximated in practice.

A test city should represent the same stage of overall market development as the national market. That is, the product should be used in similar proportions and experience the same level of competition. Snowmobiles would not be tested in Florida, or, perhaps less obvious, coffee would not be tested in Salt Lake City where the Mormon religion discourages its consumption. The demographic attributes of the test area population should be representative.

The composition of the trade is another key factor; for example, the presence of a strong grocery chain with its own dominant brands would result in an unfair test for a new food product. The availability of advertising media is important for heavily advertised products, usually meaning that at least two television networks and a Sunday newspaper supplement should be available. A test city should be of moderate size to keep costs to a minimum level, but not so small as to lose the urban character of the national market. Finally, there are issues of location. A test city should be relatively isolated from other cities, yet close to production facilities or distribution centers.

Unusual problems may be encountered in selecting test cities in international markets. Richardson-Merrill, Inc., best known for its Vick cough medi-

[28] Verne B. Churchill, Jr., "New Product Test Marketing—An Overview of the Current Scene," address to the Midwest Conference on Successful New Product Marketing Research Techniques, Chicago, Mar. 3, 1971, p. 8.

cines, is reported to have encountered particular problems in Australia and Mexico. In Australia, a heavy concentration of the population lives in the cities of Sydney and Melbourne: Sydney is characterized as "Americanized," Melbourne as "British." In Mexico, there is dichotomy between the urban population of Mexico City and the rural population of most other areas of the country.[29]

□

DURATION OF TEST MARKETS

On the average, test markets last about ten months, although the figure can vary from as little as two or three months to several years.[30] For frequently purchased consumer products, a test should be of sufficient duration to allow for measurement of *repeat purchase* experience. For products of this kind, the propensity of consumers to buy a second, third, or fourth time is a better predictor of eventual market success than are initial purchase rates.[31] *Timing* is another key factor. By extending a test too long, a company opens the possibility that a competitor will copy its product and enter national distribution ahead of it or, at worst, very shortly behind. Extending test markets also tends to increase their cost.

□

APPRAISING TEST MARKET RESULTS

To be effective, every test market must incorporate systematic procedures for collecting marketing information. Virtually all test markets involve retail store audits, and most incorporate telephone surveys and personal interviews to measure changes in levels of consumer awareness of the test product, attitudes toward it, and frequency of purchase and repurchase. (These information-gathering techniques are described more fully in Chapter 25.) Consumer panels are often employed to record more accurate data on repurchase rates, brand switching, and shopping patterns. Special studies may be conducted to ascertain trends of specific interest, such as user satisfaction or purchase intentions.

□

INDUSTRIAL TEST MARKETING

The term *test marketing* is most commonly used with regard to the testing of consumer products, but the same general process is often used for industrial products. Two aspects of the industrial test market process are apt to be dif-

[29] "Passing the International Market Test," *Sales Management,* Mar. 1, 1971, p. 21.

[30] Churchill, Jr., *op. cit.,* p. 13.

[31] A wide variety of models has been developed to predict new product success on the basis of repeat purchase rates. See, for example, Louis A. Fourt and J. W. Woodlock, "Early Prediction of Market Success for New Grocery Products," *Journal of Marketing,* October, 1960, pp. 31–38; J. H. Parfitt and B. J. K. Collins, "The Use of Consumer Panels for Brand Share Prediction," *Journal of Marketing Research,* May, 1968, pp. 131–146; and David H. Ahl, "New Product Forecasting Using Consumer Panels," *Journal of Marketing Research,* May, 1970, pp. 160–167.

ferent. For many items, specific customers, rather than geographic areas, are used because the size of the potential buying population is often so small. Industrial markets can often be classified by size of customer, type of industry, or nature of demand, and a useful industrial test marketing program tries to take such relevant customer variables into account.

Also, relationships between industrial product manufacturers and their customers are frequently direct and personal. Therefore, it is often feasible to obtain firsthand impressions of the product and the effectiveness of the test marketing program from a fairly substantial proportion of probable customers. Consumer goods programs usually do this only on a sampling basis or through sales data and store audits.

Commercialization

After the new product has been tested and any necessary changes have been made, it is ready for full-scale marketing or, as it is often called, *commercialization*. "Full-scale" does not necessarily connote nationwide marketing; many products are introduced on a region-by-region, or some other limited, basis. The rapidity with which a product is expanded to national distribution depends on a number of factors. Encouraging test market results may give cause for optimism in going immediately to full distribution, whereas mediocre consumer acceptance in testing marketing may dictate a more cautious approach. If it is feared that competitors may quickly copy the new product, rapid market expansion may be desirable. The availability of funds is a governing, and sometimes constraining, influence. A national marketing program requires large-scale production facilities to support and, as we saw earlier in this chapter, an expensive commitment to advertising, personal selling, and other introductory marketing costs.

Another major policy question is the timing of market introduction. Some products are seasonal in demand; it would be unwise, for example, to introduce a new antifreeze in May. Seasonal demand factors may be less obvious, but equally important, for products that are purchased as gifts. A substantial proportion of small electric appliances, for example, are purchased in the six-week period preceding Christmas.

Commercialization is a complex process involving the control and coordination of an enormous variety of different tasks. Product attributes and packaging must be determined in detail, new plant and equipment must be installed, advertising programs must be planned and scheduled, a selling program must be established, and meetings must be held to familiarize salesmen with the new product and win their enthusiasm for it.

To facilitate planning, controlling, and coordinating the numerous activities for the introduction of a new product, a number of companies have turned to the use of *critical path* scheduling methods.[32] These techniques, commonly referred to as CPM or PERT, identify the individual steps of the implementation process, explicitly map the sequence in which these steps are to be taken, and allow the detection of potential bottlenecks in the implementation process.

Questions

1. A leading manufacturer of cake mixes has concluded that every cake mix it brings to market has a reasonably predictable life cycle. The company believes it can maximize the profitability of each cake mix introduced by varying the marketing strategy it employs according to the position of the cake on its life cycle.
   a. What factors can you suggest which tend to support the contention that each cake mix will have its own life cycle? To refute this contention?
   b. What specific changes in the marketing strategy for a new cake mix, over the stages of the life cycle, would you expect to result in the maximum profitability? Why?

2. Under what circumstances should a firm desiring rapid new product growth avoid heavy research and development commitments? Why?

3. While new product development is accorded high importance in many firms, studies of small businesses reveal that few employ systematic approaches to new product search screening or economic analyses. Why do you suppose such firms fail to follow the approaches described in the text?

4. In many companies, product managers assigned the responsibility for managing existing products are also charged with responsibility for developing product modifications and new products.
   a. What kind of problems do you think this organizational approach may cause?
   b. What problems do you think might develop if the product manager for existing products was to be completely divorced from all new product activities?

5. Early in 1971, Brown and Forman Distillers Corporation introduced a new whiskey, Frost 8/80. The product, which looked like vodka and had a mild whiskey taste, was priced at the middle of the range for domestic whiskeys, but below imported Canadians and Scotches.

   Supported by heavy advertising and in-store promotion, Frost 8/80 was

[32] For a detailed report of the experience of one firm, Diamond Alkali Company, see Warren Dusenburg, "CPM for New Product Introductions," *Harvard Business Review,* July–August, 1967, pp. 124–139.

promoted as a unique product with dignity and a sense of quality. Its promotion was directed to affluent, well-educated urban persons in the twenty-five to thirty-five age group who were likely to be "fun-oriented, party-going people."

Brown and Forman produced a variety of liquor products, including Early Times and Old Forester bourbons and Jack Daniel's Whiskey. For some years, the company's position in the liquor market had been affected substantially by changes in patterns of liquor consumption in the United States. Between 1954 and 1969, for example, United States whiskey blends and bourbons had dropped from 70 percent to 45 percent of total liquor consumption. Vodka, Scotch, and Canadian whiskey—liquors which are generally lighter in color than bourbons or United States blended whiskeys—all had increased their share of total liquor consumption during the same period.

Most industry sources agreed that a major influence on changing patterns of liquor consumption was an increased acceptance of drinking liquor at parties, small gatherings, and similar *social* situations. Social drinkers seemed to prefer a product that did not have a strong taste, and that they could consume over, say, an evening, without getting drunk.

The introduction of Frost 8/80 involved expenditures of substantial magnitude. In addition to $2 million for first year advertising, Brown and Forman estimated it spent $2 million to build inventory, $500,000 for new bottling and production equipment, $250,000 for marketing research, as well as $250,000 for the salaries of personnel involved in product development.

a. How much of a risk is Brown and Forman taking in introducing Frost 8/80?

b. As company president, what information would you want before authorizing the marketing department to enter the market?

c. Evaluate the product positioning of Frost 8/80.

d. Commenting on the product just prior to its introduction, one competitor stated, "Whiskey drinkers might not like it because it doesn't look like whiskey, and vodka drinkers might not like it because it has that whiskey taste and it's more expensive than what they are drinking." How would you evaluate this comment and what, if anything, would you do to test it?

6. A scientist, concerned with the difficulties of teaching children to read and understand music, invented a teaching machine which, using a programmed method of instruction and an electric keyboard, could teach five- to ten-year-old children to read music, differentiate between tones, understand the essentials of harmony and compositions, and write simple tunes. The inventor believed that use of the machine would lead to a substantial improvement in music education in schools. He estimated that with volume production, the machine and accompanying program material could be sold for about $500 to $600.

a. What questions should the scientist ask and answer in order to decide what he should do with the machine?

b. In what sequence should he attempt to answer these questions? Why?

7. An automobile manufacturer received a proposal for a new type of automobile. The proposed vehicle was to be powered by a large spring, much like a mechanical toy car. Rather than a key, the motor would be wound up by a small electric motor. The proposed car would create no pollution, would have few moving parts, and would be low cost, light, and easy to handle.

a. What criteria should the manufacturer use in evaluating this proposal?

b. As a market researcher assigned to investigate this idea, how would you approach the task of concept testing the proposed vehicle?

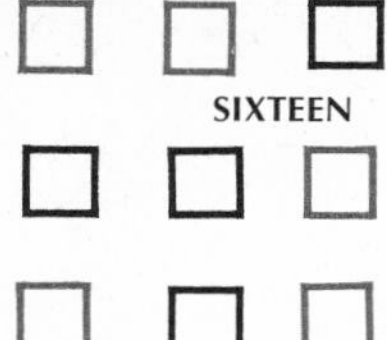

SIXTEEN

Pricing concepts

In Chapters 14 and 15, we discussed the management problems that marketing executives encounter in developing the policies that govern product management. In this chapter and in Chapter 17, we turn our attention to price as another major element of the marketing mix. The establishment of price policies and specific prices is a difficult and complex process because of the many uncertainties that attend it, and it is of major importance to companies, their channels of distribution, and to ultimate customers. Just as a large aerospace company may invest millions of dollars in research preparatory to submitting a bid for a defense contract and lose its investment because a competitor quotes a lower price, so may housewives shun an appliance or a food product because its price is too high.

BASIC CONSIDERATIONS IN PRICING

In general, the price that a company charges for a product is determined by three considerations: the competitive characteristics of the industry, the characteristics of its customers, and the company's own goals, marketing strategy, and cost structure. All three factors play a role in the decision-making process regarding price. As we shall see below, not only do these factors affect one another, but there are almost always significant uncertainties connected with each. Let us look at an example that demonstrates the importance and interplay of these several factors.

The nation's scheduled passenger airlines compete strenuously for business. Several years ago Eastern Air Lines (EAL) sought competitive advantage on the high-volume routes between New York, Boston, and Washington by petitioning the Civil Aeronautics Board (CAB), the government regulatory agency that controls many aspects of airline operations, for permission to operate what became known as an "air shuttle" service between these three cities. The shuttle service was to be a nonreservation, hourly, guaranteed-seat service, with passengers carrying their own luggage to and from airport gates. The reduced level of services, EAL claimed, made possible a substantial reduction in prices, and lower fares were thus an integral factor in the line's petition to the CAB.

Eastern Air Lines hoped that the reduction in fares and other features of the shuttle would create more business for EAL. The new business was expected to come from people currently using competitive airlines, from EAL's current passengers who would travel more frequently as a result of lower fares, and from people currently using other means of transportation who would be attracted by the lower fares and other aspects of the shuttle service.

Industry observers believed that EAL's shuttle proposal was facilitated by the airline's cost structure. Unlike other airlines operating in the three-city area, EAL had available a number of propellor-driven aircraft that could operate over the routes in question more economically than could the jets or larger propellor planes of its competitors. It seemed likely, therefore, that EAL's lower operating costs would give it a cost advantage and an opportunity to expand the demand for its services through the establishment of lower air fares.

Central to the EAL proposal, then, were assumptions regarding the behavior of competitors, customers (current and potential), and its own cost and revenue patterns.[1]

For Eastern Air Lines and its competitors, the issues raised by EAL's petition covered almost the full spectrum of questions facing executives who make pricing decisions: Will demand increase as prices fall, and if so, by how much? If a competitor cuts his prices, must we follow suit in order to hold our customers? Even if sales increase at the lower price, will the total revenue cover our costs, and if so, will we make enough profit to finance new equipment needed in the future? If demand responds to lower prices, by how much should we cut them? If competitors cut prices and trim the product (reduce the extent or quality of the service), but we do not, will it hurt our sales? By how much? What will be the effects on profit? If we do not cut our prices right away and lose customers, will we be able to get them back if we cut them later? What is our product, anyway?

[1] The service was approved by the CAB. Though EAL never released profit figures on the shuttle system, it was known to have yielded substantial increases in EAL passenger traffic between the three cities.

The price policy adopted by an airline or any other company is not entirely a matter of its own choice. In a perfectly competitive industry, where there are numerous producers of a completely undifferentiated product, say unbranded juice oranges of a given grade, selling to numerous buyers, the individual producer can have no price policy. He must sell at the prevailing market price because buyers can get all they want at the market price. Of course he can charge less, but that would hardly make sense since he can sell all he can produce at the higher price.

It is only in the presence of some degree of actual or potential product differentiation, such as in the automobile industry, where Plymouth cars are differentiated or different from Fords and Chevrolets, or when there is some other form of less-than-perfect competition, that the seller can have a price policy. To have a policy means to have a choice. Under perfectly competitive market conditions, a seller has no choice. In a perfectly competitive industry, there are numerous producers and sellers, numerous buyers, and a single standardized product. No one seller is so large that any change in his output will affect the total supply enough to influence price. This is the more or less typical situation in farm commodities.

We see, then, that industry and customer characteristics have much to do with the pricing decisions of business firms. Economists have long studied the behavior of prices, and have developed theories regarding price under differing kinds of market and competitive situations. Even though the theoretical constructs of the economist are of little direct help in the establishment of specific prices by individual companies, they are of considerable help in explaining the economic constraints that shape the pricing behavior of the business firm. We shall, therefore, begin our discussion of price concepts by looking briefly at the general characteristics of price behavior that economists ascribe to different types of industry structures.

Basic price concepts

□

INDUSTRY STRUCTURE

Both for purposes of historical description and for analysis of prices and other aspects of business behavior, economists have found it useful to develop ways of classifying industries. Their classification criteria typically focus on the number of firms and the individual importance of each firm in an industry, on the extent of product similarity among the products sold by industry members, and on the number of existing or potential customers for the industry's products. We shall look here at four industry classifications most frequently used in economic analysis, paying least attention to pure competition and monopoly, which represent extreme cases seldom found in practice, and greatest attention to oligopoly and monopolistic competition, the most important concepts.

Pure competition In an industry situation that is perfectly competitive, there are a great many small suppliers of products that cannot be differentiated from one another. The sellers sell to numerous buyers. Competition is "pure" in that no individual seller or buyer can exert any real influence in the marketplace. The seller offers his goods for sale but, in effect, can have no price policy because the market is so large and the sellers are so numerous that a price increase by an individual seller would drive him out of the market, and a price decrease would be pointless because he can sell all he produces at the regular market price. Further, since all sellers are so small, no one of them would benefit from, or be able to afford, advertising or other specialized marketing effort in behalf of his particular product.

Thus, unless there is some sort of collusion, which is usually illegal, each seller's price is at the mercy of the competitive forces that characterize the industry. The grower of Florida juice oranges and the farmer who produces wheat typify sellers in markets that fit the economist's definition of pure competition, although the government has facilitated the development of farm industry structures, for example, farmers' cooperatives, that attempt to protect individual farmers from the forces of pure competition. So far as price is concerned, the important thing is that those who sell under conditions of pure competition can have no individual price policies. In the United States, of course, we find almost no examples of markets, with the exception of some agricultural products and commodities, that are characterized by pure competition.

Monopoly A monopoly exists when one firm sells a product, or products, for which no competitive substitutes exist. Monopolies are anathema in the United States; the Sherman Antitrust Act of 1890 made both monopolies and attempts to monopolize illegal except as permitted by law, as in the case of public utilities and product monopolies based on the patent laws. Since 1890, federal authorities, with the support of most businessmen and society at large, have sought to enforce most strictly the antimonopoly provisions of the Sherman Act.

The trouble in determining whether a monopoly exists, for both lawyers and business analysts, comes on two fronts, and we shall mention each. What, for example, is an acceptable competitive "substitute"? Think, as the judiciary has had to, about a newspaper in a one-newspaper city. Is it a monopoly, or do television, radio, magazines, and out-of-town newspapers provide enough competition so that the newspaper should not be considered a monopoly in either a legal or practical sense?

The second problem, equally difficult, is in determining what is an "attempt to monopolize." Consider the paradox involved. Our laws and our value systems require that business firms compete vigorously. But suppose the firms compete so vigorously in a particular industry that only a few survive. For them, the possibility arises that a continuation of hard competition may further reduce the number of competing firms and, in the process, raise questions about attempts at monopolization.

Again, however, and even though problems of law enforcement are difficult, our national policy and attitude toward illegal monopoly are entirely clear, and so is the economist's view of pricing in monopoly situations. Since the monopolist is the only seller, and since there are no effective competitive substitutes, his price policy is easily developed. He charges what he thinks "the traffic will bear," subject only to the fears that the government will step in, that new companies may be attracted to his industry, or that people will in desperation stop buying his product. Most people would agree that the United States is fortunate to have avoided the existence of monopolies and the potentially harmful price policies available to them. There is less agreement, however, about another type of industry classification employed by economists.

□ Oligopolistic industries are characterized by (1) few sellers, (2) limited product differentiation, (3) uniformity of action in price changes, and (4) high market-entry expense.

Oligopoly The concept of oligopoly is less clear, both legally and in economic analysis, than are the concepts of monopoly and pure competition. From the practical standpoint of what exists in the United States and most industrialized nations, and in terms of our interest here in price behavior, it is a much more important concept. Though the fuzziness of the definition is apparent, an oligopolistic situation can be defined as one in which an industry has "few" sellers, at least most of whom are large, and in which the actions of each can clearly affect the others.□ The products of competing firms may be differentiated from one another in customers' eyes by some characteristic(s), but are substitutes for one another. The economist measures such substitutability in terms of *cross-elasticity of demand,* that is, the extent to which the demand for one firm's product is affected by changes in the demand for another firm's product. Though degrees of substitutability, and hence the extent of oligopoly, vary among industries, one might cite petroleum products, large electrical equipment, steel, sulfur, and many other such basic commodity industries as oligopolistic.

Note that there is almost always *some* degree of product differentiation in so-called oligopolistic industries. It is of particular importance to note, in the context of this chapter, that price is only one method of product differentiation. In this connection, the concept of the marketing mix is relevant. The companies in oligopolistic industries differentiate their products in various ways. These can take the forms of differences in product characteristics, such as quality, size, performance specifications, or color, or in the advertising messages that accompany the product, or in the type of selling and the channels of distribution used for it. In the steel industry, for example, some firms sell some of their products directly to industrial customers while others use distributors, and many steel companies use both industrial and consumer advertising in attempting to build demand for their brands of steel or steel-using products.

So far as price is concerned, there are so few sellers in oligopolistic industries that, unlike the monopolist or the seller under pure competition, price policy is a major problem. The prices of one competitor affect the prices of the others, and no single producer can be sure of what the effects of a price change on his part may be. If he raises (or lowers) his prices, competitors may, depending on what they believe to be market conditions and their own strengths and weaknesses, take any or some of the following steps: move up (or down) to meet the new price or price at a level just below (or just above) it, ignore the new price, change some of the features of their products, promote more heavily, advertise, employ more salesmen — in short, use other marketing mix strategies to counter the original price.

The competitive uncertainty and interdependence of prices in oligopolistic situations have led to a pricing phenomenon known as *price leadership*. This refers to circumstances in which, in specific industries, one firm serves, not always by choice, as the industry's price leader. The firm is usually a large one, such as General Motors or United States Steel, and one that is at least equal to the others in terms of efficiency, costs, and product quality. Not all price leaders, however, are the largest companies within their industries. Bain has suggested instances where smaller firms, because of their skill at sensing changes in demand and market conditions, have served as what are called *barometric price leaders*.[2] It should be pointed out that many economists criticize the price policies of companies in oligopolistic industries as too insensitive to the law of supply and demand (which we shall discuss below), saying that prices are "administered" by companies rather than being freely determined by market conditions, and sometimes charging that there is collusion and price-fixing by companies. There have been many occasions when companies in oligopolistic industries have been convicted of fixing or attempting to fix prices and, clearly, either is undesirable as well as illegal. But the establishment of prices in industries where there are few competitors is difficult indeed; in addition, we must remember, without condoning illegal price behavior, that there are many other ways in which business firms compete.[3]

Monopolistic competition Competitive firms are said to be in "monopolistic competiton" when they are numerous, small at least in relation to the total

[2] Joe S. Bain, "Price Leaders, Barometers, and Kinks," *The Journal of Business,* July, 1970, pp. 193–203.

[3] The difficulty of setting prices in oligopolistic industries is one major reason why prices in many cases are determined by senior executives or by committees made up of representatives of various functional interests, for example, marketing, production, legal counsel, and the company president or executive vice-president.

☐ *Monopolistic industries are characterized by (1) money sellers, (2) high product differentiation, (3) price competition, and (4) low market-entry expense.*

market they serve, and when each is able to affect demand for its product(s) by changes in price as well as other marketing mix variables.☐ Competitive reaction to changes in price by one firm is apt to be *less* sensitive than under oligopoly (note the word "less"—there are few absolutes in pricing), which in effect creates a higher degree of price competition. In addition to competing on a price basis, firms in monopolistic competition situations also use the full array of other marketing mix activities as they attempt to achieve product differentiation and market acceptance of their products. Food retailing is often cited as an example of monopolistic competition, as are manufacturers of cosmetics, hosiery, furniture, hi-fi components, and many other kinds of products.

Industries with regulated prices Our discussion in regard to industry structure and price would be incomplete without mention of the fact that there are many industries whose prices are affected not only by competition and the so-called law of supply and demand, but also by *government regulation*. The rates (prices) of telephone companies must be approved by state public utilities commissions, for example, as are those of gas and electric utilities. At the national level, there are a substantial number of regulatory agencies that set or approve prices for specific industries. To illustrate, the Interstate Commerce Commission and the Civil Aeronautics Board regulate the prices charged by railroads and airlines, respectively, and the Federal Power Commission has much to do with interstate prices on natural gas shipments.

☐

SUPPLY AND DEMAND

Thus far, our discussion of price has essentially concerned the general behavior of price in various types of industry structures. Though the nature of an industry in which a company competes does affect price, as we have indicated, definitions of industry structure are at best fuzzy. More importantly, they say nothing about specific prices and little about price ranges in the marketplace. In approaching that problem, we can again turn to economic theory as a starting point, and take a look at what people have come to call the *law of supply and demand*. Strictly speaking, the law of supply and demand, and its impact on price, was first conceived to describe the supply and/or demand aspects of what we referred to earlier as pure competition, but it has pricing implications for companies in all types of industries. The general applicability will become clear as we move through this section and the next, which has to do with the *elasticity of demand*.

In a perfectly competitive market, the price of a product depends on the relationship between the quantity supplied and the quantity demanded—in other words, on "supply and demand." What this means technically involves much more than is generally implied in such a simple statement. A more rigorous explanation is needed.

□

TABLE 16-1

Hypothetical demand schedule between price and quantity of oranges demanded (sold)

Point on demand curve	Price of oranges, per dozen	Quantity of demand, dozens in a store during one week	Revenue, price × quantity
A	$0.80	500	$400
B	0.70	550	385
C	0.60	600	360
D	0.50	700	350
E	0.40	800	320
F	0.30	900	270
G	0.20	1,000	200

In Part 2, we discussed customer decision-making units and how they behave. For the most part our discussion was presented in terms of the behavior of individual customer units. The concept of "demand" as used in the so-called theory of supply and demand is, however, related to the aggregate behavior of groups of customers. In its simplest form, the economist's generalization about demand says that as the price for a product (say oranges) falls, the quantity purchased (demanded) will rise. This relationship can be expressed numerically in the hypothetical demand schedule shown in Table

FIGURE 16-1

Hypothetical demand curve for oranges: A

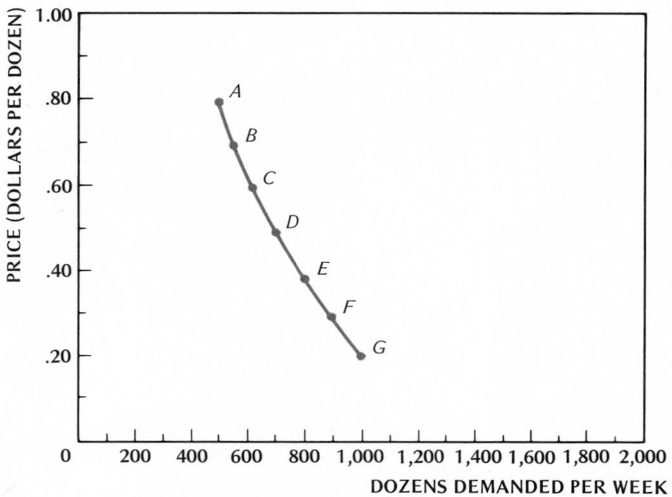

16-1. The schedule can also be presented graphically, as in Figure 16-1. The schedules show that at 40 cents, 800 dozen oranges will be bought. This is point *E* on the demand curve of Figure 16-1. This price will yield total revenue of $\$0.40 \times 800 = \$320$.

A simple relationship between price and quantity demanded, such as that shown in Figure 16-1, assumes that *all* other conditions that might affect people's behavior and the market are fixed and unchanging, *except* the price of oranges.

The concept of supply is also basically simple. All other things being equal, as the price at which a product can be sold rises, more of the product will be made available (supplied) for sale. The concept can be expressed in a supply schedule and presented graphically, as in Figure 16-2. The shape and position of the curve depend on the costs of producing the product. The curve can roughly be said to represent the seller's *marginal unit cost* curve. He will supply more products as prices rise because these rising prices cover his rising costs.

Combining the demand and supply curves of Figures 16-1 and 16-2 into a single graph yields Figure 16-3. This shows that where the two curves intersect the quantity that would be supplied at a given price is just equal to the quantity that would be purchased at that price. In this example, it is 40 cents per dozen. This is the so-called "equilibrium point." At 50 cents the quantity that would ordinarily be supplied would be 900 dozen, but only 700 would be bought.

FIGURE 16-2

Hypothetical supply curve for oranges

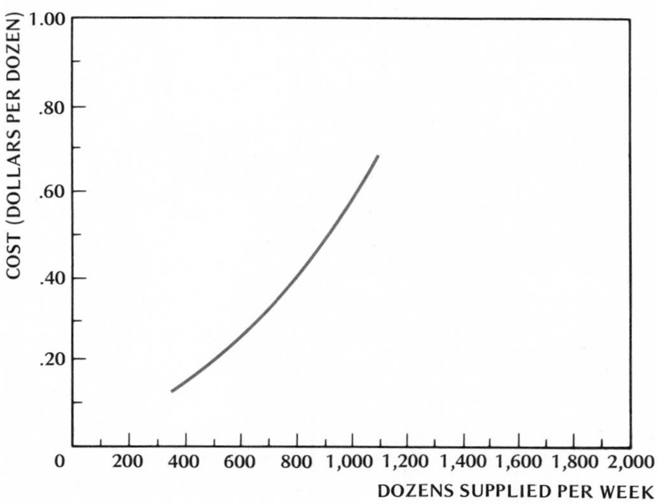

FIGURE 16-3
How supply and demand determine price and sales volume

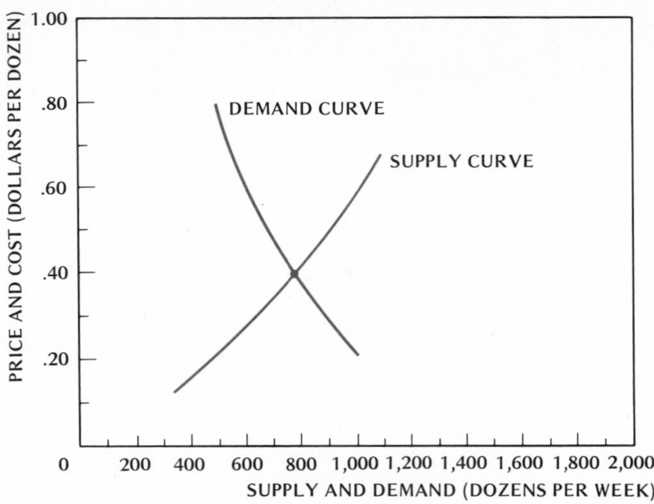

There would be 200 dozen unsold oranges. Since the cost of producing them has already been incurred, this cost represents losses because it yields no revenue. Next season (that is, in the long run), supply (that is, production) would be cut back such that the supply at 40 cents just equals the demand.

This is the price-determining model of the famous law of supply and demand. As presented here it is a highly simplified model of the conditions the theory actually encompasses. For one thing, in the discussion above we have assumed *fixed* demand and supply schedules. However, the number of customers at any given price is constantly changing, as is the number of orange growers. Hence tomorrow's schedules may be different from today's. Instead of the quantity demanded being 800 dozen at 40 cents, it may be 850. Moreover, people's attitudes may change, so that with a price reduction from 40 cents to 30 cents, the quantity demanded may rise not to 900 as in Table 16-1, but to 1,000. In that case it would be said that the demand has become *more elastic*. If with this price drop the quantity demanded had gone not from 800 to 900, as in Table 16-1, but only to 825, it would be said that the demand had become less elastic, or more *inelastic*.

Such shifts in the demand and supply curves are obviously of great interest to sellers because of their effects on prices and on the volumes that can be sold. It is useful, therefore, to turn to the concept of elasticity of demand in order to examine more directly the theoretical relationships between specific prices and specific levels of demand. The elasticity concept is useful to marketers in what we have referred to earlier as industries characterized by monopolistic competition or oligopoly.

ELASTICITY OF DEMAND

Elasticity of demand refers to the relative responsiveness of sales revenue to particular changes in price. Thus Table 16-1 shows that as prices declined, the actual number of oranges sold rose. But the total revenue, that is, quantity sold *times* price, fell. This is an example of demand that is said to be relatively price inelastic.

When total revenue falls as prices fall, or, equivalently, when revenue rises as prices rise, the demand for the product is said to be *relatively price inelastic.* When the opposite happens, that is, when revenue rises as prices fall, or when revenue falls as prices rise, the demand is said to be *relatively price elastic.* In other words, we say that there is relative price inelasticity when the direction (up or down) in the revenue associated with a given price change is the same as the direction of that price change. We say that there is relative price elasticity when the direction (up or down) in the revenue associated with a given price change is the opposite of the direction of that price change.

In Figure 16-4, which is a modified reproduction of Figure 16-1, we see that as the price fell from 60 cents to 40 cents, the revenue fell from $360 = $.60 × 600 to $320 = $0.40 × 800. A 33.3 percent price reduction caused only a 11.2 percent revenue reduction. We also see that as the price

FIGURE 16-4

Hypothetical demand curve for oranges: B

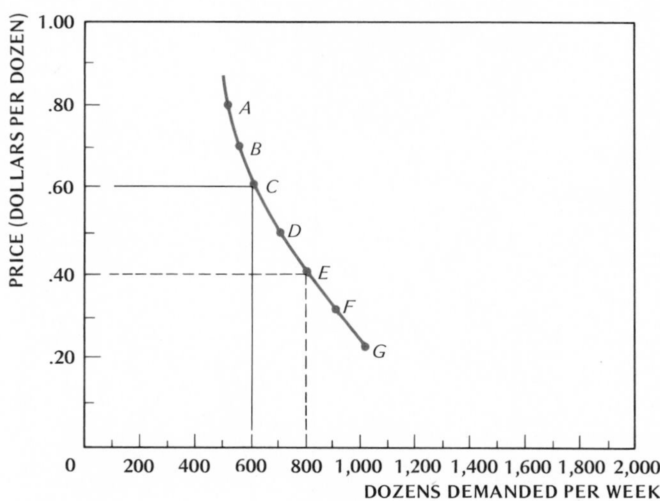

rose from 40 cents to 60 cents, revenue moved in the same direction, from \$320 to \$360. The demand is relatively price inelastic. Suppose, however, that demand is relatively price elastic. Figure 16-5 illustrates this situation. At 60 cents, total revenue equals the solid-line rectangle under the demand curve (\$0.60 × 400 = \$240). At 40 cents, the dotted-line rectangle shows a much greater total revenue (\$0.40 × 1,150 = \$460). A 33.3 percent price reduction causes a 91.7 percent revenue increase. The demand is relatively price elastic. (See the Appendix to this chapter, pages 433–434, for a mathematical formulation of the concept of elasticity.)

Ordinarily we should expect an industry with a relatively inelastic demand curve to reduce prices reluctantly and actually raise them with some equanimity. Salt used for home consumption has a relatively inelastic demand. It is essential, there are no close substitutes, and it is cheap. Neither a substantial price increase nor decrease would affect the volume sold at retail. But beef sales would respond much more, relatively, to price changes. Hence, if we assume that all other factors are unchanged, if total revenue rises rapidly as prices rise, and if total costs do not rise as rapidly as revenue, it seems reasonable to raise prices. An industry with a relatively elastic curve would ordinarily be expected to price low. Consider the case of a company manufacturing milk cartons. Suppose that it has no competitors and that its production costs per unit fall rapidly as its output increases. (In other words, there are "economies of large-scale production," which is typical within a wide range of output pos-

FIGURE 16-5
Hypothetical elastic demand curve for oranges

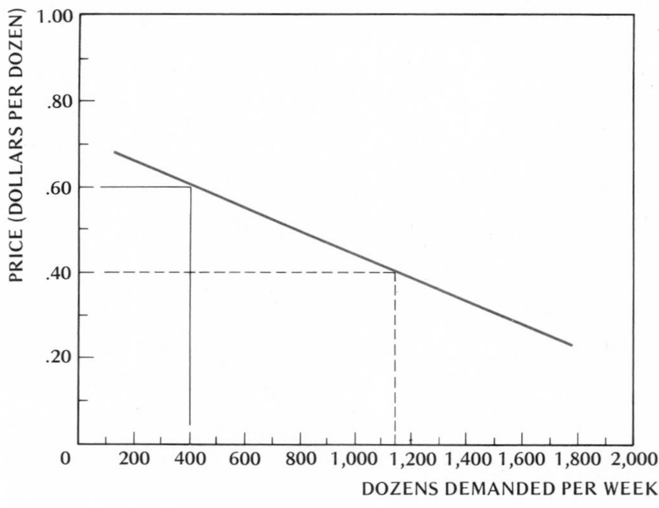

sibilities for many industries.) If the demand for milk cartons were relatively elastic, we should expect the company to reduce prices willingly, since doing so greatly increases its total revenue while its total production costs rise only modestly.

Yet this is a clearly simplified picture of the conditions facing most companies. Indeed, the whole so-called law of supply and demand, again, assumes highly simplified market conditions. It assumes that customers act *solely* on the basis of price and that "all other conditions" which might affect the market are equal, unchanged, or noninfluential.

□

ELASTICITY AND THE INDIVIDUAL FIRM

In the real world, "all other things" are seldom "equal." But demand *is* clearly affected by prices, and it pays the individual seller to have some notion of what that elasticity is for his industry and for his company's products. A price decision that does not take into account the product's price elasticity of demand can be a dangerously blind decision.

In industries characterized by monopolistic competition or oligopoly, we know that individual firms try in various ways to differentiate their products from those offered by competitors; price is, of course, only one factor that may be used for differentiating purposes. When differentiation occurs, it is evident that a particular company's demand curve, or the demand curve for a particular brand of a product, may vary greatly from the demand curve of its industry. In the case of automobiles, the demand for Plymouths varies from the demand for other cars and even from the demand for the same general category of cars, such as Fords and Chevrolets. Where the products of the various firms in the industry are differentiated from each other such that each company's cars, for example, are clearly distinguishable from the cars of the others, there is generally a distinct consumer preference pattern for each brand. The *combined* preferences form the industry curve.

Figure 16-6 illustrates the situation in a four-firm industry in which the general slope of the curve for each firm approximates that of the industry curve, but the position of each is different. Thus at a price of $2,000, the quantity that can be sold by each firm varies considerably. Also each firm has a somewhat different elasticity of demand.

While the position and the elasticity of a firm's or an industry's demand curve affect sales and prices, learning what the position and the elasticities are is no easy matter. Indeed, few companies make any serious effort to determine in detail the demand curves for their products. It is extremely difficult to do so without either making actual pricing experiments that might cause serious competitive reactions or creating artificial conditions which yield answers that do not apply in the real world. However, some careful studies have demonstrated the extent to which price elasticity of demand varies by products. Fur-

FIGURE 16-6

Hypothetical industry and firm demand curves for differential products (automobiles sold by four firms in a four-firm industry)

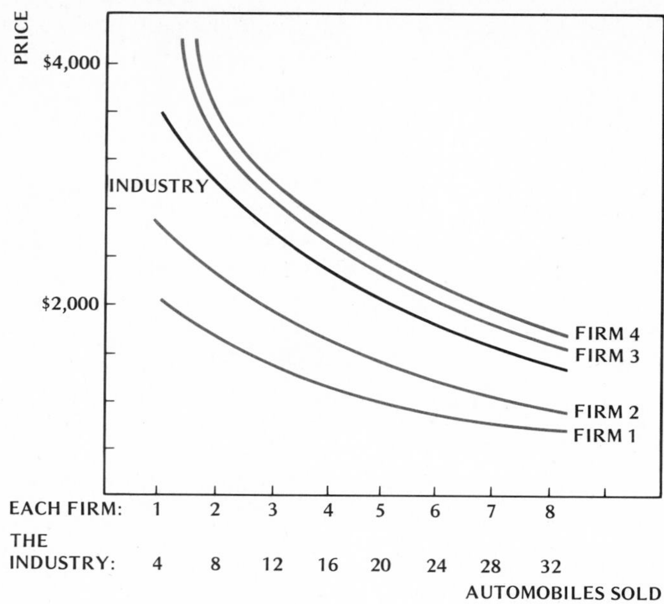

ther, some companies use computer simulations to "test" various price possibilities on proposed new products. Thus, although the determination of elasticity is a complex and costly process, some companies have found it worthwhile where major expenditures are involved.[4]

One of the conditions that affect the position and elasticity of a firm's demand curve, and may distinguish the firm's curve from the industry curve, is, as we suggested in an earlier section, the nature and composition of the industry in which the firm operates. "Real world" market conditions rarely approximate the model of perfect competition that the pure conception of the law of supply and demand assumes. The phrase *imperfect competition,* which includes oligopoly and monopolistic competition, more accurately describes the competitive status of most industries and companies in the United States and other developed nations, and it is worthwhile to look more closely at its implications for price and other forms of competitive activity.

[4] For examples of demand studies for various industries, see Francis E. Hummel, *Market and Sales Potentials,* The Ronald Press Company, New York, 1961. For specific studies of elasticities of demand for agricultural products, see Henry Schultz, *Theory and Measurement of Demand,* The University of Chicago Press, Chicago, 1938; and R. H. Williams, "Demand Functions for Merchandise at Retail," *Studies in Mathematical Economics and Econometrics,* The University of Chicago Press, Chicago, 1948, pp. 208–221 (Williams studied prices at Macy's department store).

□

IMPERFECT COMPETITION

"Imperfect" competition obviously refers to all departures from perfectly competitive conditions. The most extreme departure is legal, regulated monopoly, as we pointed out earlier, where there is only a single supplier of a particular product or service in a given market; such monopolies are subject to price regulation by public bodies. There are also, of course, legal unregulated monopolies based on product patent rights. In such cases there are no offsetting competitors to undercut the single supplier, who is therefore free to limit supply along any point on the demand curve and let the price come to rest at that point. On the other hand, where there are many competitors, the aggregate volume of the product offered by them determines the shape and position of the supply curve. If the product is undifferentiated, the price comes to rest at the point of intersection of this industry demand curve and the industry supply curve, as in Figure 16-3. Every seller then charges only the single price determined by the overall forces of supply and demand.

We know, however, that not every seller of a single category of products charges the same price as his competitors. Not all automobiles sell for the same price, nor do all brands of toothpaste or aspirin. The reason is that not all automobiles are exactly alike, as is No. 2 spring wheat. Not even all Plymouth cars are alike. In short, the products are, unlike No. 2 spring wheat, differentiated. These differences each have their own demand curves along which different prices can be effectively charged, as shown in Figure 16-6.

Companies systematically create differences in their products, such as more chrome trim on cars, or an easier to open aspirin bottle, or more foamy toothpaste. They do so both to appeal to specific customer preferences and to distinguish their particular products from those of competitors in order to be insulated from the price pressures of competitors selling otherwise identical products. This product differentiation is one type of legal imperfection in the market, and it is in the creation of, and capitalization on, such "imperfection" that a great deal of marketing activity centers.

The fact that such departures from pure competition may be labeled *market imperfections* implies nothing about the value or desirability of imperfection in the economic system. Indeed, the pure theory of price suggests that there may be at the same time both national benefits and costs associated with an economic system of extensive product differentiation.[5]

While product differentiation may be a consequence of trying to serve various special preferences of consumers, it also serves the seller's interest in avoiding severe price competition. In these cases, competition generally shifts partially to other grounds: package appeal, design appeal, taste, color, financ-

[5] See Robert Triffin, *Monopolistic Competition and General Equilibrium Theory,* Harvard University Press, Cambridge, Mass., 1940. See also J. M. Clark, "Toward a Concept of Workable Competition," *American Economic Review,* June, 1940; and *Competition as a Dynamic Process,* The Brookings Institution, Washington, 1961.

ing terms, delivery, psychological satisfactions, and a vast variety of other factors that are designed to attract customers to the seller's particular store or service or brand. In short, he is trying to create and satisfy preferences for his offerings that to some extent transcend price. He is generally trying to shift the demand curve for his offerings above the industry curve, as firms 3 and 4 have done in the situation shown in Figure 16-6, or to make them less elastic than the industry curve so that when the industry price level falls, he will hold some customers without cutting his prices, or he will lose fewer customers to lower-priced competing products, or he will have to drop his prices less than his competitors.

The discussion in the preceding two major sections of this chapter has drawn heavily on the pure economic theory of price, and is a brief summary of a vast literature on the subject. More detail can be found in most introductory economic textbooks. But the theory of price is just that: a theory based on selected facts of the real world. It is not intended to be descriptive of *all* the elements of pricing in the real world. For that, it is necessary to look also at a number of additional factors and ultimately, as we shall in the next chapter, to consider pricing policy in actual practice.

In general, business firms know less about the shape of cost and demand curves than the theory of price assumes. Moreover, each seller in one way or another is generally sheltered enough from the direct pressures of all-out price competition so that he has *some* room for independent strategy. The extent to which such independence is available to the seller, that is, the extent to which he can have a price policy, has a great deal to do with customer attitudes, with market conditions, and with his business objectives, as described in the next two sections.

Customers and market price conditions

At the beginning of the chapter, we indicated that customers, and the characteristics of the markets that they constitute, are major determinants of prices. To this point, however, most of our discussion has been concerned with structures of selling industries and the company activities that are designed to affect demand. It is obvious, however, that customer behavior and attitudes are the ultimate determinants of what actually occurs in the marketplace, and that customers are themselves affected by general price conditions in the marketplace. For that reason, we shall look at both factors.

□ THE CUSTOMER

Pricing policies and pricing discretion are deeply affected by the characteristics of the customer. In consumer goods markets, customers tend to be numerous and generally less well informed than customers for industrial goods. The latter, as indicated in Chapter 8, are generally fewer and relatively more knowledgeable. They tend to know more clearly what characteristics they want in a product; they will be able to judge more easily whether a product has these characteristics; and they will usually have more information about the prices and qualities of competitors' products. Hence, even without considering the actual activities of competitors, the pricing discretion available to sellers of industrial goods tends to be substantially less than that available to sellers of consumer goods.

This, however, is a generalization subject to important exceptions and qualifications. A prospective family car purchaser may have the competence and information that make him a better informed buyer than the purchasing agent who buys his company's janitorial supplies. The housewife who is an avid reader of *Consumer Reports* or of the woman's page of a good daily newspaper, or who carefully compares the weekly advertisements of competing supermarkets, may be a vastly wiser shopper than the purchasing agent who buys spindle lathes from the company that has romanced him most lavishly at the Playboy Club. She may also be a wiser shopper than the design engineer who recommends the instrument panels of a particular supplier because that supplier seemed so much more knowledgeable than the engineer himself. Choosing that supplier enabled the engineer to get someone else to do his job for him.

The degree of customer sophistication varies, therefore, not only with the category of product (consumer goods versus industrial goods), but also within product categories, with the education and often income of the consumer, and with many other factors. The degree of industrial purchasing sophistication sometimes varies with the industry, not necessarily because one industry is basically smarter than another, but because its problems are different. In one industry the annual requirements for nuts and bolts may be predictable, which leads to careful purchasing. In other cases, it may be unpredictable, leading to urgent "any-price-will-do" purchasing. It may also vary according to the stage of the business cycle. The appliance manufacturer may be an extremely careful and calculating sheet steel buyer when times are tough and sheet steel is in plentiful supply. When steel industry operations are running at full capacity and supply is short, the same appliance manufacturer may drastically take such measures as cutting his procurement standards, allowing his quality requirements to fall, accepting more flexible delivery dates, offering to pick up the product at the supplier's warehouse rather than insisting on delivery to his own plant.

GENERAL PRICE MOVEMENTS

A major factor that affects price in specific industries and in individual firms, and has an impact on customer behavior, is the general movement of prices over a period of time. As an example, we note that in 1931 a Chevrolet could be purchased for less than $600. In 1971, just 40 years later, the price of a Chevrolet Impala V8, with a few accessories, was in the neighborhood of $3,600. Even though it is true that American and other economies have seen rising levels of prices for many years, both total economies and individual industries encounter fluctuations in price from time to time. Such movements, in the aggregate, occur as a result of a complex of factors, among them being national and international economic problems and policies and the attitudes and behavior of customers. General movements in price levels affect specific price decisions of business firms.

Probably the most pervasive attitude of businessmen toward prices is their preference for relative price stability. Even rising prices are less than gleefully welcomed at all times. First, they produce margin calculation complications along the entire route of distribution. Second, they involve a great many bookkeeping changes in the firm itself and constantly reopen internal organizational issues regarding what the company's costs actually are. Most importantly, they raise difficult questions as to what *future* prices will be and how *competitors* will react.

Numerous studies have been made of industry pricing practices. During the late 1930s the United States Senate's Temporary National Economic Committee (TNEC) held extensive hearings that revealed evidence of the "stabilizing" attitudes characterizing most business practices in those days.[6] One author adduced five major causes for this tendency toward price stability[7]:

1. The widespread rule-of-thumb belief that higher prices generally mean higher profits because of the belief that demand is relatively price inelastic. Hence there are few "unstabilizing" price reductions.
2. With excess capacity and heavy overhead costs, price stabilization reduces the danger of cutthroat competition.
3. The belief that demand is generally inelastic, so that one price cut may encourage buyers to wait for another reduction.
4. Uncertainty as to which price policy is most profitable.
5. Price stabilization is a simple, easily understood policy compared to the complications and risks of purposely variable prices.

Firms often use variable prices without purposely setting out to do so. They are forced to make changes by competitive conditions. Patterns of price changes vary in their frequency, their amplitude, and their timing. In analyzing such patterns, it is useful to sort fluctuations into three categories: seasonal variation, cyclical change, and secular trend.

[6] For a summary and analysis of these hearings as they relate to price practices, see Saul Nelson and Walter G. Keim, *Price Behavior and Business Policy,* TNEC monograph no. 1, Washington, 1940.
[7] Arthur R. Burns, *The Decline of Competition,* McGraw-Hill Book Company, New York, 1936, p. 234.

Seasonal variations trace a recurrent pattern throughout the year from year to year. An example of such variations are the prices of fresh fruits and vegetables, which vary inversely with the volume of the current supply.

Cyclical changes are generally associated with changing economic conditions. Thus when times are good (the height of a business cycle) scrap paper prices tend to be high, and when times are bad they are low. The sensitivity of prices to general economic conditions varies by industry structure. Generally speaking, the larger the number of producers, the more sensitive are prices to business conditions. When there are relatively few producers, it generally means that the capital requirements for entry into the industry are high and the economies of large-scale production are considerable. With few producers, when times turn bad and demand falls, each seller knows that if he maintains his output at his old prosperity level, he must cut prices to sell more. But he also knows that cutting prices will cause immediate retaliation by his watchful competitors, who will be immediately affected by such a move. Hence he tends to hold the price line and, instead, cuts his output. The cyclical amplitude of prices in such industries is therefore relatively modest. It tends to be considerable, however, in industries or product situations where entry is relatively easier and sellers are many, such as with most agricultural products and in the manufacturing of women's dresses.

Secular price patterns are long-term movements that are largely independent of the general price level. Almost all manufactured products undergo a secular pattern. Thus automobiles, refrigerators, roller bearings, mylon, television sets, and hi-fi radio equipment all started out with prices that gradually, or sometimes precipitously, fell as new producers entered the field (see the product life-cycle concept described in Chapter 15), as substitute products became available, as the injured producers of existing products retaliated, as the market expanded and greater economies of mass production became possible, or as mass markets were sought by systematic price reductions.

Secular price trends can be upward as well as downward. Since World War II, the prices of Restoration antiques, and the prices of professional services of all kinds, have been on a secular rise. But within secular trends there can be modest cyclical and even seasonal variations. As an example of the former, the recession of 1970–1971 brought about a decline in the prices of corporate common stocks, even though the secular trend of such prices had been upward for a period of many years and was generally expected to resume.

Company policies and price concepts

In Chapter 17, our focus will be on the specifics of company pricing policies and methods. Nevertheless, it is appropriate in this chapter's general discussion of pricing concepts to make some mention of certain universal company-oriented factors that have much to do with choices as to specific price policies.

We shall discuss four such factors: business objectives, channels of distribution, types of products, and costs.

BUSINESS OBJECTIVES

In Chapter 13, it was noted that overall corporate strategy and the overall corporate goals that it dictates are a major determinant of marketing strategy. Thus general business objectives have great impact on the specifics of pricing objectives. If a company decides that growth is a major objective, and that such growth will have to come substantially from an increase in its market share (the *selective demand* discussed earlier in this chapter), it will adopt a marketing mix designed to achieve that objective. Within that mix, its price policy may be to price below the price of its competitors. Or, if a company has decided to maintain its share of the market for product A and not to rock A's competitive boat while it concentrates on building more share and higher profits for products B and C, then one would not expect its price policy on product A to change very much.

As a specific example of the effect of overall business objectives on price, consider the case of ball-point pens. Ball-point pens were first introduced in the United States in the late 1940s by the Reynolds International Pen Co., a new firm organized especially to manufacture and sell this new-concept pen. The introduction was launched with a massive advertising campaign claiming miracle newness. During the first week, 30,000 pens were sold at a retail price of $12.50 each. Independent analysis showed that the pen could be produced for 50 cents if production was at the rate of 10,000 per day. The first three months of Reynolds' ball-point sales (at factory prices) totaled $5,674,329. Profits after taxes were $1,558,608. The company's original investment was $26,000. Within a year numerous companies were offering ball-point pens at a retail price of around $1. Competition forced Reynolds to cut prices severely. Within a few years it ceased operations. Its owner had made and kept a fortune. Clearly this company's goal was to make a quick "killing," rather than to build a lasting business. Once ball-point-pen competition developed and the rigors of competitive life had to be faced, the company simply closed shop.

CHANNELS OF DISTRIBUTION

A manufacturer's pricing discretion also varies with the length and complexity of his chain of distribution, and so does the discretion of any organization within that chain.

The longer the chain, the less flexible the price structure. Thus, if a manufacturer sells first to a regional distributor, who in turn sells to local wholesalers, who finally sell to retailers, any change in price involves a complex series of changes throughout the chain. By contrast, a manufacturer selling direct to retailers has fewer distribution outlets to satisfy and fewer with whom to work out changes in posted invoices and accounts receivable. Hence, he is more likely to make the price adjustments that seem otherwise desirable.

The effect of distribution channels on pricing discretion has yet another aspect: the more complex the channel, the less difference minor changes at the manufacturer's level may make at the retail level.

The reason is that distributors, wholesalers, and retailers often absorb small changes in order to avoid having to make costly and frequent changes in their catalogs, price lists, and price-marked products on their shelves. For example, distributor organizations and druggists often absorb minor changes in the prices of prescription drugs and toiletries to avoid the inconvenience of small changes in price lists and already marked shelf items.

□

TYPES OF PRODUCTS

It is a generally accepted concept that the pricing policies open to a seller vary by product category in ways that may be independent of the state of customer sophistication or of market structure. There are differences between perishable and durable products, consumer and industrial products, distinctive and commodity products, new and old products.[8]

Perishable and durable products Pricing strategy for perishable commodities such as fresh fruits obviously involves important questions of inventory and storage strategy. In the case of a durable product, short-term discrepancies between supply and demand can be handled via proper production scheduling and inventory management. A factory's output can be reasonably well geared to demand estimates, but the output of a field of strawberries cannot, except within the narrowest limits. For a strawberry farmer to gear his output to demand involves the impossible requirement of having farms scattered all over the world throughout the entire range of temperature zones, or it requires a vast greenhouse (factory).

Since strawberries are perishable, they must be either sold near the point of growth or transported to distant markets by costly, rapid means. Since, in addition, they are harvested in large batches and at times that can only partially be controlled by the producer, he is forced to sell them quickly for whatever he can get. To withhold them until prices improve is to wait until they spoil. Although during the early weeks of the season high prices may be successfully charged, at the height of the season the seller has virtually no price discretion.

The retailer faces equally difficult problems. The strawberries he offers for sale on Saturday will generally have to be delivered to him on Friday or predawn Saturday. If his store is closed on Sunday, he must sell out his stock on Saturday or incur spoilage losses. To avoid spoilage or large price reduc-

[8] For numerous articles and studies on price behavior in all sectors of industry, see Jules Backman, *Price Practices and Price Policies,* The Ronald Press Company, New York, 1953.

tions on Saturday, he must buy carefully on Friday. However, if he underbuys and sells out early Saturday afternoon, he may risk driving customers to competitive stores on their next grocery shopping trips because his store did not seem to carry fresh strawberries.

Similar price practices are employed in the sale of seasonal and fashion items. Thus a department store will have winter, spring, summer, and fall sales to move out "dying" seasonal stock and make room for the next season's inventory. In fashion items, this "move out" practice would be followed even if the retailer had space and capital to store, say, ladies' spring dresses until the next season. He would move them out for fear that next season this year's stock would be out of fashion. Hence perishability is a matter of two kinds of spoilage: chemical decomposition and fashion change. Short-term price policy becomes an equalizing solvent.

Since the seller knows that he almost inevitably will have an overstocked condition at the end of the selling day or the selling season, he knows that he will have to take markdowns. Hence his original price policy must allow enough margin to offset the effects of later markdowns on the profitability of his entire operation. The systematic necessity of end-of-season sales has created customer expectations of sales such that the demand for "sale" items frequently exceeds the ordinary end-of-season supply. Hence many retailers have developed the practice of actually buying new stock especially intended for such sales, and manufacturers produce items especially to meet that demand.

Consumer and industrial products As indicated in the preceding section, industrial goods buyers are frequently better informed than the consumer goods buyers. As a result, the price flexibility or price discretion available to the industrial goods seller is often reduced. Also, sellers often know exactly who buyers are. Thus the manufacturer of fully automatic spindle lathes has a very good idea of who specifically are his prospects, including their names, addresses, and credit ratings. When this situation prevails, there is more direct face-to-face selling, and therefore more emphasis on substantive product features, on price, and on such terms of trade as credit, delivery time, and payment discounts.

Another important distinction between industrial and consumer goods is that there is greater likelihood that industrial goods are tailor-made to the detailed specifications of buyers. While a private consumer may occasionally buy a tailor-made product, say a house, the industrial consumer buys such products frequently. Many suppliers to industrial consumers sell nothing but tailor-made products. This is true of manufacturers of large electric generating turbines, and of independent parts and component suppliers to assembly-line manufacturers of such products as automobiles and electric appliances. It is also true of packaging suppliers to manufacturers of consumer packaged goods such as cosmetics, foods, and drugs.

Another distinction between industrial and consumer goods pricing procedures is in the handling of delivery costs. Most consumer goods tend to be purchased in small quantities that the buyer carries directly out of the store. In the case of heavy items, such as refrigerators or sofas, delivery to the buyer's home is generally included in the originally quoted selling price. Industrial goods prices tend to be quoted "f.o.b. (free on board) factory" or, say, "f.o.b. Milwaukee warehouse," that is, freight from the factory or warehouse to the buyer's location is to be paid by the buyer.

Such pricing procedures obviously place a nearby seller at a great advantage over a distant one, especially if the ratio of delivery expenses to the buyer's total cost tends to be high. This is precisely the case in steel and cement, for example, and in part accounted, years ago, for the development in these industries of the so-called "basing-point" system of pricing.

In April 1948, the United States Supreme Court declared this system to be a form of unfair competition and therefore illegal. It had been used by the steel industry for over half a century, and its abandonment in 1948 resulted in some major changes in plant and warehouse location strategy.

The basing-point system enabled every steel seller to quote the same delivered price to a customer, regardless of the location of either seller or buyer. The industry merely divided the nation into several geographically discrete, competitive areas. Within each area any customer was quoted the base price set for that area, plus rail freight delivery costs from the stipulated basing point appropriate to that area, regardless of the actual shipping source of the steel itself.

With price leadership being practiced in the industry, the leader established the price to be quoted at each basing point. With all sellers thus quoting an identical basing-point price, and with the published rail freight charge tacked on to this price, each seller quoted an identical delivered price to the prospect.

The outlawing of the basing-point system resulted in a vast restructuring of distribution logistics in the steel industry. The substance of this change was the establishment of more company warehouses near customer sources. The manufacturers could then make large, relatively low-cost deliveries into these warehouses and ship smaller quantities from there to customers either "f.o.b. the warehouse" or "delivered." Some companies and industries also established "delivered price zones" such that all customers within a geographic zone are quoted identical prices, but with price differences among zones.

Distinctive and commodity products A product is distinctive because it is different. It may be different because of its unique features, say, a Volkswagen or a particular heat-resistant titanium alloy. It may be different because of the aura with which it has been carefully surrounded, say, a sterling silver punch bowl sent in a gift wrapping from Tiffany's as opposed to Macy's. It may be different because it is new, say, a nontobacco cigarette; or because it is especially old, as is a marble-top seventeenth century French provincial hutch; or because it is a rare blue-period painting by Picasso.

Indeed, distinctiveness almost necessarily implies some rareness, and this generally permits the product or service to command a high price. Some products may be characterized by perishable distinctiveness, say, the nontobacco cigarette, which can be easily imitated; while others have imperishable distinctiveness, say, the Picasso blue.

The distinctiveness of a product, and therefore its ability to command a high price, usually perishes in proportion to the speed with which it achieves some sort of maturity. The seller's zone of pricing discretion fades as his distinctive specialty loses its differentiating qualities and becomes, in the customer's mind, a somewhat undifferentiated commodity. Thus when hula hoops first reached the market, they were priced at around $1.59. Rapid market acceptance produced quick market maturity, and this, combined with lack of patent or other protections, stimulated new manufacturers and produced quick competitive maturity. Since, in addition, the product itself was technically mature, that is, no new technical improvements or manufacturing processes were coming along, the market quickly became flooded and prices fell below 50 cents. Clearly this was a product with perishable distinctiveness.

Imperishable distinctiveness is rare in itself. Few manufactured products have lasting distinctiveness, even for the period of their patent monopoly. In the case of nylon, Du Pont enjoyed a patent protection, which gave it great pricing discretion. The product was for years priced as a specialty. But as substitute synthetic fibers were developed by other companies, nylon's sheltered position deteriorated and a different pricing strategy had to be employed.

Technical, market, and competitive maturity clearly mark the difference between a great many distinctive and commodity products. Maturity is also often a matter of time—the difference between a new product and an old product.

COSTS

Although in Chapter 17 we will discuss in detail the relevance of costs to specific pricing policies, some mention of cost is required here simply because cost is often one critical determinant of price. As shown in our earlier discussion of supply and demand, cost determines the *shape* of a supply curve, even though price itself is determined by the relationship between the supply and the demand curves. It is, of course, obvious that no product can survive unless it covers its costs and makes a profit, unless it is one of a family of products and must be offered to ensure the success of the other members of the family.

Beyond that, our discussion of the importance of costs and methods used in relating them to prices will be reserved for the next chapter.

Government policies and regulations

As marketing managers establish their pricing policies and methods, they do so not only against the backdrop of the theory, concepts, and general factors discussed above, but also in the context of a substantial body of governmental legislation and policy that affects the business community. We shall discuss here the most important pieces of legislation that govern pricing in the United States, but it is important to emphasize that the legal aspects of pricing are exceedingly complex, most particularly those which have to do with the Robinson-Patman Act. Most companies of substantial size employ full-time legal staffs and/or outside counsel to work on the legal aspects of pricing problems and other antitrust matters, and any businessman is well advised to seek legal assistance when questions of possible legality regarding matters of price arise. Our objective here is limited to giving a general picture of the laws and regulations that affect pricing, and some feeling for their implications.[9]

There are numerous laws and government policies that affect prices. Some are designed to protect domestic industries by keeping foreign-produced goods out of the country or by limiting their volume or their competitive effectiveness. Import quotas and tariffs are the chief examples. They help raise the general price level in the domestic market by affecting the supply curve.

Some government practices raise prices by contributing to increased or reduced demand. Thus when the federal government buys large quantities of wheat and aluminum, it tends to push prices up. Other policies raise prices by controlling the original production of the product. Federal support and acreage programs tend to limit domestic sugar beet production, and close continuing checks on market demand by state regulatory commissions result in their setting monthly quotas on crude-oil production.

Other policies discussed below, such as resale price maintenance laws, are aimed at controlling price directly. There are also policies and laws designed to preserve free-market conditions so that prices will tend to stay near competitive minimums. This, indeed, is a primary objective of the basic antitrust laws of the United States.

□ THE SHERMAN ACT

The Sherman Act of 1890 was passed to control the activities of the giant trusts that came into being in the last third of the nineteenth century, and still serves

[9] For a more detailed description of the history, content, and impact of the laws that affect pricing, see Robert A. Lynn, *Price Policies and Marketing Management*, Richard D. Irwin, Inc., Homewood, Ill., 1967.

as the keystone of antitrust legislation in the United States. Directed, as we pointed out earlier, at monopolies and attempts to monopolize, the Sherman Act, unlike most pieces of antitrust legislation, is brief and succinct. Its enforcement and interpretation by the Department of Justice and the courts over the generations since its passage make it clear that collusive activities by companies to fix prices, or to attempt to fix prices, are illegal. In addition, further to buttress the Sherman Act, the Federal Trade Commission has the authority, under Section 5 of the Federal Trade Commission Act, to take action against collusion and price-fixing activities as unfair methods of competition in interstate commerce.[10] In passing, it should be noted that both the Sherman and Federal Trade Commission acts are federal legislation and hence apply only to interstate commerce.

☐ ANTIDISCRIMINATION LAWS

In 1941 the Congress augmented the government's arsenal of antitrust laws by passing the Clayton Act, which contained a provision making it unlawful for any person or firm in interstate commerce "to discriminate in price between different purchasers of commodities . . . where the effect of such discrimination may be substantially to lessen competition or tend to create a monopoly in any line of commerce." This was followed by some statements which permitted exceptions to this broad prohibition. At about the same time, the Federal Trade Commission was established to administer the Clayton Act.

In June 1936, the Clayton Act was changed and strengthened when Congress enacted the Robinson-Patman amendment to Section 2 of the Clayton Act. Essentially, its main provisions are[11]:

It is unlawful for one engaged in interstate commerce to discriminate in prices between different buyers or goods of the same quality if such discrimination tends to lessen competition substantially or to create a monopoly. Prices may, however, differ to the extent of differences in the cost of manufacture, sale, or delivery resulting from differences in quantities sold or in the methods of sale or delivery.

A seller can justify a price or service differential by showing that the differential was made in good faith to meet an equally low price or service offered by a competitor.

Price concessions may not be given or accepted in the form of commissions; such commissions may be paid only for services actually rendered. Payments for services must be available in proportionally equal terms to all buyers.

Buyers may not knowingly induce or receive discriminations in price.

These provisions are enforced by the Federal Trade Commission. When the Commission finds a violation, it issues a cease-and-desist order, which may be appealed to a Circuit Court of Appeals and to the Supreme Court for annulment or enforcement.

[10] "Interstate commerce" is a phrase whose legal definition is exceedingly complex. In general, however, it applies not only to commerce among states, but also to commerce that affects more states than one and to commerce within a state that affects other states. It is no exaggeration to say that judicial interpretation of the phrase "interstate commerce" can be very broad indeed.

[11] This is a paraphrase of the law and not a complete statement of its provisions.

If large buyers of a given product are so few that low prices to them would be unjustly discriminatory or promotive of monopoly, the Federal Trade Commission may set the limits on quantity prices (discounts).

Under the Clayton and Robinson-Patman acts, sellers may select their own customers and change prices as often as they wish. A seller may charge different prices to different institutions in the chain of distribution, for example, wholesalers versus retailers, since they are not competitors. Under present interpretations of the law, a manufacturer may also charge a buyer, say, a supermarket chain, a different price for his branded detergent than for a private brand detergent which he also supplies that buyer. Presumably the difference must be based in some way on differences in cost to the seller, although at the present stage in the law's interpretation exactly what is permissible is not entirely clear.

Quantity discounts are permitted, but the seller must be prepared to justify them in terms of cost savings.

The law permits a seller to charge a lower price to one buyer than to another if he can demonstrate that this was done in good faith to meet an equally low price of a competitor, regardless of the legality of the competitor's price. But this has raised a further issue: the question of whether, when a manufacturer selling to many retailers in a local market area lowers his price to one of them in order to meet competition, he must then lower it to all his retailer customers in that market.

A related issue is whether a seller can cut his price to one of his customers in a local market area in order to enable this customer, not himself, to meet competition. Thus, can a petroleum refining company reduce its price to one gasoline service station in an area because that station is having competitive difficulties with an adjacent station? The refiner is not reducing his price to meet the competition of other refiners seeking to supply the station; yet unless he reduces price, his customer may either seek out another supplier or go bankrupt. In 1962, the Supreme Court ruled that the refiner *cannot* give such a price reduction to one station without giving it to all the others in the competitive region.

All concealed price concessions are illegal. Price concessions and allowances, such as advertising and brokerage allowances, are permitted provided that they are either uniformly and reasonably available to all buyers or are given for the performance of actual tasks. To give a brokerage allowance to a wholesaler who performs no brokerage services is illegal.

The process by which legality or illegality is determined in respect to the Robinson-Patman Act is generally long, complex, painful, and costly. A complaint can be made by anyone—a customer, a competitor, a noninvolved person, or a government official. A Federal Trade Commission representative will look into the situation, and if he believes there is some basis for an inquiry, a hearing is scheduled. It is an informal hearing at which he listens to evidence. He finally renders a written opinion. This can be appealed to the Federal Trade Commission (FTC) itself, which can then render its own opinion. This in turn can be appealed through the regular federal judiciary system up through the Supreme Court. But the whole procedure can be time-consuming. One famous case took 13 years from beginning to end. It involved several steps during which at various times the FTC remanded the case back to the hearing officer, and then the courts remanded it back to the FTC, and later the Supreme Court remanded it back to the Circuit Court of Appeals.

During the protracted hearings, a restraining order may be in force to halt the offending practice. In the meanwhile other companies live under considerable doubt about what is and is not permissible. Yet the business paralysis predicted by the law's opponents, both in 1914 and 1936, has not materialized. Neither has the idyllic competitive tranquillity predicted by its advocates.

□ RESALE PRICE MAINTENANCE

Resale price maintenance occurs when a seller tries to control the price at which his product can be resold. The facilitating laws are often referred to as "fair-trade" laws. These are state laws which legalize contracts for resale price maintenance within the state. Since the companies involved are generally engaged in interstate commerce, they come under the jurisdiction of the federal antitrust laws, and these, as indicated above, have historically been interpreted to prohibit any form of price fixing. Hence in 1937, Congress passed the Miller-Tydings Act, which gave federal sanction to resale price maintenance contracts that were approved under state laws.

The state laws typically provided that if one retailer of a nationally branded product in a state signed a resale price maintenance contract with the supplying manufacturer, all retailers in the state who handled the product were subject to that agreement, even if they did not sign it themselves. In May 1951, the United States Supreme Court ruled that the Miller-Tydings Act did not apply to nonsigners in interstate commerce; in July 1952, the McGuire Act, restoring the nonsigner clause to validity, became law. However, some state courts have now ruled against the nonsigner clause in the state statutes.

The manufacturer's interest in resale price maintenance generally involves at least one of the following four reasons:

1. Protection of the goodwill attached to his brand that might be dissipated if the brand were sold at lower prices.
2. Protection of certain trade channels who perform desired functions that could not be effectively performed if severe competition forced down retail and wholesale margins.

3. Protection of franchised retailers against competition from retailers who use low-price promotion of national brands to attract customers and then try to switch them to other brands.
4. Maintaining intensive distribution at retail. A brand that is perennially featured at reduced prices by some retailers is in danger of alienating other retailers. The latter will be reluctant to feature it and thereby draw attention to their higher prices. Ultimately they may refuse to carry it.

Retailer interest in resale price maintenance is probably the strongest reason for its existence on the statute books. Small retailers, chiefly druggists, have historically supported the fair-trade laws on the grounds that big chain stores with access to larger trading areas and a broad product mix will "discount" national brands on a loss-leader basis in order to attract patronage for their other products. Thus they subsidize low margins on national brands by higher margins on other products. Ultimately, it is claimed, this works against the public interest because it reduces the number of competitors from among which the public can choose to buy, and ultimately it may lead to exceedingly high prices because the discounters have destroyed the many small retailers whose presence would keep prices at a sensible level.

Opponents of the laws argue that they protect inefficient retailers and wholesalers and prevent more efficient merchants from passing the fruits of their efficiency on to the public. In short, the laws preserve the status quo, keeping the manufacturer and all the trade he deals with from facing the competitive price pressures which are an essential requirement of a free-enterprise system.

Some of the supporters of the fair-trade laws who are particularly disturbed by what they allege is the evil and unfairness of loss-leader pricing say that if more price competition is the goal of the laws' opponents they would be better advised to advocate more vigorous enforcement of the antitrust laws rather than to fight fair-trade laws.

In any case, it seems clear that the fair-trade laws have less potency now than was the case a few years ago. Whereas at one point such laws existed in 45 states, only about half the states had them in 1971. In addition to attacks upon their legality, powerful forces in the nature of economic change have been and are at work to sap their strength. The growth in the number and economic power of discount houses and other mass merchandisers, and the increasing acceptance by consumers of private brands, typically sold at prices below those of manufacturers' brands, have made manufacturers less desirous of fair-trading their products and, in any case, less able to enforce their fair-trade agreements. It seems safe to say that, though fair-trading may continue to have some potency in such areas as drugs and cosmetics, the next several years will continue to witness the decline of resale price maintenance.

UNFAIR PRACTICES ACTS

Though they are of little importance in a prosperous economy, "minimum markup" laws, also called "unfair practices" acts, exist in more than half the states. These normally require that retailers establish prices that exceed costs by at least some specific percentage, usually 6 percent; in some states, wholesalers are required to maintain at least a 2 percent markup. Where such laws exist, they typically provide a basis for determining costs, and provide also for exemptions to the law in order to permit close-out sales, sales to governmental or charitable organizations, damaged-goods sales, or court-ordered sales.

The passing of state unfair practices acts was originally brought about by retailers who wished to protect themselves against the loss-leader pricing tactics of competitors who sought to attract customer traffic by pricing some items at levels so low that they were or seemed to be priced below cost. In the economy of the 1970s, it seems unlikely that such pricing practices are of any material significance, except in regard to such products as cigarettes, which are sometimes used as "loss leaders" to attract customers, and gasoline, which often becomes the subject of price wars among filling stations. Further, critics of such legislation raise questions as to whether customers should not be permitted to purchase products at the lowest possible prices that retailers are willing to charge, and whether it is economically and socially desirable to preserve competition by protecting even the most inefficient retailers.

GENERAL POLICIES OF THE FEDERAL GOVERNMENT

As we indicated in Part 2, the government's economic policies have considerable impact on the behavior and attitudes of ultimate customers; fiscal and monetary policies, and policies regarding credit, have much to do with the money people have to spend and with their willingness to spend it. Alert marketers, therefore, must be aware of governmental policies and, as we suggested in Chapter 13, take them into account in developing marketing strategies.

The indirect impact of governmental policies on prices charged by companies can be considerable. In addition to the overall affect of monetary, fiscal, and credit policies, however, the government, particularly at the national level, has a direct interest in the levels of prices charged by specific industries and sometimes by specific companies. In the 1960s and 1970s, for example, presidential and other types of executive pressures were brought on both the steel and aluminum industries to prevent or reverse increases in prices of various types of steel and aluminum products. United States Steel, Bethlehem Steel, and the Aluminum Company of America, generally considered as influential price leaders in their respective industries, were among the targets of government pressure. Also, in the early 1970s the federal government instituted the practice of "inflation alerts," whereby the President's Council of Economic Advisors held press conferences regarding industries in which management and labor were increasing national inflationary tendencies by what were termed excessive wage-price policies. Though we shall not discuss here the merits or problems that are involved in such situations, it is apparent that businessmen, most particularly those in large companies and in basic industries, must take the possibility of government interest in their pricing policies into account as those policies are established.

Appendix: elasticity of demand

In this chapter, elasticity was defined in terms of the relationship between price and revenue. It may also be defined in terms of the relationship between a price movement and the consequent movement of the number of units sold. The demand for a product is said to be *relatively price elastic* if the percentage change in units sold is greater than the related percentage change in price. It is *relatively price inelastic* if the percentage change in units sold is less than the related percentage change in price. But in making these percentage computations, we must understand that this refers to average changes in prices and sales. Thus in Figure 16-1 when price is dropped from 60 cents to 40 cents, the percentage change is not ($0.60 − $0.40) − $0.60, or 33⅓ percent; it is ($0.60 − $0.40) − ½ ($0.60 + $0.40) = 40 percent. The percentage changes in quantity sold is (400 − 700) − ½ (600 + 700) = 46.1 percent. In this example, the percentage change in sales is more than the percentage change in price. The demand is therefore said to be relatively price elastic.

A simple formula for computing elasticity is

$$\frac{q_0 - q_1}{\frac{1}{2}(q_0 + q_1)} - \frac{p_0 - p_1}{\frac{1}{2}(p_0 + p_1)}$$

where, in Table 16-1 for example, q_0 is 600, q_1 is 800, p_0 is 60 cents, and p_1 is 40 cents. When the solution to the formula is less than 1, demand is *relatively price inelastic;* when it is greater than 1, demand is *relatively price elastic.* When it is exactly 1, there is said to be *unitary elasticity of demand.*

It will be noted that in this example $q_0 - q_1$ is a negative number. Since this kind of analysis deals with absolute numbers only, the negative sign is ignored. But the concept of elasticity is actually much more subtle than is implied here. For example, there is a considerable difference regarding the notion of elasticity "at a point" (say, at point *B* in Figure 16-7) and "arc" elasticity (say, between points *B* and *C*).[12]

Moreover, the coefficient of elasticity may change substantially between different price levels. Thus, realistically, the demand curve for oranges in Figure

[12] For more details, see George J. Stigler, *The Theory of Price,* The Macmillan Company, New York, 1947, pp. 52–59.

FIGURE 16-7
Possible realistic demand curve for oranges

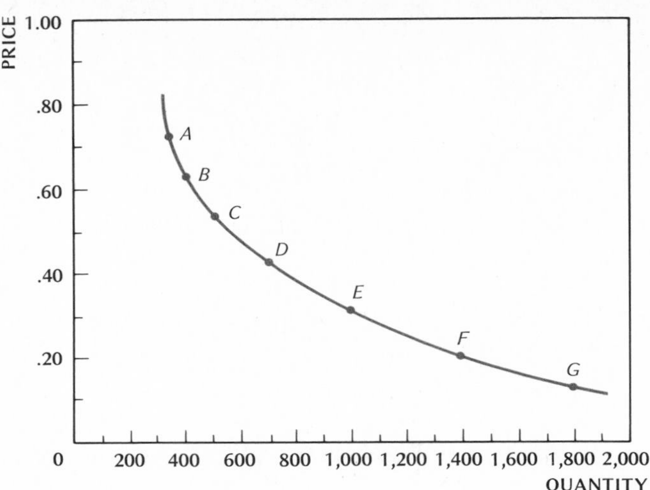

16-1 might be redrawn to look like Figure 16-7. This shows that between 60 and 70 cents the demand for oranges is relatively inelastic, but that as prices go below 50 cents, it gets progressively more elastic. In other words, there may be a solid core of people who will buy oranges whether the price is 60 or 70 cents. However, substantially increasingly larger numbers of people will buy at lower prices, and/or the same people may simply buy more as the price declines further.

Questions

1. Outline the major differences in "real world" pricing practices and economic theory. How do retailer and manufacturer pricing practices differ in this respect?

2. What are the theoretical reasons for the different behavior of prices under conditions of pure competition, monopoly, oligopoly, and monopolistic competition?

3. Would you expect the demand for each of the following products to be relatively price elastic or inelastic? Why?
   a. White bread
   b. Russian black bread
   c. Portable color television

d. Truck tires
e. Farm tractors
f. Aspirin
g. Contact lenses

4. For which of the following products do you think a drop in price would lead to an increase in primary demand? Why?
a. Portable typewriters
b. Station wagons
c. Automobile tires
d. Movie theater tickets
e. Fresh peaches
f. Office copying machines

5. For the same products, what effect, if any, would a drop in price by one firm have on its market share? Why? What factors other than price would be relevant to selective demand for these products?

6. Give some examples of industries where price leadership seems to prevail. For each industry, identify the price leader. What characteristics of the firm, its industry, and its apparent policies have led to the company becoming a price leader? Did the company have any choice in becoming a price leader?

7. Why do different kinds of distribution channels affect price policy? Can you suggest some examples to support the reasons you cite?

8. For the most part, competing brands of aerosol shaving creams are packaged in two sizes to sell at prices of $1.19 and 79 cents, respectively. Would economic theory, as discussed in this chapter, be helpful to a manager in planning the price of a new brand of aerosol shaving cream? Why or why not?

9. Faced with a severe cutback in its military business, Tech-Space Corporation, a medium-sized aerospace contractor, decided to begin efforts to diversify into industrial markets. Through trade contacts, its management learned of the need for a method of controlling vehicles by remote control using technology that did not employ radio signals.

Subsequent product development efforts using advanced electronic circuitry led to a new product which management believed to be significantly superior to any existing product on the market. After a favorable demonstration of the product's features to a large potential customer, Tech-Space devised cost estimates and, on the basis of these estimates, quoted a price of $2,475 to the customer.

The customer responded by indicating that the price quoted was at least two to three times as high as he would consider paying. Further, the product was far too complex and exacting for its needs.

□

TABLE 16-2

Tech-Space Corporation cost estimates

Raw materials	$ 250
Direct labor	250
	500
Manufacturing overhead (150% direct manufacturing cost)	750
Total manufacturing cost	1,250
Engineering overhead (20% total manufacturing cost)	250
Plant cost	1,500
General administration and selling (50% plant cost)	750
	2,250
Profit (10% total cost)	225
Selling price	$2,475

Tech-Space's cost estimates are shown in Table 16-2. On the basis of these estimates and the information presented above,

a. Evaluate Tech-Space's approach to setting prices.
b. How should the company have established its price? Why?
c. What mistakes did Tech-Space make in its overall approach to marketing the product?

10. Since the 1960s, Corning Glass Company has manufactured a patent-protected line of unbreakable dishes known as Centura Ware. These products have been sold, wherever possible, on a resale price maintenance basis. Why do you think Corning decided to utilize resale price maintenance? Was this a wise decision? Why?

11. As a consumer, how are you affected by resale price maintenance? Would your viewpoint change if you were a small retailer? A discount house operator? A manufacturer?

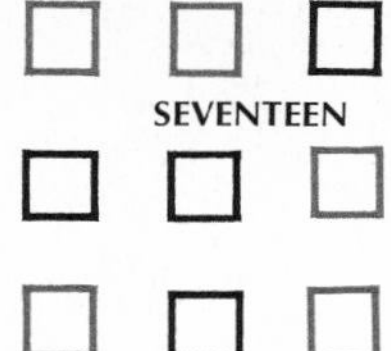

SEVENTEEN

Pricing policies and methods

In Chapter 16, which introduced the complex field of pricing, we drew upon economic theory, basic market and business factors, and governmental policies and regulations to establish an understanding of the general forces that tend to influence prices and their behavior. With that background, this chapter turns to the objectives, policies, and methods that shape the price structures of individual firms. More specifically, we shall consider the nature and usefulness of specific kinds of price objectives and policies, the relationship between pricing and various stages of a product's life cycle, different methods of pricing, and some special factors that apply to the pricing policies of retailers and wholesalers. Before moving into those areas, however, this chapter will deal briefly with prices and the marketing mix, and offer some general observations about the level and location of the price-setting responsibility within companies.

Price and the marketing mix

A central theme of this book is that successful marketing requires the employment of a well-designed marketing strategy, implemented through a well-coordinated marketing mix. This general thesis was advanced in Chapter 1, and in fact serves as the unifying thread of all the chapters in Part 4. Price, in that context, is one element of the mix. It is an extremely important one.

In Chapter 16, Eastern Air Line's shuttle service was cited as an example typifying all the general forces that impinge upon pricing. It serves also as an example of the interplay of marketing mix strategies. Eastern Air Lines had to propose a shuttle price that would satisfy the CAB, appeal to existing and new customers, and bear a relationship to competitors' prices that would presumably attract people who had been using other airlines or other forms of transportation. Price, then, was a major aspect of EAL's strategy. But, to make the shuttle service an effective marketing device, EAL had to have the right *product,* its fleet of propellor aircraft and ancillary services, in the right *place;* though wholesalers and retailers were obviously not facets of the shuttle service, the place function was served by terminals especially designed or modified to service shuttle passengers and their baggage efficiently. Eastern Air Lines also made major efforts to *promote* the shuttle. Newspaper advertisements and other media were intensively used, and the airline actively sought publicity for the service. Finally, of course, EAL had to analyze *customers* and predict their behavior regarding the shuttle, and determine its *costs* in order to appraise the profit possibilities of the new service.

Lower-than-competitive prices are, of course, not always the hallmark of a successful pricing strategy. Consider the psychological aspects of the price policy of a fur salon attempting to convince its customers that its furs are better, and therefore worth more, than the furs in a salon just down the street. The salon may deliberately price at a higher level to imply a higher quality level to women who are willing to pay more for better quality or for whatever "snob appeal" there is in paying a higher price.[1] But if this kind of pricing psychology is going to work, it will do so most effectively only if the other elements of the marketing mix are carefully thought through. It seems likely that the salon's high-price strategy will work best if its furnishings are more tasteful, its personnel more gracious, its services more satisfactory, and its promotions more decorous than those of competitors — all these features may cost money, and in turn may require higher prices to support them. Thus the operating features needed to support the "prestige pricing" may consume part of the prestige prices that the store charges. The general point, of course, is that pricing policies of any type must be consistent with the other elements of a company's marketing mix.

Organizational responsibility for pricing

If prices are an important element of the marketing mix, who sets them in individual firms? As far as medium-size and large manufacturing companies are

[1] For an interesting article on the psychology of price, for both manufacturing and retailing establishments, see Benson P. Shapiro, "The Psychology of Pricing," *Harvard Business Review,* July–August, 1968.

concerned, probably the safest generalization is that it is difficult to generalize. In small companies, it is probable that prices are most frequently established by marketing executives and company presidents. Beyond that level of size, however, one can answer accurately only in terms of specific industries and even specific firms. As we shall point out in Chapter 23, company organization charts and position descriptions seldom make explicit the organizational level and location of pricing responsibility.

It is important in this connection, however, to distinguish between pricing policies and specific prices. Studies have shown that top managements of large firms frequently concern themselves with pricing policies. In oligopolistic industries (see Chapter 16) it is likely that most top managements are involved in the establishment of price policies, as they may also be in industries where legal questions may be involved. Similarly, top managements of large companies with single products (such as Wrigley's gum) or narrow lines of products may play an active role in price policy. Marketing executives almost surely make major inputs to the policy process, but decisions on policy are likely to be joint in nature. In the largest, multidivisional product companies, such as the General Electric Company or General Motors Corporation, price policies are frequently established at the division level and reviewed by the senior corporate officials. On balance, top management's role in pricing policy is probably more active than in any other marketing areas, with the possible exception of product policy.

Prices and other terms of sale for specific products and specific customers, on the other hand, are more likely to be set at lower levels of organization. Since marketers are closest to customers, and because product planning is at least substantially a marketing responsibility, marketing executives almost always play some role in the establishment of prices. Further, field sales organizations sometimes have authority to depart from established prices, within fairly narrow limits, under conditions of competitive necessity. Again, however, we would caution that pricing practices vary so much from industry to industry and from company to company that the comments made here can at best indicate only general tendencies.[2]

Pricing objectives and policies

As companies plan their pricing strategies, they usually do so with specific objectives in mind. Pricing objectives normally derive from overall marketing strategy, and are subject to change as marketing strategy changes in response to competitive conditions and customer behavior. Nevertheless, it is essential

[2] Pricing policies of retail and wholesale organizations will be discussed in the final section of this chapter; comments here refer to manufacturing organizations.

that a company establish its prices with a specific objective or complementary objectives in mind. We shall describe a number of possible objectives in this section, reserving for later in the chapter a more detailed discussion of the methods by which some of them are implemented.

PROFIT

Economic theory typically assumes that a firm prices its product or product line so as to *maximize* its profits in the short run. Although profit is a major consideration in almost every business situation, the idea of short-run profit maximization is in most instances an oversimplification. Few firms are interested only in short-run success, and few know enough about market demand at various price levels (see Chapter 16) to price strictly on a profit maximization basis. In addition, the notion of maximum profit may normally seem to imply high prices, and the latter are apt to invite new competitors. For these reasons, most companies do not employ the objective of profit maximization in the short run. Their concern, rather, is to establish pricing objectives that hopefully will maximize *long-range* profits.

To accomplish this, many companies use a *profit target* in pricing a product or a product line. The target is usually established by specifying the *rate of return* that is desired on the company's product investment, and then pricing so as to achieve that rate of return. This type of pricing objective is commonly referred to as "ROI" (return-on-investment) pricing, which will be discussed in greater detail later in this chapter. Other companies, however, may use "satisfactory" profits as a pricing objective; the use of what is so obviously an ill-defined objective typically stems from uncertainties regarding competitive or customer reaction, or from a lack of knowledge as to costs.

MARKET SHARE

Though profit considerations underlie all marketing activity, many firms establish prices so as to achieve specific market share objectives for their products. Large food manufacturers, as well as firms in the automobile and many other industries, use market share as a major objective in establishing prices. The assumption, of course, is that in the long run an expanding or substantial market share will serve as a source of high profit.

For the most part, companies that employ the achievement of some specified market share as a pricing objective are in oligopolistic industries or monopolistic competition. For them, major price changes are apt to be dangerous or of uncertain value as competitive weapons. This is because they cannot be certain about the degree of elasticity of demand for their products, while they are usually certain that competition will react swiftly to any price changes that appear to cause fluctuations in competitive shares of the market. The tendency, then, is to price so as to achieve some specified market share, and to use service, product quality, and other marketing mix elements to protect or increase the specified share.

FOLLOWING THE LEADER

In Chapter 16, we discussed the phenomenon of price leadership in various industries, and pointed out that industry leaders are typically the largest and most efficient companies. In such industries, competitors often have little choice but to establish pricing objectives that call for following the industry leader. To charge higher prices would decrease selective demand and presumably reduce profits, while lower prices might invoke rapid and vigorous reaction from the leader and other competitors. Thus, in almost any situation where there is an industry leader, the competitors' pricing objective is to follow the top company's prices, or at least to stay "within the ballpark," and to use other competitive devices to achieve success in the marketplace. This type of pricing objective can also be defined as a *low-risk* objective. It seeks to avoid rocking the boat and bringing on retaliatory price warfare, and tends to promote the industry-wide price stability that we referred to in Chapter 16.

It is useful to emphasize that a follow-the-leader pricing objective is not necessarily permanent or unchanging, and that it does not necessarily imply a lack of vigorous competition within a particular industry. American Motors and Chrysler may tend generally to follow General Motors in price ranges, and in particular geographical markets a large oil company may have its prices followed almost slavishly by its competition, but neither situation is unchanging or noncompetitive. American Motors and Chrysler will use advertising, product innovation, and a variety of devices to fight General Motors, and the lesser oil companies will use trading stamps, station location, service, and other competitive weapons against their big competitor. Also either the leader or one of the followers may decide, at any time, that there might be a competitive advantage to be gained by a change in prices.

OTHER PRICING OBJECTIVES

Although profit, market share, and the avoidance of destructive price competition, or some combination of these, are most frequently used as pricing objectives, companies often establish prices with other objectives in mind, Many firms will price so as to create or maintain an *image* for the product or the company. Part of the mystique of a Cadillac or of expensive crystal glassware is created by its high prices; at the other extreme, discount stores and used-car dealers strive by a variety of ways to create a low-price image. As a general rule, retailers, who will be discussed in greater detail in the final section of this chapter, typically strive to create an image for their stores that derives substantially from the level of price charged for the products that they carry.

In establishing prices, companies with long marketing channels—for example, a manufacturer who sells through large distributors to smaller distributors and then to retailers—must have as a pricing objective sufficient *margins* at each level of distribution so as to make their product lines financially attractive at each level of distribution. Manufacturers of prescription drugs or home remedies, for example, often sell through several distribution levels, and a substantial portion of the prices that customers pay goes to the druggist and the wholesaler.

Trade margin considerations are important to manufacturers in another way. Where companies believe that heavy advertising or point-of-sale promotion will help to increase sales, perhaps particularly when a product is new to the market, one objective in establishing price is to make sure that the price is high enough to yield sufficient revenue for extensive promotion. As we shall see in Chapters 20 and 22, advertising and other promotional costs are high for many kinds of consumer goods, and for some industrial products, and their prices must be set with that in mind.

For companies in oligopolistic industries, it can be said that the avoidance of *governmental reaction* is sometimes a pricing objective. As Chapter 16 indicated, the executive branch of the federal government instituted the practice of so-called "inflation alerts" in 1970. In inflationary times, executives of large firms find themselves torn between what they believe to be the need for charging higher prices to cover increased costs, on the one hand, and a desire to avoid either federal pressure of direct price controls, on the other.

Price policies and product life cycles

In Chapter 15, we discussed the concept of product life cycles. Basic to that discussion was the idea that most products go through a cycle of demand that is predictable at least in general terms (see Figure 15-1). In this section, we shall examine the price objectives and policies that are relevant to products at different stages of their life cycles. We shall look first at the pricing of new products, and then move to considerations that affect pricing at the mature stage of a product's existence.

□ PRICING NEW PRODUCTS

When a product first arrives on the market, it is *distinctive* (see Chapter 16) and hence different in some way from anything else that is available. The extent and duration of a product's distinctiveness, and therefore the amount of price discretion available to its seller, depend on how well it is insulated from the competition of substitutes and how rapidly it is likely to be imitated.

Beyond that, the price decision on a new product will depend on many other factors:

What is the potential demand?
How rapidly will the demand develop?
What is the elasticity of demand?
What market segments should be selected for effort?
What are the uses of promotional tactics?
What are the channels of distribution requirements and possibilities?

As marketing managers establish tentative answers to these questions, the question of price becomes one of deciding whether to "skim the cream" off the market with a high price or to penetrate the market more deeply with a lower price. We shall discuss each of these possibilities.

Skimming the cream This approach involves setting a high initial price that skims the cream of demand at the outset and yields high profits in the product's initial on-the-market period, with the anticipation that the price will fall as competitors enter the market. It is a policy that is seldom possible except when the product is a drastic departure from previously available products, such as the original ball-point pen discussed in Chapter 16. There are several reasons why a skim-the-cream policy works:

1. Demand is likely to be relatively inelastic during a novel product's early stages, especially in consumer goods. In the case of ball-point pens, electric shavers, and television sets, customers were uncertain about their value as compared with the accustomed alternatives. When there is little basis for making a self-confident personal evaluation of the product's merits or value, advertising and promotion can do a great deal to connote a price-quality relationship and help sustain a high-price policy at the early stages.
2. A high initial price is an effective way of segmenting the market according to the differing price elasticities in that market. The initial high price captures that segment which is relatively insensitive to price. When it is exhausted, the price is cut to reach a different segment, and so forth. Book publishers often use this device, starting with hard-cover editions, or sometimes, before that, exclusive limited editions, and finally ending up with drugstore-distributed paperback editions selling for 75 cents.
3. Skimming the cream can be a conservative policy pursued in the face of great uncertainty concerning the level and elasticity of potential demand. Hence a high price is set in the hope of quickly recovering the introduction costs if it turns out that there is relatively little demand. If demand is small, such a price policy is often assumed to show that fact while covering the cost of finding out. Then the product can be withdrawn from the market without loss or with minimum loss. One of the obvious difficulties with such an approach is that a company does not really know what the size of the market is without some price experimentation. The assumption of a skim-the-cream pol-

icy that is undertaken for conservative reasons is that the rate of sales at the high price will be a good clue to the rate at lower prices.

4. Finally, skimming the cream is a way of quickly recovering the investment already in the product and of accumulating funds for a subsequent aggressive mass-marketing effort. The policy of quick recovery of the product's development costs often grows out of the expectation that there will be rapid competitive imitation which will force deep price cuts.

Penetration The opposite of the skimming policy is a penetration policy. This employs a low price as the major instrument for rapid penetration or creation of a mass market. The profit objective of a penetration-price policy is generally long term rather than short term.

An aggressive penetration-price policy is generally warranted when one or all of the following conditions exist:

1. There is high short-run price elasticity of demand.
2. Economies of large-scale output are substantial.
3. The public will readily accept the new product.
4. There is strong likelihood of quick competitive imitation.

The penetration-price policy can be aggressive in the sense that it is trying to capture a share of a market from a competing product which it hopes to replace, or that it is trying to create an entirely new market. Thus when cellophane first reached the market, it was aggressively priced to compete with the nontransparent packaging materials it was designed to replace. Henry Ford, on the other hand, offered the Model T automobile at a rock-bottom price in order to create a market, even though he was not then certain that the economies of mass production would get his costs sufficiently under the selling price.

A fourth reason for penetration pricing is the threat of potential competition. A low-price policy may be "exclusionary" in that it allows such a small profit margin that others are discouraged from entering the market. When a potential market is so small that a single plant, for example, can supply a substantial share of the expected demand, a low-price policy may be particularly wise. It captures a large market share quickly, thus discouraging other low-cost producers from entering the field. To encourage them is to encourage overcapacity, which is itself equivalent to encouraging price instability and reduced, if not negative, profits in the long run.

Where potential demand is large and quickly forthcoming, a high-price, high-margin policy is generally unwise. While it would enable a certain amount of skimming before competition forced unit profits down, the trouble with such a policy, especially for relatively undifferentiated branded consumer goods that require a great deal of promotional support, is that it sacrifices long-term market share and profit for short-term benefits. An initial low-price policy may attract numerous customers to the seller's brand quickly. Once he establishes a dominant market position, he is likely to hold a big market share for his brand when competitors enter the field. Hence in the long run he is better off. A big potential market that is likely to develop quickly is generally one that allows plenty of room for several low-cost producers. Since they are likely to enter the market as fast as possible, the original seller is probably wise to set a price at the expected long-run level, with the prime objective of entrenching himself with a large market share that pays off handsomely over a period of time. An example of this type of penetration pricing was Procter and Gamble's Head & Shoulders dandruff-preventive shampoo, introduced in the 1960s. It was believed to be much more effective than existing products and, according to some observers, could have been premium priced. But Procter and Gamble priced low in order to capture a large share of the market and head off potential competition.

PRICING MATURE PRODUCTS

As pointed out in Chapter 15, a product matures, that is, reaches a later stage in its life cycle, in various ways and for various reasons. Pricing then becomes a problem of determining whether the product has in fact reached a mature stage and, if so, what the implications of that maturity are for pricing.

For example, Du Pont first offered nylon as a high-priced specialty product, designed in part to get a quick high profit from a highly segmented market and to recover early its enormous development costs. When the product reached wider consumer acceptance, it was priced for greater market penetration. When substitute synthetic fibers appeared and Du Pont's sheltered position deteriorated, it was priced more like a commodity than a specialty item.

The decline of a distinctive product into the commodity class is generally easier to recognize among consumer than industrial goods. Brand preferences begin to deteriorate, with the leading brands being increasingly less able to command a price premium. There is often a rise of many new manufacturers and private brands. The physical features of different brands tend to become more alike as customer preferences drift increasingly toward the better features. The market gets closer to saturation, as evidenced by a rising ratio of replacement purchases. Production cost-saving opportunities decline as production methods stabilize around the most efficient ones.

The advent of a commodity stage for a product generally calls for a very low-price, low-margin policy to keep private-brand entrants, or, in industrial markets, "minimum service" producers, out of the market and to prevent the gradual market-share growth of lower-priced competitors. Generally the seller will have to decide how much room there is for price discretion. If there is room, he will have to decide what price policy to pursue—generally a low-price policy or a high-price policy. As a rule, the latter involves some efforts at product design differentiation, usually to create the appearance of exclusiveness or superiority, with more selective distribution, more attractive packaging, better retail margins, and with more product-related "free" services. Similarly, in the case of industrial goods, such differentiation might be sought by such efforts as better service, technical assistance, and more rapid delivery.

Pricing methods

Thus far, in this chapter we have been concerned with pricing objectives and policies. In this section, we shall examine some of the more important methods by which *specific* prices are determined. It is important to point out at the outset, however, that pricing methods, like pricing objectives, are not necessarily mutually exclusive. For example, we shall look at *costs* as one method of setting prices, and later at *competitive bidding,* which also involves costs, as a separate method; the reason for separate treatment, of course, is that costs can serve either as a distinct method of establishing prices or as an element of price determination in competitive bidding.

□ COST

Cost is almost universally used as a starting point in the establishment of prices. The reasons are obvious. To stay in business over the long run, any firm must cover all its costs and take in enough additional revenue, as we pointed out in Chapter 13, to make the profit necessary to attract stockholders and other sources of funds. The same statement applies to individual products in a product line. Unless a product is necessary to round out a line, there is no point in continuing to carry it if it does not cover its cost and yield a profit.

But we know also that cost, although critical, is not the only basis for setting price. You will recall from Chapter 16 that cost determines the *shape* of the supply curve, but that it is the relationship between the supply and the demand curves that determines price. The price which a particular seller may set on his product or service may deviate from what seems to be dictated strictly by the shapes and intersection of the supply and demand curves, but in setting his price, he must in some way work within a range of economically viable prices that is suggested by his costs, by customer and demand characteristics, and by competition.

The main use of cost estimates in pricing decisions should be in the determination of the profit consequences of various prices. The main problem in using cost estimates is the difficulty of determining what "cost" is relevant for a particular product in a given time period.

APPROACHES TO DETERMINING COSTS

As suggested in Chapter 13, there are many different ways of defining costs, and there are a number of useful cost concepts. A firm's accounting records describe what costs have been in the past, while the determination of price policy requires knowledge of what costs will be in the future.

Even historical records often have only limited value for cost determination. There is, for example, the problem of *joint costs.* The process of refining crude oil automatically yields gasoline, home heating oil, asphalt, heavy bunker oil, kerosene, and a variety of "light" end products. The determination of what proportion of costs to attribute to each product is far from simple. Allocating the total refinery cost to each product in proportion to the product volume is senseless in view of the big differences in the prices each product can command. But allocation in terms of the price the product can command begs the question of how cost estimates should be used to help make price decisions.

Once basic costs have been determined, the question then is should the price base be full, incremental, or marginal cost, past cost or future cost, short-run cost or long-run cost, variable cost or fixed cost, out-of-pocket cost or book cost?

Full-cost pricing reflects the average total cost of each unit of output plus a margin for profit. While this sounds sensible enough, its workability depends on the costs and practices of competitors. If a competitor's costs are lower and he used the same basis for pricing, his prices will be lower. Hence, unless the first seller has some sort of advantage, that is, some sort of differentiation, such as in product features, in delivery speed, credit, or the location of his stores, he will have to reduce his price regardless of his costs.

Indeed, perhaps the first rule in competitive pricing is that the costs that count are not your own, but those of the industry's *lowest cost (most efficient) producer*. Every other seller must get his own costs down to that level, or take a lower return on investment than that competitor, or differentiate his product and services so that customers will pay more for his brand, or go out of business.

Even if the competitor's total average unit costs are not lower, he may still undersell others because his cost basis is different. He may practice incremental cost pricing instead of full-cost pricing. *Incremental cost* is, as we said in Chapter 13, the additional variable cost sometimes loosely referred to as out-of-pocket cost, associated with an additional unit of output. Thus, suppose a chemical plant operating at 85 percent capacity is selling its current output at 30 cents per pound, 29 cents representing average total unit cost and 1 cent representing profit. Suppose now it is asked to bid on a volume of business that would utilize an additional 5 percent of its capacity. Say the 30-cent average cost consists of 20 cents variable cost and fixed costs of 10 cents per unit at present output, and that the variable cost of using the extra 5 percent of capacity continues to be 20 cents per pound. If the seller uses the 20 cents per pound figure as a basis for bidding on the additional demand, while a competitor whose total costs are only 23 cents uses full cost, the low-cost producer will still be undersold, even though both are bidding on a cost basis.

Incremental cost pricing obviously cannot be sustained forever. In the above example, other customers would ultimately insist on the lower prices given to the last customer and would shop around for sellers who would make such a deal. In time a seller would be selling an increasingly larger proportion of his output at incremental costs, forcing his increasingly smaller number of remaining customers to pay an increasingly higher price in order to cover overhead. This would drive these customers into competitive hands. However, for short periods of time, when fixed costs are covered by other sales or when there are some other long-run benefits to keeping the plant in operation at a high level, incremental cost pricing may make sense. Railroad passenger service, which has historically been priced with little regard to either consumer demand or the prices of competitive means of transportation, might be cited as an example of a failure to consider the possible use of the incremental cost concept.

The complexities of cost analysis should not make us lose sight of a point emphasized early in this subsection—that is, that costs say nothing about customer *demand* and nothing about *competitive* prices. In addition, they say nothing about profit, market share, or other objectives. Thus, although they are important, they are only a starting point in determining price.

□

RATE-OF-RETURN PRICING

Earlier in this chapter, reference was made to rate-of-return or return-on-investment (ROI) pricing. This method of pricing was pioneered in the 1920s by General Motors, and is a relatively sophisticated variant of cost-plus-profit pricing. When used with flexibility, as it is in the automobile and many other industries, this method of pricing allows the consideration of cost, demand, and general market conditions.

Rate-of-return pricing begins by assuming a "normal" sales volume, also known in the automobile industry as "standard" volume, which presumably is less than capacity. Management assumes that the normal volume will be exceeded in some years and not met in others, but that over a period of time sales will average out to the normal or standard volume. Assume that we are considering an automobile manufacturer with a capacity of 1 million units and a "normal" sales volume of 800,000 units. At the latter figure, *all* costs (variable and fixed) are estimated at $2,500 per unit. The total facilities investment is $1 billion. Thus if the target rate-of-return is 25 percent, the required return in dollars will be $250 million (25 percent of $1 billion). At a standard volume of 800,000 units, the $250 million return requires a return of about $312 per car

($250 million divided by 800,000 units). The price of the car is therefore set at, or close to, $2,812. If standard volume and costs have been properly estimated, management can anticipate that, over the years, the company's return will average out to 25 percent even though it will fluctuate on a year-to-year basis.

Rate-of-return pricing, if properly conceived and executed, yields stability in prices over a period of time by accepting lower and higher returns in poor and good years, respectively. Its use, however, must be flexible. Otherwise a company will cut itself off from profit opportunities in good times and sales opportunities in bad times.

ABILITY-TO-PAY PRICING

In the personal service sectors of business, the ability-to-pay method is frequently used as a basis for pricing. Doctors, for example, commonly employ it. A surgeon might charge a field salesman $500 to remove an ulcer and charge the company's sales vice-president $1,500 for a similar operation. Lawyers, consultants, and convention speakers often charge in the same way.

A variant of ability to pay is *benefit given* or *savings achieved.* Thus a lawyer in a personal liability suit will charge some percentage of the amount awarded his client, and some media-buying specialists (see Chapter 22) also use this method of pricing. During the early days of time-and-motion study, some of its practitioners were able to attract clients only by taking their payment as a percentage of the savings achieved, and a few men became wealthy almost overnight. This sort of pricing is now relatively uncommon, or at least is not publicized.

One area where ability-to-pay and benefits-given pricing are still common is in the entertainment business, where the method of a performer's compensation or the rental for a movie is based, respectively, on a royalty per phonograph record sold or on a percent of gross revenue basis. Agents and brokers also, in effect, operate on this basis, although it is not generally thought of in this way.

Pricing which is based on ability to pay or benefits given is obviously oriented heavily toward the problems and needs of the buyer. Cost and rate-of-return pricing are more clearly seller-oriented. In attempting to determine what his price should be, a seller may start with a minimum figure in mind, one that gives him a particular profit at an assumed sales volume, and then experiment to see how high he can go. Thus by trial and error he tries to discover the elasticity of demand for his product, which in turn presumably reflects some combination of the market's ability to pay and the market's perception of benefits received.

BASIC PRICE AND EXTRAS

For many industrial products, prices for various grades, shapes, and qualities of a product are quoted as variations from a single base price. In the steel industry, there is a quoted base price for a certain dimension of steel. Added to it will be *extras* for nonstandard shapes and sizes of the product or *quality extras* for certain performance features.

In the automobile industry, the retail price of a car is quoted for the base model, with the actual selling price dependent on the prices of various extras such as air conditioning and high-performance engines.

In these industries, price changes can take many forms, some of them more or less hidden. Thus the base price of steel may remain stable, but the prices of extras may change drastically. This frequently occurs and is a way of quietly varying the actual price in relation to different levels and elasticities of demand of various market segments without making a public announcement which might adversely affect the buying decisions of nonaffected market sectors.

DISCOUNTS AND DIFFERENTIALS

A single base price is also used to quote different prices to various channels of the trade (that is, trade discounts to jobbers, distributors, wholesalers, retailers), to vary price by the quantity of purchases (quantity discounts), to vary price by season (seasonal discounts), and to specify cash discounts.

As pointed out in Chapter 12, terminology regarding channels of distribution varies greatly from industry to industry. Similarly, pricing language in respect to channels is neither fixed, precise, nor uniform throughout business. Thus in some industries the words *discounts* and *differentials* are used interchangeably, and in others they have distinctively different meanings.

A trade discount refers to the price which, say, the retailer will pay, and it is generally quoted to him as some sort of percentage off the base or list price. Thus a manufacturer quoting an item with a retail list price of $10 will quote the price to the retailer as "$10, 40 percent." This means "40 percent off list," or $6. The price of the same item to the wholesaler may be quoted as "$10, 50 percent," or "$10, 40 percent and 16½ percent," or $5. A discount always involves some sort of reduction from a base price, which may represent a suggested or required resale price.

Discounts may also be used as temporary price cuts to retaliate against the inroads of a superior new product. Thus, when Crest toothpaste received the blessings of the American Dental Association for its claimed effectiveness against tooth decay, Colgate, the market leader, fought back at first with special "2 for 1" and "10 cents off" deals.

The types of differentials and discounts used vary by industry. They are numerous and constantly being added to. The acompanying table is a partial list:

Type of discount or differential	*Example*
Trade discount	For wholesaler or retailer services
Quantity discount	Order-size discount; package size differential
Cash discount	$10 case, with 2 percent off for payment within 30 days
Seasonal discount	Height of season versus off-season prices
Geographic differentials	Zone pricing (East versus West Coast); basing-point pricing
Load-factor differentials	Morning movies; early-week sale prices in supermarkets
Use differentials	Fluid milk versus cheese milk

The usually stated reasons for establishing price differences via discounts and differentials rather than by directly quoting a variety of different or varying prices are:

1. By quoting trade discounts off the retail list, the manufacturer communicates the retail price he believes should be charged; and when there is governmentally supported retail price maintenance (Chapter 16), he in part helps control that price.
2. Trade discounts quickly communicate what the trade is most interested in, namely, its percentage margin, not its unit dollar margin.
3. Discounts and differentials are *flexible*. They permit rapid selective adjustments of actual prices to changing conditions in different markets or trade sectors without requiring frequent and, on the downside, hard-to-reverse base-price adjustments.
4. In the case of seasonal and time-period differentials, these can regularize demand and production and thus achieve an overall operating cost reduction without endangering the profitability of the operation by varying the base price.

One other reason for an elaborate series of discounts and differentials is that it acts as a useful buffer between the base price and changing economic competitive conditions. A drop in demand often hits the discount structure first. It enables the seller to meet competitive conditions here and there without broadcasting a base-price change to the entire market and thereby setting off a spiraling competitive price decline. If adverse economic or competitive conditions are brief and light, no further cuts are required and the former discount structure can be restored in time. If conditions get worse, the gradual discount-adjusting actions of competitors can be closely watched by all sellers so that they can better judge how much of a base-price adjustment is necessary. In short, the process cuts the amount of uncertainty.

NONPRICE DIFFERENTIALS

We have said that under market conditions of oligopoly or monopolistic competition, major sellers offer highly similar products, and active price competition is largely excluded. Where it occurs, it leads to violent price wars. This does not, however, prevent powerful economic and competitive conditions from asserting pressures to which the market must yield. The most common result is an incontinent variety of allowances, deals, and services that are similar to the "price deals" discussed in a later section of this chapter.

At the retail level the most familiar forms of nonprice concessions are all designed to achieve a temporary competitive edge: "games" and puzzle-completion promotion offered by supermarkets or service stations in the 1960s; in-box or send-by-mail premiums, for example, steak knives or coupons inside boxes of detergent; combination offers, such as a toothbrush free with a tube of toothpaste; or 5 cents off coupons. Sometimes these coupons are trial offers to get people to try (sample) a new product.

The theory behind such indirect forms of price competition is that a price cut is hard to restore and can be quickly imitated. A nonprice deal looks to the customer like a "deal"—an extra dividend, a bargain, something special. Once he tries the product, it is felt that he will become habituated to it for a time and buy it the next few times even without the attraction of a deal. Generally, sellers will refrain from constantly "dealing" their products lest this "cheapen" them in the minds of consumers, lead to outright price retaliation, or become a "way of life" from which it is difficult to retreat.

With industrial goods or with wholesalers who handle consumer goods, there is a similar parade of hard-to-imitate or not quickly imitable deals such as special advertising and promotional allowances, freight allowances, margin guarantees, more generous credit terms, free warehousing, and free product applications services.

All these devices enable the seller to attract customers on terms that cannot be as quickly imitated as outright price concessions, and are more flexible than across-the-board price cuts. When competitive conditions require some sort of loosening of the existing terms of trade, these indirect measures tend to be more common at the outset than price adjustments. In many cases the competition will retaliate with a similar and often the identical tactic. But this generally takes time, and in the interval an advantage may be gained by the initiator. Even if imitation occurs, this is generally considered by all sellers to be preferable to direct price competition, with its certainty of immediate imitation and its dangers of regressive price spiraling.

PRODUCT LINES AND PRICE LINES

The existence of different market segments for the same class of product raises the question of product-line price policy. Customers differ with regard to such features as the amount of decorative trim they prefer, say, in a car; the variety of operating features they will pay for, say, in an automatic washing machine; the quality of the material they wish, say, in a suit of clothes; the service or comfort features they prefer, say, in a cross-country airplane trip; the size unit which they prefer to buy, say, the volume capacity of an automatic elevator. Because of these differences, sellers will offer types of products in a variety of sizes, designs, extra operating features, component-part qualities, and so forth. Instead of offering a single design, color, size, and weight of a car, as Henry Ford did at one time in the 1920s, the automobile manufacturer not only offers a wide line of options within a single brand, say, within the Chevrolet line, but he actually offers several lines, each with its own wide line of options.

A product-line policy that exists as a response to differences in customer wishes requires a product-line price policy that reflects and capitalizes on these differences.

There are no common or generalized criteria to show what price differences should or can go with what product differences. Clearly the relative elasticity of demand must be taken into account for each mix of distinguishing product features. Especially important are the *cross elasticities of demand* between feature mixes. Cross elasticity, described in Chapter 16, refers to the relationship between the price of one product and the demand for a possible substitute. Thus as the price of ground beef reaches the vicinity of the price of sirloin steak, the demand for the latter may rise because for a modest additional cost people can have steak instead of hamburger.

Cost to the producer cannot and should not be the deciding basis for differential product-line pricing, but it cannot be ignored. The cost of offering a wide array of product characteristics within a given product class can vary enormously, almost always requiring heavy investment. Even offering two different sized packages of laundry detergent can be costly since it may require a change to different sized package filling and closing machinery or different sized materials handling equipment.

Logically there are important reasons why a 24-ounce box of detergent should carry a price other than precisely twice the ingredient and packaging costs of a 12-ounce package. First, the cost of delivering and selling one 24-ounce package is less than the cost of doing the same thing twice with 12-ounce packages. Second, if the customer consumes 12 ounces a week, the cost of getting her to use one brand two consecutive weeks rather than trying a competitor's at the end of the first week is much less with a 24-ounce package than with a 12-ounce package. The cost of filling one 24-ounce package is less than the cost of filling two 12-ounce packages.

The relative elacticities and cross elasticities of demand among and between modestly differentiated products in the same basic line will obviously affect the price structure of the line, that is, the different prices charged for the different items. The seller's costs are the other blade of the scissors.

But price policy can itself be used to influence cost. If, all things considered, including marketing costs, the seller's per-ounce costs are substantially lower for the 24-ounce package than for the 12-ounce one, he may wish to set his 24-ounce price so low as to switch customers to the latter, thus reducing his total costs.

Another form of price lining is dictated less by differences in product features which the consumer wants than by differences in prices he is willing to pay. Hence housedresses, for example, will be produced to sell variously at $5.95, $6.95, $7.95, and $8.95. (The 95-cent ending is sometimes referred to as a "charm" price. It is said to charm the customer into thinking of a $4.95 item as largely a $4 rather than a $5 item.) There may indeed be quality differences among these different prices, but they are more the result of assumed differences in what different customers are willing to pay than in assumed differences in the product characteristics they prefer. Both types of differences cater to, and capitalize on, marginal differences in the preferences of different sectors of the market for the same generic product. It is also pointed out that such prices often serve as "price points," used for convenience and cost savings in record keeping, as well as for promotional purposes, even though the dresses sold, say, at $5.95 may have varying costs of purchase.

□

PSYCHOLOGICAL PRICING

At the beginning of this chapter, brief mention was made of a fur salon that charged high prices in order to create a quality image for itself and its product line; numerous studies have shown that customers often instinctively assume that the higher priced of two competing brands has greater intrinsic quality.[3] In the preceding paragraph, however, in our discussion of price lining, a different kind of situation was cited. In that situation, a $4.95 price was said to be a "charm" price because customers might think of the item in question as a $4 rather than a $5 item.

Both the $4.95 item and the high-priced furs are examples of *psychological* pricing. The purpose of psychological pricing, in brief, is to use price itself as a means of telling customers something about the product. The high prices of the furs in our salon and the high prices of Cadillacs, F.A.O. Schwarz toys, and Green Giant peas imply a price-quality relationship, and presumably give the customer an assurance of quality that he cannot get from visual inspection of the toy or Green Giant can, or from "kicking the tires" of the Cadillac. There is also implied a prestige of possession — not everyone can afford a Cadillac, nor can all housewives choose Green Giant rather than less expensive peas.

At the other extreme of psychological pricing are the charm prices, including the "odd" (49 cents or $1.99 or $2.99) prices so often used by retailers.

[3] Examples of this phenomenon in respect to razor blades, cooking sherry, and other products are cited in Benson P. Shapiro, "The Psychology of Pricing," *Harvard Business Review*, July–August, 1968, p. 16.

Although little is really known about the reality of customer reactions to such prices, it is generally accepted as an article of faith that charm and odd prices attract price-conscious customers to the products in question and to the stores that offer them.

Another type of psychological pricing is what might be termed *promotional* pricing. This can take many forms. Gasoline stations and tire dealers will advertise less expensive, third line tires, for example, in order to attract customers whom salesmen may then try to "trade up" to second or first line tires. The most common form of promotional pricing occurs in the price *deals* offered by food, toiletry, and other consumer packaged goods manufacturers through retailers. Price deals are used to introduce new products, to take market share from competing products, or to revive the lagging sales of a product that seems to be slipping in popularity.

There are many different kinds of price deals—a walk through a supermarket or chain drugstore will reveal most of them. "Two-for-the-price-of-one," "6 cents off," "special introductory price," "use this 10¢ coupon," "buy the blades and the razor is free"—all these are, in reality, price deals designed to appeal to customers. The ubiquitous trading stamp is regarded by many customers as a form of price deal, although trading stamp companies and retailers prefer to view it as a discount to the customer for paying cash. As in the case of the nonprice differentials discussed earlier, one of the advantages of the price deal to both manufacturer and retailer is that it can be stopped and the regular price restored more easily than if the latter had been formally reduced.

The widespread use of deals in consumer packaged goods industries is often alleged to have been accompanied by abuses of this method of pricing. In the early 1970s, on the basis of allegations that consumers had been deliberately confused or misled, the Food and Drug Administration (FDA) and the Federal Trade Commission (FTC), the federal agencies that share responsibility for administering the Fair Packaging and Labeling Act (1966), were planning new regulations to control "cents-off" promotions. Although the precise nature of the new regulations was not known at the time this book was prepared, a trade magazine listed the following probable major provisions[4]:

The cents-off claim can be made only if a normal selling price has been established for at least 20 days. Substantiating records must be available.

Package labels must state the normal price.

Shipments of cents-off goods must be in an amount not expected to exceed one month's sales. If the special price offering lasts for more than 60 days, the cents-off price automatically becomes the normal selling price.

A cents-off item cannot be the subject of a similar promotion for at least two months after the prior campaign.

[4] Adapted from "Crackdown on Cents-Off," *The Marketing Magazine*, Dec. 1, 1970, pp. 29–30. The magazine indicated that the government agencies had already received objections to the proposals from many manufacturers, wholesalers, and retailers.

A newly introduced product cannot be used for a cents-off promotion until its normal price has been established over a six-month period.

□

COMPETITIVE BIDDING

In Chapter 9, it was pointed out that a substantial proportion of the buying decisions made by business firms, institutions, and government purchasing officials is made on the basis of competitive bids submitted by firms desirous of securing orders or contracts. The idea of competitive bidding is simple—potential suppliers or contractors are asked to submit bids regarding the prices that they will charge to do the job in question. All other things being equal, such as quality, delivery time, and performance, which are often specified by the purchaser, the lowest bidder is awarded the contract.

The pricing methods of bidders, however, are in many instances exceedingly complex. Hundreds of millions of dollars, long lead times, and subcontracts may be involved, as well as intricate production and delivery schedules. Military weapons systems, supersonic planes, or atomic power plants are examples of such complex activities for which bids have to be planned.

It is evident that a substantial number of variables must be taken into account in preparing a competitive bid. A bidder must know his own costs, often at varying levels of capacity, and be able to estimate them for future periods of time. He must also take into account what will happen to his firm if he does not secure the contract. Of at least equal importance, he must make a judgment as to what his competitors will bid. To do this effectively, he must have insight into their capacities and probable commitments, their costs, and how much they want to secure the contract in question. For complicated competitive bidding situations, many firms have developed sophisticated quantitative techniques to help them analyze and evaluate their own and competitors' situations, and to develop prices.[5]

Retail and wholesale pricing

In the preceding sections of this chapter we have made occasional mention of the pricing objectives and methods of retailers and wholesalers. For example, we discussed the price-quality image sought by the fur salon, and later described the extent of price deals that food and drug wholesalers and retailers participate in with the manufacturers that supply them. Though manufacturers and their channels face some common problems in developing pricing objectives and policies, it is useful to highlight some of the factors that are of particular importance in retail and wholesale pricing.

[5] For a description of the complex techniques of analysis that can be used in competitive bidding, see Franz Edelman, "Art and Science of Competitive Bidding," *Harvard Business Review,* July–August, 1965, pp. 53–66.

THE IMPORTANCE OF PRICE

At the risk of possible overstatement, one might say that prices are even more important to wholesalers and retailers then to most manufacturers. Though all three use other elements of the marketing mix in satisfying customer needs and wants, it is probably true that price is more important in determining the *image* of a wholesaler or retail store, or chain of stores, than it is in determining the image of most manufacturers. There are two major reasons for this. First, customers often choose to shop in specific retail stores, or select wholesalers, in terms of the general price levels they believe are offered, and assume that the price levels are indicators of the quality of merchandise and services offered. Discount houses and variety chains, for example, strive to create an image of low-priced but high-quality merchandise, and giant food chains constantly attempt to perpetuate their traditional image as low-priced food retailers. Advertising and promotion, selling, and product policy are of course important, but the nature and quality of these other marketing mix activities relate to the central image that is so largely created by price policy.

The other reason for the importance of price to retail and wholesale establishments relates to the number of items that they carry. Unlike most manufacturers, they offer thousands or tens of thousands of items, and almost any retailer has at least hundreds of items for sale. Under these conditions, channels cannot give individual products or brands the sustained management attention or marketing effort that manufacturers give their products, and hence must rely heavily on their general pricing *policies* to create much of the image or character that attracts customers.

THE IMPORTANCE OF COSTS

Just as prices are of major significance to retailers and wholesalers, so are costs. Their costs are typically much less discretionary than are the costs of most manufacturers. To illustrate, the cost of merchandise that retailers purchase from wholesalers or manufacturers can range as high as 80 percent of the price that the retailer charges, and is seldom below 45 or 50 percent.[6] In addition, retailers and wholesalers find that many other kinds of costs are not very flexible. Rent, heat, and lighting, as well as the wages of sales personnel, are apt to be fixed over a large range of volumes. Hence, a substantial proportion of the costs are not discretionary.

Cost inflexibility becomes particularly important when one considers the fact that channels typically operate on low profit margins. It is generally accepted that most retail stores operate on profit margins that typically do not exceed 4 or 5 percent of sales (see Chapters 9 and 10), and most supermarkets and chain drugstores operate on even lower profit margins. Low profit margins

[6] See the gross margin data for various kinds of businesses in Chapter 10 (retailers) and Chapter 12 (wholesalers).

require, in turn, that wholesalers and retailers price carefully in respect to costs and that they exercise as much control as they can over those portions of their costs which are flexible.

THE INFLUENCE OF WIDE PRODUCT LINES

As indicated, retailers and wholesalers normally offer at least hundreds and frequently thousands of items to their customers. A large supermarket, for example, may stock as many as 7,000 different items. It thus becomes impossible to allocate costs to particular items for pricing purposes, as manufacturers often do. The typical practice, therefore, is to price items at purchase cost (cost of goods sold) plus a percentage markup.[7] In well-managed operations, however, the percentage markup is *not* the same for all items. It is lower, for example, on *price leader* items that are used to attract customers. The usual practice is to use standard markup percentages on certain classifications of items or on items destined for certain retail departments, and to vary these with special prices as required by competition or a desire to convey a particular image, for example, a low-priced one.

PRICING FOR PERISHABLE, FASHION, AND SEASONAL MERCHANDISE

In Chapter 16, we noted that there are special pricing problems for merchandise that is physically perishable, or sold only in certain seasons, or sold on a fashion basis. Strawberries, water skis, and spring dresses are examples of these three kinds of merchandise. Sellers of such items know that the time periods during which the items are demanded will be of limited duration. They know also that they will seldom be able to plan their inventories so that these inventories will be entirely sold out during the selling season, and that it will be impossible (as in the case of strawberries), pointless (the dresses), or expensive (the water skis) to carry the merchandise over into the next selling season.

As a result, sellers know in advance of their selling seasons that there is a good likelihood that they will have to hold *sales* to get rid of unsold merchandise toward the end of the selling season. To avoid losses on such merchandise lines, they typically price an entire line of merchandise at a level high enough to permit a portion of it to be sold on a sale basis late in the season. For example, a department store's entire inventory of spring dresses will be priced so as to yield a profit on the total inventory, even though a portion of that inventory will be offered "on sale" toward the end of the spring selling season. Such price reductions are referred to as "markdowns"; the mechanics of markdowns are discussed in the Appendix.

[7] Markup percentages are discussed in the Appendix.

Questions

1. Suggest some products in respect to which price might be the most important element of the marketing mix, and others where it might be of much less significance. Can you generalize as to the factors that have led to your choices?

2. It has been indicated that it is difficult to generalize about who is responsible for setting prices in manufacturing companies. Why is this so?

3. The statement is often made that a firm sets a low price in order to discourage competitors from entering the market. In what situations might a firm deliberately want to attract competitors into a market and, thus, set a high price?

4. A major study by the Brookings Institution suggested that the most common objective for pricing among large corporations is the achievement of a "target rate of return" on investment. Given this objective, how would you decide between a "skimming" policy and a "penetration" policy in pricing a new product, taking due account of the product life-cycle concept and other relevant considerations? Use a concrete example to illustrate your approach.

5. What are the major differences and similarities between manufacturers' pricing policies and methods and those of retailers and wholesalers?

6. The J. H. Trevant Company, Inc., was a leading producer of men's and women's toiletries. Its 1970 sales totaled $6.5 million, and net profit after taxes amounted to $335,000. Among the products in Trevant's line was a selection of men's toiletries sold under the Rugged Leather brand, including pre-shave lotion, after shave, deodorant, shaving cream, talc, and hair dressing. A significant portion of Trevant's men's toiletries sales was derived from the sale of a Christmas gift set consisting of deodorant, talc, and after shave.

In the spring of 1971, Trevant was approached by National Drug, a chain of 1,500 drugstores. National, which already sold most of the products in the Rugged Leather line, wished to purchase 60,000 gift sets to be sold by National under their own brand name in a specially designed gift box.

National offered to pay 80 cents per set plus the cost of designing a special package. Trevant normally sold its gift sets to the trade for $1.49, and the retail price ranged from $2.79 to $3.50.

Trevant had considerable excess capacity in 1970. Management did not believe it would be possible to utilize this capacity profitably for any other manufacturing activity in the forseeable future.

In 1970, as shown in Table 17-1, Trevant management estimated that the company made a profit of 5 cents on each of the 400,000 gift sets it sold. Prices and sales volume were unchanged since 1970, and management indicated

TABLE 17-1

Trevant Company 1970 profit and loss statement

(Gift sets and overall corporation)

	Rugged Leather gift sets		
	Total	Per gift set	Total company
Gross sales	$596,000	$1.49	$6,800,000
Less returns and allowances	16,000	0.04	300,000
Net sales income	$580,000	$1.45	$6,500,000
Cost of goods sold			
Direct labor	120,000	0.30	1,500,000
Materials	160,000	0.40	1,400,000
Manufacturing overhead	80,000	0.20	1,000,000
	$360,000	$0.90	$3,900,000
Gross margin	220,000	0.55	2,600,000
Expenses			
Selling	88,000	0.22	650,000
Advertising	40,000	0.10	450,000
Administrative expenses and general overhead	72,000	0.18	800,000
Total expenses	$200,000	$0.50	$1,900,000
Net profit before taxes	20,000	0.05	700,000

that the only projected changes in costs for 1971 were a 10 percent increase in corporate advertising expenditures and a $50,000 increase in general management overhead.

Table 17-2 elaborates on certain cost items for Rugged Leather, as well as indicating management's expectations of the costs that would be involved in the acceptance of the National Drug order. Management also knew that National Drug had an excellent credit rating.

a. Should Trevant be interested in the National offer? Why?

b. If management decided that it would be desirable to secure the National Drug business, what price per set should be established? Why?

7. Why are costs important in pricing decisions, and why should they not be the exclusive basis for such decisions? Under what kinds of circumstances might a manufacturer find it useful to price a product below its costs?

8. For a number of years, the purchasing agent of an electric appliance manufacturer had negotiated price reductions with suppliers by informing them of

TABLE 17-2

Explanation of cost items

Returns and allowances	Management expected that returns and allowances would amount to no more than 2 percent of sales to National Drug.
Direct labor	Direct labor expenses were variable, and costs for the special order were expected to be the same as those incurred on other orders for the gift set.
Materials	Material costs were variable, and costs for the special order were expected to be the same as those incurred on other orders, except that National would use a less expensive gift package. The difference was expected to be 8 cents per set.
Manufacturing overhead	This cost was allocated to product groups, that is, gift sets, at the rate of 66 ⅔ percent of direct labor dollars. Total overhead in 1971 was expected to be fixed in total.
Selling expenses	Selling expenses included a commission of 5 percent on net sales income as well as allocated sales expenses. No commission would be paid on the National Drug order. Allocated selling expenses were charged to product groups at the rate of 5 cents per sales dollar. Total allocated selling expenses would not change with the acceptance of the National Drug order.
Advertising expenses	1971 advertising expenses would not be affected by the acceptance of the National order.
Administrative expenses and general overhead	These included both fixed and variable expense items. Management expected that additional costs of $9,000 would result from the acceptance of the National Drug order.

bids entered by competitors. A given supplier, for example, might be told of a lower bid that had been submitted for a certain commodity, then asked if he wished to reduce his original bid price.

Upon the retirement of this purchasing agent, his replacement announced a change in policy. "Hereafter," he stated, "this company will no longer be involved in price jockeying. Price quotations of suppliers will be confidential. Contracts for supply will be granted on the basis of price, quality, technical assistance, delivery, and other relevant considerations."

a. What effect do you think the changes in policy would have on the prices paid for supplied items and commodities?

b. What benefits do you think the new purchasing agent expected to gain by the change in policy? Do you think the change was desirable?

c. As a supplier that had historically bid high, then reduced its prices in subsequent negotiations, how would you modify your approach to bidding after this announcement? Why?

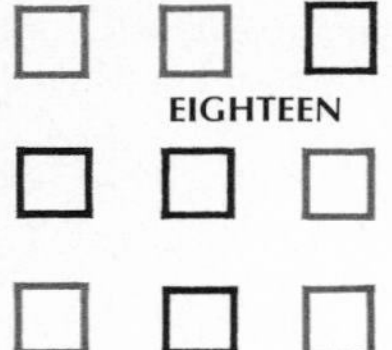

EIGHTEEN

Marketing channel decisions

An important element in the marketing mix of any firm is the system of marketing channels through which products and services are distributed to their ultimate consumers or final users. As pointed out in Chapter 2, the term *marketing channel* refers to a series of marketing institutions through which title to, or control of, a product or service is transferred from producers to consumers or business users. Terms used more or less synonymously include *channels of distribution* and *trade channels*. Note that the key element in defining a marketing channel is the passage of *title* or *control* over goods and services, not their *physical* movement. While channels are closely related to, and often identical with, physical distribution systems, the two differ in many important cases, some of which are mentioned in later sections of this chapter.

CHANNEL ALTERNATIVES

The variety and complexity of marketing channels are suggested by the schematic diagram given in Figure 18-1. In this diagram the various paths taken by manufactured goods are depicted by arrows between successive steps or levels in the channels. Note that a distinction is made between consumer goods and industrial goods. This distinction, which was introduced in Chapter 2, is useful in analyzing channels because the two types of markets differ so greatly, both in terms of logistic requirements and in terms of promotional practices. Never-

FIGURE 18-1
Schematic diagram of possible marketing channels for manufactured products.

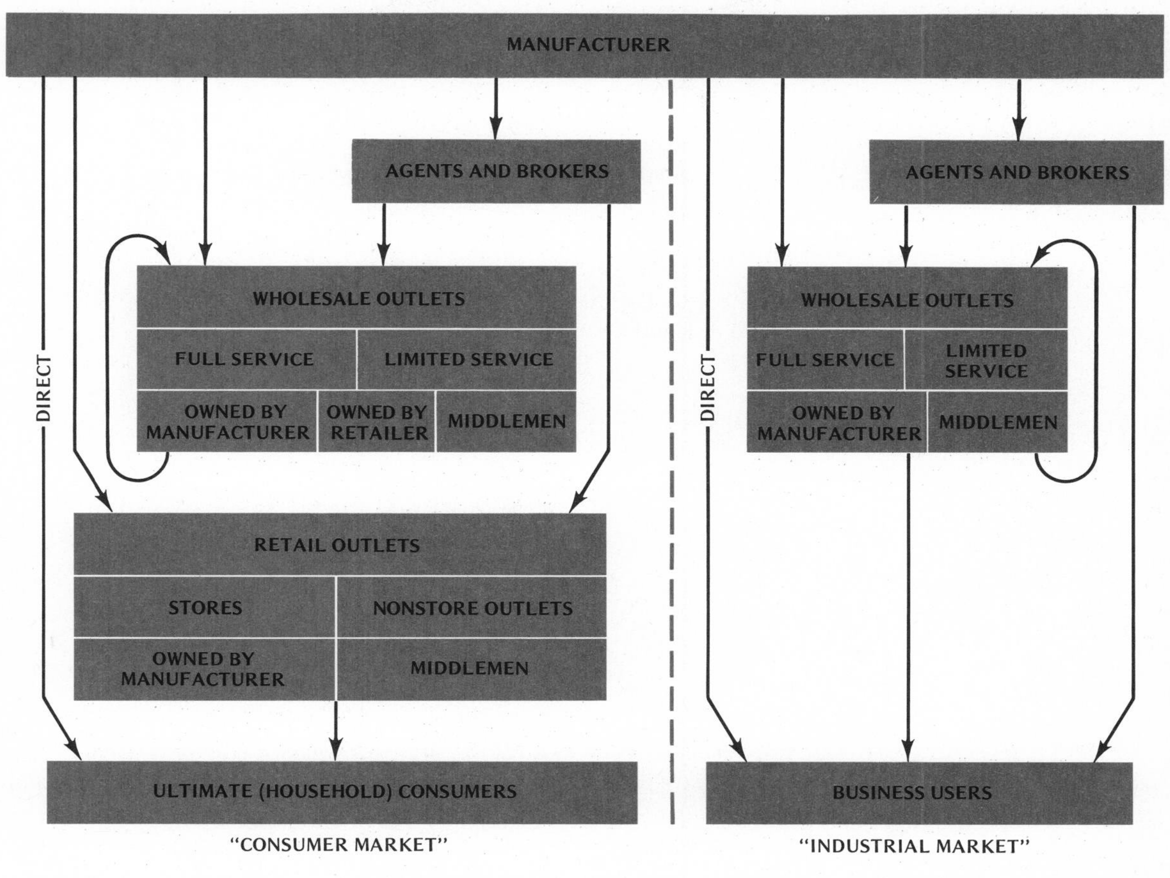

theless, it should be recognized that the separation is to some extent artificial. Many manufacturers sell in both markets, and often the same products are sold in both. For example, many parts and accessories for automobiles and electric appliances are sold to manufacturers as original equipment (OEM) and to consumers as replacements.

The marketing channels used for any particular class of products or services represent the combined effects of a series of decisions made by manufacturers, wholesalers, retailers, business users, and ultimate customers. In the long run, the pattern of these decisions is governed by underlying economic and social conditions which dictate the "best" channels for a given product. In the short run, however, firms must make a series of decisions about channels which may or may not be related to the long-run optimum. Manufacturers must decide on the number and types of dealers and distributors through which products are to be sold. Dealers and distributors, in turn, must select sources of supply for the lines they handle.

In this chapter we outline the major questions involved in channel decisions. We begin with an examination of who makes the channel decision—an issue reflecting the distribution of power among channel members. Thereafter, we will focus our attention on manufacturers' channel decisions, and the factors affecting the channel policies of manufacturers. Channel decisions by retailers and wholesalers have been discussed in Chapters 10 to 12 and will not be restated here.

Who makes channel decisions?

A marketing channel is a loosely connected system comprised of a manufacturer and various combinations of wholesalers, retailers, and ultimate customers. In the absence of single ownership or rigorous contractual agreements, it has no locus of formal power. There is, for example, no designated leader with recognized authority to reward, punish, plan, coordinate, or otherwise dictate the activities of its members. Instead, relationships among channel members are the result of negotiation and mutual agreement.

□ BARGAINING STRENGTH IN CHANNEL RELATIONSHIPS

The outcome of negotiation is invariably affected by the relative bargaining strength of its participants. Among members of a channel, bargaining strength is rarely equal. Sears, a multi-billion-dollar retailer, possesses obvious advantage in negotiating with a small garment manufacturer. Procter and Gamble, a manufacturer of comparable size, clearly deals from a position of power in negotiating arrangements with a small, independent grocery store. In other words, while a marketing channel has no figure of formal authority, it may have a *leader,* in the sense that one of its members possesses strength to influence the decisions of others.

Large manufacturers often have the potential for channel leadership. Their base of economic power permits large-scale promotion to ultimate users and, hence, a potential to establish both primary demand and brand preference. In differentiated markets, the capacity of large manufacturers to generate new products offers a source of unique competitive advantage. Large manufacturers can take the initiative in establishing channels by directing persuasive communication to wholesalers and retailers. They may possess market information, gathered by marketing research, that is valuable to channel intermediaries. In some instances, leadership can be enforced by adopting selective distribution among a limited number of available wholesalers or retailers.

A large retailer or industrial distributor, however, has the benefit of access to large markets that the manufacturer hopes to reach. The larger the franchise of a channel intermediary, the more important is its adoption decision to the manufacturer. The resources, marketing skills, and experience of a competent wholesaler or retailer enable it to reduce inefficiencies in distribution. A distributor may adopt his own brands to compete with those of manufacturers. Remember, too, that ultimate merchandising decisions—what to display, what to promote, and how to price—are made by the retailer or industrial distributor.

Who makes channel decisions therefore depends on the relative bargaining strength of a channel's members. At one extreme, a manufacturer may have almost free choice, as in the case of major oil companies dealing with service station outlets. Alternately, the manufacturer may be forced to take what he can get, as typified by the small garment manufacturer negotiating with Sears, J. C. Penney, or Montgomery Ward. Between these two extremes, manufacturers, wholesalers, and retailers vie in juxtaposition, each using its relative bargaining strength to influence the outcome of channel decisions in its own favor.

Manufacturers' marketing channel decisions

From the standpoint of a manufacturer, marketing channels are viewed essentially as means of reaching markets. In the early stages of economic development, most manufacturers operate on a small scale and sell directly to users, perhaps producing largely to customers' orders rather than in anticipation of them. Under such circumstances, which are typical even today in some of the less-developed nations, reaching the market presents relatively little difficulty and the direct manufacturer-consumer channel predominates. In contrast, large-scale specialized production requires marketing on a much wider geographic basis, and economical operation implies manufacturing in anticipation of demand. As a consequence, the producer loses direct contact with his market. He must develop some organized system for distributing his products or services to many customers scattered over a regional, national, or even international market.

□

THE IMPORTANCE OF MARKETING CHANNEL DECISIONS

The basic object of the manufacturer is to select and develop channels which, in conjunction with the other elements of the marketing program, will maximize the degree of attainment of company goals including profit, stability, and long-term growth. It should be emphasized that channel policies are an integral part of the marketing mix and must be considered in relation to other marketing decisions.

In some instances, the channel decision may be of sufficient importance to *dominate* the formulation of other mix elements. To illustrate, consider the case of the Hanes Corporation. In 1969, Hanes was a leading brand in department store sales of women's hosiery. At that time, the company decided to enter supermarkets and drugstores, where an estimated 600 brands already competed for a substantial proportion of the total hosiery market.[1] The prospective outlets raised an entire new spectrum of marketing requirements. In the self-service shopping environment of supermarkets and drugstore chains, the product would have to be sufficiently attractive to women to sell itself. In a market where hundreds of brands competed, it would need to provide adequate incentive for retailers to stock it.

Hanes's answer was a completely new product, L'eggs, with a totally different marketing program.[2] To facilitate shopping and display, the new product came only in a "one-size-fits-all" form. Its packaging was an eye-catching departure for the hosiery industry: a plastic, egg-shaped container that also reduced the danger of pilferage. An attractive display rack, the L'eggs Boutique, pictured in Figure 18-2, held 288 pairs of hosiery, yet occupied only a 2-foot circle of retail floorspace.

L'eggs were sold on a rack-merchandising basis (see Chapter 12). The display piece and its inventory were made available on consignment with no investment on the retailer's part. Display service and store delivery were provided by uniformed route saleswomen ("L'eggs Ladies") traveling in attractively painted vans. To appeal to the broadest possible consumer segment, L'eggs were priced at the midpoint of the prevailing supermarket and drugstore hosiery price range. The retailer was granted an attractive 35 percent margin.

A $13.5 million consumer advertising campaign supported market introduction. Its central theme, "Our L'eggs fit your legs," was intended to counter an apprehension by women of the one-size hosiery concept, a concern that had been revealed by Hanes's preintroduction marketing research.

L'eggs were introduced in test market in four cities in the United States in April 1970. Within six weeks of introduction, they were the leading hosiery brand. During the first six weeks, 25 percent of all women in the test areas had

[1] "Hosiery in the Supermarkets," *The New York Times*, Apr. 9, 1970, p. 72.

[2] To protect sales of Hanes's existing brands in department stores, the L'eggs package, product, and advertising contained no reference to the Hanes Corporation.

FIGURE 18-2

The "L'eggs Boutique" display rack

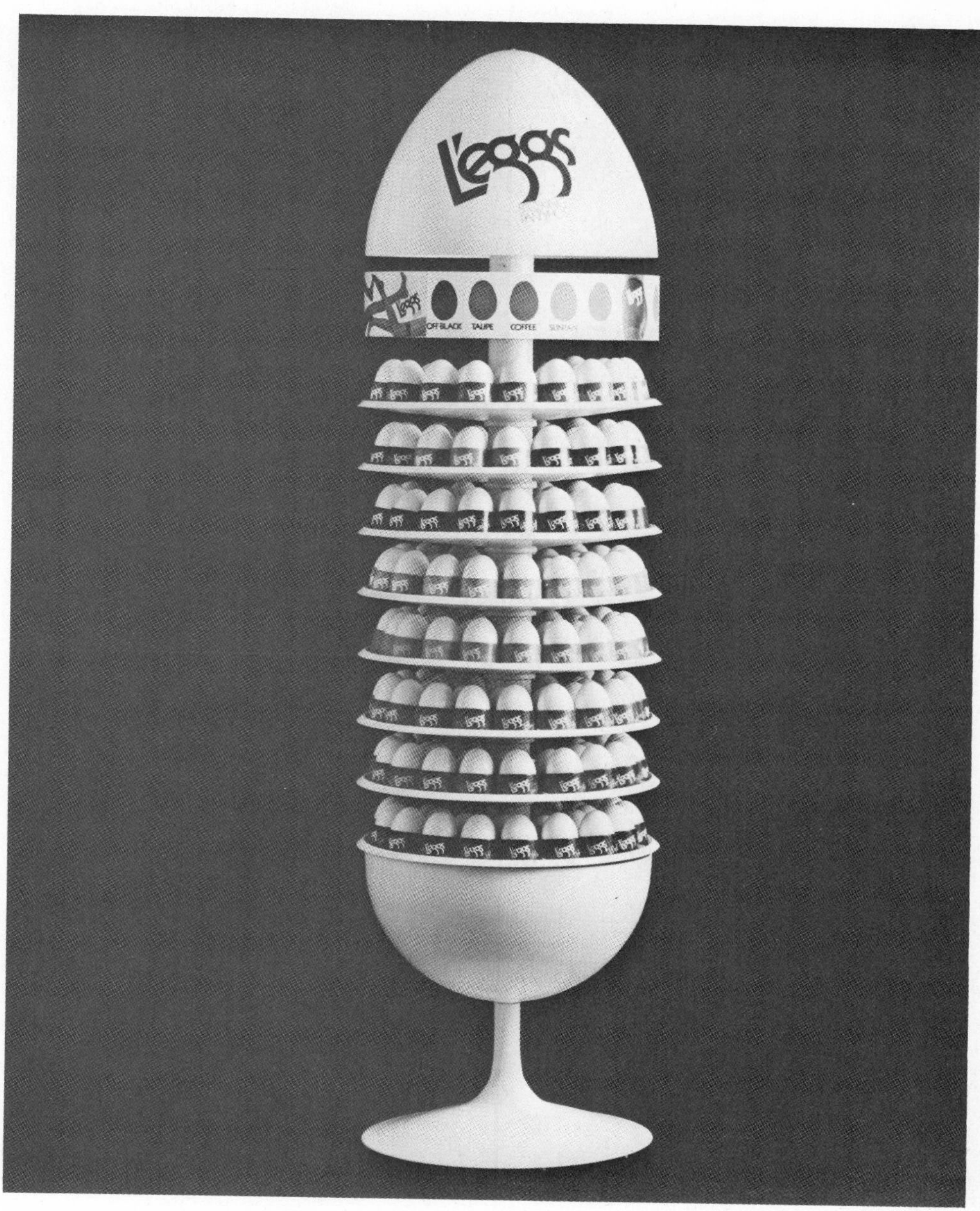

purchased at least one pair, and 50 percent of buyers repurchased within three weeks. Average sales per retail outlet amounted to 100 pairs per week. The product was moved to national supermarket and drug chain distribution in 1971.

L'eggs' marketing program was geared in its entirety to a specific marketing channel. Product, package, display, service, delivery, pricing, advertising, and sales promotion were all designed to be congruent with the purchasing environment and competitive situation in supermarkets and drug chains. Not all marketing programs, of course, are so affected by channel decisions. Nevertheless, the channel decision remains a crucial dimension of the manufacturer's marketing mix and, as such, merits close examination.

Manufacturers' channel decisions involve three general sets of questions. First, there are broad issues of channel policy pertaining to the types and number of channel intermediaries that should be employed. Second, there are questions of selecting specific members to make up the manufacturer's channel. Finally, there are fundamental issues of establishing and maintaining a working relationship with channel intermediaries.

□

CHANNEL POLICY

The channel policy decisions to be made by a manufacturer include: (1) determination of the type of retail outlets (for consumer goods) to be employed, (2) determination of the number of retail outlets, and (3) selection of the number and type of wholesale outlets to be used, if any.

Types of retail outlets For manufacturers of consumer goods, the ultimate market consists of households and individuals who buy products and services for purposes of personal benefit and satisfaction. Ultimate consumers make the majority of their purchases through retail stores, although a small percentage of the retail trade in the United States is conducted through mail-order houses, door-to-door sales organizations, and vending machines.

In Chapter 10, we described three basic criteria for distinguishing among types of retail stores. Our discussion focused on the nature and extent of merchandise lines handled, ownership, and store size. Later, in examining competition among retailers in Chapter 11, we expanded our discussion to include differences in operating methods and variations in level of services offered by different retail establishments. Together, these five dimensions form the basis on which a myriad of different retailer types have evolved in our economy, each with varying abilities to serve the needs and wants of a manufacturer's ultimate consumers.

It is from this vast assortment of types of retail stores that a manufacturer must establish a policy stipulating those which best meet his requirements. In general, the decision is determined by the degree of congruence between the manufacturer's marketing strategy and the capabilities of a particular type of retailer.

For example, many consumers cannot effectively distinguish among different quality levels in jewelry. As proxy measures of quality, they look in part to the price of an item, the image of the store in which it is sold, and the information provided by a store clerk (discounted according to their perception of the clerk's competence). On this basis, a manufacturer of expensive jewelry would seek to select only prestigious jewelry stores with competent personnel that do not generally engage in price discounting.

Toothpaste, on the other hand, is a convenience item. To maximize sales, most manufacturers rely heavily on consumer advertising to establish a brand preference for their product. This strategy cannot be effective unless the brand is readily available and adequately displayed in every type of outlet that consumers normally associate with toothpaste. This includes drugstores, supermarkets, discount drug chains, "Mom and Pop" stores, department stores, and hotel newsstands. The marketing strategy for toothpaste dictates a channel policy of maximizing extent of distribution in all such outlets without regard to other capacities they may possess. For obvious reasons, however, the toothpaste manufacturers would not seek distribution in furniture stores or sewing machine centers.

Ultimately, the importance of selecting the right type of retail outlets stems from the position of the retailer as the point of final contact between the manufacturer's product and its buyer. If the product is inadequately merchandised at this point, or if it is merchandised in a way that is inconsistent with the rest of the marketing program, no amount of effort by the manufacturer can bring about a successful sale.

Number of retail outlets With regard to the number of retail outlets to be employed in a marketing channel, manufacturers' policies may generally be characterized as (1) intensive or general distribution, (2) limited or selective distribution, or (3) exclusive distribution. A policy of *intensive distribution* is aimed at having a product stocked by as many retail outlets as possible. In its most extreme form, this would also imply as many different *types* of outlets as possible. The channel policies of cigarette manufacturers probably represent the most intensive form of distribution attainable in the United States today. It is estimated that there are more than one million retail outlets for cigarettes. At the other extreme are those manufacturers who restrict distribution to one or a few specific stores in each city or trading area, usually operating on the basis of some kind of contractual agreements with these stores or, in some cases, even owning and operating them. This policy is termed *exclusive distribution* in that each outlet or group of outlets has exclusive rights to the product or line of products in its market. In turn, the retailer devotes his efforts largely or exclusively to that product line. Examples of exclusive distribution include automobiles and some brands of men's clothing. Intensive and exclusive distribution policies represent extreme points on a spectrum of channel policies which may be depicted as in Figure 18-3.

Adoption of a definite policy on the number of retail outlets is important because, in the absence of such a policy, distribution systems have a tendency to grow and to become more complex, leading to a host of problems in pricing, selling, and physical distribution, some of which might be avoided by proper channel planning. In general, the manufacturer seeks to have enough outlets to make products readily and conveniently available to customers, but not too many to deal with in terms of reasonable cost and effective control.

Wholesale outlets Manufacturers of both consumer and industrial products must determine what channels of distribution should be used at the wholesale level. As indicated in Figure 18-1, the basic alternatives in the decision are:

1. Manufacturer direct to retailers and/or industrial users
2. Manufacturer to wholesale outlets to retailers and/or industrial users
3. Manufacturer to wholesaler via other wholesale outlets (two or more stages of wholesale distribution)
4. "Dual distribution," involving the use of two or more of the above alternatives for the same product

A manufacturer of consumer goods may choose to *sell direct* to retailers, thereby bypassing wholesalers. Bakeries and dairies adopt direct selling to ensure freshness in their product, for example. Direct selling is more prevalent in industrial markets, however, because industrial buyers often require specialized technical services, both at the time of sale and after the sale. Wholesalers are generally not qualified to provide specialized technical advice to their customers.

The decision to use *wholesalers* typically involves a series of complex tradeoffs among a number of considerations, an examination of which we will

FIGURE 18-3
Range of choice between exclusive and intensive distribution

INCREASING NUMBER AND VARIETY OF OUTLETS →			
EXCLUSIVE DISTRIBUTION	"SELECTIVE" DISTRIBUTION	INTENSIVE WITHIN GIVEN CLASS OR CLASSES OF OUTLETS	INTENSIVE DISTRIBUTION

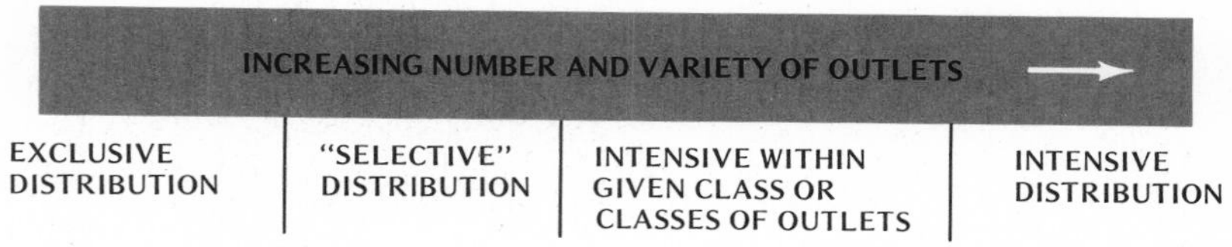

postpone to our discussion of channel policy later in this chapter. One obvious consideration is size. Small manufacturers are generally forced to use wholesalers because they cannot support an adequate selling organization and physical distribution network of their own.

Channels involving more than one level of wholesaling are limited to a few lines of trade in which special circumstances make it necessary, or more efficient, to use a multistage channel. Use of more than one wholesaling level, also called *redistribution,* occurs in the market for automotive parts and supplies, as was described in Chapter 12. Many additional examples can be found in Japan, where the use of three or more wholesaling levels is common for many commodities. There, the small size of most manufacturers, wholesalers, and retailers, plus their limited capital resources, almost dictates the need for additional wholesaling links to perform all necessary channel functions effectively. A typical Japanese channel for a consumer product is illustrated in Figure 18-4.

Dual distribution occurs when a manufacturer markets the same product through two or more different marketing channels. In its most common form, dual distribution involves selling direct to some retailers or industrial users while employing wholesalers to reach others. Note, however, that the term also extends to apply to the practice of selling through different types of retail outlets to reach different customer segments.

A typical example of dual distribution is the marketing of stainless steel by Allegheny Ludlum Steel Corporation. A majority of stainless steel is sold through independent steel warehouses that can provide users with rapid delivery on a full line of steel products. The company also has a direct sales force selling to users who require a high degree of specialized technical service or who, for unexplained reasons, simply prefer to buy direct from the manufacturer.

The Allegheny Ludlum example illustrates the most frequent reason for dual distribution: it is a strategy for reaching different customer segments with different needs or buying behavior. The practice is also used as an intermediate, or transitional, stage in the process of adjusting channels to meet changing market conditions. A second marketing channel is adopted by a manufacturer in anticipation that it will eventually displace his original channel completely.[3]

Having decided to use wholesalers, the manufacturer must also decide on the types and number to employ. The types of available wholesalers were described in detail in Chapter 12, and will not be reviewed again here. In general, the decision criteria here are directly analogous to those involved in selecting types of retailers. Similarly, channel policy as to the number of

[3] For examples of the use of dual distribution in adapting to change, see Martin R. Warshaw, *Effective Selling through Wholesalers,* University of Michigan Bureau of Business Research, Ann Arbor, 1961, Chap. II.

FIGURE 18-4
Typical Japanese marketing channel for a consumer product

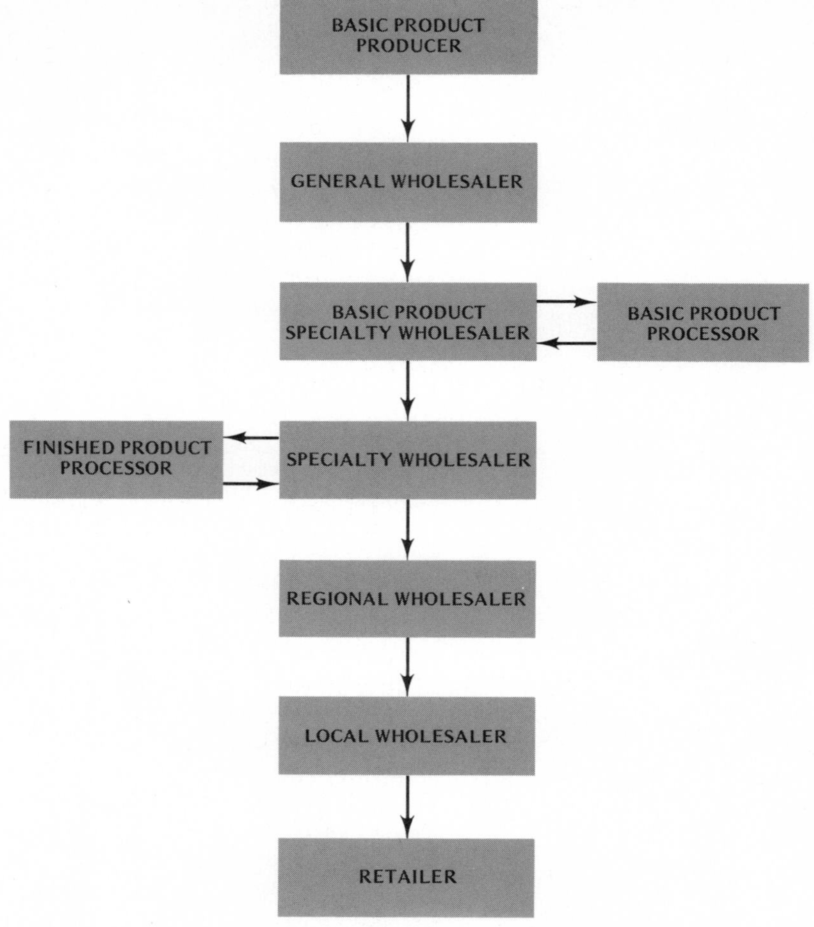

Source: G. A. Elgars and L. P. Dowd, "Wholesaling in Japan," in Robert Bartels (ed), *Comparative Marketing: Wholesaling in Fifteen Companies,* Homewood, Ill., Richard D. Irwin, Inc., 1963, p. 162.

---

wholesalers may be characterized as intensive, selective, or exclusive, just as in the case of retail outlets. To some extent, the policy at the wholesale level is dictated by that at the retail level. Intensive wholesale distribution is not required to reach a small number of retail outlets, while intensive retail distribution usually does require a similar policy at the wholesale level.

SELECTION OF SPECIFIC OUTLETS

Having specified the type and number of wholesalers and retailers to be used, the manufacturer is next faced with decisions of selecting specific outlets for inclusion in his channel. A study conducted by the National Industrial Conference Board revealed that the most important consideration manufacturers rely on in this decision is the credit rating or other indications of the financial strength of a prospective outlet.[4] Apart from protection against default in payment for merchandise, sound financial strength is regarded as an indication of potential for growth and expansion in the future.

Among the many other questions that may be asked of prospective wholesale and retail outlets are the following:

Do they have sound quality of management?
Have they a well-trained and supervised sales force?
Are their facilities neat, well organized, and (for retail outlets) well appointed?
What kind of market coverage do they offer?
Do they carry complementary lines or products?
Do they carry products that conflict with ours?
Can they be counted on to promote our products aggressively?
What kind of services can they be relied upon to extend to customers?
Do they discount prices or adhere to manufacturer's suggested prices and/or prevailing industry price levels?
What levels of inventory can they be expected to maintain?

RELATIONSHIPS WITH RETAIL AND WHOLESALE OUTLETS

In dealing with retail and/or wholesale outlets, other than those actually owned and operated by the manufacturer, a manufacturer must establish policies governing working relationships and roles in carrying out the overall marketing program. Such policies must, of course, be realistic in the context of feasible alternatives and relative bargaining strengths of the parties involved. The principal factors to be considered in this regard are territorial rights, specific services to be performed by each party, provision of facilities or equipment, prices and discount structures, and terms on which sales are made. Any or all of these factors either may be incorporated into formal, contractual agreements between manufacturers and wholesale and/or retail outlets or may simply be customary ways of doing business.

Formal contractual arrangements The most formal and comprehensive set of ground rules for working with marketing channels are those represented by franchise agreements and exclusive agency contracts. Under *franchise agreements,* the manufacturer typically develops operating plans for a line of retail or service business in complete detail. His plans may include guidance for site

[4] *Selecting and Evaluating Distributors,* National Industrial Conference Board, New York, 1965, p. 25.

location, blueprints for buildings, inventory control systems, operating manuals, guidance in financing, centralized purchasing of supplies and equipment, systems of bookkeeping and accounting, and training for employees. The franchisee furnishes capital and initiative, as well as formal agreement to abide by the terms of his contract with the manufacturer.

Franchising is considered to have been a "boom industry" of the 1960s and early 1970s. Its principal advantage to a manufacturer is the control it affords over conditions of sale of his product to the ultimate user, as well as the benefit of standardized operations as an appeal to ultimate customers. In 1969, it was estimated that there were over 800 companies engaged in franchising about 500,000 outlets and service units in the United States; their total sales were thought to exceed $90 billion. With the exception of major oil companies, however, franchise arrangements had not been adopted extensively in Europe and other areas of the world.[5]

Some of the best-known franchised outlets are in the hotel, restaurant, and automobile repair fields. Franchised outlets such as Holiday Inns, Howard Johnson, McDonald's Restaurants, Dairy Queen, Midas, Aamco, and Western Auto Supply are all familiar names to a majority of Americans. Franchising has also been adopted extensively in industrial marketing. Franchised dealers of Snap-On Tools Corporation, for example, sell a full line of hand tools and equipment to industrial plants, while Manpower, Inc., is reported to be the world's largest temporary-help service organization.[6]

In our earlier discussion of quasi-chains in Chapter 11, we mentioned that not all franchise organizations are operated by manufacturers. An example is Lafayette Radio Electronics Corporation, an electronic components retailer. In addition to its 44 company-owned stores, Lafayette also operated 265 franchise stores throughout the United States in early 1971.[7]

A slightly less intimate but still rather formal relationship between a manufacturer and wholesale or retail outlets is the *exclusive agency contract.*[8] Typically such contracts provide the wholesaler, agent, or retailer with *exclusive rights* to sell a product or line of products in a specified territory. The manufacturer may also agree to provide the outlets with various forms of marketing aid such as cooperative advertising and sales training. In return, the wholesale or retail outlet agrees to carry adequate inventories, to devote sales

[5] Charles Seroude and Grady L. West, "Franchising: A Success Package for Small Entrepreneurs," *European Business,* October, 1969, pp. 63–69.

[6] "Franchising: Big Business Destined to Get Bigger in the Industrial Scene," *Industrial Marketing,* September, 1969, p. 69.

[7] "How to Franchise Electronics," *The New York Times,* May 24, 1971, p. 47.

[8] The term *agency* does not necessarily imply that the wholesale or retail outlet acts as the manufacturer's *agent* in a legal sense, although this may be the case as with food brokers in the wholesale distribution of grocery products.

effort to the product and participate in promotional campaigns, to adhere to the supplier's pricing and other policies, to provide product service if needed, and (in some cases) not to stock competing products.

Legal constraints on formal contractual agreements In essence, both franchise systems and exclusive agency contracts represent attempts by the manufacturer and wholesaler to develop a cooperative team which competes with other similar teams, competition within the channel being reduced to a minimum.

There are limits, however, to the degree of cooperation which it is possible to achieve in such systems. Several types of legal requirements must be met. In the first place, under the Clayton Act of 1914, it is illegal to sell goods "on the condition . . . that the purchaser thereof shall not use or deal in the goods . . . of a competitor." This provision applies only in cases where the effect of the agreement "may be to substantially lessen competition or tend to create a monopoly," and it has been enforced only when the seller's market share was "substantial." In one case, for example, a producer of hearing aids had contracts preventing the sale of competitive lines with about 20 percent of all retail dealers in the United States. The federal courts sustained a Federal Trade Commission ruling to the effect that these agreements tended to lessen competition and were illegal. Similar agreements are perfectly legitimate in special circumstances. For instance, oil refiners who provide pumps and storage facilities to their dealers have a right to prevent the use of these facilities for other brands of gasoline since this would lead to deception of the ultimate purchaser.

In view of the doubtful status of exclusive dealing agreements, what benefit do manufacturers get from exclusive agency systems? The answer is that in most cases contracts call for "adequate support" of the supplier's lines by the distributor or dealer. Adequate support may be explicitly defined to include such things as amounts carried in inventory, service facilities, and cooperation in promotional programs. There may be further implicit understandings on this point. Often the agreement to provide adequate support does, in effect, prevent the outlet from engaging in the sale of competitive lines to any significant extent. Obviously the line between legitimate cooperation and illegal coercion is difficult to draw, and many complaints have been issued by the Federal Trade Commission in the attempt to stop practices that are thought to overstep this line.

A common provision of franchise and exclusive agency contracts is a territorial restriction on the distributor's or dealer's operations. This type of restriction may be lawful *unless* it is used in such a way as to restrain competition or create a monopoly. It may also be legal, subject to the same qualification, to require an outlet to handle a full line, so long as this does not involve prohibition on handling competitive lines. Both of these types of exclusive dealing *may*, however, be illegal practices, depending in large part on the context in which they appear. The Federal Trade Commission has frequently attacked so-called full-line forcing and territorial restrictions, and adoption of policies calling for such agreements must be carefully considered in the light of this.

Relationships when formal contracts are not employed When franchise or exclusive agency systems are not employed, there is no binding contractual agreement governing the channel conduct of the manufacturer, his wholesalers, or his retailers. Under these circumstances, a manufacturer must find alternate means of enlisting the cooperation of his channel intermediaries. This is usually accomplished, with varying degrees of success, by careful consideration of the different ways in which business is conducted in trading with middlemen.

Take, for example, the issue of what *price* merchandise will be sold to wholesalers or retailers. If a manufacturer sells to only one type of customer, he may find it possible to set a uniform price for his products. More often, sales are made to several different classes of customers, at both wholesale and retail levels, and in both consumer and industrial markets. This makes it necessary to differentiate prices among types of customers. Typically this is done by establishing a single list or base price—possibly the price at which sales to ultimate consumers or users are supposed to be made—and then developing a series of discounts from the list price for various classes of customers. Thus, for example, a discount of 50 percent may be offered to industrial OEM accounts, 40 percent to distributors and retail chains, and 30 percent to individual retailers. Discount structures must be designed in conformity with the provision of the Robinson-Patman Act, as explained in Chapter 16, and their proper determination presents many difficult problems. In many cases, a manufacturer must accept customary channel margins as *given* and simply allow for them in his price. On the other hand, suppliers of well-established products representing substantial volume to wholesale or retail outlets may be able to dictate lower margins without serious risk.

Terms of sale, including extension of credit, guarantees, and quantity discounts, are frequently as important as prices. *Credit* is significant because it represents the terms on which the seller will finance the buyer's inventories. For instance, if a retailer buys merchandise and forgoes a 2 percent cash discount in order to delay payment by 30 days, he is in effect borrowing money from the seller at an annual interest rate of 24 percent. In some industries, seasonal "datings" may be used (invoices are postdated by a month or more), or the goods may even be provided on consignment, in which case payment is not made until the merchandise is actually sold. Consignment amounts to complete financing of trade inventories by the manufacturer.

Price *guarantees* may be extended to protect the wholesaler or retailer against risks of price declines. Price guarantees are also common in the case of forward purchase contracts, which are advance agreements to purchase goods to be delivered in installments over a period of time. Product guarantees may be offered to protect against the risk of obsolesence brought about by model changes or competitive developments.

Quantity discounts are offered to induce wholesale and retail outlets to buy in larger lots than they otherwise would. Such discounts may apply to individual transactions or to the combined purchases during some specified period such as a month; the last are called *cumulative* quantity discounts. In view of the typical concentration of market potential in a relatively small number of customers, the effect of quantity discounts is usually to accentuate the economic advantages which larger distributors and dealers enjoy. Also, in the case of cumulative discounts, the effect is often to induce vigorous promotional efforts by dealers anxious to attain a higher discount bracket. Both types of discounts must be designed in accordance with the legal requirements of the Robinson-Patman Act, which prohibits discrimination in prices charged to customers on the same level of distribution under certain conditions.

A number of activities can encourage wholesalers or retailers to *promote* a manufacturer's product more aggressively. Cooperative advertising allowances call for the manufacturer to share the cost (usually on a 50-50 basis) of retailer advertising for his product up to some prescribed limit. Usually, the manufacturer also provides mats and other materials necessary for reproduction of the advertisement. Dealer training programs can assist retailers and wholesalers in learning to sell the manufacturer's product more effectively. Contests for dealer salesmen may encourage their selling efforts. Payments for display fixtures serve to ensure favorable presentation in a dealer showroom or retail store.

To illustrate how promotion can be used to enlist the support of channel intermediaries, consider the case of Culligan, Inc. A manufacturer of water softening equipment for household use, Culligan distributed its products through 1,039 independent dealers in 1967.[9] Dealers, in turn, earned their revenue from two principal sources. A majority of income was derived from rental of dealer-owned equipment to householders. A considerably smaller source was the outright sale of water softening equipment.

In 1967, Culligan introduced a new automatic softener, the Aqua-Sensor, specifically designed for sale (not rental) to household customers. The problem

[9] "How Culligan Taught Its Dealers to Lose Customers—at a Profit," *Advertising Age*, Dec. 11, 1967, pp. 46–48.

Culligan confronted was how to get dealers to stock the new product, then to promote it and, finally, to sell it. The problem was particularly difficult because many of the potential buyers were existing rental customers of Culligan dealers.

To encourage stocking, Culligan offered a free Aqua-Sensor (worth $300 to $400) with the first unit purchased by the dealer. Over three-quarters of its dealers responded to this offer, a large number considering that half of Culligan's dealers had sold less than 13 softening units in all of 1966.

To assist dealers in promoting Aqua-Sensor, a program was launched with the aim of identifying likely sales prospects. Cooperative advertising inviting inquiries by household consumers was intended to locate prospects among present nonusers of water softening equipment. A complete mail campaign kit was provided for Culligan dealers to send to their existing rental customers with the monthly bill, and route men were paid for providing names of customers interested in purchasing an Aqua-Sensor. A trade-in program was advertised to present owners of competitive equipment.

To aid dealers in selling to prospects uncovered by these activities, Culligan provided a complete set of merchandising aids for salesmen. These included filmstrips, flip-chart presentations, and sales brochures. The top 100 dealers in Aqua-Sensor sales were given Hawaiian holidays, together with additional sales contest prizes of sports cars and other merchandise.

Channel conflict All the types of arrangements described above are designed to promote cooperation among channel members. Sometimes, however, cooperation breaks down; and, on occasion, actual *conflict* can arise among members of a channel. Conflict may be the result of inadvertent actions of one of the channel members, or it may be brought on deliberately by one party who knowingly seeks personal gain by initiating actions hostile to others.[10]

Manufacturers can create conflict in a variety of ways. They can sell directly to a middleman's customers, thereby competing with him. They can exert undue pressures on middlemen to carry additional inventories or to provide extensive service facilities. A manufacturer may require burdensome payment terms of a middleman, or require heavy promotional support for his products. Often, actions of this kind are initiated by a manufacturer who is himself experiencing difficulties with a marketing program. To meet sales objectives or recoup lost business, the manufacturer may feel that he is forced to revise the design or implementation of his marketing strategy. An outdated or inefficient marketing channel may be the bona fide source of difficulty; it may also be the

[10] For an excellent theoretical examination of channel conflict in a behavioral science framework, see a series of five articles in Louis W. Stern, *Distribution Channels: Behavioral Dimensions*, Houghton Mifflin Company, Boston, 1969, pp. 155–224.

"scapegoat" for other fundamental problems in remaining elements of the marketing mix.

Middlemen can create conflict by their demands on manufacturers for price discounts, special promotional allowances, special deliveries, and shipping arrangements, or price and product guarantees on merchandise purchased. The decision by a retailer or wholesaler to adopt his own brands can also lead to conflict in a channel.

Almost invariably, the origins of channel conflict can be traced to changes in the market environment, many of which were discussed in Chapter 11 and the concluding section of Chapter 12. The need for change often emanates from ultimate customers. As their wants and buying behavior shift over a period of time, marketing institutions are forced to respond in order to survive. In some instances, entirely new and more efficient classes of institutions come into existence. The result is a growing tension on traditional institutions and traditional relationships within a marketing channel.

Over the long term, some degree of conflict within any marketing channel is almost inevitable. Although rendering the channel at least temporarily dysfunctional for those involved, its eventual consequence is likely to be a more efficient system of distribution within the economy.

Factors affecting marketing channel policies

The major classes of factors to be considered in formulating channel policy are the nature of the product, its ultimate buyers, the nature of available retail and wholesale outlets, competition, legal constraints, other elements of the marketing mix, and miscellaneous other factors.

□ THE NATURE OF THE PRODUCT

Marketing channel requirements are dictated in part by the nature of the product itself. Among the relevant product attributes in this connection are physical perishability, degree of product standardization, unit value, product bulk, and service requirements.

Physical perishability Perishable products are usually distributed through relatively short channels because of the obvious dangers associated with delays and repeated handling.

Thus, for example, fresh produce passes through a short channel in comparison with nonperishable farm products such as grain. Individual product farmers or cooperative associations sell to truck buyers or ship to city markets, where the goods are purchased directly by food chains or by jobbers for immediate delivery to independent food stores and institutions. This system is costly and inefficient, but no practical alternative has yet been devised. Fresh bread and milk are distributed by wholesale bakers and dairies via trucks directly to individual retail outlets, again an expensive form of marketing but seemingly necessary because of perishability.

Degree of product standardization Unstandardized goods also usually pass through short channels because of the need for direct contact between producers and users. Standardized machine tools, for instance, are commonly handled by wholesale distributors; custom-built machines or those requiring special design or installation services are typically sold direct by manufacturer to user. Among consumer goods, fashion merchandise such as women's apparel affords a similar example of lack of standardization. A rapid rate of fashion obsolescence is also analogous to perishability. For both of these reasons, it is essential for manufacturers to maintain continuous contact with retail stores, utilizing feedback information on consumer reactions as a basis for production planning. The system of retail store buyers' visiting central markets periodically to select merchandise is a cumbersome and expensive one, but meets the need for direct contact.

Unit value In Chapter 12, we described how the use of wholesalers, as opposed to selling direct, resulted in a smaller number of required *market contacts* between manufacturers and ultimate customers. In Figure 12-1, for example, it was shown that in a hypothetical market consisting of 5 manufacturers and 5 customers, 25 contacts were required for direct selling while only 10 contacts were necessary when a wholesaler was employed.

Now suppose that each of these 5 customers makes 6 purchases per year from each of the 5 manufacturers. Then the total number of transactions per year will be $25 \times 6 = 150$ if manufacturers sell directly to customers. If there is a basic cost of $10 involved for each transaction (this might include such items as the cost of a saleman's call on the customer and paperwork), then the total transaction cost is $1,500 per year if manufacturers sell direct. When a wholesaler is used, the total number of transactions per year is reduced to $10 \times 6 = 60$, and the total transaction cost is reduced to $600.

How does unit value of product enter into this situation? Suppose, in the hypothetical case we have depicted, that customers buy one unit at a time and that the value of each manufacturer's product is $30 per unit. Then, for direct selling, the transaction cost as a *percentage of sales* will be $1,500 (the total cost of 150 transactions) divided by $4,500 (the total value of the product sold) or 33⅓ percent. When products are sold through a wholesaler, this is reduced to $600 ÷ $4,500 = 13⅓ percent. On the other hand, if the unit value of each manufacturer's product were $100, the transaction cost would be 10 percent of sales under direct distribution and 4 percent of sales with a wholesaler. The wholesaler's economic advantage, while still present, is less "important" in relation to the total sales volume of the system.

In brief, the significance of unit value is in determining how important the higher costs of direct marketing are in relation to sales. Since there are almost always some benefits in having direct contact with customers, the manufacturer may be willing to incur costs of 2 percent of sales in a situation in which marketing through wholesalers would cost just under 1 percent. If the figures are 10 percent and 4 percent, however, it may not be deemed worthwhile.

Product bulk Another product attribute of some importance in formulating marketing channel policy is that of product bulk. By *bulk* is meant both the size and the weight of a product in relation to its value. A very bulky product, then, is one with very low value density, such as brick or cement, while the other extreme is represented by such goods as precious stones. Bulk affects marketing channels in two ways. First, in an indirect sense, bulk is one of the determinants of the location of industry. Very bulky products cannot afford shipment over long distances and hence are generally produced in many relatively small plants located near points of demand. This, in turn, makes it easier for producers to make direct contact with customers. A good example is the soft-drink bottling industry with local plants in many markets, distributing through truck salesmen to retail food stores, soda fountains, and vending machines. If shipment over longer distances were economical, it is a virtual certainty that soft drinks would be distributed primarily through wholesalers.

Second, bulk also affects marketing channels in that when physical handling costs are high, there is great pressure to ship goods in quantities sufficient to qualify for carload or truckload transportation rates, to utilize mechanized handling equipment, and to minimize the number of times products are loaded, unloaded, and handled. For the most part these factors tend to encourage the use of wholesalers since retailers or industrial users seldom buy in economical shipping quantities. On the other hand, when typical purchase quantities are very large, intermediate handling is eliminated as much as possible.

Service requirements For products requiring specialized sales, installation, and repair services, adequate service skills and facilities may be a prime requirement for effective marketing. It is seldom possible simply to entrust servicing responsibilities to distributors or dealers without any provision for training and controlling their activities. Coordination and quality control of product service are, in fact, a major purpose of many franchise and exclusive agency systems. In extreme cases, the inability or unwillingness of existing channels to provide service may force manufacturers to sell direct or to utilize unorthodox channels. By the same token, distributors and dealers are entitled to expect sufficient compensation for servicing activities, and this often plays a part in their decisions whether to handle a product.

THE ULTIMATE BUYERS

Since marketing channels represent links between producers and their markets, it is logical that channel decisions depend in large part on the number and types of ultimate buyers who comprise the market. An obvious consideration is the number and location of ultimate buyers. At one extreme, some food and drug products are used by virtually all households, scattered throughout a broad geographic area. In contrast, many industrial products are used by only a few business concerns with offices and plants concentrated in a few industrial centers. This point in itself goes far toward explaining the predominance of short marketing channels for industrial products, and the insignificance of direct marketing for most consumer goods.

Of major importance, too, is the typical buying pattern of customers or users. This buying pattern involves the following considerations:

1. Total average demand per time period per customer and distribution among customers
2. Frequency of purchases and average purchase quantity
3. Nature and extent of planning associated with purchases
4. Postponability of purchases
5. Relation of purchases of product to purchases of other products

With regard to total demand and its distribution among customers, it is usual to find that a small fraction of the total number of buyers account for a disproportionately large share of total purchases. In the case of industrial products, the reasons are obvious. A light machine tool, for example, may be sold to companies in many different industries; some may use it in production, others only for maintenance. If differences of this sort are sufficiently marked, it may be desirable to designate them as separate markets and use entirely different channels to reach them. Even within a single industry, a few firms will account for most of the total demand simply because of the concentration of the industry's activity. It is perhaps less commonly recognized that ultimate customer demand for many products follows a rather skewed distribution among households. The deviations from the average are not, however, so great as to dictate complete segmentation and the use of entirely different channels.

Given the level of total demand, a key factor in channel decisions is the frequency and average quantity of purchases. (For a customer with given total purchases per time period, frequency and average amount are inversely related.) The impact of purchase quantities can be seen in our previous example illustrating relative transaction costs under conditions of direct selling versus use of wholesalers (pp. 480–481). There, it was assumed each transaction involved a cost of $10 and that total dollar purchases by each customer from each manufacturer were known and equal to one unit every two months. Now suppose that some customers buy frequently in small quantities and others infrequently in large lots. Suppose, in particular, that customer 1 buys only once per year in quantities of six units while customer 2 buys six times. Serving customer 2 will involve six times as great a transaction cost per year as serving customer 1. Clearly, it is more feasible to sell direct to the customer who buys in larger quantities.

How valid is it to treat marketing costs as variable in relation to number of transactions? Clearly, not all, or even most, costs of distribution vary in this way. But many cost elements, including clerical costs associated with handling orders, shipping, and billing, as well as some components of sales and order assembly *are* roughly constant on a per transaction basis and therefore are variable in relation to the number of transactions.

The relationship between transaction costs and order size is of fundamental importance in channel policies. It is largely because of the diseconomies of handling many small orders that manufacturers of many products, including tobacco products, drugs and drug sundries, hardware, industrial supplies, and household paper goods, rely mostly on wholesalers for distribution. The wholesaler can reduce these costs by combining the products of several producers in a single transaction.

For some consumer products, the nature and extent of purchase planning may be relevant to the choice of marketing channels. The fact that some goods are often bought on impulse has encouraged an intensive distribution policy, including many types of retail outlets beyond those normally associated with a product. Quite a different problem is presented by products for which consumers want to shop, that is, compare styles, prices, etc., at the time of purchase. Such products must be sold through stores which permit efficient comparisons, either within the store, for example large department stores, or in adjacent stores, which implies stores located in downtown or suburban shopping concentrations.

Some purchases cannot be postponed for very long. Examples are prescription drugs and replacement parts for industrial machinery and automobiles. To the extent that emergency demands must be met, marketing channels must provide widespread and ready availability. The result is often high marketing costs arising from a large number of outlets selling rather small quantities in a sporadic and unpredictable pattern.

□ NATURE OF AVAILABLE RETAIL AND WHOLESALE OUTLETS

After analyzing the characteristics of ultimate customers or users of a product in relation to the product itself, the manufacturer must first decide what types of outlets are to be employed at this final stage in the channel. For most consumer goods, as indicated previously, the final stage of the channel will consist of a fairly large number of retail stores. Similarly, some industrial products, especially low-priced standard supply items, will be sold to their users by many small wholesalers, sometimes called *dealers*. In either case, whenever the final stage of the channel involves numerous small outlets spread over an extensive area, decisions must then be made regarding links in the channel between the producer and the final stage. The decision criteria are similar to those used to describe the ultimate buyers. Specifically, the decision either to sell direct to retail outlets or to use one or more levels of wholesale intermediaries should take into consideration the number, location, size distribution, product lines, buying patterns, and service requirements of retailers.

The number, location, size distribution, and product lines of retail outlets are important primarily as determinants of the distribution and average size of orders that retailers may be expected to place for a given supplier's product line. When there are many typically small outlets scattered over a national or regional market, intensive distribution is desired; and when the product line represents only a small part of the stores' total line, most retailers' orders will be too small to justify direct contact. A good example is in the drug trade. Any one manufacturer supplies only a few of the thousands of items stocked by most stores; the stores, in turn, are numerous, the vast majority are small independents, and they are widely scattered. As a result, even large manufacturers of drug and proprietary products usually rely primarily on wholesalers to cultivate their markets.

Large orders by retailers may result from any one or a combination of several factors: large outlets, dominance by chains, geographic concentration of stores, or narrow product lines. As one example, consider the musical instrument trade. There are relatively few music stores in total, virtually all of them are located in large urban markets, and their product lines are highly specialized in comparison with those of drugstores. A different combination of these factors is present in food retailing. Although there are many food stores with diversified product lines, chains, including quasi-chains, account for a large share of the total market. Many food manufacturers find that chains, voluntaries, and cooperatives, ordering in large quantities for warehouse delivery, represent three-fourths or more of their total sales. A common policy in this industry is to set some minimum standard for direct accounts and then to utilize separate channels—wholesalers or brokers—to reach the remaining outlets.

Given the number, size, and location of retail outlets, the amounts ordered by them at any one time from a manufacturer depend on the frequency with which purchases are made. The implications of purchase size and frequency have been explained in the previous section. At this point it may be added that many retailers deliberately adopt a hand-to-mouth buying policy, placing frequent orders for very small amounts of a product. Such a policy reflects concern—sometimes exaggerated—with the costs and risks of carrying goods in inventory.

In most lines of business there are fairly standard, well-recognized patterns of *services* required of, or expected by, retail outlets. These include frequency of delivery, credit (terms of sale), return privileges, and technical assistance. Service policies have been discussed from both the manufacturer's and the middleman's points of view in previous sections. With regard to the manufacturer's channel policies, the point is simply that his ability and willingness to provide the kinds of services expected by retailers may condition the decision to sell direct to them.

Essentially the same considerations as outlined above for retail outlets apply to the manufacturer's policy with respect to wholesale outlets. One should realize, however, that while a manufacturer may *want* to obtain certain outlets for his channel, they may not be available. A good example is found in the case of "Princess Housewares GmbH," the German subsidiary of a large United States manufacturer of electrical appliances.[11] A major element of the marketing strategy of the United States parent company was to place heavy reliance on wholesaler distributors to promote its products aggressively. It was unlikely, however, that German *grosshändlers* (wholesale distributors) could be relied on for aggressive promotional support of the Princess line. Accordingly, the German subsidiary had to look for alternative methods of distribution and a different marketing strategy from that adopted in the United States.

□

COMPETITION

The nature and extent of competition in an industry may have an important bearing on marketing channels. When several manufacturers offer very similar products to the same markets, it is natural that all of them should seek to employ essentially the same channels. Indeed, it may be regarded as important to have a product carried by a group of outlets partly because competitive products are stocked by them. This leads to intense rivalry in the so-called battle for shelf space, especially in the food, beverage, and drug industries. Another dimension may be added to this rivalry if retailers or wholesalers adopt their own private brands in addition to selling manufacturers' brands. In extreme cases such as dairy products, cigarettes, and fresh baked goods, the competition for space may be so great that channel policies are reduced for the most part to "getting any outlets we can get."

Competition also affects channel policies indirectly through its impact on

[11] This example is based on information contained in the case study, "Princess Housewares GmbH (A)," Harvard Business School and the Institut Européen d'Administration des Affaires (INSEAD), 1968.

promotional policies. Channels are chosen, in the final analysis, to perform certain specified marketing tasks. If the nature of competition is such as to call for a particular combination of promotional activities, channels must be selected partly on the basis of their ability and willingness to carry out this promotional program.

LEGAL CONSTRAINTS

Because relationships among manufacturers, wholesale outlets, retail outlets, and customers represent an important part of the operation of a market economy, it is not surprising that such relationships are subject to antitrust laws and other statutory and administrative regulations. In the United States, both federal and state statutes, judicial decisions, and administrative decisions impose constraints on marketing channel decisions by private business. No attempt is made to provide a comprehensive survey of these topics here; only a few of the more important legal considerations are discussed.

A basic constraint on actions by manufacturers and middlemen is that any type of conspiracy or collusion among competitors regarding channels is per se unlawful. Thus, it would be illegal for manufacturers in an industry to agree, for example, not to sell to chains. Similarly, groups of wholesalers have been found guilty of violations in several cases involving mutual agreement on definitions and lists of "qualified" wholesalers in a line of trade. These agreements were intended to discourage suppliers from selling to "unorthodox" types of distributors and/or retail chain organizations.

When a manufacturer follows any kind of *selective* distribution policy, the problem may arise that some outlets which want to handle his product line do not meet his criteria for so doing. In general, the seller in such situations has a right to *refuse to sell*. Only in cases where the refusal is employed in an attempt to attain a monopoly does the law restrict this right. As a practical matter, it may be well-nigh impossible to prevent "unauthorized" channels from getting goods. This problem has been a serious one for some manufacturers seeking to maintain fair trade resale prices on widely advertised merchandise.

The legal constraints on franchise and exclusive agency contracts were discussed in a previous section of this chapter.

Apart from the general constraints discussed above, there are various federal and state laws affecting channel policies in specific industries or trades. The licensing of alcoholic beverage outlets is a case in point.

CHANNEL POLICIES AND THE MARKETING MIX

It has been emphasized at various points in this chapter that decisions about marketing channels comprise only one part of the "mix" of marketing policies and procedures employed by the firm. As implied by the case discussion of

L'eggs hosiery, it is essential that these various policies be combined into a consistent program, the effectiveness of which depends on the collective impact of all mix elements rather than on any one of them. The relationships between marketing channels and other elements of the mix will now be considered briefly.

The starting point in planning any marketing program is *demand analysis:* the estimation of what types of products and services, in what quantities, at what times, and under what conditions, are or might be desired by consumers or by industry. Channel policies affect demand analysis in two important respects. First, to the extent that procedures rely on information about demand that is filtered through one or more middlemen, the information may become distorted in the process. Such distortion arises only partly because of inaccuracies or biases in reporting; it also reflects the very real influence that wholesale and retail outlets exert on demand. Channel outlets can be very useful sources of demand information, and their cooperation is invaluable in some kinds of marketing research, especially in marketing testing.

Second, marketing channels affect demand through their inventory and purchasing policies. This can best be explained through a simple hypothetical example. Consider the pattern of demand for a product depicted in Figure 18-5. This graph represents weekly retail sales data, and it has been assumed that variations in weekly sales are subject to cyclical, seasonal, and random (irregular) influences. If a manufacturer of this product sold direct to consumers, statistical analyses of variations in demand could be employed to determine optimum production schedules and inventory policies. But if the manufacturer sells to middlemen, who resell to consumers, his demand pattern is not the same as that depicted in Figure 18-5. The inventory and ordering policies of retailers and wholesalers tend to distort the pattern and, in most cases, to exaggerate the variations in it. When demand starts to decline, as it does from period 6 in Figure 18-5, there is a lag in the response of middlemen. Then, when the decline becomes apparent through sharply reduced rates of turnover (commonly used control measures in both retailing and wholesaling), purchases are cut back drastically. In similar fashion, when demand increases, demand by outlets will lag behind and then gain sharply as the pipelines are refilled. These effects on the demand pattern are shown in Figure 18-5. When two or more levels of outlets are involved in a channel, the discrepancies between manufacturers' sales and sales to consumers or users are even greater.[12]

[12] If middlemen's ordering policies are known and if they can satisfactorily be expressed in a few "decision rule" equations, it is possible to *simulate* patterns of demand as a basis for determining production schedules and inventory policies. For an extended illustration, see Jay W. Forrester, "Industrial Dynamics: A Major Breakthrough for Decision Makers," *Harvard Business Review,* July–August, 1958, pp. 37–66.

FIGURE 18-5

Effects of marketing channels on variations in demand

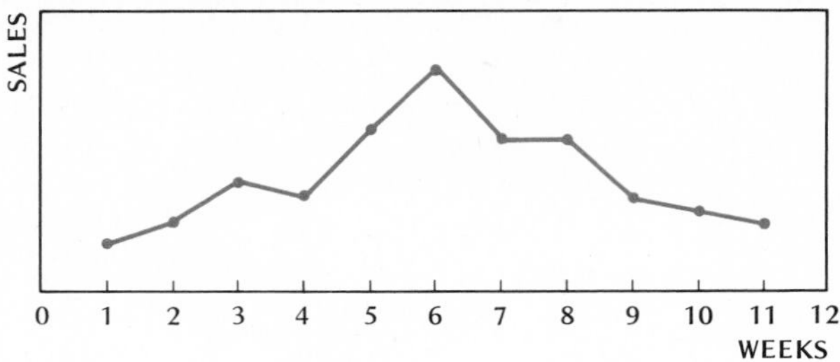

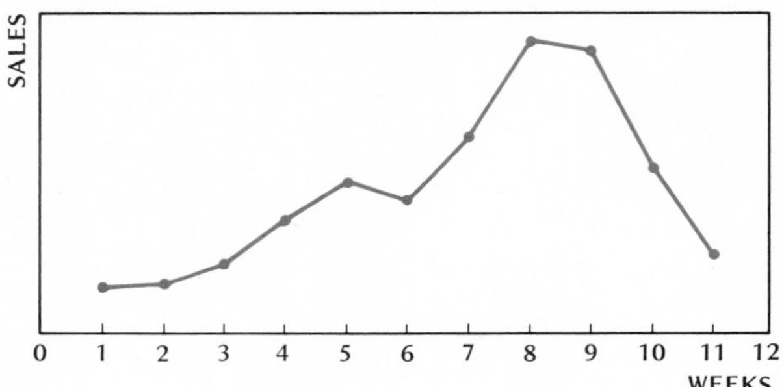

An additional complication arises if prices also vary along with sales. When this is true, channel outlets may determine their ordering policies partly on the basis of opportunities to make speculative gains on inventories. A classic case in point is that of Procter and Gamble in the early 1920s. At that time the company sought to stabilize production in order to provide regular employment to its workers—an early version of the guaranteed annual wage plan. A major stumbling block was the speculative purchasing policies of wholesalers, based on the relationships between prices of soap and those of tallow, its principal ingredient. To avoid the variations in demand caused by this speculation, the company began the development of a direct sales force and greatly reduced its reliance on wholesalers as a channel.

There is a close connection between channel decisions and product policy. As we have indicated repeatedly, one of the basic reasons for utilizing middlemen is that direct selling by a manufacturer involves numerous small transactions. Obviously the average transaction can be increased by producing and selling a broader product line. Hence, a company may diversify partly as a means of supporting a direct distribution policy, that is, a direct distribution policy may be uneconomic if the product line is too narrow. Several large, diversified food producers selling directly to retail outlets have consistently diversified their lines both through product development and through mergers; these include General Foods, Kraft, and Procter and Gamble. This consideration is so important, in fact, that common marketing channels may be more important in evaluating a new product than manufacturing technology.

Channel policies may facilitate or inhibit the development and introduction of new products within an existing line. As more and more varieties, such as models, colors, and sizes, are added to a line, inventory requirements and risks are increased at all stages of a channel. The resistance of distributors and dealers may actually prevent additional varieties from being added.

The connection between channels and physical distribution methods is fairly obvious. Manufacturers must provide for storage and delivery on the basis of channel outlets' needs; this may imply setting up branch warehouses or leasing of public warehouse space in numerous markets. Considerations of economical shipping quantities may even have an impact on plant location. For example, in the 1950s the General Electric Company relocated a number of household appliance factories at Appliance Park near Louisville, Kentucky. A partial reason for this move was the desire to facilitate shipments of appliances to distributors in mixed cars, that is, full carloads that carry several different types of products.

The requirements of wholesale and retail outlets for physical handling have affected manufacturers' decisions on packaging. In the grocery trade, standard pallet sizes have been adopted by most warehouse operators, and the dimensions of manufacturers' containers must be designed with these standards in mind. Consumer package shapes and dimensions must likewise be designed for convenience in shelf display and stacking.

Channel policies affect and are affected by the types and amounts of *promotion* used in the marketing mix. In many cases there is a real choice between the so-called push and pull strategies of promotion. The push strategy relies heavily on display, point-of-purchase advertising, and personal salesmanship by distributors and/or dealers; the pull consists mostly of consumer advertising. Clearly, the feasibility of a push strategy depends on the ability and willingness of channel outlets to implement it. Conversely, use of pull promotion usually implies narrower margins to channels and assumes that they will be forced to stock a product if customers demand it.

Finally, for many producers it is necessary to devote a major portion of the promotional budget to efforts directed *at* distributors and dealers rather than *through* them to ultimate purchasers. Some advertisements ostensibly aimed at consumers are, in fact, intended largely to influence the behavior of channel outlets.

Still another element of the marketing mix closely connected with channel policies is pricing. Manufacturers, in setting prices, must work backward from final or retail prices to a factory price, with due allowance for customary or required margins at each stage of the channel. For consumer products it is common for these margins to represent half or more of the final price. Since channel margins are almost always determined as percentages of selling prices, they are, in effect, "variable" costs in terms of total sales in the channel. Since manufacturers' field sales organizations or branch offices involve fixed cost, considerations of break-even points and stability of demand may, in turn, exert a major influence on channel policies. Thus, for example, a major reason cited for the use of manufacturers' agents is that their commissions (percentages of sales) automatically decrease with cyclical or seasonal sales declines, whereas the costs of a sales force would not.

Questions

1. Over a period of years, Paul Zorfass, an independent tailor, had developed a substantial clientele for his custom-tailored men's suits. Operating from a suite attached to his home, he had built his business through repeat sales, referrals from customers, and the occasional use of direct mail advertising.

For some time, Mr. Zorfass had been considering the possibility of expanding his business. This question became an issue of immediate concern when the representative of Pat's Mens Wear, a local chain of ready-to-wear men's clothing, offered to represent Zorfass by establishing "Custom-Corners" in his six retail outlets. Under the proposal, salesclerks in the stores would take measurements for custom-tailored suits. Zorfass would then manufacture the suits. The suits would be priced at $99 to $179, 15 percent above Zorfass's existing price schedule. Pat's would take a 25 percent commission on all sales.

Mr. Zorfass estimated that labor and material costs amounted to about 60 percent of his current revenues. Other than a slight increase in inventory, the only additional costs would be for delivery and worker supervision. He thought these expense items might average $3 to $5 per suit.

a. Assuming that Zorfass decided to expand his business, does Pat's proposition make sense?

b. Can you see any problems or difficulties the proposed arrangement might cause?

c. What alternatives might Zorfass consider to expand his sales? How would these compare with Pat's offer?

2. Hollywood Mills was a manufacturer of high-quality sheets and pillow-

cases. The company's products were distributed through wholesalers to department stores and dry-goods stores.

One of Hollywood Mills' salesmen suggested that the company should distribute its sheets and pillowcases through furniture stores, since people who buy beds are good prospects for new bed linens. Informed that retail furniture stores generally carried few accessory products, the salesman responded, "This is even more reason for adding furniture stores, since there will be little competition."

a. What action would you recommend that Hollywood Mills management take regarding the salesman's suggestion? Why?

b. Furniture store margins on accessories typically ranged between 40 and 50 percent. Hollywood Mills granted a 35 to 40 percent margin to its existing retail outlets. If the company decided to enter the new channel, should it raise its retail margins?

3. Some marketers feel that the classification of products on the basis of a single characteristic, such as how products are bought, as in the case of convenience, shopping, and specialty goods, is not of sufficient scope to aid in formulating marketing strategy. With this in mind, Leo V. Aspinwall has suggested a more extensive list of five characteristics on which to classify products:

Replacement rate. The rate at which a good is purchased and consumed by users.

Gross margin. The difference between the laid-in cost and the final realized sales price.

Adjustment. The amount of services applied to goods in order to meet customer needs.

Time of consumption. The measured time of consumption during which the good gives up the utility desired.

Searching time. A measure of average time and distance from the store where the good is normally bought.

On the basis of these characteristics, Aspinwall asserted that goods could then be generally grouped into three categories designated arbitrarily by colors:

Red goods. Goods with a high replacement rate, but low gross margin, adjustment, time of consumption, and searching time (such as many food products).

Orange goods. Goods with medium relative scores on all five characteristics (such as men's suits).

Yellow goods. Goods with a low replacement rate and high gross margin, adjustment, time of consumption, and searching time (such as refrigerators).

a. What are examples of some other products that could be classified as red goods? As orange goods? As yellow goods?

b. What implications does this system of classification have for marketing channel policy? For other elements of marketing strategy?

4. Many major tire companies operate their own retail tire stores as well as distributing tires through franchised dealers.

a. Why do you think some tire companies have decided to use both company stores and franchised dealers?

b. What problems do you think this distribution system may cause?

5. Magnus Electric, Inc., was a large, diversified electrical products manufacturer. Within its appliance division, it manufactured a line of high-price, high-quality home appliances, including refrigerators, freezers, washing machines, electric clothes driers, electric ranges, and room air conditioners.

The company sold direct to retailers, using its own national sales force. It operated its own branch offices and warehouses, and granted retailers exclusive distribution rights within specified market areas.

In 1971, Magnus decided to add a line of "traffic" appliances such as electric mixers, toasters, irons, and frying pans. In formulating a marketing strategy for the new line, the question was raised as to whether the new appliances should be sold through Magnus's existing exclusive retailers.

a. What factors should Magnus consider in deciding whether or not to use its existing distribution channels for the new line?

b. If a decision was made to seek broader retail distribution, should the new line be offered to existing exclusive retailers as well as to other retailers? Why?

6. What factors might lead a fast food franchiser to purchase the retail outlets currently owned by its franchisees, thereby operating them as wholly owned retail outlets? What risks would such a step incur?

7. What considerations might prompt a manufacturer of industrial chain saws to distribute its line through an industrial distributor, rather than directly through its own sales force?

8. "The fullest distribution support can be secured when no competing item is carried by the distributor." This statement was made by the sales manager of a large manufacturer of high-priced lawn mowers for home use.

a. Do you agree or disagree with this statement? Why?

b. Would your answer be the same if the item were a line of men's leather belts? Why?

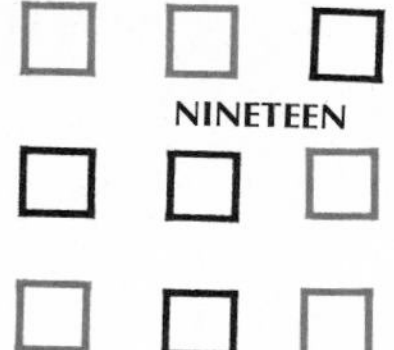

NINETEEN

Marketing logistics

Of the total cost of marketing goods, about half represents costs of physical distribution. Not only is physical distribution costly, but it has an important bearing on the total marketing program of a firm. Sales and advertising efforts will have little effect if products are not available to customers when and where they are wanted. Problems of storage and handling may also impose real constraints on product policy since proliferation of variety leads to rapidly increasing costs.

Physical distribution is closely related to manufacturing management, since inventories serve as the buffer between output and sales in any given time period; therefore, physical distribution is sometimes treated as a part of production rather than of marketing. This is in part a semantic question, but in any case effective marketing management requires a thorough understanding of logistics problems and their relationships to product, price, promotion, and channel policies.

□ *The term logistics is used here to designate the management of physical distribution activities.*

The nature and the importance of logistics

The analogy between business logistics and the problems of providing weapons and supplies at the proper times and places in military organizations should be apparent. Logistics□ comprises the following major activities:

1. Warehousing
2. Inventory control
3. Transportation
4. Overall logistics systems planning

LOGISTICS COSTS

For individual firms and industries, the importance of logistics varies greatly, depending on such factors as product bulk, fragility, perishability, the geographic dispersion of production and consumption, and the economics of production. One study of physical distribution costs, based on a survey of large American corporations, estimated that these costs amounted to 25 percent of sales in the primary metals, chemicals, and petroleum industries. The same study showed that transportation typically constitutes about 44 percent of a firm's total physical distribution costs, with warehousing and handling (20 percent), inventory carrying costs (18 percent), shipping room costs (11 percent), and administrative expenses (7 percent) making up the remainder.[1]

In some cases, logistics costs appear to exceed all other marketing costs. Despite this, relatively little attention was typically given to this area until the last two decades or so. Even now, physical distribution is frequently treated as a kind of no-man's-land between production and marketing. In too many companies, logistics decisions have been used as a kind of whipping boy to resolve organizational conflicts between sales and factory management. The result tends to be excessive cost and lack of coordination for the system as a whole.

In the 1950s and 1960s, however, some leading companies took steps to correct this situation. In some cases, distribution managers were established at a level coordinate with marketing and production, and in others, top marketing executives were assigned the responsibility for logistics planning. Whatever the organizational arrangement, the key point is that physical distribution should be recognized as a major business activity with a significant impact on the marketing program as well as on production.

LOGISTICS DECISIONS

Decisions regarding logistics must be made by all types of firms involved in the marketing of goods, including producers of raw materials, manufacturers and processors, wholesale concerns, retailers, and even, to some extent, ultimate customers. Many types of companies are engaged largely or wholly in performing distribution tasks, including railroads, truckers, and other carriers, warehousemen and specialized agencies such as freight forwarders and carloaders. The pattern of physical distribution for a given product or class of products reflects a whole series of choices made by all these participants in the

[1] Robert O. Neuschel, "Physical Distribution—Forgotten Frontier," *Harvard Business Review,* March–April, 1967, pp. 125–134.

marketing process. Although in theory it may be possible to design ideal logistics systems on an overall basis, in practice it is seldom feasible. The nearest approaches to it are the systems used by highly integrated companies such as those in the steel industry and in certain cooperative programs partially worked out among automobile manufacturers and their independent suppliers.

The viewpoint in this chapter is that of the individual firm, confronted with a set of decisions about logistics. While emphasis is placed on the problems of the manufacturer, most of the problems are very similar, if not identical, at other levels of distribution.

LOGISTICS AND MARKETING CHANNELS

Since logistics is concerned with the spatial arrangement and flow of goods, it is obviously related to the marketing channel or channels used for distributing goods. Indeed, from one standpoint channels can be regarded as logistics systems, and channels can be compared and evaluated on this basis. It must be emphasized, however, that wholesaling and retailing concerns perform many other functions in addition to those of physical distribution. Seldom should a channel decision be made solely, or even primarily, in terms of logistics considerations. The most important case in which physical distribution *does* predominate is that of a manufacturer choosing between the use of wholesalers and his own warehousing system. (This situation is discussed later in the chapter.) Apart from this, it is tacitly assumed in what follows that marketing channel decisions are made prior to the planning of the logistics system and *not* primarily on the basis of physical distribution efficiency per se. Under this assumption, a pattern of transportation, storage, and product flow must be developed at each stage in the channel to reach the next stage as effectively as possible.

The nature of logistics decisions may now be examined within each of the four major classes listed at the beginning of this chapter. At the outset it should be pointed out that this grouping is merely for convenience in exposition. Recent studies of physical distribution problems have demonstrated clearly that problems in the component areas of logistics such as inventory policy and transportation should not be treated in isolation since each is directly related to the others. This point is discussed further in the concluding section, Overall Logistics Systems Planning.

Warehousing

Storage of goods is essentially a means by which production and consumption are coordinated in time. If goods could be consumed as they are produced, as apples sometimes are by small boys sitting in apple trees, there would be no need for storage. But this is seldom practical. Most agricultural products are grown during definite seasons and must be stored if they are to be available regularly. Many manufactured goods are purchased or consumed seasonally and must be produced in advance of the times at which they are needed. Even when production and consumption are both more or less continuous, it is seldom desirable to schedule production to coincide exactly with demand. Apart from the fact that demand usually cannot be predicted accurately, the economics of production may dictate a schedule of output that deviates considerably from that of sales. High setup costs, for example, may impose a minimum run quantity greatly in excess of current demand.

For all these reasons, storage is an important element in the marketing process. The term *warehousing* is used here to denote the managerial problems associated with storage, although some kinds of goods are not, of course, actually stored in warehouses. As a matter of convenience, the discussion here is confined for the most part to warehousing of finished goods at a given stage in the production process.[2] The nature of the problems is basically the same, however, for raw materials or goods in process stocks.

The major problems involved in warehousing for the individual firm are (1) determining the number and location of distribution points and (2) deciding *who* should provide warehousing services.

□

NUMBER AND LOCATION OF DISTRIBUTION POINTS

In a competitive economy, sellers must make their products conveniently available to their customers. To this end, inventories must be maintained at a sufficient number of points, located to permit prompt delivery to buyers. Obviously this depends in part on what means of transportation are used to make deliveries; hence, decisions regarding inventory locations cannot realistically be made apart from decisions about transportation. For the time being, it is assumed that the means of transportation is given and that the time required to deliver goods from point to point can be determined. This assumption is relaxed in the concluding section of this chapter.

The number and location of distribution points required to serve a market depend, in the first place, on the locations of producing plants relative to the pattern of demand. At one extreme, a firm may serve a widely dispersed market from one or a few factories; this is the situation for some consumer goods. Bulky, fragile, or perishable goods, on the other hand, are usually produced in relatively small plants serving strictly local markets. Examples include bricks, cement, fresh produce, soft drinks, and bread. Still another pattern prevails when demand is concentrated geographically. Industries ser-

[2] The "finished" output of one industry may, however, be a raw material or a component part for another industry. For example, tires represent a component part to automobile manufacturers.

vicing oil producers find their market almost entirely in the Southwestern United States, whereas firms selling to the steel industry derive most of their sales from an area extending roughly from Chicago to Pittsburgh.

The location of producing plants is itself a logistics problem, and the analysis here could be extended to cover it as well as warehousing.[3] If, however, the locations of plants and markets are taken as given, then the problem of establishing warehousing locations may be stated as follows: to determine the location(s) of distribution points so that a required level of customer service is maintained at minimum cost. The two key elements are customer service requirements and costs.

Customer service Operationally, customer service is usually defined in terms of time required to get delivery of goods. Thus, a sales manager may say that he wants to be able to provide one-day service to all major customers, three-day service to smaller accounts, and so on. The rationale for this approach is the belief that customers (consumers, dealers, or industrial purchasers) will either refuse to order unless assured that delivery will be made by a certain time or if deliveries are late often enough—and once may be enough—will subsequently refuse to buy from the offending seller. What is late, of course, depends on competition, and standards of services expected differ among industries and trades. When a whole line of products is involved, as is usually true, the relevant measure of service may be the fraction of all items ordered that must be "back-ordered," that is, shipped separately from and subsequent to the remainder.

Most marketing executives have strong feelings about the level of service that should be provided. Implicitly, a *cost* is assigned to delays and to failures to fill orders. Ideally, this cost should be measured in dollar terms since in the final analysis it must be balanced against explicit costs of providing service. This can be done only by experimentation, however, and most companies are reluctant to experiment with their customers' goodwill. For example, an experiment might be set up in which customer service is deliberately cut back, and the results might be determined by following up the customers' responses. How many change to other suppliers? How do their opinions of the company change? The trouble with this approach is that customers may be lost permanently, making the experiment a rather costly venture.

For a given means of transportation and pattern of customer demand, the number of distribution points required varies directly with the level of service specified. One firm with extensive experience has developed some rules of thumb stating, for example, that for consumer goods: "To reach 90% of the

[3] See, for example, Donald J. Bowersox, Edward W. Smykay, and Bernard J. Lalonde, *Physical Distribution Management*, rev. ed., The Macmillan Company, New York, 1968. pp. 414–435.

market within one day will require at least 25 points; to reach 95% of the market within one day will require at least 50 points."[4]

Because of the uncertainties associated with customer service needs, the tendency in most companies has been to set up too many small distribution points. Executives have preferred to err on the side of too much service rather than not enough. These systems are very costly, however, and with the growing concern over physical distribution costs in the late 1960s and early 1970s, many firms reduced the number of distribution points and centralized storage in one or a few locations.

Costs Two conditions limit the number of distribution points used by a company. First, the greater the number of separate inventories, the greater the investment in inventory must be for a given total volume of sales; and second, warehousing costs are usually higher per unit of throughput in small warehouses than in large ones. Inventory requirements are greater because safety stocks must be provided in each of many small distribution points, and these, in most cases, will amount to more in total than the safety stocks required for one or a few large inventories. The reasons for this will be clarified in the section on inventory control. With respect to economies of scale in warehousing, these arise from two sources[5]:

1. In large warehouses, mechanical equipment such as fork-lift trucks can be employed to advantage. In many cases, specialized equipment for handling specific products can be used. Furthermore, there are usually certain fixed elements in warehouse operating expenses such as the warehouse manager's salary; in large establishments, these costs can be spread over a greater volume.
2. Transportation costs, both inbound and outbound, are related to warehouse size. If a warehouse serves a very small market, it will be necessary to ship goods to it in small quantities, thus losing the rate advantages associated with carlot and trucklot shipments. In the grocery trade, it appears that wholesale warehouses (independent and chain) are dispersed as widely as possible, consistent with the requirement of receiving most goods in carloads.

Selection of specific locations Once the number of distribution points has been set, specific locations must be chosen on the basis of the same criteria: customer service and cost. Usually a firm's total market area can be broken down into regions or districts on the basis of more of less natural divisions.

[4] John F. Magee, "The Computer and the Physical Distribution Network," in Wroe Alderson and Stanley J. Shapiro (eds.), *Marketing and the Computer,* Prentice-Hall, Inc., Englewood Cliffs, N.J., 1963, p. 70.

[5] See Theodore N. Beckman, N. H. Engle, and Robert D. Buzzell, *Wholesaling,* 3d ed., The Ronald Press Company, New York, 1959, pp. 133–134.

These divisions are often tied to major market centers, such as Boston in New England, San Francisco in California.

Within a specified market area, the optimum location for a distribution point can be chosen to minimize total transportation cost. For example, a hypothetical (and simplified) problem in warehouse location is depicted in Figure 19-1. The destinations to which goods are to be shipped, say food stores, are represented by circles. Each destination can be identified by its east-west coordinate and its north-south coordinate such as the destination at the point (3,2). The numbers in the figure represent quantities of goods to be shipped to each store, say tons of groceries per month. Thus, the number 10 indicates a shipment of 10 tons per month to the store location at (3,2). Where should a warehouse be located, that is, at what point in terms of east-west and north-south coordinates, to minimize total transportation cost if demand is as shown in the figure?

Suppose we assume that transportation costs are constant per ton per mile. Then if a warehouse is located at any given point, we can compute the cost of transportation to each store and hence the total cost of shipping to all seven stores. For instance, suppose we locate a warehouse at the point (3,3). Then

FIGURE 19-1

Hypothetical problem in warehouse location

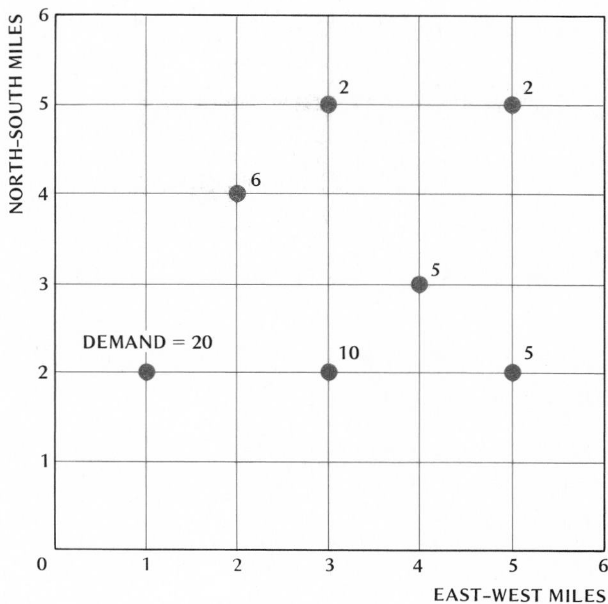

Store location	Distance from point (3,3)	Tons shipped	Tons shipped times distance
(1,2)	2.24	20	44.80
(2,4)	1.41	6	8.46
(3,2)	1.00	10	10.00
(3,5)	2.00	2	4.00
(4,3)	1.00	5	5.00
(5,2)	2.24	5	11.20
(5,5)	2.83	2	5.66
			89.12

the distance to the store at point (2,4) is 1.41 miles, and the cost of shipping to this store is 6 tons times 1.41 miles times the cost per ton-mile.[6] The costs for the other stores can similarly be computed and are shown in the accompanying table. The total transportation cost, then, if a warehouse is located at (3,3), will be 89.12 times the cost per ton-mile. Would another location be better? If similar computations are made for the point (2,3), the total ton-distance is lower, 85.8 against 89.12. By trial and error, we could find the *best* warehouse location for the demand pattern given in Figure 19-1. But in a real problem of any magnitude, this would be a lengthy process.

It is interesting to note that even a seemingly simple problem such as this cannot be solved routinely by conventional mathematical analysis. Solutions can be obtained, however, by using computers to carry out the extensive trial and error computations necessary.[7]

It should be pointed out that this approach considers only outbound transportation costs; a true solution to the problem of warehouse location would also deal with inbound freight, as well as questions of varying customer service needs in different parts of the market.

□

PERFORMANCE OF WAREHOUSING FUNCTIONS

A manufacturer who has decided that distribution points are needed at specified locations in his market is not thereby committed to establishing his own warehouses. In many cases it is not economic to do so. The principal alternatives are (1) reliance on wholesalers to carry inventories and (2) use of public

[6] The distance between any two points (x_1,y_1) and (x_2,y_2) is equal to

$$\sqrt{(x_1 - x_2)^2 + (y_2 - y_2)^2}$$

For the points (3,3) and (2,4) this is

$$\sqrt{(3-2)^2 + (3-4)^2} = \sqrt{1^2 + (-1)^2} = \sqrt{2} = 1.41$$

[7] For one solution technique, see K. B. Keefer, "Easy Way to Determine the Center of Distribution," *Food Industry*, vol. 6, pp. 450–451. October, 1934.

warehouses. If wholesalers are employed in the marketing channel, the manufacturer must still make provisions to supply them; like most other marketing problems, the design of the logistics system is a multistage one. Wholesalers are confronted with the same set of decisions that apply to their own branch warehouses, and so are retail chains with regard to their warehouses and stores.

Wholesalers In some cases the decision to use wholesalers in a marketing channel hinges in large part on relative efficiences in physical distribution. Physical distribution—storage, handling, and delivery—is a major function of most types of wholesalers and accounts for a third to more than half of their total operating costs.

Often the choice must be made between setting up sales branches and using independent wholesalers. As noted in Chapter 12, manufacturers' sales branches generally have lower operating costs than wholesalers in the same product lines, but these figures are not really comparable for a number of reasons.[8] In general, except in comparison with large and diversified manufacturers, the wholesaler *should* have a cost advantage because (1) he carries a wider line of products and operates on a larger scale in a given market, (2) he often carries lines with different seasonal patterns to minimize seasonal variations in throughput, and (3) he is a specialist in his sphere of operations, including physical handling and storage. In practice, wholesalers are not always more efficient in physical distribution, for any number of reasons. Thus, for example, in one study for a large consumer goods manufacturer it was found that distribution to dealers could be carried out at lower cost by the manufacturer himself. In this instance most of the distributors operated on too small a scale to permit realization of the theoretical advantages suggested above.

Public warehouses Frequently an alternative to either branch warehouses or wholesalers, and even more often a useful supplement to them, is the use of public warehouses. These are business concerns specializing in the provision of storage facilities on a rental basis.

Public warehouses charge for storage space on a per-unit (package, hundredweight, etc.) per-month basis. In addition to storage, many warehouses will fill customer orders, reship goods, and provide display space. The principal advantage of using public warehouses is that there are no fixed costs to the user: only the space and warehouse labor actually used in a given period must be paid for. On the other hand, beyond a certain point it is usually more economical for a firm to operate its own warehouse.

[8] Cf. Beckman, Engle, and Buzzell, *op. cit.*, pp. 199–200.

Inventory control

One of the most troublesome features of marketing logistics is effective control over inventories. During 1969, the value of manufacturers' inventories averaged about $96 billion, wholesalers' inventories were $25 billion, and retailers' inventories were around $46 billion. Not only do inventory requirements pose services financing problems to business firms, but, as pointed out in Chapter 8, fluctuations in inventories are believed to contribute substantially to cyclical variations in total economic activity.[9] Thus, from the standpoint of both proper management and general economic welfare, it is important that effective control be maintained over inventory levels.

FUNCTIONS OF INVENTORIES

As pointed out earlier in this chapter, the general role of inventories in the business system is one of coordinating production and demand. In an individual firm, the specific objectives of carrying goods in stock commonly include[10]:

1. Good service to customers, that is, the ability to fill orders within a "reasonable" period of time
2. Maintenance of a level rate of production and employment
3. Low investment in inventory
4. Avoidance of deterioration and obsolescence

These objectives obviously are conflicting when carried to extremes. For example, in the effort to provide good service to customers, large stocks of goods are accumulated; this leads to excessive investment and carrying costs. Conversely, if inventories are held to a bare minimum in accordance with objectives 3 and 4, customer service and/or regularized production may be sacrificed. Apparently it is much more common to err on the side of too much inventory than too little, for the same reasons that more companies have too many distribution points than too few (see above).

The most difficult feature of inventory management to deal with is customer service. Except when stocks are deliberately built up to permit continued plant operation during slack selling seasons, goods are carried in inventory solely to

[9] A task force of economists and businessmen reported to the Congressional Joint Economic Committee that "during periods of expansion when sales and backlogs of unfilled orders are rising, production increases both to meet higher levels of sales and to provide for accumulations of stocks. . . . Contrariwise, during periods of business contraction and falling sales and unfilled orders, production falls below levels of sales as business firms try to disgorge unwanted stocks." *Inventory Fluctuations, Price Level Changes, and Economic Growth,* Materials Prepared for the Joint Economic Committee, 1962, p. 3.

[10] Carl G. Baumes, *Inventory Management in Industry,* Studies in Business Policy no. 88, National Industrial Conference Board, New York, 1958, pp. 10–12. For a comprehensive examination of the functions of inventories, see also James I. Mugan, "Questions for Solving the Inventory Problem," *Harvard Business Review,* July–August, 1963.

meet anticipated demands during some future period. With few exceptions, forecasting methods are not sufficiently accurate to permit sales predictions without substantial risks of error. A variety of methods are available for dealing with this problem; some of these are described briefly in subsequent paragraphs.

□ INVENTORY COSTS

In any consideration of inventory management, some analysis must be made of the costs associated with carrying inventories. True carrying costs are, however, very difficult to ascertain; seldom if ever can the full cost be measured simply by adding or reclassifying the *accounting* costs shown in a firm's operating statement.

Some elements of inventory cost can be measured readily. These include charges for rented warehouse space, direct operating costs for a firm's own warehouses, insurance and taxes on stocks, and "shrinkage" resulting from deterioration or pilferage. A more difficult problem is presented by *interest* costs on the capital invested in inventories. If this capital is actually borrowed, then there is an out-of-pocket cost which can be measured. On the other hand, when funds are provided from internal sources, no cost appears in the accounting records. Because this use of equity capital is an investment, however, it is clear that some cost must be assigned to it. What rate of interest should be charged? There is considerable controversy on this point. Many companies charge no interest on inventory at all. Others use the cost that *would* be incurred if the funds were borrowed from a feasible source. Still another approach is to estimate the *opportunity cost* of employing funds in inventory, that is, the rate of return that would be earned if the capital were used in some other manner, either externally (purchase of short-term securities) or internally. The choice of an appropriate rate is, in the final analysis, a matter of executive judgment. The decision reached is of some importance because when interest costs are held to a low level, capital resources of the firm will tend to flow out of other activities into inventory. If assumed interest rates are very high, sufficient funds may not be allocated to maintain adequate inventory levels.

Another type of problem is presented by costs of *obsolescence*. For products subject to style changes especially such limited-life items as phonograph records, books, perishable foods, and seasonal wearing apparel, losses through obsolescence may be much more important than the total of all other costs. The difficulty is that obsolescence costs usually cannot be determined in advance; they are known only after the fact. But inventory decisions must be made *before* and *during* the periods in which buyer tastes or needs change, not after. Some special methods of treating this aspect of inventory cost are discussed below.

When all the costs of maintaining inventory are taken into account, total annual carrying charges may represent 15 to 30 percent of the value of average stock on hand.[11] The wide range of inventory costs (15 to 30 percent) reflects the inherent variability of these costs from firm to firm. Another source states that studies of inventory costs have shown an even wider range of 13 to 35 percent.[12] Thus, a conservative estimate of total inventory costs for manufacturers, wholesalers, and retailers in 1969 would be about $30 billion.

APPROACHES TO INVENTORY CONTROL

Considerable attention has been given to both the theory and the practice of inventory control, especially since the emergence of operations research in the late 1940s. Many of the methods that have been developed involve complex mathematical techniques and are beyond the scope of this discussion. All that is intended here is to introduce some of the basic approaches to the problem and describe briefly a few of the simpler methods used.[13]

Control with known demand If the rate of sales or usage for an item is known in advance, there is relatively little difficulty in controlling inventories. Assume, first, that stocks can be replenished instantaneously. If there were no cost associated with replenishment, goods would be produced or ordered only to meet orders as received. Usually, however, the economics of production and transportation or both along with costs of ordering dictate that orders be placed for some minimum quantity at a time. This quantity can be determined by balancing the costs of replenishment, which are minimized by ordering as seldom as possible, against inventory carrying costs, which are minimized by ordering as frequently as possible. An oversimplified model of this problem follows.

Suppose that costs of replenishment amount to R dollars per order placed. Let C represent the cost value per unit of the item and I represent the carrying charge per year, as a fraction of the value of stock on hand. Assume, further, that the total demand or usage per year is D units. If goods are ordered in a standard quantity Q, the average inventory will be $Q/2$. The total costs are de-

[11] Arthur J. Schumer, "An Approach to Inventory Management," *New Jersey CPA*, Winter, 1965, pp. 17–21.

[12] Harold D. Youell, "Inventory Management through Inventory Ratios," *Management Accounting*, August, 1967, pp. 43–46.

[13] For further discussion, see James W. Prichard and Robert H. Eagle, *Modern Inventory Management*, John Wiley & Sons, Inc., New York, 1965; and Joseph Buchan and Ernest Koenigsberg, *Scientific Inventory Management*, Prentice-Hall, Inc., Englewood Cliffs, N.J., 1963.

termined as follows:

$$\text{Total cost} = \frac{D}{Q}R + \frac{Q}{2}IC$$

What should Q be to minimize the total cost? This can be determined by means of calculus, and it turns out that costs are minimized if

$$Q = \sqrt{\frac{2DR}{IC}}$$

The replenishment quantity, determined in this manner, is designated as the *economic order quantity* (EOQ) or *economic lot* size. This approach was first developed in the 1920s, and variations of it have been used widely in industry.

In most cases, some lead time is required to replenish inventories. As long as the lead time is known with certainity, this presents no additional problem. An illustrative example is depicted in Figure 19-2, where it is assumed that the lead time is one week. Under these conditions, inventory is allowed to decline until it reaches a point just sufficient to cover the next week's sales. At this juncture, an order is placed for the standard amount (EOQ), and when the goods arrive, the stock on hand will have been exhausted.

Dealing with uncertainty Because demand is not known with certainty in advance, it is necessary to carry inventories above and beyond those required in the foregoing example. These additional stocks are known as *safety stocks,* while the goods carried to meet demands between replenishments are designated as *cycle stocks.* The distinction between these two components of inven-

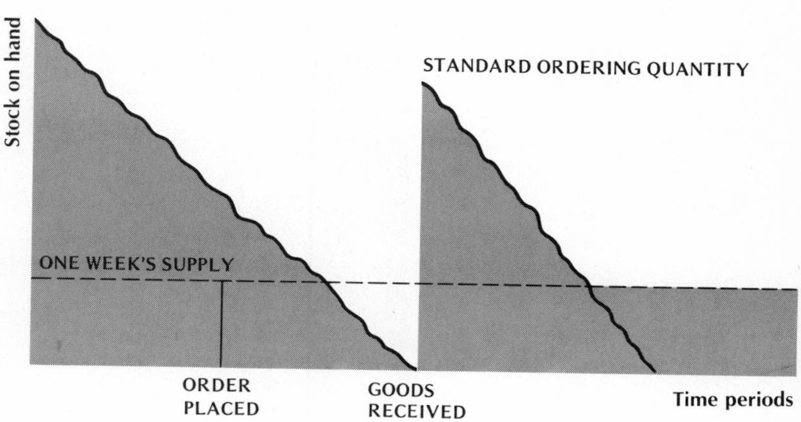

FIGURE 19-2
Variations in inventory of an item when demand is known with certainty

tory is clarified by Figure 19-3, where, as in Figure 19-2, an order is placed when stock on hand is equal to expected sales during the next week. Because demand varies, however, a safety stock is carried at all times to avoid running out. During the first cycle, actual demand equals expected demand, and when the inventory is replenished, the quantity on hand just equals the safety stock. In the next cycle period the rate of sales exceeds predictions, and a part of the safety stock must be used to fill orders. Finally, in the third cycle, sales fall below the anticipated rate, and the stock on hand when the order is received is above the safety level. A system of this kind is designated as an "(S,s) inventory policy." For each item stocked, two numbers are determined: S, the maximum stock level, and s, the minimum level. The rule of the system is simple to place an order whenever the stock on hand reaches s, the *reorder point;* the quantity ordered (EOQ) should be enough to bring the stock back up to S. When there is a delay in replenishent, as in Figure 19-3, variations in sales during the time elapsing between placement and receipt of an order lead to variations in S, as the figure shows.

How much safety stock should be carried? The answer depends on the

FIGURE 19-3

Variations in inventory of an item when demand is uncertain

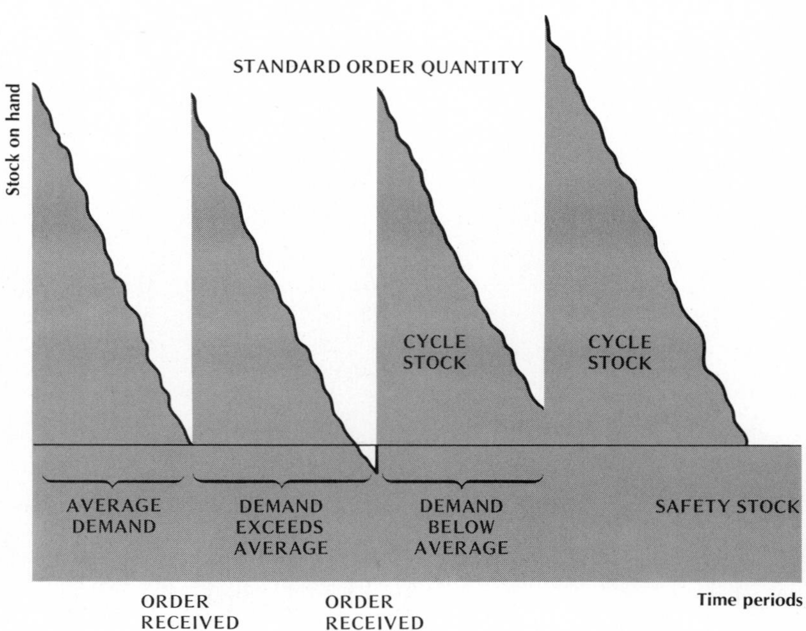

variability of sales, which is usually uncontrollable by the individual firm, and on the costs assigned, explicitly or implicity, to failures or delays in filling orders. For some products, demand fluctuates only slightly, and only a small reserve stock need be maintained. For others, such as fresh baked goods, random variations in sales are so great that a substantial fraction of the total inventory on hand at a given time is carried to provide for it. Even greater safety stocks are typically maintained for emergency items such as machine parts, without which a production line would have to shut down. In this case the cost of running out is very high.

Often it is difficult to assign meaningful measures to the costs of failures and delays in filling orders. If the effect of a failure to replace a part is to stop the production of some product, with consequences that can be estimated, then a dollar cost figure can be constructed. If "outs" and back orders result simply in lost current sales, then the cost is the dollar contribution that would have been realized from those sales. Most businessmen believe, however, that out-of-stock conditions have an impact on future sales as well as current sales, and at least implicitly they treat costs as being much greater than the dollar contribution forgone.

Assuming that realistic costs can be assigned to inventory shortages methods are available to determine proper quantities of an item to stock.[14] Essentially these methods show that safety stocks should vary directly with the cost of a shortage and with the degree of uncertainty regarding demand, and inversely with carrying charges.

INVENTORY CONTROL FOR MANY ITEMS

In the foregoing discussion of inventory control concepts, it was implicitly assumed that only a single item (*stock-keeping unit,* or SKU in operations research parlance) is involved. Most manufacturers, wholesalers, and retailers, however, sell hundreds or even thousands of distinct products. In order to implement a system of reorder points and standard order quantities, it is necessary to maintain records for each item showing:

1. Quantities ordered
2. Sales, as they are made
3. Quantity on hand, continuously updated

A system of records of this kind is called a *perpetual unit control system* since it is a perpetual record of units in stock for all items handled. True perpetual unit control systems are relatively uncommon because of the costs involved. In essence, the costs of controlling inventories must be balanced against the poten-

[14] See Robert Schlaifer, *Probability and Statistics for Business Decisions,* McGraw-Hill Book Company, New York, 1959, chaps. 4 and 15.

tial benefits to be derived. A firm such as a drug wholesaler selling many thousands of low-priced items may find the costs too great.

In the absence of perpetual unit control, a variety of compromise forms of control can be employed. One such approach is to have perpetual unit control data for *part* of the product line. Warner and Swasey Company, a manufacturer of heavy industrial machinery, is one firm reported to use such a system.[15] The company controls 20 percent of its inventory manually, and 80 percent by a computer. The 20 percent that is manually controlled consists of high-value, slow-moving items whose inventory status does not change rapidly. The computer-controlled portion consists of small, fast-moving items that need the close, tight control a computer can provide.

Another compromise is to employ some system of *periodic reordering.* Stocks of an item can be checked periodically, say, monthly, and if they fall below a predetermined level (enough to fill orders for the next month, including safety allowance), a replenishment order is placed. This type of control system involves greater risks than perpetual unit control, but is probably adequate for the majority of relatively slow-moving, noncritical items.

Although perpetual unit control systems are expensive under any circumstances, developments in real time computer technology have made such systems feasible in many situations where they previously were not. Kitchens of Sara Lee, Inc., a manufacturer of frozen bakery products, is reported to have a system in which an incoming order sets off a series of actions almost free of human involvement.[16] Two computers are used to control inventory, production, and forecasting. Each day the computers write a tape that controls daily production according to the needs of a computer-calculated forecast. The computers direct cranes to retrieve products from storage on a first-in, first-out basis, and daily reports prepared by the computer show detailed information on stock levels, number of transactions for the day, and amount of storage space available.

□

FORECASTING FOR INVENTORY CONTROL

All methods of inventory control involve some means of relating stocks on hand to anticipate sales. Consequently an essential element of all systems is a procedure for predicting sales during some future period. The predictions used in most companies are, in fact, crude projections of past experience. Thus, in a survey of inventory management policies it was found that, "The historical activity of an item (adjusted to the current year's forecast) is apparently the main consideration used in establishing the desired stock level."[17]

[15] L. James Sasanecki, "Introduction to EDP-controlled Inventory Control," *Management Services,* November–December, 1967, p. 36.
[16] *Ibid.,* p. 37.
[17] Baumes, *op. cit.,* p. 19.

A variety of statistical techniques can also be employed to make sales predictions.[18] One approach is that of *time series analysis* of historical sales data. Past variations in sales, say, on a monthly basis, can be broken down into those attributable to long-term trend, seasonal fluctuations, and random differences or "noise." A model of this type may assume that

$$\text{Sales in month } t = \text{seasonal index} \times (a + bt) + \text{error}$$

where $(a + bt)$ is a *trend* value for sales derived from statistical analysis, and the error component reflects random fluctuations.

Another statistical technique based on analysis of historical sales fluctuations is known as *exponential smoothing*. In this method, predictions are modified each period to reflect the forecasting error for the preceding period. Thus, current sales results are continuously utilized as new information to revise previous estimates. The method can be combined with trend and seasonal analysis.

□

SPECIAL PROBLEMS OF PERISHABLE AND STYLE GOODS

For staple products, that is, those for which demand continues more or less indefinitely, inventory policy depends basically on customer service objectives in relation to costs of carrying goods over a period of time. Some goods cannot be "carried" beyond a certain point, either because they are physically perishable (milk, bread, camera film) or because they are subject to losses in value (seasonal goods, apparel, newspapers). As pointed out earlier, costs of obsolescence are of predominant importance for these types of products.

Often decisions must be made about what quantity of a perishable or style item to produce or buy in anticipation of sales for some future period. The classical model for such decisions is the so-called newsboy problem[19]:

> A newsboy has, on the average, 10 customers a night who are willing to buy papers costing 5¢ each. The newsboy makes a profit of 3¢ on each paper he sells, and loses 1¢ on each paper he takes out but fails to sell. Let us suppose he has kept records, and that 40% of the time he can sell at least 10 papers and 20% of the time he can sell at least 12 papers.
>
> If the newsboy does not know how many papers he will actually sell in any given day but every day takes out 10 papers, he has a 40% chance of selling all the papers and making 3¢ each, and a 60% chance of not selling all papers and losing 1¢ on each not

[18] Forecasting procedures and techniques used in various industries and individual firms are described in National Industrial Conference Board, *Forecasting Sales*, Studies in Business Policy no. 106, National Industrial Conference Board, New York, 1963; and Louis J. Rago, *Production Analysis and Control*, International Textbook Company, Scranton, Pa., 1963, chap. 10. For an example of the computer's contribution to new techniques of forecasting, see George Schussel, "Simulation and Sales Forecasting," *Datamation*, June, 1967, pp. 40–45.

[19] John F. Magee, "Guides to Inventory Policy: Part III, Anticipating Future Needs," *Harvard Business Review*, May–June, 1956, pp. 57–70.

sold. He can expect the tenth paper to produce, on the average over time, a profit of 0.6¢ (3¢ × 40% = −1¢ × 60%). On the other hand, if he takes 12 papers every night, he can expect the twelfth paper to produce, on the average over time, a loss of 0.2¢ (3¢ × 20% − 1¢ × 80%).

It would not, therefore, be worth his while to take out 12 papers. As a matter of fact, he would probably make the greatest total profit by taking 11 regularly, since he could expect, on the average over time, to do slightly better than break even on the eleventh paper(3¢ × 30% − 1¢ × 70%, or 0.2¢).

It will be noted that this analysis of the problem relies on historical sales data. Suppose there are no applicable historical data? In the book publishing and phonograph record industries, each new item is, in some respects at least, unique. Even here, general *patterns* of sales that are useful in developing predictions may sometimes be determined on the basis of sales during the early days or weeks after a product is offered for sale. For example, in a study for a textile manufacturer, it was found that patterns of sales for items over the course of a season followed a normal growth curve. This meant that cumulative sales up to a particular point in a season could be used to forecast *total* sales for the season; if the season were three months long, predictions might be made after one week, two weeks, etc.[20]

Transportation

The number and location of distribution points for a company's products and the inventory requirements set for them together with the pattern of production and/or procurement dictate requirements for transportation of goods from factories to warehouses, warehouses to retail stores, and between other points in the overall network. Hence, an important phase of physical distribution management in most firms is that of selecting means of transportation, routing shipments, and scheduling and combining shipments to minimize total cost. Traditionally, these and related tasks have been dealt with as a separate function of *traffic management*. Only recently have serious attempts been made to coordinate traffic management with warehousing, inventory control, and production as an interrelated system.

□

TYPES OF CARRIERS

□ *Common carriers must accept goods for shipment from any person and operate over specified routes and at rates governed by regulatory bodies.*

Two major classes of carriers are used for transporting goods—common and contract carriers.□ Both are specialists in transportation. Many firms, of course, operate their own private transportation equipment. Only one-tenth of the 17 million trucks in the United States in 1970 were available for hire, the rest being privately owned. Over 85 percent of inland water transport is proprietary or

[20] D. B. Hertz and K. H. Schaffir, "A Forecasting Method for Management of Seasonal Style-goods Inventories," *Operations Research*, January–February, 1960, pp. 45–52.

☐ *Contract carriers work for one or more shippers, usually on a continuing basis, providing service between specific points at negotiated rates.*

private, and railroad cars are increasingly owned by shippers rather than by the railroad companies.☐

☐

MAJOR FORMS OF TRANSPORTATION

The major forms of transportation are railroads, pipeline networks, motor trucks, inland waterways, and air carriers. *Railroads* have long been the most important form of freight transportation in the United States, although their share of total domestic freight traffic has declined from 74 percent in 1930 to about 40 percent in 1970. For long-distance movement of bulk quantities, railroads have a clear cost advantage over other carriers, with the exception of barges where feasible. For less-than-carload (LCL) quantities, however, other modes of transportation generally provide faster and more flexible service at comparable cost. Despite the introduction of piggybacking, containerization, and freight forwarding services—all shipment methods that combine rail with trucks, ships, or other carriers—total ton-miles of less-than-carload traffic of the railroads in 1970 was only a fraction of what they handled 50 years earlier.

The United States is now covered with networks of large-diameter *pipelines* which, in 1970, accounted for one-fifth of all intercity ton-miles of freight traffic. The majority of pipeline tonnage is in petroleum or its derivatives, but lines have also been built for wood pulp, anhydrous ammonia, coal, and gilsonite (a form of asphalt).

The *trucking* industry began to develop during the 1920s and 1930s and, after limited growth during the gasoline and tire rationing of World War II, has enjoyed remarkable expansion since the late 1940s. In 1970, the trucking industry accounted for almost one-fourth of intercity ton-miles, and more than one-half of intercity traffic revenue, in the United States. Once regarded as appropriate only for distances of up to 400 miles, trucking has been given added impetus by development of the interstate highway system. In 1970, it was possible to get coast-to-coast truck delivery in as little as 70 hours.

Inland waterways have enjoyed a remarkable revival in the period since World War II. The development of "integrated barges"—large barges powered by towboats of up to 9,000 horsepower and capable of carrying up to 40,000 tons of bulk—has been a major technological development spurring this mode of transportation. In 1970, inland waterways accounted for one-seventh of intercity ton-miles in the United States. Tonnage on the Ohio River alone exceeded that of the Panama and pre-1967 Suez canals combined.

Air carriers have become a significant mode of freight transportation only since about 1950. Because of the high cost of this method of movement, its use has been restricted primarily to high-value goods requiring very rapid delivery—cut flowers, replacement parts for machinery, pharmaceuticals, and fresh lobsters, for example. Air cargo, growing at a faster rate than air passenger travel in the early 1970s, still accounted for substantially less than 1 percent of domestic freight traffic in 1970. While the new jumbo jets introduced in the early 1970s held promise of lower air cargo rates, congested air space and lagging air terminal technology represented potential barriers to the continued expansion of air carriers.

□ COSTS OF TRANSPORTATION

The rates charged by various carriers reflect differences in their costs of handling different types of goods, their perceptions of demand elasticity, and many other factors. Also, the rates charged at any given time are those approved by regulatory bodies such as the Interstate Commerce Commission; changes in costs and demand are not always reflected in the rates. Common carriers must operate under published rate lists or tariffs, which specify rates per unit of weight either for classes of goods or, in certain cases, for specific commodities. The rate structures are extremely complex and are stated in a specialized, esoteric jargon. Many so-called traffic managers are in fact primarily translators who can, through experience, decipher the rates applicable to a product, arrange for its routing, fill out forms for damage claims, etc.

The basic factors affecting freight rates are *distance* and *quantity*. Generally speaking, the rate per ton-mile is lower for long distances than for short ones, and lower for large quantities than for small ones. For instance, railroad freight rates for a carload shipment (CL) are only around one-half to two-thirds as great as for a less-than-carload (LCL) amount. A similar discrepancy exists between truckload (TL) and less-than-truckload (LTL) rates.

Because of these economies in transportation costs as well as the economies in handling shipments at both ends, shippers employ a variety of devices to consolidate small quantities of products into economical loads. On such method is the *pool car* which contains goods destined for several receivers. A manufacturer may ship products in a pool car to a public warehouse or to a trucking company, where the carload is divided and reshipped to its eventual destination.

A specialized agency engaged in consolidating small shipments into carloads or truckloads is the *freight forwarder*. Companies utilizing forwarders usually pay only slightly less than the less-than-carload or less-than-truckload rates they would pay without them, but generally get faster service than would otherwise be the case.

Overall logistics systems planning

The interdependence of the several elements of a firm's logistics system has been stressed throughout this chapter. If this fact is accepted, it follows that decisions regarding distribution points, inventory, and transportation should be made with reference to their effects on the overall functioning of the system. Because of traditional organizational barriers and because true systems planning is a complex task, this approach to logistics decisions is not widely used as yet. The principle involved is, however, gaining increasing acceptance.

Systems planning studies must be made in terms of the specific needs and problems of the individual firm. For this reason it is difficult to generalize on the subject meaningfully. A simple, hypothetical example will, however, serve to illustrate the idea.

AN EXAMPLE OF SYSTEMS PLANNING

The Froomis Company, a hypothetical corporation, manufactures three products, all of them being produced at both of the company's plants, one in Pittsburgh and one in Milwaukee. The same machinery is used to produce all three products, and only one product can be scheduled for a given week in a given factory. For each product there is a known manufacturing cost per unit; in addition there is a setup charge incurred each time the machines are changed over from one product to another. These are the basic *production conditions* within which the logistics system must operate.

Froomis sells its products to 100 wholesalers throughout the United States and Canada. The demand is seasonal, and there is a long-term upward trend in industry and company sales. Historical records show the quantities of each product shipped to each wholesaler, by month, for the past five years. The locations and past purchases of these customers, along with any anticipated changes, comprise the *demand conditions* which the logistics system must satisfy.

To plan a logistics system for the Froomis Company, it is also necessary to know its costs of storage and transportation as well as the estimated costs of failures or delays in filling orders. Given all these data, it is possible to compare a series of alternatives.

The first set of alternatives has to do with production scheduling. Facilities may be used to produce one product until enough is accumulated for the entire year, or at the other extreme, they may be shifted from one product to another weekly. Also, because demand is seasonal, the plant can be operated at a regular rate throughout the year, or the rate of utilization can be varied. The number of alternatives is very great; each alternative can be thought of as a list of 52 sets of numbers, each set showing the number of units of each product to be produced at each factory during each week of a year. Most of these alternatives are unreasonable. Suppose that the reasonable alternatives are narrowed down to as few as 50 different schedules. Then, given the setup charges and variable costs, plus any additional costs such as premium wages for overtime, costs plus any additional costs such as premium wages for overtime, costs associated with use of temporary labor, etc., it is possible to estimate production costs for each of the alternatives.

Next, the company has choices regarding the number of distribution points it will use. One possibility is to ship to distributors from the factory; if this is done, note that limitations on storage space at the factory will probably lead to the elimination of some of the production schedule alternatives. A more flexible system may be one with, say, four regional warehouses. These warehouses, in turn, can be built large enough to handle peak demand or can be supplemented by public warehouse space during busy seasons. If the field is limited only to those three choices, there are still 150 alternative *combinations* of production schedules and distribution points minus those which are inconsistent.

The third step in planning the system is to set inventory policies for each distribution point. Ideally, desired inventory levels for each item at each distribution point should be established on the basis of the expected pattern of demand and relative costs of carrying stocks versus costs of failures and delays. In addition, a system should be provided for adjusting inventory levels as information on actual sales becomes available. Note that the inventory policies depend on the number of distribution points and that desired levels are also affected by production schedules since it may be possible to reduce factory costs by carrying larger stocks than needed for current demand.

The final set of alternatives deals with transportation methods and policies. Here it is necessary to consider all reasonable alternatives with respect to types of carriers and quantities shipped from each factory to each distribution point. A decision to ship in lots of a minimum size will affect inventory levels, so that some combinations of shipping and inventory policies are inconsistent.

Out of the many alternatives of production schedules, distribution points, inventory policies, and transportation methods, the system planner seeks to find the most effective feasible one or ones. The complexity of the problem should make it clear why few companies have made studies of this kind in a literal sense. About the only way to compare so many alternatives is by simulating them on a computer, and even then the task is formidable. More often, studies of logistics are confined to *parts* of the overall system such as determining which plants should ship to which warehouses, given the means of transportation and the desired shipments to each warehouse during a period and assuming that the production schedules permit the shipments to be made.

Questions

1. Many furniture retailers maintain no inventory other than floor displays. Customers select from these displays, and their purchases are then ordered directly from the manufacturer. Delivery to the customer in many instances involves a delay of 4 to 16 weeks.

a. Is this system a reasonable one for the manufacturer, the retailer, or the consumer? Why? What benefits does the system provide to each?

b. Suppose a retailer decided that he could obtain a competitive advantage by providing rapid delivery to his customers. What are the various means by which the retailer could implement such a policy, and what are the advantages and disadvantages of each?

2. Management of physical distribution is often organized under the control of manufacturing management. In view of the importance of logistics decisions, do you think organizational control should be shifted to the marketing department? Why?

3. Identify the major logistics decisions that need to be made in each of the following businesses:

a. A farmer raising turkeys
b. A greeting card manufacturer
c. A high-fashion clothes designer
d. A spark plug manufacturer
e. A cement producer

4. Under what circumstances should warehouses be located close to end markets as opposed to close to the source of production? Why? Give examples of products in which each locational strategy seems most appropriate.

5. What factors limit or prevent manufacturers from maintaining control over physical distribution?

6. What factors should a manufacturer consider when deciding to operate its own truck fleet rather than to rely on contract or common carriers?

7. Air cargo carriers have argued that the use of air freight can actually reduce total distribution costs for certain products, in spite of the higher transportation costs involved. They support their contention by demonstrating how the use of air freight can reduce total inventory requirements, reduce obsolescence, cut the amount of inventory storage capacity required, and reduce material handling costs. In spite of these arguments, air carriers have made limited inroads in the distribution of products for which they claim these advantages. How can you explain the reluctance of shippers to switch to air freight in such situations?

8. Operations Researchers have suggested that there will be a revolution in material handling in the 1970s. They suggest that automation in materials handling, computer control and billing systems, standardization of shipping containers, and the growth of intermodal transportation systems will lead to extensive change in the transportation industries.

a. What problems or barriers can you see which may forestall this revolution?

b. What steps might management take to prepare for any major changes that may take place?

9. What are the major problems a company faces in developing and using complex computer models to aid in making logistics decisions? Attempt to cite specific examples in your reply.

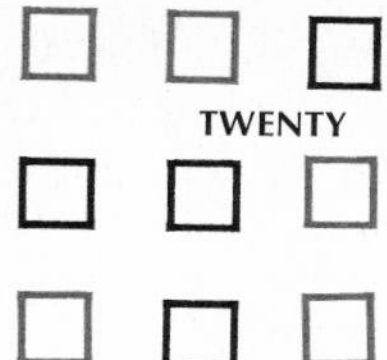

TWENTY

Marketing communications

To many, marketing communications—advertising, personal selling, and other forms of persuasion—is synonymous with marketing. This viewpoint is even shared by some businessmen, especially in traditional product-oriented firms where the "marketing function" is often defined as that of selling and advertising the company's products. Hopefully, the discussion of marketing management in the past seven chapters, and especially that in Chapter 13, has demonstrated that marketing includes much more than just promotional communications. Indeed, the most critical elements of marketing are usually those associated with determining a company's product line, in the first place, and its choice of markets in which to attempt to sell the line.

Although communication is not *all* of marketing, it is obviously an important component of the marketing process and of marketing management in a company. Promotional communication is the most visible and controversial element of marketing activity, and one of the most costly. When consumers criticize marketing practices, they almost always single out promotion, not product policies, pricing, or channels of distribution. Most of the legislation regulating marketing is likewise directed at selling and advertising activities. Communication is thus important to management because it is a subject of controversy and restrictions, and also because it has such an important bearing on success in the marketplace.

This chapter and the next two chapters deal with the management of marketing communications. In this chapter, we discuss the role of communication in marketing in general terms: the main forms of promotion, how promotional communication is thought to work, and how objectives are established for communications programs. Chapter 21 deals with personal selling, and Chapter 22 with advertising and sales promotion.

Major forms of marketing communication

We are using the phrase "marketing communication" to denote all types of communication that affect the attitudes and actions of decision-making units in a market. Our primary concern is with communications that can be controlled by a company or other organization attempting to market a product or service. It should be recognized, however, that purchases are influenced by many types of uncontrolled communications, such as informal discussions among consumers, as well as by those which a firm deliberately selects or designs.

The three broad classes of promotional communication that the marketer controls are personal selling, advertising, and sales promotion.

□

PERSONAL SELLING

□ *Personal selling is direct, oral promotional communication between representatives of marketer organizations and current or prospective customers.*

Personal selling□ communication can be literally "face to face," as when a manufacturer's salesman visits a retailer or industrial user; or it may be carried out via telephone.

Personal selling is the oldest form of promotional activity, dating from the very beginnings of exchange. It is still the most important form of marketing communication, even in the twentieth century. Estimates of expenditures for all forms of promotion in 1960 indicated that personal selling accounted for about 60 percent of the total.[1]

There can be little doubt that, in absolute terms, personal selling is the most powerful form of promotional communication. Assuming that the communications are competently designed and executed, a face-to-face conversation with a salesman will almost always have more impact on a customer than reading a printed advertisement or viewing a television commercial. One important reason is that personal communications can be "tailored" to the individual to whom the communication is directed, and to the circumstances. For example, a door-to-door salesman of vacuum cleaners can observe and comment on an individual housewife's rugs and home furnishings and on the cleaning problems created by her three-year-old son. He can also point out the special problems caused by the rainy weather on a particular day. No adver-

[1] Thaddeus H. Spratlen, "An Appraisal of Theory and Practice in the Analysis of Sales Effort," unpublished doctoral dissertation, The Ohio State University, 1962.

tisement can possibly be so specifically attuned to the needs and attitudes of each person in its audience. Moreover, the salesman has an opportunity to get "feedback" from his audience. He hears the housewife's responses, he observes her facial expressions, and he modifies his message accordingly. There is no opportunity for such feedback in advertising.

While personal selling is a highly effective form of promotion, it is also a very costly one. Depending on the type of products and customers involved, the average cost of a single sales call ranges from around $5 to as much as $100. When the potential results of personal selling are compared with the costs, it may or may not be more efficient than alternative forms of communication. For many low-priced products bought at frequent intervals, personal selling to consumers or users is too expensive even to consider.

□

ADVERTISING

□ *Advertising is paid, nonpersonal communication directed by a marketer to members of decision-making units in a market.*

The most familiar forms of advertising□ are printed messages in magazines, newspapers, and mail-delivered materials; broadcast messages delivered via television and radio; and posters and other outdoor advertising. Miscellaneous types of advertising communication include advertising "specialties" such as calendars or imprinted pencils, commercial films, skywriting, and various forms of catalogs and directories.

The key distinction between advertising and personal selling is, obviously, the absence of a human "presenter" in advertising. There are borderline forms of promotional communication, such as partially standardized sales letters signed by a salesman, but whether these belong under "advertising" or "selling" is not of much importance.

The definition of advertising includes the word "paid" to distinguish advertising from publicity, which is communication about a company or about its products and services that is not paid for—at least, not directly. This form of communication is discussed below under the heading Uncontrolled Communications.

In one form or another, advertising has been used by marketers for many centuries. However, it became a major promotional tool only after the development of mass communications—first, the newspaper in the eighteenth century, then magazines in the nineteenth and early twentieth centuries, and more recently radio and television in the 1920s and 1950s, respectively.[2] As these communication media have evolved, marketers have learned how to design standardized messages that inform and influence large numbers of prospective customers.

It is important to recognize that the basic process of communication is the

[2] For an informative and amusing history of advertising, see E. Turner, *The Shocking History of Advertising,* E. P. Dutton & Co., Inc., New York, 1953.

same in advertising as in personal selling. Although the techniques of communication have been drastically modified to fit the demands of nonpersonal media, the concepts underlying advertising have for the most part been drawn from those used much earlier in personal selling. As one of the great pioneers of twentieth-century advertising, Albert Lasker, said, "Advertising is salesmanship in print."

Because advertising is standardized communication, it is inherently less powerful, less flexible, and less costly than personal selling. But the range of possibilities within advertising is almost as great as the difference between "average" advertising and "average" salesmanship. A brief radio commercial or a printed card displayed in a bus or subway car may reach an audience at a cost of as little as a hundredth of a cent per "exposure." At the other extreme, an elaborate brochure used to reach members of a highly specialized audience, say, neurosurgeons or United States congressmen, may have a cost of $5, $10 or more per message delivered. Thus, although the distinctive feature of advertising is its ability to achieve mass communication, the size of the audience and the degree of selectivity appropriate for different marketing situations vary widely.

SALES PROMOTION

Sales promotion is hard to define clearly. The "official" definition is: "those activities other than personal selling, advertising, and publicity, that stimulate consumer purchasing and dealer effectiveness, such as display, shows and exhibitions, demonstrations, and various nonrecurrent selling efforts."[3] In effect, sales promotion is a catchall category; it includes all forms of promotion other than those falling within one or another of the major categories. Just what is included under sales promotion varies from one industry to another. Among the activities which we shall classify as sales promotion are the following:

Point-of-purchase displays and signs
Product samples
Demonstrations
Premium offers, including trading stamps and coupons
Contests and sweepstakes
Exhibits at conventions, trade fairs, etc.

Many writers also include temporary price reductions (with and without coupons), and various forms of training and assistance given by manufacturers to dealers and distributors, in the category of sales promotion. We have treated these elements of the marketing program in Chapters 17 and 18, respectively.

[3] Committee on Definitions, *Marketing Definitions: A Glossary of Marketing Terms,* American Marketing Association, Chicago, 1960.

As defined here, then, sales promotion consists of miscellaneous forms of promotional communication, mostly of the nonpersonal variety, but in some cases involving a mixture of personal and nonpersonal channels. What these activities have in common is that they are typically used to supplement the main forms of promotion, often in connection with special situations such as new product introductions or responding to the actions of competitors. From the standpoint of overall communications strategy, the key characteristic of sales promotion is its flexibility—the fact that it can be used on a temporary basis to meet short-term needs, without becoming a continuing element of the marketing program and budget.

Occasionally, the use of some type of sales promotion becomes so customary in a particular industry that the advantages of flexibility are lost. Some observers felt that this was the case, for instance, in food and gasoline retailing in the late 1960s, when "game" promotions were offered by almost every major competitor in many metropolitan areas on a virtually continuous basis.

□ UNCONTROLLED COMMUNICATION

Personal selling, advertising, and sales promotion are all designed, paid for, and controlled by the marketer. Collectively, they serve to implement a promotional strategy. But, as remarked earlier, these controlled forms of communication do not constitute all the communication that affects customers. In early 1971, the news media of the United States gave prominent attention to announcements that certain shipments of imported tuna fish had been found to contain amounts of mercury in excess of the limits set by the Food and Drug Administration. This communication, naturally enough, had a strong impact on consumers. Sales of canned tuna fish, a major item in many families' menus, declined sharply. Domestic producers of tuna, whose products had not been declared contaminated, were immediately and significantly affected. These firms clearly did not design or control the news stories, and indeed were confronted with the problem of how to counteract the impressions caused by them.

News stories about companies and products, not paid for or controlled by the marketer, make up the communications element of *publicity*. Although the marketer can seldom if ever control publicity completely, this is not to say he cannot influence it. A major purpose of the public relations activities of business firms, and other organizations, such as the Department of Defense and many civic and charitable agencies, is to stimulate favorable publicity. These efforts are sometimes defensive, as when widespread criticisms are made of automobile safety, the ecological effects of insecticides, and so forth. More frequently, public relations is aimed at generating favorable news coverage of a company's activities, mention of a new product, the use of a product in some newsworthy situation, or other information that might stimulate customers to buy.

Space does not permit extensive treatment of public relations and publicity. In connection with our discussion of the major forms of marketing communication, we point out that promotional strategy must be designed in the light of existing knowledge and attitudes about a product or service, which may come in part from publicity communications. Insofar as the marketer *can* influence publicity, he should do so in a way that will present a consistent, coordinated communications program.

Another uncontrolled form of communication is that of informal discussion among customers, so-called "word-of-mouth" communication. In Chapter 7 we mentioned some of the studies that have been done of word-of-mouth discussion; these studies show that comments made by one customer to another often have much more influence than the marketer's promotional efforts. Like publicity, word-of-mouth discussion is largely uncontrollable by the marketer, and he must simply accommodate to it as best he can. Sometimes, however, promotional programs are designed partly for the purpose of influencing customers' discussions.

Promotion as a type of communication

All types of promotional communications, whether through personal selling, advertising, or sales promotion, are intended to influence the *actions* of decision-making units. But promotion, in itself, does not produce action; instead, it affects action indirectly by changing the knowledge, attitudes, and beliefs of decision-making units. As a foundation for our discussion of promotional strategy, therefore, we shall first consider the nature of communications. In Chapters 6 and 7 we reviewed some aspects of customer behavior, including response to communications. Now, viewing the process from the standpoint of a marketer attempting to influence behavior through promotion, we shall summarize our understanding of "how communications work."

□ THE COMMUNICATIONS PROCESS

Figure 20-1 is a schematic diagram of the process of promotional communications. The key elements of the process are a communications *source,* such as company or other organization; a communications *receiver* or audience member; the *content* of the messages directed by the source to the audience; and the *channels* through which the messages flow. The end result of the process is some kind of communications *effects*—changes in the knowledge, attitudes, and beliefs of the audience members. As shown in the diagram, communications processes do not operate in isolation. The receiver's perceptions of communications are affected by other elements of the marketing program,

FIGURE 20-1
Schematic model of the communications process

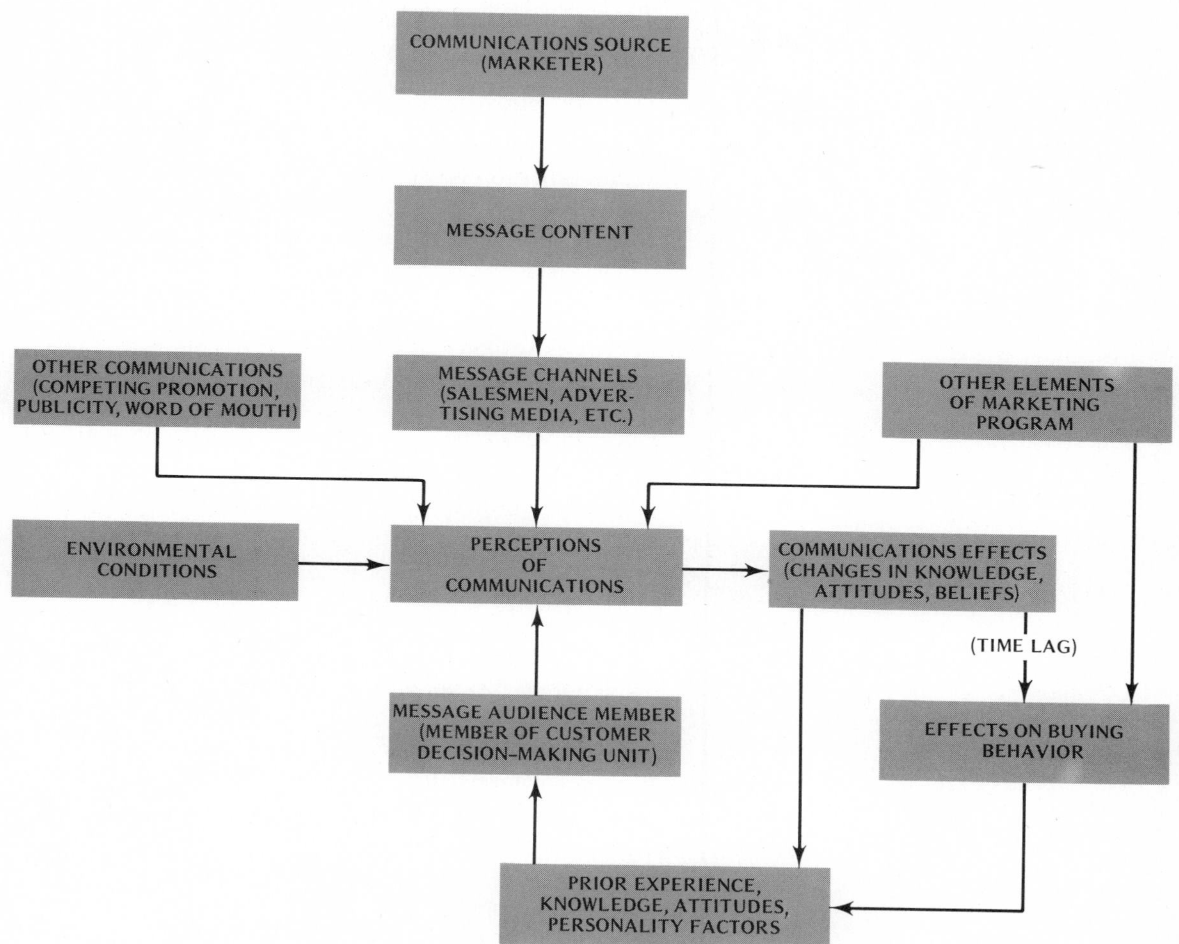

including the product itself, the package, and the price. Moreover, other sources of communications influence perceptions of a given message, and so do environmental conditions ranging from general economic conditions to time of day and weather.

There has been extensive research on the communications process and on how communications effects are related to various characteristics of messages, audience members, communications sources, and channels. In the sections that follow, we attempt to summarize some of the main conclusions of this research together with some generally accepted ideas based on the "popular wisdom" of marketing practitioners. At the outset, however, we should warn the reader that in spite of all the research that has been done, and in spite of the long history of trial and error by practitioners in the field of promotion, the process of communication is still very poorly understood.

□ THE MESSAGE AND THE AUDIENCE

The most obvious thing that can be said about promotional communications, but also the most important, is that the message must be designed so as to be relevant and interesting to a *specific* audience. As explained in Chapter 13, the starting point of any marketing plan is the definition of target markets, that is, the identification of types of individuals, households, or organizations to which the marketing effort will be directed. The target market for a men's hair grooming product might be defined, for example, as male consumers between sixteen and thirty-four years of age, with specific efforts being directed toward subgroups such as students, members of the armed services, and junior executives. Similarly, the marketing program for a scientific measuring device might be based on a choice of such target markets as research laboratories in petrochemical companies and university chemistry departments. The communications component of these marketing programs must, then, be designed with these specific types of prospective customers in mind. Advertisements for the hair grooming product, directed to young men, must appeal to the interests of young men. (To judge from the content of these advertisements, young women are judged to rank high among these interests.) These advertising messages must be expressed in terms that are meaningful and interesting to young men. The content of promotion directed to research and development directors of petrochemical companies, on the other hand, must appeal to their interests and use their language.

In brief, promotional messages must be based on a knowledge of the audience whose behavior they are intended to influence. The importance of the maxim "know your audience" is borne out by the statements of practitioners about how they design communications. Both advertising copywriters and sales managers devote considerable effort to studying *who* their audiences are:

Are they men or women? Are they young or old? Where do they live? What are their job responsibilities? What is their previous training? What language do they use in talking about the product? Answers to these and many similar questions are basic to developing effective promotional communications.

Apart from relevance to the audience, there are a number of other characteristics of the promotional message that are believed to have important effects on communications results. Depending on the subject of the communication, some of the questions that may arise in designing messages include[4]:

1. Should the basic approach be "hard-sell" or "soft-sell"? That is, should the message be an aggressive, explicit request for action, or should it be more subtle?
2. How much emphasis should be put on factual information versus creation of a "mood" or emotional tone?
3. How much stress should be put on negative appeals versus positive appeals? (A negative appeal might emphasize the costs of not replacing obsolete machine tools, for example, while a positive appeal would deal with the benefits of having new ones.)
4. How important is it for promotional messages to be entertaining? Does this make the audience more receptive, or is it a distraction from the content of the message?
5. Should the message be "one-sided" or "two-sided"? That is, should it present only the benefits of a product, or should it also recognize possible limitations or drawbacks?

The relationship of these message characteristics to communication results depends, in part, on the characteristics of the audience. For example, as explained in Chapter 6, one-sided messages are generally more effective (1) when the audience's attitudes toward the subject of the message is already favorable, (2) among those who are not very well educated, and (3) when the audience is *not* exposed to conflicting messages later on. But even when the characteristics of the audience are known, there is still considerable difference of opinion about what kinds of messages work best, and competing marketers sometimes use quite different approaches.

We have just mentioned education and existing attitudes toward the subject of a message as characteristics of the audience that help determine communication results. Other audience attributes that are believed to be important are the general level of interest in the subject of a message, the degree of familiarity with the specific subject of the message, and basic personality factors, such as the individual's degree of self-confidence. As examples of how these

[4] Cf. Thomas S. Robertson, *Consumer Behavior,* Scott, Foresman and Company, Glenview, Ill., 1970, pp. 49–51.

factors affect communications, consider these illustrations:

1. Traditionally, the introduction of new models by the major automobile producers has been an event with high inherent interest to most American consumers. Advertisements featuring these new models are almost guaranteed high readership. Many other products, such as plumbing fixtures, are of much less interest than automobiles. Advertisements for these products often employ dramatic "attention-getting" devices just to get readership from a general audience.
2. When a product is already well-known to most members of an audience, promotional messages can be designed to provide simple "reminders" of key product features. Coca-Cola, for instance, needs little explanation to most consumers in the United States and most other countries; promotion for this brand is aimed primarily at reminding consumers of its thirst-quenching qualities. Sport Cola, a new brand introduced by the Canada Dry Company in the late 1960s, was a caffeine-free cola drink, and its promotion was designed to convince consumers, especially mothers, of the merits of avoiding caffeine intake.
3. Several research studies have shown that the effects of persuasive communications are related to differing degrees of "self-confidence" on the part of audience members (see Chapter 6). If the characteristics of an audience could be determined in terms of self-confidence, promotional messages could be designed accordingly.

□

THE SOURCE

The effects of communications appear to depend, in part, on the audience's perception of the reliability of the source from which messages come. Numerous studies have shown that communications effects are greater when the source is believed to be authoritative and/or impartial than when it is seen as inexpert or partisan. For example, one of the authors conducted an experiment in which sales presentations were made to purchasing agents and engineers for a new industrial product. One audience group was exposed to presentations in which the seller was identified as a large, well-known chemical company; another group heard the same presentation but with an unknown company name. The effects of the communications, measured in terms of stated willingness to try the new product, were significantly greater for the well-known company.[5]

Marketers are, by definition, partisan sources of information about their own products or services, and they cannot legitimately overcome being perceived

[5] Theodore Levitt, *Industrial Purchasing Behavior,* Division of Research, Harvard Business School, Boston, 1965.

as such. But promotional communications can be, and frequently are, designed to include messages from other sources that may be seen as less biased. The "testimonial" is a widely used device in advertising, providing sanction for the use of a product from well-known and/or expert persons in a particular field, such as Arnold Palmer for golf equipment in the later 1960s. In both personal selling and advertising, case histories of satisfied users are often used to document promotional claims. Perhaps the most frequent use of testimonials is in the promotion of political candidates, where famous national figures spend considerable time appearing on behalf of local nominees.

THE CHANNEL

Audience perceptions of promotional messages are also affected by the channels through which communications are delivered. In the field of personal selling, there is evidence that customers are most strongly influenced by salesmen whom they perceive as being like themselves, that is, similar in age, sex, appearance, and interests.[6] These relationships have not been clearly identified through controlled experimentation, but it seems clear that the characteristics of the salesman (the channel) do influence the results of sales messages.

In advertising, likewise, the effects of promotional messages are influenced by the media in which the messages appear. Advertising practitioners speak of the "climate" of a magazine, or a television program, for advertising a given product (see Chapter 22). It is generally believed, with some support from various studies, that the same message will have different effects on the same audience member if delivered through different media.

TIME LAG

As suggested by Figure 20-1, some time typically elapses between a customer's exposure to a promotional message and any action that may be affected by the message. A housewife sees a television commercial for a detergent brand on Monday, but does not make her next detergent purchase until a week from the following Friday; an office manager talks with a salesman of duplicating equipment in March, but does not begin to consider any purchase until October. These time lags between the communications effects of promotional messages and opportunities to influence action make it necessary to consider how the passage of time modifies communications.

It is generally recognized that, even in the absence of conflicting communications, the results of a sales or advertising message "decay" rather rap-

[6] Harry L. Davis and Alvin J. Silk, "Behavioral Research on Personal Selling: A Review of Some Recent Studies of Interaction and Influence Processes in Sales Situations," Working Paper, Marketing Science Institute, Cambridge, Mass., April, 1971.

idly as time passes. If results are measured in terms of knowledge of facts about a product or other subject, for example, the average level of knowledge among those receiving a message will be highest immediately afterward. Subsequently, knowledge will decline fairly quickly and ultimately reach a level only slightly higher than that existing prior to the communication. Figure 20-2 shows the shape of a "forgetting" curve which has been shown to apply generally to promotional effects.[7]

The deterioration of effects following exposure to a communication is even more rapid when an audience member is exposed to *conflicting* communications, which is typically the case in marketing situations. As suggested in Figure 20-3, a customer who is exposed to conflicting communications, such as the visit of a competitor's salesman or negative publicity, will forget the knowledge learned from a given message even faster than one not exposed to conflicting messages.

The phenomenon of forgetting is, of course, the reason why marketers rely so heavily on *repetition* in promotion. By exposing customers to a series of messages from different sources, including salesmen, advertising, and sales promotion, the marketer can *reinforce* the effects of the original message and, to some degree, counteract the influence of competitive promotion. As an example, consider the activities of the major political parties just prior to a national election. Each party vies to deliver a maximum number of advertising messages and speeches during the period immediately preceding the voting. The object is to prevent forgetting, to reinforce earlier messages, and to offset the messages of the rival party.

[7] For a review of relevant research on forgetting, see David B. Learner, "The Repetition of Advertising," pamphlet, Batten, Barton, Durstine & Osborn, New York, 1967.

FIGURE 20-2
How communications effects decay with time

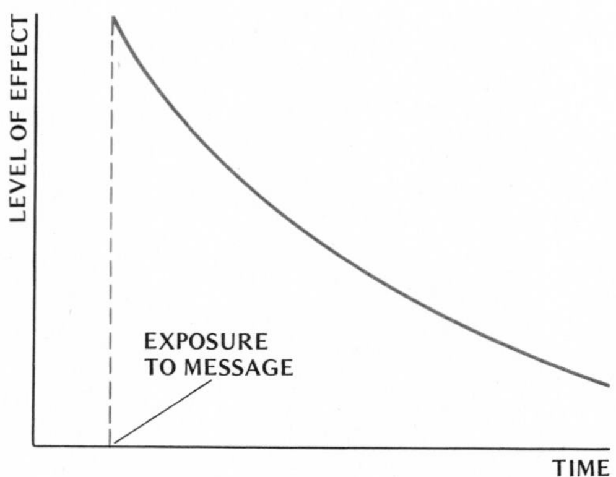

FIGURE 20-3
How communications effects decay in relation to time and conflicting communications

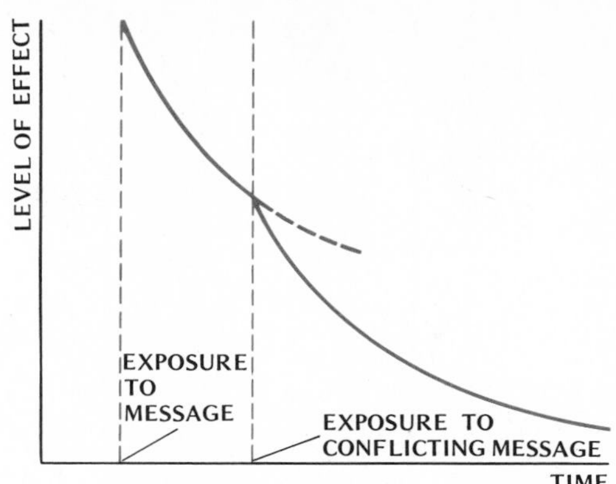

Developing the communications strategy

The foregoing brief review suggests that the role of communications in influencing customer behavior is very complex. In one way or another, selling and advertising affect customers' knowledge, attitudes, and beliefs; and these communication results, in turn, eventually lead to actions such as buying or voting. Just how all this happens is often something of a mystery. About all we can say with certainty is that "it depends"—it depends on the nature of the message, the characteristics of the audience, the source, the message channel, and on other factors. Yet somehow a marketer must design his promotional strategy, preferably in a systematic fashion, so as to achieve desired results at a reasonable cost.

In this part of the chapter, we turn to the subject of communications strategy. We shall focus on three main topics related to the design of a strategy: the establishment of objectives, the level of promotional expenditures, and the allocation of resources among major forms of promotional communication.

□

OBJECTIVES FOR COMMUNICATIONS

The objectives of an organization's marketing communications are based directly on its overall marketing objectives. As stated in Chapter 13, the starting point for the marketing program is selection of target markets. Product design, pricing, and channels of distribution must all be tailored to the characteristics of these groups of households or organizations—and so must the communications program. Communications objectives should, ideally, be stated in terms of *what* is to be communicated *to whom.*

As an example of the problems that arise in setting objectives for communications, consider the situation of the Radio Corporation of America (RCA) in the mid-1950s, when color television was still a new and unfamiliar product.[8] RCA began to market color TV receivers, and to provide color telecasting over its subsidiary, the NBC network, in early 1954. After four years of reasonably heavy promotional effort, the number of sets sold was quite small; fewer than 1 percent of households in the United States owned them. RCA's experience indicated that several obstacles stood in the way of greater sales. Consumers were generally unfamiliar with color—fewer than one-fourth had even seen a color telecast. They were also skeptical of the quality of color pictures. Dealers were apathetic about selling color TV sets, in spite of relatively high gross profit margins. Salesmen in retail stores were themselves unfamiliar with color, unskilled in demonstrating it, and felt that sales were too difficult to justify the effort required.

What kind of communications strategy was appropriate for RCA under these conditions? Obviously some effort had to be directed to both dealers and consumers. Some major objectives of marketing communication might have been stated as follows:

Objectives	*Means of achieving objectives*
Convince store owners and managers that promoting color TV is profitable	RCA salesmen: Emphasize profit margins Offer special incentives Inform dealers about the success of other dealers' programs
	Trade advertising: Reinforce salesmen's messages Convince dealers that color TV is going to be a mass-market product soon
Convince consumers that color telecasting is of high quality	Dealers: Demonstrate color reception under proper conditions Advertise special demonstrations
	RCA advertising: Inform consumers about improvements in color technology Inform consumers about dealer demonstrations

Color television did, of course, eventually become a widely accepted product in the United States, but not until the mid-1960s. RCA spent many millions of dollars on promotion of color TV, while competing manufacturers did very little, for a period of almost 10 years. Many factors other than promotion contributed to the slow acceptance of color, and to its eventual acceptance. But it

[8] The story of RCA's marketing of color TV is told in "RCA Organizes for Profit," *Fortune,* August, 1957; "Color TV: Will the Big Sales Breakthrough Come This Year?," *Printers' Ink,* Jan. 10, 1958; and "What's Wrong with Color TV?," *Electrical Merchandising,* August, 1959.

is clear that promotional communication played a major role by informing consumers and dealers and by changing their attitudes toward the product.

The RCA example illustrates the general point that communications programs should be designed in terms of specific audiences to be reached and in terms of content—what is to be communicated to these audiences. We described one of RCA's audience targets simply as "consumers." Actually, the audience would have been defined in much more specific terms. First, because color TV sets were much more expensive than black-and-white sets in the 1950s, high-income consumers were the most likely prospective customers. As suggested in Chapter 7, early adopters of new products are also likely to be better educated than average, more mobile, and relatively young. Finally, because color telecasting did not cover all areas of the United States in the 1950s, consumers in major metropolitan areas would have been the logical targets for color set promotion. Thus, the definition of the consumer audience for RCA's promotion should have taken, and probably did take, a number of consumer characteristics into account. Similarly, the promotional program for dealers would have been directed primarily at large stores in appropriate locations.

Broad communications objectives of the sort illustrated by the RCA example provide guidelines for much more specific goals for specific forms of promotion during a given period of time, down to the level of individual sales calls and individual advertisements. Detailed selling and advertising goals are discussed in Chapters 21 and 22.

COMMUNICATIONS SPENDING LEVELS

Closely related to the establishment of objectives is the matter of expenditures for marketing communications. How much will it cost, for example, to convince a given number of dealers that they should demonstrate RCA color TV sets? The cost of achieving an objective is one thing, and the company's ability to afford it is another. Given the costs of producing and distributing color TV sets, what price will have to be charged to provide margins sufficient to support a promotional program? The interrelationship of communication costs with other elements of the marketing mix means that spending levels must be determined as part of a consistent overall strategy.

Although the amount spent on communications depends on a number of factors peculiar to the individual organization and its situation at a given time, there are some broad common denominators among firms that sell similar products to similar groups of customers, through similar distribution channels. Thus, it is meaningful to talk about "typical" levels of communications expenditure in an industry, even though there are considerable variations among firms.

Manufacturers' communications expenditures Information about manufacturers' promotional expenditures is not readily available. But special studies, government investigations, and trade estimates provide some basis for making broad comparisons among industries. Rough estimates of expenditures on promotional communications, expressed as percentages of sales, are given for selected industries in Figure 20-4.

These estimates illustrate the tremendous variations in spending from one industry to another. Why do pharmaceutical manufacturers, breakfast cereal producers, and office equipment companies spend, on the average, more than 20 percent of sales on communication, while producers of primary metals and textiles spend less than 10 percent? Some products and/or some types of customers "require" more promotion, or are more responsive to it, than others. Some of the apparent reasons for these differences are discussed in the next section. Before leaving the estimates in Figure 20-4, however, we should emphasize two points. First, communications activities and costs at a given level in the channel of distribution depend in part on how promotional tasks are shared with other channel levels. A manufacturer will have lower costs if he relies heavily on distributors or dealers for promotion than if he provides

FIGURE 20-4

Approximate average promotional expenditures, as percentages of sales volume, selected manufacturing industries, 1960s

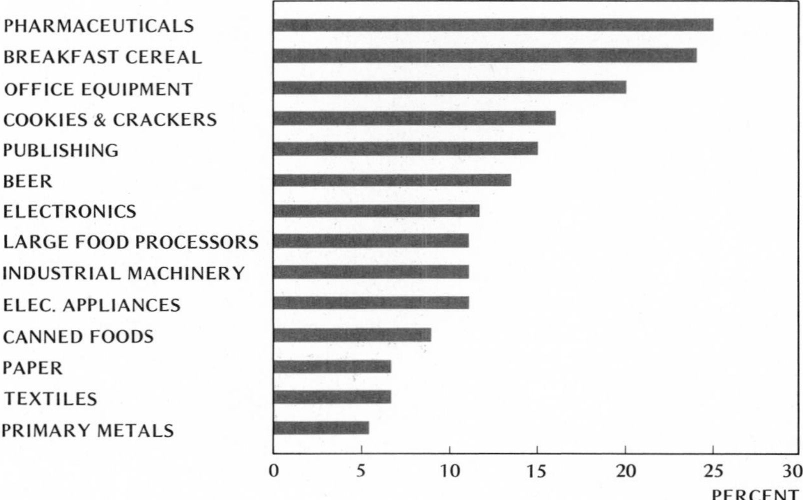

Source: Various trade estimates and special studies. Figures for breakfast cereals, cookies and crackers, and canned foods are based on studies by the Federal Trade Commission and the National Commission on Food Marketing. Insofar as possible, the figures lower personal selling, advertising, and sales promotion expeditures.

FIGURE 20-5
How sales respond to promotional communications effort

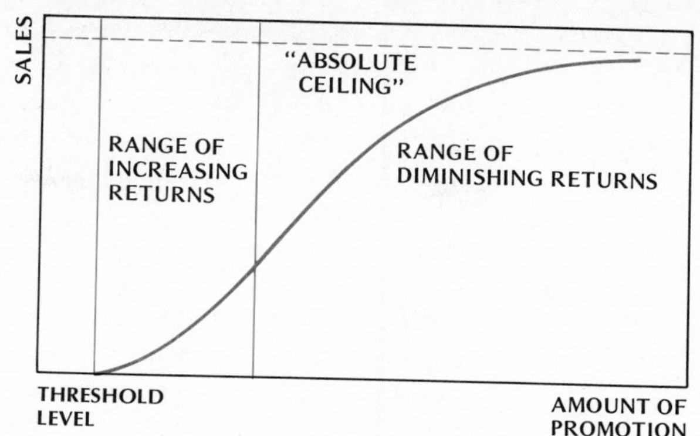

most of the effort himself. This is one of the factors, for instance, contributing to lower levels of communications spending by paper manufacturers than by industrial machinery producers.

Second, although *average* levels of spending tell us something about differences among industries, there are also big variations *within* industries. Smaller firms often spend bigger percentages of their sales on communications than large ones, because there is frequently a minimum "price of admission" in promotion. (See the discussion of "thresholds" in market response to promotion, below.) Firms within an industry also differ with respect to basic marketing strategies. Some food processors, for instance, put great emphasis on product innovation, while others are content to imitate the leaders' products and rely on price-cutting to get business. The innovative strategy requires higher spending for promotional communication than the imitative one.

MARKET RESPONSE TO PROMOTIONAL COMMUNICATIONS

Differences in promotional spending among firms and industries presumably reflect differences in how markets respond to communications effort. Let us consider, first, the general question of relationships between promotional effort, sales volume, and profits. The most widely accepted theory of how sales respond to promotional communication is depicted in Figure 20-5. As shown there, most authorities, both practitioners and researchers, believe that there is a "threshold" level of promotion for a given product or firm. Spending an amount below the threshold level will, it is believed, evoke little or no sales response. Explanations of the threshold phenomenon are varied, depending on the type of product and market involved:

1. In both personal selling and advertising, there may be a minimum "quantity" in which key forms of promotion can be bought. Hiring a single full-time

salesman, for example, may involve a minimum salary and expense allowance. Using national television advertising, similarly, requires a minimum expenditure on time and production which may be substantial in relation to the sales of a small firm. If the means of promotion that are available for smaller expenditures are much less efficient than those mentioned, then a firm spending less than the "threshold" amount will get very little sales response.
2. There may be a psychological threshold in the minds of customers. Many advertisers believe that there is a minimum "frequency" (number of exposures to advertisements) that must be achieved for a given product in order to get any response in terms of purchases.
3. There may be a minimum amount of promotion needed to induce dealers or distributors to stock a manufacturer's product line. Below this level, promotion will generate little or no response simply because customers will not have access to the product.

Some authorities deny that there are thresholds in market response to promotion.[9] Systematic research on the point is lacking, at least in published form. Until such research has been done, we believe that it must be assumed that, under most conditions, there *is* a threshold in market response.

The nature of market response to promotional communication beyond the threshold level is also the subject of some controversy. In Figure 20-5 we show a "range of increasing returns," in which increasing amounts of promotion yield more than proportional increases in sales. The reasoning for assuming that there is such a response is similar to that given for the existence of thresholds. As a firm spends more on promotion, up to a point, it can be more and more efficient. It can afford to use more and more specialized resources, such as sales training, more talented advertising agencies, and full-time marketing research personnel. Increasing specialization *should* lead to greater effectiveness in the planning and execution of promotional communications programs.

At some point, however, it is universally agreed that diminishing returns set in. Beyond this point, increasing amounts of promotion lead to *less* than proportional increases in sales volume. Once salesmen have called on all the prospective customers with high purchase potential, they must turn to less and less promising prospects. Once advertising messages have reached the primary target audiences with sufficient frequency, additional messages must be directed to audiences with lower and lower levels of response. If more and more sales calls or advertisements are delivered to the *same* customers, the incremental effect of each unit of effort must eventually start to decline. Indeed, there may be a point when additional promotional effort leads to *abso-*

[9] Julian Simon, *Issues in the Economics of Advertising,* University of Illinois Press, Urbana, Ill., 1970.

lutely diminishing returns; customers may become irritated with excessive demands on their time and actually stop buying in protest.

One last point about the general nature of market response to promotion: as shown in Figure 20-5, there is some absolute ceiling or maximum amount of sales that can be achieved for any product or service under given conditions. As sales approach this ceiling, it stands to reason that each successive increase will be harder and harder to get.

PROMOTIONAL SPENDING AND PROFITS

Managers of business firms generally try to set promotional expenditure levels so as to maximize profits. If sales volume responds to promotion as indicated in Figure 20-5, how do profits change as the amount of promotion is increased?

As explained in Chapter 13, the average per-unit costs of producing and distributing a product typically decline as sales volume increases; but beyond some point, cost reductions become smaller and smaller, and there may even be a stage beyond which unit costs increase. Even if per-unit costs continue to decline indefinitely, there will be a point where the added costs of promotion required to increase sales outweigh the contribution to profits of an added unit of sales. These cost-volume relationships are reflected in Figure 20-6, which presents a typical picture of how profits change in relation to changing amounts of promotional spending.

As suggested by Figure 20-6, a company's profits are likely to respond slowly to increased promotional spending at first, because of the threshold in promotional results discussed earlier. Then, profits rise relatively rapidly up to

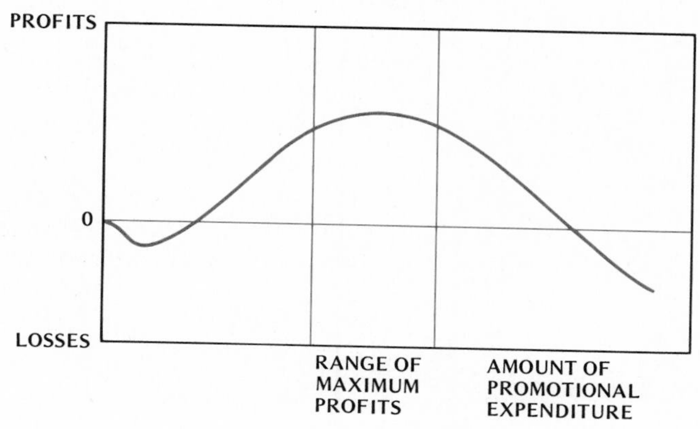

FIGURE 20-6
Typical relationship of company profits to promotional communications expenditures

a point, level off, and subsequently decline because of the diminishing returns phenomenon.

Ideally, a company seeks to set its promotional spending level somewhere in what is termed the "range of maximum profits" in Figure 20-6. We designate this as a range rather than a unique point, both because there is likely to be a fairly wide range of spending levels over which changes in promotion affect profits only slightly, and because methods for identifying the "optimal" level of spending are rather crude. (Some of these methods are described in Chapter 25.)

One important qualification must be made about the relationship of promotional spending to profits. Especially for new products, as explained in Chapter 15, promotional communication efforts are directed toward both *present* and *future* sales. Thus, many companies spend more on promotion than would be justified by current profits.

□

VARIATIONS AMONG PRODUCTS AND MARKETS

The general relationships between promotional spending, sales, and profits depicted in Figures 20-5 and 20-6 are thought to apply to companies in any industry or market. But, as suggested by Figure 20-4, some products and markets are more responsive to promotion than others.

How can these differences be explained? There is no comprehensive theory that answers this question to the satisfaction of all concerned, but some of the factors that seem to affect the "promotability" of different products and markets include the following[10]:

Number and accessibility of potential customers In some markets, there are only a few potential customers and all or most of them are located in a few well-known market areas. Industries marketing to these customers are likely to have relatively low promotional costs. Primary metals and textiles, for example, fall into this category (see Figure 20-4).

Complexity of decision-making units Promotion is much simpler and less costly for products when a single individual constitutes the decision-making unit than when a number of people participate in purchase decisions. Pharmaceutical manufacturers, for example, must direct promotional efforts to physicians, who prescribe drugs for their patients; to drugstores, who must stock them; and, to a limited degree, to ultimate consumers. Similarly, producers of office equipment direct promotion to office managers, office personnel, purchasing agents, and higher level executives in the companies that use their products.

[10] Some of the factors in this list are discussed in Neil H. Borden, *The Economic Effects of Advertising,* Richard D. Irwin, Inc., Homewood, Ill., 1942.

Standardization of products and customer needs Promotional expenditures are likely to be relatively low for products that are highly standardized and in situations where customer needs and product uses are similar—this is the case for commodities bought on a specification basis, for example. In contrast, when products are highly differentiated and/or when there is a wide variety of possible uses for a product or service, response to properly designed promotion is likely to be much greater.

Degree to which customers recognize product benefits When a product is well known to virtually all prospective customers, and its uses have been thoroughly tested and understood, there may be relatively little need for promotion and little to be gained from it. Automobile producers are presumably familiar with the properties and uses of steel, for instance, and need little information about it. On the other hand, when producers developed new types of aluminum for use in automobiles, there was a significant opportunity for expanding their markets through promotion. Similarly, most housewives are thoroughly familiar with white bread and would not change their purchases of it much even if bakeries greatly increased their promotional budgets. When "instant breakfast" products were introduced in the late 1960s, however, there was a need for high levels of promotion to inform consumers about the existence of the products and their features.

As suggested in these illustrations, customer knowledge of product benefits is partly a question of product age—the stage of the product's "life cycle" at a given point in time. As indicated in Chapter 14, promotional spending is apt to be much higher in the early stages of a life cycle than it is later on. Beyond this, some products and services seem to be inherently better or less accepted even after they have been available for a long period of time. The need for life insurance, for example, is probably almost universally recognized by adult males in the United States and other industrialized countries. But it is well known that very few consumers will buy insurance without considerable promotional effort being devoted to persuading them that concrete action must be taken.

Frequency and timing of purchases When products or services are bought frequently in relatively small amounts, opportunities for influencing behavior through promotion are apparently greater than when purchases are large and infrequent. This is no doubt the main explanation for the fact that promotional spending is generally greater for consumer goods than for products sold to industrial, institutional, and professional markets.

Product line turnover There is a greater need for promotion when the product line is modified frequently than when it remains relatively stable. Annual or seasonal "model changes" or "lines" require substantial promotion just to inform customers what is available. Examples include the book publishing, apparel, phonograph record, automobile, and major appliance industries.

THE PROMOTIONAL COMMUNICATIONS MIX

Thus far, we have discussed promotional spending without any consideration of how the total effort is divided among major forms of communication. Determining the relative emphasis to be given to personal selling, advertising, and sales promotion is, however, a key aspect of an organization's communications strategy. Typical promotional "mixes" differ among industries as much as, if not more than, total levels of promotional effort.

Some estimates of the typical distribution of total communication between personal selling and advertising and sales promotion, for selected manufacturing industries, are given in Figure 20-7. Note the great variation, ranging from very heavy emphasis on sales force effort to almost complete reliance on advertising and sales promotion. Generally speaking, consumer goods indus-

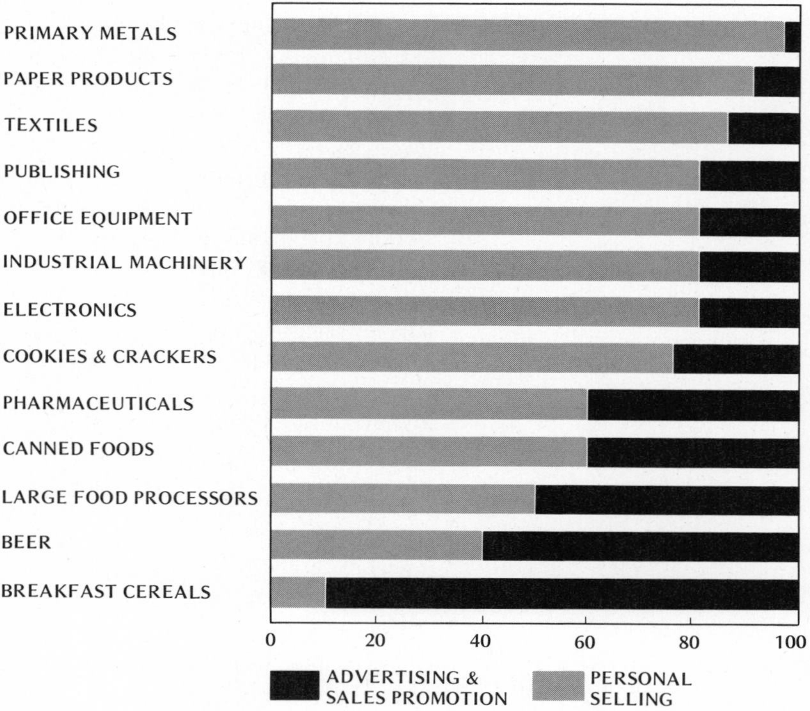

FIGURE 20-7

Approximate division of total promotion between personal selling and advertising/sales promotion, selected industries, 1960s

tries utilize advertising to a greater extent, while companies selling to intermediate customers rely more heavily on personal selling efforts. Here, too, there are great variations within industries. As mentioned in Chapter 10, most cosmetics manufacturers spend heavily on advertising; but Avon Products, a highly successful door-to-door marketer, devotes practically all its promotional budget to personal selling.

Conclusion

In this chapter, we have introduced some basic concepts related to the role of communications in the marketing programs of firms and other organizations. Promotion is basically a type of communication, and it is useful to think about it in terms of messages delivered by various communication channels to "receivers"—prospective customers for products and services. The three main forms of promotional communication—personal selling, advertising, and sales promotion—have been defined and compared.

Establishing the total level of communications effort and its allocation among the major forms are difficult but vital management tasks. These decisions, together with the determination of *what* is to be said to *whom,* constitute the communications strategy of the firm. Within the guidelines established by these strategic decisions, a wide variety of more specific decisions must be made about the number of salesmen to be used, their selling tasks, the means used to motivate and compensate them, the advertising messages to be employed, the media used to deliver them, and the methods used to measure results for both selling and advertising. These topics are discussed in the next two chapters.

Questions

1. What general combination of personal selling, advertising, and sales promotion activities would you recommend for a large manufacturer of each of the following products? Why?
   a. Cigarettes
   b. Heavy earth-moving equipment
   c. Plywood
   d. Ball-point pens
   e. Musical instruments
   f. Prescription drugs

2. In 1968, the average expenditure on advertising of manufacturers of confectionery and related products, such as candy and gum, was close to 5 percent of sales. This was a higher average percentage than that for any other food

product except soft drinks, flavoring extracts, and syrups. Yet Hershey, a leading manufacturer of chocolate bars, had never incurred any expenditures for advertising.

a. How do you account for the high degree of consumer awareness of Hershey products?

b. Do you think Hershey is likely to be more or less profitable than other chocolate bar manufacturers? Why?

3. A district sales manager voiced the following complaint at a sales meeting:

> The average salesman costs our company $20,000 in compensation and expenses. Why can't we buy two or three fewer $60,000 full-page advertisements in *Life* magazine and use the money to hire more salesmen? Surely one man working a full year can sell more product than one-third of one ad in *Life* magazine.

a. Do you agree or disagree with the sales manager? Why?

b. As marketing vice-president of the company, what action would you take? Why?

4. Avon Products has enjoyed considerable success in selling women's cosmetics door-to-door. What role should advertising have in Avon's marketing strategy? What specific communications objectives would you suggest for Avon advertising?

5. For a durable product you have purchased recently, attempt to identify *all* the communications you received which had anything to do with the purchase. How much influence do you think each communication had on your ultimate purchase decision? What could the manufacturer of the product you bought have done to influence you more effectively? What might a competing manufacturer have done to get you to buy his product instead?

6. When the communications mix of a firm includes expenditures for personal selling, advertising, and sales promotion, how can the firm measure the relative effectiveness of each?

7. Personalized Cleaning Services was a small Chicago-based firm which specialized in home cleaning services. The company's principal product was a weekly or biweekly housecleaning service. For $75 per visit, three bonded cleaners would clean and vacuum an entire house, wash the kitchen and bathroom floors, and on an alternative visit schedule, clean the woodwork and wax and polish the hardwood floors. One team could clean two homes a day. These cleaning men were paid $4 per hour, with each home visit requiring 4 hours.

The company, which originally consisted of Tom Jones the owner-manager and two assistants, had in less than four years, grown to a staff of 10 servicing nearly 50 regular customers.

Initially, Jones had built his business by calling personally door-to-door in an attempt to solicit new customers. For the past year, however, most of his time was taken in supervising the cleaning teams and in general administration. Thus, most of the firm's recent growth had developed from personal referrals from existing customers.

Jones thought that there was a large untapped market for cleaning services, and was anxious to move rapidly to exploit the opportunities. Although the firm could not afford to invest a lot of money, Jones believed he could allot \$2,000 to \$3,000 initially, and as much as \$10,000 on selling and promotion during the current year, if he could be assured of at least 25 new regular customers.

While Jones was not sure of the best approach to increasing sales, he had considered a number of possibilities and wondered how he should appraise them.

a. What communications tasks does Jones wish to accomplish?

b. What possible approaches can you think of for Jones to increase sales of his home cleaning source?

c. How would you suggest that these possible approaches be evaluated?

d. Based on your analysis of the likely customers for a home cleaning service, how well do you think each of the approaches identified in (b) above would work?

e. What should Mr. Jones do? Why?

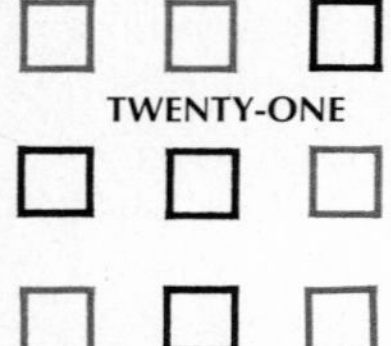

Personal selling

During the course of a recent weekday, the president of a major American company met with officials of a government agency in the USSR to discuss terms of sale for his firm's products in that country; a middle-aged lady working part-time in a suburban department store explained differences between synthetic fabrics to a teen-ager looking for a new bathing suit; an engineer representing a computer firm spent several hours discussing alternative systems designs with executives of a bank; and a Pepsi-Cola bottler's route man installed a vending machine in a new factory building.

These varied examples illustrate both the variety and the pervasiveness of personal selling in the marketing system. As mentioned in Chapter 2, about 5 million persons are employed in various forms of selling in the United States; in addition, many executives of business firms and other organizations spend part of their time in personal contact with customers. Indeed, every personal contact between a customer and any employee of an organization is potentially a "sales call." Customer attitudes and actions are powerfully affected by the efficiency and pleasantness, or lack thereof, that are displayed by representatives of a company, whether they are formally designated as "salespersons" or not.

Nature of personal selling

This chapter deals with the major tasks of managing personal selling as a component of the marketing program. These tasks include the definition of selling objectives, the design of specific selling tasks, determination of the amount of selling effort needed, recruiting and training of sales personnel, compensation of salesmen, and motivation. Because the nature of sales management problems varies greatly from one situation to another, it is helpful first to classify the major types of selling that are employed in the marketing of products, services, and ideas.

TYPES OF SELLING

Personal selling can be a major instrument of marketing strategy. Whereas advertising is typically directed at large groups of people, personal selling is the selective instrument through which a firm reaches its ultimate customers or its channels on a face-to-face basis. In Chapter 20 we gave a definition of personal selling, but no definition can capture either the variety of tasks that can be involved or the many different kinds of situations in which selling can be conducted. The examples cited below illustrate only a few of the many possible selling situations.

Cold selling The encyclopedia salesman who walks the streets and calls unannounced on people who come to the door is selling "cold." He seldom has a second chance unless invited back, and his success depends largely on his ability to interest a cold prospect in his product.

Development selling The salesman for a plastic manufacturer who offers film for packaging uses works with potential customers for long periods of time, helping them on their packaging needs and developing ways in which his product can be used by them. He develops long-run relationships in which he and his company's services and products all play major roles.

Development selling may also apply to situations in which salesmen try to create (develop) distribution of their products to the trade.

Missionary selling The salesman for the abrasives manufacturer that produces grinding wheels and other abrasive items is an example of missionary selling. The company uses industrial distributors to reach almost all its ultimate customers, and the salesman performs only "missionary" selling at that level. He calls on the distributors, and supports them by traveling through their territories visiting many of their customers. Usually he does not take customer orders, but refers inquiries to the appropriate distributors. When he does take orders, they are turned over to distributors.

New-product selling The salesman for General Foods, Procter and Gamble, or any of thousands of business firms that frequently add new products to their product lines may already have a line of products, but he must also sell each *new* one to the wholesalers, manufacturer's agents, chains, retailers, or other middlemen that handle his company's products. He has to push the special promotions (perhaps 10 cents off deals or special contests) for the new item, develop interest in the product itself, convince his customers to add the item to their lines, take orders, perhaps arrange product displays in retail stores, and file reports as to his various calls and activities. While doing all these things, and many others, for the new product, he also has to sell the remainder of his product line.

New-product selling can be both similar to, and different from, development selling. New-product selling can involve a great deal of development selling activity, but so can the selling of existing products that are sold to customers who have not previously used them. In both cases there may be a heavy element of solving customer problems in effective product use.

Service selling The salesman for an air freight company, whose responsibility is to sell his company's freight service to a variety of potential users, has to analyze their needs, make cost studies that reflect the economic advantages of air freight, and develop schedules that enable customers to meet their own or their customers' needs.

Systems selling An example of systems selling is the salesman who works for the National Cash Register Company or International Business Machines Company (IBM). The physical products sold by this salesman are computers, bookkeeping machinery, and other data-processing equipment. But since the installation of such equipment often requires the purchaser to modify his record-keeping, data-processing, and data-analysis operations drastically to suit the capacities and requirements of the machines, making a sale requires the salesman to help work out in detail the modifications required in the customer's operations before he will purchase the equipment. Hence the salesman is said to sell not just the equipment, but the entire data-processing, organizational, and operating *system* of which the equipment is the central part.

Frequently the salesman works with banks or other business firms in an attempt to sell a system of machines that handle billing and bookkeeping, payrolls and accounts receivable, or many other processes. He must have a thorough knowledge of his company's product line and its adaptability to the varied needs of many different kinds of customers. In a sense, he has to engineer a family of items whose value to his customers is determined both by the products themselves and by his own skills.

Team selling Teams are groups of men who sell, for example, weapons systems to the military establishment or complex power installations to utilities. The groups may be made up of engineers, salesmen, production technicians, and many other kinds of personnel, each of whom has a special part to play in the complex developmental and selling process. The order or orders involved may represent several millions of dollars, and the team has available to it the advisory services of hundreds of company personnel.

Retail selling Retail selling is done by the saleslady behind the counter at Macy's, the druggist in the small drugstore in Rock Springs, Wyoming, or the boy who sells score cards at a baseball stadium. Each of these people, and millions like them, is the last link in the chain between manufacturers and ultimate household decision-making units (DMUs). Some are paid a straight salary, some work on a commission basis, and others receive a combination of the two. Some are aggressive, perhaps the salesman at the used-car lot at the corner; and some are subtle, such as the saleslady who sells perfume to embarrassed men at the very chic shop in the fashionable downtown shopping plaza.

The foregoing, of course, are only brief illustrations of several different kinds of selling activity. None purports to describe fully what is involved in each situation or the many functions that may be performed by sales personnel. The latter will be described in a later section. The point here is to demonstrate the variety of personal selling activities.

These examples also illustrate the point that salesmen perform a variety of tasks, not all of which are confined to communication. They also record orders, accept payment, make deliveries, wrap packages, handle complaints, and do whatever is required to complete transactions with customers.

□ WHY SALES TASKS VARY

It is evident from the examples cited that sales forces frequently sell to different kinds of customers. Manufacturers of consumer and industrial goods use salesmen to sell their goods to ultimate customers, wholesalers, brokers, retailers, or combinations of these. The Raytheon Company, for example, sells such products as transistors directly to large customers through one sales force, but uses a different sales force to sell to distributors who, in turn, sell to small customers. Wholesalers, similarly, may sell to other wholesalers, to retailers, to institutional buyers, or to all of these.

Differences in the sizes of business firms and variations in their marketing strategies lead to vast differences in the sizes of sales forces. The differences that can be created by company size, of course, are obvious. The Fuller Brush Company, which sells on a door-to-door basis, has many more salesmen than the small manufacturer of industrial detergents whose product line is sold directly to a few hundred customers in a single metropolitan area and its environs.

The differences in sales force size that may be created by marketing strategy are less obvious. A brief example illustrates this point, although we shall discuss the general relationship between marketing strategy and personal selling in greater detail later. Assume that there are two firms of approximately equal size that produce hair tonic and other personal grooming products for men. One may have adopted a pull strategy that attempts to create demand among DMUs by heavy advertising; this firm may rely on wholesalers and other kinds of middlemen to reach its retail outlets. As a consequence, the size of the sales force is relatively small because its primary responsibility is to sell to wholesalers.

The other firm may have adopted a push strategy. Its advertising budget is far smaller, and it relies heavily on higher retail margins, extensive point-of-purchase advertising, and the work of a much larger sales force that sells directly to several kinds of retailers. The object here is to get push on the part of retailers, and the use of direct selling by the larger sales force is one major element in that strategy.

The number of salesmen employed by business firms may range from zero, in the case of firms where proprietors perform the personal selling function, to several thousands. In a study of manufacturers' and wholesalers' selling forces in the early 1950s, Tosdal and Carson reported a top figure of 18,000 salesmen.[1] We might also note that personal selling activities are not confined to salesmen alone. Sales managers and other supervisory personnel whose responsibilities are primarily of a management nature often do some selling. Frequently initial negotiations with large accounts or important new accounts are conducted at a level above that of the salesman. Senior officials may also become directly involved in the selling process. It is not at all unusual for a company president to entertain or meet high executives whose firms are potential customers. For example, the president of a large trading stamp firm estimated that nearly 20 percent of his time was devoted to relationships with potential customers.

POLICY AND MANAGEMENT PROBLEMS

Many major policy and management problems require analysis and solution if personal selling activity is to be a successful element of marketing strategy. To develop an overall view of these problems, we shall put them in the context of a hypothetical situation involving George Hoslett, recently appointed sales vice-president of the Prather Company.

The Prather Company manufactures a line of specialty food products, including tinned meats and fancy preserves, that it has been selling on almost a nationwide basis through food brokers and wholesalers to several thousand chain and independent retail food stores. The quality of the product line is excellent, and Prather prices are relatively high. Sales have increased steadily, growing faster than increases in the population or customer incomes. Mr.

[1] Harry A. Tosdal and Waller Carson, Jr., *Salesmen's Compensation*, vol. I, Harvard Graduate School of Business Administration, Division of Research, Boston, 1953, pp. 7–8.

Prather, the president, intends to add some new items to the line, and hopes that total sales will reach $30 million within a year or two. Until now, the company's sales to brokers and wholesalers have been handled by Mr. Prather, other executives, and a small sales force of four men. As part of his drive for increased sales, Mr. Prather has decided to develop a sales force that will sell directly to most retail customers. He has hired George Hoslett to serve as sales vice-president and has turned over to him the responsibility for the development and direction of the selling program and the new sales force. Mr. Hoslett has had administrative experience in sales with other firms, but has only some familiarity with the selling of food items.

Hoslett is faced with a number of major decisions. First, he must decide on a set of overall *objectives* for the sales force and make sure that these objectives are consistent with the firm's total marketing program and overall company goals. For example, how should selling activity relate to the company's advertising and sales promotion programs? Should the new sales force be used to get new retail accounts as well as hold existing accounts, or should it concentrate on building sales in existing accounts? Should the emphasis be on immediate profit results or on sales increases with the expectation that satisfactory long-range profits will follow?

Mr. Hoslett also has decisions to make about the specific *functions* to be performed by the sales force. To a large extent these will be influenced by corporate and marketing objectives. If the major objective is immediate profits, for example, he may decide that the best way to achieve them is to have his salesmen concentrate on functions that might quickly build sales in existing accounts. These might consist of frequent sales calls designed to push products, take orders, check stock levels, mark prices on merchandise, and in general to offer immediate services to retailers. On the other hand, he might decide on a somewhat different set of functions if the objective were to hold down other expenses during the period of time in which the sales force is being built. Such a program might lead to less frequent calls, less travel, and selling activities designed only to maintain rather than increase sales volume.

Having developed some ideas about selling objectives and functions, the sales manager would then have to translate them into a tentative dollars-and-cents program involving the size of the *personal selling expenditure*. He would have to determine how many salesmen are needed, how much money should be allocated for their income and expenses, and how territories are to be established and supervised. Each of these decision areas must be analyzed in terms of the number of DMUs (retailers) to be reached and the Prather Company's relationships with its DMUs. For example, the new products in the company's line probably mean that each salesman will have to spend extra time with retailers. If Mr. Hoslett decides on this approach, he may need extra salesmen and smaller sales territories at the beginning. Later, unless the company continues to add new items or actively tries to secure new accounts, adjustments in the number of salesmen and the size of sales territories will probably be required.

Mr. Hoslett faces many other policy decisions before he can start to build his sales force. The firm now has only four salesmen, and their experience has been almost exclusively in selling to wholesalers and food brokers. Should he continue to employ those men? In general, how should he go about *recruiting* the sales force and selecting men from those who apply for jobs? In recruiting and selection, should he try to find men who are similar in age and personality to the four he now has, or should he look for different characteristics? Are the requirements for successful selling to some customers, such as small independent grocery stores, different from those that apply in other customer situations, for example, the buying committees of chain store organizations? If so, what do these differences mean in terms of the kind of men he should employ for the two kinds of jobs? Mr. Hoslett might also think about the possibility of hiring a few salesmen who might later rise to sales management positions. If he decides to do this, the selection criteria for such men might differ from those applied to other sales force candidates.

Mr. Hoslett will have to decide how the new sales force is to be *trained*. The men will be new to the Prather Company, and some of them may be new to the food business. It is certain that all of them will require some indoctrination to the company, its product line, and its policies, as well as to the kinds of customers it has and Mr. Hoslett's set of selling objectives and functions. Mr. Hoslett will have to decide whether to set up a formal training program and how much time and money should be devoted to it. He will also have to decide whether the training program should be completed before the men go into the field or whether a brief training period should be supplemented by continued on-the-job training. It may be that the timing problem in hiring men and making the transition from brokers and wholesalers to a Prather direct selling force will be so severe as to necessitate very little formal training; in that case, Mr. Hoslett and other management personnel will be forced to spend time training personnel on an on-the-job basis.

Compensation presents another series of decision problems. Each of the four salesmen currently employed is paid about $10,000 per year as a straight salary. In addition, each receives an annual bonus, decided on by Mr. Prather, that ranges from $500 to $1,500. The selling activities of the men have been carefully regulated by management, and there have been little in the way of tangible criteria to govern increases in salaries or bonuses. Mr. Hoslett must decide how both the current and the new men are to be paid. There are two major problems in this regard. The first is to determine a general level of compensation. The second is to construct a method of compensation that will motivate the salesmen and make possible the effective discharge of selling responsibilities. It may be, for example, that new accounts are important enough to warrant special bonuses or a system of commission payments that encourage men to secure them. It might also appear that sales quotas should be established and that commissions should be paid on sales in excess of quotas. On the other hand, Mr. Hoslett might decide that a continuation of the salary and bonus is warranted by the need to maintain strict control of salesmen's activities. In any event, the sales vice-president also needs to recognize that financial considerations are only one contribution to motivation and that nonfinancial incentives also merit his attention.

Mr. Hoslett's two final policy problems lie in the areas of organization and control. He must create an organizational structure that facilitates the achievement of sales objectives and functions, and he must develop a system of controls that keeps sales management informed about the progress toward the achievement of these goals.

These, then, are the major policy and management problems that confront Mr. Hoslett and others in marketing and sales management positions. The rest of this chapter deals with each of these major problem areas and with some of the ways organizations have attempted to resolve them.

Selling objectives

It is axiomatic that a basic requirement for managing any activity is to establish clear objectives for it. This requirement is especially important for personal selling, because of the traditional myth that "a good salesman can sell anything." This may be true for a few gifted individuals, but most salesmen need clear-cut definitions of goals for their activity in order to be effective.

□ SELLING OBJECTIVES AND MARKETING OBJECTIVES

Personal selling objectives are the logical extensions of larger marketing objectives and strategies. This point is illustrated by the two hair tonic firms cited earlier in this chapter. The firm with the pull strategy (heavy advertising directed at DMUs) will place less reliance on its personal selling program than the firm with the push strategy (liberal trade margins and strong selling to channels by the sales force). This, in turn, affects the number of salesmen that will be required, the calls that are made, the extent of reliance on the sales force for company profits, and the activities performed by the sales force, etc.

Numerous other examples reflect the impact of marketing strategy on selling objectives. When the hula hoop became popular with children, it was essential to take immediate advantage of the fad and secure widespread distribution as rapidly as possible because the fad could be expected to last only a short time. This put great pressure on the sales forces of both manufacturers and distributors to sell the hoops vigorously to all possible retail outlets, rather than simply selecting a limited number of outlets and selling nonaggressively to them. Sales had to be made and made fast in order to yield profits before the fad was exhausted. This situation may be contrasted to that of the International Business Machines Corporation, whose selling objectives are dictated by policies designed to ensure good long-range relationships with customers. The DMUs for IBM's machines and equipment are typically well-informed business executives. Thus, both the nature of the company's overall objectives and the composition of its DMUs make it essential that IBM's selling objectives be different from those of the hula hoop manufacturer. In connection with the IBM example, it should also be noted that both the nature of IBM's customers and its line of products (computers, complex office equipment, etc.) make personal selling far more important than advertising in its promotional mix.

The impact of marketing policy, overall promotional policy, and the nature of a firm's potential DMUs on selling objectives is also reflected in the hypothetical case of the Prather Company and its line of specialty foods. Prather management may decide that its product line is such that wide distribution is necessary and that extensive displays and push by retailers will be the most effective way of securing purchase action by household DMUs. These decisions imply heavy reliance on personal selling by the Prather sales force, and comparatively less reliance on advertising. Management may also decide that continuing increases in sales volume are more important than immediate profits; as a consequence of this decision, salesmen will be instructed to call on new accounts and cement relationships with existing accounts, and less emphasis may be placed on expense control and immediate sales results.

These examples make it clear that there is no universal set of objectives that is best for personal selling programs. What is needed, rather, is a careful analysis of (1) the firm's overall corporate objectives, (2) the firm's marketing strategy, (3) the marketing strategies of competitors, (4) the nature of potential DMUs, and (5) the most effective relationships among the elements of the firm's promotional strategy.

ESTABLISHING SELLING GOALS

The objectives of personal selling programs are typically expressed in terms of sales volume, market share, or profit targets, or in terms of expense or activity controls.

Sales volume objectives are usually referred to as sales quotas, which are sales targets expressed in dollar, or sometimes in unit, terms. *Market share targets* are expressed in percentage terms, and refer to the portion of the market that the company expects to capture. Volume or share objectives may be established for an individual product or groups of products; individual salesmen; sales territories; time periods such as a month or a quarter; types of customers such as wholesale, retail, household, or institutional; or for specific sales calls or orders. For example, a manufacturer of greeting cards sets sales volume objectives for each product line sold by each of its salesmen on a monthly basis for specific large retail accounts; for classes of accounts such as gift shops, department stores, and drugstores; for individual salesmen; and for sales districts. In addition, it also establishes volume objectives for new accounts.

Profit targets normally refer to either a specified profit target or a gross margin objective. They, too, may be set for individual accounts, sales territories, sales branches or districts, products, sales calls, orders of varying size, or various time periods. An office furniture dealer, for example, may establish an overall gross margin objective of 35 percent. Salesmen may then be given some degree of flexibility in price negotiations, but their monthly commission rates may be reduced if their monthly sales do not produce the target gross profit rate.

Expense controls, or objectives, are usually established in terms of maximum amounts of direct selling expenses. The latter are typically defined as those expenses directly involved in salesmen's activities and can include such items as salaries, commissions, bonuses, meals, lodging, transportation, and entertainment allowances. Controls are often set for individual salesmen or sales territories. Indirect selling expenses such as those involved in sales supervision or perhaps those associated with credit and billing are usually controlled separately from direct selling expenses. In the Prather Company example, Mr. Hoslett might specify expense objectives such as $8 per day and $12 per day meal and lodging maximums, and a limit of $50 per month on entertainment allowances. If the billing and credit functions were under his control, he might initially establish a specific maximum amount of money to be allocated to these functions. Later, as sales increase, he might try to hold expenditures on these functions to stipulated percentages of sales.

Activity controls typically relate to the number of times salesmen are expected to perform various selling functions within a given period. For example, the Prather salesmen might be given such objectives as calling on 10 independent grocers and 3 chains per day, setting up at least 3 special displays each day, or adding 5 new accounts in a month. In general, the determination of activity objectives is based primarily on management's assumptions as to the relationship between the achievement of its other objectives, such as sales volume, market share, profit, or expense, and the specific activities that are to be performed by the sales force, such as making calls, checking inventories, or training the middleman's sales force.

SETTING PRIORITIES

The determination of personal selling objectives is complicated by the fact that objectives may be in conflict. In a given month or week, time may not permit a salesman to meet all the objectives established for him. For example, he may not be able simultaneously to increase sales volume, increase profits, and increase the number and quality of retail outlets. Similarly, a salesman selling several products may find that product objectives conflict. The objectives for a new Prather food product might heavily stress sales volume or new accounts. Objectives for Prather's established products, on the other hand, might put more emphasis on activities such as number of calls per day. The latter is not necessarily consistent with the goal of maximizing sales volume during a particular period of time.

It is thus necessary for management to determine which objectives should have priority. At times, differences in selling objectives among different products are significant enough, in conjunction with differences among DMUs and their buying habits, to affect the way in which sales forces are organized. The differences are often so great that separate sales forces are required for various segments of a product line. For example, a plastics manufacturer might find many of his markets so specialized and the selling processes so different that separate sales forces are required to sell to different industries.

Selling functions

The number and types of functions that may be assigned to salesmen are numerous. As the direct link between his company and its customers and sometimes with the customers' customers, the salesman *is* the company. It is his responsibility to carry out all the objectives and functions assigned to him by management and to show imagination and flexibility in handling situations that have not been anticipated.

□ VARIATIONS IN FUNCTIONS

In discharging these general responsibilities, the salesman typically has many things to do. In some cases, he may select appropriate DMUs for his sales calls. The Prather salesman, for example, may be asked to select the food stores that are to be visited in his company's search for new accounts. He may demonstrate and describe his product or product line, write orders, mail promotional materials to accounts before calling on them, and sometimes collect the bills. He may check prices in retail stores, mark prices on merchandise, check inventories, arrange displays, train wholesale or retail salesmen, or help in the preparation of local newspaper advertising. He may advise his distributors' customers on the advantages of doing business with Prather's distributors, take prospective clients to lunch, play golf, or spend evenings working out improved order and inventory control procedures for his clients. He may help his company merchandise its advertising campaign by showing it to wholesalers or retailers and encouraging them to coordinate the timing and content of their advertising and promotion with his company's campaign. He may help to train the new salesmen in his company, and keep his own accounts informed about prevailing prices, terms of sales, delivery dates, and product or service guarantees. He may also serve as a source of market information, keeping Prather management up to date on competitive activities, customer attitudes, and the characteristics and plans of individual customers. Finally, along with some of these and probably other activities, he may also prepare reports about his sales calls and the results of these calls, his expenses, and his lost business, plan his itinerary, travel around his territory, and wait in customers' outer offices.

There is no single appropriate combination of functions that should be performed by all selling forces. The functions of a drugstore clerk who sells a bottle of aspirin, barely looking at his customer in the process, are obviously far different from those of a heavy electrical equipment salesman who spends months in a South American country negotiating a $5 million sales with that nation's governmental and industrial representatives. The Prather Company salesman's functions, fall somewhere in between.

DESIGNING THE SALESMAN'S JOB

The most appropriate combination of functions depends on management's analysis of a number of important areas. Among them are the following:

Selling objectives A manufacturer of industrial electrical apparatus, such as fans or motors, who is interested in developing selective demand among new customers might decide to have his sales force spend a high proportion of time analyzing the needs of potential customers, planning or providing services, and making sales to them. If the same manufacturer's principal concern were simply to sustain current volume among present customers, much less time would be spent assessing needs and in face-to-face persuasive activities with new customers.

Whether inside or outside selling is involved A salesclerk selling vacuum cleaners in a department store spends more time giving information on the characteristics of various brands, checking inventories, and arranging displays than a door-to-door salesman selling the same product. A larger proportion of the latter's time is spent traveling, planning itineraries, and making sales.

The size and frequency of customer purchases A salesman selling generating and transmission equipment to utilities, which can involve as much as $20 million for one power plant, often is responsible for selling to just one company. Negotiations for a single order frequently last several years. His major function is to act as a technical consultant in all the customer's activities connected with the planning and installation of this type of equipment. In contrast, a salesclerk in a hardware store may serve primarily as an order taker, although he may give advice to "do-it-yourself" customers.

The nature and organization of the selling and distribution One manufacturer of drug products relies on wholesalers' sales forces to perform most of the selling and service functions for retailers. Its own sales force concentrates on selling the value of the company's sales promotional activities by convincing wholesalers as well as department and drugstore buyers that the company's deals are worth promoting. In many industries the servicing and/or technical assistance functions are important and involved enough to lead to the creation of a team of specialists who back up the salesmen by providing technical assist-

---

FIGURE 21-1

A salesman's job description: Veterinary Products Division of a Pharmaceutical Company

Position Title: Veterinary Sales Representative
Reports to: Veterinary Products Regional Manager
Function: Under general direction of Veterinary Regional Manager, maximize sales volume of company veterinary products in assigned territory through sales to veterinarians and to authorized distributors

Scope of Responsibilities

1. Promote the use and sale of Company products through regular calls on practicing veterinarians. In addition, implement marketing programs designed to acquaint selected producer groups with the benefits of Company products.
   Call regularly on Company veterinary distributors and work closely with their salesmen to:

   Train them to sell the product line and support special promotions.
   Keep them informed on current product information and selling techniques.
   Assure that adequate supplies of Company veterinary products are stocked in line with our minimum inventory policy.

2. Keep Home Office informed of activities and market conditions.

   Maintain prescribed records, route books and customer record sheets.
   Report daily calls and sales.
   Report competitive products, prices, and deals.
   Correspond in compliance with all Home Office requests.

3. Keep abreast of new developments in the veterinary medical field by reading and studying Home Office bulletins, literature and veterinary journals.

4. Request information from Home Office on technical questions. Request that literature, samples of information on Company's products be forwarded to veterinarians when desirable.

5. Attend State Veterinary Medical Association, Conventions as directed by the Home Office. Assemble, display, and dismantle, exhibits. Report to management any pertinent developments at conventions.

6. Inform customers of price changes, policy changes, new products, and special promotions.

7. Take inventories and arrange for credits to veterinary distributors at time of price reductions.

ance. For example, in the 1960s the FMC Corporation, a producer of inorganic chemicals, industrial equipment, and space-age products, had one technical backup man for every four salesmen.[2] Many business firms, particularly those with large sales forces, prepare detailed statements of the functions that are to be performed by salesmen. These are usually referred to as *job* or *position* descriptions. Such statements are helpful in defining responsibilities and in carrying out such related sales management functions as recruitment and selection, training, and the evaluation of salesmen's performance. One such statement of functions is presented in Figure 21-1.

The selling expenditure

One major problem area that requires careful analysis is the amount of money to be allocated to the personal selling program. Let us return to the Prather Company and the problems facing Mr. Hoslett. What is necessary in this area is a series of decisions that involve the number of salesmen and the total compensation that they are to receive; the amount to be allocated to salesmen's travel, lodging, meals, telephone, entertainment, and other expenses; and the other expenses that are related to the selling program, that is, training, supervision, clerical, and sales overhead.

The foundation of analysis in this area is, again, the firm's major marketing and promotional objectives as they are translated into specific selling objectives and functions. If Mr. Prather and Mr. Hoslett decide to sell direct to large numbers of retailers and to establish immediate high sales goals, a substantial sales force and related staff will be necessary. Similarly, other expenses will be higher than if a lower sales objective and a less immediate time target for its achievement had been set. Conversely, if the Prather decision were to place major promotional reliance on heavy trade and consumer advertising, the scale of personal selling activity would be correspondingly reduced.

□ PROCEDURES FOR DETERMINING EXPENDITURE LEVELS

After the strategic implications of the major objectives have been carefully defined, there are some fairly mechanistic approaches that can be used to translate them into expenditure estimates. These approaches are based on

1. The number of customers to be reached
2. The average number of calls required per customer per week, month, or year
3. The average number of calls that can be made by a salesman in a given period

[2] Carl Rieser, "The Salesman Isn't Dead—He's Different," *Fortune,* vol. 66, no. 5, pp. 124ff., November, 1962.

Each of these factors will be discussed below. First, however, it should be pointed out that they are less relevant in inside selling situations, such as department stores. In such situations management relies heavily on estimates of (1) the number of customers that will visit the store or its individual departments and (2) the number of customers that each salesman can handle during the relevant period of time. The amount of customer traffic varies greatly among departments in department stores, housewares versus salon furs, for example, and in other kinds of large retailing establishments, and for that reason such estimates are often made for individual departments.

Number of customers The number of DMUs available for possible selling contact varies from market to market. At one extreme, for example, might be such markets as those for shoes and similar consumer items: the salesmen's potential DMUs *could* be almost all the people in the United States. A firm selling to gasoline service stations in the United States, on the other hand, has over 200,000 possible customers, while a firm marketing to paint wholesalers has a maximum of about 1,300 possible customers (see Tables 10-1 and 12-2).

The number of customers that a firm actually solicits in a given market depends, in part, on its policies regarding market development, pricing, channels, and promotion, as well as on the potential profit associated with selling to different types of accounts. For example, suppose that a small manufacturer is about to introduce a new line of contemporary household furniture. One ultimate marketing objective might be national distribution, but because of limited resources, the manufacturer might choose to concentrate the initial marketing effort in only one or two major geographical markets. Within given cities, management might decide to limit distribution to only a few carefully selected furniture retailers in order to increase their incentive to promote the line. If a skimming price strategy (see Chapter 17) were used, this might further restrict the choice of retailers.

Still another basis for determining which retailers should carry a firm's product line is the expected profit associated with individual accounts. The profitability of an account depends on many factors, including annual volume, number and size of orders, and servicing requirements. Those accounts which are unprofitable to handle via direct selling might still be profitably reached through wholesalers. In addition, field activity might disclose that some retailers are unwilling to handle the line in spite of inducements that are offered.

Average number of calls per customer The frequency with which a salesman calls on a particular account depends on DMUs' buying habits and requirements, inventory policies, service requirements, and sales volume. Perishables and high-turnover products require more frequent selling contacts than industrial equipment bought at less frequent intervals. High-turnover items such as cookies and crackers, which require shelf rotation to ensure freshness, are usually associated with a relatively high call frequency per account. In such cases, salesmen often perform the merchandising function of stocking shelves and rotating packages.

When an analysis is made to determine the average call frequency that is necessary, it is useful to classify accounts by such factors as volume, frequency of ordering, or geographic location, that is, urban versus rural. In the Prather case, for example, Mr. Hoslett might decide that high-volume customers should be called on once each week, medium-volume customers once every two weeks, and so forth. Classifications could then be combined to derive an average.

According to one authority, customary call frequencies for selected products in the early 1960s were as follows: dictating machines sold to offices, 90 days; adding machines sold to banks and business concerns, 90 days; hardware sold to wholesalers, 60 days; candy sold to wholesalers, 60 days; air compressors sold to mill supply houses, 30 days; cheese sold direct to retailers, 30 days; soap sold to wholesalers, 30 days; and bakery equipment sold to bakers, 150 days.[3] These call frequencies should not be taken too literally, however, without further information concerning the objectives of the calls involved, such as service, missionary work, new product selling. As suggested above, selling objectives affect both the nature and frequency of sales calls.

Average number of calls per salesman The number of calls a salesman can make per week or month depends on the amount of time he spends traveling, waiting, filling out reports, attending meetings, handling claims, and performing the various selling tasks assigned to him.

The primary determinant in most situations, of course, is the *nature* of the selling job to be performed. When the product is complex or the customer's requirements are technical and highly involved, the time taken by each call is substantial. Thus, insurance or turbine salesmen normally spend considerably more time with customers than a cheese salesman who sells to retailers. In the latter situation the salesman may be primarily an order taker and inventory checker, whereas in the former a complete presentation of insurance information or detailed analyses of customer needs require much more time. Salesmen selling to firms located in sparsely settled areas obviously spend more time traveling than those in areas with a high customer density. Salesmen selling technically complex products, such as computers or missile components, where the rate of change in the company's product line is relatively high, also spend more time in training sessions that those in less complex or dynamic sit-

[3] Bertrand R. Canfield, *Sales Administration*, Prentice-Hall, Inc., Englewood Cliffs, N.J., 1961, p. 361.

uations. Salesmen introducing a new product spend more time with accounts than is normally required in later stages of a product's life cycle.

Canfield reports that meat packers' salesmen calling on retailers average 16 calls daily; office equipment salesmen selling to business concerns, 5 calls daily; insurance salesmen, 6 calls a day; stationery manufacturers' salesmen selling to retailers, 7 calls a day; and cheese salesmen selling direct to retailers, 20 to 40 calls per day.[4]

Decisions with respect to the amount of time and selling effort to be applied to a particular customer or group of customers are typically made on the basis of experience and executive judgment. However, operations research techniques have been applied to sales activity analysis to assist management in making these decisions. For example, a large commercial printing company designed an experiment in which the amount of selling effort (call frequency times length of time per call) expended on comparable groups of customers was systematically varied to see what effect such variations might have on sales. The results helped management to determine which customers to concentrate on and to what degree.[5]

The end result of analysis in these and other areas is a tentative estimate of the size of the personal selling expenditure. Later, after further discussions, the estimate will be modified into a budget that is typically called the *sales department* or *selling budget.* To see how the general estimate might be derived, we can refer again to the example of the Prather Company.

After discussions with Mr. Prather and other members of management, Mr. Hoslett might decide that the company should sell directly to 4,000 retail accounts located throughout the United States. The need for retaining existing accounts during the transition to a direct selling force and the need to give active selling effort to the new Prather products produce a decision that each account requires a call on the average of once a week, making a total of 208,000 calls each year, or approximately 800 calls per day, assuming that there are 250 selling days available. Mr. Hoslett's analysis of the desired selling objectives and functions, as well as the geographical dispersion of the Prather accounts, leads him to conclude that a salesman should be able to average 10 calls per day. This means that 80 salesmen will be required.

With as many as 80 salesmen spread over the country, Mr. Hoslett believes that it will be necessary to have a number of sales executives to serve as district or territorial managers. Both his prior experience and his insight into the Prather operation indicate that eight districts should be established, with a district manager in charge of each. With these decisions made, he is able to develop estimates of other kinds of selling expenses as shown in Table 21-1.

[4] *Ibid.*, p. 359.

[5] Arthur A. Brown, Frank T. Hulswit, and John D. Kettelle, "A Study of Sales Operations," *Operations Research*, vol. 4, no. 3, pp. 296–308, June, 1956.

TABLE 21-1

Tentative estimate of Prather annual selling expenditures

Salesmen (80): base salaries	$ 800,000
Salesmen (80): incentive compensation	80,000
Salesmen's expense	400,000
District managers (8): base salaries	108,000
District managers (8): incentive compensation	21,000
District office and clerical staffs	80,000
Headquarters sales office and overhead	50,000
Training cost (first year only—subsequent years at $3,000)	50,000
Other expenses (not including sales promotion)	70,000
Total	$1,659,000

SALES TERRITORIES

In the foregoing discussion we have mentioned the subject of sales territories. Most companies that sell over wide areas or to substantial numbers of customers use a territorial organization of some type. Although various kinds of marketing and selling organizations will be dealt with in Chapter 23, it is appropriate to say a few words about sales territories in the context of this section.

There are, as usual, no specific rules to govern either the number or the sizes of sales territories. This statement applies to the territories covered by individual salesmen and to the combination of individual territories into sales districts. There are, however, a number of areas that should be analyzed.

Customer factors How many customers are there, and what are their buying habits and procedures? How frequently should they be visited, and what are their requirements for servicing, advice, inventory, etc.? What sales volume, now or in the future, can be expected from them? Are they geographically concentrated or widely dispersed? How difficult is it to travel among them?

Organization and control From the company's standpoint, individual territories should be so organized, and combined into districts when necessary, that the management problems in selling or planning and directing the work of salesmen can be effectively carried out. For example, neither a salesman nor a district manager can operate effectively if he is required to work with too many DMUs or sales personnel. Most companies prefer that their district sales managers maintain close working relationships with salesmen and travel with them frequently in order to train or evaluate them. The extent to which a district manager can perform these and other duties depends in some measure on the number of people reporting to him. In passing, it might be pointed out that selling or supervisory activities are not always organized on geographical bases. As described in greater detail in Chapter 19, sales forces may also be organized in terms of products or portions of product lines; kinds of DMUs, for example, textile industry versus tire industry; or sometimes individual DMUs, such as a single large electrical machinery manufacturer.

Economics Any territory or combination of territories must be economically desirable, that is, either profitable or consistent with other economic criteria. The profit aspect of this statement is so obvious that it needs little elaboration. One way to analyze the economic potential of a territory in terms of selling costs is to estimate all the direct and indirect selling expenses and subtract them from anticipated sales revenue. What remains is then compared with all other projected expenses. Profits, however, are not the only economic criterion that may be applicable. Others are long-range potential and contribution to fixed costs. In rough terms, the latter phrase means that sales revenue more than covers all the costs that are incurred *directly as a result* of operations in a territory and contributes dollars that can be used to defray overhead and other costs.

Recruiting and selecting salesmen

Effective policies and procedures for the recruitment and selection of salesmen can have substantial value. They affect sales volume, customer relations, the rate of sales force turnover (the number of salesmen leaving the firm over a period of time divided by the average size of the selling force during that period), market coverage, supervision, and the ratio of selling expense to sales. In addition, the cost of hiring a salesman can be high and may come close to $10,000 in the case of firms that have elaborate systems of recruiting, screening, and testing applicants. Also involved are the unknown costs that result from customer ill will and the reduced morale among the sales force that is associated with the hiring of men unsuited for the job.

There are two major policy problems in recruiting and selecting salesmen. First, management must determine the characteristics, such as age, sex, level of income and education, and nature of personality, that typify good salesmen for the company and product line involved. Given these characteristics, management must develop a set of procedures to find (recruit) and ultimately select those applicants who come closest to meeting the firm's requirements.

□ WHAT MAKES A "GOOD" SALESMAN?

To determine the characteristics of a good salesman, management must define the objectives and functions that are used to measure performance. As discussed earlier in this chapter, the relative importance of different functions (checking inventory, stocking shelves) and objectives (sales volume) depends on the nature of the product and the selling job, the stage of the product's life cycle, and many other factors. A clear definition of objectives is required for the purpose of recruiting and selection because different kinds of people are better suited to different tasks, different objectives, and different functions. For example, aggressiveness may be more important for a house-to-house magazine salesman than for a salesclerk in the salon fur department of a department store. In many inside selling situations, a salesperson's ability to work in cooperation with others can be an important factor in successful selling in the long run.[6]

Given a clear statement of objectives and functions, management is faced with the problem of determining what individual characteristics are associated with a high level of achievement. Frequently the process of matching personal characteristics with objectives and/or functions results in a statement of the kind presented in Figure 21-2.

For many firms with small sales forces the matching process may be based

[6] For a discussion of the importance of social relations in inside selling, see George F. F. Lombard, *Behavior in a Selling Group*, Harvard Graduate School of Business Administration, Boston, 1955.

FIGURE 21-2

Duties paralleled by the personal characteristics required by an automobile salesman selling to individual customer

Duty	Characteristics
I. Locate prospect's needs by getting information about prospect's car and driving habits, using visual aids, and questioning prospect.	Initiative, tact, resourcefulness, imagination, and analytical skill.
II. Tell how car fits needs of prospect.	Voice, good English, enthusiasm, knowledge, and personality.
III. Show how car fits needs of prospect.	Imagination, sincerity, enthusiasm, knowledge, and personality.
IV. Get prospect's agreement on each point as it is made.	Persuasiveness, tact, persistence, resourcefulness.
V. Answer or forestall objections.	Confidence, knowledge, tact, and consideration.
VI. Close sale.	Persistence, aggressiveness, and confidence.
VII. Handle trade-ins.	Honesty, tact, and knowledge.
VIII. Routine reports on daily calls, interviews, prospects; prepare daily call schedule.	Orderliness, honesty, attention to details.
IX. Create good will by following up customers to see that they get service.	Friendliness, personality, helpfulness, and courtesy.

Source: Bertrand R. Canfield, *Sales Administration*, Prentice-Hall, Inc., Englewood Cliffs, N.J., 1961, p. 86.

primarily on executive experience, judgment, and intuition. In firms with large sales forces, managements often improve their predictions by analyzing existing salesmen. Frequently comparisons are made between salesmen with varying levels of performance in order to determine the characteristics possessed by successful salesmen.

□

SELECTION TECHNIQUES

The process of selecting salesmen varies greatly among companies, depending primarily on the importance of personal selling as a component of the marketing program and on the size and costs associated with the sales force. Also involved may be the past experience of management itself. Mr. Prather of the Prather Company may feel that he has been tremendously successful in picking salesmen, and perhaps he has been, simply by "staring at a man's eyes to see if he's got the stuff." Mr. Hoslett, with more experience in sales management and greater exposure to more formal techniques, may put some of his faith in psychological tests. Also, if he intends to have some of the recruiting and selection conducted by his new district sales managers, he will probably want certain formal selection tools to be used to ensure as much similarity as possible in the selection processes and criteria employed by his supervisory personnel.

Although most small companies with very few salesmen confine their selection processes to an application blank and an interview with an executive, large firms with sizable sales forces often use such steps as the following before hiring a candidate:

1. A brief application form and preliminary interview
2. A second and more detailed application blank
3. A check of references listed in the detailed application blank, and a credit check
4. Interviews with several executives
5. A series of psychological tests
6. A physical examination

Application forms and interviews are almost universally used, not only in selecting salesmen but in practically every other area of employee selection, school admissions, and other areas where individuals must be evaluated.

A somewhat more complex and controversial approach to selecting salesmen is the use of *psychological tests*. Four main types of tests are widely used—these are intended to measure mental ability, interests, "personality," and specific selling aptitude.

Mental ability tests are usually designed to measure an individual's ability to solve problems, reason clearly, and acquire information. Such tests are often used to supplement the educational record reported on the application form. A person with a poor educational record, but a high score on a mental ability test, may have lacked the motivation to be a good student. He may nonetheless be a desirable candidate for a sales force. There is no reason to believe, however, that high scores on a mental ability test are accurate predictors of selling success for *all* types of selling activity. An individual with a high score may find a highly repetitious order-taking job quite dull, whereas a man with a low score may become frustrated in a selling position where the nature of the problems and the needs of the customer are continually changing.

Interests tests attempt to match the interests of the applicant with those of successful salesmen. Presumably a sales applicant whose interests in sports, music, current events, business, etc., are comparable to those of persons who are successful in the selling field may be more highly motivated and effective than one with divergent interests. Some positive association has been found between interest scores and success in selling insurance and accounting machinery.[7]

Personality tests are used to measure such characteristics as self-confidence, aggressiveness, and capacity for adjusting to new social situations. Although such tests are used by a number of firms, there is almost no evidence that a score on any *single* personality test is highly associated with sales success.

Sales aptitude tests attempt to measure a candidate's natural capacity to sell. They try to measure such characteristics as tact, ability to remember names, and insight into personal relationships. Canfield reports some success in selecting salesmen with a test developed by him; the test has been used by over 300 companies.[8]

One possible reason for the limited success of psychological tests in predicting who will be good salesmen is that highly *standardized* tests are usually administered to applicants, although different selling situations require different kinds of individuals. As a result, people with given scores have different chances of succeeding in different situations. For example, an aggressive person may be required to sell on a house-to-house basis, but the same type of individual may not perform as well as a publisher's representative calling on college professors. As firms develop tests tailored to their own specific requirements, their ability to predict sales success will improve. A second factor that probably accounts for the limited success of psychological testing is that business firms have not had much experience with them. For the most part, their use in sales-force selection did not become widespread until after World War II.

[7] Richard R. Still and Edward W. Cundiff, *Sales Management*, Prentice-Hall, Inc., Englewood Cliffs, N.J., 1960, p. 197.
[8] Canfield, *op. cit.*, p. 123.

Sales training

Effective sales training increases the efficiency and skill with which salesmen perform their tasks. The results are increased sales, reduced selling costs, lower turnover (as a result of higher morale), and a reduction in the time taken to reach peak efficiency. Training may also increase a salesman's chance for promotion. Training programs vary greatly in content and duration, and they often contain several stages. For example, there may be an orientation stage in which the trainee is familiarized with the company's product or products and its administrative or sales procedures. This may be followed by a selling training stage, during which specific selling techniques are communicated. Finally, there may be an on-the-job training stage, which may involve selling under the close watch of a supervisor or a fellow salesman or some other member of the training staff.

The costs of training a salesman, including his salary while being trained, the trainer's time, and materials and training facilities, can be high. It can range from less than $1,000 to several thousand dollars. The time required by a training program ranges from a few days to 18 months for manufacturers of staple goods and can go as high as three years or more for manufacturers of highly technical products. At the Prather Company, for example, a training program would probably be relatively short. Mr. Hoslett might believe that the requisite information and skills could be imparted in a week or two, as long as on-the-job training procedures are used for further indoctrination and guidance.

Training is not just useful for beginners alone. It is often necessary or desirable at many times during a salesman's career. Training programs may be designed to train veteran salesmen to introduce a new product line, to select better retail and/or wholesale outlets, to improve their ability to merchandise the firm's advertising, to correct frequently made mistakes in sales presentations, to show them how to sell more products with higher margins, etc.

The nature of a training program for either beginning or established salesmen must be based on clear specifications of the functions to be performed by the individual salesmen (as discussed earlier in this chapter). Such specifications provide norms against which the activities of the existing sales force can be contrasted, as well as guides for the needs of the beginners. For example, a statement of specifications that focuses on persuading customers to order a product immediately, such as in the door-to-door selling of magazines, necessitates a sales training program that places much more emphasis on the "art" of aggressive salesmanship than would be necessary for a selling job that places more emphasis on the need for making special product modifications to suit a customer's needs. In the latter case, extensive knowledge of the flexibility of the product's characteristics and production processes may be important.

TRAINING PROGRAMS

The topics that usually receive the most attention in sales training programs are product information, company information, customer information, and selling techniques.

Product information includes information on the types, sizes, varieties, and physical and operating characteristics of the company's products. Although knowledge of these attributes is important, probably even more important is the need for developing an understanding of the potential applications and uses of the product by customers. A salesman who has sufficient empathy to understand the problems of his customers is better able to mold his sales presentation to the customer's needs. In addition, some firms have their trainees study competitive products so that they will be better able to deal with the objections and criticisms of customers who will be comparing the product against its rivals.

Company information concerns such subjects as the company's executive personnel; personnel and sales administration policies; locations of plants; sales offices and warehouses; the company's pricing, delivery, credit, and service policies; and the record-keeping procedures required for travel expenses, call reports, orders, and complaints.

Customer information is intended to help the salesmen do an effective job of tailoring products to the needs of customers. Salesmen are taught how customers make purchasing decisions, how they form decision-making units, what their purchase motives are, what attitudes they have toward the company's products and those of its competitors, the location of customers, and procedures for canvassing areas for prospective customers.

Training programs are often concerned with *selling techniques* designed to improve the salesmen's skill in making sales. There is an old saw to the effect that "good salesmen are born, not made." Whether this is true or not, most firms find it desirable to do some "making," and the trend in this direction is increasing, as the knowledge of the skills involved in interpersonal relationships grows. If Mr. Hoslett of the Prather Company hires several men without selling experience, their training program will doubtless include some selling techniques that might include securing a customer interview, opening the interview, keeping customer's attention, handling objections and complaints, and closing the sale. Salesmen might also receive training in asking questions, listening attentively, and various other matters connected with the "art of persuasion."

TRAINING METHODS

Salesmen are frequently trained in groups through the use of lectures, conferences, demonstrations, panel discussions, forums, correspondence courses, or role playing. These, with the exception of role playing, are standard educational devices. In role playing, either the salesman and the trainer or two salesmen take the roles of salesman and buyer and act out the process of making a call and/or a sale. This is usually followed by a discussion by the participants and the other trainees, evaluating the presentation and suggesting possible improvements. Role playing is apt to get the trainees more personally involved and more highly motivated than lectures. It also gives them a chance to develop skill and confidence under circumstances that are closer to actual selling situations than those associated with other methods of instruction. Role playing, however, does not teach specific facts about products or customers as effectively as do the other techniques of instruction.

Probably the most common instructional technique is on-the-job training. Together with role playing, it probably constitutes the best way to teach selling techniques. In many firms, especially small ones, it is the *only* form of sales training. Typically a trainee will accompany an experienced salesman on his calls. At first the trainee observes, but gradually he begins to increase his participation and eventually takes responsibility for the entire presentation.

Conventional training aids include manuals, texts, films, charts, models or actual product samples, and phonograph or written records of actual or hypothetical selling situations that are used as examples of selling problems and as analytical materials for the trainees.

Among the more recent training developments is closed-circuit television. This permits a firm to reach its entire sales force simultaneously with a minimum loss of travel time for both salesmen and executives. Another recent development is the use of *teaching machines*. These machines are frequently used for teaching specific types of information such as product facts or company policies. A trainee sits in front of a device that exposes him to a single piece of information and immediately tests his understanding of it. As each new piece of information is added, it builds on the answers to previous questions. This approach is being used by an increasing number of business firms.

Compensating and motivating salesmen

Careful recruiting, selection, and training can increase the degree to which a sales force has the basic capability required for its numerous and changing tasks, but they do not guarantee that salesmen will be motivated to perform them. A firm's compensation plan and nonfinancial incentives, such as pride in a job well done and the respect of a salesman's friends and associates, are the principal means by which management can help to ensure that salesmen are highly motivated.

One major problem in developing a compensation plan is the level of compensation to be paid. In general, this depends primarily on the functions the sales force is expected to perform, the earnings of salesmen employed by competing firms, and the potential profitability of the product or product line.

Adopting a level of compensation similar to that offered by competing firms is seldom as simple a solution as it first appears. As was pointed out, even within an industry the functions performed by salesmen may vary from firm to firm, thus obscuring direct comparison of wages. Additionally, specific data on competitive pay scales are difficult to obtain.

Occasionally, studies are made of compensation in various industries, but these usually lack both the frequency and detail that most companies would like to have. Trade associations in some industries collect compensation data, but these cover only a small fraction of American industry. Often the best way to get information on prevailing compensation rates is by informal contact with executives or salesmen of competing firms.

The level of sales compensation generally requires adjustment over a period of time. For example, when a product is first introduced, a high commission or other compensation rate may be set in order to ensure a compensation level adequate to attract and retain men. Later in the product's life cycle, as volume increases and the nature of the selling job changes, the compensation may be lowered in order to keep the level of compensation in reasonable relation to the product's long-run profits, to the wages paid by competing firms for similar selling functions, and to the nature of the selling functions themselves.

OBJECTIVES OF COMPENSATION PLANS

The principal objectives of sales compensation systems in business firms may be summarized as follows:

1. *Control.* To what extent does the plan facilitate management's efforts to direct the sales force toward whatever functions are deemed desirable, such as selling the company's more profitable products, putting up special displays, stocking shelves, opening up new accounts, or concentrating on accounts with the greatest profit potential?
2. *Incentive.* To what extent does the plan motivate individual salesmen to do as much as or more than is normally expected of them? Are men rewarded for surpassing assigned sales volume targets, securing new accounts, or exceeding expectations in other ways?
3. *Security and income regularity.* To what extent does the plan provide the salesman with a reasonably stable flow of income?
4. *Simplicity.* Can the plan be understood easily by sales supervisors and the members of the sales force?
5. *Economy.* Does the plan generate an adequate income for salesmen and yet contribute to the maintenance of an adequate profit or rate of return on investment for the company?
6. *Fairness.* Is the plan fair from the standpoint of both the salesmen and the company? Do salesmen who possess equal skills and opportunities tend to receive comparable rewards in relation to their performance?

7. *Flexibility.* Does the plan offer adequate differences in compensation to salesmen faced with different situations such as trainees versus experienced men, or highly skilled application engineers versus general-line salesmen?

It would be desirable if all these objectives could be achieved simultaneously. This is seldom possible, however, for the attainment of some impedes the attainment of others. For example, it is simple but often unfair to pay all salesmen identical salaries. A plan that bases a man's compensation on the gross profit derived from his sale of steel sheeting may provide incentive, but the volatile demand for steel sheeting may also create a highly irregular income pattern from year to year.

In their efforts to balance the various objectives of sales compensation, companies utilize a wide variety of compensation systems. Most of these can be classified into three broad groups: straight salary, straight commission, and combinations of the two. These three types of compensation plans are discussed in the sections that follow.

STRAIGHT SALARY PLANS

The primary advantage of a straight salary plan is that it permits management to exert a maximum degree of control over the sales force. As examples, a salary plan usually makes it easier to change the size of selling territories, to move men from one territory to another, to change the firm's selling program, or to require salesmen to provide technical service and advice not associated with immediate sales. Straight salaries provide salesmen with stable incomes from season to season and year to year. This may be particularly important in situations where product demand is seasonal or cyclical, such as for bathing suits and capital goods. Salary plans are also relatively simple to operate and easy to understand. They also simplify the task of projecting the size of the personal selling budget for the coming year.

The management that uses a straight salary plan needs to be able closely to control and evaluate the performances of its men. Because their immediate incomes play a lesser role in determining their job performances, the incentives that might be provided by some form of commission or mixed plan must be provided by supervision.

Straight salary plans are probably the *least common* of the three major types of compensation systems. They tend to be used in situations where selling tasks are so complex that it is difficult to establish explicit criteria for incentive systems. Straight salary plans are also used in situations where a firm wants to avoid undue emphasis on short-term sales results, to the detriment of longer term customer relationships. Hallmark Cards, Inc., for example, pays its 800 salesmen straight salaries because, according to the president, Mr. Donald J. Hall, "our objective is a *through* sale, not a *to* sale."[9]

[9] "Once More with Feeling," *Sales Management,* Dec. 15, 1970, p. 20.

□

STRAIGHT COMMISSION PLANS

In plans of this type, a commission is usually stated in terms of some fixed or sliding rate related to sales or profit volume. A salesman's income is therefore directly linked to the volume of sales or profits that he generates in a given time period. In this way, commission plans provide more incentive for generating immediate sales volume than salary plans. For that reason, commission plans are most typically used in situations where there is a need for aggressive selling. If the Prather Company, for example, established an immediate and substantial sales increase as its paramount selling objective, Mr. Hoslett might decide to use a straight commission plan because of its high degree of incentive.

A commission plan has the advantage of relating the amount of selling expense more closely to the funds that either are currently available or are to become available through sales revenues. The significance of this advantage depends to some extent on whether a drawing account is combined with the commission plan. A *drawing account,* in effect, permits salesmen to borrow from the company, up to some specified maximum, against future commissions. In many companies the draw becomes tantamount to a salary, because there is a tendency not to force the return of draws in excess of commissions.

Commission plans can be relatively simple to operate and understand where there is only one commission rate applied to all products. However, relatively few commission plans are this simple. Some plans use *sliding commissions* whereby a salesman is paid one rate of commission up to a certain volume; thereafter the rate may be increased in relation to sales volume. For example, a plan may call for a 3 percent commission rate on sales up to $100,000, 4 percent on sales between $100,000 and $150,000, and 5 percent on sales over $150,000. Commissions may also vary either by type of customer or by type of product. For example, commissions on sales to new accounts may be higher than those paid on established accounts. Some companies often pay a higher commission rate on items with high gross margins or on those which are overstocked. If there are a number of variations in commission rates, the plan can involve considerable clerical work in the maintenance of records for each salesman, for each group of products, or for the customers to whom the different rates apply. While these variations lead to increased clerical costs, they also may result in a more flexible plan that is more closely tailored to the needs of particular groups of customers or products.

The major disadvantage of commission plans is that they tend to complicate the problem of *controlling* the activities of the sales force. They may lead salesmen to concentrate on those functions which generate immediate sales volume or profits and to deemphasize service or other activities such as providing advice and technical service to customers that build long-run profits.

Under commission plans, salesmen tend to be more independent and less obligated to maintain specific work hours, follow specified routings for customer calls, or follow selling instructions. They may tend to stress those items which are *easiest* to sell, which often are not the most profitable. Commission plans can also create problems with respect to wage levels within the firm. Tosdal reported a situation in which a salesman on commission earned more than the chairman of the board.[10] A salesman's commission earnings can also be affected by a number of factors beyond his control such as changes in the firm's advertising, pricing, and service policies or changes in general business conditions. For example, changes in business conditions can lead to irregular variations in income, particularly for products with strong seasonal or cyclical variations in demand.

COMBINATION PLANS

The great majority of firms use some form of combination plan. The most common are those which use either a combination of salary and commission or a combination of salary, commission, and/or bonus. Combination salary and commission plans are used, for example, in many situations where both service work and sales volume are important goals. Because this is the case in a wide variety of selling situations, there was a significant trend during the 1960s toward the use of combination-type systems. A study conducted by the National Industrial Conference Board in 1966, for example, showed that two-thirds of a group of 665 manufacturing firms studied paid their salesmen both salaries and *some* form of commission or bonus incentives.[11]

Combination plans typically are used to avoid the weaknesses of straight salary or straight commission plans without losing too many of their advantages. A firm with a salary system may want to increase the degree of incentive provided by its plan without sacrificing too much of the income regularity currently provided. In contrast, a company with a commission plan may want to increase the degree of income regularity without losing too much of the incentive provided by the present plan. By varying the proportion of salary in a salesman's income, for example, management can affect the degree of control it has over his selling activities discussed in the two preceding sections.

Combination plans frequently involve a salary plus a commission based on sales volume over and above some specified quota. The *degree* of incentive provided by a combination plan depends primarily on the proportion of income that a salesman can expect to receive from commissions. Some companies set the salary level so that it provides minimum living expenses for the man and his family. This creates an element of income regularity without eliminating the incentive provided by a commission.

[10] Harry R. Tosdal, "How To Design the Salesman's Compensation Plan," *Harvard Business Review*, September–October, 1953, p. 138.

[11] National Industrial Conference Board, *Incentive Plans for Salesmen*, Studies in Personnel Policy no. 217, New York, p. 3.

It is desirable, and difficult, to find the right balance between incentive and control in a combination system of sales compensation. A study by Newton of the performance of sales forces in over 1,000 companies indicated that the "turnover rate" of salesmen (the percentage who quit or are fired, per year) is lowest when there are significant opportunities for salesmen to earn more money through increased efforts.[12] Specifically, he found that turnover was minimized when the ratio of total compensation for the highest paid salesmen to that of the lowest paid man was between 2 to 1 and 3 to 1.

□

SALES QUOTAS

□ *A sales quota is a "projected volume of sales assigned to a marketing unit for use in the management of sales efforts. It applies to a specified period and may be expressed in dollars or in physical units."*[13]

Quotas may thus be established for individual salesmen, territories or districts, divisions, or other organizational units or individuals.□ Mr. Hoslett, for example, could set quotas for the Prather Company salesmen. William Pierce, a salesman in a metropolitan area, might be given an annual sales quota of $350,000. His quota might be divided into quarterly goals and might also be divided among specific products or between existing and new products.

Quotas are often based on a variety of factors. Past sales results or projected sales forecasts play major roles. Often statistical analyses of data on national or regional economic conditions are used. Frequently management seeks the personal advice of district managers or individual salesmen in an attempt to get a good feel for specific territories and their particular economic, competitive, and selling problems. The end result is a quota that is presumably a realistic target for the salesman's or other marketing unit's performance.

Since the question of what is realistic may depend on who is giving the answer, the salesman or his supervisor, companies sometimes develop *negotiated* quotas. These are set jointly by the salesman and his supervisor. In that way the salesman in effect agrees in advance to the quota's reasonableness and therefore, in effect, makes a commitment to reach it.

Because quotas are targets, they have an important relationship to compensation plans. If commissions or bonuses are tied to quota achievement, the impact of the quota is direct and obvious. Even with straight salary plans, quota achievement may have some effect on merit increases, chances of promotion, or the general evaluation of a salesman's ability. It is important for managements to recognize that a salesman *may think that* quota achievement is a factor in any of these areas, even though management itself may place relatively little importance on it. In view of all these tangible and intangible factors, it is essential that quotas be carefully planned, thoroughly understood by salesmen and supervisors, and administered so that any factors that affect

[12] Derek A. Newton, "Get the Most Out of Your Sales Force," *Harvard Business Review*, September–October, 1969, pp. 130–143.

[13] American Marketing Association, *Marketing Definitions*, Chicago, 1960, p. 20.

sales but are beyond the control of the salesmen, such as economic conditions, strikes, or new competitive products, are taken into consideration in evaluating performance against quotas.

Nonmonetary incentives

Thus far we have concerned ourselves solely with compensation as a means of motivation. It is surely *one* vital mean toward that end, but, just as surely, it is not the *only* one. Generalizations about human behavior are dangerous, but it seems eminently reasonable to say that there are very few people whose only goals are the accumulation and use of money. Other things are involved in motivation, and we call these *nonmonetary incentives*.

Such incentives are important to salesmen. The nature of the salesman's job is such that he often is on the road or away from direct contact with his company for long periods of time. Except for periodic contacts with his supervisor, district manager, or other salesmen, he is out of touch with the organization that in large measure controls his destiny. The monthly or biweekly paycheck (sometimes his commissions are not included until the quarter is over) is neither a source of information nor a means of communication with the "world" of his organization.

The inside salesman, of course, has more frequent contact with fellow salesmen and with management. Two other factors, however, may affect him. First, his job is often more repetitious (the drug, hardware, or retail store clerk), and his physical environment certainly less subject to change. Second, he frequently finds himself in "competition" of a sort with his fellow salespeople (the furniture or appliance store salesman), even though management itself may not intend that such competition exist. Under these circumstances, boredom or personal jealousies or frictions can arise. Again, the paycheck may not solve all his problems.

The motivation of human beings is, of course, a subject to which an entire book could profitably be devoted. Our treatment of it in terms of nonfinancial incentives will nevertheless be brief, and will be presented in the context of climate, formal incentives, and behavior in the informal organization.

□

ORGANIZATIONAL CLIMATE

The word *climate* is used here to refer to the spirit and atmosphere in which a company's relationships with its salesmen are conducted.[14] Management should try to make salesmen feel that they are a part of the organization and have important roles to play in its success. Also, and particularly because

[14] See Chapter 13 for a more general discussion of climate and the importance of leadership in this regard.

salesmen often work in comparative isolation from company associates and *are* the company to many customers, it is essential that they believe in what they are doing and in the products that they sell.

The climate of a business firm is an organization-wide matter. So far as salesmen are concerned, however, it is largely dependent on the behavior of sales management and sales supervision. Most of the Prather Company sales force's internal contacts will be with Mr. Hoslett and the district managers, for example. In these relationships, salesmen can be best motivated if a spirit of cooperative effort toward the achievement of mutually shared and clearly understood goals exists. Words of private or public recognition and overt awareness of personal problems or accomplishments go far to make the company climate conducive to high morale.

FORMAL INCENTIVES

Although the climate of an organization is intangible, its beneficial effects can be enhanced by *formal incentives.* Closely tied to climate, for example, may be formal procedures for the recognition of good performance. Many firms use meetings, house organs, or other forums to acknowledge excellent accomplishment in exceeding quotas, opening new accounts, or other selling objectives. Company officers sometimes present formal scrolls or certificates in recognition of salesmen's efforts.

Other common devices whose effective use can help to motivate salesmen are *sales contests* and *sales meetings.* Sales contests typically cover brief periods of time (a week or a month) and provide prizes to winners or to all those who exceed some target. Mr. Hoslett, for example, could set up a month's sales contest in connection with new accounts or sales of a new product. The contest could be for all salesmen or for each sales district. Prizes might be offered to the top five salesmen, to the winner in each district, or to all salesmen who achieve some specified minimum objective. The prizes offered by business firms in sales contests can range from travel vacations or automobiles to a carton of cigarettes.

Sales contests are prevalent in American companies, and they are an easily overworked device. There are firms, for example, that have at least one contest in operation continuously; under such circumstances, the effectiveness of contests may be greatly reduced. They become boring and a part of normal routine, and in spite of management's exhortations the salesmen merely "go through the motions" unless the tangible rewards are great.

Another well-known and frequently used device is the sales meeting. Sales meetings serve a wide variety of purposes. They can be used to introduce new products or new personnel, report on accomplishments or objectives, realign territorial lines or selling functions, or get sales contests off to flying starts. They may also be used as opportunities to discuss company policies or programs, or to give salesmen a chance to air their grievances. The potential purposes are virtually unlimited, but in general the basic objectives of sales meetings are to generate salesmen's *understanding* of, and *enthusiasm* for, management's policies and objectives.

□

THE INFORMAL ORGANIZATION

Another important source of nonfinancial incentives is what was referred to earlier as *behavior in the informal organization*. There are informal personal relationships among employees in any business firm. This statement applies to salesmen, and particularly to salesmen who associate closely with one another in retail or other forms of inside selling situations. Such relationships can result in undue friction, lack of trust, or other problems. Conversely, they can also result in more effective teamwork or greater acceptance of objectives. Because of their potential effect on motivation and accomplishment, alert managements keep a close eye on such personal relationships and the informal organization that they create.

Questions

1. A major insurance company sold both life insurance and automobile insurance directly to consumers. Historically, the two products were sold by separate sales organizations. Marketing costs had risen rapidly in recent years, however, and the company was now considering the possibility of consolidating its two sales forces.
   a. What factors should the company consider in evaluating this possibility?
   b. Which of these factors would favor consolidation and which would not? Why?

2. "If direct selling is a significant part of the selling task, then the salesman's compensation scheme should be primarily commission to provide maximum incentive." Do you agree or disagree? Why?

3. What sales tasks and functions do you think would be most important in selling each of the following products? Why?
   a. Men's shoes
   b. Bulk chemicals
   c. Sheet steel
   d. Nuclear reactors
   e. Frozen vegetables
   f. Original sculptures

4. What personal characteristics do you think would be the best predictors of a salesman's success in selling the products listed in Question 3? Why?

5. What mix of salary and commission do you think would be most appropriate for each of the products listed in Question 3? Why?

6. (a) How might the functions performed by a salesman promoting drugs to a retail druggist differ from those involved in promoting the same drugs to doctors? (b) How might the functions of a woman selling cosmetics on a door-to-door basis differ from those of a cosmetics clerk in a retail store? (c) Based on differences in their functions, how might the content of a training program vary for personnel being trained for each of the above positions?

7. Early in 1971, Thomas Michaels, president of *Reflection Publications,* and Dominic Sorrento, sales manager of *Reflection,* were trying to decide what action to take with respect to William Daniels, San Francisco branch manager of *Reflection*.

Daniels, age thirty-two, had been with *Reflection* for 10 years. Starting as an advertising salesman for one of the company's smaller magazines, his success as a salesman had been dramatic. By the end of his third year with the magazine, he was its top salesman, producing $300,000 in advertising revenues a year. A year later, he was transferred to *Vacation,* a high-circulation monthly consumer magazine. Within four years, Daniels had moved to first place among *Vacation's* sales force, with annual sales of close to $1.5 million.

As a result of Daniel's continued sales success, he was promoted to Baltimore branch manager. Here, while continuing as a salesman for *Reflection,* Daniels also supervised the branch consisting of two other salesmen and a secretary. In spite of a somewhat depressed economic climate, Daniels continued to be an outstanding producer, raising branch sales 30 percent within two years.

Impressed with this performance, Sorrento concluded that Daniels was ready for increased managerial responsibility and, in mid-1970, appointed him San Francisco branch manager.

The San Francisco branch, *Reflection's* fourth largest office, produced close to $10 million in advertising revenues. It employed 12 salesmen and an office staff of 5. As branch manager, Daniels no longer worked as a salesman. While he was expected to help with problems on key accounts, his primary responsibilities were administrative: supervising the sales force, hiring and training new salesmen, establishing budgets, handling expense reports, and supervising the office staff.

Within six months, it became obvious to Sorrento, *Reflection's* sales manager, that Daniels was completely ineffective as San Francisco branch manager.

In discussing the situation with Michaels, Sorrento explained that revenues were already some 25 percent below quota, expenses were out of line, and that Daniels, being extremely self-sufficient and self-confident, would not listen to advice. There was also some dissatisfaction among the branch salesmen. Apparently Daniels would often bypass them and deal directly with advertisers. Moreover, he appeared unwilling or unable to sit down and discuss sales strategy or sales problems with the salesmen.

Both Michaels and Sorrento were convinced that Daniels was ineffective in a managerial capacity and that it had been a mistake to take him out of sales. Because of his successful years of service to the company and his excellent sales performance, they were reluctant to do anything which would force Daniels to leave the company. While they knew that Daniels and his family had been extremely pleased and excited by his promotion to San Francisco branch manager, neither Michaels nor Sorrento believed the company could accept continuation of the present situation.

a. What action should Michaels and Sorrento take? Why?

b. How do you expect Daniels would respond to your recommended action? Why?

c. How do you think the situation could have been avoided?

d. What recommendations would you make to Michaels regarding methods of selecting and training sales management personnel?

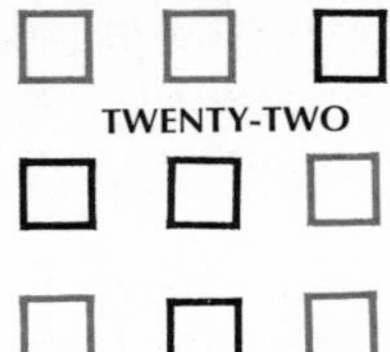

TWENTY-TWO

Advertising and sales promotion

Although personal selling is the oldest and most important form of marketing communication, advertising and sales promotion are more visible to the average consumer and, in many ways, more controversial. In 1970, total advertising expenditures in the United States reached $20.8 billion—approximately $100 per person. Reliable estimates are not available for sales promotion costs, but these probably amounted to at least another $5 billion. Thus, total advertising and sales promotion amount to about 2.6 percent of the gross national product in the United States. (Comparative figures for *advertising only* in the late 1960s were: Canada, 1.4 percent; United Kingdom, 1.1 percent; France, 0.7 percent; and Japan, 1.4 percent.)

All this effort was devoted to television commercials, magazine advertisements, billboards, counter displays, and other types of promotion in order to *communicate* information and ideas about products, services, organizations, and ideas to prospective customers, voters, employees, and other audiences.

In this chapter, we shall explore the main problems involved in managing advertising and sales promotion as elements of the overall marketing program. As pointed out in Chapter 20, advertising and sales promotion should be viewed as *means* of implementing a communications strategy, along with personal selling.

Advertising as a form of communication

The role of advertising and its relationship to other elements of a marketing program vary enormously among different types of marketing situations. Consider these examples of the ways advertising is employed:

Primary or selective demand Primary demand advertising is intended to affect the demand for a type of product, not simply one particular brand of that product. If cigar manufacturers were to attempt to increase the overall demand for cigars with an advertising campaign extolling the virtues of cigar smoking in general, this would be a primary demand campaign.

When the manufacturer of Muriel cigars, on the other hand, tries to get cigar smokers to use Muriels, this is a selective demand campaign. In the latter case, the advertiser is attempting to differentiate his brand from others, even though he may also hope, and perhaps intend, to increase the total amount of cigar consumption.

Direct or indirect action Direct-action advertising is designed to make the prospective purchaser buy the product immediately or at least get more information about it. Advertising about products intended to alleviate skin disorders is typically designed to secure immediate buying action by those interested in the products. Advertising for such higher priced items as automobiles and large appliances, which people buy infrequently, is normally of an indirect-action nature in that it attempts to create a favorable attitude toward a manufacturer's product (or brand) which will exist at the time the decision-making unit decides to make a purchase. Much advertising, however, seeks both direct and indirect effects. A full-page magazine advertisement for corn flakes may seek to build a continuing preference for the brand of the manufacturer involved, whereas the coupon in the corner of the advertisement is designed to get Mrs. Smith immediately to send in a box top and a quarter for a kitchen knife.

Consumer, industrial, and trade Consumer advertising is directed at household decision-making units; industrial advertising, at industrial customers; and trade advertising, at channels of distribution such as wholesalers and retailers. Thus, B. F. Goodrich may advertise tires to household customers and industrial belting to industrial users, and run advertisements in trade publications directed at its wholesalers and retailers.

Product and institutional Most advertising is product advertising, designed to promote the sale or reputation of a particular product or brand. This is true whether the advertising is done by a manufacturer, middleman, or dealer and whether the advertising concerns the product itself or some feature such as service, price, or quality directly associated with it. Advertisements about Shell gasoline are a case in point. On the other hand, when Shell advertisements describe that firm's general activities such as its public service work, this is defined as institutional (or corporate) advertising because it is intended to build an overall favorable attitude toward the company and its family of products.

Cooperative Many manufacturers offer retailers and wholesalers cooperative advertising allowances designed to get local advertising support for a manufacturer's brand. The manufacturer typically pays a portion of the retailer's or wholesaler's advertising costs. Allowances can be used either in connection with special promotions or as a normal part of operations. Funds are typically allocated on some proportionate basis, such as 50 cents per case purchased or 2 percent of sales during a specific period of time. Cooperative advertising often has highly specific and short-range objectives, such as getting the customer to make a buying decision in regard to a specific product at a specific location at a specific price as soon as possible.

The term "cooperative" is also sometimes used to designate advertising efforts supported by industry or trade groups or associations. Such *industry-cooperative* efforts are usually undertaken to increase primary demand for a product or service. Examples include the promotion of milk, apples, prunes, and citrus fruits by growers' or producers' associations, and advertising about "full-service banks" by a bankers' association.

Public service Some advertising is aimed at supporting charitable and public service activities, including fund-raising for the United Fund and the Red Cross, highway safety, and prevention of forest fires. Much of the time, space, and creative work for public service advertising is donated by business through the Advertising Council and by local organizations.

As these illustrations suggest, advertising is used by many different kinds of organizations to communicate a wide variety of things to various kinds of audiences. Clearly, the nature and scope of the advertising (and sales promotion) activities undertaken by the organization depend on the basic situation in which it is operating. But regardless of the situation, all organizations must deal with certain key management problems in order to use advertising effectively.

ADVERTISING MANAGEMENT: AN OVERVIEW

To illustrate what is involved in the management of advertising, it is useful to return to the example of the Prather Company, discussed in an early section of Chapter 21. Recall that Mr. Prather, president of a relatively small company producing specialty food items, was making a major shift in marketing strategy by changing from distribution through food brokers to a direct sales force. Prather was also expanding its product line and generally pursuing a corporate goal of rapid growth. What role should advertising play in this situation, and what kinds of decisions will have to be made about the advertising component of the firm's marketing mix?

The first question to be resolved is the determination of *objectives* for advertising. Prather's advertising will serve as one form of communication to housewives, retailers, and wholesalers, about the company and its products. To whom should this communication be directed? How much should be aimed at consumers, and how much to "the trade"? What kinds of housewives should be reached? Should the emphasis be on retaining present customers or getting new types of users to try Prather products? Should communication be aimed at encouraging new uses of the products, such as for children's school lunches? Note that the objectives will probably be quite different for the company's new products, with which customers are unfamiliar, than for products with established markets.

The objectives set for advertising must be carefully coordinated with those of personal selling and sales promotion, in terms of both content and timing. For example, the goals of introductory advertising for one of Prather's new products might be (1) to achieve a certain level of awareness of the product, say 50 percent among a specified group of consumers, and (2) to attain a desired level of trial of the product within a given period. Advertising designed to achieve these objectives might be supported by the use of coupons redeemable for a 10-cent discount on purchases and special in-store displays (sales promotion). The sales force, then, would be assigned the tasks of getting distribution for the new product and getting the displays assembled in stores, so that the product will be available when the advertising and promotion start to appear.

Once objectives have been established, Mr. Prather will have to decide how much to spend for advertising, and how to allocate total expenditures among markets, types of advertising, and time periods. Determining how much to spend for advertising is much more difficult than for personal selling, because the relationship between spending and results is poorly understood and hard to measure. How many messages will be needed to induce 10 percent of the housewives in an area to try Prather's new product? How long must the company maintain its costly introductory campaign? These are hard kinds of questions, to which different companies would give different answers. There are, nevertheless, some concepts and methods that have proved useful in determining how much to spend, as discussed later in this chapter.

A third major problem in building the advertising program is that of designing *advertising messages*. Within the broad framework of the objectives set for advertising and the budget available for it, what should the communication say, and how? Should Prather's advertisements present recipes for using the company's products? Should they emphasize taste appeal, or nutrition, or economy? Should the messages deal with the entire product line, or just one product at a time? Should television and radio commercials employ music? Should a slogan of some kind or a symbol (like Elsie, the Borden Cow) be employed?

Consideration of message content and execution raises a fourth, closely related, problem—that of selecting *advertising media*. What to say and how to say it depend, in part, on whether the messages are conveyed through TV, radio, magazines, newspapers, billboards, or other types of media. A decision to utilize music obviously implies a decision to use TV and/or radio; an emphasis on recipes will require some use of print media, because housewives will want "hard copies" of the instructions for reference. Thus, for Prather and every other advertiser, message and media decisions must be carefully coordinated.

In making his decisions about advertising, Mr. Prather will almost certainly rely on specialists in advertising from within his organization, from an advertising agency, or both. Agencies provide a wide range of specialized services to advertisers including, in the case of relatively small firms like Prather, considerable assistance in general marketing strategy.

Once Mr. Prather has approved a proposed advertising program, including objectives, budget, message design, and media, he should give some thought to how the *results* of the advertising will be measured. Of course, Mr. Prather and his stockholders, if any, are primarily interested in overall marketing results, in terms of sales and profits. But whatever overall results are achieved, there will be some question about the contributions of the various elements of the marketing mix to the final outcome.

Suppose sales and profits fall short of the goals set. Did this happen because the new products were unsatisfactory in quality? Or because the sales force failed to get adequate distribution? Or because prices were too high? Or did the advertising fail to inform enough consumers about the products? Even before the advertising campaign begins, Mr. Prather should take steps, again perhaps with the advice of an agency, to measure advertising results at appropriate points in time. This might include survey measures of brand awareness, measures of consumer attitudes, and other field measurements of the effects of advertising messages.

The rest of the chapter deals with the key problems of advertising management illustrated by this example: setting objectives, deciding how much to spend, designing messages, selecting media, and measuring results. In the last section of the chapter we discuss sales promotion briefly.

ADVERTISING OBJECTIVES

Advertising campaigns are most successful when individual advertisements are planned and executed with specific objectives in mind. Each advertisement should be planned in relation to other advertisements, and should also be related to the other aspects of the firm's promotional program. The definition of objectives serves two main purposes: (1) It forces marketing management to focus sharply on what it wants advertising to do, and (2) it makes the job of designing advertising campaigns and advertisements much easier.

It is not sufficient to say that the purpose of advertising is to sell products, or get customers into a store, or get votes. These statements of desired end results are too general, and do not lend themselves to the development of the specific ideas or messages that the advertisements should convey.

Advertising objectives should be stated in terms of *what* is to be communicated, to *whom,* and what effect the communication is intended to have (perhaps indirectly) on *behavior.* Some examples of possible advertising objectives for a manufacturer's product advertising are given in Figure 22-1. These examples, and the ones in Figure 22-2, are drawn from a list of over 90 specific goals actually used by a group of major companies that participated in a study of advertising management, carried out in the early 1960s.

Note that some of the objectives cited in Figure 22-1 have to do with "direct-action" results, such as announcing special promotions, which would

---

FIGURE 22-1

Examples of advertising objectives for a manufacturer's product advertising

To Increase Sales Directly, by:

1. Encouraging potential purchasers to visit dealers or distributors
2. Announcing special sales, contests, or other promotions
3. Securing new dealers or distributors
4. Inducing professional persons (e.g., doctors, architects) to recommend a product
5. Distributing coupons to be redeemed on purchases

To Create Awareness and Interest in The Company's Products, by:

6. Informing potential buyers about product features
7. Announcing the availability of new products
8. Demonstrating the benefits of a product's uses
9. Comparing a product with competing products
10. Showing how a product should be used
11. Informing potential buyers about the company's technical skills, production facilities, technical services, etc.
12. Informing purchasers about where products can be obtained
13. Announcing changes in prices, packages, labels, etc.
14. Publicizing a new brand name or symbol

Source: Adapted from Harry D. Wolfe et al., *Measuring Advertising Results,* Studies in Business Policy No. 102, National Industrial Conference Board, New York, 1962, pp. 10–11.

FIGURE 22-2

Examples of advertising objectives for a company's "institutional" advertising

1. To depict the company as a good employer and "citizen"
2. To acquaint people with a company's public service
3. To inform people about the company's industry and its role in the economy
4. To describe specific research and development activities and achievements
5. To identify the company with its overall goals or philosophy, e.g., progressiveness
6. To improve investors' evaluation of the company
7. To improve prospective employees' appraisals of the company as a place to work
8. To refute derogatory publicity
9. To explain the company's position in a labor dispute or legal issue

Source: Adapted from Harry D. Wolfe et al., *Measuring Advertising Results,* Studies in Business Policy No. 102, National Industrial Conference Board, New York, 1962, pp. 11–12.

---

presumably be reflected in increased sales more or less immediately. Most of the time, however, manufacturers' product advertising is intended to affect sales *indirectly* by changing customers' knowledge and attitudes. In this context, it may be helpful to refer to Figure 6-2 and think about the "steps in being persuaded."

Figure 22-2 gives some examples of possible objectives for a business firm's institutional advertising. The results of this kind of advertising are even further removed from an organization's ultimate goals than are the results of product advertising. For example, a company may spend substantial amounts of money on a campaign that describes its public service activities. Apart from the possibility that some members of the audience may regard such advertising as "phony"—as many did in the case of advertising featuring "clean environment" activities of paper companies in the early 1970s—there is a real question about whether it has any discernible effect, even in the long run, on the company's sales. Will any customers ever be swayed by an association between good citizenship and the XYZ Corporation? Some observers doubt it, and attribute most institutional advertising to the personal vanity of executives.

The examples of advertising objectives in Figures 22-1 and 22-2 are stated in general terms, but they can and should be made much more explicit in the context of a given situation. If the objective is to inform prospective customers about the key features of a product, for instance, then this goal should be translated into a specific statement of *how many* customers are to be made aware of *what features,* during *what period of time.* When Volkswagen first offered automatic transmissions in the late 1960s, one of its advertising objectives might have been stated as "achieving a 60 percent awareness, among a given group of prospective buyers, of the availability of the automatic stick shift, within 6 months."

Advertising expenditures

In any discussion of advertising expenditures, someone is bound to quote a classic expression of many executives' viewpoint on the subject: "I know half of what we spend on advertising is wasted; the only trouble is, I don't know *which* half."[1] This quotation reflects the near-universal difficulty of relating advertising expenditures to sales and profit results, and the consequent difficulty of evaluating the effects of change in expenditure levels. We shall have more to say about this problem in a later section of this chapter, Measuring Advertising Results. For the moment, it is sufficient to point out that determining advertising's results and consequently the amount of money to be devoted to an advertising budget is complicated by several major difficulties: (1) the effects of external variables such as population or income, changes in economic conditions, and competitive behavior; (2) variations in the quality of advertising; (3) uncertainty as to the time-lag effect of advertising; and (4) the effects of the firm's other marketing activities such as product improvement and stepped-up personal selling.

Given the complexity of the problem, many companies resort to more than one method of determining the size of their advertising budgets. Since many methods are in common use, several of them will be discussed.

□ PROFIT MAXIMIZATION

The "ideal" method for determining advertising expenditures is to identify a relationship between the amount of advertising and company profits, such as that shown in Figure 20-6, and to spend that amount of money which maximizes net profits. Since the effects of advertising may be reflected partly in *future* sales as well as *present* sales, it is necessary to take delayed results into account. Theoretically, this presents no problem: the advertiser simply maximizes the present value of all future profits associated with current advertising expenditures, discounting future profits at an appropriate rate. Instead of a simple advertising-sales relationship such as that depicted in Figure 20-6, he utilizes a *series* of relationships incorporating the effects of current advertising efforts on sales in several future time periods.

For reasons suggested above, very few advertisers are able to implement the profit-maximizing approach to determining their advertising expenditures. Some, however, can come close to this ideal. Mail-order firms who rely almost entirely on a single form of advertising, or a limited range of different forms, can, and do, employ trial-and-error methods to measure the returns from different amounts of promotion, different types of customers, and variations in media or messages.

Some companies that utilize more conventional marketing channels and

[1] This old chestnut has been attributed to John Wanamaker, a nineteenth-century American department store magnate, and to Lord Cole, one-time managing director of Unilever Ltd., in Great Britain. Its true origins are obscure.

techniques have also carried out field experiments to estimate the effects of varying amounts of advertising expenditures. In at least a few cases, advertisers have succeeded in getting plausible, consistent results from experimental studies and have based their subsequent spending decisions on the results of the studies.

Another way of relating advertising expenditures to sales and profits is for managers to make purely judgmental estimates of changes in sales for various hypothetical changes in advertising effort. This approach is used in some of the computer-based systems for marketing planning that were being developed in the late 1960s and early 1970s. Obviously, the validity of results based on subjective judgments depends entirely on the quality of the judgments employed.

Although practically all advertisers would like to be able to set advertising expenditure levels so as to maximize profits, and most of them devote considerable thought and study to the relationship between the two, very few feel completely confident that they are able to achieve this goal. As a result, the great majority of companies employ other methods in addition to, or instead of, formal procedures that relate expenditures to sales and profits.

□

ADVERTISING AS A PERCENTAGE OF SALES

Under this approach, the advertising budget is established as a percentage of anticipated sales.

The percentage-of-sales method ignores the basic question: "What is the real nature of the advertising job to be done?" It is thus not necessarily geared to the needs of the total marketing program. If advertising is viewed as a cause of sales, the use of sales to determine the size of the advertising budget is inappropriate; nevertheless, this method is widely used.[2] Its wide use reflects the prevailing uncertainty about the measurement of advertising effectiveness. Also, it is a convenient way of minimizing the difficulties of annual intracompany budgetary negotiations. It is also seemingly safe because advertising expenditures will automatically fluctuate with sales and because it provides a way of staying on a par with competition as long as competitors use a similar method.

Although the percentage-of-sales approach seems arbitrary to many people, it may be a sensible one in cases where the competing companies in an industry have tested various levels of spending over a period of time and finally "settled down" to what becomes a customary level. It is apparent that reasonably stable advertising-to-sales ratios *do* evolve in many industries, and that, apart from companies that use distinctive methods of distribution or marketing strategies, most major competitors in an industry tend to set their expenditures

[2] See David L. Hurwood, "How Companies Set Advertising Budgets," *The Conference Board Record,* March, 1968, pp. 34–41.

fairly close to the prevailing norms. These norms differ greatly among industries, however, as illustrated in Table 22-1. The figures in this table are *average* advertising-to-sales ratios for selected types of businesses. They range from ½ of 1 percent or less, in primary metals and wholesale trade, to more than 10 percent for producers of soap and related products.[3]

□

SETTING EXPENDITURES IN RELATION TO COMPETITION

The management that uses this approach ties its budget to the dollars or percentage of sales expended by its competitors. This approach is also widely used. It usually involves an estimate of industry advertising for the period in question and the allocation of an amount that makes the firm's share of that total equal to its share of the industry's sales.

[3] The figures given in Table 22-1 are understatements of *total* advertising expenditures by companies in the industries listed, because they are based on accounting data as reported to the Internal Revenue Service. It is believed that most firms adopt a relatively narrow definition of "advertising" in determining what costs to classify under this account.

□

TABLE 22-1

Advertising expenditures, percent of sales, 1967, selected industries

Industry	Percent of sales
All industry groups	1.2%
All manufacturing:	1.4
Canned and frozen foods	2.5
Bottled soft drinks	6.4
Household furniture	1.1
Soap and related products	10.9
Primary metals	0.4
Motor vehicles	1.1
Wholesale trade:	0.5
Retail trade:	1.5
Department stores	2.8
Food stores	1.2
Services:	
Banks	1.3
Motion picture theaters	6.6

Source: Internal Revenue Service data, as reported in *Advertising Age,* Jan. 25, 1971, pp. 77–78.

This is a defensive approach. It merely keeps up. It assumes that competitors know what they are doing and that competition has generally similar marketing problems and strategies. The use of competition as a yardstick makes it easy for a firm to rationalize away the need for analyzing the realities of its own competitive situation and to ignore the possibility of other and better strategies.

SPENDING ALL THE ORGANIZATION CAN AFFORD

This approach involves the income statement and the balance sheet. It asks how much the firm has available. This question is partially answered by anticipated sales and margins. These factors are relevant, but decisions based wholly on them again ignore the requirements of the advertising job. They also ignore the theoretical concept that a firm ought to be able to afford advertising dollars up to the point where an extra dollar of advertising expenditure does not yield its required rate of return on investment. In other words, the basic weakness of this approach is that, like the others already cited, it does not solve the problem of "how much should we spend" by asking, "What can we profitably spend?"

In some instances, companies adopt pricing policies or other strategies intended to yield more advertising dollars. Thus one producer of personal grooming products prices its products high enough to yield the revenue necessary for sufficient advertising impact. One of its competitors, on the other hand, uses all receipts above a minimal amount to advertise new products. In effect, the second company is borrowing from profits and other sources to push its new products during their growth phases.

THE TASK APPROACH

Whereas the methods discussed thus far determine the amount of advertising dollars by using some criterion external to the requirements of the advertising job to be done, the task approach starts by asking what the objectives of the advertising campaign are. It then moves to determine how the objectives can be effectively accomplished, that is, what media or messages, and how much it will cost to do the job. In this process, questions about decision-making units and the advertisability of the product are more sharply defined and answered within the framework of specific advertising objectives. This approach, more than any of the others, requires that assumptions about media, copy, and all other parts of a campaign be coordinated and built from the ground up to achieve a specific set of objectives.

The task approach has special merit in conjunction with the introduction of a new product. In this situation, past approaches to other products are perhaps useful as a starting place for analysis. Beyond that, however, much work remains to be done. A new product, a different competitive situation, different groups of decision-making units, and possible changes in the buying behavior of the "old" decision-making units—all these dictate that traditional approaches cannot be blindly embraced. Also involved is the likelihood that heavy initial advertising expenditures must be undertaken to introduce the new product, as indicated in Chapter 15.

Many advertisers use the task approach *together with* some of the other methods described above, to set advertising budgets.[4] For example, a preliminary budget may be developed for each of a company's products by defining objectives and building up a total amount to be spent, item by item. Then, when the individual budgets are combined into an overall divisional or company budget, the total may be adjusted after consideration of some percentage of sales guideline, as well as such other factors as the company's priorities for current earnings versus growth.

Designing advertising messages

Within the framework of a given set of advertising objectives and a given level of advertising expenditure, the advertiser faces a challenging problem in designing effective messages. Usually this task is assigned primarily to "creative" specialists in the advertising agency, although the right of final approval is almost always retained by executives of the organization that pays for the advertising.

Proper message design is very important, because the effectiveness of a given amount of advertising varies enormously. Studies of advertising readership and purchases of advertised products by Daniel Starch indicate that results achieved *per dollar* spent on advertising vary by a factor of as much as 5 to 1, depending on the quality of message content and execution.[5] Moreover, a successful basic message design can be used over and over. For example, the Olympia Brewing Company is a successful regional producer of beer in the Pacific Northwest. Olympia differentiates its product by using natural spring water; and it has used the same basic advertising theme—"It's The Water"—ever since 1902. According to executives of the company and its agency, this message has retained a high degree of interest and memorability despite more than 70 years of use.[6]

[4] See Hurwood, *op. cit.*

[5] Daniel Starch, *Measuring Advertising Readership and Results,* McGraw-Hill Book Company, New York, 1966, pp. 167–176.

[6] Barney Renderer and Thomas L. Blosl, "It's The Water—or, A Big Idea Can Go On Forever," papers from the 1970 Western Region Convention, American Association of Advertising Agencies, New York, 1971.

THE CREATIVE PROCESS

Effective copy depends initially on a thorough analysis of the product and the decision-making units who may be interested in it. It is the responsibility of the creative specialist to translate the information available to him into an advertisement, or a basic theme for an advertising campaign that will achieve the advertiser's communication objectives. Figure 22-3 depicts the inputs that combine with creative inspiration to product advertising "copy." (The term "copy" is used to designate all the various types of written material, such as artwork, layouts, scripts, that are produced as components of printed or broadcast advertisements.)

The task of translating advertising objectives into copy is neither easy nor prosaic. A direct description of a product's features is seldom sufficient, particularly in the case of consumer goods. Consider, for example, the question of how to advertise a brand of frozen orange juice concentrate. A company can anticipate little success if its full-page advertisement in *Life* sets forth only a pedestrian description of the chemical and physical content of the juice. How much more effective it will be if the advertisement conveys colorfully and

FIGURE 22-3
The creative process in advertising

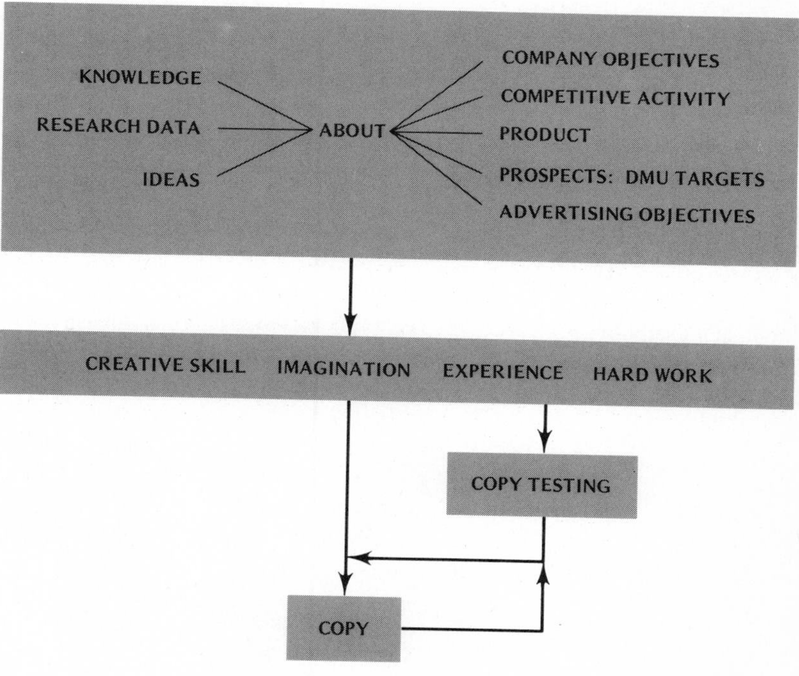

meaningfully the energy, health, vitality, pleasure, and taste that are available in the product. But even here there is a problem: should the copy emphasize all or some or just one of these attributes? Is the orange juice a treat, or a treatment, or what?

CHARACTERISTICS OF EFFECTIVE MESSAGES

What makes good copy? How should the marketing executive look at a proposed advertisement and evaluate how effectively it will create customer attention, interest, desire, conviction, and action? There is no set of rules, but there are some ideas that have fairly general acceptance.

It is generally thought that good copy should be *believable*. If it is not believable, it should be evident to the reader or viewer that he is being exposed to obvious exaggeration that is not intended to deceive. For example, no television viewer really believes that a cleanser can contains little elves who pop out to scrub a sink or scour a pan—the lack of literal believability here is so obvious that it is not offensive.

Although there are exceptions, good copy typically has the virtue of *simplicity*. It is readable, or viewable, and to the point. Where explanatory material is necessary, it is as simple and direct as possible. Product benefits are clearly portrayed, and in such a manner as to create interest.

Leading advertising practitioners put great emphasis on the importance of identifying a single, basic, motivating idea as a basis for message design. Rosser Reeves, former chairman of the Ted Bates advertising agency, used the term "unique selling proposition" to describe the basic idea he sought in developing campaigns for his clients.[7] Reeves and other highly successful agency executives seem to agree that the "proposition" or "platform" of effective advertising must be simple—and that it must be *distinctive,* so that the product or institution advertised will be differentiated from its competitors'.[8]

LEGAL RESTRICTIONS ON MESSAGE DESIGN

Legal regulations, as well as rules imposed by advertising media and industry groups, put definite limits on the content and execution of advertising messages. In the United States, the most important regulatory agency is the Federal Trade Commission, which monitors all advertising that crosses state boundaries. Under the terms of the Federal Trade Commission Act of 1914, as amended by the Wheeler-Lea Amendment of 1938, the FTC investigates cases of possible deceptive or misleading advertising. Many of the cases handled by the commission involve straightforward misrepresentation, such as stating that perfume is "imported" when it is not, or calling cheap furs "mink."

[7] Rosser Reeves, *Reality in Advertising,* Alfred A. Knopf, Inc., New York, 1961.
[8] Cf. also David Ogilvy, *Confessions of an Advertising Man,* Atheneum Publishers, New York, 1963.

A more complex area of advertising regulation is that concerned with the methods used to communicate a message. Especially in television advertising, advertisers often use devices to dramatize a claim or a product feature, and these devices sometimes involve the possibility of deception. In a classic case in the early 1960s, a commercial for shaving cream was held to be deceptive because it showed a piece of "sandpaper" being shaved off. The sandpaper used in the demonstration was, in fact, a piece of plexiglass covered with sand. In a similar case in the late 1960s, an advertiser was ordered to stop exaggerating the amount of vegetables in a bowl of vegetable soup by placing marbles in the bottom of the bowl.

These cases illustrate a general problem of defining the boundary between "showmanship" and misrepresentation. As one of the authors has suggested, both selling and the performing arts have always involved dramatization, and this inevitably leads to some degree of departure from literal "truth."[9] Advertising would be dull and ineffective if it were restricted to purely factual descriptions of product features and ingredients. On the other hand, it is clear that there are limits beyond which dramatization becomes material deception. It does not seem possible to write general rules that will encompass all situations; hence much of the work of the FTC and other enforcement agencies is devoted to resolving specific cases.

In the early 1970s, efforts were being made to extend the powers of the FTC beyond the traditional ones of preventing outright deception and stopping potentially deceptive communication devices. One proposal was to require that all advertisers be made to submit *proof of all claims made in their advertising*. Whether or not this proposal is adopted, it seems clear that legal restrictions on advertising messages will be increased in the years ahead.

At the state level, most states have laws against deceptive advertising similar in intent to those of the FTC at the national level. Also, most other countries restrict advertising content—in some instances, much more tightly than in the United States.

In addition to the general restrictions on advertising messages imposed by the FTC and by state laws, there are specific restrictions on the advertising of certain products. Cigarette advertising on television was prohibited by federal law in early 1971. Advertising of alcoholic beverages is regulated both at the national level and in each state; a book summarizing all the restrictions on liquor advertising consists of over 800 pages.

SELF-REGULATION

Above and beyond the limitations imposed by law, advertisers and advertising media have imposed various restrictions on themselves and on each other.

[9] Theodore Levitt, "The Morality (?) of Advertising," *Harvard Business Review*, July–August, 1970, pp. 84ff.

These efforts at "self-regulation," although criticized by some as hypocritical attempts to forestall more burdensome legal prohibitions, are at least in many cases sincere attempts to develop socially acceptable rules of competition.

An example of self-regulation by advertising media is the rule adopted by the National Association of Broadcasters in 1970, limiting the types of commercials that will be accepted for "mood" drug products—sleeping pills, stimulants, and calmatives. Under these rules, stations that subscribe to the NAB code will not accept commercials that depict "immediate relief" from insomnia, nervous tension, etc. The rationale for the rule was the belief that exposure to such advertising might have contributed to the acceptance of the "drug culture" among American youth in the late 1960s.

Numerous industry and trade groups have developed voluntary guides that limit advertising message content. For example, in the early 1960s the American Seat Belt Council, an organization comprised of seat belt manufacturers, adopted a Code of Advertising Practices which prohibited the use of "purely scare-type" advertising, required that proof of claims be submitted to the National Better Business Bureau, and restricted the use of superlatives such as "safest" or "strongest."[10]

Advertising media

Advertising media are the channels through which advertisers transmit their messages to the audiences they have selected as "targets" for communication. Selection of the proper media is a complex task, especially for a national advertiser, because there are literally thousands of different publications, radio and television stations, types and sizes of advertisements, times of day, days of the week, and other variations from which choices can be made.

Advertising media can be classified into several broad categories, as shown in Table 22-2. The data in this table show total expenditures by *all* advertisers in the United States in each major class of media and reflect changes in the relative importance of the media between 1960 and 1970. Each of these major classes of media is discussed briefly in the paragraphs below.

□ MEDIA AUDIENCES AND COSTS

Before we examine individual classes of media, it is useful to consider some general dimensions in terms of which advertisers compare alternative media.

Media audiences A basic consideration is the audience reached by a media vehicle: *How many* people does it reach, and of *what kinds?* Although the

[10] *Self-Regulation in Advertising,* report by the Advertising Advisory Committee of the Secretary of Commerce, Government Printing Office, Washington, 1964, pp. 28–29.

□

TABLE 22-2

Total advertising expenditures, by class of media, United States, 1960 and 1970 (in millions of dollars)

Media class	Amount spent		Percent of media total	
	1960	1970	1960	1970
Newspapers	$ 2,821	$ 4,936	34%	34%
Magazines*	824	1,061	10	7
Business publications	383	579	5	4
Television	1,269	2,853	16	20
Radio	598	1,128	7	8
Direct mail	1,658	2,548	20	18
Outdoor	239	362	3	3
Point-of-purchase displays	387	839	5	6
Total "measured media"	$ 8,179	$14,306	100%	100%
Advertising agency income	859	1,597		
Other advertising expenditures†	2,862	4,935		
Grand total	$11,900	$20,838		

* Includes farm publications.
† Includes costs of company advertising departments, advertising research, and media expenditures not separately classified.

Sources: Estimates prepared by Charles Y. Yang and others, as published in *Advertising Age*, Mar. 3, 1969, and June 7, 1971.

---

concept of the "audience" seems simple enough, there are several ways in which it can be defined and measured. These are shown in Figure 22-4. To illustrate the different concepts of "audience," suppose we are concerned with comparing the audience of an advertisement in *Playboy* magazine with that of a commercial on a network television show.

The first and simplest way in which we might compare audiences is in terms of vehicle distribution, stage I in Figure 22-4. For *Playboy*, this would be measured by *circulation*—the number of copies distributed to subscribers and newsstand buyers. For the TV show, it would be measured in terms of the number of sets tuned to the show, either for a specific broadcast or, more likely, on an average over a period of weeks. But more than one person may read, or at least look at, a copy of *Playboy*, and more than one person may watch a given television set. This leads to the second stage of audience shown in Figure 22-4, that of *vehicle exposure*. The number of persons in the total audience of a magazine or a television commercial may be two, three, or more times as great as the number of copies distributed or sets tuned in. For ex-

FIGURE 22-4

Different concepts of advertising media audience

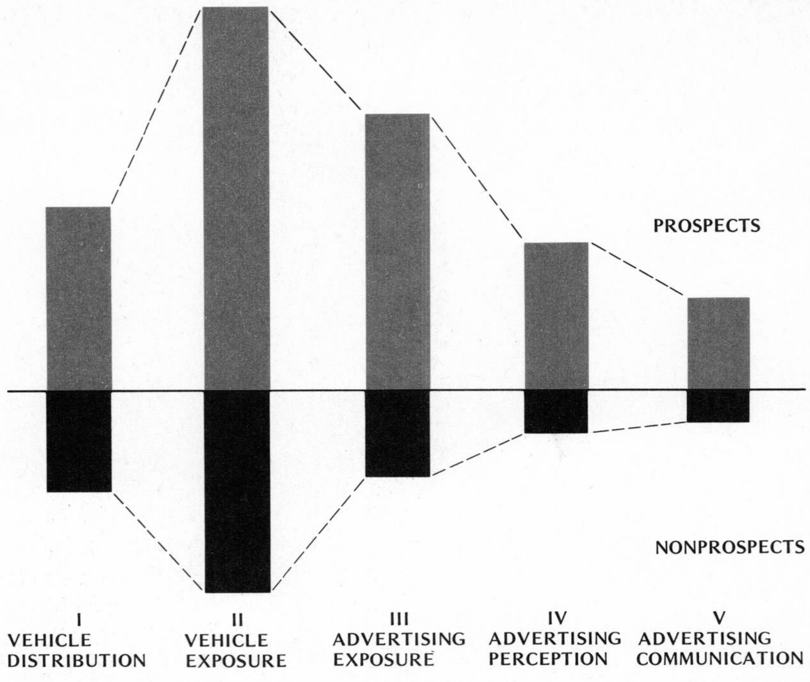

Source: Adapted from "Toward Better Media Comparisons," Audience Concepts Committee of the Advertising Research Foundation, New York, 1961, pp. 13–28.

ample, in late 1969, *Playboy's* circulation was approximately 4.8 million copies, while the average adult audience per issue was nearly 14 million.

Most advertisers are interested in *what kinds* of people are reached by media as well as *how many* are reached. In Figure 22-4, this is reflected in the division of audiences at each stage into "prospects" and "nonprospects." If an advertiser were interested in reaching only adult males, for example, then the most relevant measure of vehicle exposure would be *Playboy's* male audience—slightly over 11 million in 1969—rather than its total audience. Moreover, if some types of men were believed to be better prospects for a product than others, such as those with incomes over $15,000, then a further classification of the audience would be helpful in comparing media.

Not all the people exposed to a media vehicle are exposed to a given advertisement or commercial that appears in it. Hence, the third concept of "audience" shown in Figure 22-4, that of *advertising exposure,* will almost always be significantly smaller than total vehicle exposure. Of those "exposed" to an advertisement, not all will actually *perceive* it (stage IV), and only a fraction of those who perceive it will register any *communication effects* (stage V). Of course, the size of the audience of stages III, IV, and V will depend on the advertising itself as well as on the media vehicle. But a given advertisement will often get greater exposure, perception, and communication in one media vehicle than in another, relative to total vehicle exposure. This may be because of differences in the "atmosphere" provided by the media, or because one vehicle carries more competing advertising than another, or for other reasons.

To the extent possible, advertisers seek to compare media in terms of the audiences they expect to reach and influence with their advertising—ideally, the "stage V" concept of audience. But the information available about media is seldom adequate to permit systematic comparisons in terms of advertising communication, or even advertising exposure. Consequently, most analyses of media audiences are made in terms of vehicle distribution and vehicle exposure.

Reach and frequency Thus far we have discussed concepts and measures of "audience" for a *single* media vehicle—a given issue of a magazine or broadcast of a television show. Advertisers are concerned, however, with measuring and evaluating the overall audiences of media *schedules,* which may include dozens of different media, many of which are used periodically over a period of weeks or months.

The total audience of a series of media is not simply the sum of the audiences of each one, considered separately. If two successive issues of *Playboy* are used, part of the audience reached by the second one will be new, but part of it will duplicate the audience reached by the first issue. Similarly, there will be some duplication between the audiences of an issue of *Playboy* and of a television program.

Advertisers take audience duplication into account by estimating the reach and frequency of a media schedule, and by comparing alternative schedules in terms of these two factors. The *reach* of a schedule is its total, unduplicated audience—the number of persons exposed one or more times to any of the media used. *Frequency* is the average number of exposures per person, or per decision-making unit, among those who are reached. Both reach and frequency can be estimated for a total market, such as all households in the United States, or for each of several specific market segments.

Media costs The size of the audience reached by a media vehicle, or by a media schedule, must be related to the *cost* involved. For each of the major classes of media, it is customary to relate audience size to cost in terms of some standard *unit* of time or space. The measures used for some of the most important media are shown in the following table:

Media class	*Cost measure*	*Definitions*
Television Radio	Cost per thousand	Cost of reaching 1,000 persons, with a commercial of given length (20 seconds, 60 seconds, etc.)
Newspapers	Milline rate	Cost of a "line," one column wide by 1/14 in. deep, per *million* circulation
Magazines	Cost per thousand	Same as radio and television, but related to a given unit of space, usually one page, four-color
Outdoor	"Showing" (50 showing, 100 showing)	Cost of rental for enough displays to expose a given percentage of an area's population, a stated number of times, during a 30-day period

Because the units of time and space are different, these "cost efficiency" measures cannot be compared directly for different classes of media. For example, if the cost per thousand is $5 for a full-page advertisement in *Life* magazine and $4 for a 60 second late-evening TV commercial, which is the more efficient vehicle for advertising refrigerators? Some judgment must be made about the relative effectiveness of a printed advertisement and a broadcast commercial, and this judgment will depend on the product or service involved, the overall marketing objectives of the advertiser, and other factors.

NEWSPAPERS

The most important class of media, in terms of total expenditures, is newspapers (see Table 22-2). In 1970 there were around 1,750 daily newspapers published in the United States, with a combined circulation of over 60 million copies. Newspapers are also important media in other countries. One British paper, the *Daily Mirror,* is distributed nationally and has a circulation of nearly 5 million—much greater than that of any American paper.

From the viewpoint of the advertiser, newspapers offer several potential advantages. They are *local* in content and appeal, and provide opportunities for direct connections between a product and its local dealers or distributors. Because newspapers basically supply *news,* they offer an atmosphere of factual information and of currency that may be favorable for some advertising situations.

Advertisers can reach a very broad audience through newspapers. In the United States, over 80 percent of all adults read at least one paper each day.[11]

[11] Based on a study by W. R. Simmons, as reported in *Advertising Age,* Apr. 20, 1970, p. 100.

Newspapers also offer great flexibility: the advertiser can choose specific areas to be covered, and advertisements can be placed in newspapers on very short notice as compared with other media.

Much of the advertising carried by newspapers is local promotion by retail stores, movie theaters, and other local organizations. About half of all the advertising done by retailers is, however, paid for in part by manufacturers through cooperative advertising allowances. In a typical cooperative advertising arrangement, the manufacturer supplies prepared materials to be used in printing and reimburses the retailer for part (often half) of the cost of the space used for the advertisement.

The Robinson-Patman Act (discussed in Chapter 16) requires that companies who provide allowances for cooperative advertising, or for other forms of promotion, make the allowances available to all dealers or distributors on a "proportionally equal" basis. This is generally interpreted to mean that allowances must be on the same percentage of purchases or dollars-per-unit basis for all competing retailers or other customers. Because advertising allowances have been widely used as a means of providing sub-rosa price concessions to important retailers in some lines of business, the Federal Trade Commission has been very active in enforcing this provision of the law.[12]

Most newspapers in the United States have facilities for carrying color advertisements as well as black-and-white. During the 1950s and 1960s, great improvements were made in the technical quality of color printing for newspapers. The most advanced type of color available in the early 1970s was called "Spectacolor," and was practically equal in reproduction quality to that offered by magazines.

As mentioned earlier, newspaper space costs are often quoted and compared in terms of a "milline rate." Another way of expressing newspaper costs is on the basis of the cost of reaching 1,000 adults with a full-page advertisement. On this basis, the average range of costs in newspapers in the United States in the early 1970s ranged from about $5 to $8 per thousand persons.

□ MAGAZINES

In the early 1970s, some 8,000 magazines were published in the United States. Altogether, they accounted for about 7 percent of total advertising expenditures (Table 22-2).

The diversity of magazines is tremendous. Some offer news or other "general-interest" content to huge audiences; the *Reader's Digest,* for example, has an average audience of over 40 million persons. Others are highly specialized, technical, or even exotic. *Skin Diver,* for instance, has a circula-

[12] The requirements of the law are explained in the Federal Trade Commission's *Guides for Advertising Allowances and Other Merchandising Payments and Services,* issued in May, 1969.

tion of some 75,000 undersea enthusiasts. Audience and cost figures for some of the most widely circulated magazines, and a few special-interest ones, are given in Table 22-3.

In general, magazines offer advertisers the opportunity to reach highly selective audiences. The readers of *Hot Rod* or *Golf Digest* are "self-selected" in terms of their interests. Even among the more general-interest magazines, there are increasing opportunities to select specific areas or audience groups to be covered. Many mass-circulation magazines publish several different *geographic* editions, which are of special value to regional or local advertisers. In addition, some magazines offer "demographic" editions, that is, an advertiser can have his advertisement placed only in those copies which are distributed to a particular subset of the magazine's total circulation. *Better Homes*

TABLE 22-3

Circulation, estimated audience, and costs for some consumer magazines, 1969

Magazine	Circulation (000)	Estimated audience (000) Men	Estimated audience (000) Women	Cost for one page (four-color)
General magazines:				
Reader's Digest	17,500	19,125	21,836	$58,000
Life	8,500	18,936	17,584	64,000
Women's magazines:				
McCall's	8,500	3,167	16,138	46,000
Good Housekeeping	5,600	2,746	13,219	30,000
True Story	2,300	990	5,508	11,500
News and business:				
Newsweek	2,550	7,380	4,100	22,000
Business Week	675	2,884	745	13,000
Men's magazines:				
Playboy	4,800	11,083	2,673	36,000
Special interest:				
Hot Rod	850	3,385	650	9,600
Golf Digest	430	993	235	6,100

Sources: Circulation figures are those guaranteed by the publishers as of late 1969. Audience estimates are from the W. R. Simmons 1969 Standard Magazine Audience Report. Costs are for a single insertion, that is, "one-time" rates for full pages, four colors. Excerpted from *BBDO Audience Coverage and Cost Guide, 1970,* Batten, Barton, Durstine & Osborn, Inc., New York, 1970.

and Gardens, for example, offers a separate edition distributed to "movers"—subscribers who changed their addresses within the past year. *Reader's Digest* goes even further with its "Demo 1" edition, with a circulation of 1 million among families with incomes of $15,000 or more. These high-income families were identified by means of a questionnaire distributed with subscription renewal notices. Other magazines sell advertising space in issues reaching only doctors, students, teachers, or other identifiable groups.[13]

Magazines generally offer *high-quality printing* for advertisements. The paper used and the presses employed in magazine printing permit accurate color, sharp detail, and the possibility of special devices such as foldouts, metallic paper, or die-cuts.

Another feature of potential interest to the advertiser is the "mood" or "atmosphere" created by some magazines. Advertising may be read more carefully, and with greater depth of interest, in a magazine than elsewhere, both because magazines tend to be kept longer and sometimes read repeatedly, and because of the specialized character of the magazine's contents.

☐ BUSINESS PUBLICATIONS

Business papers are variously called trade journals, trade magazines, or business papers. They are even more numerous and varied than consumer magazines.

Business publications may be classified as general, such as *Fortune* or *Forbes;* horizontal, such as *Purchasing Week,* which is read by purchasing agents in various companies and industries; or vertical, such as *Food Topics,* which is read by executives at all levels of the food industry.

Business publication advertisements are usually specialized and have specialized appeals. Advertisers hope that their advertisements will be more carefully and thoroughly read than those in consumer magazines. Additionally, the nature of many business publications is such that their editorial content is often relevant or related to the advertisements that are carried. On occasion, editorial comment may be directly devoted to specific products that are being advertised, especially in the case of new products or processes.

Advertising rates in business publications are generally low, but smaller circulations typically mean that the cost per reader is high. From the advertiser's viewpoint, however, the latter is offset by pinpointing of very specific audience groups such as nurses, industrial designers, funeral directors, or beauty shop operators.

☐ TELEVISION

Throughout the post-World War II period the most rapidly growing class of advertising media has been television. Since the beginnings of commercial TV

[13] See *Media Decisions,* July, 1970, pp. 34ff.

broadcasting in the 1940s, expenditures for advertising in this medium have grown to 20 percent of total advertising volume (see Table 22-2).

In the early 1970s, 95 percent of all households in the United States owned one or more television sets, and television viewing occupied more time for Americans than any other single activity except work. Television ownership and usage were also high and growing in other western nations: 92 percent of British homes had sets, and ownership reached 75 percent in Germany, 60 percent in Italy, and 65 percent in France. In some countries, however, commercial television is nonexistent or severely limited.

The near universality of TV set ownership means that television offers the advertiser *mass audience coverage*. A successful program in "prime time," between 7:30 P.M. and 11:00 P.M., may reach more than 40 million persons. The cost efficiency of television varies widely, depending on the type of program, the time of day, and the nature of the audience sought. Typical cost-per-thousand figures range from $4 to $10 for adult viewers and from $10 to $40 or more for teen-agers or children.

Television's unique combination of sight and sound gives it more impact than other media, generally speaking. This is particularly advantageous for advertisers whose products require demonstration. For example, one of the most successful early large-scale users of TV advertising was the Polaroid Corporation. In the early and mid-1950s, Polaroid's "instant photography" process was unknown to most consumers. The dramatic demonstration of the Polaroid camera on television commericals played a major role in its rapid acceptance by American consumers.

Although television programming and commercials have been widely criticized, audience evaluations of TV watching are for the most part strongly favorable.[14] The pleasure derived from TV is at least potentially transferable to the advertising messages delivered through the medium.

Television time is purchased by advertisers in a variety of ways. Network programs can be sponsored, but the cost is so high that even the largest advertisers usually employ "participation," that is, partial sponsorship, rather than paying the full cost of a program throughout an entire season. A more flexible means of buying TV time is through spot announcements ("spots") on individual stations. Spot advertising offers much greater geographic flexibility and a much lower minimum investment. In both network and spot advertising, commercials are available in varying lengths, ranging from 10-second "IDs" up to 60-second announcements.

Quite apart from the cost of television time, the costs of producing commer-

[14] Evidence of public opinions is given in Gary A. Steiner, *The People Look at Television,* Alfred A. Knopf, Inc., New York, 1963; and in Raymond A. Bauer and Stephen Greyser, *Advertising in America: The Consumer View,* Division of Research, Harvard Business School, Boston, 1968.

cials can be very high. Production costs include the fees for such items as talent and filming, which must be borne by the advertiser. A single commercial produced for Heinz Great American Soups in 1971, featuring an elaborate dance number with Hollywood actress Ann Miller, was alleged to have cost $150,000 for production alone. This is an extreme case, but for even conventional commercials production costs represent 50 to 100 percent of time costs.

□ RADIO

In 1970, Americans owned an estimated 320 million radio sets—about 1½ for each man, woman, and child in the country. Advertisers had a choice of over 4,200 AM stations and 2,000 FM stations through which they could broadcast messages to radio audiences. Overall, radio is a mass medium, but no single station or program reaches more than a small fraction of the total audience.

In fact, radio is a very selective medium. Different stations aim their programming at different audiences. Some feature "hard rock" music, others news, and others classical music. Still others broadcast in Spanish, or offer programming especially designed for black audiences.

Radio messages can be prepared or changed on short notice; so advertisers have great flexibility in the *timing* of radio advertising. Radio is also a relatively *low-cost* advertising medium; cost-per-thousand figures run from around $1.50 to $4.00, depending on the type of audience sought and the time of day. (Three main time periods are designated as "drive time," 6 to 10 A.M. and 3 to 7 P.M.; "housewife time," 10 A.M. to 3 P.M.; and evening, from 7 P.M. on.)

It is extremely difficult to estimate the audience for an individual radio commercial. Estimates of average audiences for stations during given time periods are obtained by several research services, some of which collect diaries from panels of households and some of which conduct telephone interviews during broadcasting periods.

□ DIRECT MAIL

Direct mail is one of the most important classes of advertising media. As shown in Table 22-2, advertisers spent over 2.5 billion on direct mail messages in 1970.

Direct mail offers the advertiser a maximum of selectivity and flexibility. Mailed advertisements can be letters, brochures, catalogs, coupons, free samples, or premiums; they can be sent to individually selected prospects or to broad lists containing hundreds of thousands of names. Direct mail is generally much more expensive than other media, because of the high costs of delivering messages individually. It also suffers from a lack of prestige—unhappiness with "junk mail" is widespread.

OUTDOOR AND TRANSPORTATION

The costs of outdoor advertising are computed differently from those of any medium discussed thus far. In brief, the seller of outdoor advertising space studies traffic patterns in an area and estimates the number of billboards required to reach virtually 100 percent of the area's vehicular and pedestrian traffic at least once during a 30-day period. This number is defined as a "100 showing." He then quotes rates for a 100 showing, a 50 showing, or a 25 showing, or a 150 showing. The rates are typically for 30-day periods; a cost per thousand viewers can be calculated by relating the estimated traffic exposed to the cost of the advertising.

From the advertiser's standpoint, outdoor advertising is often viewed as supporting his advertisements in other media. Billboards can reach large numbers of people at relatively little cost, and they serve as reminders, means of emphasizing ideas, or prompters of impulse purchases. Messages communicated via outdoor advertising are, obviously, restricted to very brief, easily understood content.

The most familiar types of transportation advertising are the car cards, displays, and posters found in or on buses, subway cars, and other means of mass transportation. Transportation advertising is sold by specialized firms, and rates are generally based on the number of vehicles or other locations in which the advertising is to be shown. Transportation advertising is often coordinated with outdoor advertising, making use of the same or similar pictures and messages.

MEDIA SELECTION TECHNIQUES

In choosing advertising media, the marketer's objective is to achieve the communication objectives set for advertising among the greatest possible number of decision-making units, at the lowest possible cost. As indicated earlier, the total amount of money available for advertising is usually determined prior to the selection of individual media. Also, audience targets are usually defined early in the process of overall marketing planning. Working within these guidelines, media specialists in business firms and advertising agencies attempt to match media audiences and media characteristics to the marketing goals of the advertiser.

"Media analysis," the detailed estimation of reach and frequency among specific types of customers, costs, and timing of messages, is a complex task. Some companies and agencies have developed formal quantitative models for analyzing and comparing media schedules. Media models are based on quantitative audience and cost data, together with judgmental estimates of the relative effectiveness of different media. One such model, called MEDIAC, enables the analyst to test different media schedules by specifying which media vehicles are to be used on the keyboard of a computer terminal. The computer program estimates distributions of exposures for each schedule and also estimates total "effectiveness," taking into account audience size and composition, costs, media suitability to advertising objectives, duplication of audiences, and even the forgetting of messages over a period of time.[15]

By the early 1970s, formal media models were widely used by large advertisers and agencies. Experience with these models suggests that they permit more systematic and accurate analysis of media audiences and efficiency than was possible previously.

Advertising agencies

A distinctive feature of advertising, as compared with other marketing functions, is the great extent to which business firms, and other advertisers, rely on outside specialists for assistance. Advertising agencies are employed by most large marketers, and many smaller ones, to perform the tasks of designing and producing messages, selecting media, and placing advertising.

In 1967, there were more than 5,700 advertising agencies in the United States. Most of them were small firms operating on a local basis. About a third of the agency establishments accounted for 95 percent of total "billings"—the amount of money spent by the agencies for their clients. Nearly half of all advertising agencies, and three-fourths of total billings, were concentrated in four large cities: New York, Chicago, Detroit, and Los Angeles.

A few agencies are extremely large and operate on a worldwide basis. The largest agency in the world, J. Walter Thompson, had billings of $764 million in 1970; the 10 largest agencies combined accounted for billings of $4.3 billion. All but one of these 10 were firms based in the United States. (The exception, Dentsu Advertising, is a Japanese agency.)

☐ FULL-SERVICE AGENCIES

The traditional method of operation for advertising agencies, in the United States and most other countries, is to provide a wide range of services to clients. The *basic* functions of the full-service agency include:

1. Working closely with the advertiser's marketing personnel in the development of marketing plans for a product.
2. On the basis of the marketing plan, preparation of a proposed advertising plan for a year or other campaign period. The advertising plan includes basic message design, media selection, and proposals for creative execution.
3. Execution of the plan, including:
   a. Writing, designing, illustrating of advertisements, or other appropriate forms of the message

[15] John D. C. Little and Leonard M. Lodish, "A Media Selection Calculus," Working Paper 304-68, Alfred P. Sloan School of Management, Massachusetts Institute of Technology, Cambridge, Mass., 1968.

b. Contracting for space, time, or other means of advertising

c. The proper incorporation of the message in mechanical form and forwarding it with proper instructions for printing or broadcasting

d. Checking and verifying of insertions, display, or other means used

In addition to these basic functions of planning, preparing, and placing advertising, full-service agencies often provide other services to advertisers. These may include marketing research, assistance in development of marketing plans, and preparation of catalogs and other promotional materials.

The income that advertising agencies derive from the functions they perform comes from two sources: commissions and service charges (or fees). Commissions are the more important, normally accounting for at least two-thirds of most agencies' incomes. The agency usually writes a contract directly with the media, bills its client, and deducts a 15 percent commission before making the payment for the space or time to the media. The remainder of agency income comes from fees charged for special services such as those described earlier or from service charges made in connection with purchases of materials and services for clients. Fees or service-charge rates are typically negotiated by an agency directly with a client, but in the case of purchased materials or services, most agencies charge 17.65 percent of their costs.

Agency commissions are paid by all the major classes of advertising media: newspapers, magazines, business periodicals, television, radio, and standardized outdoor and transportation advertising firms. But media commissions do not apply to direct mail advertising, catalogs, or sales promotion materials. For this reason, companies that rely heavily on these "noncommissionable" media, especially industrial products manufacturers, are much less likely to use agencies than are advertisers who devote most of their expenditures to the major media.

□ SPECIALIZED ADVERTISING SERVICES

During the later 1960s and early 1970s, specialized advertising service firms increased in importance.[16] Specialists in *media buying* and in *creative services* were employed by a growing number of advertisers in place of, or in addition to, the traditional full-service agencies.

Media-buying services are specialized organizations that concentrate on buying media time and space, usually on the basis of media plans developed by the advertiser or by a traditional agency.

The opportunity for media-buying specialists to operate grew out of the increasing complexity of buying television spots in the late 1960s. Keeping abreast of ever-changing "availabilities" for spots and negotiating with stations

[16] See "Advertising That Comes à la Carte," *Business Week,* May 1, 1971, pp. 44ff.

on rates call for highly specialized skills, and these are provided by the buying services in return for a fee. Some buying services charge a commission of 1 to 2 percent of billings, while others charge a fraction of the difference between the amount budgeted for time and the amount actually spent.

Creative "boutiques" (specialists in message design) provide a specialized service in conceiving creative ideas for advertising campaigns or individual commercials. Like media-buying services, they are used by advertisers directly or by conventional advertising agencies as supplements to their own creative departments.

HOUSE AGENCIES

A few advertisers operate their own so-called "house agencies," performing some or all of the services of the independent agency. The rationale for the house agency is that if the advertiser is large enough, he may be able to perform the services he needs at a total cost less than that paid in agency commissions, and thus save money. It has also been claimed that an in-house agency facilitates coordination between advertising personnel and other marketing management personnel.

The savings theoretically possible through operation of a house agency may not materialize if advertising media refuse to grant the 15 percent commission to it. When the Monsanto Chemical Company established its own agency in late 1969, for example, it was reported that some media granted discounts while others did not. The other main limitation of house agencies is the difficulty of recruiting and keeping competent creative personnel, who (it is claimed) are generally reluctant to devote their careers entirely to a single advertiser's work.

Measuring advertising results

The effectiveness of advertising is measured by the extent to which it attains the objectives set for it. In this sense, advertising is like any other form of business activity. For example, a company may decide that its overall objective should be a particular level of profit, a specified share of its industry's market, or a stipulated rate of sales growth. Overall performance is effective to the extent that the overall objective is achieved. The overall goals of the firm determine the objectives of marketing activity, which in turn determine the objectives of advertising. Thus, the wide variety of possible advertising objectives discussed earlier in this chapter stems from broader objectives determined for marketing programs or for the firm as a whole.

SALES RESULTS AND ADVERTISING RESULTS

Many firms try to measure the effectiveness of advertising in terms of sales results. This practice is almost always misleading, although there are some exceptions. For example, direct-mail advertising for magazine subscriptions or encyclopedias can require that coupons be returned by interested customers; in this situation management can count the number of coupons returned. If the objective has been to achieve a specific number of coupon returns, the effectiveness of the campaign can thus be measured. Similarly, a television commercial's sales results can be measured if the commercial message says something like "Call 434-0666 to purchase. . . ."

In most advertising situations, it is far more difficult, if not impossible, to establish the exact relation between advertising activity and sales. Take, for example, the case of the marketing vice-president or advertising manager for a manufacturer of electric ranges. This year's advertising expenditure was $1,940,000, an increase of $440,000 over the preceding year. Sales during the year increased 13 percent, just about what had been anticipated by him and corporate management. During the year, a number of changes had been made in the company's marketing strategy and operations, including:

1. Four new models and major revisions in the remainder of the product line
2. The addition of 5 new distributors and 47 new retailers
3. A new pricing policy designed to reach lower-income groups more effectively
4. Greater margins to distributors and retailers
5. Nine additional salesmen and a new sales quota system
6. Increased use of television advertising

He is now in the process of preparing the advertising budget for next year. The budget that he had worked out, with the help of his advertising agency, amounts to $2,340,000. The president of the company says, "That's fine, but will you tell me whether the extra $440,000 that we gave you this year paid off? Can you tell me how effective the extra $400,000 for next year is going to be?"

This kind of question, asked year after year in thousands of companies, is virtually impossible to answer in any definitive way. The reason is that advertising is only one of the variables that affect sales results. There are many others both in the marketing process and in other aspects of business operations, such as those mentioned above.

It seems clear that, with few exceptions, circumstances under which all other variables can be kept constant so that the precise effect of advertising on sales can be measured are almost nonexistent. Added to this is the fact that an advertising campaign is itself made up of a variety of factors such as media, messages, colors, page or time-of-day locations, size of headline, and appeals used. Thus, even if the advertising variable could be isolated, this would still not answer questions about the effectiveness of the individual components of the advertising campaign.

INDIRECT MEASURES

Because the measurement of the direct effect of advertising on broad company goals such as increased profits or sales is so difficult, most firms rely heavily on indirect measures. These measures involve such factors as customer awareness or attitudes or customer recall of advertising messages or portions thereof. The assumption is that favorable or improved awareness, attitudes, and/or recall will lead in some way to the attainment of greater sales, profits, or whatever the primary object of the marketing and corporate strategy may be. This assumption, in turn, rests on assumptions about human behavior that are by no means firmly established or universally accepted. It seems obvious that making a housewife *aware* of a brand will not necessarily bring about a purchase. Moreover, even if she does buy the brand, it may not be due to the advertisement. It may, in fact, have nothing to do with the advertisement.

Despite the uncertainties about relationships between intermediate effects of advertising and ultimate results, there appears to be little alternative to the use of indirect measures. Among the types of measures commonly used are the following:

Exposure to advertisements In case of print media, for example, estimates are made of the readership of individual advertisements by interviewing members of the audience of the magazine or newspaper issue in which the advertisements appeared.

Recall of advertising message content A widely used measure of advertising results is recall of message content among a specified group or groups of prospective customers. Recall is usually measured within a short period of time after the appearance of advertising, within 24 hours, for example, in the case of television commercials.

Product or brand awareness Marketers who rely heavily on advertising often appraise its effectiveness by measuring customer awareness of a product or brand. This type of measure is subject to many of the same criticisms as sales measures, that is, awareness is also affected by many factors in addition to advertising. But for new products, changes in awareness can often be attributed primarily to the influence of advertising.

Attitude change Since advertising is usually intended to influence the state of mind of its audience toward a product, service, or organization, results are frequently measured in terms of expressed attitudes among groups exposed to promotional communication. Various types of attitude measures are used, ranging from questions about willingness or likelihood of buying to measures of the degree to which specific attributes, for example, "modern," are associated with a product.

All these measures of advertising results require the use of complex technical skills for the design of valid measurement procedures, selection of persons to be interviewed, and interpretation of statistical data. Some of the problems involved in these aspects of advertising research are discussed in Chapter 25.

Sales promotion[17]

As defined in Chapter 20, sales promotion consists of promotional activities of a nonrecurrent nature that are used to supplement advertising and personal selling. Sales promotion devices can include premiums, coupons, contests, free goods, and other items discussed below. Many companies exhibit their products at trade shows in an attempt to interest potential users, distributors, or dealers; such activities are also a form of sales promotion.

Sales promotion should be closely coordinated with advertising and personal selling effort to achieve maximum results. In contrast with personal selling, which is normally directed at individuals, sales promotion is aimed at groups of individuals; in contrast with advertising, which often aims at masses of people, sales promotion aims at comparatively small and well-defined groups. Such groups can be company salesmen, middlemen, and/or customers.

□ CUSTOMER PROMOTIONS

Sales promotional activities aimed directly at ultimate customers decision-making units can be divided into those which reach the customer either in the home, or place of business (in the case of business decision-making units) or in the store.

In home or in business The four principal types of sales promotional devices to which the customers can be exposed at home or in their business establishments are sampling, coupons, contests, and demonstrations. Companies using these devices attempt to presell customers on the product or brand being promoted. To the extent these are successful, they reduce the likelihood of success by competitive point-of-purchase materials.

The distribution of product *samples* to ultimate customers occurs most frequently in the case of items that have low unit value, are frequently purchased, can be easily produced in miniature, and have intensive physical distribution. Drug items, detergents, dentrifices, cigarettes, and breakfast foods are examples. Sampling is most frequently used as a means of getting consumers to try new products, or for established products that have been modified in

[17] For a more detailed discussion of sales promotion methods, see John F. Luick and William Ziegler, *Sales Promotion and Modern Merchandising,* McGraw-Hill Book Company, New York, 1968.

some way. For example, when detergents were first introduced, one of the manufacturers' most difficult problems was to teach the housewife how detergents differed from soaps. Sampling, in conjunction with advertising, played an important role in accomplishing this objective.[18]

Samples are typically distributed on a house-to-house basis, to people on mailing lists, or to people who submit requests in answer to advertisements. Advertisements that carry offers for samples often serve as a device for helping to increase the likelihood that only potential users will take the trouble to respond.

Coupons received at home usually offer either a price reduction or a free package, and are principally redeemed through grocery and drug outlets. Examples include a 10 cents off coupon for a giant size box of Duz, 8 cents off for Scott family drinking cups, or 10 cents off for a four-roll pack of Waldorf bathroom tissue. Coupons are used primarily to increase customer inventories of a product, thereby encouraging increased usage, or to induce customers to try a new product. In addition, coupons may also be used to introduce a new package, to secure increased shelf space by increasing retail sales, and to increase the readership of the advertisements in which the coupons appear.

According to trade estimates, the most frequently used method of distributing coupons in the late 1960s was through newspaper advertisements. Other distribution methods include direct mail, magazine advertisements, and insertion in packages of products.

Contests such as sentence or jingle completions are an indirect means of introducing a new product or attracting new users to an existing brand. If the purchase of a product is required for entry, regular users will probably buy the brand regardless of the contest, but new users may buy primarily because of their interest in the contest. When evidence of purchase is not required to enter a contest, the total number of entrants may be greater. Management's hope in this situation is that the product has at least been given attention by nonpurchasers, who may become purchasers in the future.

Contests are flexible in that they can be tailored to the interests of particular DMU groups through either the prizes offered or the requirements for entry. A cereal manufacturer, for example, can offer prizes aimed at children, while an automobile manufacturer might require that all contest entrants use entry blanks available only in his dealers' showrooms.

Sweepstakes are contests in which the winners are selected by essentially random methods. During the 1960s, sweepstakes were widely used in the promotion of magazine subscription sales and by mail order sellers, including book clubs, record clubs, and catalog sales companies.

[18] Cited by Alfred Gross, *Sales Promotion,* The Ronald Press Company, New York, 1961, p. 193.

In-store promotions The principal types of sales promotion devices that reach customers in retail stores include premium offers, demonstrations, and display promotions. The primary advantage of in-store promotions is that they reach the customer at the point when she (or he) is in the process of making a purchase decision. Also, the type of product covered by the promotion may already be on the shopper's list; in this case, the promotion influences the shopper's brand choice. Alternatively, the promotion may create impulse buying by customers whose shopping lists do not include the item.

Premiums can be given free with the purchase of merchandise or offered for a nominal charge. Premium promotions are based on the assumption that DMU desire for the premium will be strong enough to bring about the purchase of the product that the premium accompanies. Premiums are generally most successful when they are aimed at attracting those nonusers who are already familiar with the product and/or brand involved or where they are aimed at an increased usage rate among existing users.

Premiums are commonly used by manufacturers of low-priced, frequently purchased products such as cleansers, soaps, and cereals. One manufacturer of a bar soap, for example, frequently supplies a coupon with each bar; the coupon can be used, together with a nominal sum, to purchase a piece of silverware. A cleanser manufacturer offers plastic dispensers which can be purchased, at nominal cost, along with several cans of his product.

In-store *demonstrations* are used by many firms. Demonstrators are usually supplied by manufacturers so that any profit resulting from increased sales accrues to the store. The stores' only potential cost is the opportunity loss associated with possible alternative uses of the space. The Robinson-Patman Act prohibits allowances, such as those for demonstrations, unless they are made on proportionately equal terms to all customers. Thus a demonstration made available to a large retail store must be available to a smaller retailer on proportional terms. There is considerable ambiguity surrounding the interpretation of this restriction, and this has probably led to the use of fewer in-store demonstrations than might otherwise be economically justified.

The most common types of in-store *display promotions* include counter cards, wall signs, banners, streamers, and display bins. The importance of these devices has been steadily increasing for a number of product classes sold in retail stores, such as soft drinks, cosmetics, food products, liquor, beer, and drugs. The increase arises from the marked trend toward self-service retailing.

In addition, new brands are almost continuously being introduced in product categories such as those listed above. Customers are continuously bombarded by advertising messages, each suggesting the purchase of a different brand. Often the time between the impact of an advertising campaign and a decision-making unit's trip to the store is long enough for the advertiser's message to be forgotten or to become less important.

Manufacturers usually tie their point-of-purchase promotions to their advertising campaigns by using the same theme in both or by using copies of advertisements as part of their displays. For example, some drugstore chains use their newspaper advertisements as part of their window displays in drugstores.

Dealers are not always anxious to use a firm's display material. The common causes of rejection include:

1. Too much material supplied by too many manufacturers
2. Failure of manufacturers to design displays that will fit the dealer's needs in terms of size, durability, etc.
3. Inferior quality of display material
4. Display material that is poorly merchandised by salesmen, not seasonally appropriate, or too difficult to assemble
5. Insufficient profit potential to justify the use of scarce space[19]

In order to avoid these objections, firms should carefully plan their displays to *fit the needs of the dealers*. They should provide salesmen with presentations to show retailers how the displays can be used and why profitable use can be anticipated. Additionally, many manufacturers compensate dealers for the space required by displays. Compensation can be in cash, in discounts on merchandise, or in the form of free goods.

□

TRADE PROMOTIONS

Retailers (and wholesalers) are frequently involved in the promotions aimed at ultimate customers by manufacturers. The involvement is expensive and time-consuming (handling coupons, content entries, etc.), and manufacturers often direct additional sales promotional activities at their channels in order to secure cooperation. On other occasions, manufacturers conduct promotions at the wholesale or retail level that do not directly involve ultimate decision-making units. In either case, such promotions are referred to as *trade promotions*.

Many manufacturers run sales contests for channels. Appliance manufacturers often give prizes to retail store owners or retail store salesmen for outstanding sales accomplishments. One large appliance manufacturer spends hundreds of thousands of dollars each year on travel vacations for contest-winning dealers and dealer salesmen.

In addition to contests, there are other frequently used trade promotion devices. *Display, advertising,* and *buying allowances* are commonly used for many consumer goods such as foods and appliances. Advertising allowances for purposes of cooperative advertising were discussed earlier in this chapter. Display allowances are used to compensate middlemen for the space allo-

[19] Cf. Gross, *op. cit.*, p. 99.

cated to displays. Because displays are important to retailers, and because space in most retail establishments is a scarce commodity, there is a constant battle among manufacturers to secure it. Buying allowances, in effect, are price deals given to wholesalers or retailers. For example, the Prather Company might offer price reductions on its products if retailers purchase a specified number of cases. Such allowances are often interrelated; buying allowances can be offered in exchange for display space. Where allowances are used, the Robinson-Patman Act requires that they be proportionately available to all customers.

Merchandise premiums are an additional type of trade promotion and are comparable in general purpose to consumer premiums. Wholesalers, dealers, or dealer salesmen may be given premiums for sales results or as incentives for extra effort. An oil company might give baseball tickets to gasoline station attendants for achieving sales targets or pushing particular items. The Prather Company might offer tie clips to retailers or retail clerks in return for display space or selling effort.

Trade promotions should, wherever possible, be closely tied to customer promotions or other kinds of promotional activity. The point was made earlier that sales promotion, personal selling, and advertising are interrelated instruments of marketing strategy. Sales promotion activities in particular should be regarded by management as supplementary devices designed to complement and accentuate, but seldom to replace, personal selling and advertising. They can make important contributions, but their effectiveness is greatly increased by careful coordination with advertising and selling programs.

Questions

1. Faced with the prospect of a 15 percent decline in sales, the president of a large manufacturer of electric toasters exclaimed, "This will force us to make a substantial cut in our advertising budget for next year."

   What is your evaluation of the president's statement?

2. In what way might the sales promotional programs of a retailer selling stereo components to ultimate customers differ from those of a manufacturer selling the same products to retail outlets for resale?

3. Consider the following two statements: "The purpose of advertising is to create sales." "The purpose of advertising is to improve the buyers' disposition toward the company's products." Which comes closer to the truth?

4. How does advertising affect the price paid by consumers for goods and services which they purchase?

5. The cost per exposure of a specific advertisement in a leading national newspaper is 7 cents. The cost of a similar advertisement in *Life* magazine is 35 cents per exposure, and in a leading business magazine, the cost is $1.85 per exposure. Why would anyone ever advertise in *Life* or in the business magazine?

6. Identify the advertising appeals used to promote two different consumer products and two different industrial products. For each, what do you think the advertiser is trying to accomplish? Do you think he succeeds? Can you identify any other appeals which might be successful?

7. Starting in the early 1960s, the Schultz Brewing Company, a small family owned brewery, had suffered a continuing decline in market share and profits as the large national brewers had moved into its market area with heavy advertising and promotional support.

After a decade of declining performance, Tom Schultz, grandson of the company's founder was appointed president. One of his first actions was to fire the firm's advertising agency of 35 years and to request that a new agency make a complete study of the company's advertising approach.

Some months after, the new agency, Kidd Advertising, made a presentation to Schultz management, recommending a doubling of total promotional expenditures and a complete change in advertising strategy as the only way to save the company from extinction.

In its report, the agency recommended an increase in the total promotion budget from $370,000 (on sales of $12 million) to $700,000 as well as a $250,000 one-time investment in a new slender bottle and new package design. These recommendations are summarized in Table 22-4.

In justifying these changes, Kidd concluded:

> The market has changed. The blue-collar worker who has been your best customer has moved to the suburbs and sent his wife to college. He yearns for respectability and wants something more than Slurp or Schultz. The corner tavern is no longer the center of beer consumption. Now the wife buys a six pack or two with the groceries, and she joins her husband for a beer while they watch TV together.
>
> All your past promotion has focused on the tavern drinker who stops for one or two on the way home. You've got to reach the "now generation" who aren't so hooked on baseball. You've got to reach the wives who are accounting for a larger and larger percent of both purchases and consumption.
>
> Budweiser spends 11 percent of sales on advertising. You spend less than 4 percent. We want you to move to saturation spots on network TV to reach the buying influences and reach them enough to convince them to buy Schultz.

Discussing the proposed packaging changes, Kidd reported:

> Your bottle is seen as being old fashioned. It makes your customers feel stodgy and dull. By switching to the lighter, more slender bottle we recommend, you'll be telling them "we swing—Schultz is a modern beer for a modern family."

TABLE 22-4

Shultz Brewing promotion expenditures ,in thousands of dollars.

	Current expenditures	Proposed first year	Proposed second year
Television			
Baseball sponsorship	$160		
Network spots	. . .	$450	$500
Local sportscasts	15	25	25
	$175	$475	$525
Radio			
Baseball sponsorship	35	15	
Local sportscasts	10	10	
News and music show	. . .	75	100
	$ 45	$100	$100
Promotion	150	125	100
Total promotion	$370	$700	$725
Bottle replacement	. . .	200	
Package redesign	. . .	50	
Grand total	$370	$950	$725

The accompanying package change which calls for a stark, modern motif will reinforce this, adding a new dimension of good taste to the package as well as increasing shelf visibility and hence supermarket sales.

a. In general, what response should the company make to the agency's recommendations?

b. Would you make the recommended changes? Why or why not?

c. What information would be most valuable to you in evaluating the recommendations? How would you use it?

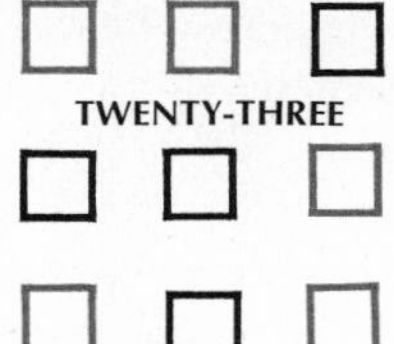

TWENTY-THREE

Marketing organization

Thus far, in Part 4, we have discussed marketing in terms of decisions confronting marketing executives as they endeavor to create and combine the elements of the marketing mix into effective marketing strategies. These decisions are seldom made, or implemented, by individuals working in isolation. Analyses and decisions must be made by people working together in organizations. Marketing strategy and marketing organization are intertwined in practice, as are the overall strategy and organization of a company (see Chapter 13). Changes in marketing strategy usually require changes in marketing organization. As illustrations, consider the following:

1. A large producer of industrial equipment found that its product line had gradually expanded to include several hundred items. Historically, the company had had over 100 sales branches, and company salesmen had been responsible for selling all the items in the line to customers in many different industries. Declining profits and the difficulties inherent in selling and servicing so many different products and industries led to a change in strategy which (a) emphasized new methods of distribution, using wholesalers rather than sales branches, and (b) concentrated on increasing the profitability of groups of products. As a consequence of this change in policy, major changes were required in the size and organization of the sales force, and product divisions with profit responsibility were established.

2. A major supermarket chain decided to open a number of general merchandise discount-type stores. This decision required the establishment of a new organization within the parent company. The new organization, which in effect constituted a new business for the supermarket chain, was charged with responsibility, within the objectives and guidelines established by the chain's senior officers, for all activities in connection with the general merchandise stores.

3. A small company that produced a single consumer product decided that its sales were increasing so rapidly in its limited geographic area that it could expand into adjacent regions. The sales manager found it necessary to set up regional sales offices to cope with the problems of wider geographical coverage. Also, in order to give the company a firm foothold in areas new to its management, the marketing manager decided to add a marketing research unit to analyze the potential of the new territories, and an advertising manager to plan and direct introductory advertising and promotion campaigns as operations expanded into new areas.

In each of these illustrations, major changes were made in marketing policies, and each change required a corresponding modification of the organization to carry out the new policies. It is clear, then, that organizations are built around, and geared to, specific strategies or policies; a corollary is that an organization ideally suited to one strategy may be inappropriate for another. By the same token, as we pointed out in Chapter 13, the choice of strategy is affected by what is feasible organizationally. The supermarket chain almost inevitably would have had great difficulty in its discount-type, general merchandise operation had it not been able to set up an organization, and staff it with competent people, that could cope with entirely new problems of buying, merchandising, and operations.

In this chapter, we shall examine some of the problems of organizing for marketing. Before turning to specific problems and ways of solving them, we shall review some basic organizational concepts. We shall then turn to the particulars of marketing organization.

Organization: concepts and purposes

There are probably almost as many definitions of *organization* as there are books on the subject, and there are good reasons for this diversity. Organizational theorists have different ways of looking at organizations, and these perspectives contribute useful insights. Some theorists emphasize the control and chain-of-command nature of organizations; others stress the relationships between pattern of organization and goals or objectives; some are concerned primarily with organizations as social systems; and still others view organization as a method of defining tasks.[1] For our purposes, the simplest definition is probably the best; so we shall define an organization as *a group of persons working together toward common goals.*

The problem of determining the best pattern of organization for carrying out tasks and achieving goals is at least as old as recorded history. In the Old Testament, Moses is described as finding it impossible to govern and judge all the people personally. Thus he was forced to organize his people. He chose "able men out of all Israel" and put them in charge of smaller groups, reserving only the hardest decisions for personal treatment.[2]

STRUCTURE

In a company, or almost any other kind of activity that involves a number of people, people work together in some sort of organization structure. This involves a division of the overall tasks of the group, the determination of objectives for individuals and subgroups, and the specification of relationships among individuals and subgroups. Structure is conveniently represented by an organization chart, often supplemented by a manual or other document that specifies objectives, responsibilities, and relationships in greater detail. An example of a chart, showing a hypothetical grouping of marketing activities in a manufacturing company, is shown in Figure 23-1. Later in this chapter, we shall discuss further the way in which marketing activities are grouped, as in Figure 23-1, and consider alternative methods of organizing marketing activity.

A chart such as the foregoing, it should be emphasized, is merely a simplified picture of an organization. What is vastly more important than any chart is the organization itself and the logic underlying it, and, of course, the people in the organization. In designing an organization structure, the businessman must keep in mind the general purposes of organizing and the limits that are placed on formal organization by the far more complex informal systems of relationships that exist in and among any group or groups of individuals; we shall have more to say later about informal systems of organization. In the specific area of marketing, it is also important to recognize that organization structure must facilitate the development, implementation, and coordination of the overall marketing program, the marketing mix, whose elements have been discussed in the preceding chapters of Part 4.

[1] For a condensed presentation of various theories of organization, see Edmund Learned and Audrey Sproat, *Organization Theory and Policy: Notes for Analysis,* Richard D. Irwin, Inc., Homewood, Ill., 1966 (paperback).

[2] Cited by James D. Mooney, *The Principles of Organization,* Harper & Row, Publishers, Incorporated, New York, 1947, pp. 20–21.

FIGURE 23-1
Marketing organization in a manufacturing company

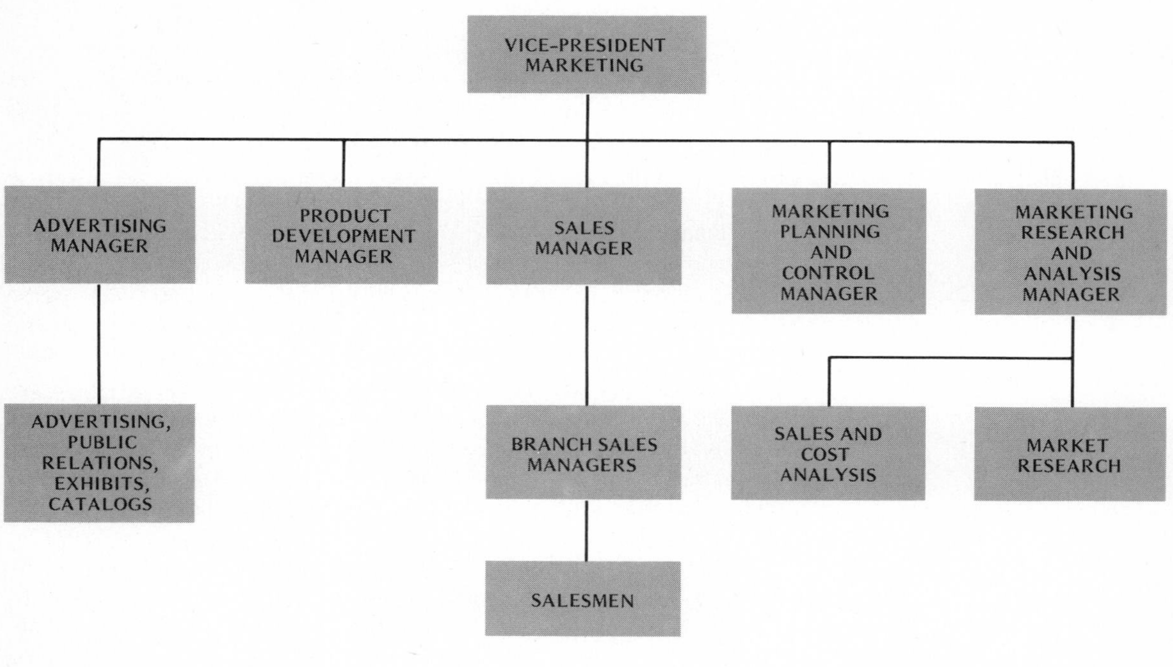

SPECIALIZATION

A major concept that underlies organizational theory, and a major purpose that the act of organizing seeks to achieve, is specialization. Tasks must be divided in a fashion that provides for their effective performance. In Figure 23-1, for example, the marketing vice-president's "box" indicates that the tasks having to do with marketing have been assigned to him and his subordinates; if the total chart were expanded to include other senior executives, it would include the president of the company and other vice-presidents in charge of such areas as production, engineering and research, finance, and administration. Note that within marketing the tasks have been further subdivided into advertising, product development, and so forth.

The principle involved in specialization is to group those activities which are similar. Tasks may be similar in various respects, including the nature of the work to be done, the skills or experience required to do it, and the time and place at which it is to be done. In marketing, for example, it is generally accepted that the tasks involved in selling different products are more similar than are the tasks of selling a product and preparing advertising copy for it. Also, the selling and advertising work are typically conducted in different places, and the skills requisite to the two kinds of activity are generally regarded as quite different. It is therefore common to find salesmen selling two or more products, but most unusual to find a single employee making sales calls and preparing advertising copy. The specialization principle, then, applies both to individual employees and to organization units.

COORDINATION

Specialists in organization theory sometimes refer to the "conundrum of organization." By this they mean that the very process of specialization (or differentiation) of tasks, which is designed to promote efficiency and effectiveness, in turn creates a new problem.

If a salesman says one thing about a product and advertising says another, confusion can easily result. If the marketing department promises delivery next week, but the production department does not have the goods available, customer goodwill and perhaps the customer himself will be lost. The tasks that have been divided for specialization must, in short, be coordinated—a second major purpose of organizing is coordination. This means that an organization must be structured and its processes developed so as to facilitate both consistency and proper timing of the various tasks that are to be performed. Throughout Part 4 we have talked of the necessity of making sure that the various elements of marketing strategy fit harmoniously. The choice of organization form is one way of helping to achieve, or of failing to achieve, such coordination.

It is important to note that problems of coordination are just as important in small companies, though perhaps easier to solve, as they are in big companies. Both General Motors and the corner drugstore will succeed or fail as they satisfy or do not satisfy their customers. In either case, customer satisfaction will not be achieved if the tasks necessary to its accomplishment are not effectively coordinated.

AUTHORITY AND RESPONSIBILITY

A third general purpose of organization is to provide for the assignment of specific authority and responsibility. As tasks are divided among organizational units and among individuals, it is necessary to determine which units, and individuals, have the authority to make decisions and carry the responsibility for results. In Figure 23-1, for example, the chart reflects the fact that the sales manager has the authority to manage the activity of the sales branches and the salesmen. He also is responsible for their activities. Note that we cannot say necessarily that he is completely responsible for their results. If poor sales results are achieved, the salesmen, and therefore the sales manager and the branch sales managers, may be to blame, but not necessarily so. The product itself may have proved to be inferior to competitive products, the advertising may have "turned off" possible customers, marketing research may have grossly overestimated the potential market, the production department may not have gotten the product out of the factory on time—a host of possible reasons may have accounted for the sales failure. It is the marketing vice-president's job to determine which organizational unit or units are in fact responsible for the poor results.

This example illustrates both the importance and the difficulty of defining authority and responsibility. An organization chart, usually in combination with some other formal mechanisms such as position descriptions and procedures manuals, normally specifies the areas in which executives have the authority to make decisions and, further, indicates their responsibility areas. But the hierarchy of decision-making responsibility implied by the chart does not absolve the senior marketing executive of the need to coordinate activities effectively and review performance accurately.

□ CONTROL AND EVALUATION

The marketing manager must also try to achieve a logical relationship between his choice of organization structure and the information processes by which he controls and evaluates the operations for which he and his subordinates are responsible. These relationships were discussed briefly in Chapter 13 in the context of overall corporate strategy, but they are of sufficient significance to marketing to merit emphasis here.

Information systems that are used for purposes of control and evaluation must be consistent with organization form if they are to be effective. An example illustrates the point. If marketing management has decided to define its sales branches as *profit centers,* that is, to hold them responsible for profit performance on the products that they sell, then the information systems by which the branches are controlled and evaluated must be designed to yield certain kinds of necessary information. Data on prices, margins, unit volumes, and inventories must be available to permit the computation of branch sales and gross profits. On the cost side, data must be accumulated that reflect all direct branch costs and whatever costs management may have decided to allocate to the branches. Only if such cost and revenue figures exist can management properly evaluate branch office performance. Thus, although Chapter 26 will have more to say about measuring and controlling marketing performance, it is important here to stress the relationship between those activities and marketing organization.

Formal and informal organization

In this chapter we are concerned with organization from the standpoint of assignments and relationships that are consciously planned and specified by management. It must be recognized, however, that it is neither possible, nor socially desirable, to specify completely what people will do or how they will behave. The relationships set forth on an organization chart reflect what is termed the *formal* organization structure of a group; there is also a system of *informal* relationships which is seldom fully known, much less charted.

In recent years, considerable research has been done on informal relationships within organizations. In a group of 20 women working in one department of a large department store, it was observed that informal but quite effective "rules" were developed by the group. For example, the older saleswomen with long tenure on the job behaved as if they "owned" specific parts of the sales area and specific merchandise lines. Also, there was a fairly clear notion of a "fair" maximum amount for one salesperson to sell per day.[3]

Now, suppose that an executive failed to recognize these informal rules and attempted to make changes in organization which involved, for example, a violation of the "private territories" of the older saleswomen. Such changes would undoubtedly be resisted, and a strong but clandestine effort to sabotage the new system might well result. Similar patterns of behavior and rules can be found in any groups of salesmen, copywriters, warehousemen, truck drivers, or other personnel.

The most important general points for a manager to recognize about informal organization are that it always exists, that its existence imposes limits on the functioning of the formal structure, and that decisions should be made to take advantage of the informal system rather than to attempt to override it since the latter is seldom possible. No matter how much care is taken in designing a formal structure, it cannot be a complete description of a group's activities. "The fact that an organization has been formally established . . . does not mean that all activities and interactions of its members conform strictly to the official blueprint."[4]

Coordinating marketing programs: a special problem

As stated above, one major purpose in any system of organization is coordination of the various tasks to be carried out. Coordination is especially important, and especially difficult, in marketing. The need for coordination arises because customers perceive a company's marketing program as a whole, not as a set of

[3] George F. F. Lombard, *Behavior in a Selling Group*, Division of Research, Graduate School of Business Administration, Harvard University, Boston, 1955, chap. 8.

[4] Peter M. Blau and W. Richard Scott, *Formal Organizations*, Chandler Publishing Company, San Francisco, 1962, p. 5.

separate and distinct operations. When a customer buys an automobile, he is interested in, and influenced by, the product itself, the manufacturer's advertising, the retail salesman, the dealer's service facilities and general reputation, credit terms, and of course the price. He evaluates all these in relation to alternatives offered by other dealers and manufacturers. All these factors act in combination to determine the success or failure of the marketing program. Not only is each factor more effective when reinforced by the others, but poor performance in just one area can be enough to negate what would otherwise be an attractive package.

The franchised dealer system used by automobile producers is designed partly to provide coordination among various elements of the marketing mix by imposing a degree of centralized control over them. For example, most of the franchise contracts used in the 1960s imposed certain limitations on the types of advertising to be used by the dealers under cooperative payment systems. This was regarded as necessary by the manufacturers because misleading, blatant, or shoddy advertising at the local level could destroy the impression sought in national advertising.

The objectives of coordinating a marketing program are to ensure that its elements are consistent, that they reinforce rather than weaken each other, and that the various tasks are performed in the proper sequence. Why is this so difficult? One reason is that the people responsible for marketing tasks are often physically separated. Salesmen are in the field, dealers and/or distributors are scattered throughout the market area, advertising is prepared at an agency, and executives responsible for product planning, marketing channel policies, and pricing are at regional and central offices. The total number of people involved in marketing decisions may be substantial even in a small company. Hence there is an inherent problem of communication among the decision makers, often accentuated by the need for quick action.

Even when physical separation is not present, there is a separation of viewpoints arising from differences in objectives and tasks within a marketing program. A specialist tends to see the performance of his specialty as an end in itself, and it is easy to lose sight of its relation to overall goals. For example, as discussed in Chapter 22, advertising men often define and measure their performance in terms of the extent to which messages have been communicated, that is, how many people were reached, how many recalled the message. Communication is not an end in itself, but it is often regarded as such, and this makes it hard to coordinate advertising with, for example, personal selling, where performance may be defined and evaluated in an entirely different manner.

Another factor in the difficulty of coordination is the dynamic aspect of marketing. The essence of most markets is change. Consumers' needs and tastes change, competitors' policies change, retail and wholesale institutions change, and technology changes. A marketing program developed to meet one set of conditions inevitably becomes obsolete. Typically, one part of the program is affected earlier or more directly than others, but it is seldom sufficient to deal only with one policy because of the interrelationships among elements of the program.

Generally speaking, changes in market conditions occur gradually, are hard to identify, and, since change is always difficult and therefore unwelcome, are often "wished away" by marketing executives. There is often a strong tendency to deny that any really basic change has occurred and to argue that a new situation is only temporary. When something is done, it is sometimes only the adoption of stopgap measures. Under these conditions, the marketing program becomes uncoordinated, inconsistent, and, at the extreme, self-destructive.

Even in the absence of major changes in market conditions, the need for coordinating the elements of a marketing program remains. The relatively simple requirement that activities be performed in proper *sequence* is more difficult to achieve than it sounds. For example, it seems axiomatic that advertisements promoting a special offer (premium, reduced price, etc.) will have little effect unless retail outlets have the merchandise in stock. But there have been many instances of failure to supply stores in time, either through delays in shipping or through failure to have salesmen solicit orders far enough in advance. Similarly, in product planning a reasonably well-defined sequence of steps should be followed (see Chapter 15). Some companies have tried to short-cut steps in the sequence, usually because of haste, and the results have often been unfortunate.

Because of the risks involved in failure to coordinate a marketing program, a prime concern in marketing organization must be to provide some means to achieve coordination. A variety of arrangements are used for this purpose, including regular written reports, periodic meetings of members of an organization, and committees made up of senior marketing executives representing such functions as advertising, line planning, selling, research, and overall marketing planning. The basic purpose of all these is to ensure that adequate *communication* takes place among the several people responsible for different phases of a program. Communication, together with understanding and acceptance of mutual overall objectives, does not guarantee coordination but does, at least, make it possible. Another common device is to make an individual or group in the organization specifically responsible for coordinating the various marketing activities. As explained in a subsequent section, product or market managers in some firms are staff executives whose primary mission is that of coordinating. In the final analysis, coordination is one of the prime responsibilities of the chief marketing executive and has been one of the main goals of the marketing concept, discussed below.

Attributes of a good marketing organization

In the light of the general purposes of organization and the special problems of achieving coordination in a marketing program, the question may now be asked, "What are the general characteristics of a good marketing organization?" There are several, including flexibility, growth potential, a central philosophy or tradition, and a comprehension of the marketing concept.

□ FLEXIBILITY

Flexibility is clearly needed to cope with the changes in market conditions that must be expected. There must be a willingness to accept new assignments and to reorganize tasks more or less continuously. The attitude that a particular job assignment will "always be here" is dangerous anywhere, and especially so in marketing. Examples of the penalties attached to inflexibility are numerous. A large company selling perishable products to distributors throughout the United States, for instance, had traditionally shipped primarily by rail. To obtain adequate quality control, the company assigned men to inspect shipments in the freight yards of major cities. Gradually trucks replaced railroads as the primary means of transportation, but in the early 1960s the inspectors were still on the payroll examining the steadily dwindling number of rail carloads.

A more serious example of inflexibility is afforded by the wholesale baking industry which supplies retail grocery stores. The bakers developed their marketing policies and organizations to meet the needs of many small independent grocery stores. Beginning in the 1920s, the small independent stores were supplanted by chains and quasi-chains and later by large supermarkets with very different needs from those of the independents. But the bakers modified their policies and organizations very slowly and with seeming reluctance. One reason was that they employed many driver-salesmen who delivered bread to the stores daily, replenished the shelves, and made collections. These jobs, and the commission system of compensation used for them, were geared specifically to the needs of small independent stores. Adoption of new policies would necessarily require modification of the drivers' duties and compensation that, it was thought, would be resisted by the men and by their unions. One consequence of this inflexibility during the 1950s was that many food chains found it increasingly advantageous from a cost standpoint to produce their own private label brands of baked goods. Thus the wholesale bakers in the early 1960s faced continued pressure to modify their marketing policies. Their traditional form of organization was a major obstacle to making changes because it was inflexible.[5]

[5] See Robert D. Buzzell and Charles C. Slater, "Decision Theory and Marketing Management," *Journal of Marketing,* July, 1962, pp. 7–16.

GROWTH POTENTIAL

Growth potential is related to flexibility. The need for it arises, in large measure, from the same causes. Because conditions change, new products and markets can be expected to supplant existing ones. This, in turn, implies the need for making provisions to let newer segments of an organization grow in size and stature. What happens instead, all too often, is that new activities lack prestige and their growth is resisted and resented. People in an organization tend to identify themselves *personally* with their products and customers, and regard it as a personal offense when other products or customers take on greater importance. These attitudes can be real obstacles in developing marketing policies and organizations suited to the new situations.

PHILOSOPHY

In most organizations there is some central philosophy or tradition underlying the specific policies and procedures used. A sound organizational philosophy is very desirable, and can provide a continuing foundation for growth even in the face of change. The J. C. Penney Company, for example, was founded with the idea of providing better values to lower- and middle-income families than did most retailers at the time (the early 1900s). The founder, Mr. Penney, stated that he sought to apply the golden rule ("Do unto others as you would have them do unto you") to merchandising. This philosophy has pervaded the organization and guided its policies through a long period of continuous change and expansion. It may be that this philosophy is more altruistic than most, but it has been a successful one.[6]

In general, it appears that any organization needs some common philosophy or tradition. The reason is that policies and programs are almost always designed in the light of market conditions at a specific time and place. When these conditions change, so must the policies and programs. A tradition or philosophy provides a more enduring guide to action than any policy. If the philosophy is well chosen, it can be a permanent basis for an organization.

THE MARKETING CONCEPT

In Chapter 1, the marketing concept was characterized as a state of corporate mind that synthesizes all marketing functions and relates them to all other business functions in the pursuit of company objectives. If the marketing concept is not fully comprehended within the marketing organization, it will certainly not be fully understood elsewhere in the company.

Thus, in developing a marketing organization, one of the key tasks of senior marketing executives is to make sure that people in organization units, such as those shown in Figure 23-1, for example, understand the interrelationships

[6] Mr. Penney died in 1971. It will be interesting to see if the Penney chain can perpetuate its founder's philosophy.

among those units. They must also understand the importance of the relationships between marketing and the other business functions. Though the marketing concept may imply that in most companies marketing is the core function of the company because of its central role in determining customer needs and desires, it does *not* imply that other business functions are not of major importance. Of direct concern to us here, in terms of organizational implications, is the fact that the marketing concept requires that (1) marketing have a major place in overall company organization, (2) its internal components be carefully coordinated, and (3) the marketing organization relate fully and effectively to other organizational components.

Manufacturers' marketing organization

Thus far, our general discussion of organizational concepts and purposes has been applicable to all kinds of companies that engage in marketing activity, whether they are manufacturing, wholesaling, retailing, or advertising firms. There are, however, important differences in the context and details of applying the concepts to various kinds of firms. For that reason, the remainder of this chapter deals separately with the organizational problems of manufacturing and of merchandising (wholesale and retail) businesses.

We deal first with marketing organization in manufacturing companies. Marketing is, of course, generally recognized as one of the three basic functional activities in almost all manufacturing concerns, the others being production and finance. We shall discuss three major issues in regard to organizing the marketing activities of a manufacturing company: (1) the place of marketing in the overall organization, (2) the scope of the chief marketing executive's duties, and (3) the grouping of major tasks within marketing organizations. Then, because there are special problems of marketing organization in large multiproduct firms, that topic will be treated separately.

□ MARKETING'S PLACE IN THE ORGANIZATION

Because marketing is so directly related, and often of paramount significance, to overall corporate objectives and to long-run success or failure, the major aspects of marketing strategy are often the responsibility, in terms of decision or at least approval, of top management, that is, the president and the board of directors. Some of the decisions discussed in prior chapters of Part 4, such as major product or price policy decisions, are typically reserved for top management. Except in very small companies, however, top management cannot assume responsibility for all or even most marketing decisions. Usually, therefore, there is a chief marketing executive who reports to either the president or the executive vice-president. He is at the same organizational level as the chief executives for production, finance, and, possibly, such other major functions as administration, engineering, and research and development.

Though this arrangement is commonplace in the business world of the 1970s, it is of more than historical interest to note that only in roughly the last two decades has *marketing* been considered of sufficient significance to merit that location. Until perhaps the early 1950s, most businesses had an executive in charge of sales, reporting to top management, who bore the title of sales manager, sales vice-president, or the equivalent. Though sometimes this executive was also responsible for advertising or dealer relations, companies typically assigned at least some other marketing tasks to other parts of the organization: product planning to production, credit policy to finance, and so forth. This arrangement often created a lack of coordinated marketing programs. Because different people in different organization units had differing amounts of authority over important elements of marketing programs, they often held different conceptions of the goals and marketing strategies involved. Policy and operating conflicts often resulted, which had to be resolved at the top management level.

Such conflicts or gaps in policy and operation were a contributing factor in the emergence of marketing as a major unified component of most manufacturing companies. The other major factors were, of course, the rapid development of what we have defined as the *marketing concept* and the increasing dominance of a customer-oriented point of view. These factors, then, gave strength to the now-accepted idea that all, or at least most, of a firm's marketing activities should be grouped and assigned to a single executive for development, coordination, and control. The chief marketing executive of a firm is usually called marketing vice-president, marketing director, marketing manager, or something similar.

□ DUTIES OF THE CHIEF MARKETING EXECUTIVE

The precise scope of the top marketing manager's job varies among companies. In some firms, he is responsible for nearly all the types of decisions that we have been discussing in Part 4, while in others there may be limitations on his authority within the marketing field. The two position descriptions reproduced below convey the scope of the chief marketing executive's job in two companies, each with a broad conception of the marketing job. Figure 23-2 shows a position description for the chief marketing official of a large consumer goods manufacturer, while Figure 23-3 describes the duties of the director of marketing of a division of an industrial products company.

These position descriptions are reasonably typical in terms of the functions and responsibilities that they encompass, at least as far as such activities as advertising, sales, sales promotion, planning, research, and many other marketing functions are concerned. Their generality in three areas, however, is open

FIGURE 23-2

Vice-president of marketing, P. Ballantine & Sons

REPORTS TO: President
SUPERVISES: Vice-President of Sales
Merchandising and Promotion Manager
Advertising Manager
Public Relations Manager
Director of Marketing Planning and Research
Market Promotions Manager

BASIC FUNCTION: Responsible for planning, directing, controlling, and coordinating the overall marketing activities of the company to meet or exceed established volume and profit goals within approved budgets.

MAJOR RESPONSIBILITIES

1. Develops for approval by the President long- and short-term marketing objectives and policies concerning

   Overall sales, advertising, promotion, public relations, and planning and research activities
   Recruitment, training, and development programs for marketing personnel
   Operating budgets to control expenses and allocate efforts for all marketing activities
   Pricing policies to market the company's products profitably and competitively

2. Directs the development of strategic and tactical marketing plans and programs regarding

   Geographic coverage
   Product-line composition
   Price schedules
   Packaging

3. Approves marketing department organization, manning levels, personnel assignments, and wage and salary programs in accordance with established policies.

4. Reviews and controls the performance of the marketing department by

   Evaluating sales performance against quotas
   Reviewing actual expenses against budgets and established standards
   Appraising the company's market position relative to that of leading competitors

5. Approves all operating systems and procedures for the collection, analysis, and dissemination of marketing information.

6. Keeps fully abreast of market developments through

   Personal contact with the trade, distributors, and industry associations
   Analysis and review of sales, research, and trade reports

7. Represents the company at appropriate industry, trade, and community functions.

PRINCIPAL WORKING RELATIONSHIPS
(Excluding direct reporting and supervisory relationships)

1. Works closely with the general counsel to insure that the marketing activities of the company are conducted in accordance with pertinent statutes and regulations.

2. Works closely with the vice-president of finance to provide all data necessary to prepare company reports and financial forecasts.

3. Works closely with the vice-president of operations to insure that production and marketing activities are effectively coordinated.

4. Works closely with the director of industrial relations to insure that the personnel activities of the marketing department are in conformance with established companywide personnel policies.

Source: Jo An Sperling, *Job Descriptions in Marketing Management,* AMA Research Study 94, American Management Association, Inc., 1969.

to some question. In most companies, the public relations function is probably *not* within the purview of the marketing executive, as it is in P. Ballantine & Sons. In most companies, unlike the chemical company cited in Figure 23-3, physical distribution (logistics) is *not* the responsibility of the marketing manager; on the contrary, decisions regarding distribution and logistics policies are typically made by production executives or by physical distribution managers at equivalent organization levels, who may consult marketing organizations where necessary.

The other areas in respect to which these descriptions cannot be assumed to be typical are *pricing* and *product planning*. Though many companies do assign these responsibilities to marketing, many others do not. As Chapter 15 has indicated, product planning can be a particularly difficult organizational problem. Frequently, the responsibility for it is shared by marketing, production, and research and development, and representatives of these organizations act as a committee to coordinate the activity.

GROUPING MARKETING TASKS

Major tasks within marketing can be grouped on the basis of one or a combination of the following four principal components:

1. Functions
2. Products or product lines
3. Geographic areas
4. Customer classes (sometimes defined as "markets")

A typical *functional* grouping of tasks in a manufacturing firm provides for the organizational separation of responsibilities for sales, advertising and sales promotion, product development, and such marketing services as research, cost control, and planning. Alternatively, in a *product* organization, responsibility for marketing decisions about different products or product lines is assigned to different persons. A *geographic* division of duties involves assignment of responsibility for specific areas, and the customers in those areas, to specific persons. Finally, a *customer class* or *market* organization is based on the idea of separate groups responsible for marketing programs for various classes of customers, such as drugstores or food stores. All four components involve the basic notion of specialization discussed earlier.

Few manufacturers organize their marketing activities solely on the basis of any one of these four factors. Typically, a combination is used. In Figure 23-1, a basic functional organization is supplemented by a geographic division of sales force activities. Many firms go one step further and utilize product groupings as a basis for further specialization in product planning and advertising.

FIGURE 23-3
Director of marketing: a chemicals company

BASIC FUNCTION
Responsible to the General Manager of a Division for management of the Division's total marketing effort and for advice and assistance in the formulation of Division marketing and sales plans. Directs all marketing activities of the Division to achieve planned and approved sales volume and profit objectives and establish the plans, policies, and procedures governing marketing activities of the Division within the general operating plans and policies of the Company and the Division.

GENERAL OBJECTIVES AND RESPONSIBILITIES
Responsibility is assigned and authority granted for the specific duties listed below, as well as those listed under the section of the *Management Guide* entitled "Responsibilities, Relationships, and Limits of Authority of Every Executive." [The section referred to is reprinted following this job description, but is not reproduced here.]

1. Develop sales and profit objectives which relate to customer needs and market opportunities and to plant capacity considerations so that the Company's return on invested capital and its competitive position may be optimized.

2. Supervise the development and execution of comprehensive marketing plans, programs, and budgets through which the Division will meet its sales and profit objectives by meeting customer needs. This responsibility encompasses the full range of marketing strategy formulation and tactical execution, including such areas as pricing, sales methods, and coverage; the nature of sales representation; physical distribution; selection of market segments for special emphasis; promotional and technical support of sales; and specifying the necessary product characteristics, breadth of product line, and means of dealing with captive markets, including forward integration. It necessitates plans in adequate detail as to the means by which sales are to be generated and the source from which they are expected. It calls for allocation of specific responsibility for generating blocs of sales volume among product managers, general line sales, and executive sales activity.

3. Seek assistance of the Vice-President of Marketing for sales tasks which are best assigned to members of management outside the Divisional marketing organization.

4. In collaboration with the Controller, supervise the development and application of appropriate measures for monitoring performance against detailed sales and profit objectives and controlling marketing actions to accommodate contingencies revealed by these measures.

5. Direct the regular review of markets and products to identify promising opportunities for creating separate specialty product businesses in areas with distinct product, service, manufacturing, and marketing requirements. Assist in executing the organizational transfer of such businesses into new divisions when decisions for such transfers have been made.

6. Select, evaluate, and develop key executives of the Division marketing organization.

7. Insure that the most effective field sales and distribution organization is maintained to serve market needs.

8. Stimulate demand through development of advertising and promotion programs.

9. Establish standards for product performance and reliability for field service necessary to compete with maximum effectiveness.

10. Participate directly in selling activities as necessary and at the appropriate level in customer organizations.

11. Provide for a field sales organization to suggest new product and other opportunities for the Company.

12. Make available professional market research, distribution, and other services for other divisions as necessary.

RELATIONSHIP WITH OTHER UNITS IN THE ORGANIZATION

1. Serves as a member of various Company committees as requested.

2. Contacts extradivision personnel as required to arrange for multilevel or top-level sales activities.

3. Works with Research, Development, Corporate Marketing, and other divisional marketing management on pertinent marketing matters affecting new-product generation or evaluation and coordination of interdivisional marketing activities.

4. Maintains close contact with the Controller in the use of accounting data for control of marketing operations.

5. Collaborates with the Director of Trade Development on matters regarding trade relations interests of the Company.

LIMITS OF AUTHORITY

1. *General*

A. Act in accordance with limits established in the general table, "Limits of Authority," and in the *Appropriation Procedure Manual.*

2. *On Purchase Contracts*

A. Approval of the Division General Manager is required on all commitments exceeding 12 months or where inventory will be raised above 3 months at current rate of disposal.

3. *On Sales Prices*

A. Full Authority to apply price schedules determined and approved by the appropriate Division General Manager. Changes in schedule or variations from established schedules of divisional products must be referred to the appropriate Division General Manager.

4. *On Sales Contracts*

A. Nonstandard contracts, including exclusive arrangements with wholesalers, or sales representatives, or special commissions, require the approval of the Division General Manager. Special contracts for divisional products require the approval of the appropriate Division General Manager.

B. Deviations from terms of existing contracts, such as modifying provisions of escalator clauses, require the approval of the Division General Manager for divisional products.

5. *On Operating Methods and Policies*

A. Any major change in distribution, or major changes in wholesale representation, or any geographical changes in the location of sales office, require the approval of the Division General Manager.

Source: Jo An Sperling, *Job Description in Marketing Management,* AMA Research Study 94, American Management Association, Inc., 1969.

Undoubtedly the most pervasive factor in marketing organization, however, is that of functional specialization. Within the major functions of sales, advertising and sales promotion, product planning, and marketing services, decisions must be made as to how tasks are to be further subdivided.

Sales force organization The sales force is typically under the direction of a sales manager responsible for selecting, hiring, training, supervising, and controlling salesmen's activities. In some companies the sales manager is also the chief marketing executive and may have responsibility for other marketing activities as well as sales. Effective management of the sales force poses some special problems because in most cases salesmen must work in the field, and communication with them must be achieved primarily through written orders and reports or telephone calls. For this reason, most companies selling on a regional, national, or international scale find it necessary to set up one or more levels of divisional or branch sales offices. These may be connected with sales branches at which warehouse stocks are maintained or the sales offices may be independent.

A large company may have an elaborate hierarchy of sales branches, divisions, and regions under its general sales manager. For example, in the 1960s, Procter and Gamble had about 2,000 soap salesmen grouped into several sales districts; the districts, in turn, were grouped into a number of divisions—all under a department sales manager for soap.

It is often difficult to decide whether a field sales force should be organized primarily by areas, products, or customers. The problem can be illustrated by a hypothetical example. Suppose an electrical equipment manufacturer sells a wide line of industrial equipment to customers in such industries as metalworking, automotive, electrical utilities, and aircraft. To some extent these customers' needs differ, and it is desirable for salesmen to specialize by learning how to meet those needs. On the other hand, specialization by product may also be desirable since the products are complex and changes are made frequently. Finally, it can be argued that the most efficient organization is to have one salesman service all products and customers in his geographic territory since in this way travel costs will be minimized and the salesmen will be able to reach customers more quickly.

How, then, should the sales force be organized? No universally applicable answer can be given. The key element is the *extent* of the differences in products and customers, and the proper answer may well be to use a combination of all three factors. Thus, the primary breakdown may be geographic, with separate sales forces for certain industries and a group of product specialists who supplement the work of the regular salesmen and make some sales calls with them.

A somewhat similar problem is involved in the organization of a manufacturer's branch warehouses. A branch may include a warehouse, a group of salesmen, and an office where orders are handled, credit arrangements made, etc. Should all these activities be under a single branch manager (geographic organization), or should sales, distribution, and office functions be separate, each reporting to a headquarters executive (functional)? One large drug manufacturer has two managers in each branch, one for sales and one for office and warehouse. Other companies have combined these assignments. The correct solution, again, depends on individual circumstances, including the personalities of the men involved.

Advertising and sales promotion A manufacturer's organization for advertising and sales promotion activities depends in part on the extent to which he relies on advertising agencies and other outside organizations. At one extreme, a company may have only a small staff to "ride herd" on the advertising agencies and/or other outside organizations that serve it. At the other extreme, some industrial concerns rely on agencies only slightly or not at all, especially when the advertising program is carried out primarily through catalogs, direct mail, or other "noncomissionable" media.

Product planning Some special problems are involved in organization for product planning (see Chapter 15). More than any other activity, product planning requires effective coordination among marketing, product, and other organizational groups. New-product ideas often originate in laboratories or grow out of technological changes. But new-product *needs* depend primarily on market conditions, and simply because a product is technologically feasible does not make it profitable, either in terms of potential sales or in terms of production costs. It follows that product decisions must be made with reference to a total company viewpoint. A common organizational arrangement is to have a product *committee* act on all proposed additions, modifications, or eliminations from the line.

One effect of the marketing concept has been for manufacturers to give marketing executives a larger role in product planning decisions. For example, product planning is regarded as a marketing function at the General Electric Company. At least in some divisions of that company, new-product proposals pass through a definite, prescribed *sequence* of decisions: first as to technical feasibility, by research and/or engineering personnel; then to market potential, by market research personnel; and finally, the development of a plan for introducing the product, assuming that it meets the earlier tests. While representatives of other groups participate in this decision sequence, the overall job of product planning is the marketing manager's responsibility.

Marketing services Staff marketing services in a manufacturing concern include such activities as marketing research, planning, budgeting, and control. Depending on the scope of the tasks, these may be assigned to separate organizational units or may be combined in one unit. In either case, personnel responsible for marketing services should report to the chief marketing executive. Only in large companies is any formal subdivision required *within* marketing services. Further subdivision, if any, may be on the basis of functions, products, or both. For example, in the 1960s the marketing research department of the Scott Paper Company was organized into separate groups for industrial and consumer products in addition to functional specialists in product analysis and market analysis.

Special problems in multiproduct firms

Companies manufacturing a variety of products have certain special problems in organization. Marketing programs must be separately developed, to some extent, for each product because of differences in markets and competitive conditions. Yet there are also advantages in coordinating the overall program for the entire line. Organizational arrangements used to meet these problems include decentralized product divisions and product manager assignments of various kinds.

□ DECENTRALIZED PRODUCT DIVISIONS

In very large companies such as the General Motors Corporation, E. I. du Pont de Nemours and Co., Inc., and the General Electric Company, each of several product lines is manufactured and sold on a scale sufficient to justify fully decentralized management. Each product division in such a corporation is, in effect, a separate company with its own general management, production facilities, and marketing operations. Often the real connection among the divisions is in ownership, central policy making, and financing, although there may also be centralized staff service activities. Under these circumstances, each product division has its own chief marketing executive and the headquarters marketing executives, if any, act largely in a staff capacity to provide overall coordination.

□ PRODUCT MANAGERS

In companies smaller than the giant corporation and *within* the divisions of the latter, an increasingly common arrangement is to assign product or brand managers to handle specified aspects of the marketing programs for a product or line of products.

The product manager has been described as a "little marketing manager," but seldom if ever is *complete* responsibility for marketing delegated to this level. Among consumer goods companies or divisions, the product manager typically is responsible for making and executing decisions in a number of areas. Luck and Nowak have described his responsibilities in the following manner[7]:

1. Furnish an intelligence center on all aspects of a product line or brand (except manufacturing details), including technical information, market situations, and so forth.
2. Create ideas for product improvement, new-product development, and promotion; or gather such ideas from internal and external sources.
3. Advise top management on marketing aspects of a new-product line or brand during its implementation through research and development phases.

[7] David J. Luck and Theodore Nowak, "Product Management—Vision Unfulfilled," *Harvard Business Review,* May–June, 1965, p. 144.

4. Prepare advertising and marketing concepts for functional management, and provide liaison with advertising and merchandising agencies in the actual development of such programs.
5. Stimulate interest in, and support for, a product line or brand among salesmen and distributors (in industrial goods, also among key buyers).
6. Prepare sales forecasts; also provide logistic guidance for production and distribution.
7. Devise product strategy and plans, and propose product goals and budgets for submission to the determining executives.
8. Assume responsibility for product strategy, campaigns, and profitability.

Industrial product managers are less concerned with advertising and concentrate instead on working with salesmen and making sales calls on key accounts. In both cases, decisions on prices, channels of distribution, logistics, and distributor and dealer relations are usually made at a higher level or by a different sector of management.

An example of a product manager organization is shown in Figure 23-4. Here responsibility for the promotional planning for each product is assigned to a product manager; product group managers supervise the work of product managers for several related products. Marketing research is a centralized staff activity, but analysts within this department specialize by product and work closely with the corresponding product managers. All products are sold by a single sales force which is organized by geographic districts. This form of organization, with variations, is used by many consumer goods manufacturers.

□ MARKET MANAGERS

An arrangement similar to the product manager setup is to assign market (customer class) managers to plan and execute marketing programs aimed at specific groups of customers. This type of organizational arrangement is particularly prevalent among large industrial products companies which sell substantial volumes of individual products or groups of products to various industries. One major division of a large multiproduct company, for example, has market managers in charge of meat products (for sale to meat packers), food products (other products sold to packers and canners), and enrichment products (sold to cereal, grain, and baking industries). Many large steel companies have market managers who develop marketing programs that are targeted toward specific industries such as automobiles, shipbuilding, and construction.

A particularly interesting organizational problem often confronts large manufacturers of industrial goods that sell different products in large amounts to different industries, each of which buys in large volume. The organizational problem is apparent. It is whether to use the product manager or market man-

FIGURE 23-4
Product manager organization in a manufacturing company

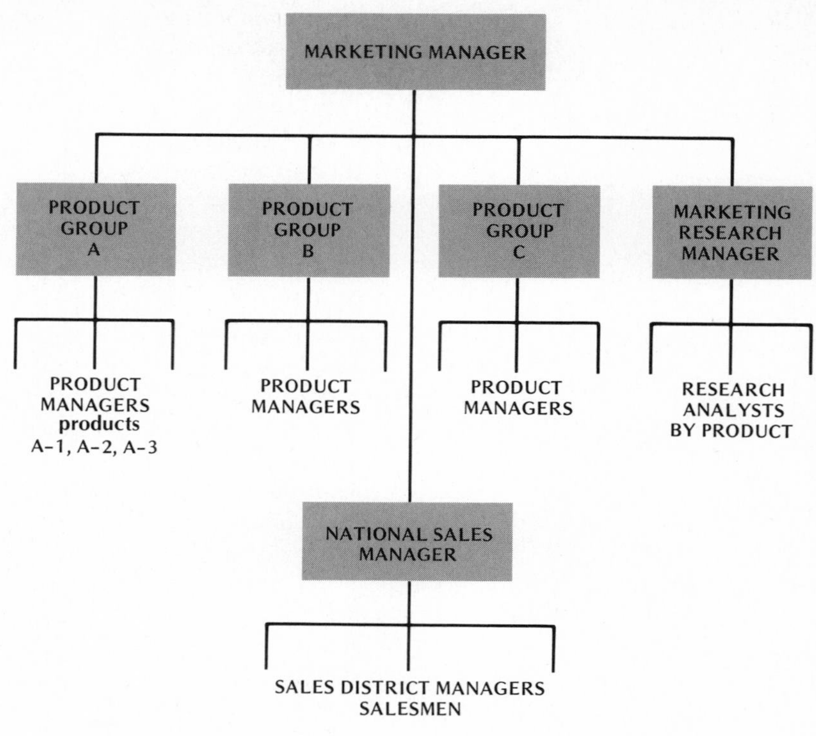

ager concept, or some *combination* of the two. In some instances, and increasingly in the late 1960s and 1970s, companies have chosen a combination of the two approaches in an attempt to ensure that both product classes and customer classes receive careful attention. Corey and Star, for example, point out that both Monsanto Company and International Business Machines (IBM) have used a combination of product and market groupings in some of their operations.[8] The organizational problems of authority and responsibility that can arise with a dual system of this type are numerous, and the chief marketing executive must be careful to define jobs, clarify relationships, and select the right people if the product and market managers are to work together effectively and discharge their responsibilities.[9]

[8] E. Raymond Corey and Steven H. Star, *Organization Strategy: A Marketing Approach,* Division of Research, Graduate School of Business Administration, Harvard University, Boston, 1971.
[9] B. Charles Ames, "Dilemma of Product/Market Relationship." *Harvard Business Review,* March–April, 1971, pp. 66–74.

Retail and wholesale organization

Although organization problems in retail and wholesale firms are similar in most respects to those of manufacturers, there are also some key differences. First, wholesalers and retailers are usually smaller than manufacturers, although there are many exceptions (see Chapters 10 to 12). Second, merchandising concerns typically service smaller and reasonably well-defined geographic areas. Third, by definition, retailing and wholesaling concerns are not engaged in manufacturing and hence have a different basic combination of activities. These differences are reflected in a different basic organizational pattern and in certain distinctive organizational issues.

□ BASIC ORGANIZATIONAL PATTERNS

The basic functions of a merchandising concern that correspond to production, marketing, and finance for a manufacturer are merchandising, operations, and control. *Merchandising* includes selection of merchandise, buying, pricing, and selling. *Operations* embraces the physical distribution and storage of goods and maintenance of store facilities. *Control* involves finance, accounting, and budgetary control of activities.

The organization structure of a retail or wholesale firm is typically built around these three basic functions. Within merchandising, organization is primarily on a product basis. Thus, large department stores have buyers and/or department managers in charge of merchandising for the goods in a department; in a large store there may be over 100 such units. Groups of departments may be assigned to division merchandise managers who, in turn, report to a general manager. A typical large department store organization is shown in Figure 23-5.

Organization in terms of product specialization is the traditional pattern in retailing and wholesaling, antedating the product manager concept for manufacturers by many years. Some merchandising activities are, however, typically organized on a functional basis, notably, advertising. Even here, the buyer usually has ultimate authority over the scheduling and content of advertisements for his merchandise.

A controversial issue among retailers concerns the extent to which responsibilities for buying and selling should be combined or separated. The two are usually separate in wholesaling firms since the sales force operates in the field and is subject to the same problems of supervision and communication as in a manufacturing company. But in a retail store the salespeople are inside. Furthermore, selling depends to a substantial extent on merchandise display as well as on personal selling efforts. For these reasons it has been traditional among department stores to combine buying and selling. Some retailing executives believe that this arrangement contributes to the generally poor quality of salesmanship in retailing, because buyers tend to concentrate on merchandise selection to the detriment of sales training and supervision activities. In addi-

FIGURE 23-5

Organization of a large department store

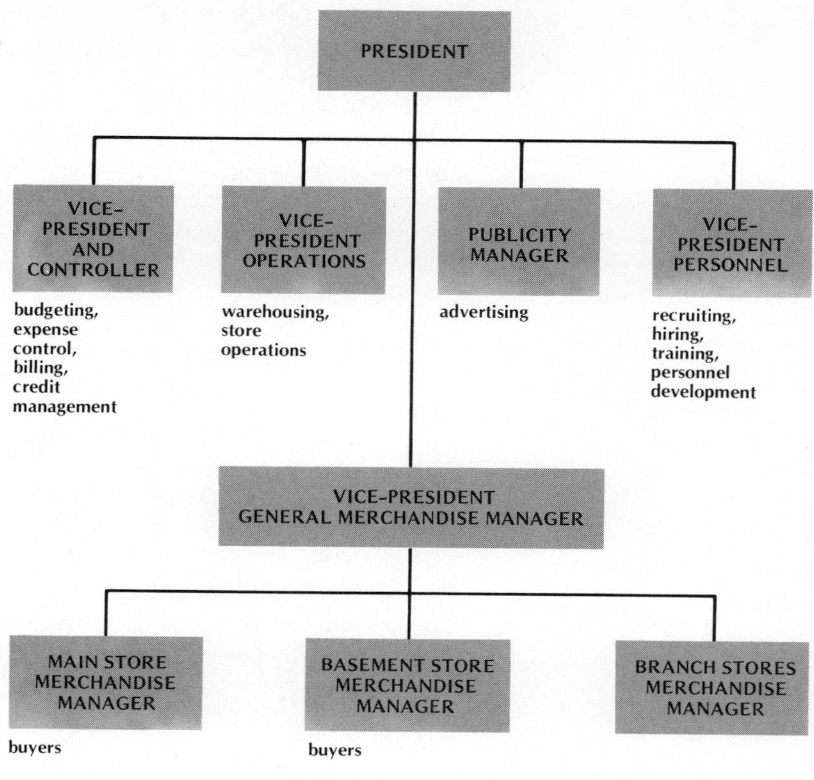

tion, expansion through branch stores since World War II (see below) has aggravated the difficulties of effectively managing both buying and selling. As a result, some stores have separated the two functions or have adopted modified versions of the traditional pattern.

CHAIN AND BRANCH ORGANIZATION

Organization problems in multi-unit retail and wholesale companies—chains and branch-store systems—are essentially similar to those of multidivision manufacturers. The key problems have to do with the manner in which authority is divided between individual store managers and headquarters or main-store executives. In large food chains there are divisional offices serving groups of stores, and most decisions are made at the divisional or headquarters level. An example of substantial decentralization is afforded by the J. C. Penney chain, in which store managers have responsibility for most decisions and are free to buy or not buy from a selection of merchandise offered by the buyers at company headquarters.

Branch department stores differ from chain-store units in that they are typically "satellites" of a large store nearby. Main-store buyers typically select goods for the branches but do not directly supervise the salespersons. As large urban stores have built more branches in suburban areas, there has been a tendency to divorce the sales management function from buying in order to get more effective control of selling activities.

Questions

1. Think of an organization of which you are a member. How is it organized? How well is it performing its functions? Do you think its success, or lack thereof, is related to its structure? Why?

2. In the text, organization is defined as "a group of people working together toward common goals." Why might that definition be described as an oversimplication?

3. What is implied by the term "conundrum of organization"? Suppose you were the marketing vice-president of a company producing a line of consumer package goods such as women's cosmetics. How might the conundrum arise for you, and how would you undertake to solve it?

4. What are the major functions of a department store?
   a. How, if at all, do these functions differ between a single-unit department store and a multi-unit department store?
   b. What problems exist in a multi-unit operation that do not exist in a single-unit store?
   c. Identify and evaluate several alternative methods of organizing to accomplish the marketing functions of a multi-unit department store.

5. Why is the *coordination* of marketing programs especially difficult? Think of some general guidelines that might be used to reduce such problems.

6. Suppose you were the marketing vice-president of Super Steel Company with sales of over $800 million. Your product line is divided into seven major product groups. You sell to a number of different industries, but five industries account for a substantial proportion of sales. Each of the five purchases at least two or three of your major product groups. What organizational problems does this present, and what might be your solution?

7. Suppose the top management of a large consumer goods company decided to sell its product line in Europe, Africa, and Australia. Heretofore, the firm has

sold only in the United States, and the company has been organized along functional lines similar to those illustrated in Figure 23-1.

a. Can you identify any new organizational problems this change would create?

b. How, if at all, would the problems differ if the firm's product line consisted of farm implements? Packaged foods? Pharmaceuticals? Why?

8. The National Grinding Wheel Company had, over the 70 years since its establishment, grown to become a $300 million company selling a variety of products ranging from fine china to ceramic components used in microelectronic circuitry. The company was organized into five divisions. Each division operated its own manufacturing facilities, had its own sales force, and, except for standardized accounting procedures and financial control, operated autonomously.

Three of the five divisions served the foundry industry: The kiln products division sold bricks used in lining foundry ovens. The abrasives division sold grinding wheels and other abrasives used in foundry operations. The pure air division sold air filtering equipment used to control pollution.

Each division had its own separate sales force consisting of about 12 men who, in turn, called on about 3,800 foundries in the United States on a regular basis. Concerned with the rising costs of direct selling, the controller's department, in a special study, suggested that a consolidation of company sales efforts in the foundry business would reduce selling costs considerably, and might also provide synergistic benefits resulting in a more effective selling job.

a. What problems might arise from such a grouping of the sales activities?

b. Could the consolidation be implemented for the foundry market alone, or would consolidation require the company to shift to an organizational structure similar to that suggested in Figure 23-4?

c. What factors would determine the desirability of each approach?

9. What is the relationship between marketing strategy and marketing organization? Why do changes in the former frequently bring about changes in the latter? Can you think of any specific examples regarding companies with which you are familiar?

10. This chapter and others have mentioned product planning as a particularly difficult problem both for marketing executives and for other company officials. Why is this so? Why would you think the product planning problem might be handled differently—and in what ways—in the aerospace industry as opposed to a consumer goods company? How would a food chain with 2,000 outlets reorganize to make decisions as to whether new products should be added in all or some of its stores?

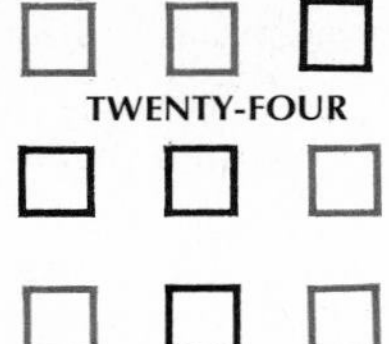
TWENTY-FOUR

International marketing

In Chapters 12 to 23 we have discussed the major elements of marketing management: the formulation of product, price, promotion, and distribution policies and the organization of the firm for implementing these policies. In this chapter, marketing policies and organization are briefly reconsidered in the somewhat different context of the firm which markets its goods and services on an international scale. The experience of many companies indicates that international marketing is not a simple extension of marketing in a single country. When a firm operates in several or many different national markets, management must deal with a new set of problems. Languages, patterns of living and consumption, institutional systems, legal restrictions, and basic attitudes toward business all vary among nation states. These variations call for special approaches to marketing strategy formulation, marketing organization, and control.

THE NATION AS A UNIT

Since this chapter is based entirely on distinctions among national markets, it is important to establish at the outset that the nation is a meaningful unit for market analysis. There are, after all, significant variations within countries as well as between them. The United States, in particular, covers a larger land area, has approximately the same population, and encompasses as wide a variety of climates as all of Western Europe. Yet the latter includes 16 separate nations. Why should these be treated as different "markets" any more than are regional areas within the United States?

It is true, of course, that no country, especially one as large as the United States, is really a homogeneous market. Some of the differences in consumer needs and tastes among regions have been mentioned in Chapter 4. There are similar variations in other countries, too; for example, there is a marked contrast between the "French" and "German" regions of Switzerland. It is also true that improvements in communication and transportation, and the evolution of supranational organizations, have tended to diminish the importance of national boundaries.

In spite of these factors, the nation is still a natural unit to employ in analyzing markets and in organizing for marketing activities. For one thing, each country has its own laws governing local business operations and imports. These laws require the establishment of separate companies, payment of tariffs, conformity with local health, safety, and license requirements, and so on, for "foreign" firms. Usually, legal regulations are designed in part to protect and encourage domestic industry, and thus act as obstacles, sometimes very important ones, to international marketing.

Apart from the fact that the nation is the basic unit of political-legal organization, there are also differences in language, culture, climate, and topography underlying most national boundaries. These variations are usually, although by no means always, greater than corresponding variations within countries.

For these reasons, companies operating internationally find it natural and desirable to organize, to plan, and to control their operations on the basis of national market units.

GROWTH OF INTERNATIONAL BUSINESS

For companies based in small countries, such as Belgium or Sweden, international business has always been of prime importance. The Nestlé Company, with headquarters in Vevey, Switzerland, could never have become a major producer of food products if it had confined its operations to its "home" market. By aggressive development of overseas markets, the company was already operating on a worldwide basis before World War II. Other major international firms based in relatively small nations include Unilever (Great Britain), Royal Dutch Shell (Great Britain and the Netherlands), and Volkswagen (Western Germany).

For United States corporations, in contrast, international business has not traditionally been of major significance. Until the 1950s, the great market potential and continued expansion of the United States economy offered greater opportunities at home than those available elsewhere. There have always been exceptions to this rule, of course. Major petroleum refiners have operated on a worldwide basis for many years, if only because prime raw material sources are located in the Middle East and Latin America. Some other companies have been marketing internationally for generations as a means of exploiting patents, secret processes, or other forms of clear-cut technological advantage. Examples include General Motors, Singer (sewing machines), and Hoover (vacuum cleaners). But these are exceptions; for the great majority of American firms, sales outside the United States were of little importance prior to the 1950s.

During the 1950s and 1960s, the volume of international trade increased rapidly. For United States–based companies, in particular, the growth of sales overseas has been dramatic.

The most important reason for the expansion of international marketing during the 1950s and 1960s was the rapid economic growth of countries outside the United States. For instance, increases in gross national product (adjusted for price changes) during the period 1950–1965 for selected countries were as follows[1]:

Country	*Percent increases*
France	67
Germany	128
Italy	108
Japan	154
Sweden	62
United States	34

Not only did incomes rise, especially in Western Europe, but in the view of many American firms, competition in foreign markets was less fully developed than at home. With some exceptions, foreign-based manufacturers were smaller, less efficient, and less aggressive than American companies. Thus, profit opportunities came to appear greater in foreign markets than in the United States itself. Moreover, early entrants into foreign markets did in fact earn greater profits overseas than on domestic operations. In 1960, Schering (pharmaceuticals) had net earnings of 23 percent on assets for its foreign operations versus 11 percent in the United States; General Foods Corporation earned 24 percent overseas, 17 percent at home; Procter and Gamble, 20 versus 15 percent; Otis Elevator, 22 versus 16 percent; and so on.[2]

Still another stimulus to the expansion of international activity during the 1950s and 1960s was the formation of trading blocs of countries. The Euro-

[1] Based on National Industrial Conference Board, *Economic Almanac, 1967–68,* The Macmillan Company, New York, 1967, p. 502.

[2] Profit comparisons reported in *Business International,* June 24, July 8, July 22, and Sept. 16, 1966.

pean Economic Community, or "Common Market," was formed by France, West Germany, Italy, Belgium, the Netherlands, and Luxemburg in 1957. Under the "Treaty of Rome," these countries agreed to a gradual reduction of tariffs among themselves and to the adoption of common external tariffs. These and other provisions of the treaty were intended to bring about, eventually, a single "market" including all six nations, within which goods and people can move freely.

Other trading blocs formed during the post-World War II period include the European Free Trade Association (Austria, Denmark, Norway, Portugal, Sweden, Switzerland, and the United Kingdom), the Latin American Free Trade Association, and the Central American Common Market. In each case, the development of a supranational organization offers at least the *possibility* of marketing operations on a much larger scale than that possible previously.

The European Economic Community, in particular, acted as a magnet to American companies. From 1950 to 1965, the value of United States private direct investments abroad increased more than fourfold, from $11.8 billion to $49.2 billion. During the same period, direct investments in the six European Economic Community countries expanded almost ten times, from $637 million to $6.3 billion.

□ SPECIAL PROBLEMS OF INTERNATIONAL MARKETING

As indicated in the preceding paragraphs, international marketing has come to be of much greater significance, for more companies, than in the past. What special problems emerge as a company passes from strictly domestic activity to the stage of truly "multinational" marketing?

One class of problems has to do with the selection of national markets and the determination of basic methods of entry and operation. Given its basic methods of operation, the firm must then decide how it should be organized for international marketing. Finally, there are questions of international strategy to be resolved. Each of these classes of problems is discussed in turn in the sections which follow.

Market appraisal and operating methods

Any firm desiring to operate in foreign markets must decide at the outset in which countries to sell its products, and what basic method(s) of operation to employ in each market.

□ APPRAISING INTERNATIONAL MARKETS

Is the potential market for ready-to-eat cereals in Germany sufficiently large to justify entry by the Post Division of General Foods? What is a reasonable estimate of sales, costs, and profits for General Electric numerical controls for machine tools in Japan? These questions are obviously fundamental in any decision to enter an overseas market, and in determining what kind of commitment should be made in a given country.

In most respects, appraisal of a foreign market involves the same logic as appraisal of a regional market or local territory in a firm's home market. There are, however, two distinctive problems in appraising foreign markets which should be mentioned. These are inadequacy of market information and the need to evaluate national political and monetary factors.

One of the most troublesome problems for an American firm is the lack of reliable information about foreign markets. In the United States and Canada, a wide variety of information about industries, products, and markets is usually available from governmental sources, trade associations, and periodicals. For example, a food processor can obtain production figures for most products from the U.S. Department of Commerce; many special studies of consumption and distribution are prepared by the U.S. Department of Agriculture. *Food Topics* magazine prepares annual estimates of retail sales for a rather comprehensive list of detailed product classes. Other trade periodicals provide still further information about such problems as distribution, brand shares, and displays. With these sources of information, a company can develop a good basic market description and can evaluate trends in sales, prices, and competition.

Even in developed countries such as France and Italy, the relative lack of information is striking in comparison with the situation in North America. Often only the crudest kinds of estimates, based on purely subjective impressions, can be obtained. Government statistical agencies are seldom extensive or well developed; trade associations and publications typically provide little or no quantitative data. In underdeveloped countries, the situation is still worse.

As a result of the lack of public or semipublic market information, the firm entering a foreign market may decide to undertake special studies of its own. Here again, facilities in most countries outside North America leave much to be desired. Marketing research firms and syndicated information services, such as those described in Chapter 26, are less numerous, less experienced, and usually less reliable in other countries. In part, this reflects the relative lack of acceptance of the "marketing concept" by indigenous companies. Traditionally, these companies have tended to be secretive, to place less emphasis on marketing considerations, and to spend substantially less money on marketing information than those in North America.

A second distinctive aspect of appraising foreign markets is the need to consider (if possible, to anticipate) political and monetary conditions. If a company is concerned with evaluating relative market potential in Michigan and California, it can almost always ignore differences in state politics; and it can certainly assume that monetary values will not differ between the two areas. In contrast, suppose that a firm is attempting to appraise potential markets in the newer independent nations of Africa. Some consideration must be given to the following factors:

1. The possibilities of radical changes in government, perhaps leading to seizure of foreign assets (as in Cuba following the success of the Castro revolution) or to substantial changes in tax rates.
2. Changes in the value of a country's money. Rapid inflation, such as that in Chile during the 1950s, can totally disrupt an economy and seriously affect a company's sales and profits. Even "moderate" inflation may require costly special financial management techniques.
3. A country's present and future balance-of-payments situation, and its possible effects on tariffs, import-export controls, currency restrictions, and domestic economic policies.

Some United States firms have developed systematic procedures, such as rating scales, for developing appraisals of foreign markets. All these procedures rely ultimately on judgments about future events; there is no way to avoid entirely the inherent uncertainty associated with international marketing.

□ BASIC METHODS OF OPERATING IN FOREIGN MARKETS

There are several ways in which a company can market its products in foreign countries. These alternative methods differ in terms of investment and organizational requirements, costs, and degree of risk.

Exporting The simplest method of reaching foreign markets is by exporting products from the firm's home country. This can be done "indirectly," by utilizing specialized export-import middlemen, or "directly," by selling to distributors and/or industrial users in the foreign market. For small firms or those without experience in international operations, sales through specialized institutions are often preferable; the import-export middleman handles all problems of shipping, customs, duties, and insurance. For these services, the middleman is compensated by a percentage commission or discount.

Even direct exporting has severe limitations as a method of operation if a firm is seeking to develop large-scale markets in other countries, especially if there is active competition from other sellers. Many firms have appointed *exclusive distributors or agents* in foreign markets, and have tried to design methods of compensation, joint planning procedures, and other arrangements so as to make these distributors serve virtually as their own subsidiaries. But even under the best conditions it is very difficult to achieve real identity of interest between a distributor or agent, in one country, and the firm he represents, in another. Thus, the manufacturer often finds that the distributor's salesmen devote "too little" effort to his products, that the distributor is unwilling to spend "enough" on promotion, etc.[3] Dissatisfaction with these aspects of marketing through distributors and agents has led many international firms to establish their own marketing subsidiaries.

Subsidiaries A much greater commitment to a market is represented by the establishment of wholly owned subsidiaries. When a United States–based manufacturer sets up subsidiary companies in Western Europe, as many did in the 1950s and 1960s, it must provide capital and personnel for their operations and must accept the risk of incurring losses. Even when the products are still manufactured in the home market, the subsidiaries will require offices, warehousing facilities, a sales force, and management.

The main purpose of establishing subsidiaries is, of course, to provide "muscle" for a company's operations in a given market. The company's salesmen call directly on retailers and industrial users, it develops local promotional programs, and it has direct access to such areas as market information and local governmental agencies. The costs of providing all this can be justified only if a company's potential sales volume to this particular market is, actually or prospectively, "large enough." (Just how large is "enough" depends, naturally, on many factors.) Many companies operate subsidiaries in larger foreign markets, such as Canada, the Western European countries, and Japan, while continuing to sell through distributors in smaller or less wealthy nations.

A further step in the development of a firm's international operations is the establishment of overseas manufacturing facilities. In principle, this might be done independently of the marketing methods it employs; but in practice, the presence of a factory, or its equivalent in a service firm, makes a subsidiary operation more nearly self-sufficient. As a result, it is likely to develop a more complete, more locally oriented marketing organization and program than if it depends on imports. In the limit, the subsidiary becomes a virtually autonomous company, whose marketing activities may have little or no connection with those of the parent company.

Licensing and joint ventures Other basic methods of operating in foreign markets include licensing of local firms and joint ventures. A licensing agreement permits a company in another country to manufacture and sell a firm's products, in return for royalty fees. (Similar "franchising" arrangements can be used by retailing companies and service firms.) This approach involves relatively little commitment and little risk if results are unsatisfactory. On the

[3] Note that these problems are also present in relationships with independent distributors and agents within the domestic market, as mentioned in Chapter 17.

other hand, it entails very substantial risks if things turn out well. Quite a few United States–based companies established long-term licensing agreements in Europe prior to World War II, and even in the late 1940s, and then found themselves blocked from entry through the more profitable route of subsidiaries when the great boom of the 1950s began.

In a joint venture, a United States–based company joins with a local firm in a particular country to form a new, jointly owned manufacturing and/or marketing subsidiary. This approach can offer great advantages in terms of local knowledge and contacts, and possibly also in terms of pooling resources and technical skills. Many joint ventures have worked out unsatisfactorily, however, because of inherent conflicts of interest regarding control of operations, cost allocations, selection of personnel, and other matters.

Comparison of basic methods The choice of a proper marketing method for a given company in a given country at a given time depends on many factors, and it is difficult to generalize about the "best" solution. During the great expansion of international trade during the 1950s and 1960s, the general trend was toward fuller control of foreign marketing activities. This generally meant:

1. Establishment of more wholly owned subsidiaries
2. Substitution of subsidiaries for distributors, including acquisitions of previously independent distributors
3. Avoidance of licensing and joint venture arrangements, except when no other approach was feasible

These general tendencies were reflected in the experience of United States firms during the early 1960s. Companies responding to a survey conducted by Booz, Allen & Hamilton in 1964 reported that 70 percent of new foreign affiliates formed since 1951 were wholly owned.[4]

Organization for international marketing

Closely related to the selection of basic operating methods is the problem of designing an effective organization within the firm itself. As their international markets grew and became more competitive during the 1950s and 1960s, many firms found it necessary to make basic changes in their organization structures.

The problems of designing an organization for effective international operations are fundamentally the same as those involved in all organizations, as discussed in Chapter 23. There is the same basic need for dividing and specializing activities, the same interplay of functions, products, and geographic

[4] Booz, Allen & Hamilton, *New Foreign Business Activity of U.S. Firms,* New York, 1965.

areas as bases for dividing and specializing. Naturally, organization on the basis of areas is more important when a firm operates internationally: there are more areas, they are more diverse, and the distances involved are greater.

THE EXPORT DEPARTMENT

Even when a company's only international business is a limited volume of export sales, some organizational specialization is required to handle the orders, documents, etc. As mentioned earlier, these functions may be performed by specialized export-import distributors or agents. Within the firm, an export department will typically be established within the marketing or sales department. In a divisionalized, multiproduct company, each division may have its own export group.

THE INTERNATIONAL DIVISION

When the volume of international business becomes substantial, a more complex organization is naturally required. A common pattern among companies in the United States has been the establishment of an international division, responsible for all operations outside the home market. In its simplest form, the international division consists solely of *marketing* groups: subsidiary companies, affiliates, and perhaps licensees. Later, if manufacturing facilities are also established in foreign countries, these too may be assigned to the division.

Within the international division, responsibility for marketing is usually assigned primarily to individual subsidiaries or other units in the various countries. The division itself may provide certain staff services at the headquarters level, including such marketing services as marketing research.

An example of the "international division" approach is the organization of the General Electric Company prior to 1964.[5] In the early 1960s, G.E. had an International Group, composed of four main elements: the separately incorporated Canadian General Electric Company, the Compagnia Generale di Elettricita in Italy, a Manufacturing Subsidiaries Department, and the International General Electric Company (I.G.E.). This last company was responsible for exporting, for supervising licensing agreements, and for headquarters services. International Business Machines Corporation followed a similar approach when it established the I.B.M. World Trade Corporation in 1950.

THE "WORLD CORPORATION"

The evolution of an international division usually reflects increased importance of international business in a firm's overall operations. Formation of such a division, usually headed by a vice-president who reports to top company

[5] Based on a description given in *Organizing for Worldwide Operations,* Business International Research Report, Business International Corp., New York, 1965, pp. 15–19.

management, implies that international activities are "important enough" to warrant attention and effort on a level roughly equivalent to domestic business.

A further stage of development is reached by some firms in which international operations become so important and so complex that a different organizational arrangement may be needed. In some cases this has led to the adoption of a "world corporation" concept.

Basically the idea of a world corporation organization is that the company "looks at the entire world as its area of operations, and reaches out everywhere for markets, techniques, ideas, personnel, processes, and products. . . . It is organized so that no single national market or group of markets draws greater attention than its size dictates."[6]

Very few companies have yet achieved the status of true world corporations, either in organization structure or top management philosophy. But many observers feel that this is the direction in which major international companies will move in the future.

PRODUCTS AND AREAS

Within either an international division or a so-called world corporation, the division of responsibility and authority is almost always based on some combination of product lines and geographic areas. As stated earlier, for a variety of reasons some kind of organization must be established on the basis of individual countries. Beyond this, many companies have established regional groupings of countries as an intermediate organizational system. For example, in 1964 the Singer Company had regional divisions for the United States, Europe, Latin America, the Far East, Africa and the Near East, and Canada.

For diversified companies, there is a basic problem in organizing so as to provide effective specialization and control for both areas and product lines. Usually, the scale of operations for various product lines in various markets differs markedly, and it is extremely difficult to design an organization which properly reflects these variations while still providing for future growth.

These problems are reflected in a reorganization which General Electric made in 1964. This company, with around 100 different, diverse product departments and equally diverse positions in various national markets, sought to develop a new structure which would permit clear assignment of responsibilities and measures of performance, and still give a basis for substantial expansion of worldwide sales. The plan which was adopted included five regional divisions (Canada, Europe, Far East, Mediterranean, and Latin America), an International Business Development Group, and the existing I.G.E. which became an export group. In addition, each G.E. product depart-

[6] *Ibid.*, p. 13.

ment was given either "primary" or "supporting" responsibility for the conduct of its business outside the United States. Supporting responsibilities were given to the product departments in cases where their activities in a given region were on a small scale, and primary responsibility then was assigned to the regional divisions.[7]

Does this sound confusing? It is, and for a very good reason. In its reorganization, G.E. was trying to achieve specialization and control on the basis of both areas *and* products. Every large, diversified company selling various products, in various countries, with varying results has the same basic problem. The solution almost always involves some *combination* of product and area groupings. The solution is also almost always unstable; after several years, conditions will change, and further changes in the organization will eventually result.

HOW MUCH DECENTRALIZATION?

Whatever pattern of organization a company adopts for its international operations, it must also determine to what extent authority and responsibilities will be decentralized within the structure. As mentioned in Chapter 23, the centralization-decentralization controversy is a perpetual theme in all organizations, and there is probably no "permanent" solution to it.

In the context of international marketing, the basic arguments in favor of decentralization are reinforced by the inherent diversity of different national markets. It is claimed, for instance, that no central headquarters executive could possibly understand the special cultural, political, and competitive conditions of Japan *and* Italy *and* Brazil. This being so, the local subsidiary managers, or other representatives, should be given substantial autonomy for pricing, sales policies, etc.

There is obviously considerable merit in the argument for decentralization of marketing responsibilities within an international firm, and most companies have in fact given their subsidiaries, distributors, or other marketing entities considerable autonomy. In a study of nine major United States–based companies' operations in Western Europe, Richard Aylmer found that nearly 90 percent of all these firms' promotional decisions, and around 60 percent of their pricing decisions, were "unique local decisions based largely on local considerations."[8] Similarly, Millard Pryor of the Singer Company[9] has written that

> Marketing is conspicuous by its absence from the functions which can be planned at the corporate headquarters level. . . . The operating experience of many international firms

[7] *Ibid.*, pp. 17–20.
[8] Richard J. Aylmer, "Marketing Decisions in the Multinational Firm," unpublished doctoral thesis, Harvard Business School, 1968, pp. 209–210.
[9] "Planning in a Worldwide Business," *Harvard Business Review*, January–February, 1965, p. 137.

appears to confirm the desirability of assigning long-range planning of marketing activities to local managers.

Although marketing decision making has traditionally been highly decentralized in international companies, there was some tendency toward centralization during the 1950s and 1960s. One reason was the evolution of supranational trading groups, especially the European Economic Community. Thus, many United States–based firms established regional headquarters offices in Europe. These offices have varying degrees of authority over individual country operations. Sometimes they are purely staff coordinating groups, and in other cases they have line authority over subsidiary managers. In either case, the establishment of regional offices reflects recognition of the potential benefits of coordinating marketing programs on a multinational basis. The value of such coordination, and some of the limitations of achieving it, are discussed in the next two sections.

Multinational marketing coordination

When a company markets its products or services on a significant scale in several different national markets, it will naturally use somewhat different marketing strategies in these markets. But experience indicates that the international marketer will find it necessary or desirable to *coordinate* the decisions or policies adopted in some or all of the countries where it operates.[10]

Coordination of the marketing programs or "mixes" used in different countries involves both *standardization,* the use of the same or similar policies in several or many markets, and *harmonization,* the development of policies which take into account interdependencies among markets. There are several significant benefits in multinational coordination, from the viewpoint of the company as a whole. These include possible cost savings, consistency with customers, greater utilization of good ideas, and improved planning and control.

□ COST SAVINGS

One important objective of coordination in multinational marketing is that of achieving cost savings. When each country is allowed complete independence, the result is often unnecessary duplication and high costs. The most obvious, and usually the most important, area for cost savings is product design. By offering the same basic product in several markets with some possible variations in functional and/or design features, a manufacturer can frequently achieve longer production runs, spread research and development costs over a greater volume, and thus reduce total unit costs.

[10] This section is based on Robert D. Buzzell, "Can You Standardize Multinational Marketing?" *Harvard Business Review,* November–December, 1968, pp. 102–113.

An example of multinational standardization in product design was the development of a new line of automatic washing machines by Hoover Ltd., the leading producer in the United Kingdom, in the mid-1960s. Hoover's previous automatic washers, introduced in 1961, were designed primarily for the British market. These "Keymatic" models featured:

An exclusive "pulsator" washing action
A tilted, enameled steel drum
Hot water provided by the home's central hot-water heater

In contrast, most European manufacturers offered front-loading, tumble-action washers with stainless-steel drums and self-contained water heaters. Either because these features were better suited to continental needs or because so many sellers promoted them, or perhaps both, Hoover saw its position in major continental markets decline. The company's situation became especially difficult in 1963–1964, when Italian manufacturers began marketing their machines aggressively throughout Europe.

During the late 1950s and early 1960s, the Italian appliance firms had installed modern, highly automated equipment, reinvested profits, and produced relatively simple, standardized products in great numbers. By 1965, refrigerator output was estimated at 2.6 million units, and washing machine output at 1.5 million units. Much of this volume was sold in Italy; home ownership of the two appliances rose to 50 percent and 23 percent, respectively. But the Italian companies were aggressive in export marketing, too; by 1965 Italian-made refrigerators accounted for 32 percent of the total French market and for 40 to 50 percent of the Benelux market. Even in Germany, the home market of such electrical giants as AEG, Bosch, and Siemens, the Italian products attained a 12 percent market share.

The success of the Italian appliance industry was a painful experience for the traditional leaders—American, British, and German—as well as for the smaller French companies that had previously had tariff protection. Whirlpool Corporation, which acquired a French refrigerator plant in 1962, subsequently leased the facility to a French competitor. Even Frigidaire decided, in mid-1967, to close down its refrigerator production in France.

To compete with this "Italian invasion," Hoover first purchased front-loading washers from an Italian producer for sale under the Hoover brand. Later in 1965, the company set out to design its own new-product line. It decided to look for a single basic design that would meet the needs of housewives in France, Germany, and Scandinavia as well as in the United Kingdom. A committee including representatives of the continental subsidiaries and of the parent company, Hoover Worldwide Corporation (New York), spent many weeks finding mutually acceptable specifications for the new line.

The resulting machine, which went on sale in the spring of 1967, was a front-loading, tumble-action machine closer in concept to the "continental" design than Hoover's previous washers, but with provisions for "hot-water fill" and enameled steel drums on models to be sold in the United Kingdom. By standardizing most of the key design elements in the new machine, Hoover was able to make substantial savings in development costs, tooling, and unit production costs.

The potential economies of standardization are not confined solely to product design decisions. In some industries, packaging costs represent a significant part of total costs. Here, too, standardization may offer the possibility of savings. Charles R. Williams cites the case of a food processor selling prepared soups throughout Europe in 11 different packages. He observes, "The company believes it could achieve a significant savings in cost and at the same time reduce consumer confusion by standardizing the packaging."[11]

Still another area for cost savings is that of advertising. For some of the major package goods manufacturers, the production of artwork, films, and other advertising materials costs millions of dollars annually. Although differences in language limit the degree of standardization that can be imposed, some common elements can often be used. For example, Pepsi-Cola is sold in 110 countries outside the United States. Part of the foreign advertising is done by films. According to one of the company's top marketing executives, "We have found that it is possible . . . to produce commercial films overseas in one market, if planned properly, for use in most (but not all) of our international markets." According to company estimates, the added cost of producing separate films for each market would be $8 million per year.[12]

All these examples illustrate the same basic point: standardization of product design, packaging, and promotional materials can offer important economies to the multinational marketer. Even if these cost savings are attained at the expense of lower sales in some markets, the net effect on profits may be positive.

□

CONSISTENCY WITH CUSTOMERS

Quite apart from the possibilities of cost reduction, some multinational companies are moving toward standardization in order to achieve consistency in their dealings with customers. Executives of these companies believe that consistency in product style, in sales and customer service, in brand names and packages, and generally in the "image" projected to customers is a powerful means of increasing sales.

[11] "Regional Management Overseas," *Harvard Business Review*, January–February, 1967, p. 89.
[12] See Norman Heller, "How Pepsi-Cola Does It in 110 Countries," in John S. Wright and Jack L. Goldstucker (eds.), *New Ideas for Successful Marketing*, American Marketing Association, 1966, Chicago, p. 700.

If all customers lived incommunicado behind their respective national frontiers, there would be no point in worrying about this matter; only diplomatic couriers and border-crossing guards would ever notice any inconsistencies in products, services, or promotion. But in reality, of course, this is not the case. The most visible type of cross-border flow is international travel by tourists and businessmen. Especially in Europe, with its relatively high income levels and short distances, the number of people visiting other countries reached flood proportions in the 1960s, and shows no sign of abating. If the German tourist in Spain sees his accustomed brands in the store, he is likely to buy them during his visit. More important, his reexposure to the products and their advertising may strengthen his loyalty back home or, at least, protect him from the temptation to change his allegiance to a competitor.

Then there is the flow of communications across boundaries. Magazines, newspapers, radio and television broadcasts—all of which include advertising—reach international audiences. For example, according to estimates made by Young & Rubicam International in the mid-1960s,[13]

> German television broadcasts are received by 40 percent of Dutch homes with TV sets.
>
> *Paris Match* has a circulation of 85,000 in Belgium, 26,000 in Switzerland, and substantial readership in Luxemburg, Germany, Italy, and Holland.
>
> On an average day, over 4 million French housewives turn to Radio Luxemburg; the same broadcast reaches 620,000 Belgian housewives, 30,000 in Switzerland, and 100,000 in Holland.

The possibility of reaching multimarket audiences with common advertising messages, and the risk of confusion that may result from reaching such audiences with different brand names and promotional appeals, has led some of the major consumer goods producers to explore ways and means of standardizing at least the basic elements of their European campaigns.

The Nestlé Company, Inc., and Unilever Ltd., probably the most experienced multinational consumer goods firms, both moved in the direction of more "unified" European advertising during the 1960s. When Nestlé launched "New Nescafé" in 1961–1962, for example, the same basic theme ("fresh-ground aroma") and very similar creative treatments were used not only throughout Europe, but also in other markets such as Australia. The value of this approach is, perhaps, reflected in the fact that several years ago Nescafé was the leading brand of instant coffee in every European country.

During the 1960s an additional argument for consistency in marketing strategy emerged: the needs of the multinational customer. Increasingly, both consumer and industrial goods manufacturers find themselves selling to companies which themselves operate on a multinational scale. Industrial users, retail chains, and wholesalers with operations in several countries may buy cen-

[13] "When Is a Frontier Not a Frontier?," Brussels, May, 1966 (pamphlet).

trally; even if they do not, personnel in one country often have had experience in other countries, or communicate with their counterparts in these countries. In either case, there is a strong pressure on the seller to offer similar products, prices, and services in each market.

Because so many of its customers are international companies, IBM has standardized the services provided to customers, the duties and training of sales and service personnel, and even the organization of branch offices, on a worldwide basis. A major reason for this policy is the need to provide the same level of service to major customers, such as international banks, in each of the several countries where they do business with IBM.

In some industries, multinational customers virtually force suppliers to standardize products, prices, and terms of sale. If a better deal is available in one country than another, the customer may find it worthwhile to transship goods and will do so.

In certain industries, trade and professional associations exert a pressure toward standardization similar to that exerted by multinational customers. Engineers, chemists, doctors, computer programmers, as well as many other groups hold conferences, publish journals, and exchange ideas on an international basis. One result is that companies selling products to professional and technical groups find it advantageous to standardize their offerings and operating methods.

□

EXPLOITING GOOD IDEAS

A third argument for standardization is that good marketing ideas and people are hard to find, and should therefore be used as widely as possible. Moreover, good ideas tend to have a universal appeal. This point of view is held especially strongly with regard to the "creative" aspects of advertising and promotional programs. Arthur C. Fatt, chairman of the board and chief executive officer of Grey Advertising, Inc., states[14]:

> A growing school of thought holds that even different peoples are basically the same, and that an international advertising campaign with a truly universal appeal can be effective in any market. . . . If an advertiser has a significant advertising idea at work in one country, not only may it be wasteful but often "suicidal" to change this idea just for the sake of change.

The key word in this statement is "significant." It is the scarcity of really good or significant ideas that encourages standardization. It may be easy to find creative concepts of average quality in each of many different national markets, but really new or unique approaches are not so easily matched.

During the 1960s there were several widely discussed examples of suc-

[14] "The Danger of 'Local' International Advertising," *Journal of Marketing*, January, 1967, pp. 61–62.

cessful application of common advertising themes:

Esso's "Put a Tiger in Your Tank" campaign, with very minor changes in art and wording, was used from Southeast Asia to Switzerland. The tiger is, of course, an internationally recognizable symbol for power.

Avis Rent-A-Car has used minor variations on its "We Try Harder" theme throughout Europe, as well as in the United States.

Magazine advertisements for Playtex brassieres in many different countries featured the same "stop-action" photographic demonstration of the product's strength and dependability. Although attitudes toward undergarments vary from country to country, Young & Rubicam, Inc., the Playtex agency, believed that there was a segment in each market for which this appeal is effective.

But even the most ardent proponents of the theory that "good ideas are universal" recognize the need to apply the concept with care. Approaches shown to be effective in one market are likely to be effective elsewhere, but they do not necessarily apply across the board.

□

IMPROVED PLANNING AND CONTROL

Flows of people and information across national boundaries may affect multinational marketing strategy in still another way. Consider the following situation[15]:

Philips Gloeilampenfabrieken, one of the world's largest producers of electrical products, found that prices of some of its appliances in Holland were being undercut by as much as 30 percent by the company's own German subsidiary. How did this come to pass? The German subsidiary had lower costs than the Dutch plant, and sold at lower prices to meet the more intensive competition of the German appliance market. Wholesalers buying from Philips in Germany had a further incentive to sell to outside customers on account of a 7 percent export subsidy given by the German government. To complete the circle, a European Economic Community antitrust ruling prohibited manufacturers from interfering with the rights of independent distributors to export freely within the Common Market. Consequently, there was little that Philips could do except to "equalize" prices in the two countries or live with the new sourcing arrangements.

Philips' experience illustrates the difficulty of orderly planning and control by top management if a subsidiary or distributor in country A is subject to the risk of unpredictable competition from his counterparts in nearby countries B, C, and D.

The feasibility of transshipments among markets obviously varies from one industry to another, depending on the value/weight ratio of the products. Thus, transshipping is common for such items as scientific instruments, cameras, and precision equipment, but relatively rare for major electric appliances. Even in the food trade, however, cross-border sales increased in volume considerably during the 1960s.

[15] Reported in *Business Europe,* Aug. 23, 1967, p. 1.

Effective control of transshipping requires *harmonization* of pricing policies in the multinational company. This does not necessarily mean equalizing prices at either the wholesale or retail level, for if a company's prices to dealers and/or distributors are the same in all countries, then the incentive for transshipping will be eliminated. Rather, it means some adjustments and compromises for the sake of consistency in pricing at the retail and wholesale levels.

Differences among national markets

Despite the potential benefits of standardization, the great majority of companies still operate on the premise that each national market is different and must therefore be provided with its own distinctive marketing program.

Why is diversity still the rule of the day in multinational marketing? In many cases, differences simply reflect customary ways of doing business which have evolved in an earlier period when national boundaries were more formidable barriers than they are today. But even if tradition did not play a role, it must be recognized that there are and will continue to be some important obstacles to standardization.

A comprehensive list of these obstacles would fill many pages, and would include many factors that affect only one or two industries. The most important and generally applicable factors are summarized in Figure 24-1. The rows in this chart represent the major classes of factors which limit standardization in multinational marketing strategies. The columns correspond to different elements of a marketing program, and the "cells" in the table illustrate the ways in which the various factors affect each program element. In effect, each cell represents a condition or characteristic which may differ sufficiently among countries, and may require variations in marketing strategies. As we shall see presently, the experiences of multinational companies afford numerous examples of these barriers to standardization. Let us look briefly at each of the four major factors limiting standardization that are listed in Figure 24-1.

□

MARKET CHARACTERISTICS

Perhaps the most permanent differences among national markets are those arising from the physical environment: climate, topography, and resources (row 1 of Figure 24-1). Climate has an obvious effect on the sales potential for many products, and may also require differences in packaging. Topography influences the density of population, and this in turn may have a strong influence on the distribution system available to a manufacturer.

The cell in Figure 24-1 labeled "Product use conditions" includes a wide variety of environmental factors affecting marketing strategies. Differences in the size and configuration of homes, for example, have an important bearing on product design for appliances and home furnishings. European kitchens are typically small by United States standards, and there is seldom any basement space available to apartment dwellers for laundry facilities. As a result, there is a great emphasis on compactness of design in automatic washers, for they must somehow be fitted into a small and already crowded area. As noted in the example of Hoover Ltd., given earlier, washing machines must also be equipped with self-contained water-heating systems to compensate for the lack of central hot-water heaters in most continental homes.

Industrial goods manufacturers also frequently encounter differences in product use conditions. The following examples illustrate this fact:

A United States producer of farm equipment found that one of his pieces of machinery could not be moved through the narrow, crooked streets of French and Belgian farm villages.

Concluding that there is more dissimilarity than similarity in industrial marketing in Europe, a chemical industry marketing researcher writes[16]: "(A factor) which would severely affect the market for surface coatings is the fact that materials used in building construction are vastly different in various parts of Europe. Brick, mortar, and tile are used predominantly in Southern Europe, whereas this is not the case in Northern Germany and in Benelux."

Many similar examples could be cited of differences in the environment which call for variations in product design and other aspects of marketing policy.

Development stage Differences among countries in stages of economic and industrial development also have a profound influence on marketing strategies. Because of the wide gaps in per capita income levels, many products or models which are regarded as inexpensive staples in the United States or Western Europe must be marketed as "luxuries" elsewhere. Even among the industrialized countries, income differences are substantial: appliance manufacturers such as Philco-Ford Corporation and Kelvinator of Canada, Ltd., find themselves with little choice but to position their products as deluxe, relatively high-priced items. This, in turn, implies a very different marketing strategy from that used in the United States.

For industrial products, differences in economic development are reflected in variations in relative costs of capital and labor. For example, General Electric Company and other companies have sold numerical controls for machine tools to United States factories primarily on the basis of labor cost savings. The same approach may be suitable in Germany, where there is a critical shortage of labor. But in most other countries it would be far more difficult to justify numerical controls on the basis of labor substitution.

[16] William Gerunsky, "International Marketing Research," in N. H. Giragosian (ed.), *Chemical Marketing Research,* Reinhold Publishing Corporation, New York, 1967, p. 258.

FIGURE 24-1

Classification of differences among national markets and their effects in marketing policies

	Elements of marketing program	
Factors limiting standardization	Product design	Pricing
Market characteristics		
Physical environment	Climate Product use conditions	
Stage of economic and industrial development	Income levels Labor costs in relation to capital costs	Income levels
Cultural factors	"Custom and tradition" Attitudes toward foreign goods	Attitudes toward bargaining
Industry conditions		
Stage of product life cycle in each market	Extent of product differentiation	Elasticity of demand
Competition	Quality levels	Local costs Prices of substitutes
Marketing institutions		
Distributive system	Availability of outlets	Prevailing margins
Advertising media and agencies		
Legal restrictions	Product standards Patent laws Tariffs and taxes	Tariffs and taxes Antitrust laws Resale price maintenance

Differences in income levels may suggest the desirability of systematic price variations. As explained earlier, many companies do charge different prices in different countries, but these variations are seldom, if ever, based solely on incomes.

Consumer shopping patterns and purchase quantities, too, tend to vary with stages of economic development. In underdeveloped countries, there are typically many small retail stores and many consumers who buy in smaller quantities than do those in highly developed nations. For instance, cigarettes and razor blades are bought one at a time in some countries. Even in England, according to one international marketing executive, "the smallest size of detergent available in U.S. supermarkets is the largest size available in the United Kingdom."

Distribution	Sales force	Advertising and promotion; branding and packaging
Customer mobility	Dispersion of customers	Access to media Climate
Consumer shopping patterns	Wage levels, availability of manpower	Needs for convenience rather than economy Purchase quantities
Consumer shopping patterns	Attitudes toward selling	Language, literacy Symbolism
Availability of outlets Desirability of private brands	Need for missionary sales effort	Awareness, experience with products
Competitors' control of outlets	Competitors' sales forces	Competitive expenditures, messages
Number and variety of outlets available	Number, size, dispersion of outlets	Extent of self-service
Ability to "force" distribution	Effectiveness of advertising, need for substitutes	Media availability, costs, overlaps
Restrictions on product lines Resale price maintenance	General employment restrictions Specific restrictions on selling	Specific restrictions on messages, costs Trademark laws

Finally, variations in wage levels may affect choices between personal selling and other forms of promotional effort. One relatively small Italian food processor has a sales force as large as that of General Foods Corporation in the United States. Presumably salesmen's salaries are proportionately less.

Cultural factors This category is a convenient catchall for the many differences in market structure and behavior that cannot readily be explained in terms of more tangible factors. Consider, for example, the figures in Table 24-1, which are taken from a recent survey made by the European Economic Community's Statistical Office. Why do French households consume more than 50 times as much wine as Dutch households, but only two-thirds as much milk? No doubt these differences could be explained historically in terms of

TABLE 24-1

Average household consumption of beverages, 1963–1964, selected nations (liters per Household)

Country	Milk	Wine	Beer
France	103	116	28
Germany	100	7	46
Holland	153	2	11
Italy	87	95	2

Source: *Le Monde,* weekly overseas edition, Feb. 15–21, 1968, p. 7.

variations in water, soil, and so on. But for practical purposes, it is usually sufficient, and certainly more efficient, simply to take differences in consumption patterns and attitudes as given, and to adjust to them.

There are many examples of cultural differences that have affected marketing success or failure. One cultural factor is the attitude of consumers toward "foreign" goods. This fact is illustrated by the following experience.

Princess Housewares, Inc., a large United States appliance manufacturer, introduced a line of electric housewares in the German market. The company's brand name was well known and highly regarded in the United States, but relatively unknown in Germany; and the brand had a definitely "American" sound. The company discovered that the American association was a real drawback among German consumers.

According to a survey, fewer than 40 percent of German individuals felt "confident" about electrical products made in the United States, compared with 91 percent who were "confident" of German-made products.

Lack of brand awareness, coupled with suspicion of the quality of "American" products, required the company to adopt a very different marketing strategy in Germany than that employed in the United States, where both awareness and a quality image were taken for granted.

INDUSTRY CONDITIONS

A convenient framework for comparing industry and competitive conditions in different national markets is that of the "product life cycle." As explained, the histories of many different products in the United States suggest that most of them pass through several distinct stages over a period of years, and that marketing strategies typically change from stage to stage.

Some products are in different stages of their life cycles in different national markets. In the late 1960s, vacuum cleaners were owned by over 75 percent of the households in Great Britain, Germany, and Switzerland, for example, but by only 10 percent of the households in Italy and 45 percent in France. Even more marked contrasts exist for some newer types of products, such as electric toothbrushes and electric carving knives, which are widely owned in the United States but virtually unknown in most other countries. Such differences in life-cycle stages usually call for adaptations of "home country" marketing approaches, if not for completely separate strategies. If products are in different stages of their life cycles in different countries, then it is tempting to conclude that marketing strategies used in the past in the more "advanced" countries should be used in other "follower" nations. There is some evidence to support this conclusion. For instance, as described earlier, the Italian appliance manufacturers have successfully employed strategies similar to those of Henry Ford in the United States automotive industry in the early 1900s. However, history does not repeat itself exactly, and past marketing strategies cannot be reapplied without some modifications.

Competitive practices Another important industry condition, partly but not entirely related to the product life cycle, is the extent of competition in each national market. Differences in products, costs, prices, and promotional levels may permit or even require differences in the strategies used by a multinational company in various markets. Even within the European Common Market, there are still substantial variations in prices of many products, reflecting in part traditional differences in the degree of competition. A survey made in 1967 by the European Economic Community's Statistical Office showed that price variations were then still substantial within the market. Typical prices were compared for some 125 different consumer products by country; on the average, the difference between prices in the countries with the highest and lowest prices was 58 percent. Even the price of a staple item such as aspirin varied from a high of $0.38 in Germany to a low of $0.22 in Holland.

MARKETING INSTITUTIONS

The multinational company's opportunities in each market depend critically on the marketing institutions available in each country, including retail and wholesale outlets and advertising media and agencies. Some of the most drastic revisions in strategy made by United States–based companies overseas have been imposed by the lack of adequate supermarkets, retail chains, and commercial television. Differences in the number, size, and dispersion of distributive outlets call for differences in promotional methods; and differences in prevailing wholesale and/or retail margins may require vastly different price and discount structures. Some of these variations in institutional systems are related to legal regulations, especially in the area of resale price maintenance.

As in the case of competitive practices, traditional disparities in marketing institutions have narrowed considerably since 1945. For instance, one element of the "Americanization" of Europe is the spread of chains, supermarkets, and other United States–style institutions of distribution. In "borrowing" these methods from the United States, the Europeans add their own modifications; their supermarkets are not as large, they rely on walk-in neighborhood trade rather than on vast parking lots, their average transactions are smaller, and there are other adaptations. But there is a clear trend toward similarity in distributive systems.

The combination of continued differences in marketing institutions now with the prospect of greater similarities in the future creates come difficult problems for multinational marketers.

□

LEGAL RESTRICTIONS

Different countries require or permit very different practices in the areas of product design, competitive practices, pricing, employment, and advertising. They also impose differing taxes and tariffs, and multinational companies often follow devious paths in the attempt to minimize the total cost effects of these levies. Obviously, such practices can be stumbling blocks for the would-be standardizer.

Some product standards, though ostensibly designed for purposes of safety, are used by governments as a device for protecting home industries. A notable case in point was the imposition of new regulations for electric appliances by France in 1967, along with delays in issuing approvals. This was generally regarded as a deliberate move to slow down the onslaught of competition by the Italian companies and thus give the domestic industry a breathing space.

But other legal restrictions are established for more legitimate purposes. The use of a 220-volt electrical system in Europe, for example, has led to a stringent set of safety standards for such products as irons—more stringent than United States standards. Cord connections must be stronger, and shielding against radio interference is necessary. These requirements, in turn, dictate modifications in product design.

Resale price maintenance and other laws designed to protect small retailers still have a strong influence on distribution policies in many countries. The trend has been away from restrictions of this kind, however, and some nations, such as the United Kingdom, have virtually abolished price maintenance.

Custom and legislative regulation combine to discourage some types of advertising and promotion. Goodyear Tire & Rubber Company, for instance, demonstrated the strength of its "3T" tire cord in the United States by showing a steel chain breaking. In Germany, this visualization was not permitted because it was regarded as disparaging to the steel chain manufacturers.[17] Such exaggerated sensitivity may be amusing, but it cannot be ignored in planning advertising campaigns.

[17] *Advertising Age,* May 9, 1966, p. 75.

CONCLUSION

Traditionally, marketing strategy has been regarded as a strictly local problem in each national market. Differences in customer needs and preferences, in competition, in institutional systems, and in legal regulations have seemed to require basically different marketing programs. Any similarity between countries has been seen as purely coincidental.

There is no doubt that differences among nations are still great, and that these differences should be recognized in marketing planning. But the experiences of a growing number of multinational companies suggest that there are also some real potential gains in an integrated approach to marketing strategy. Standardization of products, packages, and promotional approaches may permit substantial cost savings as well as greater consistency in dealings with customers. The harmonization of price policies often facilitates better internal planning and control. Finally, if good ideas are scarce, and if some of them have universal appeal, they should be used as widely as possible.

All this adds up to the conclusion that both the pros *and* the cons of standardization in multinational marketing programs should be considered, and that a company's decisions should be based on estimated overall revenues and costs. Obviously, each case must be considered on its own merits—slogans and formulas are not very helpful guides to intelligent planning.

Questions

1. How do you account for the differences in the level of wine and beer consumption shown in Table 24-1? As a French wine producer, do you think it would be possible to expand sales in Germany? What specific questions would you want to answer before making such a decision?

2. The degree of consumer use of disposable diapers ranges from over 90 percent of all "changes" in Sweden, to 30 to 45 percent in other Scandinavian countries, to 15 percent in the United States, and to only 2 percent in Great Britain.

   a. What factors do you think account for the wide variation in consumer acceptance of disposable diapers?

   b. As a major manufacturer of disposable diapers, what could you do to develop greater market acceptance? Would you use the same approach in the United States as in Great Britain? Why or why not?

3. Historically, Coca-Cola has insisted that its product specifications for Coca-Cola, such as sweetness, carbonation, taste, be identical in all markets. What benefits might the company realize by relaxing this policy?

4. Under what circumstances should a firm sell its products in export markets at a price below or above the price charged in domestic markets? Should the

price differential ever exceed extra charges for shipping costs, tariffs, and higher selling costs? Discuss.

5. As suggested in the text, Nestlé has been very successful in employing the same basic promotional theme (fresh-ground aroma) and similar creative approaches throughout Europe and other markets. What dangers do you see in this approach? How could Nestlé guard against these dangers?

6. In 1959, Ing C. Olivetti & C., S.p.A., one of the world's leading producers of typewriters, calculators, and other business machines, purchased working control of the Underwood Corporation. Underwood was a major United States typewriter manufacturer which had encountered serious financial problems during the 1950s. Discussing Olivetti's decision to acquire Underwood, Adriano Olivetti expressed the following view of the responsibilities of a multinational company[18]:

> You cannot be a business "visitor" over a certain size. It isn't fair to just take all that money out of the economy—any economy, even as strong and as rich an economy as the United States. You also have to make a contribution to the economy. Moreover, quite beyond such ethical considerations, if you ignore the responsibility of contributing to an economy, something will happen to stop you. National economies have various ways of protecting this fairness.

a. Do you agree or disagree with Adriano Olivetti's statement? Why?
b. Why is it more of a contribution to the economy of a country to manufacture products within the country rather than to export them to it?
c. Would it be more of a contribution to manufacture products within a country even if the limited volume of business available might lead to costs two or three times as high as those possible if the product were manufactured elsewhere? Why?
d. In view of prevalent attitudes of nationalism in many countries, do you think Olivetti would be wise to set up wholly owned subsidiaries as it expands its manufacturing activities around the world?

7. A number of United States corporations export products which have been prohibited from sale domestically. Chemical companies, for example, may export DDT formulations which are not salable in the United States. Similarly, pharmaceutical companies sometimes export drugs which have not been approved by the FDA. Do you think such policies should be continued? Why?

8. A certain company found that there is conflict between the laws of a

[18]Edmund P. Learned, C. Roland Christensen, Kenneth R. Andrews, and William R. Guth, *Business Policy: Text and Cases,* rev. ed., Richard D. Irwin, Inc., Homewood, Ill., 1969, p. 950.

country in which a wholly owned subsidiary operates and the laws in the country in which the parent company is domiciled.

a. What policies should the subsidiary follow? Would your answer differ if the subsidiary were only partially owned? If it were a joint venture? Why?

b. Suppose the host country was anxious to expand exports and there would be substantial economies of scale to expanded operations. Should the subsidiary attempt to build its export sales? What problems might this cause? How could they be reconciled?

Marketing information and analysis

PART FIVE

The two chapters in this part deal with the use of information in marketing management. The importance of information to marketing decision makers should be apparent from our discussion of marketing programs in Part 4. Every element of the program—product, price, distribution channels, and methods of promotion—must be designed to meet the needs of the market(s) that an organization serves. Often, one or more components of a program must be tested in order to determine how well it meets market needs. Then, after a program has been developed, its performance must be measured and periodically reappraised.

At each stage in the process of marketing program design, testing, and evaluation, the manager needs information. He needs to know who and where his potential customers are, in terms of such factors as age, sex, and family size, or in terms of industry and size of company. He needs to know what customers think of his products, where they shop, what factors they consider in making purchase decisions, what his competitors are doing—the list of information needs is long and varied. Moreover, the manager needs more than just raw facts and figures to make effective decisions. He must also analyze the facts and figures and relate them to his marketing problems and opportunities.

Throughout Part 4 we illustrated the ways in which information is used in management. We discussed product testing and test marketing, in connection with new product development; the problems of estimating price elasticity; the need to stay abreast of changes in channel networks; the difficulties of measuring advertising results; and many other examples. Now, in Part 5, we shall consider some of the general problems that arise in deciding what information is needed, how to obtain it, and how to use it.

Chapter 25 deals with marketing research—the use of formal, systematic methods to obtain information, identify relationships, and predict market behavior. In Chapter 26, we discuss the measurement of marketing "performance," and show how information obtained both from research studies and from regular company accounting and reporting systems is employed to evaluate the results of marketing activities. The division of content between the two chapters corresponds roughly to one of "before" and "after"—Chapter 25 deals primarily with the collection and analysis of information prior to management action, and Chapter 26 with the measurement of results after a program has been implemented.

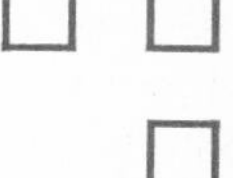

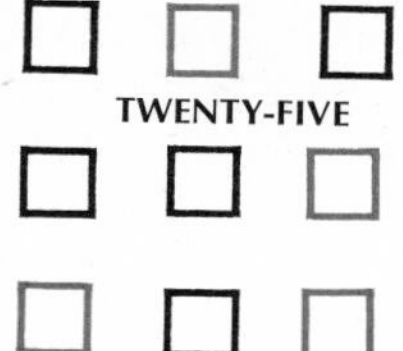

Marketing research

Throughout Part 4, we stressed the point that effective marketing management requires knowledge of the market. Every marketing decision, whether it involves the design of a new product, a price change, or the development of an advertising campaign, is based on some assumptions about how customers, distributors, and competitors will respond to a company's actions.

How does a manager know what the market needs and how it will respond? In many cases, the knowledge comes from direct observation and experience. For example, a machine tool manufacturer may learn about needed modifications in a milling machine through a salesman's direct contacts with customers. Ultimately, if the modified product is suitable for enough customers, a new product is born and becomes part of the manufacturer's regular line. In the same way, an advertising executive may get ideas for a new creative approach by hearing his own friends and acquaintances talk about a product, how they use it, and what they think of current television commercials.

Direct observation and experience are especially important means of ascertaining market needs in the early stages of an organization's history. Most businesses, and most nonprofit organizations too, are initially set up to meet needs that the founders identify by direct, personal observation. Thus, Henry Ford was convinced in the early twentieth century that there would be a large demand for a simple, low-priced, mass-produced automobile. The histories of most firms have followed a similar pattern: the perception of some basic need and the effort, often prolonged and difficult, to meet it in an economically viable way.[1]

While observation and experience are still important ways of identifying market needs, they are often insufficient, and sometimes actually misleading. Especially in large companies, the decision maker is typically too far removed from customers to observe them directly. Moreover, once an organization is faced with competition seeking to serve the same customers, it becomes increasingly difficult to find unmet needs. For these reasons, the relatively simple approach followed by Henry Ford is not adequate for his successors who manage the Ford Motor Company in the 1970s. They must concern themselves with the preferences and living patterns of millions of customers in markets throughout the world; and they must develop products and marketing programs that will gain acceptance over those of powerful, aggressive competitors. To do so, they need a much more formal and systematic way of obtaining information about the market.

This chapter deals with marketing research, the principal means by which marketing managers get and use information about customers, competitors, and distribution channels, as a basis for identifying marketing problems and opportunities and for making decisions. First, we discuss the role of marketing research in management and show how a decision-maker's information needs should be determined. Then, we review the steps involved in planning research. Finally, in the last section of the chapter, we discuss some of the most important methods for collecting marketing information.

The role of marketing research

Marketing research is one of several major sources of information for marketing management. Other important sources include an organization's accounting records, other internal reports, such as those submitted by salesmen, and, as mentioned earlier, executives' own contacts with the market. What distinguishes marketing research from these other sources of information?

□

WHAT IS MARKETING RESEARCH?

It is difficult, if not impossible, to distinguish precisely between "research" and other methods of obtaining marketing information. In many companies, the term research is applied to the activities of designated staff specialists (the marketing research department) who have special kinds of training, and who use

[1] We have mentioned other examples in earlier chapters, including that of the Head Ski Company (Chapter 1) and Michael "King" Cullen, originator of the supermarket concept (Chapter 11).

☐ *Marketing research is the use of formalized procedures, based on the principles of the scientific method, especially on statistical techniques, to collect and analyze information relevant to marketing problems.*

more complex techniques to collect and analyze data than others in the organization. The core of these methods, it is hoped, is the use of the "scientific method." But it is not always true that research is scientific, or that other procedures are unscientific.

Any definition of marketing research is, therefore, somewhat arbitrary. Granting this, we believe that the definition given is a useful one.☐[2]

☐

HOW RESEARCH AIDS MANAGEMENT

Information provided by marketing research contributes to effective marketing management in several ways. First, it can serve as an "early warning signal" to identify problems or opportunities for improved performance. To illustrate, one of the most important types of research for consumer goods manufacturers is regular, periodic measurement of consumer purchases. Because most producers of consumer products sell through wholesalers and/or chains, their own sales records do not reflect current trends in sales at the consumer level. A shift in market shares, for example in the hair grooming product category, would not be apparent to the manufacturer until some weeks after it occurred, if he waited for it to show up in his own shipments to the trade. Moreover, the manufacturer has no way of knowing what changes are occurring in the *total* market for his product, unless he obtains information from sources outside his own sales records. Thus, a company marketing a hair grooming cream would have no quantitative measure of the growth in "gel-type" products, and might miss an opportunity to enter this segment of the market, if he did not employ research to measure consumer purchases.

Most large consumer products manufacturers recognize the need to measure ultimate consumer purchases of their own and competing products, and employ one or more of several commercial services for this purpose. Some of the methods used to collect purchase data are described briefly in a later section of this chapter.

A second way in which research contributes to management is by providing *detailed information* about specific problems. Once management recognizes a potential problem or opportunity, there is usually a need to explore it in greater depth. For example, if a soft drink producer learns that "low-calorie" beverages are gaining in importance, he might seek further information about who is buying the products, what product features are important to consumers, how they respond to different advertising themes, and so forth. Some of this information may be available from informal contacts with retailers, advertising agency personnel, or other sources, but to get adequate knowledge of the situation some special effort will almost surely be required.

[2] Cf. Robert D. Buzzell, Donald F. Cox, and Rex V. Brown, *Marketing Research and Information Systems: Text and Cases*, McGraw-Hill Book Company, New York, 1969, p. 15.

Marketing research also provides managers with *forecasts* of future conditions. Estimates of past and current market situations are useful, but management action must usually be designed to meet future market requirements, especially when there is a significant "lead time" between a decision and its implementation, as in the case of new product development (see Chapter 15).

Forecasts developed via marketing research may deal only with market conditions, such as industry sales and price levels, or they may be designed to provide estimates of the results of specific marketing programs or decisions. For instance, as mentioned in Chapter 17, research may be undertaken to estimate the effects of a price change.

□

ACCURACY OF RESEARCH RESULTS

Many managers are critical of marketing research on the grounds that research results are often inaccurate. It is certainly true that the information obtained through research seldom provides complete or infallible answers to the underlying management problems. The results of research are always in the form of *estimates*. They reduce risk only to the extent that the estimates are better than those available otherwise. Moreover, although scientific methods are generally used in conducting research, there is necessarily a substantial element of subjective judgment involved too, particularly in forecasting future market behavior.

A classic illustration of the uncertainty inherent in predicting market behavior, even when research is extensively employed, is the history of Corfam, a man-made material developed by Du Pont as a substitute for leather. Du Pont introduced Corfam as a material for shoes in the early 1960s, and spent millions of dollars promoting it. Prior to the introduction, the company had conducted surveys among some 15,000 consumers who wore test versions of Corfam shoes. In addition, Du Pont's marketing researchers developed an elaborate statistical model for forecasting sales, prices, and profits. In spite of all this effort to obtain and utilize information, the forecasts turned out to be wrong. In early 1971, Du Pont announced that it was discontinuing production of Corfam because sales were insufficient for profitable operations.

Why were the market forecasts for Corfam as inaccurate as they apparently were? According to outside observers, "a number of vital assumptions made by Du Pont staffers about the product and the market . . . turned out to be erroneous."[3] Among the incorrect assumptions, it was suggested, were (1) a failure to anticipate the growth of shoe imports, which supplanted domestic United States production to a substantial degree in the 1960s; (2) failure to recognize a shift in consumer tastes, which moved away from the concept of durable shoes toward one of frequent replacement and greater emphasis on

[3] Leonard Sloane, "Du Pont's $100-Million Edsel," *The New York Times,* Apr. 11, 1971, p. F-3.

current fashion; and (3) underestimation of the competition from other, lower-priced synthetic materials.

Did the failure of Corfam reflect the futility of trying to forecast market trends through marketing research? In all likelihood, there was no way in which Du Pont could have foreseen all the changes in shoe markets that took place in the 1960s. Research techniques do not provide crystal balls. The most important moral of the story, however, is the key role of *judgment* in research. The research that the company did was based on *assumptions* about future trends. These assumptions were, in the final analysis, opinions or beliefs rather than "objective" facts. Possibly, the assumptions could have been tested more fully than they were. But no amount of research could have eliminated uncertainty about future trends completely.

THE MANAGER'S ROLE IN RESEARCH

The discussion that follows is oriented toward the needs of marketing executives as *users* of research. How much does the executive need to know about research techniques, and to what extent should he rely on the advice of experts?

Effective planning and execution of research require specialized education and experience. In most large organizations, the actual conduct of marketing research is entrusted to staff specialists and/or to commercial research firms. The manager cannot hope to become sufficiently competent in research methods to dispense with such specialized assistance entirely. But the manager can and should have enough understanding and appreciation of research problems and methods to:

1. Decide when specialized help is required
2. Work with specialists in the formulation of research investigations
3. Determine whether or not the results of a proposed study are likely to justify its cost
4. Apply research results to decision making, with proper attention to the shortcomings of various kinds of information

To deal with these questions, the manager must understand how research relates to decision problems, must be familiar with some of the rudiments of research design, and must know enough about measurement techniques to be aware of the strengths and weaknesses of various kinds of research results.

MARKETING RESEARCH ORGANIZATION

In most large companies and in many smaller ones too, a specialized staff department is used to conduct marketing research studies. In a survey conducted by the American Marketing Association in 1968, over half (55 percent) reported having a formal department of marketing research, and another quarter (24 percent) had one full-time person assigned to this activity.[4] Research departments are much more common among large companies: 82 percent of firms with sales of $500 million reported formal departments, compared with only 24 percent for companies with less than $5 million sales.

Research departments typically engage in a wide variety of activities related to information collection and analysis, including many that do not qualify as "research" by the definition given earlier. Table 25-1 summarizes the types of activities reported by the companies responding to the 1968 American Marketing Association survey, and also shows the extent to which these activities were shared among marketing research departments, other staff departments within the companies, and outside suppliers. As shown in the table, marketing research departments are frequently assigned to carry out "sales analyses" and to prepare sales forecasts, as well as to conduct more formal studies such as "determination of market characteristics."

Marketing research as a formal, separately organized activity grew rapidly in American industry, and elsewhere in the world, during the 1950s and 1960s. Of all the marketing research departments reported in 1968, nearly a third were established after 1962 and over half since 1958. On the average, the research budgets of the companies reporting to the American Marketing Association nearly doubled between 1962 and 1968.[5]

This growth, and the corresponding expansion of specialized research firms, reflected several underlying trends favorable to increased research activities:

1. Increasing acceptance of the so-called "marketing concept."
2. Greater emphasis on new products and new markets, especially international markets. Both of these types of expansion involve greater *uncertainty* for management, and consequently reduced ability to rely on prior management experience.
3. Improvements in the techniques of marketing research itself.

Determining information needs

We have defined marketing research as a means to an end—the end being that of providing needed information to managers. Given this purpose, it is clear that a vital step in making research useful is a proper determination of what information is needed, either to deal with a specific problem or, on a continuing basis, to monitor marketing performance.

□ DEFINING THE MANAGEMENT PROBLEM

The most important step in determining what kinds of research should be carried out is that of clearly defining marketing decision problems. Clear

[4] Dik Warren Twedt (ed.), *1968 Survey of Marketing Research,* American Marketing Association, Chicago, 1969.
[5] *Ibid.,* p. 28.

□

TABLE 25-1

Marketing research activities reported by 1,700 companies responding to an AMA Survey, 1968

Activity	Percent of companies in which			
	Activity performed	Done by M.R. dept.	Done by other depts.	Done by outside firms
Advertising research:				
Motivation research	32%	19%	2%	15%
Copy research	38	17	5	19
Media research	47	21	9	21
Studies of ad effectiveness	49	25	7	22
Business economics and corporate research:				
Short-range forecasting	61	45	19	1
Long-range forecasting	59	44	18	2
Studies of business trends	60	49	12	2
Plant and warehouse location studies	46	18	28	2
Diversification studies	49	28	25	2
Acquisitions studies	45	19	30	2
International studies	41	21	21	2
Product research:				
New product acceptance and potential	63	54	10	6
Competitive product studies	64	53	11	5
Product testing	53	31	22	6
Packaging research	45	23	19	7
Sales and market research:				
Market potentials	67	61	8	2
Market share analysis	66	61	6	3
Determination of market characteristics	69	63	6	3
Sales analyses	65	51	19	1
Establishment of sales, quotas, and territories	56	28	32	1
Distribution channels and cost studies	50	27	27	1
Test markets, store audits	37	26	7	7
Consumer panel operations	41	21	3	9
Sales compensation studies	43	15	29	2
Studies of premiums, coupons, sampling, deals	32	21	10	3

Note: In most cases the percentages in columns 2, 3, and 4 add to a total greater than the percentage in column 1. This reflects the fact that in many companies a given activity is performed by more than one of the organizational units named in the column headings.

Source: Based on Dik Warren Twedt (ed.), *1968 Survey of Marketing Research,* American Marketing Association, Chicago, 1969, p. 41

problem definition is an essential first step in marketing management generally, whether or not any marketing research is involved. Indeed, many problems are immediately solved once they are properly identified and made explicit.

Defining a decision problem is not as easy as it sounds; it is easy only in retrospect. For example, consider the situation faced by a manufacturer whose sales unexpectedly begin to decline. What has caused the decline? Any one, or several, of the factors in the marketing mix may be responsible—the product itself, price, inadequate or misdirected promotion, or insufficient distribution. External forces may have affected sales—general economic conditions, new or intensified competition, a shift in marketing channels, or a change in customers' needs. Probably the company's executives and salesmen have tentative explanations of the situation, but often there is disagreement even within the company. The first step in such a situation should be to make a *preliminary investigation* designed to determine what problem or problems are involved. The investigation may show that competitors are granting more attractive discounts to distributors in the face of a general industry sales decline, which is attributed to some shift in customer demand. Presumably something can be done about the first factor, but the company can exert little, if any, influence on the second.

This example illustrates an important fact in marketing research. In most firms, management does not recognize a problem until it notices a *symptom* such as unsatisfactory profits, declining sales, or customer complaints. These symptoms represent some kind of failure to achieve desired objectives, that is, an unsatisfactory level of performance. Usually the causes of symptomatic difficulties are hard to discern, and more than one management problem may well be involved.

The preliminary investigation may be made by line executives, by research specialists, or some combination of the two. It may not even be called *research*. But whatever it is called, a careful situation analysis is absolutely essential to the more formal research that may follow it. Otherwise, time, effort, and money may be wasted in solving the wrong problem.

No universally applicable procedure for conducting preliminary problem investigations can be set forth. Many managers and researchers utilize explicit or implicit checklists to ensure that factors typically found to affect marketing performance are not overlooked. Crisp suggests that in early efforts to define the problem, the following points should be examined[6]:

1. Industry elements, such as trends in total volume of sales
2. Competitive elements, such as number and types of competitors, trends in market shares

[6] Richard D. Crisp, *Marketing Research,* McGraw-Hill Book Company, New York, 1957, pp. 77–89.

3. Market elements, including characteristics of customers
4. Company elements, that is, the company's own policies

Whatever procedure is followed, it is important that this first step in the design of research be carried out as thoroughly and carefully as possible. If it is not, there is a significant risk that any research done will turn out to be irrelevant to management's real needs.

☐ ANALYZING INFORMATION REQUIREMENTS

Only after a problem has been defined as clearly as possible is the manager in a position to determine what information is needed to make a decision. In some instances, the decision can be made on the basis of experience and judgment without any systematic assembly of facts. Sometimes the needed information is already available, and it is simply a matter of assembling the information and organizing it. Only occasionally is it necessary to collect and analyze new information by means of formal research.

The information required to make a decision may be apparent from an examination of the alternatives under consideration. More often, considerable ingenuity is needed to determine what kinds of information might be of value in a specific problem. Consider, for example, a manufacturer trying to decide whether or not to invest in production facilities for a new industrial product designed for the same end use as one of his existing products. What the manager would like to know is how much of the new product could be sold and at what cost, compared with the existing product. Can information of this kind be obtained? Probably not directly. It might be possible to set up some kind of experimental marketing program for the new product, but at best this would provide only crude estimates of sales that might be anticipated under a full-scale effort.

Moreover, in a case like this, experimentation may even be dangerous; offering two products for the same use may confuse customers, destroy confidence in the existing product, and "let the cat out of the bag" to competitors. Consequently, it may well be preferable to devise some indirect way of estimating sales for the new product. Product testing, discussed in Chapter 15, is one means to this end. The company may provide samples of the new product to a few customers and ask them to make comparisons with the existing product and/or competing products. At the end of the trial period, the customers are asked to express their preferences. If a majority of customers prefer the new product (assuming that costs are the same), it may be concluded that its sales will be greater than those of the existing item.

Note carefully what is involved here. To make a decision to convert to the new product or not, we need estimates of potential sales. When this information cannot be obtained directly, we should try to establish a connection between the information we really want (estimated sales) and something that *can* be measured (customers' expressed preferences). In essence, we construct a model or set of logical relationships between what can be observed or measured and what cannot. This is one of the most critical steps in almost all marketing research activities.

To encourage careful definition of information needs, many companies require a formal *research request* from managers before any project is undertaken. An example of a written form used for research requests in one major company is shown in Figure 25-1. Note that this form calls for a summary of certain basic sales data, and suggestions for other existing sources of information, as well as requiring a statement of the management problem or opportunity and a specification of information desired. Naturally, such written requests are almost always supplemented by discussions between the managers and research specialists involved. But the use of a standardized written format has been found very valuable as a kind of discipline for thinking about information needs.

Once the information needs of the decision maker have been identified in terms of observable or measurable facts, the decision problem has been converted into one or more research problems. Up to this point, the line executive should play a major role in the analysis. Beyond this point, the tasks of designing effective measurement procedures, and of collecting and analyzing the information, are largely the responsibilities of the research specialist. Given the information requirements of the decision maker, the research spe-

---

FIGURE 25-1

Outline of a management request for marketing research used in a major corporation

The information requested below will assist the Research Department in developing a research approach which we believe will accomplish your objectives.

PRODUCT CATEGORY TO BE STUDIED: ____________________

REASON FOR REQUEST: (A precise definition of the opportunity or problem)

____

OBJECTIVES: (What do you hope to achieve from this research?)

INFORMATION REQUIRED: (List as completely as possible the questions you believe need to be answered to achieve the objectives.)

COMPLETION DATE: (By what date are results required?)

BACKGROUND DATA: Please list. . . .
1. Five-year history—company and industry
2. Reports available from other company departments on this subject
3. Any research studies you are familiar with from other sources which we might be able to obtain
4. Any other background information you believe will be of help

cialist must determine how they can best be satisfied, either by utilizing existing data or by conducting some kind of research.

UTILIZING EXISTING INFORMATION

Before considering any expenditure of time and money on original research, the specialist should evaluate the extent and quality of information already available. This may come from sources within the company or from outside agencies. Much information can be obtained free, although there is always some cost attached to assembling and appraising it. In other cases, a direct and sometimes substantial cost is involved in getting the information.

Company sources The records of most business firms constitute a valuable source of information, and one that is often woefully neglected. Among the more important internal sources are accounting records, sales reports, and various statistical summaries. Sometimes these records provide direct answers to research questions, but usually some rearrangement and analysis are also required. Thus, it is typical to find that one of the major activities of the marketing research department is sales analysis, of the kinds described in Chapter 26. Many professional researchers feel that to call this activity "research" is a misnomer, but it is clearly intended to serve the same purpose of providing information to decision makers.

Government agencies Government agencies collect and disseminate a wide variety of information of value to marketing management, especially in the United States.[7] Some of the types of information available from government sources deal with individual products or industries; examples include automobile registration data and records of tax receipts for alcoholic beverages. Other government data are of more general relevance. For example, in earlier chapters we have cited numerous facts and figures drawn from the publication of the U.S. Bureau of the Census, which conducts periodic studies of population, housing, manufacturing, agriculture, mineral production, and retail and wholesale trade. Similar information is collected and published in most other countries, although few of them provide as much detail as the United States.

Trade associations In those industries where trade associations exist, data collected by them may be of assistance both to their members and to firms outside the industry. Statistics from trade associations are not always complete, because in many industries trade association membership does not represent all the firms in the industry. Also, antitrust legislation restricts the kinds of data

[7] For a classified listing of governmental sources of information, see Paul Wasserman, Eleanor Allen, and Charlotte Georgi (eds.), *Statistics Sources*, 3d ed., Gale Research Company, Detroit, 1971.

that can be collected or disseminated. Although data collected vary among associations, they often include monthly and annual sales and production statistics on an industry-wide basis, data on individual products on an industry basis, and breakdowns of sales by geographic areas.

Trade publications In many industries and lines of business, trade publications provide regular, periodic estimates of sales, prices, and other types of marketing information. We have cited some estimates from these sources, for instance, in the discussion of different types of retailing and wholesaling institutions in Chapters 10 to 12. Often, information from trade publications has the great advantages of being relatively current and of specific relevance to an individual industry or product category. The main drawback, on the other hand, is that the accuracy of the information is hard to evaluate.

Advertising media Many advertising media, such as newspapers, magazines, and television stations, conduct research studies dealing with their audiences or local market areas. For example, Television Advertising Representatives, Inc., representing stations in eight major cities, publishes the results of periodic consumer surveys of product usage and brands most recently purchased.

Media research studies can be useful, but it should be borne in mind that they are usually intended as sales devices for the media. Especially in the case of audience studies, they may reflect a very selective approach to research.

Suppliers In some industries, suppliers of materials, packaging, or other goods provide marketing information to customers on a regular basis and/or through special studies. Information provided by suppliers, like that supplied by advertising media, must be evaluated carefully because of possible bias or selectivity. Reputable suppliers, and media, are unlikely to distort research findings. But they are likely to select subjects for research which will tend to favor their interests, and the resulting studies may give something less than the full picture for the user.

□ STANDARDIZED INFORMATION SERVICES

When existing information is insufficient to serve management needs, it may still be possible to avoid much of the expense and difficulty of original research by utilizing standardized information services. These are commercial organizations that supply the same, or very similar, types of information to many different users, typically on a contract basis.

A. C. Nielsen Company and Market Research Corporation of America are two of the best known standardized information services. A. C. Nielsen, for example, collects information on retail sales, display space, inventories, and promotional activities of competing brands of food, drug, and other consumer products. This information is secured from a sample of cooperating retail stores in the United States and in other countries where Nielsen operates. Nielsen data are made available for the nation as a whole and for various regional, city-size, and store ownership types of breakdowns.

Market Research Corporation of America operates a panel of households, each of which maintains a "diary" of its purchases in the product categories covered by the service. These records are used as a basis for projecting total consumer purchases, average prices paid, etc., on a regional and national scale. Similar panels are available in some countries outside the United States.

In the field of advertising research, Gallup-Robinson and Daniel Starch are well-known. Gallup-Robinson tests respondents' recall of advertising in mass-circulation magazines, and the Starch firm attempts to determine by various measures the extent to which particular advertisements have been seen and read by magazine readers. In the area of printed media, the Audit Bureau of Circulation has been formed by publishers to report certified data concerning magazine circulations. These data are broken down in various ways in order to permit the evaluation of possible audiences that media may reach.

The standardized information services mentioned above are only a few examples of the many types that are available. Some are designed to meet the special needs of individual industries, such as the prescription audit services used by manufacturers of pharmaceuticals. Others cover a wide range of products and/or types of information. In general, standardized services provide information at lower cost than special-purpose research. Against this must be offset the fact that, by their very nature, standardized services are not as specifically tailored to a given company's needs as special studies can be.

Planning original research

When available information is insufficient to permit intelligent decision making, it may be desirable to conduct original research in order to get additional information. The details of planning and executing research projects are the province of specialists, but the manager must understand enough of what is involved to evaluate the specialist's work. Since research costs money, the manager must also be responsible for determining whether a proposed study is likely to justify its cost.

□ HOW MUCH IS INFORMATION WORTH?

The value of information to the manager depends ultimately on three factors:

1. How much is at stake in a particular problem or opportunity
2. The degree of uncertainty involved in the situation
3. The extent to which further information is expected to reduce uncertainty

The effects of each of these factors can be illustrated in terms of a simple example. Suppose that a company is trying to determine whether or not to assign a salesman to a new territory, and that the cost of maintaining a salesman in the field is $10,000 per year. The revenue (sales minus all other costs) which he will return to the company, from which his costs must be paid, is unknown, but it is estimated that it may range from a minimum of $5,000 to a maximum of $25,000.

With these figures, it is possible to assess what is at stake in the decision. Suppose we assign a man to the territory. The maximum loss to the company is $5,000 a year ($5,000 revenue minus $10,000 cost). On the other hand, if we do not assign the salesman, we may miss an opportunity to make as much as $15,000 a year ($25,000 maximum revenue minus $10,000 cost).

Now suppose that if the manager must decide on the basis of available information, without any research, he chooses to assign a man. The most that could be lost by this decision is $5,000 during the first year; we can assume that after a year the mistake could be corrected by withdrawing. Clearly the manager would not pay more than $5,000 for research information, since otherwise it will be cheaper simply to go ahead and take a chance. If a research project were proposed at a cost of more than $5,000, the manager should reject it.

Since $5,000 is the absolute maximum that additional information may be worth, the actual value that can be expected is probably somewhat less. How much less? This also depends on the *degree of uncertainty* attached to the decision. At the extreme, management may be virtually certain that the territory will yield enough sales volume to offset the cost of a salesman. If this is so, further information has no value. On the other hand, if there is considerable doubt and controversy on the subject, information is worth more because it may help to reduce this uncertainty. In some cases it is possible to utilize the notion of "degree of uncertainty" to derive numerical estimates of the expected value of research information. Adequate explanation of this procedure is, however, beyond the scope of this book.[8]

The third factor that must be considered in appraising the potential value of research information is how much the information can be expected to contribute to the reduction of uncertainty. Some types of research are highly developed, have been used frequently, and are known to yield accurate and useful results. Others may produce only crude estimates at best. For example, referring to methods for forecasting the sales of new food supermarkets, one executive has stated that "very seldom does a store do the volume a survey shows it should do." When a research method consistently fails to yield valid results, its value to the decision maker is doubtful.

[8] See R. D. Buzzell, D. F. Cox, and R. V. Brown, *Marketing Research and Information Systems: Text and Cases*, McGraw-Hill Book Company, New York, 1969, chap. 11.

It is not intended to imply that managers should never authorize the use of new, untested research procedures. This would lead to stagnation. But when new methods are tried, part of the cost should be recognized as one of technique development as distinguished from direct contribution to improved decisions.

In brief, then, expenditures on research, either on original studies or on the purchase of information from a research organization, are justified only if they are likely to reduce some real uncertainty connected with a decision or series of decisions which involve a sufficient potential dollar gain. The manager should apply these tests before authorizing the use of the firm's resources on any research project.

□

RESEARCH DESIGN

Once it is decided that the costs of research are justified, the next major step in planning is to develop a framework that will serve as a basis for the collection and analysis of data. This framework is called the research design.

Research designs vary according to the degree to which a problem is understood and can be defined beforehand. At an early stage, when the purpose of the research is to get basic understanding of the nature of a problem, an *exploratory* design is appropriate. Later, when the elements of a situation are better known, more structured studies based on either a *descriptive* or an *explanatory* design can be carried out. Still more structured studies, aimed at predicting the effects of company actions or market conditions, are based on *predictive* research designs.

Exploratory studies An exploratory study is often seen as an initial step in a continuous process. By definition, when a researcher is at the initial step in the research process, he lacks a great deal of knowledge about the problem. If he were better informed and could develop specific hypotheses, there would be no need to conduct an exploratory investigation. Because of this lack of familiarity with the subject matter, exploratory studies are often designed in a flexible fashion that permits the investigator considerable freedom to modify his approach as he gains understanding. This freedom is reflected by the fact that exploratory studies seldom use detailed questionnaires or involve elaborate sampling plans.

In consumer goods industries, a common approach to exploratory research is to conduct one or more unstructured *group interviews* with small groups of consumers, say, 8 to 12. During the group discussions, attempts are made to elicit product (or store) *attributes* that affect buying decisions, problems encountered in purchase and use, and *terminology* used by consumers to characterize different products, brands, etc. A similar approach can be used with industrial buyers or dealers and distributors, although it is seldom convenient to assemble them in groups.

Exploratory studies sometimes reveal customer ignorance of, and/or indifference to, technical aspects of product construction; unsuspected uses of products; associations between products and stores and other activities; and other insights on the customer which would be difficult to get in any other way.

Descriptive studies A great deal of research is aimed at measuring the characteristics of some aspect of a marketing function or problem. There are studies which describe the demographic characteristics of the consumer, for example, percentage distributions of age, sex, education, location; the relative importance of different types of wholesalers or retailers; changes over a period of time in the cost and profit structure of an industry; the characteristics of successful salesmen; or the association between the amount of a product consumed by a family and its place of residence. In each of the above cases, the purpose of the investigation is to describe the distribution of some factor such as the percentage distribution of consumers by age, or to describe the relation between two or more phenomena such as the amount of a product consumed by a customer and where he lives.

There are a number of decision-making situations in which descriptive information can serve as a partial basis for action. For example, suppose a manufacturer is about to introduce a product which is superior to previous products of the same type but costs only half as much. The decision maker may at the outset be mainly interested in characteristics of present consumers of the product so that he knows *where* to distribute and advertise his innovation; he may not be immediately interested in *why* consumption is higher in Kansas than in California.

Descriptive research designs presuppose some prior knowledge of the subject to be investigated. There is need to define clearly what is to be measured and to find adequate methods for measuring it. In addition, care must be taken to specify what is to be included in the definition of a market or a population. What is needed is not so much the flexibility characteristic of an exploratory study, but a clear formulation of what and who is to be measured and of techniques for valid and reliable measurements.

Explanatory studies One step beyond description of a market is explanation of how and, to some extent, why marketing processes operate. Many research studies are intended to provide this kind of understanding. For example, a descriptive study may show that consumption of a product varies among geographic regions. An explanation of this variation might then be sought by relating consumption to other factors such as climate or consumer income.

Most explanatory studies involve the use of statistical techniques to determine *relationships* among marketing conditions and/or events. Considerable skill and ingenuity may be required to analyze such relationships, because of the inherent complexity of marketing.

Sometimes, relationships among the factors in a marketing problem are reasonably clear-cut. For example, a study conducted by a food processing company related the market share of the company's brand to the *differential* between the brand's retail price and the average price of competing "private brand" products in various time periods.[9] The principal result of this study was the following table:

Percent price differential	*Market share of company's brand*
Less than 10%	24.3%
10–11	21.3
12–13	20.7
14–15	20.6
16–17	20.5
18–19	19.5
20 or more	18.2

This table indicated clearly that, as might be expected, there is a relationship between market share and price differential: the greater the differential, the lower the market share. Even this seemingly obvious point may, however, be misleading. It is entirely possible that price differentials and market shares both varied in response to some third factor. For example, suppose that the larger price differentials reflected temporary reduced-price promotions for private brands, and that these promotions also involved allocation of more and better in-store display space to the private brand products. It could be, then, that the declines in the national brand's market share were due partly or entirely to changes in display rather than, or at least in addition to, greater price differentials.

Various techniques are used in explanatory studies to identify relationships, and to avoid incorrect conclusions.[10] None of these methods can guarantee that a study will provide a valid explanation; good judgment and knowledge of the problem which is being studied are also essential.

PREDICTIVE STUDIES

The most difficult task for marketing research is to make predictions of the effects of decisions under consideration by management, or of market condi-

[9] Adapted from an example given in R. D. Buzzell, D. F. Cox, and R. V. Brown, *Marketing Research and Information Systems,* McGraw-Hill Book Company, New York, 1969, pp. 181–182.
[10] Ibid., chaps. 5, 6, and 7.

tions which are anticipated. Predictions may, of course, be made on the basis of the results of descriptive or explanatory studies. But more "complete" answers can often be obtained by research specifically designed to estimate what effects can be obtained under a given policy.

Test marketing, which was discussed in Chapter 15, is a particularly complex and expensive form of predictive research.

In many cases, the most reliable research approach for predictive studies is that of designed ("controlled") experimentation.

The term *experiment* is used here to designate research studies in which factors believed to be causes such as advertising are *deliberately manipulated* and studies in which comparisons are made between at least two combinations or levels of the independent variables.

Experimental design There are many different patterns of experimentation that can be used in marketing research. Even a cursory treatment of the subject of experimental design is beyond the scope of the present discussion, but some of the general notions involved can be illustrated through some relatively simple examples.

One of the simplest experimental designs is called an *after-only* design. In this type of experiment, the effects of a factor, such as a price change, are estimated by measuring results, say, sales, only *after* an experimental change. A comparison is made between (1) results for an "experimental" group of customers, stores, or cities and (2) results for a "control" group in which no change was made. The difference between the experimental group and the control group is used as an estimate of the effect of the experimental change. Proper use of this design, and experiments in general, requires that the control units be chosen carefully to be comparable with the experimental group. Insofar as possible, the customers, stores, or areas in the control and experimental groups should be alike in all respects that might affect the factors being measured, *except* for the factors involved in the experiment itself.

One of the most frequent applications of this type of experimentation has been in the evaluation of direct-mail advertising campaigns. For example, suppose that we were faced with the problem of choosing one of three direct-mail pieces for use in a forthcoming mail-order campaign. We could take a sample of households from the mailing list to be used as the basis for the mailing and separate it into three groups. Each group would receive a different direct-mail piece. The orders resulting from the test mailing would then serve as the basis for comparing the relative effectiveness of the three pieces.

For problems in which management wants to choose one of a set of alternatives such as in advertisement selection or direct-mail evaluation, the after-only design can be quite useful. However, differences may still exist between the test and control groups apart from the factor which the experiment is designed to measure. To achieve greater control over these differences, or to provide ways of adjusting for them, a wide variety of more complicated experimental designs have been developed. Adequate description of the topic is beyond the scope of this discussion.[11]

Sample surveys

In all types of marketing research—exploratory, descriptive, explanatory, and predictive—the most common method of collecting information is the sample survey. In a sample survey, individuals, households, companies, or other "elements" are selected from a larger group, the "population," and some measurement procedure is used to obtain information from this sample. The most frequently used measurement method is that of interviewing. Because sample surveys are so widely used, a brief discussion of some of the major problems involved is appropriate at this point.

□ MEASUREMENT PROBLEMS

Sometimes information can be obtained by direct observation or counting of tangible events or conditions. For example, the data provided by A. C. Nielsen Company store audits (mentioned above) are obtained by counting the stocks on hand in a store and recording shipments received by the store during a given time period. Apart from errors in recording, there is no ambiguity involved in this type of measurement.

More often, marketing research is based on the use of measurement procedures which involve varying degrees of inaccuracy, systematic bias, and/or conceptual ambiguity. Generally speaking, accuracy can be improved and bias can be reduced, at a cost, but in the final analysis a certain amount of ambiguity cannot be avoided.

As a relatively simple example, consider the measurement of "readership" for advertisements. There are many different ways of interviewing a person for the purpose of determining whether or not he has read, or seen, an advertisement. All these procedures are subject to inaccuracy, but this can be reduced by such means as more careful training of interviewers, higher rates of interviewer pay, and more careful and extensive "quality checks." A more difficult problem is that of systematic bias in readership measures. Whatever the "true" reading history of a given group of persons, some measures will give systematically higher estimates than others. In a comparison of two widely used commercial methods for measuring magazine advertisement readership, conducted by an independent organization, it was found that one technique

[11] For further discussion, see Seymour Banks, *Experimentation in Marketing,* McGraw-Hill Book Company, New York, 1965.

produced a consistently higher result than the other.[12] Which method was correct? There really is no answer, because neither method necessarily corresponded to a "true" measure of readership.

In fact, there is no "true" way to measure readership of advertisements—or to measure customer attitudes, beliefs, buying intentions, and many other things considered important in marketing. All these concepts can be defined in different ways, depending in part on the purposes of a particular study. One of the most important points for the user of research to remember is the need to define the concepts and terms used in a study very explicitly, and to avoid the common error of conceptual ambiguity.

SURVEY PROCEDURES

The three major survey procedures used in marketing research are mail, telephone, and personal interview. Some of the major advantages and disadvantages of these three methods are summarized in Table 25-2.

To illustrate the effects of survey methods on the types of information that can be obtained, suppose that we are interested in studying the fertilizer consumption characteristics of farms in the United States. If personal interviews were used, it would be possible to design a study in which the universe we are interested in and the one which is sampled are the same except for refusals and not-at-homes. In contrast, suppose that the telephone is used. In 1965, only 68 percent of farm families reported having a telephone. In addition to the possibility of refusals and not-at-homes, nearly a third of the relevant population would not be included in the universe; actually the percentage would be greater than this owing to unlisted telephones. If these nontelephone owners are systematically different from owners in a way that is related to fertilizer consumption, the results of the study will be biased.

On the other hand, if we were interested in studying the market area of the island of Manhattan in New York City, where the proportion of households with telephones probably runs over 85 percent, the effect of excluding nontelephone owners is apt to be relatively trivial for many kinds of studies.

Questionnaire design If questions asked in a survey are poorly worded, asked in the wrong sequence, or simply unrealistic, the result will be distorted or perhaps meaningless answers. There is no way to eliminate this entirely, but questions should be carefully screened to avoid bias insofar as it can be foreseen. Some of the more common errors in questionnaire design include:

1. Questions that call for information not readily available to respondents. For example, a housewife may not know what brand of gasoline her husband purchases.

[12] D. B. Lucas and S. H. Britt, *Measuring Advertising Effectiveness*, McGraw-Hill Book Company, New York, 1963, pp. 78–82.

□
TABLE 25-2
Advantages and disadvantages of mail, telephone, and personal interview methods in marketing research

	Mail	Telephone	Personal interviews
Cost	Low out-of-pocket cost	Higher than mail surveys	Highest cost method
Time	Slow; replies often "trickle in"	Fastest method	Slow if large area is covered
Selection of respondents	Best way to reach many types of persons who resent intrusion of other methods Usually difficult to compile a good list with accurate addresses	Limited to telephone subscribers; may not be representative of total population Problem of compiling list similar to that in mail surveys	Hard to reach some types of persons, for example, those frequently away from home
Bias in responses	Eliminates bias created by interviewers; but persons who reply may differ from those who do not	Interviewer can get responses from two or more persons, often not possible by mail	Gives interviewer maximum control over sequence of questions, persons interviewed, etc.
Types of questions permitted	Limited to simple, clearly worded questions	Questions must be relatively short due to time limitations (generally 15 minutes is maximum)	Interviewer can use "unstructured" questions, can supplement interview with personal observations, etc. Interviews can be longer than for telephone
Other factors		Easy to pretest procedure on small sample prior to large-scale use	Requires more technical skill than other methods. Administrative problems of training and controlling interviews are substantial

2. Questions that seem to invite a particular answer. Often respondents want to please the interviewer and will give whatever answer seems most likely to do so.

3. Questions that are difficult to understand. For instance, if a housewife is asked what brand of a product she usually buys, the term *usually* can be interpreted in several ways. Usually during what period? Does it mean *most often* or *in greatest quantity?* And so on.

4. Questions that may seem objectionable or "nosy" to respondents. Many

people resent being asked about their incomes. For this reason, questions about income (if necessary) are usually asked *last* to avoid creating antagonism that might bias subsequent responses.

Interviewers In a field survey, interviewers or observers can significantly influence the information obtained, through misunderstanding of their instructions or simply by injecting their personalities into the measurement process. For example, in a quota sample design, interviewers are usually told the number or fraction of respondents that are to be interviewed who have certain characteristics (for example, interview three single male Caucasians, over age twenty-five, with incomes between $5,000 and $7,000) without being told precisely whom to interview. In one study, interviewers working with economic level quotas tended to underselect both high- and low-income classes.[13]

A respondent's reaction to the interviewer can also cause bias. For example, one researcher found that fewer drinkers were reported by interviewers who resembled the stereotype of a prohibitionist. Alternatively, under some circumstances, whether the interviewer is a man or woman, young or old, may affect the responses he gets.

The principal techniques used for estimating the extent of interviewer bias are comparison of responses obtained by different interviewers and comparison of responses against an external source such as census data. Advance planning is required in order to make the most effective use of either of these techniques. After a study is finished, it is desirable to be able to determine the extent to which differences in response are due to variations in interviewers. Suppose that there were substantial differences among interviewers. Under what conditions should one be willing to infer that these differences were due to the interviewers and not to the variations in the factors being studied?

Nonresponse A particularly troublesome problem in marketing research is nonresponse. People do not have to cooperate. They often regard being observed or interviewed as an intrusion. Two important types of nonresponse are "not-at-homes" and "refusals."

The number of not-at-homes is often surprisingly large. While some studies have shown the percentage of not-at-homes to run as low as 10 percent, others have had rates of around 45 to 50 percent. Not-at-homes tend to vary with time of year, time of week, and time of day. It is usually not sufficient merely to substitute a neighbor for a not-at-home, since this may violate the principle of choosing respondents on the basis of known probabilities (chances) of selec-

[13] A. B. Blankenship, "A Source of Interviewer Bias," *International Journal of Opinion and Attitude Research,* vol. 3, pp. 95–98, Spring, 1949.

tion. Sometimes such substitutions are made, but unless special provisions are made for this in the sample design, the result will be a nonprobability sample (as defined below).

Refusals have the same type of effect on survey results as not-at-homes. If respondents who refuse to cooperate differ from those who cooperate, distorted results may be obtained. Refusal rates have varied from 7 to 15 percent and have averaged 10 percent on surveys conducted by the National Opinion Research Center.[14]

Since refusals are often the result of personality and mood, it can be argued that they will occur randomly and will not affect overall results. There is evidence, however, that refusals tend to be concentrated among certain income groups. Different studies show a high concentration of refusals in high- and low-income groups.[15] Thus, failure to include refusal families tends to distort results influenced by income. In addition to complete refusals, there are often refusals on specific questions. Questions about incomes frequently fall in this class.

SAMPLING

A *sample* is a set of elements (persons, stores, invoices) selected from a "population" or "universe" about which information is sought. An essential first step in sample design is to define the population carefully. An appliance manufacturer, for example, may seek to determine the distribution income among new households. But what are "new households"? Are households formed within the past six months included? The past year? Should only married couples be surveyed, or are single persons also households? Precise answers to these questions are important since otherwise information may be obtained from the wrong people, while others are inadvertently left out.

There are many kinds of sample designs that can be used in marketing research. All of them can be categorized as either *probability* samples or *nonprobability* samples.

Probability samples In a probability sample, each element of the population has a known chance or probability of being included. The simplest version is the *simple random sample,* in which each element has an equal chance of selection. When a fair coin is flipped, each side has an equal chance of turning up. The same notion can sometimes be applied to marketing studies. For example, a department store could draw a simple random sample of its charge

[14] Paul B. Sheatsley, "Public Relations of the Polls," *International Journal of Opinion and Attitude Research,* vol. 2, pp. 461–465, Summer, 1948.
[15] John Harding, "Refusals as a Source of Bias," in Hadley Cantril, *Gauging Public Opinion,* Princeton University Press, Princeton, N.J., 1947, p. 120.

account customers by selecting names from a list or file by some random process.

Variations on simple random sampling include *stratified samples* and *area probability samples.* These designs may be used because simple random sampling is not feasible, because additional information is needed, or because they are more efficient. (The term *efficiency* in statistics refers to the amount of information obtained in relation to cost.)

In a stratified sample, a population is divided into two or more groups such as men and women, and each group is sampled separately. There are two reasons for doing this. First, if a factor such as sex is known to have an important bearing on the matter under investigation, then it may be important to make sure that both men and women are adequately represented in the sample. There is no guarantee that this will be true in a simple random sample. Second, stratification may be used because the researcher wants information on each group as well as on the population as a whole. Separate advertising campaigns might, for example, be directed toward male and female consumers.

Area probability samples are frequently used in consumer surveys as a means of identifying members of a population to be included in the sample. Simple random sampling requires a *list* of the population or some equivalent device. But lists may be expensive, inaccurate, or even nonexistent. While there is no list of all households in the United States, there are maps, and it is possible to identify each household by its place of residence. In an area sample, areas are selected from a map by some random selection technique, and people living within the selected areas are chosen to be studied. Often this is done in several *stages;* that is, a number of counties are chosen, then blocks within each county, and finally houses within blocks. All this can be done on a stratified basis; for instance, metropolitan areas and nonmetropolitan areas may be treated separately.

The importance of probability samples is that the theory of probability can be employed to estimate the magnitude of the sampling error involved in the research results. Only by coincidence will a figure derived from a sample agree exactly with the corresponding figure for the population. Suppose there are 10,000 manufacturing plants in which some industrial product is used, and we want to know what fraction of them has purchasing agents. If we select a sample of, say, 500 firms to study, we may find that 40 percent have them.

The sample figure of 40 percent is our best estimate of the true figure for all plants. But if another sample of 500 plants were selected, it is not likely that exactly the same figure would be obtained; we might find, instead, that 38 or 42 percent or some other fraction had purchasing agents. All measures obtained from samples are *estimates* of corresponding true values for the populations from which the samples are drawn. There is virtually always some error in these estimates; this is called *sampling error*. Probability theory permits the probable sampling error to be measured. We can say, for example, that we are 90 percent confident (or 95 percent, etc.) that the interval from 38 to 42 percent contains the true value for the fraction of plants with purchasing agents. The rationale for estimating sampling error is treated in most elementary statistics textbooks and will not be repeated here. It is important to note that probable sampling error can be determined *only* for probability samples. It should also be kept in mind that the theory does *not* provide for the measurement of any errors other than sampling error.

Nonprobability samples Sometimes it is not feasible or desirable to utilize a probability sample design. This may be true because persons selected for the sample refuse to cooperate. Even when cooperation can be secured, a probability sample may be prohibitively costly. An area probability sample, for instance, requires expensive maps, directions to interviewers or observers, and careful checking to ensure that the design is carried out. In exploratory studies, we may not even be in a position to define the population, much less to draw elements from it with known chances.

For these and related reasons, nonprobability samples are often employed in marketing research. An example is the *quota sample*. An interviewer is given quotas to be filled in his work—so many adult men, so many teen-age girls, and so on. Another nonprobability type of sample is an *opportunistic* one. An investigator may visit all hardware stores in a particular area simply because it is convenient to do so.

While nonprobability samples suffer from the drawback that sampling error cannot be estimated, they are nevertheless often more efficient than probability samples. Their usefulness must be judged in the context of the time and money available and the specific circumstances surrounding a research problem.

Questions

1. A manufacturer of industrial power tools was considering the possibility of adding a line of hand power tools including electric drills, routers, circular saws, and saber saws for sale to the do-it-yourself market. As part of its analysis, the company was interested in the likely response this new line might receive from prospective retailers, especially hardware outlets, discounters, and building supply yards catering to the homeowner market.
   a. What specific information should they look for? Why?
   b. Develop a research design suitable for obtaining the information specified in (a) above. Include as part of this design a description of the survey methodology you would employ, and prepare an appropriate questionnaire.

c. What problems or risks do you see in the research design you propose? How can management minimize or overcome them?

2. A large brewery conducted market research indicating that many women did not like the taste of beer. Subsequently, the company's product development department developed a mint-flavored beer which had none of the taste attributes normally associated with beer. Preliminary taste tests indicated that many of the same women liked the taste of this product.

a. What information would the brewery need to decide whether or not to market this new product? Why?

b. How should the brewery proceed to obtain this information?

3. The sales manager of a manufacturer of gift items sold primarily through jewelry and department stores requested an estimate of the size of the market for home barometers, as well as an estimate of the geographical distribution of barometer sales. He believed this information would be useful in measuring sales force performance. A quick perusal of secondary data sources revealed no information on dollar or unit sales of barometers. How might a market researcher provide useful figures for the sales manager?

4. A large department store located in a large metropolitan area operated three branch stores in addition to the main downtown location. The success of the branch outlets combined with the continuing shift of population to the suburbs convinced management that they should build additional suburban outlets. A critical question was how close together or far apart these stores should be. Management was uncertain how far consumers would travel to shop and hoped to develop some positive information about the size of the trading areas of branch stores to aid in deciding the number and location of new branches.

a. What kinds of internal information should be available to assist in this kind of analysis? How could this information be used?

b. What kinds of external information would you collect? Where and how would you obtain this information?

5. Long-term forecasts for the year 1980 indicate that GNP will rise 50 percent, population will increase 20 percent, college enrollments will be up 25 percent, and farm population will be down 10 percent.

a. What effects do you think these changes will have on demand for each of the following products in 1980? Why? (1) Portable typewriters. (2) Bread. (3) Frozen orange juice. (4) Kitchen cabinets. (5) Sheet steel.

b. What further information would you want to have in order to forecast demand for each of these products? Why?

6. As a means of testing the effect of varying different elements in their marketing mix, a large pharmaceutical house designed the following test procedure:

A geographical area was selected for the test, and a complete list was obtained of all physicians in private practice in the area. The area was defined so as to ensure that all doctors in the area were subject to the same environmental stimuli, that is, medical communications networks, medical journals, and advertising.

Two or more random samples were drawn from the group. Typically, each group included a minimum of 400 physicians. The expectation was that prior to the test procedure, each subgroup should write about as many new prescriptions of a given drug as any other subgroup.

Tests were conducted by taking one subgroup as a control and varying marketing activities in other subgroups. For example, to test the effect of a sample mailing for an existing product, the control group received no sample mailing, while all the test group doctors received samples by mail. In addition, the test period was preceded by a period in which neither group received mail samples.

Test results were obtained by auditing new prescriptions in a large number of pharmacies. The audit included the prescription date and the doctor's name. By using statistical means, it was then possible to determine whether the number of new prescriptions written by the test group was significantly greater than the number written by the control group.

The same procedure could be employed to measure the effects of differences in the frequency of sales calls, frequency and timing of direct mail, or many other variations in promotional activities. By increasing the number of test groups, it would be possible to compare the results of various combinations of marketing activities.

a. Can you see any serious drawbacks or limitations to this test procedure? Discuss.

b. Could the same methodological approach be used to test other products being sold to different kinds of consumers? Give some specific examples.

c. What problems or difficulties can you see in applying the same approach to different types of products or market situations?

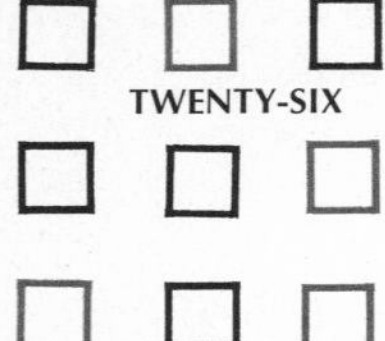

Measurement and analysis of marketing performance

A basic requirement for effective management in any field, including marketing, is some way of evaluating the performance of an organization, an individual, an activity, or a program. "Did it work?" and "How are we doing?" are questions which any manager asks almost instinctively. This need for evaluation gives rise to the requirement for a system of measuring performance, for analyzing the reasons for variations in performance, and for determining how it can be improved. In this chapter, we discuss the elements of a system for measurement and analysis of an organization's marketing performance.

Earlier, in Chapters 21 and 22, we made brief mention of the problem of measuring the "effectiveness" or performance of personal selling and advertising. We mentioned that a major obstacle to isolating the results of selling or advertising activities is the difficulty of disentangling their effects from those of other factors, especially other elements of the marketing program. Because it is so difficult to isolate the results of any single marketing function, in this chapter we shall concentrate on methods of measuring overall marketing performance at different levels in an organization.

We shall discuss, first, the relationship between performance measurement and an organization's objectives. Then, we review some of the more widely used measures of performance, based on sales volume, market share, costs, and profits. In the last part of the chapter we describe methods of analyzing sales, costs, and profits for specific components of an organization's activities.

Objectives, performance measures, and standards

The concept of "performance" in marketing is an elusive one. What does it mean to say that a retail store, a product manager, or an advertising campaign has performed satisfactorily, or failed to do so? At the outset, it must be emphasized that performance can be measured *only* in terms of some specified set of objectives which have been established for an activity or organization.

As an analogy, consider the "performance" of an automobile. For one driver, the only relevant factor may be fuel economy; his performance measure is miles per gallon of gasoline. Another driver may prize rapid "getaways," and be concerned with the time required to accelerate from 0 to 60 miles per hour. These two drivers would obviously rank a given set of automobiles quite differently. In the same way, two retail food chain companies might evaluate the "performance" of a given store very differently, and two district sales managers, even in the same firm, might differ in their appraisals of the same salesman.

Not only does the concept of performance require an explicit definition of the results desired, but these results must be somehow related to the *conditions* under which an activity is performed and to the *resources used* in their attainment. The miles-per-gallon measure of automobile performance explicitly includes fuel (resources) consumed. Implicitly, a comparison of miles per gallon figures for two cars assumes that there were no significant differences in other resources used, or in driving conditions. If an expensive gasoline additive were used in one vehicle but not the other, or if one result were obtained on a high-speed turnpike and the other in city traffic, then the assumptions would be incorrect and the comparison invalid. Similarly, in a comparison of sales by two supermarkets, some account must be taken of store size, number of employees, or investment employed (resources used), and of relevant conditions such as total food sales in an appropriate surrounding area, time of year, etc.

One other idea is usually involved in any measure of performance: an explicit or implicit comparison with some *standard*. "Performance" connotes evaluation, and evaluation connotes comparison. If your 1970 Volkswagen averages 25 miles per gallon, is that good, bad, or indifferent? Evaluation can only be relative—and the standard of evaluation must be specified. Many different standards can be used, including past performance (the car's fuel consumption last year), an *average* of some relevant group (other small cars), or some expectation (what the previous owner said when he sold the car to you).

The concept of performance, then, involves four key elements: the results desired from an activity or organization, the resources used in getting these results, the surrounding environment or circumstances, and some standard(s) of comparison.

□

THE HIERARCHY OF OBJECTIVES

□ *Performance of a marketing activity or organization is the degree to which it achieves specified results or objectives, in a given time period, relative to the resources used in attaining these results. A measure of performance is explicitly or implicitly* compared *with one or more standards. To be comparable, performance measures should be adjusted to allow for differences in conditions affecting either results attained or resources used.*

If a measure of marketing performance□ is based on "results," and results are defined in terms of objectives, it follows that meaningful performance measurement is impossible unless marketing objectives are explicitly stated. In Chapter 13, we emphasized the dependence of marketing objectives on underlying *company* objectives, and the further dependence of goals for specific marketing activities, such as advertising, on overall marketing objectives. As suggested in Chapter 23, this process of subdividing and resubdividing objectives, and corresponding activities, is at the heart of designing an organization structure. The same logical framework of objectives should underlie a system of performance measurement.

A concrete example of how marketing objectives can be derived from company objectives, and then translated into successively more specific goals for components of the marketing process, is given in Figure 26-1. This figure shows *part* of a logical analysis through which measurable goals were established for the sales force and the advertising activities of a telephone company. This kind of systematic goal setting is, unfortunately, still uncommon in practice. Its value seems hard to dispute, however, and during the 1960s and 1970s an increasing number of companies attempted to develop more explicit, consistent statements of objectives for all their major activities, including marketing.[1]

We do not mean to suggest that it is easy to establish a whole system of objectives for a company and its various subdivisions, or that doing so is a panacea. There are many problems involved in setting goals for marketing and for specific marketing activities. A prime example is the difficulty of establishing goals for consumer advertising, as discussed in Chapter 22. While most marketing executives agree that good advertising seems to yield sales "somehow," it is often unclear just what processes intervene between exposure to communications and purchasing. This obviously makes it difficult to establish concrete goals for an advertising campaign. In the example depicted in Figure 26-1, a definite goal was specified. But many companies and products confront much more complex market conditions than a telephone company; for one thing, the latter has no direct competitors.

[1] The broad application of this approach is popularly known as "management by objectives." For further discussion, see Walter S. Wikstrom, *Managing By—and With—Objectives,* Personnel Policy Study no. 212, National Industrial Conference Board, New York, 1968.

FIGURE 26-1

An example of a logical system of company objectives and marketing objectives

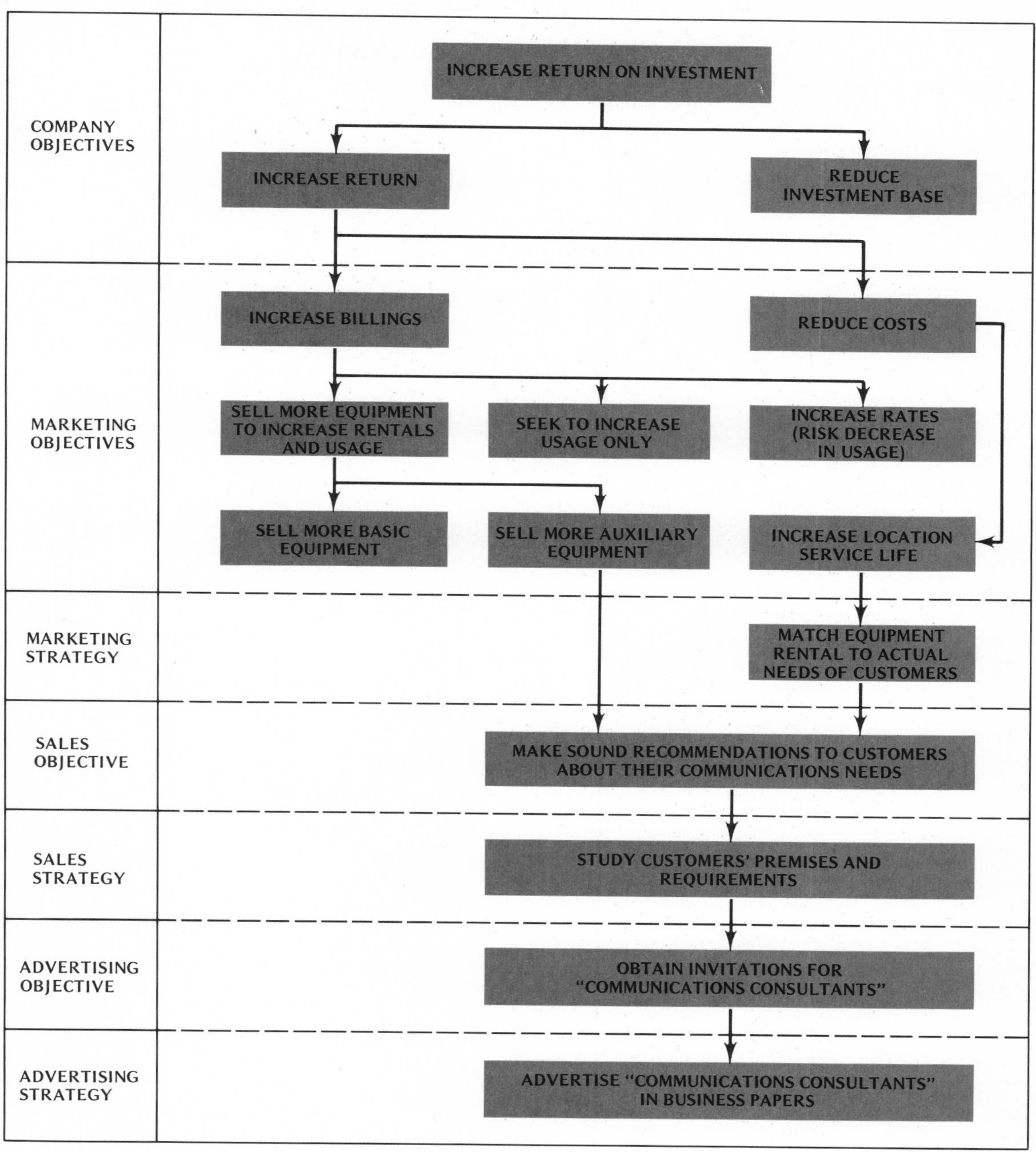

Reprinted with permission from an article by Leon Winer, "Are You Really Planning Your Marketing?", *Journal of Marketing*, American Marketing Association, January, 1965, p. 3.

Despite the difficulties involved, we believe that the foundation of effective performance measurement, and of effective marketing planning and organization, is a consistent, carefully developed framework of objectives based on overall company objectives. In the absence of such a framework, many companies have found themselves using conflicting, or at least ambiguous, performance measures for different departments or other components.

MULTIPLE OBJECTIVES

Thus far, we have discussed performance measurement as if each marketing activity or organizational unit had a single task. This is seldom the case. Typically, even when overall company objectives have been clearly defined, a marketing activity is intended to achieve several different goals. For example, a coupon promotion may be employed both to get nonusers to try a product, *and* to reinforce the loyalty of current users. Sometimes, statements of disparate objectives for a single program merely represent wishful thinking. But more generally, it is inevitable that marketing activities be assigned multiple goals. A salesman must seek new customers and also maintain existing accounts, try to increase volume and still reduce expenses, and so on.

This raises the question of *tradeoffs* among objectives which may conflict. An idealistic viewpoint is that various objectives can somehow be weighted so as to reflect their relative importance. This implies that all objectives can ultimately be reduced to a single goal; the process of assigning weights may be difficult, but only because it is hard to determine what contribution a given result makes to the "end purpose," under given conditions. The most common candidate for a single, all-encompassing business objective is "return on investment" (ROI), that is, some measure of company (or division, product, store, etc.) profits related to assets (or net worth) employed.

Both common observation and recent research on organizational behavior suggest that there probably is no single, universally applicable measure of business performance. The management of a company may agree on some one performance measure, such as return on investment, as a "most important" element of performance, if only to establish a common denominator for evaluating diverse products and activities. But no single measure is ever really sufficient to explain or guide the true motivations of managers. Ultimately, the past performance of organizational units and activities, and the estimated performance of future programs, must be evaluated in terms of an actual or estimated "package" of results, which may include sales growth, return on investment, maintenance of flexibility, and other factors.

An especially important tradeoff is that between *short-term and long-term results*. It is widely believed, for example, that most major advertisers could significantly increase short-run profits by eliminating advertising altogether.

Similarly, most retailers could probably make more money, over a period of one year, by sharply curtailing expenditures on store maintenance and improvements. But it is generally accepted that immediate profit gains "bought" by such actions would be at the expense of longer-term sales and profits. Thus, in most marketing activities, a balance must be struck between short-term results (however measured) and long-term results.

An appealing but sometimes difficult approach to evaluating performance at different points in time is that of discounting future results to an "equivalent present value." This approach was mentioned in Chapter 13 and also in connection with the discussion of new-product development in Chapter 15. As pointed out there, the concept of present value involves the use of a *discount rate*—reflecting the yield which could be achieved from an alternative use of money—to reduce expected future results, say, profits, to a level equivalent to immediate returns. A major difficulty in this approach is the inherent uncertainty associated with future operations. No one really *knows* what sales, expenses, and profits can be expected from a new product, a new store, etc., in some future time period. In principle, this difficulty can be handled, too, by assigning probabilities to different possible values of an uncertain quantity such as "sales of product X three years in the future."

Discounting of estimated future results and the use of probabilities provide a consistent logical framework for analysis and decision making. But the problem of maintaining a proper balance between current and future performance remains.

□

DESIGNING A PERFORMANCE MEASUREMENT SYSTEM

We have suggested that measures of performance for marketing and for its component activities should be derived from an explicit statement of company objectives. Over a period of time, some company objectives remain constant and others change. Marketing objectives should reflect both types of company goals, termed "permanent objectives" and "program objectives."

To illustrate, many companies attempt to meet or exceed a certain rate of return on investment. This goal may underlie *all* the firm's activities over an extended time period. It is a "permanent" objective. During a given year, the firm also establishes more specific objectives, related to particular programs or projects. One such goal may be "to obtain contract awards for at least six major new electric utility facilities." Objectives that are established for specific time periods, usually in connection with annual company plans, obviously should not conflict with permanent objectives. Instead, program objectives are the *means* by which permanent objectives are achieved over a period of time. As pointed out above, attainment of program goals *may* involve temporary sacrifices in, say, return on investment. But such a temporary reduction in performance is intended to yield greater long-term results, just as a "strategic retreat" in military operations may contribute to ultimate victory.

The determination of marketing objectives for specific programs obviously depends on the nature of those programs. These program objectives vary greatly among companies, and from year to year in a given firm. For this reason, it is difficult, if not impossible, to compare the performance of different groups, managers, etc., in terms of program goals. Some kinds of continuing standardized performance measures are also needed, if only to permit comparisons.

Virtually all *continuing* measures of marketing performance are directly or indirectly related, or at least thought to be related, to return on investment. Figure 26-2 depicts the logical connections between return on investment and some of the more commonly used measures of marketing performance. As shown in this figure, commonly used measures of marketing performance include:

- Sales volume
  - Dollar sales
  - Market share; sales relative to "potential"
  - Sales to specific customers or customer groups, in specific areas, for products and product lines
- Asset utilization
  - Inventory turnover
  - Accounts receivable relative to sales
- Gross margin
  - Gross margin less controllable expenses ("contribution margin")
- Operating expenses
  - Individual expense items
  - Productivity
  - Expenses for specific products, customers, areas

Each of these types of performance measures is discussed in the sections that follow.

Sales and market share measures

In most companies, the first and most important purpose of marketing activities is conceived to be that of "selling the merchandise." Although this viewpoint can lead to a dangerously narrow approach to marketing, as suggested in Chapter 1, it is still reasonable to measure marketing performance partly in terms of sales results achieved, compared with some standard.

□ STANDARDS OF SALES PERFORMANCE

The most commonly used and best understood standard of sales performance is a company's own past sales and forecasts of future sales. Figure 26-3 shows

FIGURE 26-2
How marketing performance measures are related to return on investment

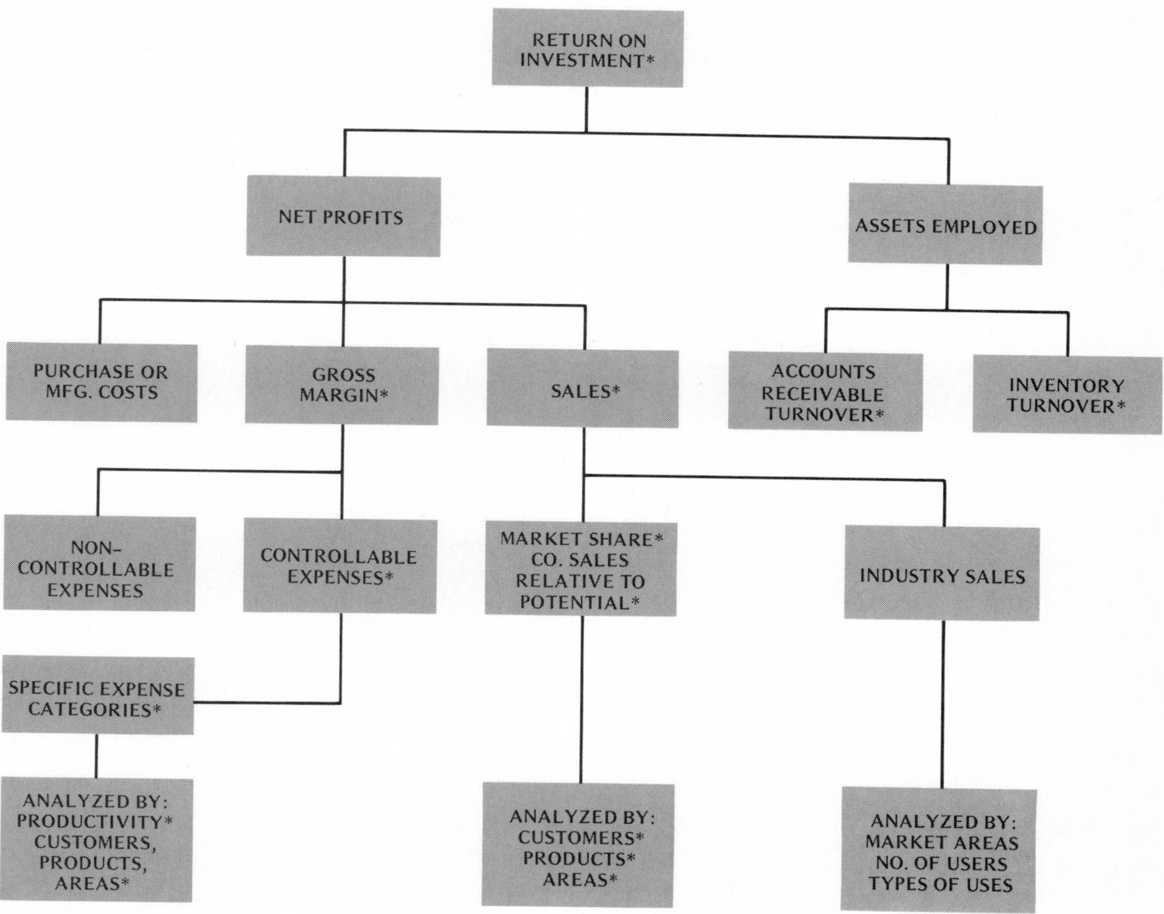

*(* = commonly used performance measures)*

FIGURE 26-3

Typical format for a monthly sales report

		Monthly sales			Year to date			Actual % of forecast	
		This year	Last year	Increase (decrease)	This year	Last year	Increase (decrease)	Month	YTD
Product Group	1								
Product Line	11								
	12								
	13								
Product Group	2								
Product Line	21								
	22								
Division Totals									

a common report format for comparison of actual sales with those of past periods and with forecasts. Such reports may be prepared monthly, weekly, or even daily, depending on the frequency of changes in a company's situation and on the costs and problems of obtaining reliable sales information.

Usually, sales reports show results for the current "period," for example, the month just ended, and also cumulative results for some longer period, such as "year to date." The main reason for showing cumulative results is to avoid overemphasis on short-term fluctuations, which may have little or no significance. Sales may fluctuate greatly from week to week, for instance, but this may simply reflect delays in processing orders, holidays, or other "static" not relevant to a meaningful appraisal of performance. Over a longer period of time, these fluctuations are assumed to "average out."

With few exceptions, a company's short-term sales figures are significantly affected by seasonal variations. One way to allow for this factor is to compare sales in a given period with sales in the corresponding period of the preceding year (see Figure 26-3). Another alternative is to adjust actual sales figures by some kind of seasonal index. This is feasible, of course, only if there is enough sales history to permit determination of a reliable seasonal pattern.

The most meaningful standard of sales performance is the sales *forecast* for a given product line and/or market area. Virtually all well-managed companies prepare sales forecasts, which serve as the basis for expense budgeting as well as for appraisal of actual sales results. Some of the more commonly used methods of sales forecasting are described in the next section.

SALES FORECASTING METHODS

Some firms forecast crudely: by hunch, "feel for the market," and rough guesses. In these situations the forecasters may not even be aware that they are forecasting. Others forecast by elaborate economic studies, consumer surveys, correlation and regression analysis, mathematical formulas, distributor and trade surveys, and so forth. In some cases, a crude approach is sufficient. There may be no time for a sophisticated forecast, as with a fad item like hula hoops or a seasonal fashion item where the question is, "What will be the most popular color of women's blouses next summer?" In other cases, the required degree of forecast accuracy is so low relative to the speed and ease with which a company can organize itself to meet the demand effectively that the cost of sophisticated forecasting would not justify itself. This is frequently the situation in ladies' fashion goods.

Sales forecasts are generally of two kinds: short-term operating forecasts that predict sales for 1 to 12 months ahead and long-term forecasts that predict sales for 1, 5, to 10 years in advance. The latter are primarily projections of fundamental trends affecting sales, and are most generally used for planning long-term financing and plant improvement and expansion. Short-term forecasts are often broken down by sales territories and become the basis for allocation of marketing effort and for evaluation of territorial performance (see below).

There are numerous methods of sales forecasting. Each in turn has many variations and refinements. Roughly speaking, the major methods can be categorized as:

1. Jury of executive opinion
2. Sales force composite
3. Regression analysis
4. Statistical analysis of trends and cycles
5. Market surveys

Jury of executive opinion In its simplest form, this method secures demand estimates for a given future period from a group of executives and then averages the results.

The system is obviously crude, and it has both advantages and disadvantages. Its advantages are as follows: (1) It can be made easily and quickly. (2) It may not require the preparation of elaborate statistics, some of which might themselves involve a lot of guesswork. (3) It brings a variety of specialized viewpoints together into a pooling of experience and judgment. (4) It may be the only feasible means of forecasting in view of the absence of adequate data.

The disadvantages of the system are as follows: (1) It may not give proper weight to measurable conditions, since it is based almost wholly on personal opinion. (2) It requires costly executive time. (3) It disperses responsibility for accurate forecasting. (4) It presents difficulties in making breakdowns for operating purposes by product, time intervals, or markets. (5) It often gives equal weight to well-informed opinions and poorly informed opinions.

Sales force composite This method combines the views of numerous segments of the sales organization, in a manner similar to the executive opinion approach. There may, however, be at least three superior virtues in the sales force composite opinion method: (1) The various segments of the sales organization are closer to actual field experience and hence speak more knowledgeably, especially in providing detailed estimates for individual products and sales districts. (2) The estimates of the various segments can be more meaningfully compared with the estimates of other segments; that is, a regional manager's estimates for his region can be compared with the composite estimates of his subordinate district managers. (3) The estimates submitted by the salesmen become a more acceptable basis to them for setting their sales quotas.

The starting point in the composite method is generally for each salesman to estimate probable future sales in his territory. Sometimes he makes these estimates alone, and at other times he makes them in consultation with his branch or district manager. Estimates are then progressively consolidated, first at branch offices, then at district and regional offices, and finally at headquarters. It is common practice to check the sales force estimates against independent estimates made by a headquarters marketing research department.

One of the clear advantages of this grass-roots buildup of estimates is that it forces each level to think carefully about its territory, its accomplishments, and its prospects. The estimate often becomes an effective basis for consultation between superior and subordinate concerning the subordinate's activities, and it gives the superior a better picture of what is happening in his scattered territory.

There are some obvious disadvantages in basing sales forecasts on salesmen's estimates: (1) Salesmen are poor estimators, since they are often more optimistic or more pessimistic than conditions warrant. (2) If estimates are used as a basis for setting quotas, salesmen are inclined to understate demand in order to get more favorable quotas. (3) Salesmen are often unaware of broad economic patterns which are shaping future sales, and are thus incapable of forecasting trends for extended periods. (4) Sales forecasting is generally a subsidiary function of salesmen, whose primary duty is to sell; hence, they may not exercise the care needed for accuracy. (5) The method requires an extensive expenditure of time by executives and salesmen. (6) Elaborate precautions are sometimes needed to keep estimates realistic and free from bias.

Regression analysis Regression analysis is a statistical approach to forecasting sales by relating the quantity or amount sold to other variables, such as disposable personal income, awards of construction contracts, or changes in quarterly automobile sales. Thus, a study of past sales trends of shoes may show a relationship to disposable personal income. A closer study may show that on the average, the percent change in shoe sales is 0.8 times as great as the percent change in income.

In order to make a shoe sales forecast based upon the discovery of such a historical relationship, a forecast of personal disposable income is needed. Because the sales of so many different kinds of products are clearly dependent in part on income, numerous banks, governmental agencies (especially the President's Council of Economic Advisers), business consultants, and various business firms make and publish forecasts of personal disposable income at least annually. Hence a shoe manufacturer might base his sales forecast on a disposable personal income forecast developed by someone else.

Sales volume for a product or a company is often correlated with factors other than income. For example, analysis may show that fertilizer sales correlate with agricultural commodity prices, farm output, and the previous year's rainfall. Instead of the forecaster using just one variable on the basis of which to predict sales, he may use many variables. In the case of fertilizer, a multiple regression analysis might be made to show the relationship of all the variables, taken together, to fertilizer consumption rates.

Regression techniques are used in many industries for many purposes. For example, sales of residential heating oil are known to vary inversely with temperature. A regression analysis of the relationship between heating oil sales and "degree days" (one degree day equals one degree below normal for one day) yielded a correlation coefficient of .98. Since allegedly better long-run forecasts of degree days were available than of sales per se, this made it possible to forecast sales reasonably accurately on the basis of predicted temperatures.[2]

Regression analysis has various advantages and disadvantages. The advantages are: (1) This approach describes in measurable, objective terms the relationships influencing the course of sales. (2) The results of the analysis indicate the degree of reliability that can be attached to such relationships. (3) Such analysis reveals relationships affecting sales that casual inspection or intuitive reasoning may not uncover. (4) If sales are correlated with a well-known barometer, such as disposable income, the forecaster gains by the antecedent opinions of other forecasters. (5) If the correlation is made to a statistical series which leads his company's sales, he need not forecast any antecedent statistical series; he need examine critically only anything that may upset the past relationships on which his correlation is based.

But there are powerful disadvantages also. One of these is the danger of relying too heavily upon statistical methods, and a tendency to use them to

[2] George P. O'Donnell, "The Marketing of a Petroleum Product by Probabilities," *Proceedings, Operations Research Conference,* Society for the Advancement of Management, New York, January, 1954.

avoid making an independent appraisal of the future. This is especially important in situations where new influences constantly enter the picture and possibly alter previous relationships. Another disadvantage is that extensive research and good sales records are usually required for making reliable analyses, and these may be costly. Finally, experts are usually required, which also may be costly, although perhaps no more costly than other methods which may make heavy drains on executives' and salesmen's time.

Statistical analysis of trends and cycles A company's sales will usually be affected in some way by at least three basic influences: long-term economic trends, cyclical business fluctuations, and seasonal variations. In some industries the patterns are sufficiently well defined that the influence of each major force can be statistically studied. By estimating the probable course of the business cycle or of basic economic growth trends and by incorporating historical patterns of seasonal fluctuation, a "time series model" can be developed for sales forecasting.

For short-term forecasting, a widely used method is that of "exponential smoothing." Space does not permit a full description of this technique here, but it is essentially a model for projecting observed trends in sales data into the future, taking account of errors in previous forecasts.

Market surveys For entirely new products, for a company entering an established industry with a new brand, or for a company entering a new territory or building a sales outlet at a new location, forecasts sometimes have to be made from scratch. A common approach is to base the forecast on data obtained via surveys, using methods like those described in Chapter 25.

Suppose that a company is considering whether to open a new supermarket in an established community. Suppose, too, that several sites are available. From experience, it knows how large a store should be. It must now determine which of the available sites is best. For this it will make a "trading area" study for each site. Such a study analyzes automobile driving patterns in the city, traffic conditions around the proposed sites, population density and family income figures around these locations, competitive store locations, customer attitudes toward these stores, and the ethnic composition of the population.

Consumer-attitude studies might include questions designed to determine the probability of consumers' switching from their present stores to the proposed new one. They might attempt to discover areas of dissatisfaction, say the meat department or inadequate parking space, with present stores which indicate the possibility of high customer draw for a properly operated and laid-out new store.

In the case of an entirely new product, such as a home knitting machine, interviews might be conducted among a properly selected sample of people to gauge the likelihood of their buying the product. Or the product might be test-marketed in one or more cities to see what the expected national volume is likely to be. A similar indication might be secured from home interviews by asking people whether they would buy it at a given price. Such surveys can be complemented and reinforced by surveying the trade (wholesalers, agents, retailers) to get their impressions of probable sales, and whether they would handle and support the product.

Business firms can also be surveyed on other types of questions such as their planned capital expenditures over the next year, their inventory plans, their expectations of sales during a given period, their credit policies over the next year. Surveys of this kind are published periodically by several research and publishing firms.

MARKET SHARE MEASURES

Obviously one of the major determinants of an individual company's sales is the total amount of business potentially available to it in the industries, product lines, and market areas where it competes. In many situations, it is reasonable to assume that the size of the total market is uncontrollable by the individual competing firm, and to focus attention on the firm's market share as a primary measure of sales performance.

Many firms use year-to-year or quarter-to-quarter changes in their market shares to (1) appraise sales performance and (2) express market targets or set market goals. A year-to-year decline in market share, from say 25 percent to 22 percent, will be considered an ominous sign. A marketing department's statement that it plans to raise its market share over the next three years from 25 percent to 28 percent is one kind of sales target.

Market share information is also frequently used as an aid in sales forecasting. Thus a petroleum company may look at its past market share performance and observe that it has been growing by an average of 1.1 percentage points per year. In forecasting sales for next year and for five years in the future, it may make the rough estimate that at its historic rate next year's share will rise from 8.9 percent to 10.0 percent, and that in five years it will be 14.4 percent, that is, $8.9 + (5 \times 1.1)$.

Market share figures can also be divided according to sales territories and product subcategories. Thus, while a television set manufacturer may have a 25 percent national market share, it may be 15 percent in the New England region, 30 percent in the West Coast region, and 28 percent in the Southeast region. On the other hand, its national share may be 40 percent for portable sets, 10 percent for console sets, and 23 percent for table-model sets.

There is strong disagreement in the business community about the values and uses of market share information. The most obvious problem is that while, say, a rise in market share may indicate more sales than competitors are making, it does not indicate anything about profits. In other words, what was the cost of getting a larger share? Perhaps the increase was achieved by giving bigger dealer discounts, hiring more salesmen, expensive sales contests, more advertising expenditures, or "borrowing from the future," that is, merely selling more to dealers this year without any corresponding increase in retail sales. Next year dealers will buy less because they have so much inventory on hand.

In spite of these and many other problems, market share figures are often used to help control and measure marketing effectiveness because they are relatively simple and easy to understand and are a convenient way of comparing one company with another. But there is great variation between industries in the ease with which these data can be obtained. To determine its share in each of its markets, the firm must obviously have estimates of the total size of each market. For some products, such as automobiles, published industry sales figures are readily available. For others, information must be purchased from commercial sources or estimated by complicated methods (see Chapter 25).

Perhaps the chief technical argument made for using market share as a method of appraising performance is that it helps avoid holding management accountable for forces over which it has no control. If the economy goes into a recession, the demand for television sets declines. Hence even though a company's sales fall, its marketing management can still be effectively evaluated by looking at the proportion of industry sales it captured. Other, so-called external forces might be those which affect all competitors equally such as a generalized shortage of critical materials (such as copper), national prosperity, an industry-wide change in the price structure, or a shift in foreign demand.

Arguments against this reasoning are that a market share drop may be unavoidable if a new company enters the business; that because one company may emphasize a low-priced model, it is naturally less adversely affected by recession and less favorably affected by prosperity; and that a merger by two competitors may, without added effort, greatly strengthen their combined effectiveness and injure that of the remaining companies.

Most companies use market share data in some way. The better managed ones try to combine them with profit standards and/or expense control mechanisms and with other information about the market, distribution channels, and competitive conditions.[3]

□

SALES ANALYSIS

Measures of performance in terms of sales and/or market share are usually employed on a regular basis only for *major components* of a company's opera-

[3] For further discussion see Alfred R. Oxenfeldt, "How to Use Market-share Measurement," *Harvard Business Review*, January–February, 1959.

tions, such as product divisions, major product lines, or sales regions and territories. These regular measures are supplemented in many firms by less frequent, more detailed analyses of sales for specific products, individual customers, and small geographic areas.

Traditionally, sales analysis was a laborious process involving costly hand tabulation of many individual invoices or salesmen's reports. Consequently, it was infrequently employed in most firms. Since computers came into widespread use in the 1960s, it has become relatively simple and inexpensive to tabulate sales in as much detail as may be desired. There is still a limit, however, on the amount of detail that an executive can absorb. For this reason, regular sales analyses are still confined primarily to major categories of products and customers, with further breakdowns of these categories being available only on request.

A major purpose of analyzing sales into progressively more detailed components is to determine the *reasons* for an observed sales performance record. Suppose, for example, that sales in a particular sales territory fell below expectations. Further analysis might show that the problem lies in unsatisfactory sales of certain products, or in the loss of one or two key customers. This process of isolating a problem clearly makes it much easier to determine what corrective actions, if any, should be considered.

Expense measures

Since a company's profit is the difference between its revenue and its costs, a second major class of performance measures is directed toward operating expenses. Actual expenses, classified in various ways, can be compared with various standards including *budgeted* amounts and *industry averages*.

□ EXPENSE BUDGETING

The marketing budget is a detailed statement of planned expenses for a specified future period, generally a year or a selling season. The amounts stated in a budget are generally assumed to be maximum, not required, expenses. The budget, therefore, is a means of controlling actual expenses, because deviations from the budget will direct management's attention to potential problems and the individuals responsible for them. A company can have a corporate marketing budget as well as marketing budgets for each of its divisions, products, and sales territories. A retail store can have a budget for each of its merchandise lines. This forces careful advance planning of expenditures on the part of the individuals responsible for each of the centers of activity that are budgeted, and fixes responsibility for deviations on the individuals who directly control or manage these expense centers.

BUDGETING PROCEDURES

The first step in preparing the marketing budget, regardless of the particular center of marketing activity involved, is a forecast of sales volume. Since certain classes of expenses vary with sales, a reasonably accurate sales forecast is a prerequisite to determining the maximum expenses that must or can be allowed to achieve these sales.

The corporate marketing budget can be created either on a ''top-down'' basis or on a ''bottom-up'' basis. Bottom-up budgeting involves the preparation of a separate operating budget on the part of each division, or each product group, each sales territory, and each functional segment of the marketing organization. The top-down procedure flows in the opposite direction, with each department receiving an overall budgetary allocation from the vice-president. Then the general sales manager, for example, allocates his department's budget among the managers of the three sales divisions, who in turn make allocations to their respective territories. In practice, the bottom-up and the top-down procedures both involve lengthy discussions and negotiations among such groups as the various managers and department heads, the division managers and territory managers, the territory managers and salesmen. Frequently a company will use bottom-up and top-down procedures simultaneously, with each procedure helping to guide the content developed in the other.

While budgeting for a forthcoming year starts with a sales forecast, it also starts with the expense record of the present year or of past years. Thus if sales next year are expected to equal those of this year, there is some justification in looking to this year's expenses as a starting point in estimating next year's expenses; this is precisely where the role of planning and management comes in with its questions. Can we achieve the same sales next year with less expense? How might we do it? Would a restructuring of effort and expenses actually produce more sales?

Therefore, the next step in budgeting is generally to plan fixed, variable, and discretionary expenses separately. As explained in Chapter 13, fixed expenses are those which vary little or not at all in relation to sales volume, given a particular marketing organization. The expenses of the headquarters staff or warehouse rents are fixed in the short run. Little can be done in the short run to avoid or change them. It is in the manipulation of the variable and discretionary expenses that the budgeting process assumes its important short-term planning and control role. Variable expenses include a large proportion of salesmen's expenses, physical distribution expenses, and some record-keeping expenses. Discretionary expenses include those of advertising, sales promotion, and new product development.

BUDGETS AS CONTROL MECHANISMS

The budget can be employed as a control mechanism in a variety of ways. The very process of requiring various groups in the marketing organization to develop their own budgets is one way of exercising control over them. It provides management with some assurance that their expenditures and activities are well planned, and gives management a standard against which to judge their effectiveness.

But beyond that, if a budget is detailed enough, it provides specific information about where to look for performance improvement. Suppose that the branch manager of a regional office submits an expense budget for a given year and that at the end of the year he must submit a statement comparing it with his actual costs. Obviously, his superior will expect explanations for the variances, and presumably the division manager will have them; but regardless of how good these appear to be, if such variances are repeated year after year while other branches get much closer to target, this particular division manager may find himself unemployed.

On the other hand, when these variances are compared with the gross margins which his sales produced, they might show a very attractive picture of performance, thus excusing the variances themselves. A well-managed budgetary system will have required divisional *pro forma,* that is, expected, profit and loss statements as well, so that the results of the expense budget will be subtracted from the gross margin to yield a net profit, or net *contribution* to unallocated costs and profit, on the basis of which the division's performance can also be evaluated.

□ INDUSTRY AVERAGES

Another standard against which actual expense performance can be compared is some kind of typical or average figure for an industry. Trade associations in many lines of retail and wholesale trade publish such figures periodically, and they are widely used as standards of performance. Few manufacturing industries have similar statistics, partly because such items as manufacturers' activities and product lines are typically much less standardized than those of distribution companies.

□ COST ANALYSIS

Analysis of the profitability of sales effort, customers, product lines, and salesmen requires knowing the expenses associated with each segment of a business. This requires cost studies and some way of allocating marketing costs to the functions, products, customers, and salesmen involved. Since the operations and problems of manufacturers and wholesalers, on the one hand, and of retailers, on the other, are somewhat different, it is necessary to discuss their situations separately.

□ COST ANALYSIS FOR MANUFACTURERS AND WHOLESALERS

Manufacturers and wholesalers must make decisions not only about what items to carry and emphasize, that is, their product lines, but also about which customers and territories to cultivate or deemphasize. They wish to know whether their business would be more or less profitable if they dropped or deemphasized certain classes and sizes of customers, certain territories, and certain types of orders. In order to obtain this information, they must make cost analyses, which require procedures for allocating expenses to marketing functions, to customers, to products, and to territories.

Their first step is generally to determine the gross margin and directly assignable expenses associated with each segment of the business whose effectiveness is to be measured. The remaining unallocated expenses can be treated as overhead, with a "contribution to overhead and profit" then figured for each segment. The basic procedure for doing this is as follows[4]:

1. Direct expenses are measured and assigned directly to products.
2. The indirect expenses are assigned to functional categories: storage, physical handling, delivery, promotion, and inventory cost. A functional category puts together all the expense items that have been incurred for the same marketing activity. A functional classification, therefore, permits the allocation of an entire cost group by means of a single measure of functional activity.
3. Allocations to the functional cost categories are made for products on the basis of their utilization of the variable activities giving rise to these costs. The actual allocation of costs is, in effect, made in proportion to some measure of each product's responsibility for the cost-creating activity. If, for example, the average inventory value of product X is one-hundredth of the total average inventory value of all products, then it is charged one-hundredth of the inventory "investment" cost for the period.
4. The excess of dollar gross margin over the sum of the direct expenses and the shares of the various functional cost groups which are allocated to a commodity indicates its relative profitability.

Four main functional cost groups are generally used in analyzing manufacturers' marketing costs; these are shown in Figure 26-4, together with suggested bases of allocation when costs are analyzed both by product and by customer. The specific functional cost groups used should generally coincide with organizational centers of responsibility, since the primary purpose of cost classification is cost control. The specific functional categories used and the extent to which they are subdivided will also depend on the degree of specialization of functions in a given firm or on its particular operations and needs.

One manufacturer developed a more detailed classification for use by his distributors that included the following categories[5]:

[4] Charles H. Sevin, *Marketing Productivity Analysis,* McGraw-Hill Book Company, New York, 1965, pp. 12–25.
[5] "Distribution Cost Accounting for Net Profits," *Industrial Distribution,* July, 1957, pp. 106–136.

FIGURE 26-4

Bases of wholesaler's allocation to commodities and customers

Functional costs	Bases of allocation	
	To products	To customers
I. Maintenance:		
A. Investment	Average inventory value	(Not allocated)
B. Storage	Floor space occupied	(Not allocated)
II. Movement:		
A. Physical handling	Number of standard handling units	Number of invoice lines (weighted by classes of customers)
B. Order routing	Number of invoice lines	Number of invoice lines
C. Delivery	1. Number of standard handling units 2. Bulk or weight	Number of deliveries (weighted by delivery zones)
III. Promotion	Amount of time spent in promotion (where allocated)	Number of sales calls
IV. Reimbursement:		
A. Payments	(Not allocated)	Number of payments
B. Collections	(Not allocated)	Average amount outstanding

Source: Charles H. Selvin, *Marketing Productivity Analysis,* McGraw-Hill Book Company, New York, 1965, pp. 13–15.

1. Stock investment
2. Stock storage
3. Order handling and accounting
4. Outgoing material handling (including delivery)
5. Incoming material handling
6. Customer financing
7. Buying costs
8. Building costs (occupancy)
9. Administrative costs
10. Selling costs

It should be noted that in Figure 26-4 the same costs can be allocated to the commodity in connection with which the functions are performed, *and* to the customers for whom the functions are performed. Thus, if the purpose of the analysis is to determine the costs of handling certain products, the allocations are made to products. If the object is to determine the costs of reaching and servicing certain customers or categories of customers, the allocations are made to customers.

Analysis of marketing costs may also be profitably done on the basis of sales territories. This can become an important step in selecting areas to be covered, determining the amount and type of sales effort needed in each area, setting salesmen's quotas, and controlling operating costs.

The extent of detailed breakdown of costs that is employed depends on the degree of specialization in the firm, on the needs and the operations of the firm, and on the firm's estimation of the relative value of keeping such detailed records. The cost of such record keeping has been substantially reduced in recent years by the introduction of high-speed computers in the operations of both large and small companies. Each cost category can be given a numerical code so that the tabulation and printing of expense records for given periods can be done quickly. Few companies install computers for this use alone, but companies that have computers generally use them for a great many purposes, and detailed marketing-cost record keeping can be one of these. Smaller companies which may not be able to own such equipment can rent computer time from computer service centers.

COST ANALYSIS FOR THE RETAILER

The retailer is generally not in a position to select his customers, his order sizes, or, once his store is located, his territory. Hence his major object in cost analysis is to adjust his inventory, his space allocations, and his merchandising efforts to sales possibilities in order to maximize profits.

Most retailers have less space than they would like to display their products. Beyond that, new products are constantly being offered them to compete with present ones for display space. In 1969, manufacturers, distributors, and brokers offered one large supermarket chain over 5,000 new products, or differently packaged versions of presently carried products. It accepted less than 200, and within a year had dropped half of these. Hence the questions which face most retailers are: Shall I add this new item to my line? Which of the brands of item X should I carry? How much space should I give to item Y, and how should this be distributed among the various brands of Y? Is department A as profitable as it should be? Which items should get preferred end-of-aisle display this week? Is it more profitable to advertise item A or item B?

Some merchants simply use an item's markup percentage to help answer these questions. Some combine markup percentages with actual or estimated stockturn rates. Some rank their products according to their dollar gross margins. But none of these is as useful as other methods that are available, and cost analysis is frequently involved in these methods.[6]

[6] An appraisal of the usefulness of product cost and profit information in food distribution is given in R. D. Buzzell, W. J. Salmon, and R. F. Vancil, *Product Profitability Measurement and Merchandising Decisions,* Harvard Business School, Division of Research, Boston, 1965.

For example, suppose that two items sold in a department store contribute the same dollar gross margins, but item A occupies twice the space and requires twice the inventory investment as item B. By careful cost analysis the merchant might find that if A were eliminated, the space and capital thus made available could be used to carry two new items, C and D, so that the dollar gross margin yielded by B, C, and D would exceed that formerly obtained by A and B. Hence, to look at an item's gross margin contribution is not enough. Costs have to be examined too.

The chief problem in cost analysis is allocating costs to particular products, departments, and activities, as noted above. Most of the costs in a retail store, such as rent and wages, are incurred in common for all the store's items. If a single item is eliminated, there is not likely to be any cost reduction. Similarly, some costs represent activities and functions that may be drastically underutilized during various parts of the day. In a typical store a large proportion of employees' time is normally idle time, used neither for selling nor for necessary nonselling activities.

Accordingly, the expenses that a cost allocation system can easily charge to various categories of commodities are those involved in the maintenance of, and investment in, inventory. These are occupancy costs such as rent (or its equivalent), heat, light, and the depreciation, maintenance, and costs of specialized fixtures and equipment such as soda fountains, refrigerators, special wrapping supplies and equipment, and taxes and licenses for specific commodities. All these can be traced directly to the lines or departments benefited. Inventory carrying costs can also be allocated by specific commodities and departments. In some cases, it may also be possible to allocate physical handling costs to items which differ in terms of weight, size, fragility, and other physical characteristics.

When these costs are subtracted from the gross dollar or percentage margins of the products or departments in question, they yield a contribution to overhead and profit which becomes the basis for evaluating the products or departments in question.

Well-managed retail operations generally break down these contribution analyses in terms of the space occupied by specific products and departments. Thus they make analyses of contribution per square foot of floor space or per lineal foot (or cubic foot) of shelf space. Further analysis is also useful to take into account the inventory investment in each product.

Allocation of costs to individual items is generally impractical when the number of items is large or when the store is small. Allocation to departments or broad categories of products may be more practical for these situations.

Questions

1. James Dwyer was Mid-Atlantic district sales manager for the Eastern Machinery Corporation. As part of his job, he was required to complete a salesman performance evaluation for each of his salesmen on an annual basis. The performance evaluation shown below was prepared for Charlie Barr who has worked in Dwyer's district for the past four years.

The company paid its salesmen a straight 3 percent commission on sales and reimbursed them for authorized expenses. Quotas were set on an annual basis equal to dollar sales for the preceding 12 months.

Products A and B shown in the performance evaluation form are established lines. Product B has been suffering sales declines throughout the company as a result of technological advances made by competition, but not matched by Eastern. Product C is a new product introduced by Eastern in 1968. This product has very high profit margins and faces little direct competition.

a. What is your evaluation of Charlie Barr as a salesman? Why?

b. What further information would you like to have in evaluating Barr? Why?

c. What value do you see in the performance evaluation form? How should it be used?

d. What other information would you want included in the evaluation form?

e. How can evaluation ratings be used to motivate and direct salesmen?

2. Most firms which employ salesmen establish sales quotas of one kind or another. Very few firms, on the other hand, establish profit quotas for salesmen.

a. If both sales and profit are important corporate goals, why do so few firms consider profit at the salesmen level?

b. Can you think of any reasons why it would be undesirable to establish profit quotas for salesmen—even if appropriate cost data were available? Discuss.

3. Two forecasters working for the same automobile manufacturer arrived at substantially different estimates of next year's demand. Does this variance imply that forecasting is largely guesswork? Why or why not?

4. "After all, in the final analysis the best (sales) forecasting method is obviously the one that yields the highest percentage of correct predictions." Comment.

5. Given the limitations of regression analysis, as identified in the text, would you be more likely to use regression in making short-term forecasts or long-term forecasts? Why? Would your answer differ for different types of products? Explain.

Salesman performance evaluation form

1. Personal characteristics

   Date: Feb. 1/1972

   Salesman name: Charlie Barr

   Years with company: 7

   Positions with company:

2. Job performance

Positions with company	Start	Finish or current
1. trainee – 1 year	6,000	6,900
2. salesman – Maine 2 years	8,200	11,500
3. salesman – Baltimore 4 yr.	12,000	15,700
4.		

3. Sales performance (thousands of dollars)

Year	Product A	Product B	Product C	Total sales	Percent quota	Total selling expenses
1968	$240	$175	$ 5	$420	120%	$17,600
1969	280	185	25	480	114	20,400
1970	306	70	45	521	109	22,600
1971	300	145	80	525	101	24,500

Evaluation rating

	Score	Weight	Points
(1) Personal characteristics	26	10	260
(2) Job performance	29	20	580
(3) Sales performance			
(a) Sales volume	525	1	525
(b) Percent of quota	101	5	505
Total			1,870

Rating points:

Excellent	2,000 and over
Good	1,750–1,999
Fair	1,600–1,749
Poor	Under 1,600

Rating for year: Good

Ranking in district: 3/8 (based on total points)

Signatures: ____________________

Salesman

____

District Sales Manager

6. How should firms attempt to measure the effectiveness of their market research departments?

7. In many firms, new product development is an area of major expense and relatively poor performance. What possible performance measures could be applied by a manufacturer of packaged grocery products to measure the success of each of the stages of new product development listed below? What advantages and disadvantages do you see to each of the measures you identified?

a. Search for new product ideas
b. Screening
c. Concept testing
d. Economic analysis
e. Product development and testing
f. Test marketing
g. Commercialization

8. Several years ago, a major typewriter manufacturer was trying to broaden his distribution channels to include variety stores. Many of these stores were reluctant to take on the line because it provided only a 30 percent margin, whereas they traditionally required a 35 to 40 percent gross margin to operate profitably.

a. Does the use of gross margin percent seem to be a reasonable criterion for deciding whether or not to stock an item?
b. How would the method of allocating overhead among departments within the variety store affect the appropriateness of gross margin amount as a criterion?

The public environment of marketing

PART SIX

In this book we have discussed the problems that marketing managers face in trying to define and meet the needs of consumers, and the policies and actions they employ in solving these problems. Our perspective has been that of the marketing manager who is responsible for solving the marketing problems of his individual firm.

Since marketing, more than any other business function, requires knowledge of, and response to, the environment of the firm, emphasis has also been placed throughout on knowing as much as possible about competitors, about customers, about social and economic trends, and, in general, about all external forces that have an impact on marketing. Such forces serve as guides and as constraints to the marketing manager's decision making.

One type of external influence that has been cited frequently is government regulation. Laws and regulations passed by government represent one means by which society seeks to control and influence the behavior of its members, including the behavior of business firms. A few of the specific examples we have discussed include the product liability laws that affect product policy (Chapter 14); the Robinson-Patman Act and other laws, as well as the activities of regulatory agencies, that affect prices (Chapters 16 and 17); the Clayton Act and its effect on relationships within marketing channels (Chapter 18); and the various statutes and regulations that influence or control many aspects of marketing communications (Chapters 20 to 22).

Important though specific laws and regulations may be, they represent only one of the ways in which society governs behavior. In essence, laws are a formal expression of society's attitudes, and they change as society re-

defines its goals and the method of their achievement. Of at least equal importance are the less structured and continuously evolving forces that shape attitudes and behavior. These less formal expressions may be manifested, for example, through the economic policies of government, the moral suasion of its leaders, or the sheer force of public opinion.

Here in Part 6, we will be concerned with the effects of all means, formal and informal, by which society seeks to attain its general objectives. In other words, our concern is with public policy. In the ensuing chapter, we will look at what public policy is, the mechanisms through which it operates, the goals it seeks to attain, the ways in which it is implemented, and the complexities involved in rationalizing different perspectives of public policy issues. Ultimately, our principal concern is with the influence of public policy forces on decision making in marketing.

Public policy is, of course, a very broad area of investigation, so broad that we must caution at the outset that our treatment can only be general. It is designed as an introduction to the nature of public policy and its evolutionary character, to those aspects of it which are particularly important to marketing managers, and to the complexities of the problems that confront marketers as they try to assess the implications of public policy for their decisions.

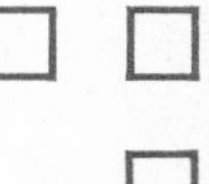

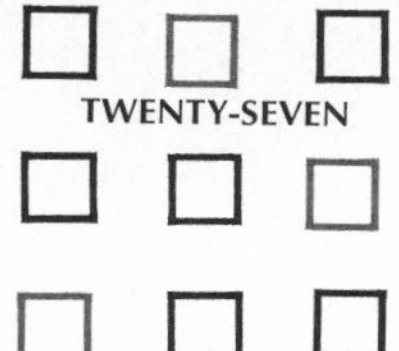

Marketing and public policy

In the early 1970s, advertisers of proprietary drugs could not avoid looking to the future with marked apprehension. Gradually, public opinion seemed to be moving in a direction that might eventually curtail or constrain their advertising practices in significant fashion. The underlying public concern appeared to be that proprietary drug advertisements promoted the euphoric effects of their products, and that extensive promotion of this kind would eventually lead to acceptance of all mood-inducing drugs and, consequently, drug abuse.

Earlier, the matter had already reached proportions sufficient to attract the attention of legislators. Senator Frank Moss of Utah had publicly expressed his concern about proprietary drug advertising. As mentioned in Chapter 22, the Code Authority of the National Association of Broadcasters had responded in 1970 by volunteering to tone down television advertisements for nonprescription sedatives and stimulant mood drugs. But public criticism continued and, in early 1971, had manifested itself in five separate legislative resolutions that would affect proprietary drug advertising.

Each resolution varied in its approach. Hawaii's congressional delegation proposed legislation to ban outright radio and television advertising of prescription and proprietary drugs or, alternately, to encourage the Federal Communications Commission to control such advertising by rule and regulation. A

Maryland congressional delegation proposed similar approaches to curtail "excessive" mass media advertising for medicines and drugs. A Connecticut proposal would require all drug advertising by retailers to gain prior approval by a health commissioner. In Massachusetts, it was proposed that a commission be appointed to study the matter. From the Michigan congressional delegation came a resolution that called upon the news and advertising media "to use judicious restraint in the sponsorship of drug messages to the public, bearing in mind the possible harmful effects on public attitudes."

What was the real nature of public opinion about drug advertising? Was the mood of criticism a transient whim of a vocal minority or a genuine complaint of a majority of consumers? Was it justified? Did any of the proposed resolutions have a chance of gaining legislative approval? If complaints were legitimate, what should drug advertisers themselves be doing? If advertising were to be curtailed or banned, what would be the effect on sales and profits and on incentives to develop and introduce improved products?

These are but a few of the many questions that might be asked by marketing managers affected by the proposals, and by those responsible for formulating and administering governmental restrictions. They were also questions surrounded by a high degree of uncertainty. Until the late 1960s, the majority of marketers had rarely been asked to consider questions of this kind. They were, however, increasingly typical of questions involving the influence of *public policy* on marketing decisions.

□

WHAT IS PUBLIC POLICY?

It is the purpose of this chapter to look broadly at the nature of public policy and its influences on marketing. For our purposes, public policy is defined as that body of guidelines, developed by a society to achieve its general objectives, and formulated in a manner that is partially but not completely expressed by governmental bodies in the form of law and regulation. Less formally, we might say simply that public policy is the current expression of what society believes it wants, expressed only partially by government.[1]

This statement is, of course, deceptively simple. Any society is comprised of a diversity of groups. In the United States, for example, some picture of our diversity is reflected in the following partial list of groups (whose components are not mutually exclusive) that comprise our society: young, middle-aged, and old people; poor, middle-income, and rich people; large and small businessmen; Catholics, Protestants, and Jews; unionized and nonunion workers; clergy; blacks and whites, Westerners, Southerners, and Easterners;

[1] For more detailed discussions of public policy and the process of public policy making, see Gordon Tullock, *Private Wants, Public Means,* Basic Books, Inc., New York, 1970; and Yehezkel Dror, *Public Policy-Making Re-examined,* Chandler Publishing Company, San Francisco; 1968.

parents and children; public and private employers; men and women. Just as the individuals within each of these and countless other groups have their own desires and wishes, so in diverse ways do the groups that they make up. Also each group, in ways large or small, has a voice in the determination of public policy.

Another major characteristic of public policy is its variation over *time*. What society determines as its objectives in the 1970s will not necessarily be what it wanted in the 1930s, or the 1870s. For example, what many people call "the quality of life" is increasingly emphasized as a major social goal in the 1970s. Forty years earlier the nation was primarily concerned with recovery from a severe economic depression, and in the 1870s major goals were to resurrect economic, political, and social structures that had been strained to the breaking point by the Civil War.

Public policy, then, varies over time in response to events and to changes in the diversity and relative strengths of the groups that shape it. How then, given the pluralistic nature of society, and the diversity of goals among its many subgroups, does public policy find expression?

Public policy mechanisms

Our broad definition of public policy implies that, of necessity, it is formulated by a variety of processes. Some processes are formal, such as political elections and collective bargaining; and some, such as lobbying, discussion, and "protest marches," are informal. Some processes lead to results in terms of nationally expressed policies, while others do not. It is our purpose in this section to examine the most important mechanisms through which public policy is expressed.

□ GOVERNMENT LEGISLATION AND REGULATION

The most clear-cut expression of public policy is through government regulation. In the United States, as in other democratic societies, the multitude of groups and the welter of their interests and desires submit themselves to the political process at local, state, and national levels, and some form of governmental policy ultimately results that is binding on the total society or on the group that it directly affects. Such governmental policy is formally expressed in either of two ways: direct legislation or the establishment of regulatory agencies.

Direct legislation as a form of government regulation needs little elaboration. We have discussed elsewhere, and mentioned again in the introduction to Part 6, some of the laws that affect business activity in such marketing areas as pricing, channels, communications, and product policy.[2] Such laws or regulations exist at federal, state, and local levels. Direct legislation can be regarded as roughly analogous, in a "thou shalt not" sense, to nine of the Ten Commandments. For the most part, it states what people (or businessmen) can*not* do under given circumstances.

In general, direct legislation proscribes certain kinds of behavior, but is silent beyond the specific kinds of behavior it articulates. The work of *regulatory agencies,* on the other hand, is broader and more encompassing. The Federal Communications Commission (FCC) has broad legislative mandate to regulate the behavior of the communications industry. Similarly, the Federal Trade Commission (FTC) has extensive legislative authority to establish rules and regulations for business conduct.

Because they are established under broad-based mandates, regulatory agencies have been able to respond to growing concern with public policy issues in the 1970s by enlarging the scope of their regulatory activities. Consider, for example, how the Federal Trade Commission altered its regulations of marketing practices with a span of just over one year. As recently as late 1969, the FTC was known as "the little old lady of Pennsylvania Avenue."[3] Its performance was argued to have little impact on the marketing practices it was supposed to police. But under a new chairman, Casper W. Weinberger, and his successor, Miles W. Kirkpatrick, the FTC undertook a number of unprecedented actions in 1970 and 1971. It allowed consumers to intervene in proceedings once reserved only for the FTC and the company accused. This step first occured when a group of law students called SOUP (Students Opposing Unfair Practices) were allowed to present evidence in a case in which Firestone Tire & Rubber Company was charged with misrepresenting the price and safety of its tires. In the Firestone case, as in an earlier case involving Chas. Pfizer & Company's "Un-Burn" sunburn lotion, the FTC also served notice to all advertisers that future advertising claims would be banned unless documented by "adequate and well-controlled studies."[4] Essentially, the FTC was shifting the burden of proof in advertising claims from itself to the marketers.

Subsequent actions in 1971 extended the FTC's stance of toughness. In attacking advertising claims made by the three largest enzyme-detergent manufacturers, the FTC proposed a ban on all stain removal claims unless the *limitations* of these products were also stated. Finally, the concept of "corrective advertising" was introduced in cases involving Coca-Cola Company's "Hi-C"

[2] For a summary of government legislation affecting marketing, and its interpretation by the courts, see John R. Grabner, Jr., "Legal Limits of Competition," *Harvard Business Review,* November–December, 1969, pp. 4ff.

[3] "Marketers Who Staved Off Old FTC Now Find 'Little Old Lady' has Teeth," *Advertising Age,* Dec. 14, 1970, p. 74.

[4] "The New FTC—So Good It Hurts," *Sales Management,* Jan. 15, 1971, p. 30.

drink and Standard Oil of California's F-310 Chevron gasoline. Both cases involved alleged deceptive advertising, and each accused company was asked to sign a consent order promising that future advertisements would "clearly and conspicuously disclose" that the FTC had found prior claims deceptive.

Direct legislation and regulatory agencies exist also at state and local levels of government. Although we cannot describe their activities at any length, they can affect the work of marketing managers in such diverse areas as pricing (state resale price maintenance laws), advertising (state and local outdoor advertising commissions), and physical distribution facilities (local real estate zoning regulations). The passage in 1971 of a Massachusetts law requiring unit pricing in supermarkets (see Chapter 14) and a proposal for a similar law in Maryland are examples of a growing state and local presence in marketing and public policy in the 1970s.

FISCAL AND MONETARY POLICY

A second major public policy influence on marketing activity lies in the fiscal and monetary policies of the federal government. In Chapter 5, we mentioned that fiscal policy refers to actions taken by the national government in respect to taxation and public expenditures, while monetary policy consists of government action regulating the total supply of money and interest rates.

These public policy tools, by virtue of their powerful impact on the economy, have pronounced effect on markets in general, and on specific industries in particular. We shall cite two examples. When the Federal Reserve System decided on expansionary monetary policies in 1970 to counteract a general economic slowdown and depressed conditions in the construction industry in particular, these policies resulted in greater economic activity because mortgage rates dropped and because more money was available to builders and potential homeowners. In terms of fiscal policy, reduced income tax rates during the recession of 1958–1959 helped to make a sluggish economy more vigorous by leaving more money in the hands of the private (consumers and business) sector.

MORAL SUASION

We use the phrase "moral suasion" here to describe another mechanism by which public policy is expressed. Direct regulation and monetary/fiscal policies are formally developed through a political process, either by law or by governmental regulation. Moral suasion, however, consists of attempts to persuade a party (typically a business firm) to take a course of action, based on the presumed moral rectitude or social desirability of that action, that the party might otherwise not have taken. The most prominent uses of moral suasion have already been mentioned in Chapter 16, wherein members of the executive branch of the federal government succeeded in convincing companies in basic industries that contemplated price increases would not be in the public interest. The "inflation alerts," also mentioned in the pricing chapters, serve as a further example of moral suasion.

Critics of these uses of executive power would argue that "moral suasion" is a euphemism, and that in reality such procedures are power tactics not justified by legal sanction. Certainly businessmen and marketers, whose discretionary power to make decisions is thereby constrained, would argue that moral suasion is too often a cloak for unjustified governmental pressure. In this contention, they find support from many nonbusiness observers who object to the extra-legal expansion of governmental authority.

Arguments of this type become increasingly vehement, and more frequent, as the line between the public and private sectors of American society become more blurred. It is not our purpose here to present opposing arguments on this important question. Our concern, rather, is with the fact of the existence of moral suasion—and there is no doubt that it exists. Its implications for the marketer are obvious. He must take into account the possibility of governmental intervention in those instances where governmental authorities feel that such intervention is justified by the public interest. It is likely, however, that such intervention is not apt to occur unless public authorities also believe that the weight of public opinion is on their side.

PUBLIC OPINION

In a democratic society, public opinion is a potent force in the shaping of public policy. Those who study the behavior of nondemocratic societies would argue that decisions in those societies are also affected by public opinion, even though the latter is less freely expressed and less publicized in those societies.

Public opinion, as a concept, is hard to define. In general, it consists of the expressed or believed-to-exist attitude of the public at large, or at least a substantial segment of the public at large, on any given issue. In our society, it is best known for its impact on the political process. But the marketing concept, with its espousal of the "consumer as king," is itself an indication that marketing activities must be attuned to public opinion. Hence, a nationwide sentiment against polluting the environment forced automobile manufacturers to redesign "cleaner" cars while, on a lesser scale, a poster company stated on its wares that they were made of "biodegradable" paper.[5] It is probable that public opinion was at least an influencing factor in the 1970 decision of a large New York City bottling company voluntarily to collect and recycle used bottles to conserve resources and reduce the city's trash problems.

[5] "Ecology Is In," *The Wall Street Journal,* Feb. 18, 1971.

Discernible trends in public opinion can, of course, serve as indicators of future market opportunities. The Westinghouse Electric Corporation devoted a full page of its 1968 annual report to opportunities for profit in "Attacking Public Problems," citing its explorations in the fields of housing, transportation, education, and health care.

Public opinion is seldom unanimous on a given issue. It is, rather, what is believed to be the *prevailing* opinion of society, or at least of those members of society who have an opinion on a topic. Public opinion is, however, often difficult to measure with any real degree of precision. Our society is diverse in its values and aspirations. Many people are unsure of what their opinions are, or prefer to express them privately. Nevertheless, in spite of the many uncertainties that attend its measurement, public opinion can have a powerful impact on many kinds of marketing decisions.

□

PRESSURE GROUPS

Public opinion and public policy are substantially affected by the activities of pressure groups. Pressure groups abound in pluralistic societies, and exist to attain objectives that are believed to be in their own best interests. Though almost any kind of group that seeks to influence public policy is definable as a pressure group, in our context the best known examples are labor unions and such collective business associations as the National Association of Manufacturers, the chamber of commerce, and various trade associations.

Critics of our social and political system, who might themselves be said to be a pressure group, decry the existence and influence of pressure groups as a distortion of, or disservice to, the best interests of society at large. There are numerous instances of pressure group tactics that are illegal or morally indefensible, and these are clearly undesirable from society's standpoint. Equally undesirable are those instances when the objectives of pressure groups are so selfishly and narrowly defined as to be detrimental to society's best interests.

The problem, of course, lies in the determination of what society's "best interests" are. In democratic societies, we discover "best interest" by permitting pressure groups to exist and operate in a free society while we, through political processes and through education, strive to achieve public policies that serve the interests of the general public and the diverse groups that comprise it. This challenge, in a society such as ours, is an endless one.

At a less philosophical level, the impact of pressure groups on public policy is an important fact of life for businessmen. Organized groups of citizens, for example, have been successful in bringing about changes in the nature of Saturday morning children's television programs. In Canada, consumer groups were instrumental in gaining passage of legislation in 1969 aimed at lowering prices for prescription drugs.

In addition, it should be noted that the business community is affected by the activities of pressure groups within the business community. For example, the efforts of small retailers and druggists had much to do with the passage of resale price maintenance laws and the Robinson-Patman Act, respectively. To cite a more recent example, representatives of the domestic shoe and textile industries sought in the early 1970s to secure the protection of the government against rising imports of these products from Asia.

INDIVIDUALS

An important phenomenon of the 1970s is the impact of individuals on public policy. Ralph Nader has been the most prominent example of a "one man pressure group." Hailed by some as a benevolent crusader and by others as an ingenuous do-gooder, Nader has served as a conspicuous example of what one man can do to influence public policy and affect the business community thereby. It is probably accurate to say that Nader's activities regarding automobile safety have had more to do with changes in that field than those of any other individual. In passing, it should be pointed out Nader's interests have not been confined to product and other improvements in industry; alleged inefficiencies and other shortcomings of various governmental agencies have not escaped his attention.[6]

THE END RESULT

So far, our discussion of public policy has dealt with the diversity of forces that contribute to it, and the various mechanisms that shape it and give it expression. It is clear that the process by which public policy is determined is neither simple nor clear-cut; yet, somehow, public policy emerges out of these diverse groups and mechanisms. It is expressed, as we said early in this chapter, in the forms of goals and guidelines for national action. These have to do with many areas of national life. We shall now discuss only those public policy goals which have direct and immediate application to business and marketing managers. Other goals, for example, those with respect to such vital areas as peace, equality of opportunity, defense, and education, are important to the business community but less directly related to it, and we shall not discuss them. The next three major sections of this chapter, then, will be addressed to public policy goals in three areas: the maintenance of competition, basic economic goals, and the quality of life.

Public policy and the maintenance of competition

The American economy, like that of most free world nations, operates under a *market system*. Under this system, producers and consumers are for the most

[6] For an examination of Nader's accomplishments, see "The Passion That Rules Ralph Nader," *Fortune*, May, 1971, pp. 144ff.

part left to make their own decisions in freely competitive markets, each participant seeking to make the best of the market conditions he confronts.

The key to successful functioning of the market system rests in the phrase "freely competitive market." Absolute freedom in competition is rarely attainable. Nevertheless, to maintain the viability of the market system, a major goal of public policy in the United States is to ensure that competition among business firms is as vigorous as possible. In this section, we will examine various means by which public policy seeks to attain this goal.

MARKET PERFORMANCE, CONDUCT, AND STRUCTURE

To understand how public policy toward maintenance of competition is formulated, it is useful to begin with a brief discussion of the modern economic framework within which competition is viewed. We refer to the field of study known as *industrial organization*.[7]

The framework of industrial organization is based on three central concepts: performance, conduct, and structure.

Performance Questions of performance relate to how successful an industry is in attaining goals judged desirable by society. How efficiently does its marketing system work in distributing goods and services to the public? What kinds of marketing services are provided, and at what costs? How well are consumers' desires met by the system? How flexible is it in responding to growth and changes in technology? In other words, these and related questions relate to how well an industry's marketing system works.

In the United States, the term *antitrust* is used to describe the bulk of the body of law and public policy that has emerged to regulate the performance of industry.[8] Antitrust does not act directly on performance, however. Its objective is to regulate those activities which cause or determine good or bad performance.

Conduct How well a marketing system works is obviously determined by prevailing marketing practices, or conduct, within the system, including these elements: (1) how prices are set, and how they relate to costs; (2) how much is

[7] The term "industrial organization" is somewhat of a misnomer, since it has little or nothing to do with how one organizes and directs a particular industrial firm. For a comprehensive review of industrial organization, see F. M. Scherer, *Industrial Market Structure and Economic Performance,* Rand McNally & Company, Chicago, 1970.

[8] For a comprehensive examination of United States antitrust legislation and its interpretation, see Richard E. Low, *The Economics of Antitrust,* Prentice-Hall, Inc., Englewood Cliffs, N.J., 1968; and H. Lee Fusilier and Jerome C. Darnell, *Competition and Public Policy: Cases in Antitrust,* Prentice-Hall, Inc., Englewood Cliffs, N.J., 1971. A review of comparable legislation in other countries can be found in *Market Power and the Law,* Organization for Economic Cooperation and Development, Paris, 1970.

spent on selling, advertising, and other forms of marketing communication, and how these amounts are determined; (3) how many new products are introduced, and what kinds of products; (4) to what extent firms in the industry compete with one another, and in what ways.

Because conduct determines performance, public policy, through legislation or regulation, seeks to encourage those patterns of conduct which are likely to result in the "best" performance. For example, collusive behavior among competitors is prohibited under the Sherman Act or Section 5 of the Federal Trade Commission Act. There are numerous laws and regulations governing pricing behavior, some of which were described in Chapters 15 and 16. Patent restrictions, trademark restrictions, and the Fair Packaging and Labeling Act all govern the product policies of business firms, as do the activities of agencies such as the Food and Drug Administration. The Federal Trade Commission is empowered to ensure that products and prices are not misrepresented in advertising. Numerous laws and regulations, as were described in Chapter 18, place conduct restrictions on the marketing channel policies of business firms.

Structure Assuming that it is possible to obtain an accurate picture of an industry's marketing performance, and the patterns of conduct which lie behind it, the most difficult question of all is *why* firms in the industry behave as they do.

Any attempt to improve performance by changing behavior through antitrust legislation, voluntary industry action, or otherwise is likely to be ineffective unless it has some impact on the basic underlying factors which are thought to govern conduct. The most important of these factors, in the opinion of most industrial economists, is the *structure* of an industry, that is, the number of competing firms and the degree of concentration of total industry sales among these firms. At one extreme, an industry made up of many small firms, no one of which accounts for more than a small fraction of total industry sales, is supposed to be characterized by active price competition and low promotional expenditures. At the other extreme, an oligopoly consisting of a few large, powerful firms is generally thought to behave in just the opposite fashion, that is, to avoid price competition and to spend excessive amounts of money on promotion.

We find, then, that public policy also seeks to govern the structure of an industry by legislating or regulating to discourage oligopolies or monopolies. This body of legislation, and its interpretation by courts of law, is too complex to be discussed adequately here. It should be recognized, however, that its essential goal is to prohibit mergers, acquisitions, and other business actions which might lead to undue concentration of market power in any industry.

THE EXCHANGE PROCESS

The integrity of the exchange process, that is, of transactions between buyers and sellers, is protected by public policy in several ways. A principal method is through the legislation and regulation of market structure and conduct, as outlined in the previous section. By discouraging high concentration (a structure element), for example, it is hoped to preserve the relative bargaining strength of buyers. By prohibiting specific kinds of business conduct, for example, unfair pricing practices, it is hoped to provide the buyer with the opportunity and ability to make a fair and reasonable choice in his buying decision. False and deceptive advertising claims are prohibited for the same reason.

Another means of facilitating exchange is *product standardization*. Many products are classified by quality, size, and other criteria, and marketed on the basis of such standard classifications. Food items, drug items, and many other consumer and industrial products are subject to standardization by governmental regulation. In still other instances, standardization is voluntarily undertaken by industry itself. Many kinds of electrical products are a case in point: the National Electrical Manufacturers Association (NEMA) establishes standard size, weight, and performance criteria for many electrical products.

Related to this are attempts to simplify product lines, undertaken either voluntarily or under regulation. The National Electrical Manufacturers Association, for example, does much that is designed to simplify the product lines of its member manufacturers. In other industries, most particularly those producing consumer packaged goods, the Fair Packaging and Labeling Act (discussed in Chapter 14) has sought to increase product simplification by reducing the number of package sizes that manufacturers offer.

The viability of the exchange process is also protected by attempts to make sure that customers have adequate *information* about products. This is a major goal of the so-called "consumerism" movement. Consumer groups, for example, were a major force behind passage of the Fair Packaging and Labeling Act. Many consumer organizations have also undertaken extensive education programs to teach buyers how to use information in making more effective buying decisions. Consumer demands for adequate information also extend to adequate information on service and repair. In response, some business firms have adopted unique consumer communications systems. Whirlpool Corporation's "Cool Line," for example, is a nationwide toll-free telephone system that enables customers to speak directly to factory-based customer service representatives.

"CUSHIONS" FOR SPECIAL GROUPS

In order to preserve a high order of competition in the economy, public policy has required for many years that certain kinds of enterprises be afforded some protection from the ultimate rigors of competition itself. Thus, farm prices have been supported by national action to protect farmers, and tariffs have been selectively applied to protect "infant," sick, or essential industries. Small retailers have theoretically been protected from large competitors by resale price maintenance. In recent years, the government has taken steps through the Small Business Administration (SBA) to encourage the development of small enterprises.

Public policy and national economic goals

Most people would agree that several major goals shape public policy actions regarding the national economy: economic growth, full employment, price stability, and a more equitable distribution of income.[9] A full discussion of these goals is impossible here. We shall discuss them briefly, however, in order to convey an impression of their nature, possible conflicts among them or between them and other goals, and their impact on marketing managers.

□ GROWTH

The American economy, except for a few periods in its history, has been conspicuous for its continued growth. By 1971, the gross national product (GNP) had reached one trillion dollars. Up until the early part of this century, growth was largely unplanned in the sense that public policy did little to stimulate it in any direct way.[10] It is only in the last several decades, however, that we have realized the continuing importance of public policy as a weapon to offset cyclical economic downswings and maintain an upward growth rate.

The so-called "Keynesian revolution" in economic theory brought awareness that public policy, as manifested in fiscal and monetary policy, can powerfully affect economic activity. In addition, such other public policy devices as tariffs (or the lack thereof), farm price supports, unemployment insurance, the social security system, and effective planning regarding the use of natural resources are helpful not only to those most directly affected by them, but also to the general economy. The objective, of course, is *real* growth, that is, continuously expanding supplies of goods and services on a per capita basis, rather than the illusory growth reflected in the expansion of the gross national product through inflation.[11]

What influence does the public policy goal of economic growth have on

[9] An interesting discussion of national economic goals, and their relationship to other goals, can be found in *Joint Economic Report, 1971, the Report of the Joint Economic Committee of the U.S. Congress on the February 1971 Economic Report of the President,* Government Printing Office, Washington, 1971.

[10] An outstanding exception to this generalization might be the national homesteading policies of the nineteenth century and tariff laws, designed to protect infant industries, at various times.

[11] For example, 1970's GNP of almost one trillion dollars amounted to only $720 billion in 1958 dollars.

marketing managers? Obviously, an expanding economy generally implies increasing real incomes and expanding markets for goods and services of all kinds. In the event of recession, it means that there is a high probability of some type of government action to invigorate the economy. Astute marketers, therefore, keep a close eye on overall economic developments, knowing that their industries and their companies may well be affected by public policy actions.

FULL EMPLOYMENT

Since the passage of the Full Employment Act of 1946, it has been public policy to manage the economy, in terms of various kinds of government action, so as to achieve a high rate of employment. The objective, of course, is jobs for all who want them, and various measures are employed to work toward that objective. The most prominent are, again, monetary and fiscal policies, but many others, such as loans to small businesses or minority enterprise, government aid in education and training programs, and the encouragement of business investment through changes in depreciation regulations, are designed to stimulate employment opportunities as well as overall economic growth.

For marketers, there is some assurance in knowing that public policy is designed to keep employment high. Where specific instruments of full employment policy affect particular classes of potential customers, those who supply goods and services to such groups have increased opportunities available.

PRICE STABILITY

If prices fluctuate widely, either upward or downward, individuals and groups suffer. Uncertainty as to what the future may hold can lead, variously, to speculation, inaction, or retrenchment. Therefore, the national economic goals of most countries include the objective of avoiding or dampening drastic changes in price levels.

Moral suasion, one of several means employed by governments to bring about price stability, has sometimes had direct impact on marketers. For example, in 1969, the Canadian government established a Prices and Incomes Commission in a major effort to hold back price and wage increases, and to help break a prevailing pattern of "inflationary society." The commission had little real authority; its role was to bring about agreement among government, business, and labor unions on means to combat inflation. After a conference with the commission in February 1970, major Canadian business firms agreed to be restrained by price guidelines for the remainder of the year. In most instances, the stipulated price increases did not fully reflect increases in production costs. The Prices and Income Commission was generally *not* successful in its efforts to control inflation, however, primarily because it was unable to enlist the cooperation of labor unions. Nevertheless, it continued to take an active role in restraining price increases, primarily by the use of moral suasion. In a 1971 report, for example, the commission severely criticized four major oil companies—Imperial Oil Ltd., Shell Canada Ltd., Texaco Canada Ltd., and Sun Oil Company Ltd.—for refusing to take "remedial action" after being charged with "unduly increasing prices" during 1970.[12]

□ INCOME DISTRIBUTION

A public policy goal that has assumed increasing importance in recent years is the more equitable distribution of income. Along with economic growth and full employment, most Americans endorse the concept that a country as rich as ours should see to it that all people should share the bounty that our technology affords. Although many difficulties are involved, public policy has evoked a number of programs in recent years that are designed to assist the less fortunate sectors of society in their attempts toward betterment. Federal and state governments have increased their efforts in the field of manpower training, with the hope that such training will lead to better employment, and hence to larger incomes and a higher standard of living. Private industry, both at its own expense and with governmentally provided funds, has done much to provide jobs for minority groups. For example, several associations of businessmen, such as the National Alliance of Businessmen (NAB), have put together programs to seek out and train individuals who have previously not been able to find or hold jobs.

Attempts to broaden the distribution of income are not limited to ethnic and minority groups. Regional efforts are also being made. For the last several years, to cite an example, efforts have been under way to assist the economically depressed Appalachian region as well as other parts of the country where the loss or absence of industry has caused economic difficulty.

If the nation is successful in achieving, at least to some extent, a wider distribution of income, such a move will have major implications for marketers. Markets for consumer goods will be wider and deeper. Depressed areas of the country will become more viable marketing targets. There will be an upsurge in the need for industrial goods that are used in the process of producing the consumer goods for new customers.

The quality of life as public policy

In the late 1960s and early 1970s, a relatively new public policy goal emerged as a major factor in the American society, one that we refer to here as improvement in the *quality of life*. Though related to the economic objectives dis-

[12] "Four Oil Companies Scored in Canada in '70 Price Rise," *The New York Times*, June 5, 1971, p. 37.

cussed above, many Americans would assert that this goal transcends economic goals, and almost all agree that it is of major importance.

The public policy goal envisaged in the words "quality of life" refers to a desire to define our mutual objectives in terms of a life that is culturally, aesthetically, and environmentally rewarding. It has become evident that our physical environment has suffered greatly under the impact of expanding population and the abuse and rapid depletion of our natural resources. In addition, many Americans charge that, as a society, we have become too engrossed in the material aspects of existence, and that as a result its human and qualitative aspects have suffered. Still others argue that our national priorities are out of order, and that we have become absorbed in "getting ahead" rather than in enjoying and enriching our national existence.

Whatever the claims and their merits, the quality of life has become an important public policy objective. It finds its most evident expression in governmental and private attempts to improve the quality of life, but beyond that it manifests itself in a variety of ways. Many diverse groups, not limited to elected or regulatory bodies, are involved in the effort to shape public policy in this realm. As of the early 1970s, the specific nature of public policy was as yet undefined. But the absence of specificity does not detract from the interest that has been shown, and it is worthwhile to touch briefly upon some of the more important current efforts in the area.[13]

A CLEAN ENVIRONMENT

The focal point of efforts to create a better quality of life has been the attempt to bring about a cleaner environment. Beginning in the late 1960s, a variety of activities directed to the attainment of this goal were undertaken. Governments at national, state, and municipal levels established regulations and implementing bodies to reduce the degree of pollution of air and water. Private groups and business firms undertook similar efforts.

Among many examples was federal government legislation to control the emission of harmful gases and materials from combustion engines. The emission standards that this act required to be met by 1975 were so stringent that representatives of the automobile industry expressed serious doubt as to their technical feasibility.

Soft drink bottling companies were subjected to severe public pressure to discontinue sale of nonreturnable bottles, or to adopt new types of containers that would dissolve in soil over a period of years.

Another major issue was that of phosphates in detergents. Reduced phosphate levels were required by federal legislation in the United States, and in

[13] For a more complete exposition of public policy issues relating to the quality of life, and their impact on business, see John J. Corson, *Business in the Humane Society,* McGraw-Hill Book Company, New York, 1971; and *Public Affairs Challenges of the '70s,* National Industrial Conference Board, New York, 1970.

Canada, phosphates were banned entirely in 1970. Suffolk County in Long Island went even further, banning the sale of all detergents early in 1971; well-known brands such as Tide, Fab, and All literally disappeared from supermarket shelves.

Attainment of a clean environment is, of course, a costly undertaking. It is representative of the complexity of public policy issues for which many consumers, though espousing the clean environment cause, were paradoxically unwilling to pay the cost. In 1970, for example, most major United States oil companies introduced new lines of low-lead gasolines. Selling at a 1 or 2 cent premium, these gasolines were heavily advertised at the time of their market introduction. One estimate showed that major refineries with low-lead gasolines were spending 50 percent of their combined promotional budgets on the new gasolines in the latter part of 1970. Yet low-lead gasolines, initially at least, were market failures, accounting for only 2 to 5 percent of each firm's total gasoline sales.[14]

PUBLIC HEALTH AND SAFETY

Allied to environmental issues are others that relate to public health and safety. Starting in the late 1960s, a variety of activities emanating from direct legislation, regulatory agencies, public opinion, pressure groups, and individuals combined to spur marketers into action. The Child Protection and Toy Safety Act of 1969 gave the Secretary of Health, Education, and Welfare authority to declare a toy an "imminent hazard," and to ban it from sale immediately. The Accident Prevention Committee of the American Academy of Pediatrics expressed doubts that this law went far enough and, in its publicity releases, continued to warn parents of the need for caution in purchasing toys.

In 1971, the Federal Trade Commission acted for the first time in an issue of public safety by seeking an injunction to halt an advertising campaign by the American Safety Razor Company involving distribution of sample razor blades in newspapers. Food additives such as cyclamates came under close scrutiny or outright prohibition by the Food and Drug Administration, and the sale of swordfish was temporarily banned because of the high mercury content of the fish. Ralph Nader rose to prominence by writing *Unsafe at Any Speed,* a book concerned with automobile safety. Publicity surrounding this book assured passage of the Motor Vehicle Safety Act of 1966 establishing a government agency to set mandatory vehicle safety standards.

CULTURAL AND AESTHETIC ISSUES

Not all concerns regarding the quality of life are physical. Many are cultural or aesthetic. By their inherent nature, these public policy concerns tend to have greatest impact in the quality and content of advertising.[15]

[14] "Gasoline: Low Lead Bombs at the Pump," *Marketing Communications,* April, 1971, pp. 52–54.

[15] For a spirited defense of the use of "dramatic license" in advertising, see Theodore Levitt, "The Morality (?) of Advertising," *Harvard Business Review,* July–August, 1970, pp. 84–92.

In part, the goal of attaining cultural or aesthetic beauty has been manifested through legislation or regulation. Outdoor advertising, for example, has been regulated by both national government (on interstate highways) and state and local authorities. In general, however, this public policy goal has had its greatest influence through the media of public opinion. In the early 1970s, prevailing public opinion was not generally favorable to the cultural effects of advertising. A 1971 survey of 2,700 subscribers to the *Harvard Business Review* (presumably nearly all businessmen) found, for example, that 41 percent felt advertising downgraded public taste, while 57 percent felt advertising had an unhealthy influence on children.[16]

At this stage, the ultimate expressions of these public policy questions are impossible to predict. So far as marketers and other businessmen are concerned, it seems clear that they will continue to grow in importance. In some instances, such as systems for the provision of cleaner air and water, they may provide excellent and useful marketing opportunities. In other instances, they may create restrictions or constraints on the businessmen's latitude of action. It will be the purpose of the next sections of this chapter to examine in greater detail the implications for marketing managers of these and other public policy goals and issues that have been discussed above.

Public policy and marketing management

Throughout this chapter, we have dealt with an assortment of issues and topics characterized, above all, by their diversity. We have seen that public policy is a broadly defined concept operating through mechanisms ranging from individual actions to federal government legislation. Its goals are complex, sometimes amorphous, often conflicting, and always changing. Its impact is seemingly universal, at one moment questioning the advertising practices of proprietary drug manufacturers and, in the next, protecting infant industries in order to foster competition.

Public policy has not always been of front line concern to marketers. Few textbooks on marketing published before 1970, for example, made specific reference to the topic as such. At best, reference was made to the basic legislative framework within which marketers had to operate. From the tone of this chapter, however, we have indicated that, in the late 1960s and early 1970s, public policy influences on marketing increased enormously.

At this point, it is significant to ask if public policy has really "come of age" for marketers. Is it truly a matter that merits close attention and scrutiny by the marketing manager?

In our view, the answer to this question is clearly affirmative. To illustrate, let us examine the case of the Talbot Company—a hypothetical, but not

[16] Stephen A. Greyser and Bonnie B. Reece, "Businessmen Look Hard at Advertising," *Harvard Business Review*, May–June, 1971, pp. 18ff.

unrealistic, business firm—as one of its product managers prepares a 1972 marketing plan. Hopefully, this illustration will demonstrate just how pervasive, yet significant, can be the impact of public policy on contemporary decision-making in marketing.

THE TALBOT COMPANY

Ralph Gordon had been an employee of the Talbot Company for five years, the last two as product manager for Glossex furniture polish. Hence, in August 1971, as he began to prepare a 1972 marketing plan, the task should have been an easy one. Not only had he done it before, but Glossex, with annual sales in excess of $20 million, was well established as a leading product in its field.

Nevertheless, Mr. Gordon was somewhat uncertain about what the coming year held in store for his product. A number of events during the past year, most of which were beyond his control, had caused him to wonder if particularly close attention to the marketing plan might not be appropriate. To begin with, there was all that bad publicity the Talbot Company had attracted in the last year. Talbot was a large company with annual sales of over $200 million. Its products included cleaning compounds, polishes, starches, and insecticides sold in consumer, industrial, and agricultural markets. It was the insecticides, not Glossex furniture polish, that had started all the trouble.

As a term project, a group of students at a Midwestern agricultural college has tested several agricultural insecticides for their polluting effect on the environment. Talbot's products were among those severely indicted. Somehow, the matter got into the press, and a reporter from *The New York Times* was soon at the head office seeking an interview. Statements by a company official that the matter was "poppycock," that the tests were not properly conducted, and that "there was no other way to kill the (blank) bugs anyhow" only added fuel to the fire. Soon after, a group of women began to picket supermarkets calling for a boycott of all Talbot products until the insecticide was withdrawn. The effect on the sales of Glossex was minimal and temporary, however.

Mr. Gordon was concerned by his company's apparent indifference to the whole affair. There had been a transient concern when students at a few colleges refused to sign up for employment interviews, and even talk about establishing an "office of public responsibility" as automobile manufacturers had done within the past year. But then the matter died down, and everyone seemed to look on it as a mere temporary aberration. Mr. Gordon wondered, however, if one more incident leading to adverse publicity might not cause more serious damage to sales and profits.

For 1972, it was planned to reformulate Glossex to include a new synthetic additive that resulted in a higher furniture luster. New labeling had already been designed for both the aerosol and plastic containers in which Glossex was sold. Because the new ingredient was poisonous when consumed in large quantities, the label contained a health warning. Mr. Gordon had been surprised when the company's lawyers advised the warning. Who would be fool enough to *drink* furniture polish? The answer, of course, was children, and under recent court decisions involving product liability, the company could be sued if it had failed to warn parents to this effect.

One of Mr. Gordon's main problems involved how to advertise Glossex in the coming year. The advertising agency's suggestion of a "50% Brighter" theme was questionable. In a 1971 Federal Trade Commission hearing involving Firestone tires, the commission served notice on all advertisers that performance claims would be banned unless documented by "adequate and well-controlled" studies. Talbot had no studies that could document its brightness claim, although Mr. Gordon was confident such a claim was true. On the other hand, it also seemed inadvisable to continue the present theme of "Cleans Stubborn Furniture Stains." In a 1970 case involving enzyme-detergent manufacturers, the commission had barred any implication that a specific ingredient removes a stain if, in fact, the stain would likely be removed by washing without the ingredient. Glossex was not unique in its stain-removing qualities. Just what could a company advertise? Mr. Gordon was no longer sure, but when he did find an appropriate theme, he knew it would have to clear the legal department.

In reformulating Glossex, the Talbot Company's objective was to gain sales by attracting present users of inferior competitive products. To Mr. Gordon, this meant the 1972 marketing plan would need to include ways of inducing users of competitive furniture polishes to *try* Glossex. A suggestion had been made for a nationwide sweepstakes contest in which entry forms would be attached to Glossex on supermarket shelves. The contest seemed like a good idea; a similar promotional device six years earlier had helped propel Glossex to prominence at the time of its market introduction. But in 1971, many marketers had become wary of contests. The Coca-Cola Company had been required by the Federal Trade Commission to award $100 prizes to many persons said to have been wrongfully deprived in a 1969 contest in which they were not told that more than one answer was required to questions used in the contest. Unless a contest were very carefully designed, it could end up costing the company a lot of money.

In 1971, for the first time in several years, Glossex posed some unusual questions of pricing. In its aerosol version Glossex sold in two sizes, 6 ounce and 18 ounce. Because of the cost of aerosol containers, the 18-ounce size retailed at a price less than double that of the 6-ounce size, even though it contained three times as much polish. But within recent months, unit pricing had become widespread in supermarkets, either through legislation or voluntary adoption by food retailers. With the difference in unit price now being so fully disclosed to consumers, Mr. Gordon wondered if some change in pricing policy were not called for.

The pricing issue was also made more acute by some bad publicity that had fallen directly on Glossex in 1970. In August, a professional journal called *Antitrust Law & Economic Review* had published a survey of competitive prices of manufacturers' brands and private (distributors') label products. Glossex was one of the items selected for the survey and, among A & P stores in Washington, D.C., was found to be priced 48 percent higher than "comparable" distributors' brands. When the journal article was submitted as testimony before a Senate consumer subcommittee, it was widely publicized in the news media. As a result, the Talbot Company had received over 9,000 letters complaining that its products were overpriced, a figure that astounded Mr. Gordon.

As he looked back at the past year, Mr. Gordon found it hard to point to any one event in the public forum that had significant impact on Glossex' sales and profits. Yet many events had occurred, and many similar events seemed likely to arise in the year ahead. Mr. Gordon wondered if it did not add up to something significant in the way of change. He was concerned, too, about his company's lack of a well-defined position on public policy matters. Should it fight public policy encroachments on its latitude of action? Should it support activities that were "in the public good," whatever that was? Mr. Gordon did not know, and no one else in the company seemed to know either.

HOW SHOULD MARKETERS RESPOND?

In a sense, the most significant aspect of the Talbot Company case is not the many different dimensions on which public policy matters infringed on its marketing decisions. In the 1970s, almost any company could document a similar case history. Different problems might be cited, to be sure, but the same compelling forces of public policy would be in back of these problems.

Instead, the crucial need of most companies on matters of public policy is the development of a *strategy* by which the firm will consistently approach such issues. Just as a marketing strategy is necessary to bring overall effectiveness to the diverse elements of a marketing mix, so also is consistency required in approaching the diverse elements of public policy. The Talbot Company apparently had no such strategy. Its response was to fight one bush fire after another, as each arose.

An obvious question is what strategies are appropriate in addressing issues of public policy. The answer, of course, depends on the specific circumstances of each individual firm. Consider, for example, the case of General Motors Corporation. As the world's largest corporation and manufacturer of a product that pollutes and sometimes kills, General Motors was an obvious target of emerging quality of life goals in the late 1960s. Its initial defensive responses to Ralph Nader's accusations were judged by many as inappropriate and clumsy. But by the early 1970s, General Motors had assumed a position of leadership in addressing issues such as automobile safety and pollution. Accordingly, the company undertook a strategy that stressed and acknowledged its social responsibilities, but at the same time refused to shoulder excessive blame for problems it did not create alone, or to accept excessive responsibility for solving these problems alone. Thus, in addressing the Executive Club in Chicago in March 1971, General Motors chairman James M. Roche attacked those who would place *too much* responsibility for public policy problems in business:

> Business didn't create discrimination in America, but business is expected to eliminate it. Business didn't bring about deterioration of our cities, but business is expected to rebuild them. Business didn't create poverty and hunger in our land, but business is expected to eliminate them.[17]

The rationale for this approach presumably rests in the reality that, despite its size, General Motors cannot be expected to solve all the nation's contemporary social problems. To the extent that sectors of the public have unrealistic expectations in this regard, it would be folly to adopt a passive strategy of appeasement to their demands.

The public policy strategy of General Foods Corporation, on the other hand, was very different from that of General Motors in 1971. In a speech to advertisers given in the same week of March, General Foods' president Arthur Larkin reflected his company's position of advocating self-regulation in the advertising industry. He stressed that criticisms of advertising were logical, natural, and healthy. Unlike General Motors, however, General Foods had not been an object of attack, criticism, and expectation. By advocating self-regulation, the company presumably hoped to avert any such occurrence.

Questions

1. Considering the case of the Talbot Company described in the latter part of this chapter:
   a. Should Gordon recommend the use of a sweepstakes contest in 1972? Why?
   b. As Mr. Gordon, what additional information would you want prior to establishing your 1972 marketing plan? Why?
   c. Assuming that the Glossex profit contribution in 1971 was running at a rate of 7 percent of sales before taxes, how much would you be willing to spend to gather the information you want?
   d. Do you think the Talbot Company should have a well-defined position on public policy matters? Why? If so, how should management approach the task of developing such a position?

[17] "Roche, Larkin Views Differ on Consumerism," *Advertising Age*, Mar. 29, 1971, p. 113.

2. In early 1968, a "Door-to-Door Act" was introduced in the United States Congress. According to the text of the proposed legislation (Senate Bill 1599, 90th Congress, 1st Session), it was designed, "to assist the consumer by enabling him, under certain conditions, to rescind the sale of goods and services when the sale is entered into at a place other than the address of the seller." (The bill specifically exempted mail-order and telephone sales.) Under the provisions of the act, any contract to buy goods or services involving $25 or more could be canceled by a customer who so notified the seller by midnight of the day following the transaction. According to the authors of the bill, the consumer needs a "cooling-off" period to reconsider purchases from door-to-door vendors because he "is frequently induced to purchase goods or services which he does not need or desire through the unsolicited and often unethical persuasion of certain door-to-door sellers."

Proponents of the Door-to-Door Sales Act cited examples of allegedly unfair practices in door-to-door selling such as the following (taken from testimony before the Hearings of the Consumer Subcommittee, Committee on Commerce, United States Senate):(1) Fraudulent "contests" in which consumers are lured into purchases by claims that they have won prizes, which turn out to be certificates redeemable only as partial payment for the seller's merchandise. (2) Bogus "surveys" used as a means of gaining entry to consumers' homes. (3) False statements that a buyer can obtain discounts in return for supplying names of friends as prospects for the salesmen. (4) Keeping buyers, especially persons dependent on public welfare payments, in perpetual debt. Failure to maintain adequate records of amounts paid and balances due, and in some instances, falsification of payment records.

Not only were these practices basically undesirable, according to supporters of the act, but "they are geared to those most easily duped: the poor, the uneducated, the unsophisticated, and the elderly." Concern over abuses in door-to-door selling had already led to passage of statutes in several states, as well as a national law in Great Britain, with provisions similar to those of the Door-to-Door Sales Act.

Executives and attorneys representing door-to-door sales companies opposed the proposed legislation. Their major objections can be summarized as follows: (1) Singling out door-to-door selling for special restrictions would damage the reputation of ethical companies in the field. Moreover, there was no evidence to indicate that dishonest practices are more prevalent in this method of sale than in conventional retail stores. (2) Enabling a buyer to cancel a contract, without necessarily having a good reason to do so, would "undermine the foundation of the law of contracts," and make it much more difficult to do business. (3) It would become more difficult to recruit and retain good sales persons, and this would result in higher costs of doing business. (4) Existing state, municipal, and federal laws, if adequately enforced, already prohibited deceptive practices in door-to-door selling as well as in other types of retailing.

Do you think the Door-to-Door Sales Act should be passed? Why or Why not?

3. If you were a tobacco company executive, what position would you take on government proposals to limit the amount that cigarette companies can spend on advertising, prohibit brand endorsements by athletes and celebrities, and forgo advertising in college publications? How do you see your ethical responsibilities if you were privately convinced cigarettes were harmful to health? Why?

4. Executives who participate in illegal price-fixing agreements often feel they are doing what is necessary to stabilize sales and jobs in the industry. Would it be better if industry price-fixing agreements were legally recognized, as is the case in many European countries? Or should such agreements continue to be created as illegal per se and the executives made personally subject to jail sentences and fines?

5. During the summer of 1970, Robert B. Choate presented a brief to the United States Senate's Consumer Subcommittee charging that the nation's cereal marketers were heavily promoting their least nutritious products. According to Choate's figures, which were concerned with 60 brands of advertised cereals, only two of the 20 best-selling brands were among the 20 products having highest nutritional content. In his testimony, Choate particularly chided cereal manufacturers for promoting the least nutritious products heavily in children's television programs, stating: "It would seem that the worst cereals are huckstered to the children on a totally antinutritional basis equating sweetness with health and ability, while the very few good cereals are sold to adults in a manner all but defying cost analyses."[18]

General Foods Corporation, manufacturer of the Post brand of cereals, refuted Choate's testimony, insisting that it contained "a great many technical errors" and "a number of wrong assumptions." The company pointed out that Choate's testimony ignored the very important factor of taste preference. "You can't force a youngster to eat a breakfast food he doesn't like, no matter how loaded it might be with nutrients," the company said, adding it did not specifically advertise nutrition to children because it "isn't meaningful to them."[19]

a. Evaluate General Foods' response to Choate's testimony.

Some of the top products in Choate's ranking were fortified with vitamins and minerals, and promoted on the basis that they contained 100 percent of

[18] "Many Top Dry Cereals Have Little Nutritional Value, Consultant Says," *Wall Street Journal*, July 24, 1970, p. 12.

[19] *Ibid.*

the minimum adult requirement of certain nutrients. Discussing this, a General Foods spokesman noted that his firm limited fortification to 33 percent of the minimum adult daily requirement. This was done, he said, because nutrition experts claim it is best to get required daily nutrients in three separate mealtime doses. "If we exceed these levels, someone might say we're trying to preempt other meals as a selling technique and find us guilty of deception."[20]

b. Evaluate this statement by the General Foods spokesman.

c. Do you think that cereal manufacturers who fortify their products to 100 percent of the minimum adult daily requirement should reduce the vitamin or mineral content of their products? Alternately, should they stress this feature in their promotion and advertising?

6. Many book and record clubs, as well as other business firms, utilize a selling approach known as *negative option selling*. Under this system a prospective customer, such as a club member, is automatically shipped merchandise and billed for it, unless he specifically instructs the seller not to do so.

Supporting this procedure at Federal Trade Commission hearings on a proposed rule to ban the negative option, a psychologist representing the Columbia Record Club stated that the approach offered "unique psychological advantages" to the consumer. He explained that busy consumers were attracted to the negative option as a form of "guidance" in selecting purchases and as a "defense against human weaknesses." The consumer "cannot be exploited if he is aware," he said.[21]

a. What is your evaluation of the psychologist's testimony?

b. Do you think the FTC should oppose negative option selling?

c. Regardless of the FTC decision, should firms such as the Columbia Record Club use the negative option? Why?

7. Evaluate the following statement made by economist Milton Friedman: "There is one and only one social responsibility of business—to use its resources and engage in activities designed to increase its profits so long as it stays within the rules of the game, which is to say, engages in open and free competition without deception or fraud."[22]

[20] "Cereal Nutrition Doesn't Crackle or Pop," *Marketing/Communications*, March, 1971, p. 39.

[21] "Negative Option Lets Consumer Outwit His Own Character Traits, FTC is Told," *Advertising Age*, Nov. 23, 1970, p. 1.

[22] Milton Friedman, "Social Responsibility of Business Is to Increase Its Profits," *The New York Times*, Magazine Section, Sept. 13, 1970, p. 126.

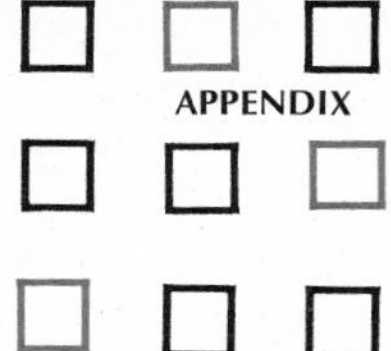

Accounting concepts and marketing analysis

This appendix is intended to provide an explanation of some accounting concepts and methods that are of special importance in the analysis of marketing problems. It covers four topics: (1) cost analysis for evaluating specific projects or expenditures, including so-called "break-even" analysis; (2) operating statements; (3) analytical ratios based on financial statements; and (4) terms of sale. Reference has been made to these topics throughout Parts 4 and 5, particularly in connection with the introduction to marketing management in Chapter 13. The material in this appendix may be used to supplement the applications of accounting concepts to specific problems given in that chapter and elsewhere.

At the outset, it should be emphasized that the same basic accounting principles and procedures that are used in business generally are equally applicable to marketing. But certain concepts are of particular relevance in the analysis of marketing problems, and the ways in which analyses of costs, volume, and profit are carried out are sometimes slightly different than in other areas of accounting.

Cost analysis

Costs or expenses may be classified in many ways, as Chapter 13 shows. For many analytical purposes it is customary to distinguish them along the following lines: (1) total costs and unit costs and (2) variable, fixed, and discretionary costs.

TOTAL COSTS AND UNIT COSTS

Total costs are all the costs associated with an activity. The total cost of manufacturing 1,000 widgets is, say, \$480. It is divided into the following cost categories:

Direct material	\$180
Direct labor	210
Factory overhead	90
Total	\$480

The *unit cost* of producing these 1,000 widgets is \$480 ÷ 1,000, or 48 cents per unit. The direct-labor cost per unit is 21 cents, or \$210 ÷ 1,000.

Unit cost is often a convenient and more meaningful way of expressing costs. The total cost of a family reunion picnic may have been \$150. But if it was attended by 100 persons, it was only \$1.50 per person (unit).

VARIABLE, FIXED, AND DISCRETIONARY COSTS

Fixed costs (FC) are costs whose total amount remains unchanged during a given period of time or over a specified or relevant range of output. A store's annual rental payments of, say, \$100 per month are a fixed cost. If the store's sales in January are 100 units and in February are 50, its rent is fixed at \$100 in each of these months, although its rent per unit of sales rose from \$1 in January to \$2 in February.

For a manufacturing plant, fixed costs generally include the depreciation and amortization of investment in machinery, most of the cost of a mainte-

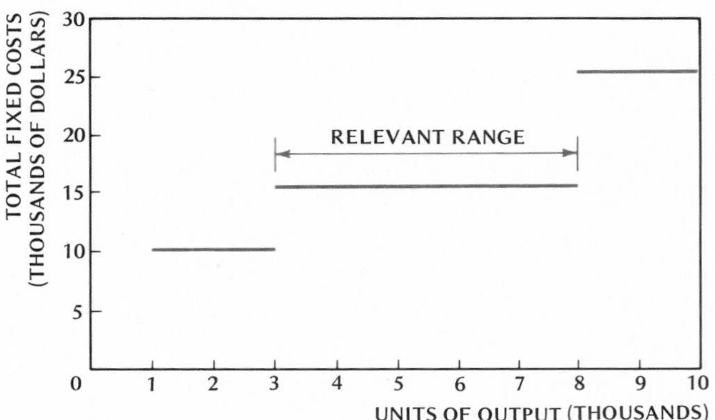

FIGURE A-1
Fixed costs and relevant range

nance crew, most of the management and supervisory payroll, real estate taxes, depreciation on the building, and similar expenses. These are costs which remain unchanged over a fairly wide range of plant output and over a given period of time. This range of output is generally called the *relevant range*. In Figure A-1, fixed costs are $10,000 between 1,000 and 2,999 units of output, $15,000 between 3,000 and 7,999, and $25,000 between 8,000 and 9,999. The relevant range is between 3,000 and 7,999 if that is the output range within which the firm will most commonly operate. Although *total* fixed manufacturing costs may be low under 3,000 units, *unit* fixed costs are relatively high in this range. Thus at 2,999 output, unit fixed costs are $10,000 ÷ 2,999 = $3.333. The lowest fixed costs per unit are at 7,999 output: $15,000 ÷ 7,999 = $1.885.

Variable costs (VC) are fixed *per unit* of output but vary in total amount directly with output. Suppose a toothpaste packager buys his empty tubes and bulk dentifrice at a total cost of 10 cents per tube. If he fills 10,000 tubes per day, his total materials costs will be $1,000, or 10 cents per tube filled. If he produces 100,000, it will be $10,000, also 10 cents per unit. Thus a variable cost is generally uniform (or fixed) per unit, but fluctuates in total in direct proportion to change in total business. Figure A-2 shows this relationship.

Discretionary costs (DC) are costs which, unlike fixed or variable costs, arise

FIGURE A-2
Variable-cost chart

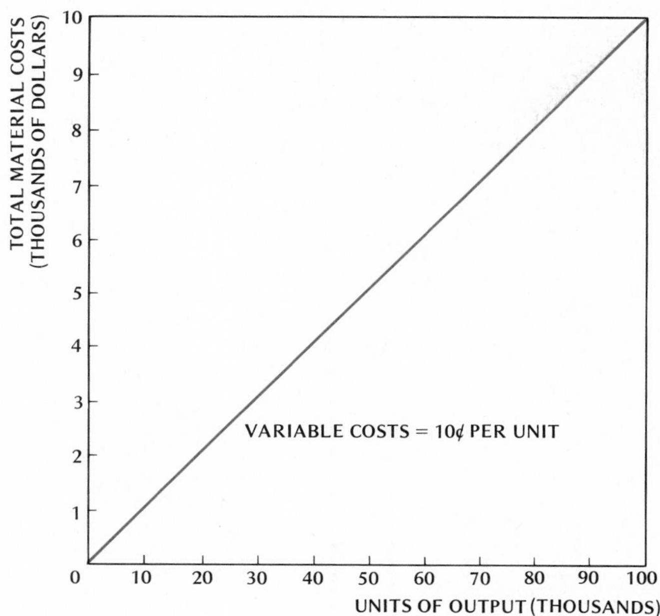

mostly at the discretion of the management. Variable costs are caused by changes in output. Fixed costs are caused by the fact that a company has decided to go into business, but discretionary costs are different. Advertising expenditures are discretionary costs. Research and development expenditures are discretionary costs. They are distinguished by the fact that management *wants* to incur them. Instead of being caused by changes in production and sales volume, their object is to *cause* changes in sales volume. A company advertises more in order to sell more. Hence although successful advertising expenditures may *seem* to be like variable costs in that they vary with output and sales, they are different in that they are causes of volume changes, not caused by volume changes.

BREAK-EVEN ANALYSIS

Break-even analysis attempts to determine the volume of sales necessary (at various prices) for the manufacturer or merchant to cover his costs, or to break even between revenue and costs. Break-even analysis is useful in a variety of ways: to help set prices, estimate profit or loss potentials, and to help determine the discretionary costs that should be incurred.

Our toothpaste packager had direct material costs of 10 cents per unit. Suppose that his other variable costs were 5 cents. His total variable costs therefore would be 15 cents. Suppose that he had annual fixed costs of $50,000 and intended to sell his toothpaste to wholesalers for 20 cents. How many tubes must he sell to break even, that is, just exactly to cover all costs? The question can be answered simply by using the following formula:

$$\text{Break-even units} = \frac{\text{fixed costs}}{\text{unit contribution}}$$

Unit contribution is the difference between unit selling price and unit variable cost:

$$\underset{(\$0.20)}{\text{Unit selling price}} - \underset{(\$0.15)}{\text{variable cost}} = \underset{(\$0.05)}{\text{unit contribution}}$$

The word *contribution* refers to what this difference (5 cents) contributes toward covering fixed costs and producing profits.

The break-even formula yields the following:

$$\text{Break-even units} = \frac{\$50{,}000}{\$0.05} = 1{,}000{,}000 \text{ tubes}$$

In other words, the toothpaste manufacturer must produce and sell 1 million tubes to break even.

This relationship between fixed costs, variable costs, revenues, and the

FIGURE A-3
Variable cost

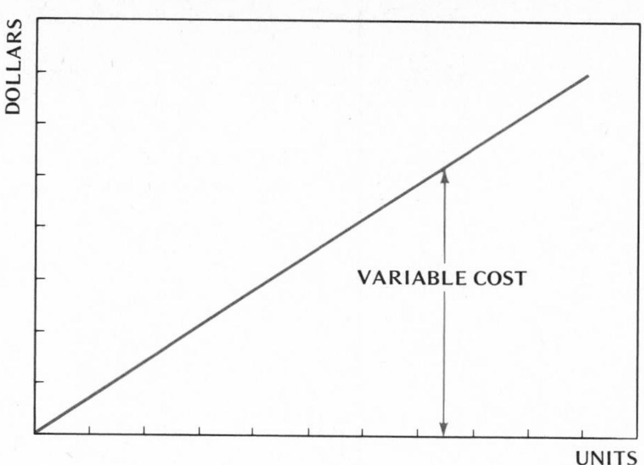

break-even point can be shown graphically. Figure A-3 is a plot of total variable costs against units of output.

Figure A-4 plots total fixed costs against units of output. It is the relevant range cost segment of Figure A-1 stretched out to cover the full range of possible outputs. Thus, for the purposes of this illustration, we assume that fixed costs are constant over the whole range of possible outputs.

Figure A-5 is merely the fixed cost of Figure A-4 added to the variable cost of

FIGURE A-4
Fixed cost

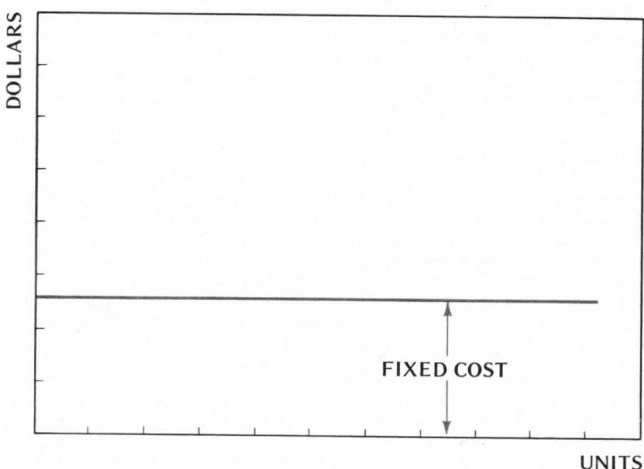

FIGURE A-5
Total cost

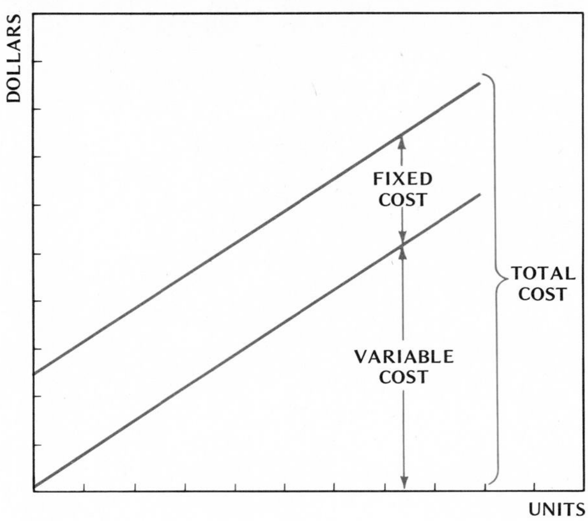

Figure A-3. This gives a combined graph of total cost at various levels of output. (Discretionary costs are ignored for the moment.)

Superimposing a revenue curve (total sales times unit price) on Figure A-5 yields Figure A-6, or a break-even chart.

The point of intersection of the lines of total revenue and total cost in Figure A-6 is the break-even point. The chart also shows the volume of losses and profits at various output and sales levels, given present cost curves and present prices.

It is important to recognize that the break-even volume is strictly an arithmetic concept. It assumes that this volume is both produced *and sold.* In Figure A-6, if 1,300,000 units are produced but only 900,000 are sold, the firm does not break even because no revenue has been received for the 400,000 unsold units for which production costs have been incurred. The total cost curve will lie above the total revenue curve.

The break-even logic can also be used to determine the volume of sales needed to yield a specific profit objective. Thus, the question might be, "At present prices (20 cents wholesale), what volume of sales is needed to earn a net profit of $30,000?"

Using the break-even formula as a basis for answering this question, we get

$$\text{Break-even units} = \frac{\text{fixed costs} + \$30{,}000}{\text{unit contribution}}$$

$$= \frac{\$80{,}000}{\$0.05}$$
$$= 1{,}600{,}000 \text{ units}$$

Proof:		
	$1{,}600{,}000 \times \$0.20$	$= \$320{,}000$
	$VC = 1{,}600{,}000 \times \$0.15 =$	$240{,}000$
	Difference	$= \$\ 80{,}000$
	FC	$= \ 50{,}000$
	Net profit	$= \$\ 30{,}000$

Suppose that the question is, What volume of sales do I need to yield a 10 percent profit, that is, a 10 percent profit on sales? Using the break-even approach again, we get

$$\text{Break-even units} = \frac{\text{fixed costs} + 10 \text{ percent } (\$0.20 \times \text{break-even units})}{\text{unit contribution}}$$
$$= \frac{\$50{,}000 + 0.10\ (\$0.20\ \text{BE})}{\$0.05}$$
$$= \frac{\$50{,}000 + \$0.02\ \text{BE}}{\$0.05}$$
$$\$0.05\ \text{BE} = \$50{,}000 + \$0.02\ \text{BE}$$
$$\$0.03\ \text{BE} = \$50{,}000$$
$$\text{BE} = 1{,}666{,}666 \text{ units}$$

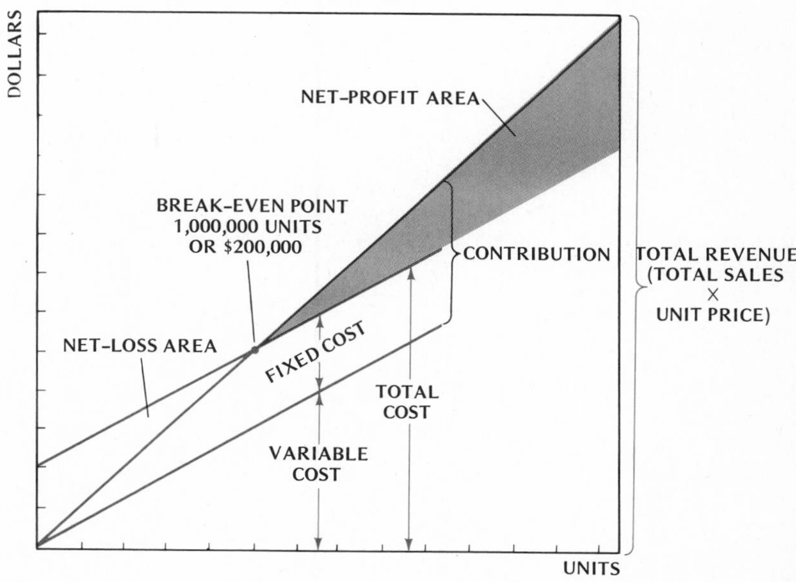

FIGURE A-6
A break-even chart

Proof:	1,666,666 × \$0.20	= \$333,333
	VC = 1,666,666 × \$0.15 =	249,999
	Difference	= \$ 83,334
	FC	= 50,000
	Net profit	= \$ 33,334

$$\frac{\$33{,}334}{\$333{,}333} = 10 \text{ percent profit}$$

The break-even formula is also useful in answering a variety of other questions, such as

1. If fixed costs rise *x* dollars and the price remains the same, how much sales increase is needed to break even?
2. If fixed costs rise *x* dollars and unit sales remain the same, how much of a price increase is needed to break even?
3. With an expected variable cost increase of *y* cents per unit, how much of a sales increase is needed at the present price to yield an operating profit of \$40,000?

With products that the seller believes may respond favorably to advertising and other promotional efforts, he may try to achieve sales expansion via advertising expenditures. Thus in Figure A-7 he adds discretionary advertising expenditures (DC) to his present total costs (FC + VC). With total costs now higher, he must either sell more to break even (raising sales from *OA* to *OB*) or

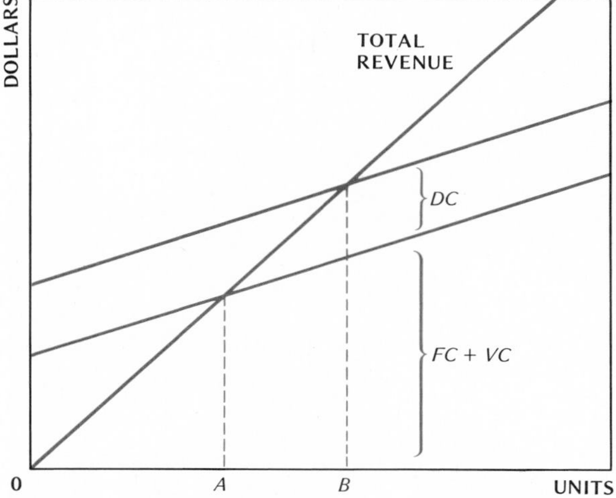

FIGURE A-7
A break-even chart showing how the addition of a discretionary expenditure affects the break-even point

raise his prices at the present volume. But the advertising expenditure was made in the expectation that sales would rise in response to that expenditure. Examination of a chart like Figure A-7 shows *how much* sales must increase to justify the increased expenditure, and permits the analyst to estimate the profit consequences of different changes in sales volume that might follow from the advertising effort. It does not, of course, say anything about what sales result it would be reasonable to expect (see Chapter 20).

□

COSTS AND MARKETING STRATEGY

It was pointed out earlier that fixed costs are actually not fixed over the entire range of output, but variable costs are also seldom as stable and linear as shown in the break-even chart. For example, if a recession occurs, management is likely to tighten controls and cut variable costs. During good times it may be indulgent and careless and allow variable costs to rise. When competitive activity is severe and sales are endangered, advertising and selling expenditures might be raised to stem the downturn and recoup sales losses, although in practice the reverse is frequently done in order to "conserve cash." When the latter is done, management's assumption is obviously that sales will not adequately respond to advertising.

The bigger the unit contribution, the more likely marketing management is to spend more on sales-building promotions. This is not only because it is more likely to have the resources to spend this way, but also because high unit contributions will produce large total profits if sales are high.

The relative sizes of fixed and variable costs are also important in their other effects on marketing strategy. A high variable-cost ratio, and therefore a low fixed-cost ratio, makes getting into an industry (that is, *entry*) relatively easier than when the ratios are reversed. This produces extremely competitive conditions in the industry. Good examples are the garment manufacturing industry and the restaurant business. Because the variable-cost ratio is high, nobody is likely to "win" the competition (that is, destroy his competitors) because of his willingness to charge substantially lower prices. The reason is that a high variable-cost ratio generally means that there are few economies of scale, that is, there is little or no high-volume, low-cost productivity that is facilitated by mass technology or mass selling. Higher volume sales do not produce proportionately lower unit costs with which to out-compete the competition. Prices will tend to be low, and where they are substantially above variable costs, they reflect the seller's other advantages such as, in the garment industry, good styling or workmanship and in the restaurant business, quality food, service, and entertainment.

A relatively high initial fixed-cost ratio will not only tend to limit the number of producers who will enter the industry but may offer an enormous profit potential. Thus our toothpaste packager, whose equipment could fill thousands of tubes an hour, broke even at 1,000,000 units of output. At 1,600,000 he had net profits of $30,000. But at 2,000,000 units, with only a 25 percent increase in output, his profits would rise to $50,000 or 67 percent. That is one reason why he is more willing to spend money for advertising. It is also the reason why machine-produced consumer goods are more heavily advertised than handicraft-produced consumer goods. A rising volume of output is spread over fixed costs, and this reduces the average total cost per unit. Even if variable costs rise directly with output, average total costs per unit may fall substantially, as shown in column 5 of Table A-1.

Table A-1 is illustrated graphically in Figure A-8. Had the fixed-cost ratio been lower, the average-cost curve would have descended less steeply. In other words, the higher the fixed-cost ratio, the greater the benefits of full utilization of productive capacity.

The fact that some costs are fixed does not mean that unit costs will fall indefinitely. There comes a point when the average-cost curve begins to turn back up—when an increase in the ratio of variable input (say, direct labor and materials) to fixed input begins actually to yield a *lower* output costing more per unit. Thus, beyond some point, the addition of more men and material to a fixed plant may result in costly congestion, loss of proper supervision, and wasteful mistakes. The result could actually be that total output falls absolutely or relatively. A rising "tail" on the average-unit-cost curve in Figure A-8 would illustrate this point.

□
TABLE A-1
Cost relationships

Quantity (1)	FC (2)	VC (3)	Total cost (4)	Average total cost per unit (5)
1	$100	$ 10	$110	$110.00
2	100	20	120	60.00
3	100	30	130	43.33
4	100	40	140	35.00
5	100	50	150	30.00
6	100	60	160	26.33
7	100	70	170	24.28
8	100	80	180	22.50
9	100	90	190	21.11
10	100	100	200	20.00

FIGURE A-8
Graphic representation of Table A-1

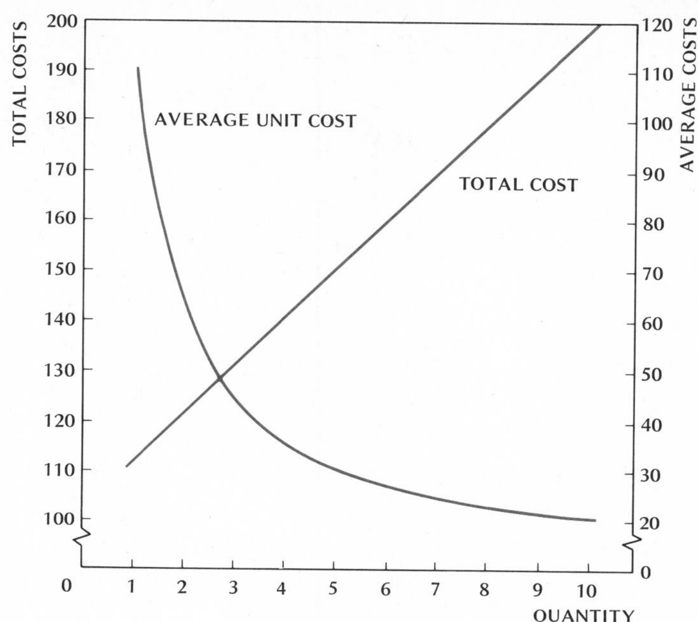

Operating (or profit and loss) statement

An operating, or profit and loss, statement is a financial summary of business operations during a period of time. It shows how the various elements of the operation contributed to the final outcome. Like cost analysis, it is one measure of the effectiveness of the firm.

A retailer's operating statement is composed of the following major elements:

SALES less COST OF GOODS SOLD equals
GROSS MARGIN less EXPENSES equals PROFIT

Each element of the operating statement can be expressed as a ratio of sales, and these ratios can be compared with those of other retail outlets of like size and product line to appraise the relative effectiveness of a retailer. Various trade associations and trade publications regularly publish detailed operating statistics and ratios of department and specialty stores, retail food chains, and other types of retail and wholesale firms.

A retail operating statement is much more detailed than the above example. Table A-2 is typical. Since accounting statements are governed by conventions that tend to reflect the peculiarities of the industries or business functions they portray, such a statement requires some explanation.

1. *Gross sales* represent the total value of sales made during the period.
2. *Returns* are the value of credit or cash given to customers for merchandise purchased but subsequently returned. (This may be resold and the revenue of that sale then appears a second time under gross sales.)
3. *Allowances* are the value of a price adjustment that is given customers who have brought back defective or other merchandise. The adjustment generally keeps the item from becoming a return.
4. *Net sales* are gross sales less returns and allowances. This represents the merchant's real volume of business out of which all expenses must be met.
5. *Cost of goods sold* is the cost to the merchant of the goods he sold during the period. The merchant who has been in business before the year of the current statement will have started the year of the current statement with a carryover of last year's leftover stock, that is, his "beginning inventory."

When he adds the cost of goods purchased during the year to the cost of transporting them into his establishment, he gets gross cost of goods handled. Subtracting his *ending* inventory at the close of the accounting period, he gets gross cost of goods sold.

The final net cost of goods sold is obtained by subtracting cash discounts earned from gross cost of goods sold. A cash discount is a reduction in the price of merchandise offered by a supplier for prompt payment. (Discount terms are discussed below.) The reason for stating cash discounts earned separately as a subtraction from gross cost of goods sold rather than merely stating purchases at a lower figure is for control and analysis purposes. It shows how well the firm's financial management is capitalizing on a particular kind of profit or money-saving opportunity.

There is some difference among businesses as to whether these discounts are to be treated as merchandise discounts and therefore subtracted from gross cost of goods sold, or as "other income earned" and therefore added to operating profit. Most retail merchants use the former treatment.

While the net profit outcome is identical, treating it as "other income" results in a higher "cost of goods sold" and therefore a lower operating profit. Thus, in Table A-2, what would happen to "cost of goods sold" and "operating profit" if "cash discounts earned" were treated differently?

VALUATION OF INVENTORIES

The value placed on the "ending inventory" in the operating statement can obviously have a profound effect on the level of operating profits. A high ending inventory valuation reduces the cost of goods sold figure for the period and

TABLE A-2

Retail operating statement

Gross sales		$7,580,340
Returns and allowances		745,325
Net sales		$6,835,015
Beginning inventory	$ 810,055	
Purchases	4,225,017	
Inward transporation costs	55,013	
Gross cost of goods handled	$5,090,085	
Ending inventory	907,153	
Gross cost of goods sold	$4,182,932	
Cash discounts earned	251,192	
Cost of goods sold		3,931,740
Gross margin		$2,903,275
Expenses:		
Payroll	$ 998,765	
Supplies	83,073	
Repairs and maintenance	55,073	
Advertising	184,111	
Delivery	33,582	
Interest	43,700	
Pensions and insurance	129,709	
Depreciation	37,853	
Losses and bad debts	6,211	
Real estate costs	191,403	
Utilities	11,382	
Taxes (other than income taxes)	53,052	
Services purchased	58,491	
Miscellaneous	4,011	1,890,416
Operating profit		$1,012,859
Other income		61,511
Net profit before income taxes		$1,074,370

therefore raises the gross margin dollars and gross margin percentage, as Table A-3 shows.

Since the ending inventory of one period is the beginning inventory of the subsequent period, the effect on profits of a high or a low valuation tends to cancel out between the two years. This depends, however, on how inventories

□
TABLE A-3
Inventory valuations

	Low inventory valuation		High inventory valuation	
Net sales		$5,000,000		$5,000,000
Gross cost of goods handled	$4,500,000		$4,500,000	
Ending inventory	1,150,000		2,150,000	
Cost of goods sold		3,350,000		2,350,000
Gross margin		$1,650,000		$2,650,000
Gross margin, percent		33		53

are in turn valued in the subsequent period and on what has happened to the price level in the interval. If the prices at which the store buys its merchandise are consistently rising and it values its closing inventory at the last prices it paid for the goods (even though some of them were purchased earlier at lower prices), then a high valuation may continue from year to year. But suppose that prices fall drastically during the year and the merchant again values his inventory at the last prices he paid. He will have valued them high the previous period and low in the present, with quite opposite gross margin consequences.

One alternative to all this is to value inventory by a "cost audit," that is, to trace back the actual prices paid by the retailer for each item in inventory. For department stores, supermarkets, hardware stores, variety stores, and drugstores, all of which carry thousands of different items and make new purchases constantly throughout the year, a cost audit of each item is more costly than its value. Hence records are kept on an aggregate dollar basis, and this creates the opportunity for using a variety of valuation methods.[1]

When purchase costs have varied throughout the accounting period, so that the same type of product was purchased at one price early in the period and at higher prices later or vice versa, the question arises as to which figures to use for inventory valuation purposes. If the ending inventory is based on the higher costs of the most recently acquired merchandise, it means that the cost of goods sold is recorded at the lower earlier costs. This results in a relatively higher gross margin and higher taxes. If the firm's objective is to minimize taxes, it will therefore use the so-called LIFO (last in first out) method of inventory valuation. Thus the last goods purchased are assumed to be the first ones sold. If the most recent purchases were the most costly, then the ending inventory is based on lower costs. The opposite of LIFO is FIFO (first in first out). Which of these methods is most appropriate obviously depends on whether

[1] For a discussion of the various systems and their advantages and disadvantages, see Malcolm P. McNair and Anita C. Hersum, *The Retail Inventory Method and LIFO*, McGraw-Hill Book Company, New York, 1952.

purchase costs and retail prices are stable or clearly moving in one direction or another, and on the firm's objectives.

VARIETY IN OPERATING STATEMENTS

Although the purposes, format, and analytical approaches of operating statements are broadly the same regardless of the type of business, there are some differences among those of retailers, wholesalers, and manufacturers, and differences among types of each of these.

The statement in Table A-2 is typical of a medium-sized department store. Among the distinguishing ways in which certain elements of the statement are treated in different types of business are the following:

1. Smaller stores generally use a "natural classification" of expenses such as payroll, supplies, repairs. Larger stores—department stores and supermarkets—generally use functional or expense-center systems. Thus instead of *payroll* they may have categories such as administrative expense, selling expense, and handling and shipping expense, each of which includes a portion of total payroll expenses.
2. Wholesalers use both natural and functional expense classifications.
3. Manufacturers' operating statements are much less standardized. Moreover, they generally include in "cost of goods sold" the salaries and wages incurred in processing the goods into the final manufactured products.

Retailers and wholesalers also process their goods before they are ready for the sales counter. For example, they may be labeled, repackaged, priced, pressed, sorted, etc. But these costs cannot easily be segregated from other costs of doing business, and in most lines of business are of relatively little importance in terms of cost. Hence they are handled in broad natural categories such as "payroll."

A manufacturer's operating statement generally breaks down into the broad categories shown in Table A-4. Internal statements used for management con-

TABLE A-4
Manufacturer's operating statement

Net sales	$5,000,000
Cost of goods sold	3,500,000
Gross margin	$1,500,000
Marketing, general and administrative, and overhead expenses	1,000,000
Operating profit	$ 500,000
Other income	500
Gross profit	$ 500,500

trol will, of course, show detailed breakdowns of each of the broad categories of expenses.

CASH DISCOUNTS

Retailers earn cash discounts, and their treatment has been described above, but wholesalers and manufacturers both earn and give cash discounts. Cash discounts given are generally deducted from gross sales to yield net sales.

Analytical ratios

A firm is interested not only in how much it sells and how much profit it makes but also in how efficiently various aspects of its operations are being managed compared with some previous time period or with other firms of a similar type and size. Such comparisons are facilitated by looking at various operating ratios or analytical ratios, that is, by stating certain elements of the operating statement as percentages of net sales. Commonly used analytical ratios are gross margin percentage, expense ratio, profit ratio, and markup.

In nearly all cases such ratios use *net sales* as the base. Thus in the operating statement of Table A-2:

$$\text{Gross margin} = \frac{\$2{,}903{,}275}{\$6{,}835{,}015} = 42.5 \text{ percent}$$

$$\text{Expense ratio} = \frac{\$1{,}890{,}416}{\$6{,}835{,}015} = 27.7 \text{ percent}$$

$$\text{Returns and allowances} = \frac{\$745{,}325}{\$6{,}835{,}015} = 10.9 \text{ percent}$$

MARKUP COMPUTATION

Markup is the amount by which the selling price of an item exceeds its cost to the seller. Thus an item which the merchant buys for 60 cents and sells for $1 has a markup (or markon) of 40 cents. For a manufacturer, markup is the difference between his fully allocated cost of producing the product and his selling price.

As pointed out above, operating or analytical ratios are generally expressed as percentages of net sales. In the preceding example, the markup percentage is $0.40/$1.00 = 40 percent. It is *not* $0.40/$0.60 = 66⅔ percent.

In ordinary business parlance the term *markup percentage* is generally shortened simply to markup. Hence the answer to the question "What is the markup on that $1 item?" is "40 percent." If there are no returns, allowances, or markdowns on the sale of that item, and no inward transportation costs, we would also say that its gross margin is 40 percent.

Many retailers use markup formulas in deciding how to price an item. Thus, in view of his expenses and profit objectives, a retailer may have a standard practice of using a 50 percent markup for certain classes of furniture, 40 percent for men's suits, and 33⅓ percent for linens.

Suppose that the retailer buys a suit for $100 and uses his 40 percent markup formula. What will be his selling price? Not $140. Since the markup percentage is based on *selling* price, he must price the suit such that the difference between that price and his cost is 40 percent. Therefore, to find the selling price of a $100 suit with a 40 percent markup, the merchant makes the following calculation:

Let

$$\begin{aligned} X &= \text{selling price} \\ \$100 &= \text{cost} \\ 40 \text{ percent} &= \text{markup} \end{aligned}$$

Therefore,

$$\begin{aligned} X &= \$100 + 0.4X \\ X - 0.4X &= \$100 \\ 0.6X &= \$100 \\ X &= \$100 \div 0.6 \\ &= \$166.67 = \text{selling price} \end{aligned}$$

since

$$\text{Selling price} = \text{cost} + \text{markup}$$

and

$$\begin{aligned} \text{Markup} &= 40 \text{ percent of selling price} \\ \text{Cost} &= 60 \text{ percent of selling price} \end{aligned}$$

Hence given a desired markup, to find his selling price the merchant divides his dollar cost by his percentage cost, that is, the difference between 100 percent and his desired percentage markup. Therefore,

$$\begin{aligned} \text{Selling price} &= \frac{\text{cost}}{(100 \text{ percent} - \text{ markup percent})} = \frac{\text{cost in \$}}{\text{cost in percent}} \\ &= \frac{\$100}{0.6} \\ &= \$166.67 \end{aligned}$$

Proof that $166.67 is a 40 percent markup:

$$\begin{aligned} \$166.67 &= \text{price} \\ -\ 100.00 &= \text{cost} \\ \hline \$\ 66.67 &= \text{margin} \end{aligned}$$

$$\frac{\$\ 66.67}{\$166.67} = 40 \text{ percent}$$

If the merchant knows his selling price and his markup and wishes to recall what his costs were, the reverse formula holds:

$$\begin{aligned}\text{Cost} &= \text{selling price} \times \text{cost percent}\\ &= \$166.67 \times 0.6\\ &= \$100.00\end{aligned}$$

To convert a markup expressed as a percentage of selling price into one expressed as a percentage of cost, the following formula applies:

$$\begin{aligned}\text{Markup percent on cost} &= \frac{\text{markup percent on price}}{\text{cost percent on price}}\\ &= \frac{40 \text{ percent}}{60 \text{ percent}}\\ &= 66\tfrac{2}{3} \text{ percent}\end{aligned}$$

To convert a markup expressed as a percentage of cost into one expressed as a percentage of selling price, the following formula applies:

$$\begin{aligned}\text{Markup percent on price} &= \frac{\text{markup percent on cost}}{100 \text{ percent} + \text{markup percent on cost}}\\ &= \frac{66\tfrac{2}{3} \text{ percent}}{166\tfrac{2}{3} \text{ percent}}\\ &= 40 \text{ percent}\end{aligned}$$

Hence a 40 percent markup on selling price is equivalent to a 66⅔ percent markup on cost. A 33⅓ percent markup on selling price is equivalent to a 50 percent markup on cost.

Often a product passes through several hands (channels of distribution) on its path from the manufacturer to the consumer. In such cases the markups to the individual members of the distribution chain are stated in terms of their individual selling prices. If a manufacturer with a cost of goods sold of $75 decides to sell to wholesalers via brokers[2] at a 25 percent markup to himself and a 4 percent commission to the broker, the selling price to the wholesaler is $104.04. This is computed as follows:

1. A 25 percent markup on $75 cost of goods sold equals $75/0.75, equals $100 net to the manufacturer.
2. A 4 percent brokerage commission on the quoted price to the wholesaler equals $100/0.96, equals $104.04, the quoted price to the wholesaler.

If the wholesaler sells it to retailers at a 20 percent markup, his selling price equals $104.04/0.80 = $130.05.

If the retailer sells it to ultimate consumers at a 40 percent markup, his selling price equals $130.05/0.60 = $216.75.

In such a case the manufacturer will usually stipulate the percentage brokerage commission and may suggest the markups for each other channel. The customary method is to quote the suggested retail price ($216.75) and list the

[2] Brokers work on a *commission* that is stipulated by the manufacturer, not on a markup (see Chap. 12).

markups and commission as a series of discounts. Hence in the above illustration it would be stated: $216.75 less 40, 20, and 4. (The series of figures 40, 20, and 4 mean 40 percent, 20 percent, and 4 percent. In practice the percentage signs are omitted.)

□ MARKDOWN COMPUTATION

A markdown is the amount by which a merchant reduces the original selling price of merchandise in order to sell it more easily. Clearance sales, for example, generally involve heavy markdowns.

Just as markup is computed on net selling price, so is markdown. If a merchant buys an item for 60 cents and prices it at $1, his markup is 40 percent. If he subsequently reduces the price to 90 cents, he has taken a 10-cent markdown. The percentage markdown is based on the *net* sales price, or 90 cents. Hence the markdown percent is $0.10/$.90 = 11.11 percent.

Markdowns do not appear on the operating statement, except for that portion which represents allowances made to customers who have already bought the item.

While regular markdowns do not appear on the operating statement, they are a significant measure of retail efficiency. All retailers *expect* to incur markdowns. The reason is that they must keep a relatively large inventory and assortment of all classes of goods, even toward the end of a regular buying season (say winter clothes during February), or run the risk of alienating and losing customers to stores that have a good selection at such times. At the end of February and early March, however, many people begin shopping for spring clothes. Hence, at some point the winter supply must be cleared out to make room for the spring supply. Marked-down prices are one way to encourage people to buy this end-of-season stock.

Although markdowns are an expected part of retail life, maintaining the proper balance between adequate near end-of-season stock and the markdown percentage is a sign of good management. Both high and low markdowns percentages suggest some possible management shortcoming.

Most progressive merchants keep separate markdown records, broken down by departments. This is not only for control and evaluation purposes but also for pricing. The fact that markdowns must be incurred requires that this be taken into consideration in the original pricing of the product. Therefore the amount of typical markdown usually has some effect on the size of the original markup. Hence the initial markup generally exceeds the expected rate of gross margin.

The markdown percentage of a store or a store department is computed on total net sales of the store or department, not just on the marked-down goods themselves. Thus, if a department buys 50 dresses for $10 each and prices them to yield a markup of 33⅓ percent, its selling price will be $15. If it sells 40 at $15 and marks the remaining 10 down to $12 each and sells these, its gross sales will be

$$
\begin{aligned}
40 \times \$15 &= \$600 \\
10 \times \$12 &= \underline{120} \\
\text{Gross sales} &= \$720
\end{aligned}
$$

If one of the $15 dresses is returned and then resold for $12, the final calculation will be

$$
\begin{aligned}
40 \times \$15 &= \$600 \\
11 \times \$12 &= \underline{132} \\
\text{Gross sales} &= \$732 \\
\text{Returns and allowances} &= \underline{15} \\
\text{Net sales} &= \$717
\end{aligned}
$$

$$\text{Markdown} = 11 \times (\$15 - \$12) = 11 \times \$3 = \$33$$

$$\text{Markdown percent} = \frac{\text{markdown, \$}}{\text{net sales, \$}} = \frac{\$33}{\$717} = 4.6 \text{ percent}$$

STOCKTURN

Stockturn refers to the number of times a store's average inventory is sold during a given period, generally a year. A common synonym of stockturn is *turnover.*

The stockturn rate may be computed in several ways:

1. By dividing the cost of goods sold by the average inventory at cost
2. By dividing the net sales by the average inventory at selling price
3. By dividing the net sales in physical units by the average inventory in physical units

Average inventory is computed as follows, using consistently throughout the calculation either cost, selling price, or physical units:

$$\text{Average inventory} = \frac{\text{beginning inventory} + \text{ending inventory}}{2}$$

If the above equation were to use cost, the figures from Table A-2 would show:

$$
\begin{aligned}
\text{Average inventory} &= \frac{\$810{,}055 + \$907{,}153}{2} \\
&= \frac{\$1{,}717{,}208}{2} \\
&= \$858{,}604 \\
\text{Stockturn} &= \frac{\text{cost of goods sold}}{\text{average inventory at cost}} \\
&= \frac{\$4{,}182{,}932}{\$858{,}604} \\
&= 4.9
\end{aligned}
$$

The stockturn rate can be an important measure of retail or wholesale efficiency in several ways:

1. It indicates that the merchant is minimizing his investment in merchandise inventory. Instead of having, say, $1 million of net sales on $200,000 in average inventory investment, he may do it on an average investment of $100,000, or a stockturn of 10 instead of 5.
2. A lower average investment in inventory probably means that the merchant's investment in warehouse and perhaps display space is lower.
3. High stockturn is generally associated with reduced markdowns. High turnover means more frequent purchasing by the store. This allows better management of near end-of-season stocks and lower markdowns.
4. High stockturn generally is an indication of the store's or department's buying skill. It generally means that the store is especially adept at selecting items or fashions or sizes or colors, etc., that are high in public favor and therefore move rapidly off the shelves. In other words, a high stockturn generally means a low ratio of slow-moving stock.

But a high stockturn is not an automatic sign of superior management. On the negative side it might suggest the following:

1. The stock might be unbalanced. That is, the store is concentrating on fast-moving items and not providing customers with the breadth of selection or assortment which might be necessary to keep them coming back.
2. The stock might be too shallow. That is, there is so little inventory in each item that it becomes quickly sold out. A high frequency of stockouts will disappoint and alienate customers.
3. High stockturn may produce high expenses because:
   a. It requires a better and perhaps more costly inventory control system in order to keep low inventories from quickly becoming stockouts.
   b. Frequent reordering is necessary, and this consumes the time of buyers and of clerks who process orders and invoices.
   c. It will raise the number of incoming packages that must be handled.
   d. Buying in smaller amounts may raise the cost of incoming transportation.
   e. Buying in smaller amounts may prevent being able to take advantage of quantity discounts.

What a "proper" stockturn rate is depends not only on the industry but also on the strategy of the company in question and on the particular department in the company. Thus in a supermarket the meat department's stockturn may be low at 30 times a year but the canned food department's stockturn may be high at 15 times a year. A Dun and Bradstreet, Inc., study of average annual stockturns is shown in Table A-5.

□
TABLE A-5
Average annual stockturns

Line of retail trade	Average number of stock turns
Bakeries	18.7
Small department stores (under $250,000 annual volume)	2.5
Drugstores	3.9
Dry goods and general merchandising	2.4
Furniture stores ($200,000–$300,000 annual volume)	2.5
Gasoline service stations	21.3
Grocery and meat stores	17.2
Meat markets	53.3
Restaurants	35.5
Women's ready-to-wear	4.1

Terms of trade

Terms of trade, also called *terms of sale,* refer to the conditions of sale and purchase governing a product. These vary greatly over the entire spectrum of business operations. Generally they include two major factors:

1. *Dating* refers to the time that payment for the merchandise is due and the time (or date) before which the specified amount of discount may be taken by the buyer.
2. *Discount* generally refers to the reduction in price offered to the buyer by the seller. The most common types of discounts are cash discount, trade discount, quantity discount, and various forms of special or arbitrary discounts.[3]

A cash discount is a reduction in price allowed the buyer for prompt payment. It is most frequently expressed as a percentage of the gross amount due the seller, that is, of the billed price after deduction of trade, quantity, and arbitrary discounts. A very common type of cash discount is illustrated by the terms "4/10 net 30." These terms mean that the purchaser may take a 4% discount if he pays the bill within 10 days after the date of the invoice, and that, if he does not pay the discounted bill within 10 days, he is expected to pay the full amount within 30 days. After 30 days, the bill will be considered overdue and may be subject to an interest charge.

Sometimes the date before which a discount may be taken is reckoned not from the date of the invoice but from some other date specified in the terms. For instance, the terms might have read "4/10 EOM," in which case the 4% discount would be allowed not only for 10 days after the date of the invoice, but for 10 days after the end of the month in which the invoice was made out. Whereas an invoice dated March 5 with terms 4/10 net 30 must be paid by March 15 if the discount is to be taken, on an invoice

[3] The remainder of this discussion of terms of trade is reprinted by permission from Malcolm P. McNair, Elizabeth A. Burnham, and Anita C. Hersum, *Cases in Retail Management,* McGraw-Hill Book Company, New York, 1957, pp. 61–65.

of the same date with terms 4/10 EOM the discount may be taken up to April 10. When terms are written EOM, purchases billed after the twenty-fifth of any month are regarded by many sellers as of the following month, so that on an invoice dated March 27 with terms 4/10 EOM the discount may be taken as late as May 10 instead of April 10.

Convenience is the reason for EOM dating, as it is for another type of dating called ROG (receipt of goods) dating. EOM dating is practical because it is convenient for purchasers to pay a number of bills, or all bills from a single resource, on the same day of the month. ROG dating is used when a purchaser is located at a considerable distance from his resource, since, in this event, if terms are based on the date of invoice, payment may become due before the merchandise is received. Payment before receipt and inspection of the merchandise may lead to dissatisfaction and to the need for adjustment. Under ROG dating, therefore, the days for allowing discount are numbered from the date the goods are received by the purchaser instead of from the date of the invoice.

A similar type of dating is seasonal dating, in which the terms specify the date from which the period for allowing discount is to be computed. For example, seasonal merchandise purchased July 1 may be billed 3/10–Sept. 1, in which case the discount will be available until September 10. Seasonal dating is advantageous to the seller in that it saves warehousing expense, induces early buying of seasonal goods, and enables the producer to keep his plant operating in slack seasons. It is advantageous to the buyer because he may purchase early in the season but defer payment until after his own sales of the merchandise have begun.

The date of payment for merchandise may also be affected by another practice called "extra dating." Extra dating means that the discount will be allowed for a certain period in addition to that first mentioned in the terms; for example, 4/10 60x (extra) means that the 4% discount may be taken not only for 10 days, but for 60 extra days, or 70 days in all from the date of the invoice.

These types of dating are commonly called "advance" or "post" dating; that is, the date of payment is advanced into the future, so that payment need not be made until after the time indicated by the date of the invoice.

When a purchaser pays his bill before the discount date, he may be entitled to deduct, after the allowed discount, interest for the days by which he "anticipates" the discount date. In actual practice, anticipation is allowed by a majority of the resources with which department stores and other large retailers deal. A purchaser has no legal right, however, to take anticipation unless it is part of the contract express or implied, that is, unless the right to take anticipation is noted on the invoice, or unless anticipation is an established custom of the trade, an established practice of the parties concerned, or otherwise a part of the agreement between purchaser and seller.

Anticipation is usually computed at 6% per year (360 days), and for convenience it is calculated on the face amount of the invoice. Thus in paying on May 25 an invoice for $780 dated May 20 with terms reading "4/10 EOM–net 30," the purchaser will deduct the 4% discount which he is entitled to take for payment any time before June 11, and he will deduct also anticipation, at the rate of 6% per annum, for the 16 days between May 25 and June 10, or an additional $2.08. His check therefore will be written for $746.72.

A quantity discount is a reduction in price allowed the buyer for a purchase of or above a specified amount. There are three types of quantity discount. The discount may depend on (1) the quantity of a single item purchased, (2) the total quantity of all items purchased on a single order, or (3) the quantity purchased during a season or over some other specified period of time. In either of the first two cases, the discount is referred to as a quantity discount and may be deducted before the invoice is entered as a purchase for the store or department. Such a discount sometimes consists of free goods. In the third case, the discount is designated as a period discount, a patronage discount, a deferred discount, or a cumulative quantity discount, and may take the form of a cash rebate, a merchandise credit, or free goods.

A trade discount is a reduction in price given to a certain category of customer to cover the cost of performing a particular trading function. The amount of the trade discount may or may not appear on the face of the invoice. If it does not, then the trade discount has already been deducted from the manufacturer's catalogue or list price to arrive at the price billed on the invoice. If, on the other hand, the merchandise is billed at the manufacturer's catalogue or list price, then the discount may appear at the foot of the invoice as a percentage of the billed price. This billed price is the list price and frequently the manufacturer's suggested retail price.

Arbitrary discounts are ordinarily allowed purchasers by sellers either to vary selling prices without changing quoted or catalogue prices or to differentiate among individual customers within a trading group. If a manufacturer publishes a catalogue listing merchandise with constantly changing costs, he may adjust his catalogue prices easily by adding a new discount percentage when costs decrease or by rescinding a previous discount when costs rise. An arbitrary discount is also a convenient way of giving individual customers advantages over other customers within a trading group, a practice which the Robinson-Patman Act seeks to restrict. These arbitrary discounts are accounted for as trade discounts, being either deducted from list price to arrive at the billed price appearing on the invoice or noted as a percentage of list price if the list price is the billed price.

If a series of trade, quantity, and arbitrary discounts are allowed on the same invoice, they are computed separately in the order in which they are listed [as shown on page 557 in the example of 40, 20, and 4], the second being computed on the net after deduction of the first, and so forth. If a cash discount also is allowed, it is deducted after all other discounts have been deducted.

Shipping instructions are not, strictly speaking, part of the terms of sale, but they accompany every buyer's order and may affect the amount of payment. If a violation of shipping instructions causes an increase in shipping charges paid by the retailer, he may deduct from his bill the difference between the expected and actual amount paid. The term F.O.B. when used as part of the shipping instructions means "free on board" and refers to the point to which the seller will pay transportation charges.

INDEX